D1631609

Applied Accounting Theory
A Financial Reporting Perspective

The Willard J. Graham Series in Accounting

Consulting Editor **Robert N. Anthony** *Harvard University*

Applied Accounting Theory
A Financial
Reporting Perspective

Philip E. Meyer, D.B.A., C.P.A.

Associate Professor and Chairman
Department of Accounting
Boston University

 1980

Richard D. Irwin, Inc.   Homewood, Illinois   60430
Irwin-Dorsey Limited   Georgetown, Ontario   L7G 4B3

Material from the Uniform CPA Examinations and
Unofficial Answers, copyright © 1961, 1971,
1974, and 1977 by the American Institute of
Certified Public Accountants, Inc. is adapted
with permission.

ISBN 0-256-02360-3
Library of Congress Catalog Card No. 79–89956

Printed in the United States of America

1 2 3 4 5 6 7 8 9 0 MP 7 6 5 4 3 2 1 0

D
657.3
MEY

Preface

The objective of this book is to provide an understanding of corporate financial reporting in light of contemporary accounting theory and practice. It offers the perspective with which to appreciate the nature of existing and emerging issues in accounting and financial reporting. This work addresses the conceptual, institutional, and policy elements of accounting as it examines major components of generally accepted accounting principles, conventions, and practices. Users of this book will include two types of audiences—prospective accounting practitioners *and* potential users of accounting information.

Persons studying to become accountants are exposed to the near-encyclopedic orientation of intermediate and advanced principles of accounting volumes, an integral element of which is a strong emphasis on procedural rules and techniques. The proliferation of pronouncements by standard-setting bodies results in considerable effort by students just to be aware of which rules apply to particular sets of circumstances. Hence, accounting concentrators will benefit from a work whose nature is to integrate accounting theory, institutional dimensions of accounting, and their relationship with the financial reporting environment. This volume would therefore be used in a senior-year capstone course in accounting theory as well as in an MBA, MS, or "five-year track" accounting theory seminar which examines applied accounting problems at a conceptual level.

The second audience to which this work is directed is that of prospective *users* of accounting information. In a college and university context, such persons will have completed an introductory financial accounting course and might be pursuing a course of study leading to a career in fields such as corporate finance, securities analysis, or the legal profession. At the post-collegiate level, this book will be useful in executive education programs for middle and upper echelon corporate personnel and in training programs for financial analysts, loan officers, securities brokers, and corporation lawyers. In addition, this volume will be beneficial as a review medium for persons preparing for professional certification tests such as the CPA, CMA, CFA, and CIA examinations, and as a basis for independent study by investors in stocks and bonds who wish to become intelligent readers of published financial statements.

There is an increasing awareness among accounting academicians and practitioners that it is important that both prospective preparers and prospective users of accounting information be exposed to sophisticated accounting courses whose scope extends beyond a concern with only technical aspects of accounting. Indeed, there is a need to appreciate conceptual, institutional, and policy dimensions of accounting and financial reporting to an extent that has not been traditionally covered in the accounting curriculum. This volume aspires to enable its readers to appreciate and evaluate alternative points of view in accounting as they relate to existing and emerging issues in the area of corporate financial reporting.

In proceeding to achieve the book's objective, an effort is made to synthesize seemingly disparate financial accounting questions by identifying pertinent points of harmony and of contention. The text also presents at an applied level salient features of noteworthy contributions to financial accounting thought. In addition, the titles of more than 250 works, selected on the basis of the contribution they have made to accounting theory and financial reporting practice, are provided in end-of-chapter bibliographies.

Although the conceptual orientation of the book means that its primary concern is not with procedural, how-to-do-it aspects of accounting, this work is not a mere theoretical treatise. It has an applied thrust, and indeed many illustrative examples are presented. The presentation is descriptive and analytical; there is more concern with providing balanced points of view than with proving the rightness of the author's own personal beliefs. The book's first three chapters focus on the financial reporting environment by considering the nature of accounting and financial reporting, and identifying pertinent institutional and conceptual characteristics. Chapters 4 through 15 examine particular accounting issues and facets of financial reporting.

This volume contains 45 cases, keyed to particular chapters, to be used as a basis for understanding more fully the textual portion of the book. These class-tested cases give readers an opportunity to deal with extensions of the chapters' material, contemplate applications, explore theoretical issues, and consider what-if type of questions—in the process of solidifying their knowledge of particular accounting and financial reporting issues. All the cases can be analyzed on the basis of (1) the related chapter's narrative, (2) prior accounting knowledge, and (3) a general understanding of the business environment. Therefore, although students in an accounting theory course would be more inclined to approach the cases on the basis of their previous accounting knowledge, MBA students who have a limited accounting background are equally able to respond to the cases in an intelligent and skillful manner.

I express appreciation to the following persons who provided invaluable assistance with their constructive comments on all or a part of this work: Robert N. Anthony, Harvard University; Gary F. Bulmash, American University; Pieter T. Elgers, University of Massachusetts; Robert Hampton III, Price Waterhouse & Co.; T. Lincoln Morison, Jr., The First National Bank of Boston; R. F. Salmonson, Michigan State University; Donald R. Simons, Boston University; Phyliss Barker Webster, University of North Carolina at Greensboro; and Earl A. Spiller, Jr., Indiana University. I am also grateful to Evelyn Felder whose exemplary secretarial skills contributed significantly to the successful completion of this book.

Last, and by no means least, I am indebted to my wife, Ricki, whose support and encouragement enabled me to devote to this volume many of the hours and much of the attention which were rightfully hers.

January 1980   ***Philip E. Meyer***

Contents

Contents

come Statement Effects. Monetary Assets and Liabilities—Gains and Losses from General Price-Level Changes. Monetary and Nonmonetary Assets—Balance Sheet and Income Statement Effects.

CASES

Contents

Financial Statements and Financial Reporting

$\mathbf{A}$ccounting has been defined as the process of identifying, measuring, and communicating economic information to permit informed judgments and decisions by users of the information.[1] Two types of information have, in turn, been identified: information about financial position and information about performance. Financial position refers to a given point in time, and performance relates to change over a period of time. Financial position can be viewed as a static notion while performance suggests a dynamic dimension. The two are related in the sense that the referred-to performance is that of changes in financial position over a period of time, i.e., how or why financial position is different at one date from what it had been at some earlier date.

Once the types of information to be accounted for are identified, the second stage of the definition is approached, namely, measurement. Accounting measures financial position not by concentrating only on an entity's cash, or for that matter, only on the economic resources it possesses for future use, i.e., all of its assets. It also considers the entity's existing obligations, that is, its liabilities. The excess of assets over liabilities is called owners' equity, and is the measure of an enterprise's book value.

Accounting has traditionally measured the change in an entity's financial position by directing attention to those transactions which underlie the change in its owners' equity. More specifically, it is recognized that changes

---

[1] Committee to Prepare a Statement of Basic Accounting Theory, *A Statement of Basic Accounting Theory* (Sarasota, Fla.: American Accounting Association, 1966), p. 1.

in owners' equity are of two types: investment/disinvestment and operations. The former refers to the investment by the entity's owners and distribution of the entity's assets to its owners as a return on their investment. *Operations* refers to the transactions that represent the purpose of the entity's very existence, namely, its sales and related expenses.

The traditional measure of an entity's performance has revolved around this latter aspect of changes in owners' equity. The underlying belief is that if owners' equity constitutes accounting's concept of wealth, then it should be those changes in owners' equity which result from the entity's ongoing business activity which should be the focal point of measurement. In 1971, the accounting profession adopted yet another approach to measuring performance, namely, one whose orientation is not limited to changes in owners' equity resulting from operations. The nature and objectives of this additional measure of performance, whose focus is on changes in financial position in terms of *liquidity,* complement rather than supplant the traditional approach; it is examined in depth in Chapter 11.

Accounting has identified wealth and performance as phenomena for which measurement and communication are warranted. Wealth is measured by directing attention to an entity's owners' equity, and performance is measured by focusing on the effect of an entity's operating transactions on its owners' equity. The medium through which such information is communicated is financial statements. The financial statement used to communicate information relating to an entity's wealth is a balance sheet, or statement of financial position, and that which conveys information about the effect of operations on an entity's owners' equity is called an income, or earnings, statement.

The balance sheet identifies all an entity's assets and all its liabilities at a given point in time defined by consensus as to which resources and obligations shall be measured and recorded. Owners' equity is, in fact, nothing more than the excess of its assets over its liabilities. In other words, owners' equity is but a mathematical residual having no inherent qualitative significance as such. Thus, an important feature of the communication process is that rather than merely presenting the one composite amount of *owners' equity,* primary attention is directed to the component elements of owners' equity.

In addition, within the asset and liability sections of balance sheets, the various amounts are further classified into homogeneous categories. Parenthetical and footnote disclosures are also included to provide details which place the presented amounts in an appropriate perspective, or to furnish additional information which would not otherwise be disclosed.

With respect to the income statement, rather than merely reconciling a fiscal period's amounts of beginning and ending owners' equity to derive net income, the communication process is considerably broader in scope. Transactions representing inflows of assets as a result of selling goods and rendering services are *revenue* transactions. Those in which an outflow of assets occurs or will occur pursuant to the generation of revenue are *expense* transactions. The income statement presents a summary of an entity's revenue and expense transactions as well as income from investments, gains, and losses—with the resulting excess identified as either net income or net loss. An important feature of the communication process is that the component amounts are set forth explicitly. This means the resulting net income or net loss is merely a mathematical difference, that is, the amount by which owners' equity changed during a fiscal period as a result of events and circumstances other than investments (such as the sale of its stock) and disinvestments (such as a dividend distribution).

The communication of performance measurement typically requires additional disclosures as well. Certain quantitative or descriptive information may be presented parenthetically within the earnings statement, or as footnotes to the financial statements. In addition, many companies also prepare a statement of retained earnings through which readers can appreciate how income for a period affects owners' equity as of the end of the period.

Accounting information can be classified into two categories: financial and managerial. Financial accounting includes information disseminated to parties that are not part of the enterprise proper, but it is of interest to the company's officers and top managers as well. Financial accounting encompassses information relating to an entity's financial position, earnings, liquidity, and profitability. External users may include present and prospective stockholders and creditors, competitors, customers, suppliers, regulatory commissions, financial analysts, and trade associations. The Internal Revenue Service would typically not be included in such a grouping because the data it receives from taxpayers are based on income tax laws which differ in many respects from general-purpose financial accounting data.

Managerial accounting relates to aspects such as data processing, efficiency and productivity, planning and control, and capital budgeting. Managerial accounting data are not generally dissiminated to persons outside the company. They differ from financial accounting in that whereas a set of general-purpose financial statements is assumed to meet the needs of all the external users, the nature of managerial accounting is that different kinds of specialized reports are prepared for particular persons. Users of managerial accounting data can include department heads, project managers, section supervisors and factory foremen. The scope of this volume is limited to financial accounting or, more descriptively, accounting and financial reporting.

THE FINANCIAL REPORTING ENVIRONMENT

As indicated in the previous section, a set of general-purpose financial statements is the medium through which accounting information is communicated to external users. The data which appear in such reports are based on measurements made by accountants. Although there is a popular conception that the hallmark characteristic of accountants and accounting is an unswerving propensity to be exact and accurate at least as far as financial statement data are concerned, this is not an entirely accurate assumption at all.

The very nature of accounting measurement is that it includes the effect of estimates as well as discretion as to which one of several acceptable accounting methods to use in any particular case. For example, the recognition of annual depreciation expense relating to a particular asset involves estimating both the asset's expected useful life and its eventual salvage value, and selecting from among several different methods an appropriate depreciation system, e.g., an equal amount each year, an accelerated approach, or one which is based on units of service rather than the passage of time.

The matter of alternative acceptable accounting methods is one which attracts much attention from practicing accountants, corporate officers, financial analysts, and rule-making bodies. With each passing year, the number of acceptable alternative methods is reduced through the promulgation of restrictive new rules. But there is an ever-present belief that somehow considerable discretion seems to persist. This phenomenon is aptly set forth as Shank's Axiom which states that "no matter how detailed the rule, the mind of the enterprising entrepreneur will conceive a transaction consistent with the rule and inconsistent with the spirit behind it."[2]

The dilemma can be viewed in terms of a spectrum with uniformity at one extreme and flexibility at the opposite end. On the one hand, having uniform rules, which may appear to be an attractive state of affairs, could result in like rules being applied in unlike circumstances. Moreover, there is an understandable, natural reluctance by accountants to reduce every conceivable transaction to the level where the availability of "chapter and verse" citation would become a substitute for the exercise of professional judgment. At the other extreme, if flexibility were to predominate, some persons are fearful the resulting state of affairs might turn out to be one of accounting anarchy. The ensuing debate has been in existence for decades, and in all likelihood it will continue for many years.

One additional comment is warranted with respect to the role of account-

---

[2] John Shank, "The Pursuit of Accounting Standards—Whither and Whence," *Journal of Contemporary Business* (Spring 1973), p. 89.

ing data. By no means is accounting information the sole or even necessarily the primary basis used to make investment or business decisions. Although financial statements do tend to provide increasing amounts of information which in an earlier era may not even have been considered to be within the province of accounting, there are many critical factors for which external users may seek information which are not included within the financial statements, e.g., competence of management, new product development, product quality, prospects for growth, competitive position, and production efficiency.

And even for those aspects of an enterprise's financial condition and operating results disclosed in financial statements, users should recognize that rather than providing answers, financial statements at best serve the function of identifying areas and issues for which questions should be raised. For instance, although it is enlightening to observe an increase in income as a percent of revenues, this information alone is inadequate; it should be the basis for inquiring what were the relevant underlying factors, whether their nature suggests the increase is temporary, permanent, or capable of further improvement, and what effect such a change had on other aspects of the company's financial condition.

In any case, a set of general-purpose financial statements is but one of many inputs to which an informed decision-maker can turn. Its insights can be significant, but in some circumstances its contribution may be minimal. Financial accounting is a reactive phenomenon in the sense its objective is to identify, measure, and communicate the outcome of events that have occurred and of situations which exist as a result.

THE NATURE OF INCOME

The traditional accounting definition of income is that it is the increase in an entity's owners' equity resulting from operations and other causes. At the implementational level, expenses are subtracted from revenues and the excess is the measure of income (or loss). Criticism has been directed toward this classical approach on the grounds it fails to account for (1) the effect of changes in the general purchasing power of the dollar and (2) the impact of resources' specific price changes. Although a considerable degree of controversy has ensued as a result, the differences of opinion are invariably traceable to varying perceptions of the objectives of accounting. Rather than suggesting this is in any way a trivial matter, it should be noted the debate by and large exists *within* the context of the basic *accounting* model. That this model differs from that of traditional economic theory is noteworthy, and the nature of the difference is a matter which warrants our attention.

Economic Theory and Accounting Theory

Economic theory perceives a business enterprise as the medium through which parties who own and employ factors of production can earn a return on their investments. Workers contribute services to the firm and earn wages in return, suppliers furnish needed raw material for which remuneration is received, creditors offer funds for which interest accrues, and owners of real property provide land in exchange for rental payments. One other party providing a needed factor of production is the entrepreneur, namely, the one or more individuals who assume the ultimate risks of ownership. It is such persons who conceive of the role for the enterprise to play, invest their own funds and, either themselves or through hired managerial personnel, marshal together the other needed input factors and assume the responsibility of shaping the entity into a going concern.

Whereas the relationship between the enterprise and each of the parties providing factors of production is one in which the amount of return to be realized is usually well-defined, this is not the case for the entrepreneurial input. To the extent entrepreneurs' investment consists of money, their contribution is similar to that of creditors. But entrepreneurs' investment has an additional dimension; beyond the contribution of managerial skill and/or specialized knowledge, they contribute an intangible ingredient as well, namely, an element of risk assumption.[3] As the entity's residual owners, not only do the entrepreneurs enjoy no guarantee of a positive return *on their investment*, but they may not even realize a return *of their investment* either.

Economic theory expresses some interest in the matter of the positioning of the entrepreneurial factor relative to the other factors of production. The focal point of the concern is with the fact that in a legal sense, the entire excess of revenues over payments to owners of the other factors accrues to the enterprise's residual owners. Accordingly, even though the entrepreneurs' return is *not* predetermined or negotiated in a transactional sense as it is in the case of their counterparts, economic theory envisions a "normal" return being earned by the provider of this factor as well. Although the imputed dollar amount of this return may not be disbursed immediately or even in the foreseeable future, it is nevertheless viewed as being earned, i.e., it constitutes a return on the entrepreneurs' investment in the form of unrealized capital appreciation.

In practice, all the excess of an enterprise's revenues over payments made to owners of the other factors of production does indeed accrue to the entrepreneurial owners. Such an amount can and often does exceed the presumed normal return that the entrepreneurial factor "should" earn, rec-

---

[3] This is not to suggest that entrepreneurs are the only risk-takers; it is the degree of risk they assume which is substantially greater than that affecting their counterparts.

ognizing that in practice it would be difficult, if not impossible, to determine what constitutes a "normal" return. In economic theory, this additional sum is sometimes referred to as *excess* profit or *pure* profit, attributable to the fact that profit—income or earnings—is the term used to signify the return to the provider of one of the several factors of production, namely, the entrepreneurial factor. In a purely technical sense, the entity itself might even be viewed as incapable of earning a profit, because by definition it is merely an inanimate medium through which factors of production are combined to provide goods and services in an output market. Only the parties who own such factors are able to earn a profit, and they do so by receiving a return on *their* investments. The enterprise itself makes no investment as such and therefore cannot earn a profit—a return—on its non-existent investment.

Accordingly, from the point of view of the entity, that amount accountants refer to as income is merely another one of the various costs which it, the enterprise, incurs in the process of generating revenue through the sale of goods and services. The only time it would be appropriate to view the entrepreneurs' return as the income of the entity is if and when there is an assumption the enterprise and the providers of its entrepreneurial input are one and the same. Economic theory rejects this approach because it envisions the entrepreneurs as inherently no different from other providers of input factors and thus having no more kinship or mutuality of interests with the enterprise than any of their counterpart contributors.

Current accounting theory views the designated measure of income as the amount which accrues to the entrepreneurs, as well as being the entity's earnings. This reflects the belief that not only does income measure the return on the entrepreneurs' investment of funds, but it also relates to the risk-assumption quality innate to the entity's residual owners. Because of this distinctive feature, accounting theory has deemed it appropriate to equate the interests of the entrepreneurs with those of the entity. But even within the realm of accounting theory, there have been instances in which this traditional orientation has been subjected to criticism.[4] Nevertheless, much to the consternation of persons who maintain there should be greater affinity between economic theory and accounting practice, the structure of the accounting model as it currently exists does reflect the notion that the equity interest of entrepreneurial owners is paramount. Instances of this bias include the measurement and disclosure of earnings per share of common stock, the preparation of consolidated financial statements whose nature is to reflect the effective equity of parent company stockholders, and the treatment of declared dividends as a distribution rather than as a determinant of an enterprise's income.

---

[4] This point is discussed in Chapter 3.

The Role of Profit

Use of the expression *bottom line* as part of the general vernacular is, of course, based on the accounting convention that an earnings statement's format entails disclosing revenues and expenses, and that the difference between these two sums appears as its last number—on its bottom line. In its popular usage, *bottom line* would appear to embody a very precise and qualitatively significant message in the sense that it evokes an image of a succinct yes/no-good/bad capstone summary of what would otherwise be a vastly complex issue.

It is ironic that it is accounting, or more specifically, accountants—the term's progenitors—who recognize the misleading nature of a one-line/bottom-line means of expression. Persons who are able to appreciate the dynamics of a business enterprise, indeed of any organization or individual human being, realize that substantive understanding of phenomena and circumstances are obtainable only through critical analysis of underlying component elements. To obtain a meaningful appreciation of an enterprise's performance, attention should therefore be directed to those factors which are the determinants of the so-called bottom line amount.

This, in turn, suggests that the accounting concept of income revolves around an examination of the pertinent characteristics of transactions. At a computational level, the excess of revenues over expenses is a quantitative measure of the increase in the owners' equity of the entity resulting from operations. On the one hand, the one bottom line number represents the interrelationship between an enterprise's flow of transactions and the resultant effect on its financial position. On the other hand, the amount of income also signifies the return on investment that accrues to the enterprise's entrepreneurs, i.e., its stockholders. Such a return manifests itself in increased owners' equity—owners' equity in its own right being a measure of the entrepreneurs' investment in the enterprise.

CORPORATE FINANCIAL REPORTING

Although many business enterprises operate as sole proprietorships or as partnerships, the corporate form of organization has become increasingly predominant in the United States. The traditional attractions of operating an enterprise as a corporate entity are owners' limited liability, the relative ease of ownership transfer, and the availability of certain income tax incentives.

Close to 400 corporations have annual sales in excess of $1 billion, and the annual revenues of the 22 largest companies exceed $10 billion each.[5]

---

[5] *Forbes* (May 14, 1979), pp. 234–38.

And not only are the largest corporations big and becoming bigger in absolute terms, but their size has been increasing in a relative sense as well. Whereas in 1966, the 100 largest American companies had sales of $250 billion, accounting for 33 percent of the nation's $753 billion gross national product, at the end of 1976—ten years later—the hundred biggest corporations had sales of $745 billion, accounting for 44 percent of the $1.7 trillion gross national product.[6]

Practically all large corporations in the United States are publicly held, that is, the shares of their stock are traded on stock exchanges or in organized over-the-counter markets. The typical nature of publicly held corporations is that the stockholders and board of directors delegate day-to-day administrative responsibilities to hired professional managers. This is different from most privately held enterprises where it is not unusual for management functions to be carried out by the very same persons who are also the company's stockholders/owners.

The Changing Orientation

The traditional function of financial reporting had been one of providing proprietors with information about their companies, that is, the enterprises which they both owned and managed. Once it became virtually a universal practice for managerial responsibilities to be delegated to hired personnel, *stewardship* emerged as the focal point of financial reporting. The nature of such an orientation is to direct attention to accountability aspects of the manager-owner relationship, i.e., "how effectively have the owners' assets been managed" being set forth in terms of both its capital preservation and profit generation aspects.

With the pervasiveness of the corporate practice of employing professional managers to conduct the enterprise's affairs on behalf of absentee owners, the focus of financial reporting began to change. Although the importance of stewardship continues, financial reporting recently has become somewhat more oriented toward the presumed needs of investors. Lay and institutional investors alike view stock ownership as but one of various investment alternatives to pursue, and as a result the type of information they seek is much more future-oriented than that which characterizes the traditional stewardship frame of reference.

As a result, it is primarily the predictive ability of financial statements which has become the focal point for investors. Rather than being viewed strictly as a means of assessing how well the enterprise's managers fulfilled

---

[6] *Forbes* (May 15, 1977), p. 45.

their stewardship responsibilities, the financial reporting process is assumed to have much more of a future-directed nature. This investor orientation has been well-stated as follows:

> Financial reporting is the culmination of the accounting process, being the distillation of innumerable transactions and decisions of the past into the presentation of historical facts—it is an accountability for the past. Nevertheless, the principal use of such data is as a springboard for making operating or investment judgments about the future; a record of the past and a picture of present financial strength are critical ingredients to such judgments. While the principal role of the public accountant in this process is reporting on factual information about the past and the present, he must bear in mind that investment decisions involve an appraisal of future prospects. Thus, information which financial statements present should be geared to provide maximum assistance in and the springboard for making judgments about the future.[7]

The "future" orientation of accounting has been specifically cited by the Financial Accounting Standards Board, viz.,

> Financial reporting should provide information to help present and potential investors and creditors and other users in assessing the amounts, timing, and uncertainty of prospective cash receipts from dividends or interest and the proceeds from the sale, redemption, or maturity of securities or loans.[8]

The shifting emphasis from the primacy of the stewardship frame of reference to one of increased sensitivity to the future-oriented informational needs of persons who make investment and disinvestment decisions has had two effects on accounting and financial reporting. One of these consequences has been the emergence of the question whether the existing conceptual framework is responsive to the environment accounting aspires to service. The most provocative of the question's many aspects is probably that which addresses the very validity of the traditional historical cost basis of accounting. Depending on how one defines the objectives of financial reporting, it might be appropriate to supplant the existing system with one that reflects current value information. It would not be unreasonable, for instance, for someone to suggest that the cost basis system was adequate when stewardship was the principal objective, and that a current value approach is more suitable if the predictive ability of financial statements were to emerge as their primary function. The other consequence wrought by the emergence of

---

[7] Harvey Kapnick, *Financial Forecasts and the Role of the Independent Accountant*—a statement presented to the Securities and Exchange Commission on March 22, 1972 (Chicago: Arthur Andersen & Co., 1972).

[8] *Statement of Financial Accounting Concepts No. 1*, paragraph no. 37. Copyright © by Financial Accounting Standards Board, High Ridge Park, Stamford, Connecticut 06905, U.S.A. Reprinted with permission. Copies of the complete document are available from the FASB.

the "predictive ability" phenomenon has been the expansion of the realm of financial statement disclosure; some of these are cited below.

Expanded Disclosures

The proliferation of footnotes to financial statements is a particularly visible manifestation of the trend toward expanded disclosure. Their function is to disclose information not included in the body of the financial statements proper. A summary of the enterprise's significant accounting policies is stated in one of these footnotes; its purpose is to identify those accounting methods used in instances in which (1) acceptable alternative methods are also available, or (2) the unique nature of the company's business justifies using an otherwise unconventional approach. The theme underlying this type of disclosure is that it enables the reader to appreciate the nature of biases, if any, that affect the resulting amounts. This kind of insight, in turn, could be helpful when comparing different companies' accounting data.

A second type of disclosure that appears in a footnote is that of pro forma data. This refers to those instances in which it is deemed important for the reader to be aware of what a particular accounting result would have been if certain alternative circumstances had been in effect; in other words, cases in which a calculation is made under specified assumptions contrary to fact. For example, a pro forma calculation sometimes must be made under the assumption a business combination that actually occurred during a period had occurred at the beginning of the immediately preceding period. The purpose of making a pro forma disclosure in this case is to enable the reader to be in a better position to predict future earnings for the combined enterprise, even though in actuality the constituent companies had not operated in a combined state during any preceding period.

Footnotes also disclose matters relating to lease commitments, contingent liabilities, pension plans, stock options, income taxes, foreign currency transactions, and long-term debt (interest rates and maturity dates). And either among the footnotes or elsewhere in the corporate annual report, data about quarterly stock market prices of the company's shares of common stock are provided, social responsibility disclosures are made, and information about the relative contribution of the enterprise's different segments are presented. Such disclosures enable readers not only to appreciate the company's performace to date, but also to be better able to predict the prospects for its future profitability, liquidity, financial position, and so forth.

As a result of the increase in disclosure requirements in both quantity and scope, the level of technical understanding needed to read and comprehend financial statements has increased dramatically. This phenomenon is perhaps most poignantly demonstrated by the Securities and Exchange Commission's recognition that certain financial disclosures are indeed prepared with the knowledge they will be appreciated only by reasonably sophisticated readers such as professional financial analysts. The trend toward increased disclosures is one which has not been confined only to those publicly held companies within the Commission's jurisdiction, however. Most of the requirements promulgated by private sector rule-making bodies—whose authority is sanctioned by the accounting profession and the business community—apply to all enterprises that distribute their financial statements to external parties. In fact, this trend toward expanded disclosure has inspired the observation that instead of financial statements' traditional caveat that "the accompanying footnotes are an integral part of the financial statements," the time may be near when the message will be restated to appear as "the accompanying financial statements are an integral part of the footnotes!"

FINANCIAL STATEMENTS AND FINANCIAL REPORTING

Although the movement toward expanded disclosure has been accelerating ever since its initial response to the increased interest on the part of securities investors during the 1960s, the actual promulgation of official financial statement requirements has occurred on a somewhat piecemeal basis. In response to the resulting criticism of such an approach, there emerged the proposition that improvements would result if accounting measurements and disclosure practices were to be based on an articulated set of well-defined objectives. In turn, the American Institute of Certified Public Accountants published a study group report in 1973 which bore the title *Objectives of Financial Statements*.[9]

Subsequently, the Financial Accounting Standards Board assumed the responsibility for defining such objectives, and in 1978 it issued Statement of Financial Accounting Concepts No. 1. The title of the 1978 document was *Objectives of Financial Reporting by Business Enterprises*.[10]

Note the difference between its title and that of the study group report that had been published five years earlier: what had originally been viewed as being objectives of *financial statements* had become objectives of *financial reporting*. This variance in terminology was intended to convey a very distinct message, namely, that financial statements are but one aspect, albeit an important if not the predominant one, of financial reporting. Indeed, the Board stated its concept of the distinction as follows:

---

[9] Study Group on Objectives of Financial Statements, *Objectives of Financial Statements* (New York: American Institute of Certified Public Accountants, 1973).

[10] *Statement of Financial Accounting Concepts No. 1.* Copyright © by Financial Accounting Standards Board, High Ridge Park, Stamford, Connecticut 06905, U.S.A. Reprinted with permission. Copies of the complete document are available from the FASB.

Financial reporting includes not only financial statements but also other means of communicating information that relates, directly or indirectly, to the information provided by the accounting system—that is, information about an enterprise's resources, obligations, earnings, etc. Management may communicate information to those outside an enterprise by means of financial reporting other than formal financial statements either because the information is required to be disclosed by authoritative pronouncement, regulatory rule, or custom or because management considers it useful to those outside the enterprise and discloses it voluntarily. Information communicated by means of financial reporting other than financial statements may take various forms and relate to various matters. Corporate annual reports, prospectuses, and annual reports filed with the Securities and Exchange Commission are common examples of reports that include financial statements, other financial information, and nonfinancial information.[11]

The significance of the Board's 1978 choice of terms is that it formally acknowledged the validity of the notion that accounting information cannot be communicated through financial statements alone. This means that what had previously been viewed as an obligation to prepare financial statements as such would subsequently be more broadly defined, i.e., in terms of the financial reporting responsibility at large.

The important distinction between financial statements and financial reporting notwithstanding, it should be recognized that the presentation of an enterprise's financial statements lies at the heart of its financial reporting obligation. Quantification of operating results and financial position has been the hallmark of accounting throughout its long and distinguished history. Certainly in the contemporary milieu—as corporations' transactions become more complex and as the economic environment poses greater challenges to both the business enterprise and the investor in its securities—the role of financial reporting becomes increasingly important. In turn, the need to obtain a reasonably sophisticated understanding of its whys and wherefores as well as its strengths and weaknesses is a critical one.

By identifying pertinent institutional and conceptual characteristics of accounting, the next two chapters provide a comprehensive orientation to the financial reporting environment. That overview is followed by chapters 4 through 15 in which particular accounting issues and facets of financial reporting are examined. The broad range of subjects encompassed by such an examination and the variety of possible approaches to resolving financial reporting issues will give meaning to the proposition that the environment of accounting and financial reporting is a dynamic one. As significant, it will also provide the insight and understanding needed to appreciate their impor-

---

[11] Ibid., paragraph no. 7.

tant implications for both business corporations and investors in such enterprises' securities.

Additional Readings

Arnett, Harold E.   "What Does 'Objectivity' Mean to Accountants?" *The Journal of Accountancy* (May 1961), pp. 63–68.

Backer, Morton, and Gosman, Martin L.   *Financial Reporting and Business Liquidity.* New York: National Association of Accountants, 1978.

Benjamin, James J., and Stanga, Keith G.   "Differences in Disclosure Needs of Major Users of Financial Statements." *Accounting and Business Research* (Summer 1977), pp. 187–92.

Bernstein, Leopold A.   "In Defense of Fundamental Analysis." *Financial Analysts Journal* (January–February 1975), pp. 57–61.

Boulding, K. E.   "Economics and Accounting: The Uncongenial Twins." In *Studies in Accounting Theory,* edited by W. T. Baxter and Sidney Davidson. Homewood, Ill.: Richard D. Irwin, Inc., 1962, pp. 44–55.

Chatfield, Michael.   *A History of Accounting Thought,* rev. ed. Huntington, N.Y.: Robert E. Krieger Publishing Co., Inc., 1977.

Crum, William F.   "Causes That Underlie Changes in Corporate Earnings." *Management Accounting* (February 1972), pp. 38–40.

Duff and Phelps, Inc.   *A Management Guide to Better Financial Reporting: Ideas for Strengthening Reports to Shareholders and the Financial Analyst's Perspective on Financial Reporting Practices.* Chicago: Arthur Andersen & Co., 1976.

FASB Research Report.   *Economic Consequences of Financial Accounting Standards: Selected Papers.* Stamford, Conn.: Financial Accounting Standards Board, 1978.

FASB Statement of Financial Accounting Concepts No. 1.   *Objectives of Financial Reporting by Business Enterprises.* Stamford, Conn.: Financial Accounting Standards Board, 1978.

Hatfield, Henry Rand.   "An Historical Defense of Bookkeeping." *The Journal of Accountancy* (April 1924), pp. 241–53.

Johnson, Charles E.   "Management's Role in External Accounting Measurements." In *Research in Accounting Measurement,* edited by Robert K. Jaedicke, Yuji Ijiri, and Oswald Nielsen. Sarasota, Fla.: American Accounting Association, 1966, pp. 88–100.

Mautz, R. K., and May, William G.   *Financial Disclosure in a Competitive Economy.* New York: Financial Executives Research Foundation, 1978.

May, Robert G., and Sundem, Gary L.   "Research for Accounting Policy: An Overview." *The Accounting Review* (October 1976), pp. 747–63.

Norr, David.   "What a Financial Analyst Wants from an Annual Report." *Financial Executive* (August 1970), pp. 20–23.

Rice, C. D.; Ford, H. C.; Williams, R. J.; and Silverman, G. W. *The Businessman's View of the Purposes of Financial Reporting.* New York: Financial Executives Research Foundation, 1973.

Rosenfield, Paul. "Stewardship." In *Objectives of Financial Statements—Selected Papers,* vol. 2. New York: American Institute of Certified Public Accountants, 1974, pp. 123–40.

Study Group on the Objectives of Financial Statements. *Objectives of Financial Statements.* New York: American Institute of Certified Public Accountants, 1973.

Zeff, Stephen A. "The Rise of 'Economic Consequences'." *The Journal of Accountancy* (December 1978), pp. 56–63.

2
The Institutional Framework of Accounting

THE AUDIT FUNCTION

Financial statements are prepared on behalf of an enterprise by its in-house accountant(s) for dissemination to external parties. For such users to be satisfied the statements are fairly presented, a certified public accountant (CPA) is engaged to conduct an examination and to attest to the statements' fairness. Attestation is a communicated statement of opinion (judgment), based on convincing evidence, by an independent, competent, authoritative person, concerning the degree of correspondence in all material respects of accounting information communicated by an entity with established criteria.[1]

Attestation, in turn, is the communication dimension of the specialized area of accounting known as *auditing*. Auditing is the systematic process of objectively obtaining and evaluating evidence regarding assertions about economic actions and events to ascertain the degree of correspondence between those assertions and established criteria, then communicating the results to interested users.[2] The relationship between accounting and auditing has been expressed in terms of accounting being essentially a *creative*

---

[1] Committee on Basic Auditing Concepts, *A Statement of Basic Auditing Concepts* (Sarasota, Fla.: American Accounting Association, 1973), p. 6.

[2] Ibid., p. 2.

process of generating information while auditing is a *critical* process of evaluating information.[3]

The Audit Opinion

The attest aspect of auditing is effected by the issuance of an audit opinion. This opinion is a letter which describes the scope of the audit, and the auditor's opinion as to the fairness of the financial statements. As a result of the audit examination, the auditor may issue (1) an unqualified opinion that the statements are fairly presented—sometimes called a *clean* opinion, (2) a qualified opinion which states that the statements are fairly presented except for one or more cited factors, or that it is subject to the outcome of a particular uncertainty, or (3) an adverse opinion which declares that the statements are not fairly presented. Alternatively, it is possible the auditor may disclaim an opinion either because of a lack of independence or because the limited scope of the audit examination does not permit an opinion to be rendered. A model unqualified opinion appears below.

> We have examined the balance sheet of CZY Company as of December 31, 19x4 and 19x5, and the related statements of income, retained earnings, and changes in financial position for the years then ended. Our examinations were made in accordance with generally accepted auditing standards and, accordingly, included such tests of the accounting records and such other auditing procedures as we considered necessary in the circumstances.
>
> In our opinion, the financial statements referred to above present fairly the financial position of CZY Company at December 31, 19x4 and 19x5, and the results of its operations and the changes in its financial position for the years then ended, in conformity with generally accepted accounting principles applied on a consistent basis.

It is important to note that the issuance of an audit opinion does not absolve management of its responsibilities regarding financial statements. This point is sometimes expressed in a *management report* that a corporation may include in its published annual report to stockholders. An excerpt from such a management report appears below:

> The integrity and objectivity of data in these financial statements . . . are the responsibility of management. . . . The auditors' report . . . expresses an informed judgment as to whether management's financial statements, considered in their entirety, present fairly in conformity with generally accepted accounting principles the Company's financial condition and operating results. This judgment is based on procedures . . . sufficient to provide reasonable

---

[3] Robert K. Mautz, *Fundamentals of Auditing,* 2d ed. (New York: John Wiley and Sons, Inc., 1964), p. 2.

assurance that the financial statements neither are materially misleading nor contain material errors.[4]

And with respect to the auditor's role, there is *no* assertion—either explicit or implicit—that the financial statements are correct or accurate, nor that the auditor's role is to certify the statements. The auditor merely makes an informed judgment, and no generalized or specific affirmations are made regarding the statements being precisely right or true. The use of expressions such as *fairness* and *in our opinion* are intended to denote a degree of attestation which is reasonable, practicable, and meaningful.

The Audit Examination

One of the focal points of an audit examination is the enterprise's internal controls. *Internal controls* encompass the systems and procedures used to safeguard assets, effect the recording of accounting data, encourage adherence to prescribed company policies, and foster efficient operation of the business. In the course of an audit, there is a determination (1) whether the company has an adequate internal control system in a normative sense, and (2) if it is adhered to at the implementational level. This kind of testing is referred to as compliance testing—as opposed to substantive testing which relates to tests designed to substantiate specific amounts.

Evidence is a critical feature of the audit examination. It relates to the auditor's need to have a sufficient basis for rendering an audit opinion. Evidence manifests itself in a variety of forms which include physical observation, oral corroboration, written documentation, inferences, and calculations. It is the relative merit of particular elements of evidence which auditors consider in rendering professional judgments.

Another critical aspect of auditing is the relationship between the risk and materiality of reported amounts. This can be illustrated by considering a manufacturing enterprise's different types of assets. A company's cash relative to its total assets may be relatively immaterial in size, and if materiality alone were the criterion, it would require minimal audit work. But the high degree of risk associated with cash has a countervailing effect, namely, that cash should be given a substantial amount of attention. In addition, it is possible a small balance might actually be the residual of large amounts of increases and decreases that had occurred during the period, e.g., a $3 million increase in cash may be the result of a $150 million inflow of cash and a $147 million cash outlay. On the other hand, consider plant assets such as buildings and machinery. The relative risk of theft is minimal even

---

[4] *American Telephone and Telegraph Company 1978 Annual Report*, p. 25.

though the dollar amounts involved are likely to be large. Audit concern is therefore apt to be more a reaction to such assets' size rather than their risk exposure.

This interactive relationship is manifest in auditors' increasing use of statistical sampling techniques. Two of the most critical statistical concepts of importance to auditors are *confidence* and *precision*. Consider the challenge confronting auditors with respect to selecting an appropriate sample size to test the reasonableness of the enterprise's cost of inventory on hand. In pursuing a statistically based solution, the issue would be expressed in terms similar to the following: What is the estimated dollar value of a particular enterprise's end-of-year merchandise inventory which the auditor can be 95% confident is within $300,000 of the actual value?

To even reach this stage, the auditors will have had to exercise their judgment with respect to both risk and materiality. The selection of a 95% confidence criterion as opposed to one of 98% or 90% reflects the auditors' perception of the relative risk; that is, the greater the risk, the higher the degree of confidence. And the choice of an answer which falls within $300,000 of the actual value is a reflection of the auditors' need for precision. Precision is the companion concept of materiality in the sense the auditor makes a decision that as much as a $300,000 variation is tolerable in a particular case. This means that for the purposes at hand $300,000 is deemed to be relatively immaterial. A greater degree of precision—such as a variation of only $25,000 in our case—in an auditing sense reflects a lesser tolerance for inexactness, that is, a more restrictive notion of what constitutes a material amount.

The parameters of auditing extend far beyond the realm of tracing transactions, corroborating balances, observing inventory counts, and confirming outstanding receivables. Although the matter of searching for fraud had traditionally been viewed by auditors as beyond the scope of their responsibilities, the incidence of lawsuits against auditors suggests that readers of auditors' reports may have a different perception. Indeed, in both this area and that of *illegal acts* by enterprises, the rule-making bodies are continually contemplating what the auditor's role is and how the resulting responsibility might be discharged.

Internal Audit

Although an independent CPA is engaged to perform an audit as the basis for rendering an opinion as to the fairness of an enterprise's financial statements, most large corporations maintain a staff of internal auditors as well. Typically such persons are positioned in the organizational structure in a manner which gives them relative autonomy, so to minimize any conflict of interest. The head of a company's internal audit group may even report directly to the chief executive officer, or to the board of directors.

Whereas the CPA is concerned with an enterprise's financial representations to third parties, an internal auditor's orientation is more managerial in nature. There is less of a concern with financial statements' fairness than with the company's operational efficiency. The CPA's audit occurs periodically while that of the internal auditor is continual; the CPA is apt to be satisfied with the determination that the enterprise has a satisfactory or adequate accounting system, whereas the internal auditor is likely to be more thorough and comprehensive in documenting strengths and weaknesses.

Internal auditors do not simply analyze expense accounts; they analyze activities and groups of accounts which reflect the results of these activities in order to evaluate profit-improvement or cost-reduction aspects. Internal auditors tend to apply deeper and broader analysis to their tests, and seek to think like an operating executive. Moreover, whereas a CPA's audit concentrates exclusively on matters having direct and unambiguous financial accounting implications, studies conducted by an internal audit group may look beyond conventional measures of performance and focus attention on non-financial and not easily quantifiable factors. Such a study is called an *operational* or *management audit*. Indeed, there even exists the notion of a *social audit* whereby the human dimension of activity becomes the focal point of the audit study.

The importance of granting independence to an enterprise's internal audit staff can be appreciated by considering the organizational structure of the Federal government whose internal audit agency is the General Accounting Office (GAO). The GAO is continually engaged in audit activities encompassing all facets of the Federal government. Organizationally, however, the GAO is accountable to the United States Congress, not to the President. Since it conducts audit examinations with a congressional mandate, it operates with relative impunity.

A noteworthy development during the 1970s was companies' creation of audit committees consisting of several non-management members of their boards of directors. Such a committee is vested with responsibilities related to the company's audit. An audit committee provides other directors with assurance that steps are being taken to objectively review managerial performance. Audit committees can also concern themselves with auditor selection, reviewing audit results, reviewing internal accounting and control procedures, selecting and establishing accounting policies, monitoring internal audit activity, and providing the independent CPA and the internal audit staff with access to the company's board of directors.

The Public Accounting Profession

To practice as a certified public accountant (CPA), candidates must be licensed by the board of public accountancy in the state in which they practice. Such boards are part of the state government, and they have the exclusive right to grant, suspend, and revoke CPA certificates. The eligibility requirements which must be met to become a CPA vary among states. They include educational background, and the required number of years of work experience, if any. Each of the jurisdictions requires that all prospective CPAs successfully complete a 2½-day uniform national examination. Many states also have mandatory continuing education requirements for CPAs as a prerequisite for renewing their licenses to practice.

The American Institute of Certified Public Accountants (AICPA) is a voluntary professional society whose activities include promulgating rules and guidelines for auditing, conducting continuing professional education programs, and serving as a spokesman for CPAs at large. Each of the states has a counterpart professional organization concerned with addressing state and local issues, interacting with the state's board of accountancy, and providing professional journal and/or technical meeting forums for members to exchange insights and ideas. These groups tend to call themselves associations, societies, or institutes, e.g., Maryland Association of CPAs, Massachusetts Society of CPAs, and Pennsylvania Institute of CPAs.

Auditor-Client Relations

A set of professional ethics exists for most CPAs at two levels. The AICPA code of professional ethics is probably the most visible ethics document, and it is promulgated on a national basis. Violation of any of its rules could result in the revocation of a CPA's membership in the AICPA—which says nothing about the individual's ability and right to practice public accounting per se. Thus, we come to the second level, namely, that of the rules of professional conduct incorporated into the statutes of the states. Typically, a state legislature uses the AICPA code of professional ethics as a model for its rules of conduct, but sometimes differences occur.

An important feature of CPAs' role as auditors is that, rather than acting as an advocate, their position is more akin to a jurist's. Whereas attorneys represent their clients' best interests, independent auditors in effect are dispatched by society to determine that companies' and other entities' presentations to external parties are made fairly. The awkward aspect of this relationship is that the auditor's fee is paid by the enterprise being audited, and therefore literally the enterprise is the auditor's client—although at a conceptual level it is unnamed third parties who are the auditors' ultimate client.

Some CPA firms, in addition to their traditional audit practice, also provide other client services. Tax planning and management consulting are notable types of activities in which CPAs strive to act in their clients' best interests. There are critics who question whether a CPA firm can simultaneously "wear two hats"—those of independent auditor and supportive counsellor.

The need for external auditors to be independent of their clients relates to a concern that they not subordinate their professional judgment to the views of their clients. As a result, if the auditor has a financial interest in a client enterprise, an audit opinion cannot be rendered. Another noteworthy aspect of the auditor-client relationship is that of privileged communication. Auditors are required to respect the confidentiality of data and information obtained in the course of carrying out their professional responsibilities. However, the courts have not extended to auditors the privilege of refusing to repeat communications of a client obtained in confidence. Cases in which the courts do respect confidentiality include those of physician-patient, lawyer-client, husband-wife, and clergyman-parishioner. Indeed, in 1975, a CPA cited by a Federal judge for contempt of court, was jailed for refusing to give to a Federal grand jury certain documents relating to possible tax fraud by a client.

Similar to the situation encountered by other persons who render professional services, CPAs are subjected to malpractice suits. A few CPAs have been indicted and convicted in criminal cases. With respect to civil suits, CPAs are liable for ordinary negligence—but the liability extends only to the client. In instances in which litigation is instituted by third-party users of client's financial statements, gross negligence or fraud must be proved.

Whereas fraud is the willful misstatement or omission of a material fact with the intent to deceive, gross negligence is the unintentional but nevertheless flagrant violation of generally accepted auditing standards. Three critical elements must occur: existence of misleading financial statements, incurrence of a loss by the plaintiff, and plaintiff reliance on the financial statements as the basis of the loss.[5] It appears that gross negligence would occur if the CPA expresses an audit opinion that financial statements are fairly presented when actually there is no basis for rendering such an opinion, or alternatively that the basis is so weak it is in fact unwarranted. Thus, it would be the rendering of an audit opinion for which there is inadequate underlying basis that would suggest the presence of gross negligence.

---

[5] Different criteria apply when federal securities laws are involved.

REGULATORY INFLUENCES

The accounting rules and practices which now prevail do so because they have the endorsement of the current private sector rulemaking body. This organization is called the Financial Accounting Standards Board (FASB) and it is located in Stamford, Connecticut. It was created in 1973, and operates as an autonomous entity. Although the FASB is acknowledged to be the premier rule-making body in accounting in the private sector, there are a number of other organizations which have assumed and/or are concurrently carrying out an active role in the promulgation of rules and regulations affecting accounting and financial reporting. The following examination of institutional influences on accounting considers the emergence and directions to date of the FASB, the traditional and current role of the Amercian Institute of CPAs, and the direct and indirect impact of governmental interest in financial accounting issues.

Financial Accounting Standards Board

Prior to 1973, the acceptability of particular accounting principles and practices was a matter in the jurisdiction of committees of the American Institute of CPAs (AICPA). The Financial Accounting Standards Board was created as a result of the recommendation of a blue-ribbon task force the AICPA itself had commissioned. Disillusionment in both the business and accounting communities had handicapped the AICPA-sponsored rule-makers—focusing on the fact that rule-making was vested solely in the AICPA and that its committee consisting of 18 part-time persons made it too unwieldy to be effective—so an autonomous organization was created.

Operational Aspects

The FASB consists of seven persons selected by the Financial Accounting Foundation. They serve on a full-time basis having severed all employment relationships with other organizations. Several of the members will generally have had extensive experience as practicing CPAs, and the other persons' backgrounds are in industry, government, and academe. The Board employs a research staff, and invites the input of interested parties on all matters.

Prospective topics for Board consideration are initially examined in a published discussion memorandum whose purpose is to identify all relevant facets of the matter at hand. It attempts to catalogue the different points of view and arguments, and on occasion it endeavors to recognize implications or possible consequences of different courses of action.

Position papers are solicited from interested parties followed by public

23

hearings where persons who wish to make an oral presentation have the opportunity to do so. The Board then considers these various inputs as well as research findings it may have commissioned. An exposure draft of a proposed Statement is then circulated among CPAs, investors, financial executives, and academicians. Responses to the exposure draft are considered, and either another draft or the final pronouncement is then disseminated. Copies of the various Board publications, including interpretations released from time to time, can be obtained from the FASB—either by subscription or on a piecemeal basis.

The power of FASB pronouncements manifests itself in the following manner. Companies desiring an audit by an independent auditor must engage the services of a CPA. CPAs, in turn, must adhere to the code of professional ethics incorporated into the statutes of the states which grant licenses to practice. One of the features of the AICPA code, which is the model on which states pattern their statutes, is that the pronouncements of the FASB constitute generally accepted accounting principles. Therefore, for CPAs to be able to express an opinion that financial statements are fairly presented, they must be prepared in accordance with FASB issuances; a departure can be justified if the CPA "can demonstrate that due to unusual circumstances the financial statements would otherwise have been misleading."[6]

Substantive Considerations

During the first six years of its existence, the FASB issued 29 Statements. Not unexpectedly, the FASB has been criticized by some for issuing too many pronouncements while others complain it has not been productive enough. Some maintain the Board is too conceptual in its approach to issues, while others claim that it is oblivious to time-honored accounting theory. Some assert the Board has been too drastic in effecting change, and others believe it has been too timid in imposing its views. Some feel the FASB's pronouncements are too broad, and others are critical because its Statements are too specific.

In addition, questions are raised whether the Board does in fact engage in a research-oriented approach to resolving accounting issues, whether it is sufficiently sensitive to the nuances of enterprises other than large, publicly-held corporations, and whether the Board is mindful of particular industries' apparent need for special accounting rules. Moreover, concern has been expressed about the absence of an appeal mechanism. The FASB's charter does not provide for appeal to some separate body that would formally hear, and possibly reverse, final pronouncements containing flaws. Underlying the

---

[6] *Restatement of the Code of Professional Ethics* (New York: American Institute of Certified Public Accountants, 1972), p. 22.

FASB concept is a philosophy that good-faith pronouncements, issued after deliberation, exposure, and comment, should stand as issued; subject to ongoing reconsideration by the Board itself in the light of experience.

The trend of FASB pronouncements during its first six years was toward leaner, more conservative balance sheets with immediate, rather than postponed, income statement recognition of events—particularly those which adversely affect earnings. Since 1975, research and development expenditures, rather than being reflected as assets, are recognized immediately as an expense. The introduction of formal "probable" and "estimable" tests when accounting for loss contingencies has resulted in sooner rather than later recognition of the earnings impact.[7] Foreign currency exchange gains and losses are recorded on the basis of the effect on monetary items of rate changes which may not even be realized as of the end of a fiscal period. A decline in the market value of marketable equity securities requires immediate loss recognition, and introduction of the *capital lease* concept resulted in more lease obligations disclosed among balance sheet liabilities than had been the pre-FASB experience.

Such issuances might be viewed as constituting a "back to basics" approach. The balance sheet may have been strengthened, and the income statement includes the effect of more happenings than had been the case in 1973. The impression one might well receive is that of a series of seemingly disparate pronouncements which in fact reflect the one common theme—of more stringent rules and more detailed disclosures.

American Institute of Certified Public Accountants

The American Institute of Certified Public Accountants (AICPA) is a professional society whose members comprise more than two-thirds of the nation's certified public accountants. Prior to 1973, the Institute had been vested with exclusive responsibility for the determination of what constitutes acceptable accounting practices and procedures. And with respect to the auditing standards to which CPAs adhere in the course of conducting audit examinations and rendering audit opinions, the AICPA has been and continues to be the sole organization exercising rule-making power in this area. The AICPA's authority to assume such responsibilities is derived from its membership's implicit desire to see it happen.

Accounting Research Bulletins

An Institute committee had issued some 42 Accounting Research Bulletins (ARBs) when in June, 1953 it published a restatement and revision of the

---

[7] Interestingly, the pronouncement, FASB Statement No. 5, had a different effect on accounting recognition of self-insurance provisions; this subject is discussed in Chapter 5.

earlier pronouncements: ARB No. 43. During the next six years, additional Bulletins were promulgated with the result that most of the matters contained in Bulletin Nos. 43 through 51 remain in effect today. Among the accounting practices and procedures set forth in these ARBs, which to this day remain as their definitive source, are the required lower-of-cost-or-market rule for inventory valuation, the recommended preparation of consolidated financial statements, and the alternative methods which may be used to account for long-term construction-type contracts.

Accounting Principles Board

In 1959, the AICPA created a new committee called the Accounting Principles Board (APB). This group, whose size varied from 17 to 21 persons, was founded on the premise it would adopt more of a research-based orientation than had been the practice of its predecessor. Indeed, the Board proceeded to commission the preparation of Accounting Research Studies with the intention of using particular studies as the basis for issuing pronouncements. Some 15 Studies were published in the series, and a number of these dealt with topics on which the Board subsequently issued pronouncements.

The APB's pronouncements were called Opinions, of which there were 31 issuances during its 14-year life. The FASB views APB Opinions as constituting "generally accepted accounting principles" although some have since been superseded by other official pronouncements. In addition to Opinions, the Board also issued Statements, and the staff of the AICPA published Interpretations, neither of which were official requirements. However, it was the APB's Opinions which had to be adhered to by AICPA members that represented the primary purpose of its activity.

Even though the Board consisted exclusively of AICPA members, the professional orientation and mode of full-time employment of these individuals were varied. Early in the history of the APB, it was decided each of the eight largest international CPA firms (hereafter, the Big Eight firms) would be represented on the Board. Looking at its membership during its later years gives us an indication of the APB's average "mix": eight of the members represented the Big Eight firms, six men represented CPA firms other than the Big Eight, two members were in industry, and two were university professors.

The APB did make some very substantive contributions to the development of accounting and financial reporting. Among its most momentous pronouncements, which remain in effect in virtually unaltered form to this day, are those which introduced definitive rules in the areas of pension cost accrual, disclosure of extraordinary components of income, interperiod tax allocation, earnings per share, intercorporate investments, the statement of changes in financial position, accounting changes, and disclosure of accounting policies. The demise of the Board was in large part attributable to an increasing belief by members of the business and investment communities that the promulgation of accounting principles was too critical an activity to be delegated to a large, part-time committee of CPAs.

AcSEC and AudSEC

With the 1973 advent of the Financial Accounting Standards Board, the AICPA created a senior technical committee to serve as its official policy-setting body on financial accounting and reporting matters. Known as the Accounting Standards Executive Committee (AcSEC), this group issues Statements of Position on an intermittent basis, and submits to external rule-making bodies input to assist in the development of official pronouncements.

In the area of auditing rules—for which the AICPA has exclusive private-sector authority to issue official pronouncements—it maintains a senior committee called the Auditing Standards Executive Committee (AudSEC). This group publishes Statements of Auditing Standards—the first of which is an edited compilation of a predecessor committee's many pronouncements. AudSEC's issuances tend to spell out guideline approaches and procedures for auditors to follow in conducting an audit examination and rendering an audit opinion. Some of the issues it considered in recent years have included responsibility for the detection of fraud, disclosure of illegal acts by clients, the requirement to obtain a client representation letter, and required communication of material weaknesses in internal accounting controls.

Federal Government

The direct influence of the Federal government on accounting and financial reporting comes primarily from three sources: the Internal Revenue Service (IRS), the Securities and Exchange Commission (SEC), and the Congress. Their influence on accounting differs in the sense that the IRS influence is probably inevitable, the SEC impact is actually mandated by statute, and the Congressional involvement is the most ominous in its implications.

Internal Revenue Service

Contrary to the popular misconception among many lay persons, accounting is a significantly distinct area of interest from that of tax law. Because the determination of a taxpayer's income tax liability is necessarily based to a large extent on accounting data, it is not unusual for some accountants to also render tax-related professional services. However, whereas accounting is based on rules for which there are presumably conceptually valid underlying reasons, the regulations comprising the Federal tax system are the end result of a variety of factors which can include, but are not limited to, public policy, equity, subsidization, the creation of incentives and disincentives, legalities, and accounting principles. As a result, the mere presence of a particular regulation in the fabric of tax law does not in any way suggest it is equally appropriate in an accounting context as well.

Accordingly, tax law has relatively little direct influence on accounting. Probably the most notable instance of cause-and-effect is the Last-in, First-out (LIFO) method of estimating the cost of an enterprise's inventory as of the end of a fiscal period. Although this is a subject afforded considerable attention later in this volume (in Chapter 6), suffice it to observe that this method became an acceptable method for accounting purposes only after it had been incorporated into tax law; in other words, LIFO's roots are in Federal tax regulations. Interestingly, the reason LIFO did eventually become acceptable for financial reporting as well is because the tax law mandated it be that way. Using LIFO for tax purposes in a period of price inflation results in lower taxable income and, therefore, a lower tax obligation than if another estimation method were used, and simultaneous use of some other approach for financial reporting purposes would result in relatively higher reported earnings. The tax law, therefore, requires that taxpayers who elect LIFO for tax purposes use it for financial accounting as well.

Indirect influences of the tax law on accounting is generally limited to two types. First, there is the case of a specific method acceptable for tax purposes which taxpayers, in turn, elect for financial accounting as well; such as the double-declining method of measuring depreciation expense. The other influence of tax law is even more indirect, namely, the effect income tax considerations can have on the manner in which accountable transactions are structured. As an example, for a business combination to qualify as a tax-free exchange, certain characteristics must be present—features which can also affect the applicability of the pooling of interests method of accounting. Alternatively, if a combination is recorded by the purchase method, the excess of purchase price over owners' equity acquired poses the challenge of having to assign the excess to assets whose subsequent use would generate tax reductions—as opposed to either (1) land, for which there would be no tax benefit until its disposition, or (2) goodwill, which has no favorable tax consequences at all.

Securities and Exchange Commission

The Securities and Exchange Commission (SEC) was created during the 1930s to administer laws designed to protect the general public in securities transactions. Although the scope of its jurisdiction extends far beyond that of accounting, our concern is limited to the impact of the SEC on accountants and accounting rules. The Commission's primary medium for issuing accounting-related rules is through its Regulation S–X, amendments to which are issued in the form of Accounting Series Releases.

When a corporation proposes to issue securities to the general public, it must file a *registration statement* with the SEC, and it must provide each prospective investor with a *prospectus*. Once issued, the company must annually submit a *Form 10-K* report to the Commission, and it must give each of the investors an *annual report*. All four of these documents must include financial statements prepared in accordance with generally accepted accounting principles (GAAP) audited by an independent CPA.

The SEC is legally empowered to impose accounting principles on publicly held companies in its jurisdiction. However, with respect to financial statements given directly to investors, it has as a general rule deferred to existing generally accepted accounting principles (GAAP), as promulgated by the FASB. But with respect to registration statements and annual Form 10-K submissions made directly to the SEC, its Regulation S–X sets forth specific accounting requirements typically more rigorous than those of GAAP. The Commission also specifies certain disclosure rules for prospectuses and annual reports as well as rules governing auditor-client relationships.

With respect to the SEC's oversight relationship with accounting, there is an important distinction between its *macro* and *micro* dimensions. At the *macro* accounting profession/accounting discipline level, the Commission's role encompasses expressing its approval or disapproval of particular practices and modes of operation. But at the *micro* level, which entails reviewing particular corporations' financial statements, the SEC does not perform an endorsement or ratification function, that is, that a company is financially sound or that its securities represent a good investment opportunity. Instead, the SEC merely satisfies itself as to the adequacy of the disclosures—in terms of their completeness and their lucidity.

With respect to accounting principles and methods, three types of SEC involvement can be discerned. First, there are instances in which the Commission introduces requirements when the private-sector rule-making bodies had failed to do so. Examples include preparation of the statement of changes in financial position prior to the issuance of APB Opinion No. 19, reporting of product line revenue and profit data prior to the issuance of FASB Statement No. 14, and causing prior period adjustments to be restricted for all intents and purposes to the *correction of an error* prior to the issuance of FASB Statement No. 16.

A second manifestation of SEC influence is that of superimposing additional reporting requirements on existing GAAP. For example, APB Opinion No. 31 had set forth certain disclosure requirements whereby long-term lessees were required to identify the dollar amount of subsequent years' rent expense commitments, on a year-by-year and five-year groupings basis. The SEC added the requirement that for SEC-submission purposes, there also be disclosure of the present value of the future lease liability as well as the current year's earnings on the basis of the leases having in fact been capitalized. Another example of the SEC proceeding beyond a private-sector pronouncement also concerned accounting for leases. FASB Statement No. 13 established an approach to accounting for leases which had a rather pervasive effect on the way many existing leases had to be accounted for. The FASB therefore provided a four-year gestation period with respect to applying its pronouncement retroactively, only to have the SEC reduce the interval for SEC submissions to one year. A third example is the SEC requirement, relating to accounting changes (the subject of APB Opinion No. 20), that the company's independent auditor submit a letter to the Commission stating whether or not its change to an alternative acceptable accounting principle is preferable under the circumstances.

The third type of SEC involvement is that of issuing a pronouncement which for all intents and purposes preempts an official position adopted by the private-sector rule making body. There have been only two instances of this. One is the case of the financial Accounting Standards Board's 1974 issuance of an exposure draft of a proposed Statement establishing accounting and disclosure rules with respect to constant dollar accounting. As the FASB was conducting its deliberations, the Commission issued a rule which required qualifying large publicly held companies to disclose selected "current cost" data as part of their annual submission to the SEC. The other relates to the matter of accounting for oil and gas exploration costs. The SEC in August, 1978 issued a set of rules having the effect of supplanting FASB Statement No. 19 which had been promulgated eight months earlier.

The interface between the SEC and accountants in the private sector reflects several different but interrelated phenomena. The Commission, as a matter of policy, is supportive of private sector rule-making despite its being legally empowered to regulate accounting practices. At the time the Financial Accounting Standards Board was created in 1973, the SEC issued Accounting Series Release No. 150 which reaffirmed its traditional position that financial statements based on accounting methods for which there is no substantial authoritative support are presumed to be misleading. The Release also stated that pronouncements of the FASB would be viewed as constituting "substantial authoritative support."

The SEC has expressed the opinion that different readers published financial statements have need for different types of information. Whereas the lay investor's need for information can be satisfied with rather basic types of disclosure, a sophisticated analyst demands and is capable of assimilating a greater degree of detail. Causal readers presumably limit their understanding to that which appears in a company's annual report to stockholders while more discriminating users are prepared to expose themselves to the more extensive data which are contained in accessible Form 10-K type of material. Given the validity of this distinction, the SEC apparently feels obligated to require that more extensive disclosures be available for persons for whom additional insights would result.

The Commission's oversight responsibilities with respect to accounting are not limited to financial statement principles and procedures. The scope of its activity encompasses the auditor-client relationship as well. For instance, the SEC has established rules which define what constitutes an auditor's independence—rules which are more rigorous than those set forth in the AICPA code of professional ethics. The SEC is also empowered to issue sanctions against companies and their independent auditors for irregularities in financial statements, which in the case of CPAs can result in temporary or permanent suspension from practicing before the Commission.

The SEC has also embraced the concepts of *continual reporting* and *auditor of record*. *Continual reporting* refers to the obligation of publicly held companies to report to pertinent external parties on a regular and continuing basis. This is accomplished through media such as quarterly reporting of selected accounting data and submissions to the SEC to disclose on a current basis the recording of extraordinary charges and credits. *Auditor of record* refers to the notion that a company's independent auditor, rather than merely attesting to the fairness of its annual financial statements, is viewed as associated with its continual reporting obligation. The SEC also established a rule in 1971 which states that when a company changes independent auditors, it is required to report to the Commission any disagreements over accounting or auditing matters that occurred before the change.[8]

Congress

When the Securities and Exchange Commission was created, Congress delegated to it the authority to establish accounting principles as they should apply to publicly held enterprises. The SEC, in turn, delegated authority to private sector rule-making bodies although in continues to exert oversight responsibility. Despite this modus operandi, Congress has become involved on an ad hoc basis with selected accounting issues affecting American companies.

One notable instance was that of the 1971 investment tax credit controversy. When this question had risen in 1962, the Accounting Principles Board (APB) issued a pronouncement which for all intents and purposes was subsequently amended largely because of SEC pressure. The investment tax

---

[8] During the first four and one half years that the rule was in effect, about 10 percent of the 1,667 changes were associated with disagreements, and over half of the disagreements related to the recoverability of the cost of some or all assets and to timing of revenue or expense recognition.

credit ceased to exist several years later only to be reintroduced in legislation proposed in 1971. This time, the APB obtained the support of the SEC, whereupon it proceeded to issue an exposure draft of its proposed Opinion. Many financial executives and accountants were disappointed to learn of the APB's action. When the United States Senate enacted the legislation reestablishing the investment tax credit, it included a provision stating that no taxpayer could be required to account for the credit in accordance with any particular method to the exclusion of all other approaches. The obvious effect of this Congressional action was to preempt the APB—needless to say, much to the Board's consternation.

Congressional involvement in accounting principles surfaced again in 1975 when the Energy Policy and Conservation Act was enacted. In part, the Act empowered the SEC either to prescribe accounting rules for companies which produce crude oil or natural gas, or to decide to rely on rules promulgated by the Financial Accounting Standards Board; such rules would have to be determined within a 24-month period. The SEC, in turn, indicated it would defer to the FASB to develop accounting procedures in this area.

Within the designated time interval, the FASB issued an exposure draft of a proposed pronouncement which set forth definitive rules in this area. The gist of the proposal was that an existing method of accounting for unsuccessful exploration expenditures would no longer be acceptable; it was an approach which had the potential of significantly reducing some companies' reported earnings. The SEC indicated shortly thereafter that it endorsed the FASB's conclusions and, in fact, it proceeded to make plans for immediate implementation of the new rules.

Fifteen days after the conclusion of the exposure period of the proposed FASB pronouncement, the United States Senate passed by voice vote on amendment to its earlier Act. The amendment stated the accounting rules envisioned by the Act would apply only to the development of accounting practices required for the preparation of reports to be filed with the Department of Energy for use in compiling a reliable energy data base, and that it should not be construed to establish or to affect the establishment of generally accepted accounting principles for financial reporting purposes.

Although the amendment was never actually incorporated into law,[9] its potential impact was momentous. In the view of some persons, its effect threatened to undermine the very integrity of the FASB, indeed of rule-making by private sector as well as public sector bodies in general. The message it conveyed was that, irrespective of what rules are promulgated through recognized and accepted media, the United States Congress is, in effect, a court of last resort. Parties whose vested interests are threatened by

---

[9] The accounting sequel to this episode is described in Chapter 7.

the FASB, the SEC, or any other official body, need only look to Congress for vindication.

This involvement by Congress was particularly anomalous in light of staff reports that had been issued by two of its subcommittees. An October 1976 report published by a House of Representatives subcommittee chaired by Congressman John E. Moss had been especially critical of nonuniformity in generally accepted accounting principles. Two months later, a Senate sub-committee, chaired by the late Senator Lee Metcalf, distributed a staff report bearing the title "The Accounting Establishment."[10] The report's general tone questioned the structure of accounting institutions—most pointedly the FASB, SEC, American institute of CPAs, and the eight largest international CPA firms. In addition, there was criticism of corporations having substantial discretion in choosing among alternative accounting standards to report similar business transactions. The report recommended that government bodies should establish accounting principles and auditing standards, gov-ernment agencies should inspect CPAs' work and set ethical standards, and CPAs' exposure to litigation should be broadened. After hearing 39 witnesses testify at its public hearings, the subcommittee issued a report in 1977[11] which proposed changes considerably more palatable to most CPAs and the various organizations responsible for the development of accounting rules.

Private sector reaction to the Metcalf and Moss subcommittees' reports ranged from indignation to acknowledgement that certain institutional re-forms warranted consideration. Despite what changes in substance or in form may have resulted, the most significant aspect of these two reports was that accounting and financial reporting had been initiated into the realm of public policy.

SUMMARY

The theme of this chapter's coverage of the institutional framework of accounting might best be summarized by the following observation of the aforementioned U.S. Senate subcommittee:

> The position of independent auditor is vital to the successful functioning of the Nation's economy, with its many competing interests. Confidence in finan-cial information is a key element in our economy's operation. The independent auditor's role is especially important for publicly owned corporations because

[10] Subcommittee on Reports, Accounting and Management of the United States Senate Committee on Government Operations—A Staff Study, The Accounting Establishment (Wash-ington: U.S. Government Printing Office, 1976).

[11] Subcommittee on Reports, Accounting and Management of the United States Senate Committee on Governmental Affairs, Improving the Accountability of Publicly Owned Corpora-tions and Their Auditors (Washington: U.S. Government Printing Office, 1977).

33

investors and other interested parties are generally far removed from the actual operations of such businesses, and must rely heavily on information reported publicly under the Federal securities laws to support their economic decisions.

The role of independent auditor for publicly owned corporations is analogous to that of an umpire in sports. Like the umpire, an auditor must perform his or her responsibilities in a manner which assures all interested parties that the opinion given is competent and unbiased. The independent auditor provides that assurance by applying standards established fairly, by forming an opinion using professional expertise and judgment, and by strictly maintaining his or her independence.

Standards that are established fairly may not satisfy everyone affected by their application, but all interested parties should be able to agree that the process of establishing such standards is sound and does not favor any particular interest.[12]

The rule-making environment is as dynamic as the institutions and circumstances with which it is concerned. Dramatic changes have occurred in the manner in which accounting rules are formulated—in terms of who promulgates the rules, the constituencies whose interests are considered, and the very means through which their conclusions are communicated. Although each passing year's developments may provide more insightful understanding of the dynamics of rule-making, increasing numbers of new issues invariably present themselves—but this too is an integral part of the situation's vigorous nature. It is in this sense that rather than considering this chapter as a description of the current *state of affairs,* it should be viewed as the presentation of a historical perspective, that is, a framework with which the nature and thrust of subsequent changes might be better appreciated.

Additional Readings

American Accounting Association Committee on Basic Auditing Concepts. *A Statement of Basic Auditing Concepts.* Sarasota, Fla.: American Accounting Association, 1973.

Beaver, William H. "What Should Be the FASB's Objectives." *The Journal of Accountancy* (August 1973), pp. 49–56.

Benston, George J. "The Value of the SEC's Accounting Disclosure Requirements." *The Accounting Review* (July 1969), pp. 515–32.

Benston, George J. *Corporate Financial Disclosure in the UK and the USA.* Lexington, Mass.: Lexington Books, 1976.

Burns, Thomas J., ed. *Accounting in Transition: Oral Histories of Recent U.S. Experience.* Columbus, Ohio: College of Administrative Science of The Ohio State University, 1974.

---

[12] Ibid., pp. 6–7.

Carmichael, D. R. *The Auditor's Reporting Obligation.* New York: American Institute of Certified Public Accountants, 1972.

The Commission on Auditor's Responsibilities: Report, Conclusions and Recommendations. New York: American Institute of Certified Public Accountants, 1978.

Keller, Thomas F., and Zeff, Stephen A. "'Postulates' and 'Principles': Research Methodologies." In *Financial Accounting Theory II–Issues and Controversies,* edited by Thomas F. Keller and Stephen A. Zeff. New York: McGraw-Hill Book Co., 1969.

Kripke, Homer. "A Search for a Meaningful Securities Disclosure Policy." *The Arthur Andersen Chronicle* (July 1976), pp. 14–32.

Mautz, R. K., and Newmann, F. L. *Corporate Audit Committees: Policies and Practices.* Cleveland: Ernst & Ernst, 1977.

Mautz, R. K., and Sharaf, Hussein A. *The Philosophy of Auditing.* Sarasota, Fla.: American Accounting Association, 1966.

Meyer, Philip E. "The APB's Independence and Its Implications for the FASB." *Journal of Accounting Research* (Spring 1974), pp. 188–96.

Moonitz, Maurice. *Obtaining Agreement on Standards in the Accounting Profession.* Sarasota, Fla.: American Accounting Association, 1974.

Previts, Gary John. "The SEC and Its Chief Accountants: Historical Impressions." *The Journal of Accountancy* (August 1978), pp. 83–91.

Skousen, K. Fred. *An Introduction to the SEC.* Cincinnati: South-Western Publishing Co., 1976.

Solomons, David. "The Politicization of Accounting." *The Journal of Accountancy* (November 1978), pp. 65–72.

Spacek, Leonard. "The Need for an Accounting Court." *The Accounting Review* (July 1958), pp. 368–79.

Storey, Reed K. *The Search for Accounting Principles.* Houston: Scholars Book Co., 1977 (originally published—New York: American Institute of Certified Public Accountants, 1964).

Study on Establishment of Accounting Principles. *Establishing Financial Accounting Principles.* New York: American Institute of Certified Public Accountants, 1972.

Subcommittee on Reports, Accounting and Management of the Committee on Government Operations of the United States Senate—A Staff Study. *The Accounting Establishment.* Washington: U.S. Government Printing Office, 1976.

Vatter, William J. "Obstacles to the Specification of Accounting Principles." In *Research in Accounting Measurement,* edited by Robert K. Jaedicke, Yuji Ijiri, and Oswald Nielsen. Sarasota, Fla.: American Accounting Association, 1966, pp. 71–87.

3

The Conceptual Basis
of Accounting

The most widespread term used to signify the body of accounting dicta and rules is *generally accepted accounting principles,* which is
sometimes referred to simply as *GAAP.* From a historical point of view, one
could characterize much of *generally accepted accounting principles* as
having a common-law type of origin, with only the accounting developments of recent decades being statutory in nature. In fact, the system as we
know it today might well be viewed as a conglomeration of assumptions,
doctrines, tenets, and conventions. As particular elements are examined below, their respective qualities are identified accordingly.

Writers in the professional and academic literature of accounting have
attempted to define and examine the various components of the GAAP
model. Such endeavors have proceeded in two directions: (1) intensive anal-
yses of particular elements and (2) extensive examinations of the aggregate
collection of elements. With respect to the latter approach, the typical
contribution has been cast in the form of a pyramid-shaped hierarchy of
broad postulates, less expansive principles, and a series of well-defined procedures.

To engage in a review of the relative merits of classifying a particular
element as a postulate or a principle, or as a subset of another element,
would not yield the insight needed to realize our objectives. As a result, the
ensuing discussion identifies and examines the particular roles played by the
key elements of GAAP. It affords no attention as such to whether the inclusion
or exclusion of a particular item conforms to or can be reconciled with each
and every classification scheme set forth at one time or another. Moreover,

the component elements of GAAP are not mutually exclusive. Indeed, the very fact a particular transaction may be cited as exemplifying two or three of its different elements indicates the dynamic nature of GAAP. Equally important is the recognition that in certain instances, inconsistencies may exist among GAAP's components. Ten elements of *generally accepted accounting principles* are now examined to provide an understanding of the concepts underlying accounting and financial reporting.

THE ACCOUNTING ENTITY

The entity concept of accounting relates to the identity of the matter or activity for which an accounting is to occur, and the relationship assumed to exist between the entity and external parties. An entity is any area of economic interest to a particular individual or group whose identity and essential character are separable from those having an interest in it. The concept of an entity can transcend the individual business firm. A nation's economy can be viewed as constituting an entity with its resulting gross national product, balance of payments statement, and so forth; and each of the economy's various sectors—business, consumers, government, and foreign interests—can be viewed as distinct entities. An industry can also be viewed as an entity, e.g., automobile manufacture, aerospace, steel production, airlines, and so forth.

Although the legally constituted business corporation is the entity which generally receives most attention, a hierarchy can be identified within a single business firm. At the base of the hierarchical pyramid are *accounts* where the effect of specific transactions are segregated into homogeneous groupings. At the apex of the hierarchy is the notion of an *economic* entity composed of a legally distinct parent corporation consolidated with autonomous subsidiary companies in which it holds controlling interests. As will be discussed in Chapter 9, by consolidating the financial statements of these affiliated companies, a single all-inclusive financial report can be, and often is, prepared for users external to the economic entity.

Contained within the hierarchy are various *responsibility centers,* each a defined area of responsibility. The center may be responsible for performing some function, which is its output, and for using resources to perform this function. Responsibility centers may consist of a number of cost centers; a cost center being a meaningful organizational unit for which costs are accumulated, such as a department within a manufacturing plant. A responsibility center could also be a specific long-term contract, a factory job order, a product line, an operating division, a sales office, or even particular sales personnel.

A critical aspect of the concept of the accounting entity is that the defined unit be viewed as autonomous. Parties interacting with the entity are independent of it, whether their relationship is one of stockholder, employee, or customer. To illustrate, although it has been suggested that there is a mutuality of interests between a business organization and its owners, the concept of a self-contained accounting entity would preclude such an approach affecting accounting practices. For example, even though a corporation's earnings represent an increase in its stockholders' equity in the corporate assets, individual stockholders may not recognize their proportionate share as income.[1] Shareholders are distinct from the business entity and can therefore recognize as income only those assets distributed as dividends. Similarly, when existing shareholders sell their shares of stock to other parties at amounts which differ from that which the corporation itself realized upon the shares' initial issuance, the corporation does not recognize the changed market value of its shares. This is because the corporation is distinct from its stockholders, and from an accounting point of view it is not affected by transactions in which it is not a direct party.

Even in the realm of the closely held corporation, the concept of accounting entity has relevance. Salary payments to employees who are also owners are properly accounted for as a business expense, that is, as a determinant rather than as a distribution of income. This is because the enterprise—as an independent entity—has well-defined transactions with a variety of other entities. Each owner, in effect, becomes two entities: an employee entity and an investor-in-capital entity.

To make the point at an even more personalized level, consider the case of a person who was unable to reconcile his monthly bank statement balance with the end-of-month amount appearing in his check register because of his belief there was some kind of contradiction in recording checks payable to himself—with the result such checks were never even recorded. What the person overlooked was that his cash-in-bank balance was one self-contained entity, that the amount of his cash-on-hand constituted a separate entity, and the transactions between these two entities require an accounting. Reference to the accounting literature indicates the entity is variously regarded as a proprietary unit, an economic unit, a managerial unit, a social unit, and a collection of rights and restrictions on their exercise.

DUALITY

Duality is a term used to signify that an important feature of accounting is the double character or nature of many of its pervasive conventions. This

---

[1] Although in theory, sole proprietorships and partnerships are also distinct accounting entities, some accounting conventions that are used in practice do reflect the notion of "mutuality."

gives rise to the double-entry bookkeeping format. Its nature is that every accountable event is perceived to have two dimensions—as reflected by a debit and a credit. There is nothing inherently "good" or "bad" about an item being a debit or a credit. Indeed, the very notion of a debit denoting the left side of an account and a credit pertaining to its right side is merely a convention. Its validity is neither superior nor inferior to that baseball convention which states that on hitting the ball, the batter runs to first base rather than toward third base. The terms *debit* and *credit* have become part of the vernacular in the sense a retail establishment *credits* accounts when merchandise is returned. Customers view this as being "good—as the retailer has thereby reduced its accounts receivable asset because the amount due has declined. A credit memorandum received from one's bank is also looked upon favorably—because the bank thereby increases its deposits liability to the customer.

At a more substantive level, consider the apparent anomaly resulting from the fact only asset and expense accounts are increased with debit entries. One might question this commonality on the grounds that asset growth is "desirable" while expense growth is "undesirable." Such a conclusion results from imputing "good" and "bad" qualities to debits and credits. In fact, assets and expenses do have a common focal point, a subtle one.

Both assets and expenses refer to economic resources in the entity's domain. Whereas an asset represents an economic resource having future service potential, an expense measures an economic resource whose service potential has already expired. This, in turn, suggests most assets have the potential to become expenses and that expenses at one time had been assets. Both these observations have merit. Whereas monetary assets' utility lies in their ability to buy economic resources and to reduce liabilities incurred to acquire economic resources, the function of nonmonetary assets is to provide the wherewithal to engage in revenue-producing transactions which will earn a profit and increase the enterprise's owners' equity. As these assets are used, that is, as their future service potential is consumed, they are reclassified—transformed, as it were—into expenses.

By the same token, any amount categorized as expense will have been an asset at one time. Sold merchandise is an example of this: what was once an Inventory asset, upon sale appears as Cost of Goods Sold among an income statement's expenses. Less evident perhaps is the case of wages expense, for it too had been an asset. This can be appreciated if one recognizes the work performed by an employee creates the wherewithal for the enterprise to earn revenue. That intangible contribution is therefore an asset, because it is an economic resource having service potential. Once that service potential is exhausted through the generation of revenue, the service potential's "future" quality expires and an expense is recognized. This is the case whether the transformation from future to past happens immediately, such as a technician repairing one's electrical appliance for a fee, or whether the transformation is postponed, such as a technician working on an assembly line in an automobile plant.

The Accounting Equation

The basic accounting equation is Assets equal Equities. It relates to an entity's economic resources having future service potential, that is, assets, and is used to express pertinent aspects about an entity's financial position. One of the objectives of accounting is to measure financial position whose components of wealth might include only very liquid assets such as cash and investments in marketable securities or it might include other types of assets as well, such as real estate holdings, diamonds, and durable goods.

The fact of the matter is that the mere possession or formal "ownership" of such economic resources does not necessarily define the entity's owners' equity, because it only sets forth the "gross" worth. In other words, to the extent that an entity has liabilities, its owners' equity becomes its gross worth net of its liabilities. The equities side of the accounting equation depicts the respective equities of various equityholders in the entity's assets.[2] Under the traditional proprietary conception of the accounting equation, the relationship is expanded as follows:

1. Assets equal Equities
2. Assets equal Liabilities plus Owners' Equity
3. Assets less Liabilities equal Owners' Equity

Other conceptions include:

4. Assets equal Sources of Assets
5. Assets equal Restrictions upon Assets
6. Resources over Which Managers Have Command equal Resources over Which Investors Have Command

The notion of an accounting equation is a basic feature of the accounting model. That a variety of conceptions as to its precise nature should exist by no means detracts from the equation's innate importance. If anything, the very fact a diversity of viewpoints does exist only reinforces the central role the equation does indeed play in the structure of contemporary accounting.

Position and Flow

The accounting equation becomes the focal point for communicating information about an accounting entity's financial position. Indeed, insight

---

[2] See Philip E. Meyer, "The Accounting Entity," *Abacus* (December 1973), pp. 116–26.

into an enterprise's financial position as of a particular point in time is one of the functions of accounting. A balance sheet is analogous to a snapshot in the sense it is static rather than dynamic; it conveys an impression of phenomena as they exist at one particular moment—with no message whatsoever about how or why they differ from what had been the situation previously.

As a result of the nature of a balance sheet, or any snapshot-type of information, there is a need to also have financial statements which relate to changes over time and performance during particular time intervals— a movie-film type of communication medium. The two primary flow-type financial statements prepared therefore to complement the balance sheet are the income, or earnings, statement and the statement of changes in financial position. The income statement, unlike the balance sheet, has a *dynamic* quality in the sense it depicts the enterprise's performance over a defined time period. Its objective is to set forth revenues, expenses, gains, and losses in a manner which permits the derivation of net income—the measure of the net increase in owners' equity resulting from operations and other causes. Conversely, the net loss is a measure of the net decrease in owners' equity resulting from operations and other causes. The statement of changes in financial position, on the other hand, relates to how a period's transactions affect the enterprise's liquidity; the statement is discussed at length in Chapter 11.

THE GOING-CONCERN ASSUMPTION

The accounting model assumes the business entity is a going concern. This means there is an expectation the enterprise will continue to operate in perpetuity; it is therefore sometimes referred to as the *continuity* assumption. Its presence within the framework of GAAP accounting has a variety of implications. Perhaps its most pervasive contribution is that of justifying the inclusion of non-cash assets in the balance sheet. In the definition of an asset—that it is an economic resource having future service potential—the feature which distinguishes an asset from an expense is its expected service potential in the future; this of course assumes there will be a future during which the enterprise will realize the said service potential.

The going-concern assumption is sometimes cited to counter proposed modifications of the existing cost method of recording and disclosing an entity's assets. In particular, some advocates of a current value basis of accounting suggest that current value might be measured in terms of assets' realizable value. Proponents of a historical cost basis, in turn, argue the notion of realizable value would violate the going concern assumption because to view all assets at their realizable value would imply that the enterprise would

41

no longer be an ongoing entity. A counter argument is that since "going concern" relates to the entity at large, it does not preclude valuing a particular asset at its realizable value.

Another ramification of the going-concern assumption relates to the attest function performed by independent auditors as a result of which an audit report is rendered containing the CPA's opinion as to the fairness of the financial statements. One of the factors traditionally the basis for either a qualified opinion or a disclaimer of opinion is whether the company can be characterized as a going concern. This can be best understood by considering the following example.

A company operated a commercial television station as one of its primary lines of business. At the time it sought to renew its operating license, the Federal Communications Commission decided to grant the broadcasting rights to another corporation. The existing licensee contested the matter through litigation, and was permitted to continue operating the station until a final verdict was rendered. As subsequent appeals were denied, serious doubt arose whether the company would win its case and thus continue to operate as a viable enterprise. Accordingly, even though all the components of its financial position and operating results were fairly presented, the CPA's audit opinion was qualified. The nature of the qualification was that the financial statements were fairly presented subject to the favorable outcome of the litigation. If an adverse verdict were to occur with the result that the operating license would be relinquished, the assumption of being a going concern, underlying the financial statements, would be invalid.

It is apparent the assumption of going concern is one of the pervasive elements of the traditional accounting model. In one context, it suggests certain things about the capitalization and valuation of particular assets. Yet, at the organization-at-large level, it introduces a dimension to auditing which requires consideration of factors other than those which are solely technical in nature.

CONSERVATISM

The word *conservative* suggests a certain predisposition in attitude or a sense of cautiousness in one's behavior, but it has somewhat different connotations when applied to different aspects of life. It is a designation which might apply to one's wardrobe style, political persuasion, fiscal management habits, or appreciation of traditional values. Although the term is associated with accountants and accounting, there is often a reluctance to acknowledge it as an integral part of accounting, at least in a normative sense. However, on examining the whys and wherefores of accounting assumptions, conventions, and practices as they have evolved, a distinctive conservative nature can be discerned.

Accounting conservatism has been portrayed by the expression "anticipate no profit and provide for all possible losses." This characterization might be viewed as the reactive version of the *minimax* managerial philosophy, that is, minimize the chance of maximum losses. The concept of accounting conservatism suggests that when and where uncertainty and risk exposure so warrant, accounting takes a wary and watchful stance until the appearance of evidence to the contrary. Accounting conservatism does not mean to intentionally understate income and assets; it applies only to situations in which there are reasonable doubts.

The required use of the historical cost basis of accounting is viewed by some as being the classic example of accounting conservatism. When the current value of an economic resource exceeds its historical cost, companies are not permitted to revalue upward the original recorded amount. It is accounting conservatism, among other considerations, which precludes recognizing appreciation of value until it is realized in an arm's length transaction. However, conservatism also says that if an asset's current value is *less* than its historical cost, a downward adjustment can be required, most notably, use of the lower-of-cost-or-market method in accounting for both inventory and investments in marketable equity securities.

The very definition by which expenditures qualify for capitalization as balance sheet assets suggests a conservative orientation. The requirement than non-reimbursable research and development costs may not be recorded as assets irrespective of a company's belief that future benefits will result, the rule that development stage enterprises may not use less rigorous criteria for determining whether an expenditure is to be treated as an asset or as an expense than those which apply to relatively mature enterprises, and the FASB's intention that exploration costs associated with unsuccessful efforts to develop oil and gas reserves not be capitalized as part of the cost of successful efforts, all have as their common theme the conservative notion that unless and until an investment has demonstrable benefits extending beyond the current fiscal period, treatment as an asset is inappropriate.

This conservative strain is alo evident in the manner in which corporations account for the deferred benefit of an income tax operating loss carryforward balance. The U.S. Federal tax laws permit a taxpayer to reduce subsequent years' taxable income by an amount equal to the given year's tax loss. Unless a company is "assured beyond a reasonable doubt" it will realize the carryforward benefit before its expiration (currently of seven-year duration), it may not reflect this economic resource as an asset in its current balance sheet.

Financial statement recognition of *appropriated* retained earnings is an example of conservatism relating more to disclosure than to accounting measurement. Its role is to signify to readers of a company's balance sheet that a certain amount of its assets are earmarked for some restricted purpose—either at the company's discretion or imposed by an external party such as bondholders. The disclosure of such a restriction indicates that although retained earnings may be a valid measure of cumulative internal growth of owners' equity, assets equal to the designated *appropriation* may not currently be available for distribution as dividends.

There are instances of transactions whose required accounting reflects conservative influence, although a variety of other components of generally accepted accounting principles are relevant, if not dominant, as well. Required early recognition of expected bad debt losses, mandatory expense recognition of pension costs prior to cash disbursement, and compulsory amortization of capitalized intangible assets are examples of a conservative strain, although one could simply attribute these practices to the inherent nature of accrual accounting discussed later in this chapter.

With respect to loss contingencies, the presence of prescribed "probable" and "estimable" tests means that stringent rules now characterize an area which at one time afforded an opportunity for much discretion and variation among companies. The definitive rule now in effect means that the earnings impact of certain *future* losses is to be recognized sooner rather than later.

With regard to the measurement and disclosure of earnings per share, the average number of shares used to determine the per-share result includes not only actual outstanding shares, but *common stock equivalents* as well, and its effect is to generate an even lower per-share result. In addition to this primary disclosure, a second calculation is made to determine what the result would be on a fully diluted basis. And generally, only if each of the required additional considerations results in a lesser amount, is its effect included. Thus, in the interest of conservatism, earnings per share is, in effect, portrayed on a "worst possible case" basis, i.e., if each and every potentially dilutive share were in fact outstanding, how small the resulting earnings per share would be.

In summary, the phenomenon of *accounting conservatism* is an integral aspect of generally accepted accounting principles, having implications for both accounting measurement and financial statement disclosure practices. Whether CPAs, their clients, and readers of financial statements support and approve of accounting conservatism is an issue whose various dimensions may be worthy of debate, e.g., What are the benefits *and* the costs of conservatism? Suffice it to say, however, that accounting conservatism may well be one of the most pervasive conventions of accounting as it now exists.

THE COST BASIS

Transactions are recorded on the basis of the dollar amounts exchanged because at the moment a transaction occurs, the exchange price, by its nature, is a measure of the value of the economic resources being transacted.[3] This approach to valuation is viewed by accountants to be objective in nature. Objectivity, in turn, is considered desirable because it suggests verifiability, a notion which has sometimes been expressed in terms of "any two accountants should be able to arrive at the same conclusion."

Objectivity as a goal or criterion can have shortcomings as well. Even though similar, if not identical, determinations may be reached by different accountants, this may not generate a very useful result. To illustrate this point, consider the question of evaluating the book you are now reading. If ten evaluators agree to independently reach conclusions about the book using only objective measures while a second group of readers were to make subjective assessments, their respective conclusions would probably differ.

The respondents using the objectivity criterion would be able to make observations only about verifiable phenomena, namely, factors with which any other reader could agree. These might include the number of chapters in the book, the color of its cover, the physical dimensions of each page, the average number of words in each chapter, and so forth. These data are objective, and the evaluators would likely generate agreement among themselves.

On the other hand, the readers who assess the volume on the basis of subjective criteria are able to offer opinions on the book's scope of coverage, sophistication, readability, and general usefulness to accountants and users of accounting information. It is likely that no two opinions would coincide, because each evaluator uses his or her own subjective standards and measurement criteria.

The distinction between objectivity and subjectivity might be characterized as follows:

Rather than viewing the matter as two absolute notions, the issue is viewed in terms of a continuum. As one moves in the direction of objectivity, the resulting measurements may become less and less useful, and when proceeding in the direction of subjectivity, the insights may become increasingly useful.

---

[3] The *cost* basis might therefore be more aptly called the *exchange price* basis.

Of course, the presumed greater relevance of information on the subjective end of the spectrum is offset to some extent by its not being objective. In other words, given the likelihood that ten different persons will offer ten different views, the user of such individual or collective input must bear the responsibility of determining how much weight should be given to each. In the case of receiving only objectively determined evaluations, the matter of accuracy and reliability is not an issue.

The cost basis of accounting is probably the most distinctive feature of accounting as it has been practiced throughout its history. Accordingly, it has been the most impregnable of all the elements comprising generally accepted accounting principles. In its own way, the historical cost principle has exemplified the plight and indeed the the perserverance of accounting itself—both as a profession and a discipline.

Formidable opposition to the historical cost basis has come from some users of accounting information, and in the 1960s many accountants, both academicians and practitioners, also began to seriously reassess the whole framework of accounting. Not surprisingly, much of their attention was directed toward the historical cost basis. Even before 1960, there had been efforts by some accountants to explore the implications of alternative valuation bases, and in some cases positions were advanced which advocated departures from the cost basis of accounting. However, such earlier works were most often confined to treatises directed to persons for whom accounting theory was of paramount concern, with the result that there was little or no effect on the practice of accounting per se.

In summary, the overview discussion of the cost basis of accounting has been set forth in a more philosophic manner than that of the other elements of GAAP. Illustrations of its applicability and its exceptions are not given here because the subject is afforded significant attention in context of an extensive examination of valuation issues in Chapter 13. The purpose of this introductory section has therefore been to point out that the historical cost basis of accounting denotes a methodology which uses data that are objective and verifiable as a basis for measuring the value of economic resources.

REALIZATION

The accounting concept of realization is closely related to the cost principle. *Realization* means that accounting is effected for only those economic events which have transpired in a transactional sense. It states that until an economic resource whose value has appreciated is sold or exchanged in an arm's length transaction, recognition of changes in its value may not be reflected in the enterprise's financial statements.

This transaction orientation precludes recognizing holding gains or losses related to investments in plant assets, intangible assets, inventory, and marketable securities. There are, however, some exceptions, the most notable of which is that of the lower-of-cost-or-market method. Applicable to inventory and marketable equity securities, deference to the doctrine of conservatism justifies downward revaluations only. In the case of marketable equity securities, however, a written-down stock whose market price subsequently increases is revalued upward, but not beyond its original cost basis. Depreciation of plant assets and amortization of intangible assets are sanctioned because their use over time is viewed as tantamount to realization, that is, their diminished utility associated with use constitutes the realization of their expected benefits.

In addition to prescribing in a general sense that a change in an economic resource's value is not an accountable event, realization in a more definitive context sets forth the guidelines for when revenue is recognized. Revenue is defined as an entity's inflow of assets resulting from operations, and is typically earned by selling merchandise or rendering services.

Revenue is recognized only when it has been realized; this means revenue is recorded when it has been earned. The question which therefore arises is when revenue is considered to have been earned. In a typical buyer/seller situation, revenue is realized at the point of sale, that is, when legal title passes; but it is the many, less clearcut cases which pose the more taxing challenge for accountants. Notions of *substantial performance* and *critical event* have been set forth in an effort to determine when to recognize revenue, and they are explored in depth in context of Chapter 4's exclusive concern with revenue realization and its implications for income measurement.

MATCHING

The matching principle of accounting refers to the manner in which income is measured. As opposed to an accretion approach whereby comparison between a period's beginning and ending financial position is the basis for imputing the period's income, the generally accepted approach used by accountants is transactions and events oriented. Its specific nature entails defining certain events as revenue transactions while others are viewed as expense transactions. The excess of revenues over expenses, in turn, becomes the measure of a period's income.

The matching principle, when considered in isolation, does not indicate how revenues and expenses are defined. It merely states that once these terms are defined, matching will yield a measure of income. In fact, there are two different ways to define what amounts shall be subjected to the matching principle. The first approach is the cash-basis method, and its focal point is

47

the cash asset, that is, any inflow of cash related to operations is revenue and any cash outflow related to operations is an expense. Two examples are described briefly.

The first case is that of most individuals' understanding of their own financial position and earnings. When asked to estimate the amount of one's personal wealth, a person's initial reaction is likely to focus on only cash holdings—cash on hand, checking accounts, savings accounts, and certificates of deposit. And when the need arises to discuss a family's budget for a particular period, individuals are likely to respond by citing their salary and interest income, and their anticipated expenditures of cash. Indeed, the one financial statement that most American adults prepare annually—the federal income tax return—is basically a cash-basis document: salary and wages are taxable when *received,* interest earned on U.S. Savings Bonds, Series E, is includible when *redeemed* (although one can elect to pay tax as the interest accumulates), and medical expenses and charitable contributions are deductible when *paid.*

The second example of a cash-basis orientation is the financial statement presentation of many government bodies at the state and municipal levels. This cash-basis tradition relates to the nature of the appropriations/ expenditures framework under which governments operate. The budget report emerges as the dominant performance-oriented document of governments, and its resulting surplus or deficit becomes a focal point, if not a rallying point, for politicians, civil servants, and citizens alike. An example of its cash-basis orientation is that the *entire* dollar cost of constructing a government office building may appear in the government's performance statement—its budget in the year the expenditure is made—irrespective of the fact its presumed benefit extends beyond that one year.

The inherent weakness of cash-basis accounting is that it matches cash-in and cash-out rather than focussing on the more substantive issue of relating benefits and costs to one another. The accrual-basis alternative overcomes this weakness. The accrual basis approach to income measurement focuses attention on the flow of total assets, not just the cash asset. It defines *revenues* in terms of inflow of total assets related to operations, and *expenses* as the revenue-related outflow of assets—either an immediate reduction or through the creation of a liability. Since *cash* is not the all-important criterion, the growth and decline of most other balance sheet components can affect income measurements as well.

It is this phenomenon that is implied by the word *accrual,* since to *accrue* means to arise or to accumulate. Specifically, it refers to the notion a transaction is accounted for even though its physical dimension may not have yet transpired. The seven accounting "transactions" which require end-of-period recognition using accrual accounting and the matching principle are:

48

Transaction	Example
1. Accrued revenue	Interest earned but not yet received.
2. Accrued expense	Wage cost incurred but not yet paid.
3. Unearned revenue	Earning subscription revenue which had been collected in advance.
4. Prepaid expense	Expiration of a prepaid insurance premium.
5. Depreciation	Recognizing the cost of a machine as expense over its useful economic life.
6. Inventory	Recording the cost of goods sold on the basis of a period's purchases and the change between beginning and ending inventory balances.
7. Receivables	Recognizing bad debt expense on the basis of expected uncollectible amounts.

At this point, it is important to recognize the interrelationship which exists among the realization, matching, and accrual elements of generally accepted accounting principles:

Realization determines when revenue is earned so as to qualify for accounting recognition.

Matching identifies the expenses which relate to, and are therefore to be matched with, recognized revenue.

Accrual assures that the revenues and expenses being matched properly reflect increases and decreases in the pertinent asset and liability accounts.

Income measurement is examined in depth in Chapter 4 (revenue recognition) and Chapter 5 (expense recognition), and the interrelated realization-matching-accrual elements of GAAP play an all-important role in both of those chapters.

CONSISTENCY

Consistency refers to the notion that the current use of an accounting method or procedure should conform with the entity's previous practice. The importance of interperiod consistency can be appreciated in light of the need to have an appropriate frame of reference, a focal point as it were, when reading and analyzing financial statements. In that context, using prior periods' data as a benchmark is a valid and oft-used means to understand and interpret accounting data.

The term *consistency* should not be confused with the expression *comparability,* as the latter denotes conformity with the accounting practices of comparable companies. Although comparability is important as far as a particular entity is concerned, so long as it adheres to GAAP, there is no explicit mandate to select principles and adopt practices paralleling those of similar enterprises.

The importance of consistency derives from the fact there are a number of transactions whose measurement can be effected with any one of several different, but equally acceptable, accounting approaches. The understandable concern that exists is that a particular method be used consistently among fiscal periods. Another aspect of the need for consistency relates to the existence of much estimation even within the confines of a particular method which is itself applied consistently. For instance, even though all a company's machines might be depreciated on a straight-line basis over an eight-year period, there are estimates present—that each year derives an equal amount of benefit from the asset, the useful economic life will be eight years, and there will be salvage value of a particular amount after eight years. Since none of these estimates is necessarily correct in its conclusions or amounts, there is an obligation to use methods and procedures which at least have the virtue of being consistent among fiscal periods.

To appreciate how consistency can help overcome the deficiency of inevitable inexact accounting data, consider the following analogy. A person seeking to know what her weight is, gets on a scale and thereby learns she weighs 50 kilograms (kg.). In fact, the scale is in error, and she really weighs 55 kg.—the scale has understated the weight by (55 − 50 =) 5 kg. Thirty days later, this person returns to the same scale at which time there is generated a reading of 48 kg.—a decrease of (50 − 48 =) 2 kg. from that of a month earlier. In fact, the person's weight is really 53 kg. which is (55 − 53 =) 2 kg. less than the true weight of 30 days earlier—again a 5 kg. understatement by the scale. Even though the scale in our illustration provided wrong amounts on both occasions (50 kg. instead of 55 kg., then 48 kg. rather than 53 kg.), by virtue of its internal consistency over the thirty-day period, the individual in question has at least obtained meaningful and correct information about her true (50 − 48 = 2 kg. versus 55 − 53 = 2 kg.) loss of weight during the month.

The relevance of this illustration is self-evident. So long as the measurement technique, the scale as it were, is applied consistently throughout each period and as of each end-of-period reading date, the user of the resulting information is at least able to obtain some relative insights. The user is thereby in a position to make some valid interperiod comparisons.

The virtues of consistency notwithstanding, companies are able to make accounting changes if and when the underlying circumstances so justify. Accounting changes are classified into four categories: changes in accounting principle, changes in accounting estimate, changes in accounting entity, and prior period corrections. Although the nature of, and differences among, these different types of accounting changes are discussed in Chapter

50

15, it is important to observe that when an accounting change occurs, appropriate disclosures must be included in the financial statement presentation. Depending on the particular type of change that occurs, readers of financial statements are thereby able to recognize the effect of an accounting change in interperiod comparisons.

DISCLOSURE AND MATERIALITY

Recall the key words contained in the definition of accounting which was introduced in Chapter 1: "Accounting is the process of identifying, measuring, and communicating economic information. . . ." The elements of generally accepted accounting principles identified and examined up to this point have had accounting *measurement* as their focal point. Indeed, measurement has traditionally been the most substantive aspect of accounting and of what accountants do. However, with the proliferation of publicly held corporations, increasing interest in financial statements by professional financial analysts, credit-grantors, and stockholders who sometimes use companies' published financial statements as a basis for instituting litigation against managers and independent auditors, the importance of disclosure has practically emerged as an area unto its own. It commands the attention of all persons who view financial statements as a relevant, if not the primary, source of information about a company.

Contrary to the lay notion of "the more the better," a distinction is made between *maximum* and *optimal* disclosure. It is considered almost as dysfunctional to overwhelm readers of financial statements with data in excess of their needs as it would be to provide an inadequate amount of pertinent information. *Optimal* is intended to denote a degree of disclosure which is netiher too voluminous nor too sparse. This concept has been expressed as follows: "Accounting reports should disclose that which is necessary to make them not misleading."[4]

An integral aspect of optimal disclosure is that of *materiality*. Although this is one of the most cited terms, it is also the least definitive term that affects accounting and financial reporting; indeed, each FASB Statement contains the caveat, "the provisions of this Statement need not be applied to immaterial items." A definition follows:

> A statement, fact, or item is material, if giving full consideration to the surrounding circumstances, as they exist at the time, it is of such a nature that its disclosure, or the method of treating it, would be likely to influence or to

---

[4] Robert T. Sprouse and Maurice Moonitz, *A Tentative Set of Broad Accounting Principles for Business Enterprises* (New York: American Institute of Certified Public Accountants, 1962), p. 7.

"make a difference" in the judgment and conduct of a reasonable person. The same tests apply to such words as significant, consequential, or important.[5]

It is because of materiality that a sole proprietor of even a small corporation would not capitalize and therefore subsequently not depreciate a wastebasket costing $19, or that some companies with sales of billions of dollars might round off amounts in their financial statements to the nearest thousand dollars. On the other hand, even though $900,000 relative to earnings of $750 million may not be material in a purely arithmetic sense, if the $900,000 pertains to an ominous expenditure such as an illegal political contribution, it might still be significant and, therefore, be worthy of disclosure in a footnote to the financial statements.

To appreciate why it is virtually impossible to formulate a universal measure of materiality, consider the following analogy. When asked how old their newborn baby is, proud parents tend to respond in terms of weeks—2, 3, and so forth. As the infant begins to crawl, the parents' response is apt to be expressed in broader terms, namely, 6 months or 7 months. Once the child is a toddler, the frame of reference becomes half-years—2½, 3, 3½. And when the youngster enters grade school, the focal point is likely to be whole years—7, 8, 9. Before long, the children's ages are stated in terms of pre-teens, teenagers, and "college age." With advent of the third decade of their children's lives, parents are likely to use half-decade spacing —early 20s, late 30s. Soon it becomes an entire decade such as "in her 40s," then the ultimate—combined decades of the "middle aged" and "senior citizen" variety.

The reason parents of a 2½-year-old child express themselves differently from those of a 42½-year-old child is that each six-month period is material in the former instance but is not so in the latter situation. This is the case even though there is no book which states what is a material time period as far as ages are concerned. The respondent—the parent, or in our case the accountant—makes a judgment as to what can be assumed to be material for the party to whom the information is being communicated.

Perhaps the oldest recorded reference to materiality is that which appears in the Book of Genesis which states, with respect to Joseph's stockpiling operation in anticipation of seven years of famine, that "Joseph laid up grain as the sand of the sea, very much, until they left off numbering; for it was without number." In speculating why additional numbers could not be created so that readers of that text might have a better understanding of the situation, in the parlance of 20th century accounting it might be observed the

---

[5] Paul Grady, *Inventory of Generally Accepted Accounting Principles for Business Enterprises* (New York: American Institute of Certified Public Accountants, 1965), p. 40.

sheer volume of the grain being stored was such that disclosure of an exact amount would have had no material effect on readers' appreciation of its magnitude.

SUBSTANCE OVER FORM

In noting that *substance over form* is a basic feature of existing financial accounting, the Accounting Principles Board stated the following:

> Financial accounting emphasizes the economic substance of events even though the legal form may differ from the economic substance and suggest different treatment. Usually the economic substance of events to be accounted for agrees with the legal form. Sometimes, however, substance and form differ. Accountants emphasize the substance of events rather than their form so that the information provided better reflects the economic activities represented.[6]

A review of the numerous events and circumstances encompassed by official FASB and pre-FASB pronouncements indicates there are a variety of instances when economic substance does indeed prevail over legal form. In a few of these situations, an explicit statement to this effect appears in the text of the pertinent pronouncement. However, in most cases, the *substance over form* characteristic of a required or recommended accounting approach is only implied.[7] In cases in which it is implied, substance over form is discernible only after probing further into the apparent conceptual underpinnings of the particular approach being set forth.

The notion that economic substance should prevail over legal form is one with which virtually all accountants agree at the important conceptual level. But it is the implementational issue of determining what is the economic substance underlying a particular event or set of circumstances which can and does pose real challenges for accountants, with much of the ensuing dilemma revolving around honest differences of opinion as to what economic substance is.

SUMMARY

For purposes of explication, the components comprising generally accepted accounting principles have been set forth as ten seemingly distinct elements. It must be emphasized that even among accountants, persons can and do visualize and conceptualize these principles differently from one

---

[6] *Accounting Principles Board Statement No. 4,* paragraph no. 127.

[7] See Philip E. Meyer, "A Framework for Understanding 'Substance over Form' in Accounting," *The Accounting Review,* January 1976, pp. 80–89.

another. As important, it should be recognized that these elements are not mutually exclusive; indeed, a critical aspect of their nature is their interdependency. Similarly, to assert that some are postulates, others are principles, and the rest are conventions is not relevant to the objectives of this volume.

Whereas Chapter 2 exposed the reader to institutional and environmental aspects of accounting as a profession, Chapter 3 has offered a framework with which to appreciate the nature of accounting as a discipline. Its discussion revolved around the conceptual underpinnings of accounting and financial reporting. As a result, one's understanding of the issues and problems to be discussed in subsequent chapters will be enhanced. As important, as particular elements of GAAP are modified and refined—by official pronouncements or by a general consensus—greater appreciation of particular whys and wherefores should result.

Additional Readings

Abdel-khalik, A. Rashad, and Keller, Thomas F., eds. *The Impact of Accounting Research on Practice and Disclosure.* Durham, N.C.: Duke University Press, 1978.

Alexander, Sidney S. "Income Measurement in a Dynamic Economy." In *Five Monographs on Business Income,* edited by Sidney S. Alexander, Martin Bronfenbrenner, Solomon Fabricant, and Clark Warbuton. Houston: Scholars Book Co., 1973, pp. 1–95.

American Accounting Association Committee on Concepts and Standards for External Financial Reports. *Statement on Accounting Theory and Theory Acceptance.* Sarasota, Fla.: American Accounting Association, 1977.

American Accounting Association Committee to Prepare a Statement of Basic Accounting Theory. *A Statement of Basic Accounting Theory.* Sarasota, Fla.: American Accounting Association, 1966.

Anderson, James A. *A Comparative Analysis of Selected Income Measurement Theories in Financial Accounting.* Sarasota, Fla.: American Accounting Association, 1976.

Bedford, Norton M. *Income Determination Theory: An Accounting Framework.* Reading, Mass.: Addison-Wesley Publishing Co., Inc., 1965.

Chambers, Raymond J. *Accounting, Evaluation and Economic Behavior.* Englewood Cliffs, N.J.: Prentice-Hall, Inc., 1966.

FASB Discussion Memorandum. *Conceptual Framework for Financial Accounting and Reporting: Elements of Financial Statements and Their Measurement.* Stamford, Conn.: Financial Accounting Standards Board, 1976.

FASB Discussion Memorandum. *Criteria for Determining Materiality.* Stamford, Conn.: Financial Accounting Standards Board, 1975.

Hagerman, Robert L.; Keller, Thomas F.; and Petersen, Russell J. "Accounting Research and Accounting Principles." *The Journal of Accountancy* (March 1973), pp. 51–55.

Ijiri, Yuji. *The Foundations of Accounting Measurement—A Mathematical, Economic and Behavioral Inquiry.* Englewood Cliffs, N.J.: Prentice-Hall, Inc., 1967.

Ijiri, Yuji. *Theory of Accounting Measurement.* Sarasota, Fla.: American Accounting Association, 1975.

Mautz, R. K., and Gray, Jack. "Some Thoughts on Research Needs in Accounting." *The Journal of Accountancy* (September 1970), pp. 54–62.

Meyer, Philip E. "A Framework for Understanding 'Substance over Form' in Accounting." *The Accounting Review* (January 1976), pp. 80–89.

Meyer, Philip E. "The Accounting Entity." *Abacus* (December 1973), pp. 116–26.

Moonitz, Marurice. *The Basic Postulates of Accounting.* New York: American Institute of Certified Public Accountants, 1961.

Moore, Michael L. "Conservatism." *The Texas CPA* (October 1972), pp. 41–47.

Paton, W. A., and Littleton, A. C. *An Introduction to Corporate Accounting Standards.* Sarasota, Fla.: American Accounting Association, 1940.

Paton, William Andrew. *Accounting Theory.* Houston: Scholars Book Co., 1972 (originally published—New York: The Ronald Press Company, 1922).

Pattillo, James W. *The Concept of Materiality in Financial Reporting.* New York: Financial Executives Research Foundation, 1976.

Solomons, David. "Economic and Accounting Concepts of Cost and Value." In *Modern Accounting Theory,* edited by Morton Backer. Englewood Cliffs, N.J.: Prentice-Hall, Inc., 1966, pp. 117–40.

Sorter, George H. "The Partitioning Dilemma," in *Objectives of Financial Statements,* vol. 2, *Selected Papers.* New York: American Institute of Certified Public Accountants, 1974, pp. 117–22.

Sprouse, Robert T. "The Importance of Earnings in the Conceptual Framework." *The Journal of Accountancy* (January 1978), pp. 64–71.

Sprouse, Robert T. "The Measurement of Financial Position and Income." In *Research in Accounting Measurement,* edited by Robert K. Jaedicke, Yuji Ijiri, and Oswald Nielsen. Sarasota, Fla.: American Accounting Association, 1966, pp. 101–15.

Sterling, Robert R. "Conservatism: The Fundamental Principle of Valuation in Traditional Accounting." *Abacus* (December 1967), pp. 109–32.

Sterling, Robert R. "The Going Concern: An Examination." *The Accounting Review* (July 1968), pp. 481–502.

Storey, Reed K. "Cash Movements and Periodic Income Determination." *The Accounting Review* (July 1960), pp. 449–54.

Study Group on Business Income. *Changing Concepts of Business Income.* Houston: Scholars Book Co., 1975 (originally published—New York: The Macmillan Company, 1952).

Watts, Ross L., and Zimmerman, Jerold L."'The Demand for and Supply of Accounting Theories: The Market for Excuses." *The Accounting Review* (April 1979), pp. 273–305.

Yu, S. C. *The Structure of Accounting Theory.* Gainesville, Fla.: The University Presses of Florida, 1976.

Income Measurement: Revenue Recognition

In this chapter and in the following one, attention is directed toward various elements of income measurement. The traditional accounting model uses a "transactions" approach to determine an enterprise's earnings or loss for a specific period. Not unexpectedly, a particular transaction has either a favorable, unfavorable, or neutral effect on the company's well-being, i.e., its owners' equity. *Revenue* and *expense* are terms used to signify these aspects of companies' transactions.

Accounting perceives each revenue transaction as having a related expense aspect which occurs concurrently. For instance, recognition of the revenue character of a sale of merchandise requires concurrent recognition of the cost incurred to effect the revenue. Thus, the sale of merchandise for $500 requires simultaneous recognition of the forfeiture of particular goods having a cost of, say, $300, because it represents a diminution of the seller's assets available for future sale transactions. Concurrent recognition of both the revenue and expense dimensions of the sale transaction is a critical feature of income measurement because it represents the most meaningful basis of measuring the net benefit or net cost of the transaction. This essential characteristic of income measurement is called the matching principle of accounting.

Before the matching process can be effected, that is, before implementing the procedures which result in a reasonable matching of expenses with related revenues, particular revenue transactions must be examined to ascertain that revenue has in fact materialized. Earnings statements are prepared for finite fiscal periods while the inflow of assets—which revenue mea-

57

sures—occurs continually. In other words, accountants must determine which portion of an ongoing stream of revenues is associated with particular fiscal periods.

The problem is complicated because the revenue-earning process occurs in phases. A case could be made for focusing attention on the period or periods in which either the production process occurs, the production phase is completed, the goods are delivered to customers, or the sales proceeds are collected. There is also the possible implication of the sale price being collected prior to the delivery of the merchandise, or that of a post-sale "warranty" relationship between vendor and customer.

As a general rule, revenue is recognized at the time legal title is transferred from the seller to the buyer. This reflects the belief that in most cases, the passage of legal title is the critical event in the earning process. It is critical in the sense that before it occurs there is no assurance that revenue will be realized, and once it occurs the seller is precluded from obtaining alternative benefits from the merchandise thus sold. If instead of selling goods, revenue is earned through rendering services for particular customers, completion of the component elements of such a service constitutes the critical event and is the basis for recognizing revenue.

THE TIMING OF REVENUE REALIZATION

In this chapter, attention is directed toward revenue realization instances which present variations of the conventional "passage of legal title" criterion for recognizing revenue. The ensuing discussion is intended to demonstrate the adaptability of the traditional accounting model to situations whose business nature does not conform with the basic revenue-earning case of selling merchandise with the expectation that the sales proceeds will be collected within a specified number of days.

By observing the unique features of different revenue recognition approaches, one is able to further appreciate and understand some of the intricacies of accounting. Furthermore, the discussion will serve as a frame of reference that will be useful when one is confronted with a novel revenue-earning transaction. As particular revenue realization cases are examined, the conceptual underpinnings of alternative accounting approaches are considered. Just as the accounting questions in these cases have been resolved with the aid of earlier cases, so too one can expect that future issues in financial reporting will be decided with the benefit of insights of earlier precedents.

A critical feature of the discussion that follows is that as each revenue realization case is examined, its implications for the matching principle of accounting are considered as well. To examine revenue issues in isolation would preclude obtaining the insight needed to appreciate the effect of revenue recognition on income measurement. Only by integrating both the revenue and related expense dimensions can one obtain the requisite bases for understanding the issues at hand, as well as their broader ramifications.

Revenue Received in Advance

Revenue is received in advance when a company collects cash from a customer for future delivery of goods or services. Examples include magazine publishers which sell multi-year subscriptions to their periodicals, health spa organizations which sell service contracts to use athletic and weight-reducing facilities, and correspondence schools which offer home-study courses through the mail. The pertinent question is: Does the seller earn the revenue in the period in which the money is collected or during the subsequent period in which the goods or services are delivered?

The answer is that the revenue should be recognized when the critical event occurs. This, in turn, raises the question of what constitutes the critical event. On the one hand, it can be argued that the critical event is the customer's remitting the required fee—that once this event has occurred, revenue has been realized. The alternative point of view is that the critical event is the actual performance of the requisite contractual duties. It is during the period in which the goods or services are delivered to the customer that the revenue benefits should be recognized. It is argued that despite its importance, the mere collection of cash is relatively incidental to the company's earning of revenue. In other words, the distinction between the collection of, and the generation of, revenue emerges as the paramount consideration.

To demonstrate the applicability of the matching principle of accounting, consider the following example. A magazine publisher receives $20,000 in 19x1 for long-term magazine subscriptions, one-fifth of which is delivered in 19x1. It is estimated that expenses related to fulfilling the subscription commitment of $12,000 are incurred proportionately (income tax aspects are ignored).

As shown in Exhibit 4–1, under the approach which recognizes revenue on receipt of the cash, the full $20,000 appears as revenue in 19x1's income statement. The matching principle requires that the related ($12,000) estimated expense also be reflected in 19x1's income statement. Since for purposes of this example we are assuming that expenses are incurred proportionately, the remaining four-fifths of the estimated expense, or $9,600, appears as a liability in the end-of-year balance sheet.

The alternative approach recognizes revenue as the magazines are delivered. Since only one fifth of the subscriptions' lives expires in 19x1, only one fifth of the ($20,000) cash received is recognized as revenue in 19x1. It is

Exhibit 4-1
Accounting for Revenue Received in Advance

| | 19x1 | |
	Collection of Cash	Delivery of Magazines
Income Statement:		
Revenue	$20,000	$ 4,000
Expenses	12,000	2,400
Income	**$ 8,000**	**$ 1,600**
Balance Sheet:		
Deferred liability	$ 9,600	
Revenue received in advance		$16,000
Retained earnings	8,000	1,600
Total	**$17,600**	**$17,600**

matched with one fifth of the expected ($12,000) expense which we assumed was the related 19x1 expense. The remaining four fifths of the cash collected is reflected in the balance sheet as a liability because it represents the dollar amount of goods the company is obligated to give to the subscribers.

Had either the "cash collection" method included only 19x1's actual $2,400 expense in its income statement, or had the "magazines delivered" approach included an expense amount other than one which is causally, or at least proportionately, related to 19x1's $4,000 revenue, there would have been an improper matching of revenue and expense. In practice, the cash collection method is generally deemed to be unacceptable because it is believed it is the delivery of goods or services which is the critical event.

Precious Natural Resources

In most revenue transactions, the critical event is the passage of legal title from seller to buyer. The reason accountants concentrate on this event is that until such title passes, it cannot be assumed the merchandise has actually been sold to a willing buyer. Thus, although a company's financing, purchasing, production, and warehousing functions may be operating satisfactorily, uncertainty surrounds the issue of salability until legal title passes. This uncertainty refers not only to whether or not a willing buyer will emerge, but also to the amount of the sale price, the collectibility of the receivable which might thereby be created, and the possibility that additional selling or delivery costs would be incurred to effect a sale. Recognizing revenue—together with the related expenses—before the emergence of a bona fide customer would yield a measure of income which would at best be tentative. To avoid such measurement uncertainties, recognition is deferred until it is known that at least the possibility of uncertainties happening is minimized. The accounting model does, however, provide for exceptions.

Thus, if there is a commodity for which the passage of legal title is a relatively inconsequential aspect of the operating cycle, revenue may be recognized at some other point in time. One of these cases is that of "precious metals having a fixed monetary value with no substantial cost of marketing" such as "inventories of gold and silver when there is an effective government-controlled market at a fixed monetary value."[1]

In such cases, the usual uncertainty of locating a buyer, incurring marketing costs, estimating the sale price per unit, and collecting the resulting receivable are for all intents and purposes trivial. There are numerous buyers, no marketing costs will be incurred, the current sale price is known, and the receivable's collectibility is assured. Therefore, what emerges as the critical event is the extraction of the resource from the ground. As soon as extraction happens, the critical event in the earning process has occurred, and revenue may be recognized.

An understanding of the resulting financial statement effects can best be obtained in context of the example that follows. Assume that discovery of a precious metal called *Mep* has far-reaching ramifications for a variety of strategic military purposes. As a result, legislation has been enacted which makes it illegal for any person or business entity to possess even the least amount of Mep. However, rather than merely confiscating any Mep that might be extracted from underground reserves, the Federal government is required to purchase the commodity at a price of $3 per gram.

Exhibit 4–2 shows an income statement and a balance sheet for a company that is in the business of extracting Mep—in its first year of operation. These financial statements are prepared on the basis of the two different approaches that might be used to recognize revenue. The assured revenue per gram is $3, and the cost of extraction is $2 per unit. 40,000 grams of Mep were extracted during 19x1, of which 25,000 grams have been delivered to the government and cash has been received. Administrative expenses are a fixed cost of $12,000 per annum; the December 31, 19x1 balance sheet

---

[1] *Accounting Research Bulletin No. 43*, chapter 4, paragraph nos. 15–16.

Exhibit 4-2

Accounting for Precious Natural Resources

	Delivery	Extraction
Income Statement:		
Sales revenue:		
25,000 @ $3	$ 75,000	
40,000 @ $3		$120,000
Cost of goods sold:		
25,000 @ $2	(50,000)	
40,000 @ $2		(80,000)
Administrative expenses	(12,000)	(12,000)
Net income	**$ 13,000**	**$ 28,000**
Balance Sheet:		
Cash	$ 90,000	$ 90,000
Inventory:		
15,000 @ $2	30,000	
15,000 @ $3		45,000
Plant assets (net)	180,000	180,000
Total	**$300,000**	**$315,000**
Liabilities	$187,000	$187,000
Common stock	100,000	100,000
Retained earnings	13,000	28,000
Total	**$300,000**	**$315,000**

amounts for Cash, Plant Assets (net of accumulated depreciation and depletion charges), Liabilities, and Common Stock are given; and no dividends were declared during the year.

Under the conventional "delivery" method of revenue recognition, the 25,000 delivered grams comprise the company's sales revenue. In light of the matching principle of accounting, the cost of goods sold includes only the costs relating to these 25,000 grams. After considering the fixed administrative expenses, the resulting net income is $13,000. The (40,000 − 25,000 =) 15,000 grams that were extracted but not delivered during 19x1 comprise the year-end inventory, and are so reported on the December 31, 19x1 balance sheet at $2 per gram. Since this is the first year of operation and given that no dividends were declared, the end-of-year Retained Earnings reflects the year's $13,000 net income.

The alternative method—which focuses attention on extraction rather than on delivery—includes as revenue for 19x1 the sales proceeds related to all 40,000 grams which were extracted during the year. Under the matching principle, the costs incurred to generate such revenue—in this case the $2 cost per gram—are reflected in the same (19x1) income statement in which the revenue appears. Therefore, cost of goods sold is (40,000 @ $2 =) $80,000, and net income for the year is $28,000.

The only balance sheet differences between the two approaches are the amounts of Inventory and Retained Earnings. The balance sheet based on the "extraction" method of recognizing revenue contains an inventory amount of $45,000—based on the 15,000 grams on hand at year-end *at a rate of $3 per gram*. It seems somewhat incongruous that inventory should be reflected on the basis of its higher selling price rather than its historical cost. It is also anomalous that the 15,000 grams, having "flowed through" the earnings statement by virtue of their being considered elements of revenue, should still even be considered part of the company's year-end Mep inventory.

The explanation to these two anomalies is that indeed the 15,000 grams of Mep are *not* units of ending inventory in the sense they have the potential to generate future revenue benefits. Instead, the nature of the $45,000 "inventory" is more akin to that of "unbilled receivables." That it is of a receivable nature is a direct result of its having already been recognized as revenue in 19x1's income statement. As a quasi-receivable, its future service potential to the company lies in its prospective conversion to the more liquid state of cash. To refer to the $45,000 as a receivable with no qualification, however, would be misleading since the customer does not yet have knowledge that a receivable-payable relationship has been created—inasmuch as an invoice has yet to be rendered. Being more "receivable" than "inventory" also explains why it is appropriate to reflect the 15,000 grams at a rate of $3 rather than $2 per gram.

The ($28,000 − 13,000 =) $15,000 difference in net income between the two methods is attributable to the 15,000 grams on hand at year-end. Whereas these 15,000 grams do not affect earnings under the "delivery" method, they do have a $15,000 impact on income determined by the "extraction" approach. The reason for the $15,000 effect is that under the latter method, there is (15,000 @ $3 =) $45,000 more included in Sales Revenue and (15,000 @ $2 =) $30,000 more reflected in Cost of Goods Sold, which yields a net effect on earnings of [15,000 @ ($3 − 2 =) $1 =] $15,000. This $15,000 variation underlies the differences in the end-of-period balance sheets' amounts of Inventory and Retained Earnings.

The pronouncement which sanctions the "extraction" method also states that "a similar treatment is not uncommon for inventories representing agricultural, mineral and other products, units of which are interchangeable and have an immediate marketability at quoted prices and for which appropriate costs may be difficult to obtain."[2] In any case, appropriate disclosure is required. This may be accomplished by including in the company's summary of significant accounting policies a statement to the effect that consistent with industry practice, the corporation has recorded as bullion revenue the estimated net realizable value of unsold bullion produced prior to the year-end.

Long-Term Construction Contracts

The case of revenue earned from the extraction of precious natural resources is one for which the passage of legal title is not deemed to be the critical event in the earning process. As a result, revenue may be recognized at that point in the earning process considered critical, namely, its extraction from the ground. A similar case is that of the long-term construction contract, that is, in which a company's operations entail constructing specific projects for particular parties with which it has entered into a contractual agreement.

When the duration of the construction extends beyond one fiscal year, the following accounting question arises: During which year or years shall the income earned on the contract be recognized? More fundamentally: In which period or periods shall the contract revenue be recognized, for which there arises an obligation to promptly match with it the related expenses of fulfilling the contract?

No contract is consummated when the contract is signed; instead, the signing of a contract merely signifies that certain obligations and events are expected to occur in the future. Consequently, the period the contract is entered into is not a viable candidate for revenue recognition. The two accounting approaches that do present themselves are the completed-contract and the percentage-of-completion methods. The completed-contract method is the conventional, point-of-delivery approach. It reflects the traditional belief that only after all of the components of revenue and expense are ascertained can one meaningfully proceed to measure the resulting income. In other words, the case for deferring revenue recognition until the very conclusion of the construction period is that it is only then that the matching principle of accounting can be applied with an expectation of yielding an accurate measure of income.

The percentage-of-completion method, on the other hand, represents an effort to recognize revenue systematically over the life of the construction

---

[2] Ibid., paragraph no. 16.

process. And given the matching principle of accounting, the percentage-of-completion method also accepts the commitment to measure the related expenses over the life of the contract. There is of course a serious obstacle that must be overcome, namely, that of dealing with uncertainties during the construction period—uncertainties which cannot be resolved until the completion of the particular project. The types of uncertainties that surround such an undertaking include whether the contractor is able to complete the contract, the reasonableness of the contractor's estimates of the project's stage of completion at the end of each intervening fiscal period, the reliability of projected cost data, and the collectibility of the receivable thereby created.

The nature of the two methods is shown in Exhibit 4–3. As a result of a contract signed on October 1, 19x1, Babel Co. began to construct an office

Exhibit 4–3

Accounting for Long-Term Construction Contracts—Income Statement Effects

Contract Price—$25,000,000
Expected Cost at the Outset—$18,000,000

	Billings to Date	Collections to Date	Costs Incurred to Date	Estimated Cost to Complete
December 31, 19x1	$ 4,000,000	$ 3,000,000	$ 4,500,000	$13,500,000
December 31, 19x2	$19,000,000	$14,000,000	$12,000,000	$ 8,000,000
April 1, 19x3	$25,000,000	$23,000,000	$19,500,000	-0-

	Completed Contract Method 19x3	Percentage of Completion Method		
		19x1	19x2	19x3
Revenue	$25,000,000	$6,250,000[1]	$8,750,000[2]	$10,000,000[4]
Expenses	19,500,000	4,500,000	7,500,000[3]	7,500,000
Income	**$ 5,500,000**	**$1,750,000**	**$1,250,000**	**$ 2,500,000**

Supporting computations:
[1] $25,000,000 \times \left(\dfrac{\$4,500,000}{\$4,500,000 + 13,500,000} = \right) .25 = \$6,250,000$

[2] $25,000,000 \times \left[\left(\dfrac{\$12,000,000}{\$12,000,000 + 8,000,000} = \right) .60; .60 - .25 = \right] .35 = \$8,750,000$

[3] $12,000,000 - 4,500,000 = \$7,500,000$

[4] $25,000,000 - (\$6,250,000 + 8,750,000 =) \$15,000,000 = \$10,000,000$

65

building complex for Tower, Inc. The contract price was $25,000,000, and Babel expects its costs to be $18,000,000. Although construction is expected to be completed by April 1, 19x3, progress bills are presented to Tower periodically on the basis of which it remits payments to Babel.

As shown in Exhibit 4–3, under the completed-contract method, all of the revenue and expenses are recognized in 19x3 because that is the year during which the contract is completed. The percentage-of-completion method, on the other hand, involves recognizing revenue, related expenses, and resulting income during all three contract years. Its three-year totals, however, equal those reported by the completed-contract method entirely in 19x3.

In 19x1, the percentage-of-completion approach reflects one-quarter of the contract's total fee as revenue because as of year-end one-quarter of the contract's expected costs had already been incurred. The 19x2 income statement includes as revenue for the year 35 percent of the total contract revenue for the following reason: As of December 31, 19x2, 60 percent of the total expected costs had been incurred which, when compared to a 25 percent stage of completion one year earlier, yields the indicated increment. Note that although the $12,000,000 of costs incurred as of year-end is 66⅔ percent of the $18,000,000 contract cost estimated at the outset, it is only 60 percent of what is now a revised total cost of ($12,000,000 + 8,000,000 =) $20,000,000. 19x3's income statement reflects the earning of the remaining 40 percent of the contract revenue and its related ($7,500,000) cost.

Although this discussion is directed primarily toward the differential income statement effects of the completed-contract and percentage-of-completion methods, the related balance sheet effects are presented as well, in Exhibit 4–4. The amount of outstanding receivables as of the end of each of the three years is identical under the two methods since it reflects the excess of actual billings over actual collections to date. The balance sheet difference between the two approaches emanates from the varying income statement approaches. The completed-contract method is concerned with disclosing on the balance sheet the spread between billings and cumulative costs, while the percentage-of-completion approach depicts the difference between the amount billed and that which has been recognized as revenue.

Under either method, if during the construction period it becomes apparent a loss will occur because estimated total costs exceed the contract price, there should be immediate income statement recognition. This would cause some variation in each method's resulting balance sheet as well. In this respect, there is no difference between the case illustrated and that of conventional sales transactions.

To summarize, the difference between the two methods of accounting for long-term construction contracts revolves around the timing of revenue recognition, that is, is it necessary to wait for the entire earning process to be

Exhibit 4-4

Accounting for Long-Term Construction Contracts—Balance Sheet Effects

	Completed Contract Method			Percentage of Completion Method		
	19x1	19x2	19x3	19x1	19x2	19x3
Balance sheet debits:						
Receivable	$1,000,000[1]	$5,000,000[3]	$2,000,000[5]	$1,000,000[1]	$5,000,000[3]	$2,000,000[5]
Excess of costs over billings	$ 500,000[2]					
Excess of revenue over billings				$2,250,000[6]		
Balance sheet credits:						
Excess of billings over costs		$7,000,000[4]				
Excess of billings over revenue					$4,000,000[7]	

Supporting computations:

[1] $4,000,000 − 3,000,000 = $1,000,000
[2] $4,500,000 − 4,000,000 = $500,000
[3] $19,000,000 − 14,000,000 = $5,000,000
[4] $19,000,000 − $12,000,000 = $7,000,000
[5] $25,000,000 − 23,000,000 = $2,000,000
[6] $6,250,000 − 4,000,000 = $2,250,000
[7] $19,000,000 − 15,000,000 = $4,000,000

completed, or should revenue be recognized as progress is made toward completion? Although two of the uncertainties plaguing conventional sales do not exist, namely, identifying a willing buyer and ascertaining the sale price, uncertainty may exist with respect to the collectibility of the contract price. However, the more significant uncertainty is the reliability of expense data based on costs incurred continually throughout the construction period. The issue thus becomes a practical one. There must be a determination that, given the conceptual applicability of the percentage-of-completion method, a particular set of circumstances has the qualities that are sufficiently dependable to produce reliable expense measurement.

Television Movie Rights

Once a motion picture has been exhibited in theaters, telecast rights are sometimes sold to television networks or individual television stations. The accounting issue that arises is during what period or periods should the owner of a film—the licensor—recognize the resulting license fee revenue.

In the earlier discussion of distinctive revenue recognition situations, the obligation to match such revenues with their related expenses was emphasized. Indeed, in the case of long-term construction contracts, it was observed that the difficulty of developing reliable expense data could possibly jeopardize a company's ability to use what may actually be the conceptually superior percentage-of-completion method.

In the film case, however, the challenge of achieving a proper matching of revenue and expenses as such is relatively uncomplicated because the related expenses, if any, are generally not material in amount. The cost of producing a motion picture will have been determined and already matched against revenues derived from theater showings. And even if part of the production costs are to be deferred and matched with television revenues, the *measurement* of costs as such does not pose a serious problem. It is identification of the appropriate revenue period or periods which must be determined; attention is directed toward the matter of when to recognize the revenue rather than its resulting consequences for matching revenues and expenses.

The various revenue recognition avenues are illustrated in Exhibit 4–5. On July 1, 19x1, Spectacle Films signed a $9,000,000 contract with the JKL television network giving JKL the exclusive license to televise the motion picture "Bottom Line." The movie can be shown only one time between January 1, 19x3 and July 1, 19x4. Beginning in 19x1 and continuing through 19x4, JKL is to remit $2,250,000 to Spectacle each July 1. Spectacle delivered the movie reels to JKL in November, 19x2, and the telecast occurred on April 15, 19x4. (The long-term receivable's implicit "interest" is not consid-

Exhibit 4-5

Accounting for Television Movie Rights

	19x1	19x2	19x3	19x4
1. Inception of contract: July 1, 19x1	$9,000,000			
2. Collection of cash: Each July—19x1 . . . 19x4	$2,250,000	$2,250,000	$2,250,000	$2,250,000
3. Delivery date: November 19x2		$9,000,000		
4. Date of telecast: April 15, 19x4				$9,000,000
5. License period: January 1, 19x3—July 1, 19x4			$6,000,000	$3,000,000
6. Inception of license period: January 1, 19x3			$9,000,000	

ered in this illustration.) Six different revenue recognition possibilities are identified in Exhibit 4–5, and each of these is considered in turn below.

Recognizing revenue as of the date the contract is entered into reflects the belief that the signing per se represents the revenue transaction's crucial event. In other words, once the contract has been affirmed, the uncertainties which normally cause revenue recognition to be deferred are effectively non-existent. The method's primary shortcoming is that a contract in which the parties merely exchange promises, would usually not be treated as an accounting transaction.

Focusing on the collection of cash—or alternatively on the dates the installment payments become receivable—might be viewed as superior to the first approach at least because an arm's length transaction occurs. Its deficiency, however, lies in that the mere collection of cash has no causal relationship to the revenue earning process. The only time the receipt of cash becomes relevant for revenue recognition purposes is when collectibility is so uncertain that its ultimate collection is viewed as constituting the critical event, which is not so in our case.

The delivery date basis for recognizing revenue might be justified on the basis of its almost universal usefulness in conventional sales transactions. However, in the case of motion pictures licensed for television exhibition, mere delivery is of relatively no consequence since the television network or station—the licensee—is not permitted to use the movie until the date stipulated in the contract.

For the licensor to recognize revenue on the basis of the date the licensee actually televises the motion picture can be questioned as well. It results in the licensor's recognition of revenue being arbitrary and, more important, there is no direct involvement by the licensor. An enterprise's operating results and financial position should be affected only by events and circumstances to which the enterprise is a direct party. The showing of the movie—on April 15, 19x4 in our example—is an event totally beyond the licensor's sphere of accountability.

The license period—in our illustration, the 18 month period during which the film may be exhibited—probably emerges as the approach most consistent with accrual accounting. Because it is over the license period that the licensor foregoes the opportunity to derive alternate benefits from the motion picture encompassed by the license agreement, the resulting benefit can be said to occur over this entire period.

This method can be viewed as analogous to that of leasing tangible property, i.e., irrespective of when lessees use leased property or facilities, lessors recognize rental revenue over the entire lease period. But, in rejecting the license period method, the applicable pronouncement of the American Institute of CPAs (AICPA) states that "the license period is not intended to provide continued use of the film throughout the term but rather to define a reasonable time period within which the licensee can exercise his limited rights to use the film.''[3]

It is the sixth method identified in Exhibit 4–5 which has received the endorsement of the accounting profession. The AICPA committee concluded that a licensing agreement should be considered the sale of a right and that the revenue should not be recognized until the beginning of the license period. It listed five conditions that must be met: a known sale price, determinability of costs, assured collectibility, film acceptance by the licensee, and physical availability of the film.[4]

Some accountants maintain that revenue recognition spread over the entire license period is conceptually superior to recognizing revenue at the license period's inception. Prior to the issuance of the AICPA's pronouncement, it was not uncommon for revenue to be recognized in its entirety when a licensing contract was originally signed.

Initial Franchise Fee

A franchise is an agreement between two parties who are known as the franchisor and the franchisee. The franchisor grants to the franchisee the exclusive right to engage in a specified business activity as part of its organization. For example, nationwide motels and restaurants often operate on a franchise basis. Each of the operating outlets is viewed by the general public as an integral part of the well-known company with which it is identified. When a franchise system is used, however, each operating unit is actually an autonomous enterprise operated by its owner, the franchisee.

The aspect of franchise agreements with which the following discussion is concerned is that of the initial franchise fee. This fee is paid by a prospective franchisee to the franchisor to establish the franchise relationship. It provides the franchisee with the exclusive privilege of operating a particular franchise, and generally entitles the franchisee to receive from the franchisor specified "start-up" services. Such services typically relate to site selection, financing, advertising, management training programs, and other types of pre-opening assistance.

Usually the franchisee is also committed to remit to the franchisor ongoing fees. Such amounts are usually based on a formula under which a specified percentage of sales revenue and/or earnings is periodically paid to the franchisor. This payment may also entitle the franchisee to receive from

---

[3] Committee on the Entertainment Industries, *Accounting for Motion Picture Films* (New York: American Institute of Certified Public Accountants, 1973), p. 6.

[4] Ibid., p. 7.

the franchisor aid in the areas of quality control, advertising, operating supplies, etc.

There are various ways a franchisor might account for the recognition of the "up-front" revenue. Since we are dealing with revenue realization, the question really being asked is when is such revenue earned—or better yet, when does the critical event occur? Alternative approaches to recognizing revenue are shown in Exhibit 4–6, based on the following illustration.

Exhibit 4–6
Accounting for Initial Franchise Fee

		19x1	19x2	19x3
1.	Cash collection:			
	July 31, 19x1—80%	$48,000		
	January 15, 19x3—20%			$12,000
2.	Franchise period:			
	15-year amortization	$ 2,000	$ 4,000	$ 4,000
3.	Franchise inception:			
	July 1, 19x1	$60,000		
4.	Substantial performance:			
	December 16, 19x2		$60,000	

On July 1, 19x1, Yummy Yogurt Co.—the franchisor—signed a franchise agreement with Robert Brown—the franchisee. Under this agreement, Mr. Brown has the exclusive right to operate a Yummy Yogurt store in Coolidge, Massachusetts for fifteen years, effective immediately. Mr. Brown is required to remit an initial franchise fee to Yummy in the amount of $60,000. Of this amount, 80 percent is due 30 days later (July 31, 19x1) with the remaining 20 percent due 30 days after the yogurt store opens for business. In return, the franchisee is provided with certain preopening services.

Mr. Brown opened his Yummy Yogurt store on December 16, 19x2, and remitted the initial franchise fee's two installment payments on their respective due dates. The franchisor incurred costs directly associated with providing Mr. Brown with the required preopening services of $4,000 in 19x1, and $9,000 in 19x2. Exhibit 4–6 identifies four distinct approaches to recognizing Yummy Yogurt Co.'s initial franchise fee revenue.

The cash collection method recognizes revenue in the periods the franchisor receives cash payments from the franchisee 19x1 and 19x3. This approach suggests the receipt of cash is the critical event in the earning process. Despite the fact that a high degree of uncertainty pervades franchise-granting, or for that matter the starting-up phase of any business undertaking, focusing attention on cash collection does not appear to be very realistic. Presumably the franchisor renders important services to the franchisee, and their costs must be matched against revenues. The amount of such expenses is not known when the cash is collected, with the result a proper matching of revenues and expenses would not be effected.

Recognizing initial franchise revenue ratably over the franchise agreement's 15-year life overlooks that invariably this fee is to a significant extent compensation for preopening assistance as contrasted with the establishment of the continuing relationship. Indeed, the universal inclusion of a series of ongoing fees be paid to the francishor suggests it is such payments that pertain to the relationship-solidification phase of the franchisor-franchisee relationship. In addition, because the initial fee is typically not refundable if franchisees never actually begin to operate their businesses, the fee has little, if any, "life of the franchise" quality about it. Hence, even if the franchisee's business does become a going concern, it is difficult to make a strong case for amortizing the initial fee over the franchise period.

The franchise inception approach assumes implicitly the crucial event in effecting a franchise agreement is the signing of the franchise agreement. Such a premise is not valid because the signing of a contract is merely an exchange of promises. In addition, the many uncertainties whether the franchise operation will actually come to fruition are so important, they mitigate any attempt to meaningfully match revenue with related costs. Duties must be performed by both franchisor and franchisee before an accountable transaction can be viewed as having occurred.

A committee of the American Institute of CPAs addressed the question of accounting for franchise fee revenue. The resulting pronouncement identifies *substantial performance* by the franchisor as the recommended approach. This is said to have occurred when the franchisor has no remaining refund obligation, has performed the required initial services, and has fulfilled any other conditions bearing on the franchise sale's consummation. In addition to substantial performance, there must be reasonable assurance as to collectibility of the fee.[5] With respect to our illustrative example, it is assumed that once the franchisee opened the store's doors for business on December 16, 19x2, the franchisor will have substantially performed the specified preopening services and is reasonably assured the remaining (20 percent) portion of the initial fee will be collected when due.

With respect to the important matter of applying the matching principle of accounting to measure income, the same AICPA pronouncement offers the following guideline. "Costs directly related to specific revenue-producing

---

[5] Committee on Franchise Accounting and Auditing, *Accounting for Franchise Fee Revenue* (New York: American Institute of Certified Public Accountants, 1973), pp. 8–10.

transactions, usually incremental costs, should be deferred pending recognition of revenue, and costs not directly related to specific revenue-producing transactions, including fixed costs, should be expensed as incurred."[6] Applied to the case at hand, the $13,000 of costs incurred in 19x1 and 19x2 which pertain directly to the establishment of Mr. Brown's Yummy Yogurt store, appear as an expense in 19x2's income statement to be matched with that year's recognition of the $60,000 initial franchise fee revenue.

Installment Sales

When a seller of goods or provider of services grants credit to a customer, there is of course an expectation the resulting amount due will be collected. If serious doubt exists in a particular case, presumably the "receivable" relationship would not even be entered into. Yet there are invariably certain outstanding amounts which prove to be impossible to collect. Vendors who grant credit generally expect a certain portion of their outstanding receivables to be uncollectible. Consequently when charge sales are made, bad debt expense is considered one of the normal and recurring expenses of doing business. Indeed, too low a bad debt amount might even suggest too rigid a credit policy which may be "chasing away" potential credit-worthy customers.

In such conventional sales transactions, the overwhelming majority of the resulting receivables are collected in their entirety and in a somewhat timely manner. The case of installment sales is, however, a different set of circumstances. Installment sales are sales whereby the resulting amount due, instead of being collectible as one amount, is receivable through a predetermined number of "installment" payments of specific amounts and collectible on designated due dates.

Many retailers use the installment sales approach. Responding in particular to customers' desire to purchase durable goods bearing retail price amounts in excess of what they are able to pay immediately or even 30 days later, vendors have created collection plans whereby customers remit their payments in a manner comparable to making monthly payments on a home mortgage loan. Even though each payment is of a like amount, earlier remissions contain proportionately higher interest and lower principal, while an opposite effect occurs as later payments are made. Installment receivables generally have a greater degree of uncertainty surrounding their collectibility than do conventional receivables.

The accounting issue that arises is when to recognize revenue from installment sales transactions. As contrasted with conventional sales, in which

---

[6] Ibid., p. 17.

the passage of legal title constitutes the critical event, with respect to install-ment sales the subsequent collection of the installment receivables may be the critical event. The question is closely related to the matching principle of accounting as well. The unusually large exposure of collection costs and bad debt losses which can characterize installment receivables suggests that all the pertinent expenses that should be matched with the sales revenue may not even be known at the time income would be measured for conventional sales.

Thus, the concern is whether to recognize installment sales revenue prior to collection, given the possibility that significant amounts of the resulting receivables will never actually be realized in the form of cash. Alternatively, for those receivables which are collected, material amounts of collection costs may be incurred, costs which need to be matched with related reve-nue. Two alternatives to conventional sales recognition have been devel-oped: the cost recovery method and the installment method. Both these approaches include in the income statement of the year of sale (i.e., when legal title is transferred from seller to buyer) both the sales revenue and its related cost of goods sold. However, both methods defer recognition of the resulting gross profit. The deferred gross profit appears as a credit on the equities side of the balance sheet until its subsequent transfer to an income statement of some future period. The basis for making such transfers is differ-ent for the two alternative methods, as illustrated in Exhibit 4–7.

In 19x1, Fancy Furniture Co. sold merchandise having a retail price of $200,000; the cost of the furniture was $120,000. The sales were made on an installment basis: a down payment is required and payments are due over a three-year period. As of the end of 19x1, 19x2 and 19x3, 25 percent, 65 percent and 80 percent of 19x1's installment sales had been collected. To simplify this illustration, assume that no interest cost was charged or im-puted.

Exhibit 4–7 shows the amount of realized gross profit for each of the three years under the conventional sales method, the cost recovery method, and the installment method. Under the conventional sales method, the entire gross profit appears in the income statement in the year of sale. Under the cost recovery method, no gross profit is recognized in an income statement until collections of the outstanding receivable are equal to the cost of goods sold. This means that in the illustration, gross profit is not recognized until collections exceed $120,000. The first year's collections were ($200,000 × 25% =) $50,000, and the cumulative amounts collected as of December 31, 19x2 and 19x3 were ($200,000 × 65% =) $130,000 and ($200,000 × 80% =) $160,000 respectively. The critical $120,000 point was surpassed in 19x2 and, as a result, gross profit recognized in that year is ($130,000 − 120,000 =) $10,000. In 19x3, $30,000 of gross profit appears in the

75

Exhibit 4–7

Accounting for Installment Sales—Realized Gross Profit

		19x1	19x2	19x3
1.	Conventional sales method:			
	$200,000 − 120,000 =	$80,000		
2.	Cost recovery method:			
	$120,000 − ($200,000 × .25 =)			
	$50,000 = $(70,000)	–0–		
	$200,000 × .65 = $130,000;			
	$130,000 − 120,000=		$10,000	
	$200,000x.8 = $160,000; $160,000			
	− ($120,000 + 10,000 =) $130,000 =			$30,000
3.	Installment method:			
	$200,000 − 120,000 = $80,000:			
	$80,000 × .25 =	$20,000		
	$80,000 × (.65 − .25 =) .4 =		$32,000	
	$80,000 × (.8 − .65 =) .15 =			$12,000

earnings statement because cumulative collections exceed the cost by ($160,000 − 120,000 =) $40,000, of which $10,000 had already been recognized in 19x2.

The installment method is not as conservative as the cost recovery method. It does not require that all of the merchandise's cost be recovered before proceeding to recognize gross profit. Instead, it views each collection of installment receivables as proportionately a recovery of cost and the realization of gross profit. Accordingly, since 25 percent of the receivable is collected in 19x1, 25 percent of the $80,000 gross profit, or $20,000, is recognized. Similarly, in 19x2 and 19x3, the respective collection of 40 percent and 15 percent of the total receivable results in proportionate gross profit recognition of $32,000 and $12,000 respectively.

Both the cost recovery and installment methods focus attention on the collection of cash, because the circumstances surrounding the sale transaction suggest that their collection constitutes the crucial event. Each method reflects the amount of installment sales and their cost of goods sold in the income statement in the year of sale. But their effect on income measurement is deferred until there is realization in the form of cash receipts. Interestingly, the official stance of the Accounting Principles Board on this matter is that only ". . . where receivables are collectible over an extended period of time and, because of the terms of the transactions or other conditions, there is no reasonable basis for estimating the degree of collectibility . . . when such circumstances exist, and as long as they exist, either the installment method or the cost recovery method of accounting may be used."[7]

Electric Utility Fuel Surcharge

In light of the significance of fuel costs in the production of electricity, utility companies are sometimes allowed to impose an automatic fuel adjustment surcharge on the amounts they charge their customers for electricity. This practice is sanctioned by rate-setting regulatory commissions to compensate for the long lead time which would normally transpire between when utilities incur such added costs and when they would be able to increase their rates after regular rate hearings.

In practice, utilities' additional fuel cost incurred in one month becomes the basis for including an adjustment in the next month's billing to their customers. The accounting issue that arises concerns the propriety of utilities including the added fuel cost as an expense of a period which is not the same period the fuel adjustment is included as an element of their revenue.

Exhibit 4–8 shows the different approaches that could be employed. Assume that in late December of 19x1 an electric utility determines it has sustained a cost of $400,000 because of the increasing price of fuel needed to generate electricity that month, which it in turn pays during December. The company is permitted to shift the burden of this cost to its customers, and it does so by including it in bills mailed to customers in January, 19x2.

The first method is the traditional approach. It recognizes the additional fuel cost as an element of 19x1 income in the same way that other costs of generating that year's power affect 19x1's earnings. The fact that the company's billing process causes it to include the surcharge in invoices distributed in a subsequent month is not a basis for treating this one element of cost differently from all others. As a result, 19x1's income is adversely affected by the fuel adjustment, only to be neutralized by an opposite effect in 19x2. Revenues and expenses are not properly matched, however.

The second method involves deferring recognition of the $400,000 as an expense until the period in which the related revenue is recognized. It reflects the belief that if the resulting revenue is only recognized in 19x2, the matching principle requires its related expenses be so recognized in 19x2 as well. As of December 31, 19x1, the $400,000 cost acquires an "asset" quality, that is, its payment in 19x1 results in a prepaid expense. Although this method results in revenues and expenses being matched in 19x2, the timing of the revenue recognition can be questioned. Is the $400,000 revenue earned in 19x1 or in 19x2?

---

[7] *Accounting Principles Board of Opinion No. 10,* footnote no. 8.

Exhibit 4–8

Accounting for Electric Utility Fuel Surcharge

(credit)	19x1	19x2
1. Costs when incurred, revenue when billed:		
Revenue		$400,000
Expense	($400,000)	
Effect on income	**($400,000)**	**($400,000)**
2. Costs deferred . . . , revenue when billed:		
Revenue		$400,000
Expense		($400,000)
Effect on income	**–0–**	**–0–**
3. Costs when incurred, revenue as anticipated:		
Revenue	$400,000	
Expense	($400,000)	
Effect on income	**–0–**	**–0–**

The third approach reflects the belief that if the cost incurred in 19x1 relates to the sale of electric power in 19x1, the question becomes one of revenue recognition, with the matching principle as a secondary consideration. In other words, 19x1's $400,000 cost signifies this same amount is billable to the company's customers because of electrical power they receive in 19x1 and for which they are, in an accrual sense, immediately liable. Accordingly, the utility's legal right to recover the $400,000 from its customers is recognized when that right materializes in 19x1 with complementing balance sheet disclosure of an "unbilled receivable" asset.

In summary, the case of an electric utility shifting to its customers the burden of its added fuel cost further demonstrates the accounting dynamics of revenue recognition and income measurement. The deficiency of the traditional approach lies in its failure to properly apply the matching principle of accounting. The other two methods, on the other hand, reflect a strict application of the matching principle. When considering when to recognize the revenue aspect of a fuel adjustment surcharge, the "revenue when earned" feature of the third method emerges as the most appropriate approach.

Sales and Net Sales

In addition to the revenue recognition questions examined thus far, there are two other revenue-related matters which also warrant attention. Both relate to determining the appropriate amount of revenue to include in an earnings statement in light of two nuances: vendors' involvement with collection of taxes and the presence of a "right of return" provision.

Collection of Taxes

With the increasing number and magnitude of sales and excise taxes imposed by various governments, a question arises as to what effect, if any, such sums should have on revenue amounts appearing in earnings statements. For certain goods and services, a tax is paid by the customer to the seller, and this tax is then remitted to the government. The seller is the collection agent for the particular taxing authority. Several different methods of accounting for such amounts have been adopted in practice.

Exhibit 4–9 will facilitate an understanding of the issues and four alternative approaches. Assume that the company in question has sales of $100,000 on which it collects an 8% sales tax from its customers. Its cost of sales is $40,000 and its other expenses are $50,000.

Method A excludes the $8,000 sales tax from the income statement altogether. It reflects the belief that the company serves merely as a collection

Exhibit 4–9

Accounting for Sales Tax Collections

	A	B	C	D
Gross sales	$100,000	$108,000	$108,000	$108,000
Less sales taxes		8,000		
Net sales	$100,000	$100,000	$108,000	$108,000
Cost of sales	40,000	40,000	48,000	40,000
Gross profit	$ 60,000	$ 60,000	$ 60,000	$ 68,000
Expenses	50,000	50,000	50,000	58,000
Net income	$ 10,000	$ 10,000	$ 10,000	$ 10,000

agent such that the receipt of the tax from customers immediately creates a liability to the taxing authority, and nothing more. Method B includes the sales tax collected in the period's gross sales from which it is then subtracted to arrive at net sales. This is analogous to the procedure used for sales returns, allowances, and cash discounts as such amounts are included in gross sales but excluded from net sales.

Method C includes the sales tax in net sales as well, and also includes it as one of the elements comprising the period's cost of sales. This approach yields the same ($60,000) gross profit amount that is generated by the two preceding methods. Method D includes the tax collected in net sales but does not consider it a component of cost of sales. The resulting gross profit therefore exceeds that of the other three approaches by the ($8,000) amount of the tax. However, because the tax is then included among the company's other expenses, net income for the period is the same ($10,000) as that reported by the other three methods.

The fact that net income is identical under all four approaches might suggest that determining which method is superior is unimportant. This is not the case, however, because understanding an earnings statement is a process which demands more effort than merely looking at its bottom line. Having like companies measure gross or net sales using unlike concepts of revenue causes havoc.

Although this accounting question is discussed in context of the collection of sales and excise taxes, the issues it raises have widespread applicability. Consider the case of a consulting firm which bills its customers not only for the fees it earns, but also for the reimbursement of specific out-of-pocket costs, such as those relating to travel. The potential materiality of these costs could have a significant effect on the amount of total revenue that would be reflected in the firm's earnings statement—irrespective of there being no effect on net income.

Right of Return

When vendors sell merchandise to their customers, a right of return privilege may exist—either contractually, on the basis of industry practice, or as a matter of law. Upon broadening one's concept of "customer" beyond that of the end consumer, certain seller-buyer relationships require definitive guidelines for recognizing revenue when a right of return is present. Publishers of newspapers, magazines and books, producers of perishable foods (such as baked goods), manufacturers of phonograph records and tape cartridges, and producers of seasonal children's toys are the kinds of enterprises whose exposure to merchandise returns can be significant.

Three different methods of accounting are described below, and illustrated in Exhibit 4–10. A company had gross sales of $90,000, $150,000 and

Exhibit 4-10
Accounting for a Right of Return

		19x1	19x2	19x3
1.	Disclose actual returns:			
	Gross sales	$90,000	$150,000	$240,000
	Less returns	10,800[1]	23,400[4]	37,800[7]
	Net sales	**$79,200**	**$126,600**	**$202,200**
2.	Unconditional acceptance:			
	Net sales	**$49,200**[2]	**$106,600**[5]	**$172,200**[8]
3.	Allowance for expected returns:			
	Gross sales	$90,000	$150,000	$240,000
	Less expected returns	16,200[3]	27,000[6]	43,200[9]
	Net sales	**$73,800**	**$123,000**	**$196,800**

Supporting computations:

[1] $90,000 × .18 × ⅔ = $10,800
[2] $90,000 × ⅔ × .82 = $49,200
[3] $90,000 × .18 = $16,200
[4] ($150,000 × .18 × ⅔ =) $18,000; $18,000 + ($90,000 × .18 × ⅓ =) $5,400 = $23,400
[5] (150,000 × ⅔ × .82 =) $82,000; $82,000 + ($90,000 × ⅓ × .82 =) $24,600 = $106,600
[6] $150,000 × .18 = $27,000
[7] ($240,000 × .18 × ⅔ =) $28,800; $28,800 + ($150,000 × .18 × ⅓ =) $9,000 = $37,800
[8] ($240,000 × ⅔ × .82 =) $131,200; $131,200 + ($150,000 × ⅓ × .82 =) $41,000 = $172,200
[9] $240,000 × .18 = $43,200

$240,000 in 19x1, 19x2 and 19x3 respectively. It has been the company's experience that 18 percent of these sales are eventually negated as a result of merchandise returns. Of a year's sales that will eventually be returned, two-thirds generally occur in the year of sale, and the remaining one-third of the returns take place in the following year. Refer now to Exhibit 4–10 which presents the income statement effects of the three different methods of accounting for merchandise returns.

The first method recognizes the full amount of each year's gross sales, and subtracts from it the revenue relating to the goods actually returned during the year. The amount representing a year's returns includes both merchandise included in that year's gross sales and merchandise sold in prior years. The reported net sales is not truly a valid measure of the year's net sales performance, however, because it contains the effect of returns of earlier years' sales and omits the impact of the current year's revenues which will be returned in subsequent years.

The second method includes as revenue only those sales for which the company no longer has exposure to merchandise returns. In our example, it is assumed that, as of year-end, two-thirds of the year's unreturned sales will no longer be returned and that one-third of the immediately preceding year's unreturned sales are no longer returnable. This method is more conservative than the first method inasmuch as it does not even recognize a sale until a point of unconditional acceptance has been reached.

The third method recognizes the entire amount of a year's gross sales, similar to the first method. Unlike the first method, it recognizes in the year of sale that portion of its revenue which, on the basis of past experience, is expected to be returned. In this regard, the method draws on the strong point which characterized the second method, that is, a concern that amounts included in net sales not be susceptible, at least in a probabilistic sense, to subsequent return.

From the point of view of accounting theory, the allowance approach represents the most appropriate method of accounting for returns. It is consistent with the matching principle of accounting since a period's revenues reflect the pertinent events surrounding the revenue transaction in the first place. Noteworthy is the fact that a balance sheet result ensues as well. The nature of the method entails creating an allowance for expected returns—a balance sheet contra-asset account similar to an allowance for bad debts.

SUMMARY

In light of the need to identify the critical event in an enterprise's revenue-earning process, attention in this chapter was directed toward various distinctive cases. Among these were: during production (long-term construction contracts), completion of production (precious natural resources' extraction), delivery of goods or services (revenue received in advance), transference of legal title (conventional sales), beginning of a licensing period (television movie rights), substantial performance of preopening services (initial franchise fee), and collection of resulting receivables (installment sales). In addition, attention was directed toward revenue recognition implications of electric utility fuel surcharges, vendor collection of sales and excise taxes, and accounting recognition of sales returns.

The underlying theme of the discussion has been that a fundamental aspect of traditional transactions-oriented income measurement is revenue recognition. It is the cornerstone of income measurement in the sense that application of the matching principle of accounting builds on revenue—so intricately at times it may be difficult to even discern where one concept ends and the other begins.

Additional Readings

American Accounting Association 1964 Concepts and Standards Research Study Committee. "The Realization Concept." *The Accounting Review* (April 1965), pp. 312–22.

Bowers, Russell. "Tests of Income Realization." *The Accounting Review* (June 1941), pp. 139–55.

Calhoun, Charles H., III. "Accounting for Initial Franchise Fees: Is It a Dead Issue?" *The Journal of Accountancy* (February 1975), pp. 60–67.

Graese, Clifford E., and Demario, Joseph R. "Revenue Recognition for Long Term Contracts." *The Journal of Accountancy* (December 1976), pp. 53–59.

Heilman, E. A. "Realized Income." *The Accounting Review* (June 1929), pp. 80–87.

Horngren, Charles T. "How Should We Interpret the Realization Concept?" *The Accounting Review* (April 1965), pp. 323–33.

Mobley, Sybil C. "The Concept of Realization: A Useful Device." *The Accounting Review* (April 1966), pp. 292–96.

Myers, John H. "The Critical Event and Recognition of Net Profit." *The Accounting Review* (October 1959), pp. 528–32.

Paton, William A. "Premature Revenue Recognition." *The Journal of Accountancy* (October 1953), pp. 432–37.

Spiller, Earl A., Jr. "The Revenue Postulate—Recognition or Realization." *N.A.A. Bulletin* (February 1962), pp. 41–47.

Storey, Reed K. "Revenue Realization, Going Concern and Measurement of Income." *The Accounting Review* (April 1959), pp. 232–38.

Windal, Floyd W. "The Accounting Concept of Realization." *The Accounting Review* (April 1961), pp. 249–58.

5

Income Measurement: Expenses and Losses

C hapter 4 identified a number of issues revolving around revenue realization and its accounting recognition. Because income is determined by matching revenues with their related costs, expense ramifications were considered as well. There are, however, a number of income measurement questions which exist not as a direct result of the revenue earning process. Indeed, it is precisely because of their *indirect* relationship with revenue generation that such questions arise. Some of these expense and loss situations are therefore examined in this chapter in light of the need to measure an enterprise's income in accordance with the matching principle of accounting.

EXPENSES, COSTS, AND LOSSES

Net income is the net increase in owners' equity resulting from operations and other causes, and it is measured by matching revenues and expenses. The nature of gains and losses is discussed later. Revenues are increases in owners' equity from the sale of goods or the performance of services, and expenses are the decreases in owners' equity related to producing the revenues. As a reduction in owners' equity, an expense manifests itself as a decrease of an asset and/or an increase in a liability. Remember, owners' equity equals total assets less total liabilities.

Assets are economic resources having future service potential, and expenses are economic resources whose service potential has been exhausted.

Hence, during the fiscal period in which the service potential of an asset expires, the appropriate portion of the asset's original cost is transformed into *expense*. Before being matched with revenues, the service potential underlying income determinants such as cost of goods sold, insurance expense, and depreciation expense, would be reflected as merchandise inventory, prepaid expense, and plant assets, respectively.

When the occurrence of an expense is accompanied by the simultaneous payment of cash or the creation of a liability, one might conclude that no asset is acquired to be subsequently transformed into an expense. Understanding at a conceptual level, however, yields a different result. Consider "wages" whose expense nature is recognized at the time the Wages Payable liability is recorded. In fact, the services performed by employees do represent the creation of an asset, because they *are* economic resources having future service potential.

In the typical case in which the perceived resulting revenue benefit occurs during the same period, no useful purpose would be served by initially recording an asset only to recognize the consumption of the service potential in the very same period. Accounting procedures for manufacturing enterprises, on the other hand, actually do recognize that certain types of wages are economic resources with *future* service potential. Specifically, this is the case when manufactured products which benefit from the employees' input will not generate a revenue benefit until a subsequent period. In these circumstances, the wage cost is accounted for as an element of the cost of inventory units thus being created, i.e., as an asset until the goods are completed and sold.

The key point is that an expense in an earnings statement is the recognition of the exhaustion of an economic resource's past service potential, and that an economic resource having future service potential appears in a balance sheet as an asset. Thus, any expense, prior to its income statement recognition as such, will have been—at the conceptual level—an asset. One could even say that not only were all expenses assets at one time, but also that all assets, other than cash and receivables which are monetary in nature, are prepaid expenses in the sense that once their service potential is exhausted—through use, sale or time expiration—they will become determinants of income.

Given this overview of the interrelationship between expenses and assets, we can now appreciate why the terms "expense" and "cost" are not synonymous. Whereas *expense* refers to a particular type of economic resource, namely, one whose service potential has been exhausted in producing revenue, *cost* is the basis on which any type of economic resource is generally accounted for. Both economic resources having future service potential, which are called assets, and those whose service potential had existed in the past, which are called expenses, are accounted for on the basis of their cost.

As a result of this distinction, one can also appreciate why double-entry bookkeeping provides similar debit/credit rules for assets and expenses, and the opposite of these for revenues, liabilities, and owners' equity. The former are increased with debits and are reduced with credits; the latter increase with credits and decrease with debits.

The one additional matter to be considered is that of losses, whose effect on income determination appears to be identical to that of expenses. What is a loss and how does it differ from an expense? Like an expense, a loss is a diminution of an economic resource's service potential, but unlike an expense a loss is not even expected to generate revenue. Thus, a loss is an involuntary expiration of an asset while an expense is a voluntary expiration of an asset in pursuit of revenue. For example, if merchandise were destroyed in a fire, the service potential of an economic resource is reduced, and a loss is recorded. Unlike the conscious sale of merchandise for which a revenue benefit is the result, no parallel outcome is present in the destruction situation.

Consider the case of bad debts. One of the required end-of-period adjustments made by accountants is that of recognizing in the current period's income statement the effect of the outstanding receivables management estimates will never be collected. Irrespective of whether the estimate is based on year-end receivables or credit sales during the year, the amount of expected loss that emerges appears as a negative component of earnings. Although such bad debts are, in a sense, losses since they relate to expected diminution of the receivables asset with no apparent (revenue) benefit, they are usually reported as an expense.

The reason for this is that when making sales on account, a company recognizes it is inevitable that a certain portion, hopefully small, of the resulting receivables will not be collected. Such bad debts are therefore viewed as an expense that must be incurred to generate credit-sales type of revenues. Some accountants, rather than reporting the amount of expected bad debts either as a loss or as an expense, take the position that the expected bad debts should be shown instead as a direct reduction from gross sales. This reflects the belief that such reporting in effect corrects the amount of sales which had ostensibly been made during the year.

Loss is used in a second context as well. When an economic resource which is not the type of asset that the company is in business to buy and sell is disposed of, the difference between its book value and the proceeds received appears as a gain or loss in the earnings statement. Whereas both the revenue and expense amounts are disclosed in the case of revenue transactions, only the resulting gain or loss is set forth for a non-revenue transaction. A third use of the term *loss* is that of signifying that the aggregate effect of all revenues, expenses, gains and losses has caused a net decrease in owners' equity.

MEASUREMENT ISSUES

Given this overview discussion of the nature of expenses, costs and losses, selected aspects of the income measurement process are now examined. Our frame of reference continues to be the matching principle of accounting, and the challenge of isolating meaningful relationships between segments of revenue streams and expenses which are incurred continually or sporadically, and whose related expenditure may be prepaid or deferred.

Stock Option Compensation

In this section, two aspects of stock option compensation are examined. The first revolves around measuring the cost of such employee compensation, and the second is concerned with "cost" aspects of a stock option plan established or financed by a principal stockholder.

The Measurement Date Issue

Although a stock option compensation plan can appear in a variety of formats, its basic nature is that a company grants to selected employees the opportunity to purchase at a future date shares of its capital stock at a predetermined price. It is the expected relationship between the shares' option price and their market price at the time the options are exercised that makes the option valuable to the employee. Companies often establish the option price at an amount less than the grant date's market price. The plan may provide that if the grantees are still employed at some future date such as two years hence, they can exercise their options during the subsequent six-month period. The grantor implicitly assumes the grantees will work diligently and their efforts will be translated into increased income, which in turn manifests itself in the form of increased market value of the company's outstanding shares of stock; an example follows.

On January 1, 19x1, options were granted providing that each of the company's four top executives would have the opportunity to buy 10,000 shares of its common stock for $25 per share any time between December 31, 19x2 and December 31, 19x3. Annual executive compensation expense in the form of a cash salary commitment is $1,000,000. On December 1,

19x3, three of the grantees exercised their options; pertinent dates' market prices are as follows:

January 1, 19x1	$30
December 31, 19x1	$39
December 31, 19x2	$36
December 1, 19x3	$38

The accounting question is, What is the compensation expense that should be reflected in each of the three years—19x1, 19x2 and 19x3?

Although six different approaches are identified in the accounting literature, the two are accorded most attention are the date-of-grant and the date-exercisable methods. Under the date-of-grant method, the difference between the option price and the date-of-grant market price is the measure of compensation expense. In our example, this amount is ($30 − 25 =) $5 per share; therefore, (4 grantees each having the option to buy 10,000 shares =) 40,000 shares at a cost of $5 per share yields a total cost of $200,000. Half of this is recognized in 19x1 and the remaining $100,000 in 19x2 because the options represent compensation for services rendered between January 1, 19x1 and December 31, 19x2. Because one-fourth of the options were not exercised in 19x3, (10,000 @ $5 =) $50,000 of the expense that had been recorded for these options becomes a change in an accounting estimate. It therefore reduces the company's executive compensation expense for 19x3 by $50,000. The three years' total executive compensation expense amounts are therefore $1,100,000, $1,100,000 and $950,000 respectively.

Under the date-exercisable method, the difference between the option price and the market price at the time the options are exercisable is the basis for measuring the compensation cost. Accordingly, any interim fluctuation of the shares' market price is deemed to have an immediate impact on the grantor's cost. Thus, in 19x1 whose year-end market price of $39 exceeds the $25 option price by $14, the outstanding options cause recognition of [40,000 @ ($39 − 25 =) $14 =] $560,000 additional compensation, for a total of ($1,000,000 + 560,000 =) $1,560,000. In 19x2, the market price declined to $36 with the result that [40,000 @ ($39 − 36 =) $3 =] $120,000 is the amount which reduces that year's compensation expense to ($1,000,000 − 120,000 =) $880,000. 19x3's compensation expense reflects the lapse of one-quarter of the options; [10,000 @ ($36 − 25 =) $11 =] $110,000 of previously recorded expense is "corrected" with the result that the year's expense is ($1,000,000 − 110,000 =) $890,000.

The three-year cumulative compensation expense recognized by these two methods is shown on the next page.

	Date of Grant	Exercisable Date
19x1	$1,100,000	$1,560,000
19x2	1,100,000	880,000
19x3	950,000	890,000
	$3,150,000	**$3,330,000**

Note the date exercisable method recognizes ($3,330,000 − 3,150,000 =) $180,000 more total compensation expense than does the date-of-grant method. This difference is attributable to the 30,000 exercised options bearing a $6 greater cost per share—$6 being the difference between the $36 market price at the exercisable date and that of the $30 at the date of grant.

Support for the date-of-grant method, which is the approach required by existing authoritative pronouncements, is based on the belief that ". . . it was the value at that date which the employer may be presumed to have had in mind. . . . The date of grant also represents the date on which the corporation foregoes the principal alternative use of the shares. . . ."[1] It has also been argued that once an expense has been calculated, it should not be modified on the basis of subsequent developments. In addition, there exists the distinction between accountable transactions affecting a company directly and those involving only external parties which are not accountable. A key aspect of this notion is that fluctuation in the market price of its own outstanding shares should not be allowed to have any effect on the measurement of the company's earnings.

Advocates of the date-exercisable method maintain it is precisely because a grantor expects a significant difference between the option price and the market price at the exercisable date that the plan was created in the first place. It is only if such a situation can be expected to occur that an adequate incentive is provided. The date-of-grant difference is relatively inconsequential, and should therefore not be construed to be a measure of cost. In addition, because grantees must remain in the grantor's employ until the exercisable date to be able to avail themselves of the plan, it is only then the grantor becomes obligated to make the shares available. The cost should therefore be the difference between the proceeds that would be received in the open market and that accepted from the grantees which meaningfully measures the sacrifice sustained by the grantor as a result of its option plan commitment.

Principal Stockholder Involvement

Apart from the matter of identifying an appropriate date in order to measure the compensation expense of a stock option plan, a question can also

---

[1] *Accounting Research Bulletin No. 43,* chapter 13, paragraph nos. 10 and 11.

arise whether the granting corporation recognizes an expense if it incurs no cost at all. Specifically, when a plan is either established or financed by a principal stockholder, with no direct cost accruing to the company as such, is it appropriate or necessary to impute an expense in the process of computing the enterprise's earnings? For example, a stockholder provides the corporation with 3,000 of its shares, whose market value is $40 per share, for the express purpose of distributing them to employees as compensation.

Such a set of circumstances provides a good example of how economic substance prevails over legal form in the realm of financial reporting. The intent, if not the result, of such involvement by a principal stockholder (e.g., one who either owns, controls, or influences 10 percent or more of the corporation's common stock) presumably is to generate benefits which would accrue to the enterprise as well as to the shareholder. The economic substance of such a situation is effectively the same as that of a stock option plan offered by the corporation proper. Therefore, unless special circumstances exist, such as an indication that no benefit would accrue to the corporation as such, an option plan structured in this manner would become an accountable transaction.

When measurement of the (3,000 @ $40 =) $120,000 compensation expense is effected, the offsetting credit is treated as an addition to the company's (invested capital component of) owners' equity. Such a credit parallels that which is recognized if a company receives gratuitously an economic resource whose substance demands accountability, e.g., donation of a plant site from a municipality seeking the creation of new employment opportunities for its citizens. Thus, the mutually beneficial outcome of the situation at hand indicates the principal stockholder is effectively an extension of the enterprise. The economic substance of such a relationship overcomes what, in legal form, is but a gratuitous gift by an external party and a no-cost distribution of shares by the corporation.

Contingent Losses

A loss was defined earlier as a diminution in an asset for which there is no resulting benefit. It can be assumed that for most types of losses—just as for most types of expenses—the dollar amount can be derived when financial statements are prepared. However, there are instances when the exact amount of an expense or of a loss is not known, and an estimate must be made.

An example of an estimated expense is the recognition of income tax charges. At the time end-of-period financial statements are prepared, it is possible the company may not know its exact income tax cost for the year. Even if it has made the calculation, the Internal Revenue Service may disallow some expenses. Therefore, the amount which appears as an expense in the earnings statement is likely to be an estimate. The fact that an amount is an estimate does not affect its status in financial statements; recall that the amounts representing both depreciation expense and bad debt expense are estimates.

An example of an *estimated* loss would be the loss that arises on applying the lower-of-cost-or-market rule to merchandise inventory and to marketable equity securities. The nature of this accounting requirement is that on the basis of market value information, the estimated loss in asset value is recognized even though the exact amount of the loss will not be known until subsequent realization in an arm's length transaction.

In addition to losses that have occured for which there are either actual or estimated amounts, the accountant may also encounter a "contingent" loss, that is, one whose existence depends on the occurrence of future events. More specifically, such a loss arises when there is already an existing condition involving uncertainty as to its outcome which will be resolved on the basis of the occurrence of particular future events. An example is the outcome of pending litigation.

The distinction between an estimated loss and a contingent loss is that, whereas in the former the underlying event has already occurred and only the *amount* of the loss has yet to be ascertained, the contingent loss situation is characterized by uncertainty even as to the existence of the loss. The accounting issue surrounding the recognition of contingent losses centers on identifying the criteria which must be met to warrant loss recognition. FASB Statement No. 5 establishes two such criteria, probability of occurrence and estimability of amount. More specifically, "information available prior to issuance of the financial statements indicates that it is probable that an asset had been impaired or a liability had been incurred at the date of the financial statements . . . (and that) future events will occur confirming the fact of the loss (and that) the amount of loss can be reasonably estimated."[2]

In effect, the FASB states that meeting these two conditions requires a contingent loss to be accounted for as though it were an estimated loss, that is, as an expense. Examples include bad debt losses, product warranty costs, uninsured casualty losses, threat of expropriation loss, and, in certain cases where underlying factors so indicate, losses resulting from litigation or assessments. The FASB specifically excluded from the scope of its pronouncement the matter of accounting for contingent gains, such as sums the plaintiff expects to recover in a suit for monetary damages.

---

[2] *Financial Accounting Standards Board, Statement No. 5,* paragraph no. 8. Copyright © by Financial Accounting Standards Board, High Ridge Park, Stamford, Connecticut 06905, U.S.A. Reprinted with permission. Copies of the complete document are available from the FASB.

Specifically not qualifying for formal loss recognition are losses from expected future inventory declines because the underlying condition does not exist as of the current balance sheet date. Similarly, expense recognition of the "cost" of self-insurance is precluded. Self-insurance means that because the company itself will absorb any ensuing losses, an "insurance" cost is borne implicitly by the uninsured company. Rather than disclosing the full amount of such a cost in the period in which a loss occurs, the matching principle of accounting would suggest that the "cost" should be shared by each fiscal period similar to what would happen if premium payments were actually remitted to an insurance company. By including such self-insurance costs in its earnings statement, a company's financial statements would be comparable to those of other enterprises that do incur the cost of insurance coverage and therefore account for such costs. The counter argument revolves around the empirical fact that there is no arm's length transaction with a third party for which to account.

The cited FASB criteria preclude expense recognition of self-insurance costs because losses that may occur subsequent to the end of the fiscal period do not reflect existing conditions during the period. The essence of the self-insurance concept is that recognition is made prior to the emergence of the loss circumstance. The FASB requires that such circumstances must exist even though the precise impact of a particular outcome will be based on future events. The alternative acceptable means of disclosing the presence of a self-insurance system is through earmarking retained earnings. This is effected by creation of an "appropriated" segment of retained earnings, typically by parenthetical or footnote disclosure. When this is done, a company identifies the amount of dollars it has "earmarked" for purposes of absorbing uninsured future losses. This has no effect on net income, however.

Income Taxes

Although the calculation of income taxes can require considerable effort in its own right, a number of tax-based issues raise questions for financial reporting as well. In other words, once a company's current tax obligation is determined, making adequate balance sheet and earnings statement disclosures is not a perfunctory matter.

There is no consensus among accountants whether income tax charges are a determinant of earnings or a distribution of earnings. The conceptual pros and cons notwithstanding, income taxes in practice are treated as determinants of income, and accordingly the term *expense* is associated with such charges. Perhaps in an effort to emphasize they are not expenses over which management can exercise any substantive degree of control, income taxes are sometimes isolated in the earnings statement by presenting Earnings before Income Taxes, followed by the income tax charge and the resulting Net Income. But this, in its own right, has no bearing on the accounting *measurement* of income taxes.

One of the important income measurement ramifications of treating income taxes as an expense and not as a distribution of profits is that the accrual and matching principles of accounting must be adhered to. If they were not applicable, the amount of income tax that would appear in an earnings statement would be that which would actually be due the governmental tax authority. But because accrual and matching are the focal point of accounting for expenses, several measurement and disclosure questions pervade the area of accounting for income taxes. The three major issues with which the ensuing sections are concerned are timing differences between accounting income and taxable income, tax loss carryforward benefits, and the investment tax credit. Because the issue in all three cases ultimately revolves around which fiscal period should reflect, or to which should be allocated the recognition of, the income tax cost, the subject is referred to as *interperiod tax allocation.*

Timing Differences between Accounting Income and Taxable Income

While income computed for financial reporting purposes is prepared in conformity with generally accepted accounting principles, taxable income on which a company's income tax liability is based is calculated in accordance with the prevailing income tax laws. Because transactions are sometimes treated differently for purposes of determining accounting income and taxable income, these two ''income'' amounts will usually differ from one another. Some of the differences are permanent in the sense that once each system records the particular transaction according to its requirements, there will always be a difference between them; for example, interest earned on a municipal bond is excluded from Federal taxable income, but is included as revenue when computing accounting income.

As opposed to a permanent difference, a timing difference exists when there is a difference between the periods in which transactions affect taxable income and the periods in which they enter into the determination of pretax accounting income. For example, a company might concurrently use the straight-line method of computing depreciation for accounting income purposes and an accelerated method in calculating taxable income. Over the life of the asset, the cumulative depreciation will be identical, but particular years' depreciation expense amounts will differ. And because they differ in any given year, the tax expense is derived from applying the pertinent tax rate to the different resulting amounts of income may vary as well.

As an illustration, assume a company's accounting and taxable income before considering depreciation expense are both $50,000 in 19x1 and the tax rate is 40 percent. Depreciation is $5,000 per year for 19x1 through 19x4 for accounting purposes, and for tax purposes the amounts are $8,000, $6,000, $4,000 and $2,000 respectively. The actual tax due in 19x1 is computed as follows: $50,000 − 8,000 = $42,000; $42,000 × 40% = $16,800. Had the tax liability been based on accounting income, the $18,000 amount currently payable would have been based on the following calculation: $50,000 − 5,000 = $45,000; $45,000 × 40% = $18,000. It is because the actual tax is ($18,000 − 16,800 =) $1,200 less than that which the accounting records alone would indicate, that many companies maintain separate records for financial reporting and income taxation purposes.

For purposes of measuring accounting income, the question that arises is whether the $16,800 tax currently due is a valid measure of the company's tax expense. Given that pretax accounting income in 19x1 is ($50,000 − 5,000 =) $45,000 and not the ($50,000 − 8,000 =) $42,000 taxable income, the resulting tax obligation would be $18,000 and not $16,800. Moreover, this $1,200 difference will eventually be remitted to the government; it is just being deferred by virtue of the company's being able to use a different depreciation method for tax purposes. From the point of view of financial accounting, therefore, the full $18,000 tax does accrue during 19x1. Because only $16,800 of it is immediately payable does not detract from the need to recognize the full amount of the accrued expense. The $1,200 not recorded as a current liability is reflected as a deferred income tax on the equities side of the balance sheet and is usually identified as a noncurrent liability.

Implicit in this approach to measuring income tax expense is the belief it matches revenues and expenses. It of course assumes an income tax is a determinant of income even though one could argue that an income tax payment is a distribution of profit and therefore not subject to the matching principle. But given the assumption an income tax is an expense, consistency suggests that the presence of income taxes in a particular period's income statement should be directly related to the various revenue and expense elements whose aggregation is the very basis of calculating the income tax charge in the first place.

Our depreciation expense illustration exemplifies but one of four types of timing differences that can occur. It is a case of an expense deducted for tax purposes earlier (or faster) than it is being recorded as an expense for accounting purposes. A second category consists of revenue transactions included as a component of accounting income earlier (or faster) than parallel recognition in computing taxable income. An example of this would be profit on installment sales which for financial reporting might be recognized in full at the date goods are delivered but which for tax purposes are reported only as subsequent collections are made. From a managerial point of view, these two types of timing differences are desirable because they effectively postpone the payment of taxes even though for financial accounting purposes, there would be a tax accrual.

The other two types of timing differences encompass situations where actual tax payments are initially larger than the tax expense to be recognized in the measurement of accounting income. One category comprises expense items that are recognized earlier (or faster) for accounting purposes than for tax purposes. For example, warranty costs may be recorded as an expense component of accounting income on the basis of estimates made during the year merchandise is sold. For tax purposes, warranty costs must be deducted only as they are paid, and thus at a slower pace than they are being recorded for accounting purposes.

The other group of transactions whose timing differences can cause taxable income to be higher than financial reporting's earnings before taxes is that of revenues included in taxable income earlier (or faster) than they are recognized for accounting purposes. An example would be revenue received in advance of performing a service contract: a health spa that includes all enrollment fees in taxable income upon receipt while for accounting purposes it recognizes the revenue over the life of the enrollment period.

In both these latter cases, the income tax that accrues on the basis of the amounts comprising accounting income is less than the amount actually payable, which is based on the higher taxable income. Because the amount currently payable exceeds that which is recorded as being the proper tax expense, a deferred tax *debit* results. Being the counterpart of the deferred tax credit which emerged earlier, its inclusion among the balance sheet assets has the nature of the equivalent of a prepaid expense. This is because it will eventually be reflected in a subsequent period's income statement as part of its tax expense without simultaneously creating a liability, i.e., because it was "prepaid."

The conceptual pros and cons of accruing an income tax expense amount that varies from that which is currently payable, because of timing differences, can be summarized as follows. Such interperiod allocation is based on the presumption that income taxes are an expense and, as such, matching is best achieved if the tax accrual is based on the revenue and expense elements comprising accounting income, rather than taxable income. Creation of a deferred credit does not signify a permanent savings, but rather indicates a tax payment has merely been postponed. It is therefore included among liabilities, and not as part of owners' equity.

A primary counter argument points out that the concept that income tax is a determinant, rather than a distribution, of profit is not universally accepted. If taxes were regarded as a distribution of income, the accrual and matching principles would not apply. The establishment of a deferred liability is also questioned on the grounds that no legal liability exists. The governmental taxing authority is satisfied with the amount of tax that was computed on the basis of taxable income; therefore, recognition of an amount due to a party which does not expect to so receive it is said to be a questionable exercise at best.

A third point centers on the observation that as old plant assets are retired, they are replaced with new assets having a greater dollar cost. Since depreciation-induced timing differences are generally the largest component of deferred income taxes, the result is that annual and cumulative amounts of accrued tax expense invariably exceed the tax amounts actually remitted. As a consequence, a company's deferred tax liability would continue to grow *ad infinitum*. Readers of financial statements in turn would encounter a paradoxical situation. On the one hand, if they accept the assertion that a *bona fide* liability exists, they can ask why does its size only increase. On the other hand, if it is to be viewed as a *de facto* element of owners' equity, they can ask what purpose will have been served by initially reducing after-tax earnings if readers of the balance sheet add it back to the very owners' equity whose growth is presumably measured by earnings in the first place.

Accounting recognition of a deferred income tax credit can have substantive implications for public utility companies whose rates are regulated by Federal or state commissions. A basic principle of rate setting is that the rate customers can be charged by a utility is set to produce the total amount of revenue it needs to achieve a predetermined rate of return. The rate of return, in turn, is based on two factors: *income* and *asset base*. For example, if an electric power company is allowed to earn a 9 percent return on its $100,000,000 asset investment, its after-tax earnings would be expected to be $9,000,000. If the company projects expenses (including income taxes) to be $206,000,000, rates would be calculated to achieve a level of revenue equal to ($206,000,000 + $9,000,000 =) $215,000,000.

If a regulated utility uses an accelerated depreciation approach to compute its tax liability and the straight-line method for measuring accounting income, the question that arises is how shall tax expense be measured for financial reporting purposes. If only the lower current tax due "flows through" the earnings statement—the flowthrough method—there will be lower expenses which, given the "fixed" amount of allowable income, results in lower revenues needed. Assume the $206,000,000 of expenses in our example includes $4,000,000 of income tax currently due plus a deferred $2,000,000 tax. If only the $4,000,000 were to flow through the income statement, total expenses would be $204,000,000 which, together with the $9,000,000 allowed income, indicates a revenue need of $213,000,000 rather than $215,000,000. The result is that the full benefit of using accelerated depreciation for tax purposes is effectively passed on to consumers. This result also gives an added dimension to the term denoting the method; namely, the flow-through method is the one which allows the entire benefit to flow through to the consumer.

Alternatively, if for rate-making purposes the $2,000,000 deferred taxes are included in the earnings statement—the "normalization" approach—the higher amount of recognized tax expense would result in higher total expenses. And given the "fixed" allowable income, this in turn would generate greater revenue needs—in our example, the original $215,000,000 rather than $213,000,000. Higher revenue needs, borne by consumers, means the benefits of using accelerated depreciation for tax purposes are *not* being passed on to the consumer.

Although the relative merits of the flow-through and normalization methods in a rate-setting context involve issues which transcend the realm of accounting theory and financial reporting *per se*, the controversy is nevertheless worthy of our attention. It illustrates the ramifications of accounting for a milieu whose nature, at least in the minds of some persons, might be oblivious to phenomena as remote as the machinations of accrual accounting. But the issue is real, and to a significant extent, it was wrought by principles and standards designed to render a meaningful measurement of the cost of income taxes.

Tax Loss Carryforward Benefit

In determining its taxable income, a corporation may discover that rather than having earned profit for which it incurs an income tax obligation, it instead sustains a loss. The key term used in making such calculations is "net operating loss"—a technical expression which for our purposes can be assumed to be the computed negative taxable income. A company that incurs such a loss sustains no Federal income tax obligation. There is, however, a provision in the tax law which permits such a taxpayer to reduce the computed income tax liability of designated prior or subsequent years by an amount equal to the net operating loss. An example follows.

Assume that in its first year of operation, 19x1, a company has a $10,000 net operating loss. In the following year, 19x2, it earns taxable income of $15,000 on which it incurs a 40 percent income tax. There is no tax obligation in 19x1, but the income tax liability for 19x2 is ($15,000 × 40% =) 16,000. The loss carryforward feature of the tax law allows the company to reduce its 19x2 tax obligation by $4,000—equal to 40 percent of 19x1's $10,000 loss—so the amount actually due for 19x2 is ($6,000 − 4,000 =) $2,000. this can also be understood as follows: as a result of carrying forward 19x1's $10,000 loss, 19x2's $15,000 taxable income is effectively reduced to $5,000. The 40 percent tax on $5,000 yields a $2,000 tax obligation.

In our example, 19x1 is referred to as the year of the loss and 19x2 is called the year of realization. The reason for this terminology is that although a loss occurred in 19x1, the income tax benefit it generates is only realized in the following year. The issue that arises for financial accounting is how to account for the tax loss carryforward benefit. One approach is to reflect its effect only if and when realization occurs in a subsequent year. The alternative point of view is to account for its prospective benefit as soon as the loss occurs. The accounting results generated by these two methods are presented in Exhibit 5–1.

When recognition of the carryforward benefit is made only in the year of realization, the full amount of the $10,000 loss is so depicted in the year it was incurred, 19x1. The subsequent realization of the carryforward benefit

Exhibit 5–1

Accounting for Tax Loss Carryforward

	Recognition of Tax Loss Carryforward Benefit in	
	Year of Realization	Year of Loss
19x1 Partial income statement:		
(Loss) before income tax	($10,000)	($10,000)
Income tax ($10,000 × 40% =)		4,000
Net (loss)	**($10,000)**	**($6,000)**
19x2 Partial income statement:		
Earnings before income tax	$15,000	$15,000
Income tax ($15,000 × 40% =)	(6,000)	(6,000)
	$ 9,000	$ 9,000
Tax loss carryforward ($10,000 × 40% =)	4,000	
Net income	**$13,000**	**$ 9,000**
Cumulative net income:		
19x1 Net (loss)	($10,000)	($ 6,000)
19x2 Net income	13,000	9,000
Total	**$ 3,000**	**$ 3,000**

in 19x2 causes that year's income to be affected by income taxes only to the extent that the current obligation is not offset by a carryforward. In the case at hand, 19x2's $6,000 tax is partially offset by the $4,000 benefit carried over from 19x1. As a result, it is only the net ($6,000 − 4,000 =) $2,000 effect that distinguishes *Earnings before Income Tax* from *Net Income*. Unless the ($6,000 and $4,000) components of the $2,000 are so disclosed, as they must be, readers of the income statement would conclude that only a $2,000 tax was incurred, but this of course is not the case. The tax on $15,000 was $6,000; something less than that amount was actually payable because of special circumstances totally unrelated to the (19x2) year's operations. As a result, the carryforward benefit must be identified as an extraordinary component of Net Income.

The alternative year-of-loss approach maintains that since 19x1's loss generates a future benefit for the company, the full impact of the loss on 19x1's earnings is not $10,000. Instead, the loss year's income statement should disclose the loss as affected by (i.e., net of) the expected future benefit; thus the ($10,000 − 4,000 =) $6,000 net loss result for 19x1.

Before proceeding to the earnings statement results for the subsequent period, it is important the end-of-19x1 balance sheet effect be considered as well. Recognition during the loss year of a future carryforward benefit results in the creation of an asset, to reflect the expectation the company will be relieved of part of a future period's tax obligation. In terms of journal-entry recognition, consider the following:

Dr. Future Tax Loss Carryforward Benefit   4,000
     Cr. Income Tax Expense   4,000
     To record carryforward effect of the 19x1 loss.

The nature of such as asset at first glance would appear to be akin to a receivable. But, in fact, money is not going to be received from the Internal Revenue Service; rather, money that would otherwise be payable will not be due. It would therefore be more appropriate to view the future tax benefit as similar to a prepaid expense, in the sense that because of its existence, an expense appearing on some future period's income statement will not create a liability of a like amount. This asset is categorized as current or noncurrent on the basis of when the future benefit is expected to be realized.

In 19x2, the earnings statement reflects the full impact of the 40 percent tax on that year's $15,000 income, or $6,000. As a result, the after-tax income is ($15,000 − 6,000 =) $9,000. The fact the amount actually payable is also affected by the realization of the previous year's carryforward benefit would have no effect on income in 19x2; its effect is only on the balance sheet. This is depicted in the journal entry that follows.

Dr. Income Tax Expense	6,000	
Cr. Taxes Payable		2,000
Cr. Future Tax Loss Carryforward Benefit		4,000
To record 19x2 tax expense and tax liability.		

The result is that despite earnings statement recognition of a $6,000 tax, only $2,000 is actually payable, because the benefit capitalized as an asset in 19x1 is being realized in 19x2.

The conceptual difference between the two approaches is as follows. The year-of-realization method is based on the belief that no benefit can be assumed to exist until the company actually earns taxable income which qualifies for reduction. An operating loss carryforward expires after a specific number of years, and sometimes a company is unable to use all of the benefit. At the implementation level, the value of the benefit is therefore created only when qualifying income is earned, that is, in the year of realization, and accounting conservatism suggests that a company should not record as an asset a future benefit which may never even occur.

On the othe hand, the year-of-loss method is based on the notion the benefit which the company expects to realize is in substance created in the loss year. The loss burden shouldered by that year should therefore be reduced by the benefit which will occur subsequently. And to counter the "conservatism" argument, advocates of this method maintain it is the only approach which reflects the spirit, if not the intent, of the going-concern principle. This tenet of accounting states that it is assumed that the enterprise will continue to operate indefinitely with the implicit assumption it will earn income, and therefore be able to realize the benefit of the tax loss carryforward.

As far as generally accepted accounting principles are concerned, the Accounting Principles Board ruled in favor of the year of realization method, but the year-of-loss approach may be used in certain cases, viz., ". . . the tax benefits of loss carryforwards should not be recognized until they are actually realized except in unusual circumstances when realization is assured beyond any reasonable doubt at the time the loss carryforwards arise."[3]

Investment Tax Credit

With respect to the payment of Federal income taxes, an investment tax credit is available to businesses which invest in certain qualifying property such as machinery and equipment. The taxpayer is able to reduce its current income tax *obligation*—not merely the taxable income on which the obliga-

---

[3] *Accounting Principles Board Opinion No. 11*, paragraph no. 45.

tion is based—by a statutory percentage of the capital outlay, which in recent years has been set at 10 percent.

The financial reporting question that arises is, How is the benefit of the investment credit to be accounted for? One point of view is that the full amount of the benefit should be reflected in the income statement in the year the tax reduction is realized, that is, in the year the related asset is acquired. The alternative position is that recognition of the benefit should be spread over the useful life of the pertinent asset. Before proceeding to examine the two approaches at a conceptual level, an example is provided to illustrate the different accounting results that would occur.

Assume that 19x1 is a particular taxpayer's first year of operation, and that during the year it purchased qualifying equipment at a cost of $400,000. The estimated useful life of the equipment is 8 years with no expected salvage value, and the straight-line method of depreciation is used. For both 19x1 and 19x2, income before depreciation and income tax is $233,000, and the income tax obligation is computed to be $85,000 before consideration of the 10 percent investment tax credit. The amount actually payable appears as a current liability in the year-end balance sheet, and no dividends are declared. The relevant portions of the 19x1 and 19x2 income statements and end-of-year balance sheets—under the two methods—appear in Exhibit 5–2.

The method which recognizes the full impact of the investment credit in the income statement in the year the taxpayer's tax obligation is reduced is called *the flow-through method.* This title signifies the entire benefit of the credit flows through the income statement immediately. On referring to the exhibit, note first that the ($50,000) depreciation expense is based on the ($400,000) cost of the equipment divided by the eight years of its expected useful life. The ($40,000) amount of the investment credit is equal to 10 percent of the qualifying asset's $400,000 cost. The resulting ($85,000 tax less the $40,000 credit, or) $45,000 net tax obligation appears as such in both the 19x1 income statement and the year-end balance sheet. Because the entire credit appears as a component of 19x1's earnings, it has no additional effect on subsequent years' income.

The theory underlying the flow-through approach is that the investment tax credit is a selective rate reduction. In addition, the legislative history of the investment credit—both the Revenue Act of 1962 underlying the original law and the Tax Reduction Act of 1975 which increased its rate from 7 percent to 10 percent—indicates its objective is to stimulate business investment. Such stimulation occurs by having more after-tax (cash flow) dollars to reinvest in the business which is, of course, independent of the accounting method used to record the tax credit. Advocates of the flow-through method contend that the very recognition of the credit in its entirety in the income statement—with its necessarily favorable effect on net income—is stimula-

Exhibit 5–2

Accounting for Investment Tax Credit

	Flow-Through Method	Deferral Method
19x1 partial income statement		
Income before depreciation and income tax	$233,000	$233,000
Less depreciation expense ($400,000 × ⅛ =)	50,000	50,000
Income before tax	$183,000	$183,000
Income tax	$ 85,000	$ 85,000
Less investment credit:		
$400,000 × 10% =	40,000	
$400,000 × 10% × ⅛ =		5,000
	$ 45,000	$ 80,000
Net income	**$138,000**	**$103,000**
12/31/x1 partial balance sheet		
Taxes payable	$ 45,000	$ 45,000
Deferred investment credit		35,000
Retained earnings	138,000	103,000
Total	**$183,000**	**$183,000**
19x2 partial income statement		
Income before depreciation and income tax	$233,000	$233,000
Less depreciation expense ($400,000 × ⅛ =)	50,000	50,000
Income before taxes	$183,000	$183,000
Income tax	$ 85,000	$ 85,000
Less investment credit ($400,000 × 10% × ⅛ =)		5,000
	$ 85,000	$ 80,000
Net income	**$ 98,000**	**$103,000**
12/31/x2 partial balance sheet		
Taxes payable	$ 85,000	$ 85,000
Deferred investment credit		30,000
Retained earnings	236,000	206,000
Total	**$321,000**	**$321,000**

tive in its own right. It is argued this is the case because being able to report higher earnings can have a favorable effect on the market value of the company's common stock and in turn on its prospective cost of additional capital.

To appreciate the nature of the alternative approach, called *the deferral method,* refer again to the Exhibit 5–2. The only difference between the company's 19x1 income statement under the deferral method and that which reflects the flow-through method is that only one eighth of the $40,000 tax credit, or $5,000, is recognized as a determinant of 19x1 earnings. Recognition of the other seven-eighths of the $40,000 credit, or $35,000, is deferred and its income effect is spread over the remaining seven years of the equipment's estimated eight-year useful life. As a result, the deferred $35,000, instead of being a credit in the 19x1 income statement, appears as a credit in the end-of-year balance sheet. The year-end retained earnings is therefore $35,000 less than that produced by the flow-through method, but total equities and total assets are the same $183,000.

In 19x2, the income statement contains another one eighth of the investment tax credit ($5,000) causing the year's tax cost to be ($85,000 − 5,000 =) $80,000. Reference to the year-end balance sheet, however, indicates that $85,000 is the amount of taxes actually payable for 19x2. The $5,000 of tax credit recognized as a component of earnings represents the accounting realization of the second eighth of the credit whose full cash impact had been realized in 19x1. Thus, the Deferred Investment Credit as of the end of 19x2 is $5,000 less than it had been at the beginning of the year, and the difference between the two methods' end-of-year amounts of Retained Earnings is the same $30,000 of yet-to-be recognized credit that appears as the "deferred" balance.

Advocates of the deferral method believe this approach best reflects the accrual principle of accounting. Because a company benefits by using an asset, not by acquiring it, the cost of a depreciable asset is not treated as an expense in the year of acquisition, but is depreciated over the asset's estimated useful life. Similarly, a tax benefit resulting from the acquisition should be recognized over the same time period. This notion can be conceptualized further by viewing the tax credit as being tantamount to a rebate, even though it is granted by the government rather than by the vendor. In the case at hand, the $40,000 investment credit has the effect of reducing the equipment's cost basis to ($400,000 − 40,000 =) $360,000. The resulting annual depreciation expense, given the expected eight-year useful life, would be ($360,000 ÷ 8 =) $45,000, and this is effectively what does result when the income statement for each of the eight years includes both $50,000 of depreciation expense and $5,000 of recognized investment credit.

Accounting for the investment tax credit has had an eventful history, and a brief review follows. When the investment tax credit was first created, the Accounting Principles Board (APB) issued *Opinion No. 2* which concluded that an investment tax credit ". . . should be reflected in net income over the productive life of acquired property and not in the year in which it is placed in service."[4] That position reflected the belief that ". . . earnings arise from the use of facilities, not from their acquisition. . . (and that) . . . the credit is contingent to some degree on future developments."[5] The Opinion was supported by 14 of the 20 voting members of the Board.

Some fifteen months later, the APB issued *Opinion No. 4* which stated that ". . . the alternative method of treating the credit as a reduction of Federal income taxes of the year in which the credit arises is also acceptable."[6] Fifteen of the 20 voting members supported this position.

A number of observers felt that the subsequent action by the APB was in response to opposition by both accountants and businessmen, and indicated the Board did not have the power to impose accounting principles. However, the APB did manage to sustain itself, and its stature and ability to promulgate official pronouncements was not immediately threatened. When the investment tax credit went out of existence several years later, the haunting specter of the conflict between Opinion Nos. 2 and 4 became somewhat academic. Before long, however, the viability of the Board was again questioned, and early in 1971 the American Institute of CPAs commissioned a task force ". . . to study the establishment of accounting principles and to make recommendations for improving that process."[7]

Later that year, the Federal government indicated its plan to reinstitute the investment credit, and the House of Representatives passed its version of the bill on October 6. The APB believed this would be an opportune time to reimpose its original (Opinion No. 2) approach to accounting for such a credit. On October 22, it released an exposure draft of a proposed Opinion which effectively restated the provisions originally set forth in APB Opinion No. 2, namely, that ". . . benefits arising from investment tax credits should be accounted for as reductions of income tax expense over the periods in which the cost of the related property is charged to income. . ."[8]

The subsequent Senate version of the enabling legislation contained a provision which states no taxpayer could be required to use any particular

---

[4] *Accounting Principles Board Opinion No. 2*, paragraph no. 13.

[5] Ibid., paragraph no. 12.

[6] *Accounting Principles Board Opinion No. 4*, paragraph no. 10.

[7] Report of the Study on Establishment of Accounting Principles: *Establishing Financial Accounting Standards* (New York: American Institute of Certified Public Accountants, Inc., 1972), p. 1.

[8] Accounting Principles Board: *Exposure Draft of Proposed APB Opinion "Accounting for Investment Tax Credits,"* paragraph no. 4.

method in accounting for the investment tax credit in reports subject to the jurisdiction of any Federal agency. This provision effectively precluded APB action of the type set forth in its exposure draft. Obviously concerned by this development, the Board announced it "has had to defer its efforts to develop a single uniform method. . . (and that it) unanimously deplores congressional involvement in establishing accounting principles for financial reports to investors. . . (and) congressional endorsement of alternative accounting methods especially since there has been strong demand by congressmen and others for the elimination of alternative methods which confuse investors."[9]

It is perhaps ironic that the investment tax credit which had threatened the APB's existence early in the 1960's reappeared less than a decade later during the period when the committee established by the American Institute of CPAs was deliberating the matter of how accounting rules should be established. In March 1972, the committee recommended the abolition of the APB, and this course of action was adopted. The Financial Accounting Standards Board began operating in July, 1973.

SUMMARY

In this chapter, five topics of an expense/loss nature were examined. The stock option compensation case posed two questions, identifying the appropriate date for measuring the cost of granting stock options to employees, and the need to look to the economic substance, rather than legal form, of principal stockholder involvement in stock option compensation. The matter of accounting for loss contingencies was also examined with the focus on how financial reporting deals with uncertainties such as whether an accountable event has even occurred.

Three seemingly different questions were raised with respect to accounting for income taxes: timing differences between accounting income and taxable income, when to recognize the potential future benefit generated by a tax loss carryforward, and how to account for the benefits from using an investment tax credit. Although the matter of whether an income tax is a distribution or determinant of income remains a question in its own right, it was acknowledge that official accounting pronouncements assume income tax charges are to be treated as an expense.

Although the matching and accrual principles of accounting permeated the examination of all three tax related issues, particular nuances make each question distinctive. For instance, in the case of the carryforward, there is the issue of uncertainty as to ultimate realization of the tax benefit. On the other

---

[9] *Statement of the Accounting Principles Board on Accounting for the Investment Tax Credit,* December 9, 1971; paragraph nos. 1 and 5.

hand, upon discussing the timing difference situation, it was pointed out that although the notion of reversing/offsetting effects presumed to occur in subsequent periods may well be true for particular transactions, its validity can be questioned when applied to a going concern as a whole.

It is apparent that a variety of conceptual considerations pervade the measurement and disclosure of particular expense/loss amounts, even those which at first glance might appear to be well-defined and relatively unambiguous. In the next chapter, attention is directed to accounting for the cost of inventory which not only significantly affects income measurement, but has important balance sheet implications as well.

Additional Readings

American Accounting Association 1964 Concepts and Standards Research Committee. "The Matching Concept." *The Accounting Review* (April 1965), pp. 368–72.

Arthur Andersen & Co. *Accounting for Income Taxes*. Chicago: Arthur Andersen & Co., 1961.

Beams, Floyd A. "Income Reporting: Continuity with Change." *Management Accounting* (August 1976), pp. 23–27.

Black, Homer A. *Interperiod Allocation of Corporate Income Taxes*. New York: American Institute of Certified Public Accountants, 1966.

Devine, Carl Thomas. "Loss Recognition." In *An Income Approach to Accounting Theory*, edited by Sidney Davidson, David Green, Jr., Charles T. Horngren, and George H. Sorter. Englewood Cliffs, N.J.: Prentice-Hall, Inc., 1964, pp. 162–72 (originally published—*Accounting Research*, October 1955, pp. 310–20).

FASB Discussion Memorandum. *Accounting for Future Losses*. Stamford, Conn.: Financial Accounting Standards Board, 1974.

Hylton, Delmer P. "On Matching Revenue with Expense." *The Accounting Review* (October 1965), pp. 824–28.

Price Waterhouse & Co. *Is Generally Accepted Accounting for Income Taxes Possibly Misleading Investors?* New York: Price Waterhouse & Co., 1967.

Stanley, Curtis H. "Cost-Basis Valuation in Transactions between Entities." *The Accounting Review* (July 1964), pp. 639–47.

Thomas, Arthur L. *The Allocation Problem in Financial Accounting Theory*. Sarasota, Fla.: American Accounting Association, 1969.

Thomas, Arthur L. *The Allocation Problem: Part Two*. Sarasota, Fla.: American Accounting Association, 1974.

Throckmorton, Jerry J. "Theoretical Concepts for Interpreting the Investment Credit." *The Journal of Accountancy* (April 1970), pp. 45–52.

Wheeler, James E., and Galliart, Willard H. *An Appraisal of Interperiod Income Tax Allocation*. New York: Financial Executives Research Foundation, 1974.

6

Inventory Costing and Valuation

Inventory accounting is one of the most important aspects of accounting and financial reporting. In the case of an enterprise operating in a service industry, the scope of inventory accounting is generally limited to the area of accounting for supplies. For a merchandising company—one which buys a finished product and resells it without additional processing—the scope of inventory accounting extends to the area of merchandise as well. And for a firm which purchases material and processes it by adding labor and overhead input thereby increasing its value, a variety of additional inventory-type accounting issues emerge.

Inventory is a facet of business which requires the attention of virtually all segments of management. Particularly when considering the mercantile or manufacturing company, one can visualize inventory implications for management functions as diverse as sales, production, purchasing, warehousing, finance, data processing, quality control, physical security, transportation, and insurance. And one of the very real dilemmas posed by inventory is that of conflict among organizational units.

For instance, the marketing organization desires a wide variety of merchandise lines with each line having an adequate quantity available for sale. The production department, on the other hand, may be more interested in achieving an efficient level of operation which would likely be attained if large quantities of relatively few items were produced. Concurrently, the finance function may be concerned with the buildup of inventory levels and its implications for the company's liquidity position. What is suggested therefore is that inventory plays a vital role in virtually all merchandising and manufacturing enterprises. There are a variety of accounting problems that warrant consideration.

Inventory is one of the current assets which appear in a balance sheet. A current asset is defined as an asset management can reasonably expect to convert to cash within one year or one operating cycle, whichever is longer. The operating cycle is the interval of time from when cash is expended to purchase inventory until cash is received from customers to whom the goods have been sold. Typically, the operating cycle is less than one year, but in industries such as tobacco or whiskey whose processing times are relatively long, the operating cycle extends beyond one year. By so defining current assets, accountants in effect say that inventory by definition is a current asset.

As a current asset, inventory is quite prominent in the balance sheet. In addition to using total assets as a frame of reference in financial analysis, such as when calculating asset turnover or rate of return, current assets, and therefore inventory as one of its components, are considered when computing an enterprise's working capital.

In the earnings statement, one of the primary determinants of income is the cost of goods sold. The derivation of this amount is one of the objectives of inventory accounting. Companies are continually buying and selling merchandise such that a measurement system must be devised and used to assure a reasonable determination of periodic earnings. A direct connection exists between the balance sheet and the income statement. Indeed the nature of the basic accounting equation and the double-entry bookkeeping system alerts us to the close association between, and the complementary qualities of, these two financial statements.

INVENTORY COSTING

The first dimension of inventory accounting to be considered is that of inventory costing. This refers to determining the costs of inventory, and when specific identification of particular inventory units is not practicable or feasible, the accounting methods available to allocate inventory costs between units sold and goods on hand.

Inventoriable Costs

The cost of inventory includes but is not limited to the amount remitted to the vendor. Other costs associated with its acquisition also represent elements of inventory cost and are therefore called inventoriable costs. For example, transportation costs paid by the company to bring the merchandise to its premises are inventoriable, but the cost of delivering goods *to* a buyer when absorbed by the seller is not inventoriable.

Discounts

Another aspect of inventory accounting is that of discounts. There are generally three types of discounts that might be available to a buyer: a trade or professional discount, a quantity or volume discount, and a cash discount. The trade or professional discount is offered to selected customers such as a registered technician who buys parts from an appliance manufacturer or a member of a professional organization who purchases literature from the association's continuing professional education department. Such a discount is reflected neither in accounting for the seller nor for the buyer. The invoice price (net of the discount)—and not the (pre-discount) list price—is the only accountable amount. The accounting approach to quantity or volume discounts is identical. Merely because the price per unit would have been higher had less units been exchanged is not consequential for accounting purposes; only the net invoice price is significant.

A cash discount, however, is accounted for differently. This is the discount sometimes available to a buyer if payment is made within a designated time period. If the buyer takes the discount, the cost of the goods thereby acquired is recorded at the net-of-discount amount similar to what happens in the other discount cases. But if the buyer does not pay within the qualifying time interval, the question arises as to how to account for the forfeited discount.

One point of view states the purchase should be recorded at the full amount actually remitted. The reasoning is that the specific payment made, irrespective of what might have happened had the discount been exercised, is the pertinent measure of the sacrifice experienced by the buyer. The alternative point of view maintains the purchase should be recorded at the net-of-discount price because this is the amount the seller was prepared to accept in exchange for the goods sold. The fact that the buyer remits a larger amount is not related to the purchase of merchandise per se, but rather it represents in effect the interest cost incurred by the buyer to use the seller's money for an additional period of time.

The disagreement about the treatment of cash discounts points out the significance of the notion of "inventoriable costs." Recall the discussion in Chapter 3 of the common thread which exists between assets and expenses—assets are economic resources which have future service potential while expenses are economic resources whose service potential has been exhausted. While inventory is on hand, its future service potential—as a generator of revenue—still exists. Once it has generated revenue, its service potential no longer exists and it is therefore no longer an asset. It becomes transformed into an expense, that is, its ultimate purpose—to generate revenues—has occurred, and it is therefore included in the earnings statement in the same period in which the revenue it generated is included.

To properly effect the matching process, it is important to identify the elements comprising inventory's cost which are therefore not to appear as an expense in an income statement until the related revenue is recognized. It is equally important to include in the current income statement those costs which are properly determinants of *its* income rather than that of subsequent periods. Thus, we are dealing with possible errors of both omission *and* commission. In this light, we can therefore appreciate the different results that occur when accounting for items such as an unexercised cash discount.

Variable Costing

The costs comprising a manufacturing company's inventory are sometimes categorized as either variable or fixed. This distinction relates to whether or not a particular cost element varies as production volume changes during a given time interval. Another type of categorization relates to whether a particular cost is incurred for the benefit of several cost objectives or for the exclusive benefit of a single cost objective; these are referred to as indirect and direct costs, respectively. For a business which operates as several divisions, the president's salary is a direct cost of the company at large, but the share "borne" by a division is treated as an indirect cost of the division. This categorization does not suggest anything about whether the amount in question is fixed or variable. The president's compensation may either be fixed or variable depending on how it is computed. If it is a predetermined dollar salary, it is fixed; if it varies with volume, it is variable.

That portion of inventory costs which is "fixed" represents costs which do not vary with volume, but are incurred irrespective of volume. Such costs arise in each period such that their having been incurred in one period will have no effect on their recurring in subsequent periods. Yet, inclusion of such costs as an element of a company's inventory cost suggests that, similar to all other asset costs, their occurrence in the past does allow the company to avoid incurring them again in the future—and this just isn't the case. Thus, if future cost incurrence will be unaffected by the fixed cost of a prior period, that prior period's fixed cost has no relevance to future events and therefore does not represent any benefit to such a future period. Thus, some argue that fixed costs should be excluded from inventory.

This point of view is sometimes referred to as "direct costing," but this is a misleading title because the matter of direct versus indirect costs is not at issue. It is more appropriate to refer to this approach as "*variable* costing." The traditional method which makes no distinction between the fixed and

110

variable elements of a company's inventory cost is called "absorption costing." This title signifies that all of the inventory costs are "absorbed" by the product rather than having its fixed costs treated as an expense of the period during which they were incurred.

Although "variable costing" is not permitted by generally accepted accounting principles, there are some accountants who believe it should be permitted. It would match fixed costs with revenues in the period such costs are incurred, and it would mitigate the effect on income of changes in inventory quantities. On the other hand, the method's drawbacks include the practical difficulty of segregating the fixed and variable elements of a company's costs, as well as the conceptual issue of whether a portion of an enterprise's total manufacturing cost should be an income determinant prior to the period in which the resulting product generates revenue for the company.

COST METHODS

Once inventory is recorded, there exists the challenge of determining what portion of the cost of the goods available for sale during a period can be attributed to merchandise sold, as opposed to those units which remain unsold at the end of the period. If each item of merchandise is purchased for the very same price as every other unit of inventory, there would be no difficulty in assigning costs. But invariably, the price paid for merchandise fluctuates, as units which are alike in appearance and quality may be bought on different dates or from different suppliers. Ideally, each unit could have its own distinguishing mark such as a serial number, but to have to refer to such a notation each time a unit of merchandise is handled is cumbersome and unproductive. In fact, for products which are fungible goods (such as gasoline when quantities are commingled in tanks), it is impossible to physically separate "units" on the basis of their different costs.

Average Cost

In those circumstances in which specific identification of the components of the aggregate inventory is impossible, accountants have devised several alternative cost measurement approaches. Perhaps the most obvious system is one which uses an average of the various unit costs comprising goods available for sale. A weighted average is used rather than a simple average. This means that each unit's cost influences the determination of the average proportionate to the quantity purchased at that per-unit cost.

111

FIFO Costing

A second approach to measuring inventory costs is the First-in, First-out (FIFO) method. It assumes that goods are sold in the same order they are acquired, that is, older units are sold before newer units. When a company buys inventory at progressively higher unit costs, the cost of goods sold appearing in its income statement reflects cost amounts based on the lower prices of earlier inventory purchases since it is those units that are assumed to be sold. Concurrently, the inventory which appears as an asset in the balance sheet reflects the relatively higher prices paid for the most recent purchases since it is these newer units that are assumed to be on hand.

Inspired by the significant price inflation of the 1970s, questions were raised about the desirability, if not the propriety, of using the FIFO method. The fact that older, lower inventory unit costs comprise cost of goods sold in an accounting period when the current replacement cost of those goods is considerably higher has several questionable consequences. First, revenue reflecting current prices is being matched with costs representing earlier years' dollar amounts, dollars whose current purchasing power is less than that of current revenue. Second, such an income statement's resulting profit can be deceptive to the extent it is used as a basis for predicting future earnings. Its effectiveness as a predictor would be impaired were there to be a reduction in the rate of inflation. This is the case because a portion of the current profit, the so-called "inventory profit," exists only because of the spread between the current price level reflected in revenues and the older price level embodied in the cost of goods sold. If the rise in a future period's prices should recede, the spread between its revenues and cost of goods sold would become smaller, with the result that earnings, rather than growing or remaining constant, would actually be less than the apparent trend would have suggested.

To demonstrate the phenomenon of "inventory profits," consider the following example. A retailer incurred the following inventory (unit) costs over a five-year period:

	Unit Costs	Increase Absolute	Increase Percent
19x1	$.48		
19x2	$.50	$.02	4%
19x3	$.60	$.10	20
19x4	$.65	$.05	8
19x5	$.69	$.04	6

Assume that once the retailer learns at the beginning of a year that higher merchandise cost will be incurred in subsequent purchases, there is an immediate adjustment in selling price, a pricing policy sometimes referred to as Next-in, First-out (NIFO). In our illustration, the following retail prices result:

	Sale Price	Increase	
		Absolute	Percent
19x2	$1.00		
19x3	$1.20	$.20	20%
19x4	$1.30	$.10	8
19x5	$1.37	$.07	5

Refer now to Exhibit 6–1. It presents the company's sales, FIFO-based cost of goods sold, and resulting gross profit for years 19x2 through 19x5. Assuming that both sales volume and units purchased increase by 10,000 units each year. Listed below are pertinent data relative to the increase in gross profit.

	Gross Profit	Increase	
		Absolute	Percent
19x2	$50,800		
19x3	$71,000	$20,200	39.8%
19x4	$81,000	$10,000	14.1
19x5	$91,200	$10,200	12.6

The point that needs to be made is that in 19x3, when the retailer experienced a 20 percent increase in merchandise cost, the resulting gross profit exceeded that of the proceeding year by 39.8 percent. Readers of the 19x3 earnings statement, which appears to depict management's ability to cope with the adversity of inflation, might conclude that the "favorable" performance suggests equally impressive increases in profit in subsequent years. And if and when inflation recedes and managers can concentrate on those matters over which they have control, profits would then increase even more significantly. In fact, however, as inventory costs increase by only 8 percent and 6 percent in the next two years, the rate of growth is significantly lower—14.1 percent and 12.6 percent, respectively—than the 39.8 percent experienced in 19x3.

Perhaps the most criticized aspect of the "inventory profits" issue is that FIFO-based cost of goods sold does not adequately "recover" the number of dollars needed to replace the sold units. The result is that part of the asset growth ostensibly resulting from profitable operations and thus technically available for dividend distribution is in fact not truly asset growth. Instead, some of these "earnings" dollars will be expended to purchase the same quantity of merchandise which has a larger dollar cost than that which was allowed to flow through current cost of goods sold.

113

Exhibit 6–1

	19x2	19x3	19x4	19x5
Sales: 100,000 @ $1.00	$100,000			
110,000 @ $1.20		$132,000		
120,000 @ $1.30			$156,000	
130,000 @ $1.37				$178,100
Cost of goods sold:				
Beginning inventory				
40,000 @ $.48	$ 19,200			
50,000 @ $.50		$ 25,000		
60,000 @ $.60			$ 36,000	
70,000 @ $.65				$ 45,500
Purchases:				
110,000 @ $.50	$ 55,000			
120,000 @ $.60		$ 72,000		
130,000 @ $.65			$ 84,500	
140,000 @ $.69				$ 96,600
Ending inventory:				
50,000 @ $.50	(25,000)			
60,000 @ $.60		(36,000)		
70,000 @ $.65			(45,500)	
80,000 @ $.69				(55,200)
Cost of goods sold	$ 49,200	$ 61,000	$ 75,000	$ 86,900
Gross profit	**$ 50,800**	**$ 71,000**	**$ 81,000**	**$ 91,200**

LIFO Costing

A third approach to measuring inventory costs is the Last-in, First-out (LIFO) method. This method assumes that the units purchased most recently are the goods which are sold first. In terms of actual physical flow, it may not suggest as many actual case situations as the FIFO method. The assumed flow of inventory costs need not correspond to the actual physical flow of goods. The conceptual justification for the method lies therefore in its resulting income statement effect. By treating the most recent (last-in) costs as the cost of goods sold most recently (i.e., the first-out units), the period's revenues are matched with amounts which reflect the goods' current cost, even though the goods may have physically been acquired during a prior period.

To appreciate the nature of the different results generated by the three inventory costing methods, refer to the illustration presented in Exhibit 6–2. It can be observed that the illustration's data are characterized by a progressively upward movement of prices (from $4 to $6). It is therefore not surprising to observe that FIFO generates both lower cost of goods sold and higher ending inventory than LIFO. The very nature of FIFO is to include (1) the older (first-in) costs, which in this case are the relatively low amounts, in cost of goods sold and (2) the more recent, in this case higher, costs in ending inventory. When LIFO is used, (1) the recent, higher costs comprise cost of goods sold and (2) the older, lower costs are included in ending inventory. It is therefore understandable why companies concerned with the presence of inflation-induced inventory profits might turn to LIFO as a possible alternative approach to inventory costing.

Because LIFO is also an acceptable method for computing taxable income, a tax benefit can result as well. In a period of rising inventory prices, by basing cost of goods sold on the recent, higher costs, the resulting taxable income is lower than if the FIFO method is used. With the payment of lower taxes than would be payable under FIFO, the company retains more after-tax cash. Lest one contemplate using LIFO for tax purposes to achieve the favorable after-tax cash flow while concurrently adopting FIFO for financial reporting purposes whereby higher net income would result, be aware this is specifically prohibited by the Internal Revenue Service. Its rules require that a taxpayer using LIFO for tax purposes must use it for financial accounting as well. It was this cash-saving result which gave considerable impetus to the use of LIFO in financial reporting, much to the consternation of some accountants who felt the method should be accepted on the basis of its conceptual qualities and not because it is permitted by the taxation authorities.

Another characteristic of LIFO which has generated concern is the balance sheet effect it generates. Because the most recent inventory costs appear as the cost of goods sold in the earnings statement, it is the older, typically lower costs, which comprise the inventory amount appearing in the balance sheet. It is possible this amount contains costs several decades old. Such a result can therefore be questioned on the grounds that with the normal turnover of merchandise in actual business operations, it is difficult to justify the numbers thus reflected in the balance sheet.

However, in response to this concern, there exists the notion that the layers of inventory costs of earlier years represent in effect a company's "involuntary" investment in inventory, a quasi-permanent investment analogous to that which is made in plant assets. This in turn might suggest that

115

Exhibit 6–2

Inventory Costing Methods

The circumstances:	Units	Cost per Unit	Total
Beginning of period balance	10	$4	$ 40
July 8—purchase	+ 8	$5	$ 40
July 17—sale	− 12		
July 26—purchase	+ 7	$6	$ 42
End of period balance	13		
Cost of goods available for sale			**$122**

The results:
FIFO:
  Ending inventory $72
  Cost of goods sold $50
Average:
  Ending inventory $63
  Cost of goods sold $59
LIFO
  Ending inventory $55
  Cost of goods sold $67

Supporting computations:
1. FIFO

Cost of goods sold:		Ending inventory	
10 units @ $4 = $40		6 units @ $5 = $30	
2 units @ $5 = $10		7 units @ $6 = $42	
Total	$50	Total	$72

2. Weighted average*

Cost of goods available for sale	$122
Number of units available for sale	25
Average cost per unit ($122 ÷ 25 =)	$ 4.88
Ending inventory (13 @ $4.88 =)	$ 63.44
Cost of goods sold (12 @ $4.88 =)	$ 58.56

3. LIFO*

July 31—balance	10 units @	$4 =	$ 40
	3 units @	$5 =	15
Ending inventory	13 units		$ 55
Cost of goods available for sale			$122
Less ending inventory			55
Cost of goods sold			$ 67

* Assumes that the periodic method of inventory recordkeeping is used.

what is tantamount to safety stock can justifiably be reflected as the amount expended when it was initially acquired even, or especially, if it happened many years earlier.

Interestingly, there have been some cases of companies whose customers bought unusually large amounts of inventory in anticipation of a labor strike. The companies then found themselves selling quantities of larger magnitude than their normal volume with the result there was a reduction of inventory quantities at the end of the period. In the ensuing accounting under LIFO, their cost of goods sold included "old" units accumulating in "inventory" at significantly lower amounts which in turn resulted in an unusually wide spread between their "cost" basis and the current period's revenues which of course reflected current prices.

If ever there were a situation which dramatizes the interrelationship between the income statement and the balance sheet, it is the case when examining the relative merits of the FIFO and LIFO approaches to assigning inventory costs. Continuing with the assumption of an upward trend in inventory unit costs, one can appreciate that LIFO-based inventories have little or no susceptibility to writedowns caused by a decline in market value. As will be discussed in the next section, when the market value of ending inventory is below its cost basis, a loss is recognized immediately in the earnings statement, and the carrying value of the balance sheet asset is reduced accordingly.

When LIFO inventory costing is used, the ending inventory contains the oldest costs, which are typically below current market value. An interesting question arises when there is a decline in current value relative to the higher original cost: Would the current income statement, which already absorbs the impact of high current costs, also be required to include the effect of a high historical cost relative to lower current value? On the grounds the effect would be tantamount to a Highest-in, First-out (HIFO) system, some accountants might not accept the notion of "lower of LIFO-cost or market."

Of course, the basic argument in support of LIFO costing during inflation is its income statement result. The quality of LIFO-based earnings is viewed as better than that of FIFO, which suffers from increasing earnings by inventory profits in a period of rising prices. Its countervailing aspect is the balance sheet effect. Consider for example the contention that a secret balance sheet reserve is created by LIFO. This results from the fact that lower LIFO-induced income manifests itself in the balance sheet through a lower inventory asset and lower retained earnings. To the extent retained earnings is "understated" relative to FIFO-based earnings, it can be argued that in effect a "reserve" has been created. And "reserves," as such, are not permitted by generally accepted accounting principles, largely because of their discretionary nature and the resulting fear of manipulation by management.

117

When LIFO is used, the mere purchase of merchandise at the end of the period has an effect on the period's cost of goods sold and therefore on earnings. Had FIFO been used, there would be no effect on the period's cost of goods sold nor on the resulting income. The reason for this contrast is that because LIFO treats the most recent "last-in" costs as components of the current cost of goods sold, the end-of-period purchase affects income. In the illustration in Exhibit 6–2, the inventory asset in the balance sheet does not reflect the eight new units' full impact. It was affected only to the extent that eight units available earlier in the period which had been acquired at unit costs of less than $7 are added to the ending inventory at an amount which was less than their actual $56 cost.

On the other hand, if FIFO is used, the $56 is included in both cost of goods available for sale and ending inventory, and they are offsetting amounts. The reason for this is that the only units whose costs affect Cost of Goods Sold are those which were "first-in;" the purchase of merchandise which remains unsold can affect only the cost of the ending inventory.

Because of the effect of purchases on LIFO-based cost of foods sold (an effect which is not present under FIFO), LIFO might lend itself to managerial manipulation. To "attain" earnings at an amount less than that which would emerge through the normal processes, the purchase of more expensive merchandise increases cost of goods sold and decreases prospective net income. In any case, apart from the manipulative aspects of this issue, many opponents of LIFO argue the method's validity should be questioned if the mere purchase of additional units can possibly affect earnings.

In summary, the distinction between FIFO and LIFO raises the question of what criteria should govern in this area. Some persons believe in FIFO's supremacy because it reflects the physical flow of units, while advocates of LIFO contend that LIFO's notion of a "base stock" of inventory is similarly consistent with sound business practice. FIFO advocates point to the need to depict meaningful current balance sheet amounts while LIFO supporters place more emphasis on the need to match revenues with current costs to measure income. FIFO proponents criticize LIFO's "secret reserve" and LIFO backers deplore the presence of FIFO-induced "inventory profits." FIFO cannot be "manipulated" to manage earnings, but LIFO can legally be used to reduce income tax payments.

INVENTORY VALUATION

The nature of the matching process for determining net income requires that the cost of merchandise being held for sale be treated as an asset until the goods are sold. In the period in which the sale occurs, the cost of the goods sold appears in the earnings statement and is matched with the revenue its sale generates. While awaiting sale, the disclosure of inventory as an asset has two characteristics: first, its cost measures the sacrifice made by the company to have such an economic resource and second, the economic resource has future service potential at least equal to the amount of the said sacrifice.

Lower of Cost or Market

When it can be determined that the future service potential of the inventory asset is less than the cost incurred to own the inventory, this fact must be reflected in the financial statements. The procedure with which this is implemented is called the "lower-of-cost-or-market" rule, and it entails recognizing a loss in the earnings statement to account for the decline in the balance sheet's inventory carrying value. As the method's title suggests, the focal point for making such an adjustment is the market value of the merchandise in question.

The expression "market value" in its own right raises the question of how to define "market." A retail company deals in two markets: an input market in which it purchases merchandise from wholesalers or directly from manufacturers, and an output market in which it sells goods to consumers. Prices will usually be lower in the input market, and it might be argued that these amounts, which reflect the replacement cost of merchandise, are the pertinent market values to consider. Yet once the company has inventory on hand, a case can be made for measuring value on the basis of what it expects to realize upon sale of the goods. Realizable value is related to the expected sales price; to the extent that additional costs will be incurred to complete and sell the units, they are subtracted from the sales price to yield net realizable value. It is then the lower of this amount or the replacement cost which was used at one time as a measure of market value.

At the present time, however, there exists an additional feature whose objective is to preclude recognizing a loss of a magnitude which would possibly result in a gross profit upon sale in excess of the company's normal profit. The specific provision now in effect states that replacement cost shall not be used to represent market value if it is less than "net realizable value less the company's normal profit." In other words, the accountant subtracts from the net realizable value the amount of profit normally earned, and that amount is established as the lower limit (floor). Therefore, although market is the lower of replacement cost or net realizable value with the stated lower limit, it can also be viewed as being replacement cost with an upper limit (net realizable value) and a lower limit (net realizable value less normal profit). Even more simply, market is the middle amount of (1) replacement cost, (2) net realizable value, and (3) net realizable value less normal profit.

119

Exhibit 6–3 provides an illustration of the lower-of-cost-or-market method. This illustration is intended to demonstrate how the lower-of-cost-or-market rule is effected at the present time. We shall later reconcile its current nature with the rule as it existed previously. That discussion will enable us to understand the purpose and accounting result of the method as it is presently constituted. Each of the four cases assumes different replacement costs and sales prices.

The example assumes the cost of the inventory is $100, the estimated cost to complete and sell the goods is $20, and the company normally earns a profit equal to 30 percent of the sales price. Case A's replacement cost is $93 and the sales price is $140. Net realizable value is the $140 less the $20 cost to complete and sell, or $120. The normal profit is 30 percent of the $140 sales price, or $42, and when subtracted from the $120 net realizable value, a lower limit of $78 is established. The lower of replacement cost or net realizable value, is the $93 replacement cost. Since it is not less than the $78 floor, it becomes the basis for recognizing a $7 loss because it is $7 less than the $100 cost basis. In other words, the company has lost the $7 of gross margin that might have resulted if the goods had been sold at their normal markup.

Exhibit 6–3

Cost incurred to date			$100	
Cost to complete and sell			$ 20	
Normal profit relative to sales price			30%	

	Case A	Case B	Case C	Case D
1. Replacement cost	$ 93	$110	$ 95	$ 85
Sales price	$140	$150	$110	$160
Less cost to complete and sell	20	20	20	20
2. Net realizable value	$120	$130	$ 90	$140
Net relizable value	$120	$130	$ 90	$140
Less normal profit (which is 30% of sales price)	42	45	33	48
3. Net realizable value less normal profit	$ 78	$ 85	$ 57	$ 92

Note: A different replacement cost and sales price is given for each of the four cases.

120

In Case B, we again have a situation in which replacement cost of $110 is less than net realizable value ($130), but not less than the $85 lower limit. Because $110, the measure of market value, is more than the $100 historical cost, market value is not recognized in either the income statement or the balance sheet.

Case C is an instance in which net realizable value of $90 is less than the S95 replacement cost. Because it is impossible to violate the lower limit in this case, the $90 becomes the measure of market value. It, in turn, becomes the basis for recognizing a $10 loss in the income statement resulting from the $10 reduction in the balance sheet inventory balance.

In Case D, the $85 replacement cost is less than the $140 net realizable value. However, whenever replacement cost emerges as the propsective measure of market value, there is also a need to consider the "net realizable value less normal profit." In this case, the normal profit is 30 percent of the given $160 sales price or $48 which, when subtracted from the $140 net realizable value, yields a lower limit of $92. Since the $85 replacement cost is less than this floor amount, $92 supplants $85 as the measure of market value. The $8 difference between $92 and the $100 cost of the inventory is therefore recorded both as a loss and a diminution of the balance sheet asset.

Comparing these results with those generated by both a system with no lower limit provision and one which uses only replacement cost as the measure of market value will help to explain the accounting issues at hand. This comparison is demonstrated with use of accounting journal entries set forth in Exhibit 6–4.

In Case A, as noted above, a $7 loss is recognized in the period in which the market decline occurs. The writedown of the inventory asset to $93 means that when the units are sold in a subsequent period for (the given sales price of $140, the resulting profit will be [$140 − ($93 + 20 =) $113 =] $27. The identical result occurs if there is no "floor" provision and if realizable values are excluded from consideration altogether. This $27 profit together with the earlier $7 loss yield a net profit of $20, which would be the year-of-sale profit if the lower-of-cost-or-market method were not used at all. By segregating the two amounts, we are able to isolate what might be called the "holding" gain or loss from the "trading" gain or loss. In Case B in which there is no decline in market value, the sale-date profit of $30 is based on the difference between the $150 sale price and the $120 cost; this result occurs under all three approaches to "lower of cost or market."

Case C is not affected by the lower limit because net realizable value emerges as the measure of market value. Because the ($100 − 90 =) $10 loss is recognized when the market decline occurs, inventory is written down to $90. In the year of sale, this $90 and the $20 cost to complete and sell add

121

Exhibit 6–4

	Upper and Lower Limits (system now in effect)		No Lower Limit (previous system)		Replacement Cost Only	
	Period of Market Decline	Future Period of Sale	Period of Market Decline	Future Period of Sale	Period of Market Decline	Future Period of Sale
Case A:						
$100 – 93	$7 loss		$7 loss		$7 loss	
$140 – ($93 + 20)		$27 profit		$27 profit		$27 profit
Case B:						
$150 – ($100 + 20)		$30 profit		$30 profit		$30 profit
Case C:						
$100 – 90	$10 loss		$10 loss			
$110 – ($90 + 20)		–0–		–0–		
$100 – 95					$5 loss	
$110 – ($95 + 20)						$5 loss
Case D:						
$100 – 92	$8 loss		$15 loss		$15 loss	
$160 – ($92 + 20)		$48 profit		$55 profit		$55 profit
$100 – 85						
$160 – ($85 + 20)						

up to an amount equal to the $110 sale price and there is no profit or loss in that year. The $10 loss appears as a holding loss; were it not to surface until the year of sale, it might incorrectly be construed to be a trading loss.

If only replacement cost were to be considered in determining market value, the amount of loss recorded initially would be ($100 − 95 =) $5. The additional $5 loss, which is the difference between the $95 replacement cost and the $90 net realizable value, would only appear in the period of sale; this would incorrectly suggest that there was a $5 trading loss. Note that under this unacceptable alternative, the ($5 + 5 =) $10 loss for the two-year period is the same as the loss reported when realizable values are considered in applying the lower-of-cost-or-market method.

Case D points out the impact of the lower limit. When this "floor" feature is considered, an $8 loss is recognized because the $100 cost basis is compared with the $92 "net realizable value less normal profit." Had the floor not been used, or for that matter had realizable value not been considered, the loss would have been $15 because that is the difference between the $100 historical cost and the $85 replacement cost. When the merchandise is sold subsequently for $160, the resulting profit would be [$160 − ($92 + 20 =) $112 =] $48 if the lower limit had defined market value and [$160 − ($85 + 20 =) $105 =] $55 if either of the other approaches had been used. Note that the cumulative (two-period) results are identical, that is, the $48 profit less an $8 loss yields a net $40 profit, and the $55 profit less a $15 loss yields a net $40 profit.

The essential difference between the two approaches is that under the system in which market value is subject to a lower limit, the amount of profit that could possibly result in a subsequent year of sale can never exceed the company's normal profit, assuming the sales price does not increase. This is demonstrated in the case at hand. The 30 percent normal profit on the $160 sales price is $48; when there is a lower limit, the year-of-sale profit is $48. However, when there is no floor, a greater-than-normal profit is recognized in the year of sale. It can therefore be observed that the validity of the "lower limit" feature is contingent on one's position regarding possible year-of-sale profit in excess of "normal" profit. Apparently, the authors of the current rule were concerned with preventing abnormal profit amounts to such a degree that they were willing to limit the amount of loss which could be recognized when there is a significant decline in inventory's replacement cost.

The "lower-of-cost-or-market" method is applied to certain marketable equity securities as well; and this is discussed in detail in Chapter 11. Thus, the method, when used either for inventory or for marketable equity securities, can be examined in context of various accounting principles. Although it represents a departure from historical cost, this can be defended on the basis of the conservative accounting outcome it generates. It is further justified on the grounds that recognition of a loss in the income statement in the period during which the decline in market value occurs provides a better matching of revenues and expenses. Implicit in this argument is the premise that a holding loss is a bona fide determinant of earnings.

There is, however, criticism of the "matching" argument. It can be argued that if matching is important enough for purposes of measuring and recognizing *holding losses,* its proponents should be as concerned with disclosing the effect of *holding gains* as well. Given that objectivity is not compromised when recognizing market values lower than historical costs, not to use such market values when they exceed recorded historical cost is inconsistent accounting treatment. The counter argument is that only holding losses are recorded because of accounting conservatism.

Another manifestation of inconsistent application is that when applying the method to merchandise, once the inventory is written down to market, it cannot be written back up to cost if there is a subsequent increase in market value. When the method is applied to marketable equity securities, however, subsequent write-up can occur, although not to more than the original cost of the securities.

Another difference between its use for inventory and for marketable equity securities exists when a variety of different items comprise the asset balance. The question is whether the lower of cost or market is determined for each item and then these lower amounts are added together, or alternatively whether to use the lower of all the items' total cost or all the items' total market value.

For inventory measurement, either approach may be used, but when applying the method to marketable equity securities, only the latter procedure is permitted. The resulting difference is that under the former approach there is no offsetting effect among items. Consider the following example:

	(1) Cost	(2) Market	(3) Lower	(4) Difference
Item				
A	$10	$12	$10	$ (2)
B	14	11	11	3
C	16	23	16	(7)
D	39	23	23	16
Total	**$79**	**$69**	**$60**	**$10**

Under the "individual" approach, Column 3's $60 is the resulting balance sheet amount resulting in a ($79 − 60 =) $19 loss. The "aggregate" approach, based on the sums of Columns 1 and 2, yields a lower amount of $69, and only a ($79 − 69 =) $10 loss is recognized. The disappearance of the ($19 − 10 =) $9 difference between the two methods occurs because the $9 excess of market over cost for items A (of $2) and C (of $7) depicted in Column 4 is offset by the $19 excess of cost over market of items B (of $3 and D (of $16).

Other Losses

The discussion until this point has been concerned exclusively with accounting for losses in value which have already occurred. There are two other types of inventory losses that warrant our attention.

A company may make a commitment to buy goods at a particular purchase price. Under normal circumstances, when the merchandise is received, its cost is recorded to reflect the purchase price agreed on earlier. However, if the price of the goods decreases after the purchase commitment was made but before the goods are received, the buyer is required to recognize immediately the loss that will ensue. This rule is similar to that of the conventional application of the lower-of-cost-or-market rule. The buyer must recognize the impact of a decline in market value in the period in which it occurs. An illustration will show how there can be accounting recognition even though the goods in question are not yet reflected in the buyer's inventory records.

Assume that the buyer has made a commitment to purchase certain merchandise for $5,000. Prior to receipt of the goods, it is determined the value of the merchandise has fallen to $4,000. An accounting entry is made as follows:

Loss on Purchase Commitments	1,000	
Accrued Loss on Purchase Commitments		1,000

The loss account is included in the current period's earnings statement as a determinant of income, and the "accrued loss" amount appears among the liabilities in the buyer's balance sheet even though there is no creditor to whom the buyer is in debt. When the merchandise is received, assuming there has been no further change in its value, the following accounting entry is made:

Purchases (or Inventory)	4,000	
Accrued Loss on Purchase Commitments	1,000	
Accounts Payable (or Cash)		5,000

As a result, the loss is recognized in a timely manner, and the goods are recorded at their current value when received.

125

The second situation that warrants attention is that of a company whose inventory already appears in its financial statements in accordance with the lower-of-cost-or-market rule. However, its management believes that there is likely to be a further decline in market sales value in the future, and that this expectation should be reflected in the current financial statement.

It would be incorrect to recognize such a contingent loss in the current earnings statement if the required "probable and estimable" criteria (discussed in Chapter 5) are not met. The company could, however, "appropriate" retained earnings by making the following entry:

Retained Earnings	20,000	
Reserve for Future Inventory Losses		20,000

Such an approach would alert readers of the financial statements to the contingency. Whether or not the future loss occurs, the "reserve" would eventually become unnecessary: either the amount of an actual loss would appear in a future income statement or the loss just never materializes, and its balance would then be "reinstated" in retained earnings.

SUMMARY

In this chapter, the two most pervasive aspects of inventory accounting were examined: inventory costing techniques and financial statement valuation. For merchandising and manufacturing enterprises, *inventory* is a significant component of both operating results and financial position. The method of inventory costing used by a company can have a material effect on its earnings. Because specific identification of inventory unit costs is a difficult, if not an impossible task, costing procedures are approximations of the inventory's actual cost. Since the results generally differ among the alternative methods, companies tend to adopt that approach which yields amounts compatible with particular objectives, such as to maximize reported earnings or to minimize taxable income.

Inventory *valuation* refers specifically to the rule that inventory be reflected in financial statements at the lower of its historical cost or its current value. *Current value* in turn is based on either replacement cost or realizable value, and various factors are considered in the process of determining which amount to use to measure *value*. In addition to questions of what constitute the cost and the value of inventory, inventory's very nature lends itself to misstatement—through poor recordkeeping, inadequate physical control, and possible deliberate manipulation of its component amounts. It is therefore evident that inventory accounting is a topic which warrants lucid understanding by persons aspiring to appreciate the nature of the financial reporting environment.

Additional Readings

Barden, Horace G. *The Accounting Basis of Inventories.* New York: American Institute of Certified Public Accountants, 1973.

Buckley, John W., and Goode, James R. "Inventory Valuation and Income Measurement: An Improved System of Analysis." *Abacus* (June 1976), pp. 34–48.

Fess, Philip E. and Ferrara, William L. "The Period Cost Concept for Income Measurement—Can It Be Defended?" *The Accounting Review* (October 1961), pp. 598–602.

Holmes, William. "The Market Value of Inventories—Perils and Pitfalls." *The Journal of Commercial Bank Lending* (April 1973), pp. 30–35.

Johnson, Charles E. "Inventory Valuation—The Accountant's Achilles Heel." *The Accounting Review* (April 1954), pp. 15–26.

McAnly, Herbert T. "How LIFO Began." *Management Accounting* (May 1975), pp. 24–26.

Moonitz, Maurice. "The Case against LIFO as an Inventory-Pricing Formula." *The Journal of Accountancy* (June 1953), pp. 682–90.

O'Connor, Stephen J. "LIFO: Still a Valid Management Tool?" *Financial Executive* (September 1978), pp. 26–30.

Skinner, R. C. "Combining LIFO and FIFO." *The International Journal of Accounting: Education and Research* (Spring 1975), pp. 127–34.

Sorter, George H., and Horngren, Charles T. "Asset Recognition and Economic Attributes—The Relevant Costing Approach." *The Accounting Review* (July 1962), pp. 391–99.

7

Accounting Dimensions of Long-Lived Assets

There may be an inclination to view the subject of accounting for assets as one whose questions are limited to issues such as selecting an inventory costing method, estimating uncollectible accounts receivable, and determining whether an expenditure to extend a machine's useful life or to improve the quality of its output is capitalizable or reflected immediately as an element of current income. In fact, there are several topics relating to assets which are not as well-defined or as well-understood as some of these above-cited accounting matters. Therefore, attention in this chapter is directed to several such accounting issues including depreciation, nonmonetary transactions, intangible assets, capitalized interest costs, oil and gas exploration costs, executory contracts, and long-term leases.

THE NATURE AND ROLE OF DEPRECIATION

Assets are economic resources having future service potential, and this potential manifests itself in one of two ways. Those assets which represent an enterprise's ability to expend cash to acquire goods and services and/or to reduce its liabilities through cash payments are called monetary assets. They include cash, as well as receivables and certain investments in marketable securities that give them the quality of being "near-cash" in nature.

Assets that enable an enterprise to engage in a revenue transaction are nonmonetary in nature. Such assets' service potential is consumed in the revenue-generating process in the sense that the asset is forfeited, such as through the transfer of merchandise to the customer. Even if an asset is not surrendered in a physical sense, however, a portion of its service potential may also be consumed. For instance, a delivery truck is ostensibly the same vehicle after a cross-country round trip it had been beforehand. But from an accounting point of view, the revenue generated by the 6,000 mile excursion has as one of its costs the fact that the truck's future service potential has been reduced—for it is now 6,000 miles closer to the end of its useful economic life.

Depreciation is the term used to describe the process of recording the expense nature of tangible capital assets such as buildings, machinery, equipment, furniture and fixtures, and motor vehicles. The same conceptual justification exists for intangible assets, namely, the need to account for the consumption of such assets' service potential. The term used to denote the process is *amortization*. In a purely etymological sense, depreciation is a form of amortization. Accounting parlance has, however, adopted the word *depreciation* to signify the expense nature of tangible assets while allowing *amortization* to apply to the expense character of intangible assets.

Depreciation is a technique through which the cost of an asset is matched against resulting revenues on a systematic basis. The mere fact that an asset is acquired during one year or that cash is expended for it during another year is of no consequence when contemplating how and when to reflect its cost in an income statement. This is because its inclusion as a determinant of earnings is based on the role it plays in the generation of revenue. By its very nature, an enterprise incurs a cost because it expects thereby to be able to generate revenues which will provide not only a return *of* capital, but a return *on* capital as well. The cost of assets measures the capital an enterprise has invested in a particular revenue-potential opportunity.

To measure the return on the capital investment, the accountant matches the cost of acquired assets whose service potential has since been consumed (expense) with the benefits derived (revenue). The resulting excess represents the enterprise's profit, that is, the return on its capital investment. It is because of this that depreciation is so vital to the accounting process.

It is significant to note there is an accounting requirement that there be explicit disclosure of each fiscal period's depreciation expense, while virtually all other determinants of income before income taxes can be set forth in very broadly or very narrowly defined expense categories. Moreover, the nature of the balance sheet disclosure requirements conveys a significant message in its own right. As a tangible plant asset is "depreciated," a lesser portion of its original cost still awaits being depreciated in subsequent fiscal periods. The cumulative depreciation charges therefore have the effect of reducing the carrying value (also called the book value) that appears in each ensuing balance sheet.

Rather than disclosing only the asset's progressively lesser carrying value in the balance sheet, there is an accounting requirement that there be disclosure of the asset's cost as well as its cumulative depreciation to date. Therefore, disclosure of assets' carrying value and parenthetical disclosure of their accumulated depreciation permits the analyst to derive their original cost. Although the benefit of such a disclosure policy may be nominal, its objective is intended to be educational.

Depreciation charges do not convey information about changes in assets' value. Accordingly, the resulting carrying values do not identify the current value of the assets. Indeed, at one time such cumulative charges were described as constituting a *reserve* or an *allowance* for depreciation. These terms, however, had misleading implications, suggesting perhaps that a fund of depreciation monies had been set aside and was therefore available to be spent. Such a connotation is furthest from the truth, and accountants continue to encounter misunderstanding on the part of persons who are uninformed or misinformed. Indeed, in the context of identifying an enterprise's sources and uses of cash or of working capital, the distinctive role of depreciation charges can provoke further misunderstanding That dimension of depreciation is discussed in the context of Chapter 11's examination of differences between the objective of income determination and that of measuring the effect of operations on an enterprise's liquidity.

NONMONETARY TRANSACTIONS

The practice of accounting for transactions in terms of their cash equivalent reflects the underlying assumption that all transactions are in fact expressed in such monetary units. In fact, most business transactions do reflect agreements whose consummation does involve cash, and they are referred to as monetary transactions. However, there are transactions not expressed in terms of cash, and they are referred to as nonmonetary transactions. The resulting question is whether to reflect such transactions in financial statements on the basis of their component elements' historical cost (book value) or to account for such items in terms of their transaction date fair value. "Fair value. . . should be determined by referring to estimated realizable values in cash transactions of the same or similar assets, quoted market prices, independent appraisals, estimated fair values of assets or services received in exchange, and other available evidence."[1]

The answer to this question depends on the nature of the particular circumstances. It is desirable there be first an appreciation of what such different circumstances are. Exhibit 7–1 identifies four different types of nonmonetary transactions.

---

[1] *Accounting Principles Board Opinion No. 29,* paragraph no. 25.

Exhibit 7–1

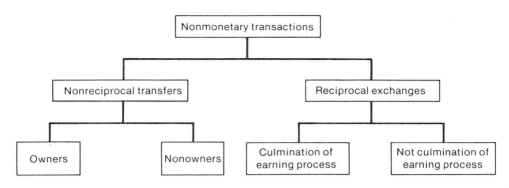

An example of a nonreciprocal nonmonetary transfer *to an owner* would be the declaration of a dividend payable in the form of the enterprise's merchandise. An example of a nonreciprocal nonmonetary transfer *from an owner* would be stockholders donating some of their shares to the corporation. An example of a nonreciprocal transfer *to a nonowner* is a contribution of a company's merchandise to a charitable organization. An example of a nonreciprocal transfer *from a nonowner* is the receipt of a parcel of land from a municipality as an incentive to build a plant and thus create employment opportunities for the local labor force. All of these nonreciprocal transfers are accounted for in terms of the asset's fair value.

The right side of the diagram indicates that for a *reciprocal* exchange there is distinction between whether or not there has been a culmination of the earning process. The earning process is not considered to have been culminated if goods held for sale are exchanged for comparable goods being held for sale. For instance, the earnings process has not been culminated if automobile dealer A gives a red Buick to automobile dealer B in exchange for a blue Buick which A needs to satisfy a customer who is unwilling to wait several weeks for delivery from the manufacturer's assembly plant. By contrast, if automobile dealer A sells a red Buick to an appliance retailer and in lieu of cash receives in exchange air conditioning units for the showroom premises, this transaction would be a culmination of the earning process.

The same distinction applies to assets other than merchandie. If an appliance manufacturer gives a lathe to a machine and equipment dealer in exchange for another lathe, the earning process is not viewed as having been culminated. But if an appliance manufacturer gives a lathe to a manufacturer of lighting fixtures and instead of cash accepts a new lighting system, this transaction would constitute culmination of the earning process. In those instances in which the circumstances indicate the earning process has been culminated, the transaction is recorded on the basis of fair value. This means that both the automobile retailer who sells a car for air conditioning units and the appliance manufacturer who exchanges a lathe for a lighting system record the newly acquired asset at fair value.

Assets acquired in exchange transactions which do *not* constitute a culmination of the earning process are accounted for either on the basis of the fair value or the surrendered asset's book value—depending on (1) whether there is an apparent loss or gain and (2) if a gain, the extent to which cash is also involved. As a general rule, the new asset is recorded at an amount equal to the book value of the surrendered asset. But if on the basis of the fair value there is an indicated loss, the fair value amount prevails. The nature of this and the other exception to the general rule is explained through several examples below.

Exhibit 7–2
Accounting for Reciprocal Exchanges

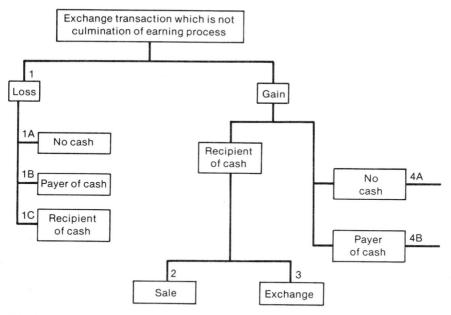

Valuation Basis of New Asset:

Cell 1–A—Fair value	Cell 3 —Book value
Cell 1–B—Fair value	Cell 4–A—Book value
Cell 1–C—Fair value	Cell 4–B—Book value

Exhibit 7–2 presents a diagram which identifies the various resulting possibilities; it serves as the basis for the following three illustrative examples. In all three cases, Z gives Y an asset whose recorded book value is $32,000 in exchange for a similar asset having a recorded book value of $26,000. The exchange is not a culmination of the earning process. As each of the examples is discussed, readers who are interested in having the resulting accounting treatment presented in "journal-entry" form should refer to Exhibit 7–3.

In Example 1, the fair value of both assets is $30,000 and no cash is exchanged. Since Y's asset's ($26,000) book value is less than the ($30,000) fair value by $4,000, there is an indicated gain. As signified by Cell 4–A, however, no gain is recognized, and the new asset's accounting basis corresponds to the book value of the surrendered asset, i.e., $26,000. From the

Exhibit 7–3

Three Illustrative Examples of Reciprocal Exchanges

Example 1

	Y—Cell 4–A		Z—Cell 1–A	
New Asset	26		30	
Loss			2	
Old Asset		26		32

Example 2

	Y—Cell 1–B		Z—Cell 1–C	
New Asset	25		20	
Loss	6		7	
Cash			5	
Cash		5		
Old Asset		26		32

Example 3

	Y—Cell 4–B		Z—Cell 2	Z—Cell 3	
New Asset	31			28	
Cash			5		
Cash		5			
Old Asset		26	4		28
Gain			1		

133

point of view of Z, because it surrenders an asset whose book value ($32,000) is greater than the ($30,000) fair value, a $2,000 loss is recorded and the new asset's accounting basis is therefore its $30,000 fair value; this is depicted in Cell 1–A in the diagram. In other words, the new asset may *not* be recorded at an amount greater than fair value.

In Example 2, the fair value of Z's asset is $25,000, the fair value of Y's asset is $20,000, and Y also gives Z $5,000 cash. Because Y surrenders $5,000 cash and an asset having a book value of $26,000, receiving in exchange an asset whose fair value is $25,000, it records a loss—in the amount of ($5,000 + 26,000 = $31,000; $31,000 − 25,000 =) $6,000. The "Cell 1–B" nature of the exchange causes Y to record the new asset at its $25,000 fair value. Z surrenders an asset having a $32,000 book value in exchange for $5,000 cash and an asset whose fair value is $20,000. Because there is a resulting [$32,000 − ($5,000 + 20,000 =) $25,000 =] $7,000 loss, Z's "Cell 1–C" circumstances require that the new asset be recorded at its $20,000 fair value.

In Example 3, the fair value of Z's asset is $40,000, the fair value of Y's asset is $35,000, and Y gives Z $5,000 as well. Because Y forfeits $5,000 cash and an asset having a $26,000 book value in exchange for an asset whose fair value is $40,000, there is an indicated gain of [$40,000 − ($5,000 + 26,000 =) $31,000 =] $9,000. Y's "Cell 4–B" situation results in the gain not being recorded, and the new asset's accounting basis equals the book value of the two assets surrendered which is ($5,000 cash + 26,000 =) $31,000.

Let us summarize what has been observed thus far. Example 1's and Example 2's accounting by Y and Z and Example 3's accounting by Y encompass the five different situations depicted in Cells 4–A, 1–A, 1–B, 1–C, and 4–B respectively. The Cells 1–A, 1–B and 1–C cases resulted in an exchange loss being recognized and the new asset being recorded at its fair value. The Cells 4–A and 4–B situations involved no recognition of the indicated gain, and the new asset was recorded at the book value of the asset(s) surrendered.

We can now understand the nature of the accounting rules relating to nonmonetary transactions. Both nonreciprocal transfers and also reciprocal exchanges which are a culmination of the earning process result in accounting recognition based on fair value. When the earning process is not culminated, fair value is not used, unless use of fair value amounts result in the recognition of an indicated loss, depicted in Cells 1–A, 1–B and 1–C.

With this frame of reference we now return to Example 3 and the accounting requirements facing Z. From an accounting point of view, Z's surrender of its noncash asset for cash and a noncash asset constitutes two transactions: the sale of a portion of the asset for cash, and the exchange of the other part of the asset for another (noncash) asset. The accounting is effected by allocating the old asset's $32,000 recorded book value on the basis of the relative value of the assets received. Z receives $5,000 cash and another asset whose current value is $35,000, or a total of $40,000. Since the $5,000 cash is [$5,000 ÷ ($5,000 + 35,000 =) $40,000 =] ⅛ of the total, ⅛ of the old asset's $32,000 book value, or $4,000 is viewed as being sold for $5,000—resulting in a recordable $1,000 gain (Cell 2). The remaining ⅞ of the $32,000 old asset, or $28,000, is exchanged for the new asset with the result the new asset has an accounting basis equal to ⅞ of the old asset's recorded book value, or $28,000 (Cell 3).

At a conceptual level, Cell 2 is not viewed as a nonmonetary transaction. Z, as the recipient of cash, recognizes a gain or loss in the same manner that characterizes conventional sales transactions. In our illustration, the implicit gain of ($40,000 − 32,000 =) $8,000 is deemed to be realized in the same proportion as cash is received to the total consideration received: $5,000/$40,000 × $8,000 = $1,000. Cell 3, on the other hand, is similar to Cells 4–A and 4–B in the sense the new asset is recorded on the basis of the old asset's book value. Therefore, in summary, Cells 3, 4–A, and 4–B represent the exception to the "fair value" rule normally in effect for nonmonetary transactions. Cells 1–A, 1–B, and 1–C, on the other hand, represent the exception to the exception—to assure that the new asset is not recorded at an amount which exceeds its fair value.

INTANGIBLE ASSETS

One definition of an intangible asset is that it is "a capital asset having no physical existence, its value being limited by the rights and anticipative benefits that possession confers upon the owner."[2] Some of the primary elements of this definition are examined below.

For an asset to be classified an intangible asset, it must first of all be a capital asset. This means that although its primary function is to aid in the generation of revenue, its expected benefit does not lie in its ability to be sold in a revenue transaction, nor in its ability to allow the enterprise to meet its monetary obligations. Instead, an intangible asset provides a benefit by allowing, if not causing, a revenue transaction to occur—in the same sense that tangible fixed assets such as factory buildings, machinery, and delivery vehicles allow revenue transactions to occur. And, as in the case of tangible fixed assets, accounting recognition of the asset must be justified by its expected future service potential to the company.

---

[2] Eric L. Kohler, *A Dictionary for Accountants—4th Edition* (Englewood Cliffs, New Jersey: Prentice-Hall, Inc., 1970), p. 235.

A second characteristic of an intangible asset is that it is not physical in nature. The asset's existence or identity is defined by the rights it grants to its holder/owner since it is such rights that represent the future service potential quality of the asset. In a broad sense, it is the future service potential of any asset which defines its asset character. In the case of tangible assets, the intangible nature of such future benefits notwithstanding, the asset itself is typically visible, that is, the evidence of such assets' existence is readily apparent. Consider *cash*, which might be considered the ultimate tangible or physical asset. Certainly, a ten-dollar bill has physical existence; indeed the presence of a tray of diamonds comprising an enterprise's merchandise inventory is a very tangible type of phenomenon as well.

Recognize, however, that ten-dollar bills are just pieces of paper—they are merely representations of value. The true benefit of possessing a handful of currency lies in the potential it represents to buy goods and services and to reduce one's monetary indebtedness to others. Similarly, the possession of tangible goods such as diamonds is merely a representation of the true benefit that could be realized. It is the wherewithal to exchange such items of inventory in a revenue transaction for monetary proceeds greater than the diamonds' original cost which really defines the value, indeed the very identity, of the inventory. Thus, whereas all assets' value is defined by the perceived intangible, future service potential, most assets have a physical dimension as well. Those assets which do not have such a physical quality as part of their basic nature are called intangible assets.

An important aspect of this discussion is the recognition that on considering the expected future service potential quality of intangible assets, the accounting criteria are no more or less demanding than those which permeate the case of tangible assets. Thus, there must be an expectation of future service potential as well as evidence the asset was acquired as a result of an arm's length transaction between independent parties. The basis on which the asset is recorded must conform to the same historical cost criterion used to account for all other acquired assets. The essence of an intangible asset is therefore no different from that of any other asset.

Well-Defined Intangibles

One type of intangible asset is that which has a relatively finite expected life. A prime example of such an intangible asset is a patent. A company or an individual may obtain government-sanctioned patent protection for seventeen years. The cost of obtaining the patent can include a registration fee, legal fees, and the cost of compensating an external inventor to transfer his or her rights to the new patent holder. The future service potential of the patent lies in the owner's right to exclusive use of the patented item. There may be a vast difference between the amount of dollars that represent the value of the future service potential and the number of dollars that constitute the recordable cost for accounting purposes, but this has no bearing on the manner in which the patent is recorded by accountants.

The finite-life feature of patents has importance for purposes of measuring income. Since each passing year indicates there is proportionately less patent protection remaining, this decline in future service potential must be recognized as a cost of generating that year's revenue. Merely because the legal life of patent protection is 17 years does not necessarily mean amortization must occur over this entire period. Instead, management must make an estimate of the expected useful life of the patent, and this estimate may be less than 17 years. If the state of technology is such that a superior product will likely be developed by the company or by its competitors during the 17 year period, and that the new product will render the current product obsolete, it is the expected shorter time period that prevails.

A company may sometimes purchase a new or existing patent solely to protect an existing patent. Even though the new patent has its own 17-year legal life, it is amortized over the years it will provide benefit for the company's existing patent. This allows the cost of the additional protection to be matched against the benefit it provides; preventing a competing product from reaching fruition during the existing product's expected useful life benefits only the existing product.

A copyright is an exclusive protection for written material such as books, magazine articles, and lyrics of a song. It protects its owner from infringement or plagiarism by other parties. Either the author of the work or some party, such as a commercial publisher to whom the author has assigned the copyright, is thereby entitled to any resulting benefits. Until recently, the life of a copyright was 28 years and was renewable for one additional 28-year period. Under the current law, the protection extends until 50 years after the author's death. The accounting procedures discussed relative to patents apply to copyrights as well. The cost of a copyright is capitalized as an intangible asset, and is amortized over its expected economic life. Merely because the copyright remains in force for a certain number of years does not necessarily mean that is also the appropriate amortization period.

A franchise is an exclusive right to sell designated goods or services. Examples of franchises could include operators of motels that are part of national chains, and professional sports enterprises operating competitive teams by virtue of an exclusive agreement of an organized league. The granting of a franchise by the franchisor provides the franchisee with the assurance that no competing franchise will be given to other parties within a designated geographic area. To obtain the franchise right, the franchisee pays the franchisor a fee at the outset which may also entitle the franchisee to receive some "start-up" assistance from the franchisor. Invariably the franchisee must also remit annually to the franchisor an amount equal to a portion of its revenues and/or profits—in accordance with some predetermined formula. The initial preoperating fee paid by the franchisee to the franchisor is capitalizable and subject to amortization by the franchisee whether the franchise is established for a well-defined time interval or if the agreement remains in effect indefinitely.

The opposite of a franchise is a noncompetition agreement. This refers to a contractual understanding between two parties that in exchange for bargained consideration, the recipient is *not* permitted to engage in specified business activity. For example, part of the purchase price for an amusement park may be identified as compensation paid to the seller not to operate a competing facility within a designated radius for a specified time period. From the point of view of the new owner, part of the price paid to purchase the amusement park is the cost of acquiring an intangible asset, which in turn would be amortized over the life of the noncompetition period.

The cost of purchasing a trademark, a brand name, a secret process or formula, or an operating license (such as to operate a radio station or a taxicab) is capitalizable as an intangible asset. However, it is only the cost of *acquiring* such exclusive rights from external parties which is capitalizable. Costs incurred internally, such as advertising and promotion costs, are specifically excluded from the capitalized amount.

Goodwill

Perhaps the most enigmatic and misunderstood intangible asset of all is *goodwill*. Goodwill can be portrayed as an asset by a corporation only if it results from a qualifying business combination. Laymen often impute goodwill to an enterprise simply on the basis of the presumption of innate favorable factors. Some of the phenomena believed to constitute goodwill include special technical skills and knowledge; strong managerial ability; possession of a monopoly, near-monopoly, or mere large share of particular selling markets; good name and business reputation; established clientele and good customer relations; favorable geographic location; superior quality merchandise; and desirable labor relations.

Indeed there may sometimes be a tendency to attribute special consideration to public utility companies for enjoying a relative monopoly, to those industrial firms which have captured more than 50 percent of the market for their products, to companies that have been able to withstand efforts to unionize their employees, and to enterprises whose visible owners or managers are celebrated sports or show business personalities. Such perceptions implicitly assume the companies in question possess some unique ingredients which thereby allow them to earn more than the "fair" return on investment that would otherwise accrue.

However, for corporate accounting purposes goodwill exists only if it is paid for as part of a business combination.[3] If a business combination's underlying circumstances require the purchase method of accounting be used to record the transaction, goodwill may result. The acquiring company must first attribute the purchase price paid for the acquired company's assets and liabilities to the current value of those assets and liabilities already recorded by the acquired company. Purchased goodwill is then derived by subtracting from the purchase price the current value of the acquired recorded assets less liabilities assumed. Implicit in this approach is the assumption the acquiring company had paid this additional amount to acquire the heretofore unrecorded goodwill.

Goodwill is thought of in several ways. Some accountants maintain that goodwill is only a composite for a variety of unrecorded intangible assets. Such presumed assets, in turn, would include some of the items listed earlier in our discussion of laymen's perceptions of goodwill. Others assert goodwill is a measure of the momentum factor that characterizes the purchase of a going concern, e.g., the avoidance of starting-up costs. Another view, set forth in an Accounting Principles Board-commissioned study, is that goodwill is not an asset at all. Instead, the residual (debit) is a diminution of the acquiring company's owners' equity, a premium as it were that its stockholders sustain to effect the business combination.[4]

Goodwill must be amortized over a period not to exceed 40 years. Prior to the time amortization became a requirement, some companies did not amortize purchased goodwill at all, often because they felt there was no meaningful basis for selecting an amortization period; while other companies did amortize goodwill over different time periods. The amortization requirement is based on the view ". . . that the value of intangible assets at any one date eventually disappears and that the recorded costs of intangible assets should be amortized by systematic charges to income over the periods estimated to be benefited."[5]

The amortization rule applies to goodwill, as well as to the other intangible assets discussed earlier. With respect to the method of amortization, ". . . the straight-line method of amortization—equal annual amounts—should be applied unless a company demonstrates that another systematic

---

[3] This subject is discussed in greater depth in Chapter 9 as part of a comprehensive examination of accounting for business combinations.

[4] George R. Catlett and Norman O. Olson, *Accounting for Goodwill* (New York: American Institute of Certified Public Accountants, 1968) pp. 105–107.

[5] *Accounting Principles Board Opinion No. 17*, paragraph no. 27.

method is more appropriate."[6] In addition, "a company should evaluate the periods of amortization continually to determine whether later events and circumstances warrant revised estimates of useful lives."[7]

Organization Costs

Certain costs incurred by a company at its inception are collectively called organization costs. Such costs would include incorporation fees, the cost of "start-up" accounting and legal services, promotion costs related to the sale of shares of stock, and the cost of printing stock certificates. Although these costs are incurred at the beginning of a corporation's life, their related benefits occur during subsequent periods. The accounting principle of measuring earnings by matching revenues and related expenses suggests that such costs should therefore not be recognized as an expense when they are incurred. Were there to be immediate expense recognition, the first fiscal period's income statement would absorb an undue burden while those of subsequent periods would not reflect their share even though they would reflect the benefits then being realized.

It is therefore acceptable to account for organization costs as an asset, and to include this item as an intangible asset. The matching principle suggests that amortization is warranted. However, the period benefited encompasses the entire expected life of the corporate entity which is assumed to be infinite. Consequently, organization costs need not be amortized, that is, it is permissible to carry organization costs as an intangible asset, without any downward adjustment. In practice, some companies do amortize these costs over an arbitrary time period, while others do not even capitalize organization costs in the first place. Such approaches can usually be justified on the basis that the amounts involved are not of sufficiently material size to warrant perpetual asset recognition.

Another manifestation of the "organization costs" notion is that of preoperating costs. Whereas organization costs relate to the creation of a company proper, preoperating costs are those incurred by an existing company when it introduces new operating facilities or sales locations. The company may wish to account for pertinent preoperating costs as an investment in an asset—to be amortized over an appropriate subsequent time period. For instance, a company which opens new retail outlets might justify capitalizing the cost of finding sites, recruiting and training employees, preopening rentals and salaries, and initial advertising and promotional campaigns.

---

[6] Ibid., paragraph no. 30.

[7] Ibid., paragraph no. 31.

Interest Cost

Recall that the criterion governing whether an expenditure may be accounted for as an asset is that it must represent an economic resource having future service potential. When accounting for the purchase of an asset, cost is not only the amount paid to the vendor; it also includes related costs such as freight charges and installation fees. The term "product cost" is sometimes used by cost accountants to signify the relationship between assets and their related elements of cost. By contrast, the expression "period cost" signifies those costs not causally related to particular assets, and therefore would be recognized as expense in the period in which they are incurred."[8]

One of the costs practically all enterprises incur is interest. Interest represents the cost of borrowing money from another party (called a creditor). It is viewed by many accountants as a *cost of capital* rather than a *cost of an asset* inasmuch as it is a general cost incurred by an enterprise to have the means to conduct its operations. Because it is viewed not as an element of any particular asset's cost, these accountants maintain that interest cost should be accounted for as a period cost. This means it is an expense in the period in which it is incurred, that is, the period during which the creditor's funds are used. This would be the case even if the expected life of the financed asset were longer or shorter than the period for which the money was borrowed.

The reasons underlying this approach are varied. On the one hand, it is not practicable to trace borrowed funds to specific assets once a borrower begins to actually use them in enterprise activities. Moreover, the effective cost of borrowed funds is difficult to determine because the apparent cost of incremental borrowings would be expected to be tempered by existing debt obligations, if not by the borrower's entire financial structure which includes equity capital as well. And at a more conceptual level, interest is not a cost of using an asset, rather it is a cost of acquiring an asset. Two companies acquiring an identical asset for which a like amount is remitted to the vendor should not reflect the asset in their respective balance sheets at different amounts merely because of the financing arrangements—one company having used internally generated funds while the other enterprise used borrowed money.

A particular accounting dilemma arises in the case of interest cost related to funds borrowed during the period in which assets are constructed. As mentioned earlier, costs incurred during a preoperating period are capitalizable because their revenue-generating effect can be expected to occur only once operations have begun. Such capitalized expenditures are then amor-

---

[8] This distinction parallels that which was made in context of Chapter 6's discussion of the notion of inventoriable costs and the variable-costing approach to accounting for the cost of inventories.

tized over an appropriate time period. When a company engages in construction or preoperational testing of "plant" assets, it may borrow a significant amount of money which can result in a substantial interest cost. On the one hand, the traditional accounting view of interest as a period cost rather than a product cost would suggest that capitalization is not warranted. On the other hand, accounting's recognition that preoperating costs may be capitalized would intimate that expense recognition of construction period interest can be deferred and in turn spread over the related asset's useful economic life.

FASB Statement No. 34 stipulates that interest cost be capitalized as part of the cost of certain assets requiring a period of time to prepare them for their intended use. Qualifying assets include those that are constructed for a company's own use, such as buildings, and those intended for sale or lease which are constructed as discrete projects such as shopping centers. The amount of the capitalized interest is based on actual borrowings, and therefore does not encompass imputed interest on equity capital. The capitalized amount is included as part of the cost of the related asset, that is, it is not disclosed separately in the balance sheet. However, in the period when the interest is capitalized, there is required disclosure of the total interest cost incurred during the period as well as the portion that was capitalized.

NON-RECOGNIZED INTANGIBLES

The preceding section identified those items which can be recorded as intangible assets. There are, however, other expenditures made by enterprises for which there is controversy whether the costs can be capitalized. Much of the debate surrounding these issues revolves around the question of what should constitute an asset. Questions are raised not only with respect to the asset status of costs which have already been incurred, but also with respect to the status of events and circumstances for which costs have not yet even been incurred.

Research and Development Costs

"Research and development costs" (R&D) is a term which embraces a variety of expenditures a company can make with the objective of generating future revenue benefits. It encompasses different types of expenditures in the sense that different purposes are served by each. Basic or pure research pertains to efforts to investigate heretofore unexplored areas for purposes of generating insights into a particular sphere of knowledge. Included in this category is experimentation having no specific revenue-earning objectives.

142

New product development refers to activity oriented toward producing a viable product. It is the link between pure research and achieving a salable product. Whereas the discovery of a new chemical preservative might be an example of pure research, experimentation designed to incorporate it into salable food products would exemplify new product development.

A third type of effort falling within the research and development category is product improvement. This class encompasses expenditures relating to goods already being produced and marketed. The purpose of such an effort is to improve the quality of the enterprise's output or to enhance the potential uses and applications of particular products. Another type of R&D cost is that of expenditures designed to improve or supplant existing production or distribution processes. The objective of such endeavors is to introduce efficiency by reducing production costs, and to increase productivity by expanding capacity, consolidating work assignments, increasing mechanization, and so forth. Expenditures may also relate to the company seeking ways to improve working conditions within its plant by increasing safety standards, eliminating health hazards, and introducing other factors which contribute to employee welfare. Such amounts might be viewed as being investments which could ultimately, if not indirectly, have a favorable effect on the firm's revenue-earning ability.

Prior to 1975, it was acceptable to account for research and development costs either as an expense in the period during which the expenditure occurred or as an asset investment. If the asset capitalization approach was selected, it became necessary to amortize the asset over an appropriate time period, based on management's estimate when the revenue benefits were expected to occur. The inherent difficulty in the capitalize-and-amortize method lies in the high degree of uncertainty associated with the useful life of such expenditures. Initially, management would be required to identify the expected revenue-benefit to be generated, as well as its expected duration. There would then be recognition of the risk of failure in light of factors such as whether a salable product would in fact be produced, whether it could be produced at a reasonable cost, whether the product would be marketable, and whether there existed the organizational ability, structurally and financially, for such an endeavor to reach fruition.

The Financial Accounting Standards Board in October 1974 issued Statement No. 2 whose scope included only those costs which are demonstrably of a research and development nature. The pronouncement states that all R&D expenditures must be recognized as an expense of the period during which the cost is incurred.[9] Reasons for the Board's prohibition of

---

[9] *Financial Accounting Standards Board Statement No. 2*, paragraph no. 12. Copyright © by Financial Accounting Standards Board, High Ridge Park, Stamford, Connecticut 06905, U.S.A. Reprinted with permission. Copies of the complete document are available from the FASB.

capitalization of research and development costs were uncertainty of future benefits, lack of causal relationship between expenditures and benefits, its understanding of the accounting definition of economic resources, a concern with matching revenues and expenses, and the perceived usefulness of the resulting information.[10]

Proponents of capitalization were not satisfied with the FASB's reasoning. In particular, they contend that the expenditure of money for R&D activities does meet the traditional test of what constitutes an asset. The investment of a company's funds expected to provide revenue benefits in future periods constitutes an asset. If the revenue benefit is expected to occur during the period the cost is incurred, immediate expense recognition is warranted, and if an expenditure is expected to generate no revenue benefit, it is treated as a loss as soon as such a determination is made. The very nature of research and development activity is that immediate revenue benefits are not expected; what is expected is that revenue benefits will occur in subsequent periods.

Because immediate revenue benefits are not feasible, it is argued the matching principle of income measurement would preclude immediate expense recognition. The FASB's prohibition against capitalization which thereby results in immediate income statement recognition in effect forces R&D expenditures into the category of "loss." Such an accounting result is said to run counter to the business nature of such expenditures, namely, that in fact they are investments in the enterprise's future—investments in the same sense that dollars are expended to acquire merchandise, machinery, investment securities, and patent protection.

The primary substantive difference between R&D and other expenditures is that of uncertainty. Expenditures recorded as assets have, on the basis of past experience and their relatively well-defined nature, high degrees of probability as to their expected future service potential. The revenue-benefit potential of R&D expenditures, on the other hand, is significantly less likely. It is therefore the matter of expectation which emerges as the governing criterion. Whereas management, by its very action, expects future benefits to occur, the FASB apparently believes the subjectivity inherent in R&D expectations is just too tenuous to justify accounting for such expenditures as enterprise assets.

Oil and Gas Exploration Costs

Companies which produce crude oil and natural gas encounter significant exploration and drilling costs before even reaching the development and production phase of their operations. The nature of the exploration process is

---

[10] Ibid., paragraph nos. 39–50.

144

such that expenditures made in the hope of discovering reserves may lead to nothing. In other words, a company must drill a number of prospective wells in orcer to yield one well having revenue-earning potential. A substantive financial reporting question arises about how to account for the costs incurred in drilling operations which result in "dry holes."

The traditional point of view is that the costs associated with dry holes constitute an expense in the period in which the expenditures are made. This is based on the belief that since no reserves result, there is no product with which such costs can be associated. In effect, such expenditures are treated as period costs, that is, because no future revenue-benefit is expected, they are an expense of the period in which they are incurred. As a result, the only costs which are treated as product costs and are therefore capitalized (as an asset investment) are those associated with exploration and drilling operations which turn out to be successful efforts.

An alternative accounting approach is to treat the costs associated with dry holes as an element of the cost of discovering commercially productive reserves. The nature of oil and gas operations is that companies, in the process of locating reserves, expend funds for what they know will result in a number of failures. To reflect such circumstances, some companies began during the 1950's to treat the cost of dry holes as elements of the cost of productive holes. Such costs were therefore capitalized, and amortized over the expected useful life of the "related resulting" revenue stream. Because the nature of this approach is to treat the cost of dry holes as part of the full cost of productive holes, it was called the *full cost method.* Its emergence created a need to assign a name to what had previously been the only existing approach, and it was therefore dubbed the *successful efforts method.*

In December 1977, the Financial Accounting Standards Board issued its Statement No. 19 which rejected the full cost approach and endorsed the successful efforts method. The FASB noted that under full costing, even "costs that are known *not* to have resulted in identifiable future benefits are nonetheless capitalized as part of the cost of assets to which they have no direct relationship.[11] Therefore, it was the Board's opinion that "costs that are known *not* to relate directly to the discovery of oil and gas reserves or in the development of a system for the extraction of previously discovered reserves should not be capitalized. To capitalize them would be inconsistent with the existing accepted accounting framework based on measuring the historical cost of an asset."[12]

---

[11] *Financial Accounting Standards Board Statement No. 19,* paragraph no. 144. Copyright © by Financial Accounting Standards Board, High Ridge, Park, Stamford, Connecticut 06905, U.S.A. Reprinted with permission. Copies of the complete document are available from the FASB.

[12] Ibid., paragraph no. 145.

In addition to considering the issue in context of accounting theory, the Board also addressed the matter in light of financial reporting objectives by observing that "in the production of oil and gas, significant risks and returns arise in the search for reserves. In other words, discovery of oil and gas reserves is a critical event in determining failure or success, for assessing risks and returns. Because it capitalizes the costs of unsuccessful property acquisitions and unsuccessful exploratory activities as part of the costs of successful acquisitions and activities, full costing tends to obscure failure and risk. Successful efforts accounting, on the other hand, highlights failures and the risks involved in the search for oil and gas reserves by charging to expense costs that are known not to have resulted in identifiable future benefits."[13]

There is some similarity between the resolution of the research-and-development-costs question and that of oil-and-gas-exploration costs. The FASB has adopted positions which yield an identical result, namely, that the costs in question are not treated as investments in assets. But the two cases are different. R&D expenditures may or may not result in future revenue-benefits, while the costs associated with dry holes definitely have no future revenue-benefit potential. Even though the two cases appear to be different, in fact their business natures are sufficiently similar and like accounting treatment results. One might observe that if the FASB initially determined that R&D costs were not capitalizable, certainly the no future revenue-benefit aspect of dry holes would have a similar accounting treatment.

However, better insight into the parallel might be obtained if the R&D case were viewed in context of the dry hole situation. From a business management vantage point, funds are expended to drill unsuccessful wells because this is the only feasible way to discover commercially productive wells. Despite this fact of life, the cost of the dry hole is not capitalizable because there is no *direct causal relationship* between such expenditures and the revenues to be generated by discovered reserves. Similarly in the case of R&D expenditures, some profitable and some non-profitable outcomes will ensue. It is the problem of no apparent *direct causal relationship* which precludes capitalization. The notable difference therefore is that the cost of successful oil and gas drilling efforts is capitalized because of the demonstrated direct causal relationship between it and future revenues, whereas that portion of R&D expenditures which will result in future revenues is not capitalized because it cannot be definitively differentiated from the non-revenue generating portion.

Despite the FASB's resolution of the matter, a Securities and Exchange Commission pronouncement (ASR No. 253) issued nine months later had the effect of superseding the FASB Statement. The SEC established a new method

---

[13] Ibid., paragraph no. 151.

of accounting called Reserve Recognition Accounting. Its nature is to treat all exploration costs as expenses when they are incurred, and to recognize immediately, as an asset and as income, the present value of the resulting reserves' expected future revenue stream. This approach is a dramatic departure from the traditional means of measuring assets and income, and the SEC's implicit position was that the nature of the circumstances justified introduction of the distinctive new method.

Non-Transaction Events

The remaining sections of the non-recognized intangibles area are concerned with the question of whether there should be asset recognition for resources which exist, but for which an enterprise has yet to incur costs at a transactional level. There is first a discussion of certain kinds of executory contracts, and this is followed by an examination of financial reporting aspects of human asset accounting.

Executory Contracts

To the extent contracts deal with acts and promises to act, three kinds of situations can exist. A contract under which each party has performed an act is one which falls within the realm of accounting, e.g., the purchase of inventory for cash. Similarly, if only one of the parties performs an act while the other merely promises to carry out an act in the future, there is a need to account for such a transaction, e.g., the purchase of inventory on account. However, if both parties merely exchange promises, this is generally not considered to be an event which warrants accounting, e.g., the promise to deliver inventory in exchange for a promise to remit a particular amount of money thirty days later.[14]

By contrast, consider the case of prepaid expenses, the term which refers to items such as insurance, rent and advertising. Using insurance as an example, advance payment of an insurance premium constitutes the acquisition of an asset, namely, insurance coverage over the life of the policy. The important factor to note is that to be an accountable transaction, the policyholder must make the prepayment. Because the insurance company only promises future coverage, the insured party cannot just make a reciprocating promise—to remit a premium payment at some future date.

Other examples of executory contracts which do not qualify for accounting recognition include employment contracts whereby a company promises

---

[14] Even though the commitment to purchase the merchandise is itself not an accountable event, if a decline in the goods' realizable value were to occur prior to delivery, the buyer would record the loss. Even though the commitment itself is not reflected as a balance sheet asset, the loss is reflected as a determinant of income.

to pay an employee a specified salary if the individual were to perform services over a particular time interval, the "value" of having a union contract, and contracts with price hedging characteristics such as commodity contracts or forward foreign currency exchange contracts.

Human Assets

The possibility of accounting for human assets was first introduced in the early 1960's. It is a subject not yet well defined although some accountants perceive it to be a concept that might offer some real analytic possibilities. One of the basic premises implicit in human asset accounting is that for an economic resource to be considered to be an asset, it need not necessarily be *owned* by the enterprise. "Ownership" of a resource is in effect supplanted by the notion of exclusive "rights."

To demonstrate the nature of human assets, consider the case of a professional sports team. To the extent the worth of such an organization is inextricably based on its player personnel, one encounters a very real *human asset* situation. Because it is such individuals' performances that constitute the primary source of teams' revenue-producing efforts, these persons represent human assets to their employers even though *they* are not "owned" in the usual sense. A team only owns the right to be the exclusive party to negotiate a performance contract with a player.

There are of course other enterprises for which human assets are the organization's principal resources, e.g., CPA firms, universities, and advertising agencies. Indeed, any organization is ultimately only as good as its individual members. But the nature of a professional sports team in particular lends itself to the phenomenon of accounting for human assets. The "output" of athletes is presumed to be measurable in terms of sports statistics reflecting home runs, touchdowns, goals, assists, and so forth. Furthermore, trading the right to negotiate a contract for particular players among the various professional teams occurs frequently. The nature of such trades suggests an implicit valuation of athletes' future services. It would appear therefore that the accounting procedures relating to human resources might possibly even parallel those which apply to inanimate assets such as plant, property and equipment.

There is no provision within generally accepted accounting principles for disclosure of human assets *per se* unless they are acquired by purchase. Some research efforts have been undertaken to determine the extent to which human assets are identifiable and how they might be measured.

Much of the impetus for human resource measurement comes from persons with a behavioral science orientation who wish to study business enterprises. Such individuals tend to engage in interdisciplinary inquiries which may encompass the work of sociologists, economists, and accounting

148

theorists. Although persons actively pursuing research in this area are relatively few in number, many individuals acknowledge that human asset accounting is an intriguing and a provocative question. The very concept raises the question of whether conventional financial statements' portrayal of economic resources may be ignoring the most vital resource an organization possesses.

Its scope is even broader, however. An American Accounting Association report stated the objective of human resource accounting is not just recognition of the value of all resources used or controlled by the firm, but also includes improvement of the management of human resources so the quantity and quality of goods and services are increased.[15] It is therefore not surprising that virtually all the research being conducted in this area is done in context of managerial accounting issues. Perhaps once substantive concepts and measurement techniques are developed, some definitive ramifications for the financial reporting realm may emerge as a result.

LONG-TERM LEASES

A lease is a contractual agreement between parties called the lessor and the lessee. The lessor agrees to rent property it owns to a lessee, usually for a specified time period. If the rental agreement extends beyond one year, it is referred to as a long-term lease. The lease specifies the time period during which the lessee has the exclusive right to use the lessor's property, and identifies the amount of compensation the lessee is obligated to remit to the lessor, the due dates, and which party pays maintenance and insurance costs where applicable, and describes renewal or purchase options available to the lessee during or at the end of the lease period. Leasing activity is found in virtually every phase of business operations involving capital assets, including land, buildings, machinery, motor and other transportation vehicles, and computer hardware.

Earlier in this chapter, it was pointed out that an executory contract is not generally an accountable transaction. The mere exchange of a promise for a promise is not sufficient to warrant accounting recognition. A long-term lease is an executory contract because it represents an exchange of promises: the lessor promises to give the lessee exclusive access to a particular asset for which the lessee promises to remit rental payments to the lessor. Accordingly, the mere existence of a lease did not traditionally warrant accounting recognition by either lessees or lessors in the body of their respective financial statements. Of course, each period's rental expense and rental revenue

---

[15] "Report of the Committee on Accounting for Human Assets," *The Accounting Review*— Supplement to Vol. XLIX, 1974, p. 116.

did appear in their respective income statements. Footnote disclosure as to the existence of long-term leases might also have occurred, but this of course is quite different from inclusion in the financial statements proper.

As leasing activity became increasingly widespread during the 1950s and 1960s, accountants reevaluated their stance with respect to this matter. Although the matter of when a lessor should recognize revenue from a long-term lease attracted much attention, most of the concern was directed to the accounting and disclosure requirements facing the lessee. Indeed, among the many presumed benefits of leasing rather than purchasing assets was the very fact that lessees would experience no resulting balance sheet effect; this phenomenon caused leasing to be referred to sometimes as "off balance sheet financing." The property's presence would not be reflected among a lessee's assets, which means that resulting rate-of-return type of data would yield relatively larger amounts. More important, excluding the lease's future monetary obligations from its recognized liabilities allowed a lessee to reflect its debt at an amount less than what it would otherwise have been.

In 1962, the American Institute of CPAs published a research study whose author concluded that rather than using "ownership" as the criterion for what constitutes a recordable asset, it was "property rights" which should be the basis for requiring capitalization as an asset and recognition of the resultant liability.[16] In other words, the traditional notion of the primacy of legal ownership would yield to the economic substance embodied in the exclusive right to use property. The Accounting Principles Board eventually issued four pronouncements dealing with leases (*Opinion Nos. 5, 7, 27,* and *31*).

With respect to lessees, the APB stated that "the right to use property and a related obligation to pay specific rents over a definite future period are not considered by the Board to be assets and liabilities under present accounting concepts . . . (but) leases which are clearly in substance installment purchases of property should be recorded as purchases."[17] Whereas for lessees the APB focused its attention solely on whether the lessee had equity in the leased asset, for lessors it concentrated on which party had the risks of ownership. As a result, when the nature of a lease placed the lessor more in the position of financier because the risks of ownership had effectively been assumed by the lessee, the Board permitted a method whereby a lessor could account for a lease as though it were a sale. The leased asset would be replaced in the lessor's balance sheet by the amount receivable from the lessee and its income statement would reflect lease-related revenue on a

---

[16] John H. Myers, *Reporting of Leases in Financial Statements* (New York: American Institute of Certified Public Accountants, 1962), pp. 4, 38–42.

[17] *Accounting Principles Board Opinion No. 5,* paragraph no. 14.

more accelerated basis than that which merely records the receipt of cash lease payments.

Because the rules applicable to lessors and lessees were based on different criteria, a lease which a lessor accounted for as a sale would not necessarily be treated as an installment purchase by the lessee. That such an anomaly did arise in particular lease situations was no coincidence. Lessees would generally try to structure lease agreements so that they would not have to be capitalized, and lessors sought to arrange to have the conditions of a lease permit accounting recognition as a sale. It was possible to devise lease contracts which allowed each party to use the accounting method it desired, precisely because of the lack of symmetry between accounting rules for lessors and lessees. Indeed, the result was that leased assets were sometimes omitted from the balance sheets of both parties to the lease agreement.

Although subsequent issuances of the APB sought to clarify its basic approach, the matter remained unresolved until the Financial Accounting Standards Board issued a comprehensive pronouncement in 1976. As the FASB considered the various directions it might take to establish definitive criteria, it in effect reopened the entire issue of the nature of long-term leases and the approach to financial statement disclosures that should be adopted. A fundamental question was whether footnote disclosure would suffice or whether the more revealing inclusion in balance sheets and income statements was warranted.

The FASB took the position that "a lease that transfers substantially all of the benefits and risks incident to the ownership of property should be accounted for as the acquisition of an asset and the incurrence of an obligation by the lessee and as a sale or financing by the lessor."[18] The pronouncement was intended to remove "most, if not all, of the conceptual differences in lease classification as between lessors and leases . . . (by providing) . . . criteria for such classification that are more explicit and less susceptible to varied interpretation . . ."[19] than had been the case previously.

Probably the most critical aspect of the FASB's resolution of the leasing question was its notion of a "capital lease." It is such a lease which requires a lessee to reflect in its balance sheet the leased property as an asset and the resulting obligation as a liability. To qualify as a capital lease, at least one of four criteria must be met. The criteria relate to end-of-lease-term ownership, bargain purchase option, length of lease life versus economic life, and the

---

[18] *Financial Accounting Standards Board Statement No. 13,* paragraph no. 60. Copyright © by Financial Accounting Standards Board, High Ridge Park, Stamford, Connecticut 06905, U.S.A. Reprinted with permission. Copies of the complete document are available from the FASB.

[19] Ibid., paragraph no. 62.

relationship between the minimum lease payments' present value and the asset's fair value when the lease term begins. Leases which meet none of these criteria are accounted for as operating leases by lessees, and rental expense is recorded as lease payment obligations accrue.

A capital lease is recorded by a lessee as an asset and as a liability at an amount which reflects the minimum lease payments' present value not to exceed the property's fair value; executory costs such as insurance, maintenance and property taxes paid by the lessor are excluded. The asset in turn is amortized, similar to depreciating owned assets, over the lease life or economic life depending on which criteria (cited earlier) were met. Each lease payment is viewed as both a reduction of the liability and the remission of interest, and allocation is effected in accordance with the "interest" method set forth in *APB Opinion No. 21* (discussed in Chapter 8). Disclosure requirements of capital leases include separate financial statement or footnote disclosure each period of the asset, the liability, and the amortization expense. In addition, the lessee must disclose the gross amount of capital leases by major classes according to nature or function, future minimum lease payments in the aggregate and for each of the next five years, minimum sublease rentals to be received, and total contingent rentals for each operating period encompassed by the financial statements.

For operating leases, there are disclosure requirements regarding future minimum rental payments, minimum rentals to be received in the future under noncancellable subleases, and each period's rental expense broken down for minimum rentals, contingent rentals, and sublease rentals. And for either type of lease—capital or operating—there must be a description of the leasing arrangements such as the basis on which contingent rental payments are determined, the existence and terms of renewal or purchase options and escalation clauses, and restrictions imposed by lease agreements such as those concerning dividends, additional debt, and further leasing.

Lessor Accounting

In accounting for a lessor, a lease can be classified as being in one of four categories. First, there is a sales-type lease whose nature is it gives rise to (manufacturer's or dealer's) profit or loss to the lessor, based on the difference between the asset's fair value and its book value. A sales-type lease meets at least one of the same four criteria a lessee uses to determine if a capital lease exists. In addition, collectibility of the minimum lease payments is reasonably predictable and no important uncertainties surround the amount of unreimbursable costs which would be incurred. A lessor accounts for a sales-type lease by recording as unearned revenue the difference between the gross investment and its present value; the unearned revenue, in turn, is amortized as interest revenue to yield a constant rate of return. The Statement identifies rules which apply to determining an appropriate discount rate, annual review of the estimated residual value, residual guarantees, and changes in the provisions of a lease, renewals, extensions, and terminations.

The second type of lease is called a direct financing lease. It meets the same criteria as a sales-type lease, but it does *not* give rise to (manufacturer's or dealer's) profit or loss to the lessor. The difference between the gross investment and the book value is recorded as unearned revenue. Initial direct costs are recognized as they are incurred, and in the same period unearned revenue of a like amount is recognized as being earned. The remaining unearned revenue is amortized as interest revenue over the lease life at amounts that result in a constant rate of return. The accounting difference between a sales-type lease and a direct financing lease is illustrated below.

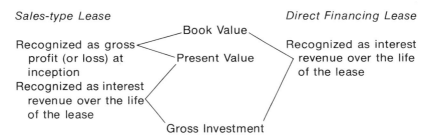

The third category is the distinctive case of a leveraged lease similar to the direct financing lease except that it must meet three additional conditions as well: having at least three parties, financing by the long-term creditor being non-recourse as to the general credit of the lessor, and the lessor's net investment initially declining and subsequently rising. A description of how to account for a leveraged lease is very complicated, and is beyond the scope of this book. The fourth type of lease is an operating lease and is entered into by a lessor which does not qualify for the other three categories. For an operating lease, the lessor records depreciation expense if the asset is depreciable, and it recognizes rental revenue as the payments become receivable. Initial direct costs are deferred and amortized over the life of the lease proportionate to the recognition of rental revenue.

Long-term leases can have so many procedural variations that any attempt to deal with particular aspects or nuances must be done within the context of a work whose objectives are far more technically oriented than those of this volume. For our purposes, a few general conclusions will suffice. First, the FASB has taken the position it is "the benefits and risks incident to ownership" which serve as the focal point for accounting for long-term leases. Second, certain long-term leases therefore are accounted for by a lessee as the acquisition of an asset and the creation of a liability. And third, there are extensive disclosure requirements which must be met by both lessees and lessors for all types of long-term leases irrespective of how they might be accounted for in the financial statements proper.

SUMMARY

Accounting for long-lived assets is a multi-faceted subject. Enterprises are continually expending funds and incurring debt in their effort to acquire the resources to produce goods and services. Such resources have costs associated with them, and these costs in turn affect the amount of income that will be earned by the company. It should therefore come as no surprise that almost all the accounting questions relating to long-lived assets ultimately relate to the measurement of earnings as well. As a result of examining long-lived assets in light of their related income ramifications, one can appreciate the extent an entity's balance sheet and earnings statement complement one another.

It was also pointed out that in the case of some resources which traditionally had not been viewed as being accountable assets, the additional question exists of possible direct effects on the equities side of the balance sheet. Lessees' capitalization of long-term lease agreements can significantly affect the amount of liabilities which appear in an enterprise's balance sheet. The possible recognition of human resources among an enterprise's assets raises a question as to the nature of their effect on recorded balance sheet equities. Even with respect to purchased goodwill, it has been argued that rather than being an asset, the elusive "debit" should be treated as an immediate contraction of the company's owners' equity.

Although a discussion of an enterprise's assets has implicit ramifications for the right side of its balance sheet as well, there are a variety of issues involving liabilities and owners' equity which warrant discussion in their own right. Such matters are examined in the next chapter.

Additional Readings

Anthony, Robert N. *Accounting for the Cost of Interest.* Lexington, Mass.: Lexington Books, 1975.

Bierman, Harold, Jr., and Dukes, Roland E. "Accounting for Research and Development Costs." *The Journal of Accountancy* (April 1975), pp. 48–55.

Caplan, Edwin H., and Landekich, Stephen. *Human Resource Accounting: Past, Present and Future.* New York: National Association of Accountants, 1974.

Cramer, Joe J., Jr., and Neyhart, Charles A., Jr. "A Comprehensive Accounting Framework for Evaluating Executory Contracts." *Journal of Accounting, Auditing and Finance* (Winter 1979), pp. 135–50.

Dieter, Richard. "Is Lessee Accounting Working?" *The CPA Journal* (August 1979), pp. 13–19.

Dixon, Robert L. "Decreasing Charge Depreciation—A Search for Logic." *The Accounting Review* (October 1960), pp. 590–97.

FASB Discussion Memorandum. *Accounting for Interest Costs.* Stamford, Conn.: Financial Accounting Standards Board, 1977.

FASB Discussion Memorandum. *Accounting for Leases.* Stamford, Conn.: Financial Accounting Standards Board, 1974.

FASB Discussion Memorandum. *Financial Accounting and Reporting in the Extractive Industries.* Stamford, Conn.: Financial Accounting Standards Board, 1976.

Gellein, Oscar S., and Newman, Maurice S. *Accounting for Research and Development Expenditures.* New York: American Institute of Certified Public Accountants, 1973.

Goldberg, L. "Concepts of Depreciation." In *Studies in Accounting Theory,* edited by W. T. Baxter and Sidney Davidson. Homewood, Ill.: Richard D. Irwin, Inc., 1962, pp. 236–58.

Hawkins, David F., and Wehle, Mary M. *Accounting for Leases.* New York: Financial Executives Research Foundation, 1973.

Hermanson, Roger H. *Accounting for Human Assets.* East Lansing, Mich.: Michigan State University Bureau of Business and Economic Research, 1964.

Imhoff, Eugene A., Jr., and Janell, Paul A. "Opinion No. 29: A New Valuation Method." *Management Accounting* (March 1979), pp. 50–53.

Lamden, Charles W.; Gerboth, Dale L.; and McRae, Thomas W. *Accounting for Depreciable Assets.* New York: American Institute of Certified Public Accountants, 1975.

Lasusa, Peter R., and Larsen, John W. "Accounting for Hedged Transactions." *The CPA Journal* (June 1978), pp. 17–21.

Myers, John H. "A Set of New Financial Statements." *The Journal of Accountancy* (February 1971), pp. 50–57.

Myers, John H. *Reporting of Leases in Financial Statements.* New York: American Institute of Certified Public Accountants, 1962.

Paton, William A. "Depreciation—Concept and Measurement." *The Journal of Accountancy* (October 1959), pp. 38–43.

Schachner, Leopold. "The New Accounting for Leases." *Financial Executive* (February 1978), pp. 40–57.

Schiff, Michael. "Benefits of Immediate Writeoffs." *Management Accounting* (December 1976), pp. 11, 12, and 26.

Schiff, Michael. "Cheers for Thirteen." *The CPA Journal* (December 1978), pp. 21–27.

Whittred, G. P. "Accounting for the Extractive Industries: Use or Abuse of the Matching Principle?" *Abacus* (December 1978), pp. 154–59.

Wyatt, Arthur R. "Leases *Should* Be Capitalized." *The CPA Journal* (September 1974), pp. 35–38.

Zises, Alvin. "Disclosure of Long-Term Leases." In *Financial Accounting Theory I: Issues and Controversies.* 2d ed., edited by Stephen A. Zeff and Thomas F. Keller. New York: McGraw-Hill Book Co., 1973, pp. 448–64.

Accounting Dimensions of Balance Sheet Equities

One of the objectives of accounting is to measure an entity's financial position. Lay persons may tend to think of financial position in terms of cash and perhaps selected other property such as securities or real estate. Accounting takes a more comprehensive approach in that it considers all the economic resources held by an entity. Those which have future service potential are called its assets. As an entity enjoys exclusive use of its assets, it is ever aware of its relationships with various external parties. In particular, it interacts with employees, suppliers, customers, creditors, taxing authorities, and stockholders, among others. Its relationship with each of these groups tends to be different.

In the parlance of economics, external parties are referred to as the providers of the factors of production. For example, employees' return on their investment is called wages, creditors' return is interest, suppliers are compensated for materials, residual owners earn profit. Although each of these parties invests in the business to earn a return on its investment, the nature of their investments differs. An employee for example invests services, a landlord invests access to facilities, and government contributes the franchise, as it were, to be able to operate and possibly earn a profit.

Creditors and stockholders are unique in the sense they invest amounts of money which give the entity the wherewithal to acquire noncash assets and engage in revenue-generating activities. Such investments' existence is deemed worthy of accounting measurement and balance sheet disclosure. In the case of creditors, it is understandable that the presence of such sums being owed denotes that a portion of assets are committed. Therefore, from the point of view of accounting, an entity's assets less the amount of its liabilities to creditors might be referred to as its net assets, that is, its assets net of its liabilities.

Net assets is actually only a mathematical residual—it does not pertain to amounts owed, explicitly invested, or for that matter even the *value* of the enterprise. However, because the corporate form of business requires the entity's ownership be vested in parties which own its shares of stock, such shareholders in effect have equity in the enterprise's net assets. As a result, *net assets* is sometimes called *stockholders' equity* or *owners' equity;* in this volume, the term *owners' equity* is the preferred expression. That owners' equity in an enterprise's assets is measured by net assets derives from the fact that at a transactional level, the amounts which legally comprise net assets can be traced to stockholders' own investments, donated capital, and internal asset growth. If and when the entity were to be dissolved, those assets which remain after creditors' claims are met would accrue to stockholders. Thus, because it is stockholders who ultimately benefit from profitable operations and who have no priority in the event of liquidation, their equity is often equated with an enterprise's owners' equity.

In an era characterized by the proliferation of professional managers and widespread absentee ownership, however, the legal distinction between creditors and stockholders has become somewhat less definitive than previously. The "I-thou" notion which had once characterized the stockholder-bondholder relationship may well be a more apt characterization of that which exists between a hired top-level management team and external investors (i.e., stockholders and bondholders) taken as a whole. Indeed as a more behaviorally oriented view is adopted, the classical distinctions may lose some of their practical importance, although not in a legalistic sense.

This chapter examines selected items which appear on the equities side of the balance sheet. These liability and owners' equity amounts are collectively referred to as *equities* because they are a measure as it were of the creditors' and stockholders' equities in enterprise assets. There may be an inclination to view balance sheet equities as merely a repository for what remains after accounting for assets and earnings. This is not so. The following discussion focuses on substantive issues having significant conceptual and practical implications for preparing and understanding financial statements.

BONDS VERSUS STOCK

An enterprise has basically four sources of funds: earnings, sales of capital assets, borrowings, and owners' investment. Generating funds internally through profitable operations is certainly a desirable source, but may be inadequate. Selling plant assets is not usually a viable alternative since such assets are used to facilitate the revenue-generating process. As a result, the two most critical sources to which enterprises invariably turn are debt capital and equity capital.

Before examining pertinent accounting and financial reporting issues, it is appropriate to review some of the relative advantages of pursuing each of these financing alternatives. Our perspective in the following discussion is that of the existing common stockholders, for it is they, through the corporate officers employed by them, who consider and select from among the various available sources of funds. In the case of long-term financing, this basically means either selling bonds or issuing additional shares of stock.

Among the relative advantages of obtaining funds through the sale of bonds are the following. Bondholders typically do not have voting rights, with the result the existing stockholders experience no dilution of their voting power. The fixed interest cost of bonds gives the issuing company an opportunity to engage in "trading on the equity" which is sometimes called financial leverage. This refers to borrowing at a given interest cost if the incremental return on the resulting investment is expected to exceed the cost, e.g., borrow at 14 percent if the funds can be used to earn 20 percent.

The interest cost associated with borrowed funds is a deductible expense in computing the issuing corporation's income tax obligation, which is not so in the case of dividends distributed to stockholders. The only effect bonds (other than convertible bonds) have on a company's earnings per share is lower income because of the resulting interest cost, while the issuance of new shares of stock increase the earnings-per-share denominator's number of outstanding shares which can often have a far more dilutive effect. Bonds can provide yet another attraction in the sense they may contain a call feature which gives the issuing corporation the right to call in and retire the securities at a predetermined price and thereby reduce the outstanding debt virtually at its discretion.

There are also relative advantages in issuing new shares of common stock instead of selling bonds. Common stock typically has no dividend requirement. Moreover, if and when a dividend is declared, the amount distributed is not predetermined as is the case with interest on bonds. Another feature of common shares is that they need not be redeemed at a designated maturity date, that is, they can remain outstanding as long as the corporation exists.

Although bondholders generally do not have voting rights, they are sometimes able to impose certain restrictions on the issuing corporation, e.g., they may require that a specified minimum amount of working capital be on hand at all times, limit the size of cash dividends which may be declared, or restrict the creation of additional debt. Another point favoring the issuance of stock is that in the event of dissolution, existing stockholders' rights parallel those of additional shareholders but are subservient to those of new creditors. One other noteworthy benefit of issuing shares of stock is that the corporation would be in a better position to obtain debt capital at a later date than if it had sold bonds.

BONDS PAYABLE

The issuance of a bond generally means that the corporation assuming debt—hereafter, the issuer—incurs a dual obligation. The principal or face value is due on a specified maturity date, and interest payments are remitted periodically over the life of the debt—annually, semiannually, or quarterly. The combined present value of these two obligations at the issuance date determines the bond's value, and thus the amount of proceeds which the issuer realizes.

Discounts and Premiums

In anticipation of selling bonds, the issuer selects an interest rate which identifies the amount to be disbursed at each interest payment date. For instance, if a bond having a $1,000 face value is assigned a 10 percent interest rate, this means the issuer promises to remit ($1,000 × 10% =) $100 of interest each year. The 10 percent rate is called the nominal, or coupon, rate. Since preparing to issue bonds is a process which can encompass several months, it is likely the interest rate prevailing in the market at the issuance date will differ from the nominal rate. The prevailing rate is called the yield, or real, rate, and it reflects a variety of factors relating to both the particular issuer and general money market conditions.

Let us now consider how an issuer accounts for a difference between a bond's nominal rate, which defines the amount of annual interest payments the issuer is committed to make, and the yield rate, which reflects prospective bondholders' expected interest return. As of the issuance date, the bond certificate's pre-printed nominal rate is fixed while the different yield rate in effect tells the issuer that the nominal rate is not appropriate in the particular circumstances. To resolve this apparent impasse, instead of selling the bond for its face value, the proceeds will reflect the market-based interest cost, i.e., the yield rate. Accepting proceeds which differ from the bond's face value means the issuer incurs an interest cost based on actual market conditions. It also means that bondholders thereby earn a rate of return that is likewise the result of a market transaction.

Consider the following example. Assume a bond whose face value is $1,000 and matures in 20 years is issued with a nominal rate of 10 percent with interest to be paid annually. If the prevailing market interest rate at the issuance date is also 10 percent, the proceeds are $1,000 because the bond-holder is paying for the following two things:

1.	The present value at 10% of 20 annual interest payments of ($1,000 × 10% =) $100 each	$ 851.36
2.	The present value at 10% of the $1,000 face value 20 years hence	148.64
	Total present value assuming 10% yield rate	**$1,000.00**

Consider the case if the prevailing market conditions demand a yield rate of 12 percent, namely, higher than the 10 percent nominal rate. Instead of $1,000, the proceeds would be $850.61 because the bondholder is ac-quiring:

1.	The present value at 12% of 20 annual interest payments of ($1,000 × 10% =) $100 each	$746.94
2.	The present value at 12% of the $1,000 face value 20 years hence	103.67
	Total present value assuming 12% yield rate	**$850.61**

Because we are dealing with a 12 percent yield rate rather than one of 10 percent, less money is required at the issuance date to generate the twenty required $100 interest payments and the $1,000 principal at the maturity date.

The issuer is prepared to accept $850.61 instead of $1,000 because the resulting ($1,000 − 850.61 =) $149.39 discount is in effect the cost of incurring an interest rate of 12 percent rather than one of 10 percent. The effect of the additional $149.39 interest cost is in turn spread over the 20 years during which the issuer benefits from the use of the bondholders' funds. It means that although $100 cash interest is *paid* annually, the total interest expense each year is ($149.39 ÷ 20 years =) $7.47 higher. This approach to accounting for the issuance discount is called the straight-line method of amortization. Each year, $7.47 is transferred from the balance sheet discount account to the earnings statement as an element of interest expense. The resulting balance sheet disclosure is as follows:

Bonds payable	$1,000.00
Less: Discount on bonds payable	149.39
Net liability	**$ 850.61**

One year later, the discount is $7.47 lower, or $141.92; this also means the net liability is $7.47 higher, or $858.08. As of the maturity date, the discount will have been fully amortized and the net liability will have risen to the bond's face value of $1,000.

Although the notion of spreading the additional $149.39 interest cost over the 20 year life of the bond in *equal* amounts appears to be a reasonable means of measuring the total interest cost, there is a conceptually superior alternative approach known as the effective interest method. Its nature is described with the use of Exhibit 8–1 which contains an illustration using the same circumstances and data with which we have been dealing until now.

Exhibit 8–1

The Effective Interest Method

End of Year	(1) Effective (yield rate) Interest	(2) Cash Interest	(3) Amortized Discount	(4) Present Value
				$ 850.61
1	$ 102.07*	$ 100	$ 2.07†	852.68‡
2	102.32	100	2.32	855.00
3	102.60	100	2.60	857.60
..	..	..	..	..
18	114.24	100	14.24	966.20
19	115.94	100	15.94	982.14
20	117.85	100	17.85	1,000.00
	$2,149.39	$2,000	$149.39	

* $850.61 × 12% = $102.07
† $102.07 − 100.00 = $2.07
‡ $850.61 + 2.07 = $852.68

Recall that $850.61 was identified as the combined present value of the $1,000 face value to be repaid in 20 years and the $100 interest payable at the end of each of the intervening years. Because $850.61 therefore represents the principal outstanding during Year 1, 12 percent of it or ($850.61 × .12 =) $102.07 is the effective interest cost for that year—as seen in Column 1 in the Exhibit. Since $100 is the cash interest payment, the ($102.07 − 100.00 =) $2.07 excess is the additional cost resulting from the 12 percent yield rate being higher than the 10 percent nominal rate; this amount appears in Column 3. Because $2.07 will be paid when the bond matures, it becomes part of the principal owed to the bondholders. Thus, the principal to which the 12 percent interest cost is applied in Year 2 is the sum of the previous $850.61 principal and the accrued $2.07 interest cost, or a total of $852.68, as reflected in Column 4.

162

The issuance date discount was $149.39, that is, the difference between the bond's $1,000 face value and its $850.61 present value. As a result of adding the $2.07 accrued interest to the principal owed, the $149.39 balance of the discount is reduced by $2.07 to $147.32. This reduction in the amount of the discount is referred to as amortization—similar to what was encountered when the straight-line method was applied. As shown in column 3 in the Exhibit, each succeeding year experiences progressively larger amortization of the original discount. Each year's principal owed is larger by a like sum, and the resulting total interest cost is proportionately higher as well. It is this feature which causes the effective interest method to yield a more meaningful result than the straight-line method; namely, with the passage of time, the principal owed grows, and progressively larger interest costs are incurred which in turn warrant expense recognition.

When the yield rate is greater than the nominal rate, there is an issuance discount. To consider the reverse case, we continue to assume a 10 percent nominal interest rate but now use a lower yield rate of 8 percent. Recognize the issuance date proceeds are again based on the following two items:

1. The present value at 8% of 20 annual interest
   payments of ($1,000 × 10% =) $100 each $ 981.82
2. The present value at 8% of the $1,000 face
   value 20 years hence   214.55

Total present value assuming 8% yield rate   **$1,196.37**

The company will therefore realize proceeds of $1,196.37, and there is a ($1,196.37 − $1,000.00 =) $196.37 premium to be amortized over the bond's 20 year life. The resulting balance sheet disclosure would be as follows:

Bonds payable	$1,000.00
Premium on bonds payable	196.37
Total liability	**$1,196.37**

Under the straight-line method, ($196.37 ÷ 20 =) $9.82 is amortized each year with the result that interest expense will be ($100.00 − 9.82 =) $90.18 annually. This reflects the fact that although the cash interest is based on a 10 percent interest rate, a lower yield rate actually prevails. Being able to repay $1,000 at the maturity date rather than the larger $1,196.37 received on the issuance date indicates that $9.82 of the $100 cash interest disbursed each year to the bondholders is in effect not interest per se but rather a partial return of the premium received on the issuance date.

In the effective interest method, the same kinds of calculations made in context of the earlier *discount* case apply to premiums. For Year 1, the

effective interest is ($1,196.37 × 8% =) $95.71. When compared with the
$100.00 cash interest payment, the resulting ($100.00 − 95.71 =) $4.29
difference is the amount of premium to be amortized, thus reducing the
bond's present value (by $4.29 from $1,196.37) to $1,192.08. The amount
of premium to be amortized increases each period because the continuing
reduction in the bond's value as it approaches its $1,000 face value causes

Exhibit 8–2

Yield Rates with Different Bond Lives

	(1)	(2)	(3)
	Assume Prevailing Market (yield) Rate of		
	10%	8%	12%
A. 20 years			
1. Present value of annual interest payments of $100 (the nominal rate of 10% of $1,000) for 20 years	$ 851	$ 982	$747
2. Present value of payment of the face amount of $1,000 at the end of year 20	149	215	104
Present value and proceeds at date of issuance	**$1,000**	**$1,197**	**$851**
B. 15 years			
1. Present value of annual interest payments of $100 (the nominal rate of 10% of $1,000) for 15 years	$ 761	$ 856	$681
2. Present value of payment of the face amount of $1,000 at the end of year 15	239	315	183
Present value and proceeds at date of issuance	**$1,000**	**$1,171**	**$864**
C. 25 years			
1. Present value of annual interest payments of $100 (the nominal rate of 10% of $1,000) for 25 years	$ 908	$1,067	$784
2. Present value of payment of the face amount of $1,000 at the end of year 25	92	146	59
Present value and proceeds at date of issuance	**$1,000**	**$1,213**	**$843**

the effective interest to be less each year. As opposed to Year 1's $95.71 interest expense, the cost for Year 20 is ($1,018.52 × 8% =) $81.48; the resulting ($100.00 − 81.48 =) $18.52 amortization of premium reduces the $1,018.52 principal down to the $1,000 face value.

An additional noteworthy aspect of bond premiums and discounts is the importance of the length of the bond's life. Exhibit 8–2 illustrates the effect of time on the bond's value and thus on the amount of proceeds to be realized on the issuance date. The same interest rates (8 percent, 10 percent and 12 percent) are used, and all of the resulting amounts are expressed in terms of whole dollars.

As shown in Column 1, when the yield rate and the nominal rate are identical, the present value of the bond is always $1,000, irrespective of the bond's life. Note, however, the reason it is $1,000 in each case is different in the sense that the relative present value of the bond's two components varies. In Column 2, there is also variation among the two elements' present values with the result that the amount of the resulting premium increases as the number of years increases, viz., $171 versus $197 versus $213. In Column 3, the size of the discount also increases as the length of the bond's life increases, viz., $136 versus $149 versus $157.

Even though the discussion to this point has been in context of the relationship between the market yield rate and the issuer's selection of a nominal rate, it provides an important insight into the effect of any change in interest rates such as the subsequent increase in the market interest rate from 12 percent to 13 percent. If this change occurred one year after issuance, the bond's value in the market would decrease from $852.68 (which appeared in Exhibit 8–1) to $791.86 as indicated below:

		12%	13%
1.	The present value of 19 annual interest payments of ($1,000 × 10% =) $100 each	$736.58	$693.80
2.	The present value of the $1,000 face value 19 years hence	116.10	98.06
	Total present value	**$852.68**	**$791.86**

This is the phenomenon of the inverse relationship between the market interest rate and the value of a bond. As the interest rate increases, the value of the bond decreases, as seen in Column 3 of Exhibit 8–2, which shows the effect of an increase in the interest rate from 10 percent to 12 percent. Similarly, the decline in the interest rate depicted in Column 2 results in an increase in the value of the bond.

It is important, however, to note that once a bond is issued and recorded by the accountant, the amount at which it is reflected in financial statements

165

is unaffected by subsequent changes in market yield rates. This means issuers of bonds may not recognize gains or losses in the market value of outstanding bonds unless they are realized in an arm's length transaction. The one type of transaction which thus qualifies is an early extinguishment of debt, and it is examined in the next section of this chapter.

Early Extinguishments

Although every bond has a maturity date, the issuer may wish to effect an early extinguishment of the debt. This can be done by using available cash to retire the bonds or by financing the retirement with a concurrent issuance of either different bonds or shares of stock. The term *refunding* is sometimes used to denote the latter approaches. Note, however, that when a bondholder exchanges convertible bonds for shares of stock, it is not treated as an early extinguishment; the accounting treatment for such a conversion is discussed later.

To effect an early extinguishment, the issuer disburses a sum of money which is not necessarily equal to the amount at which the bonds are reflected in its balance sheet. This is because for accounting purposes, the bond is disclosed on a basis which reflects either (1) its face value net of unamortized issuance discount or premium or (2) the present value of both the maturity date face value and the stream of interest payments. The amount paid to the bondholders, on the other hand, is based on either a predetermined call price, or the bond's current market value. As a result, it is likely that the bond's accounting basis value will differ from the amount that is expended to retire it. If the amount paid exceeds the bond's carrying value, a loss is recognized; and if the payment is less than the accounting basis, a gain is recorded.

Prior to 1973, the gain or loss had been accounted for differently if the retirement was part of a refunding plan involving the issuance of new bonds. Based on the belief the two sets of bonds were related, the portion of the gain or loss resulting from the retired bonds' unamortized premium or discount could be amortized over what would have been the remaining years of the old issue or what were in fact the years of the new debt's life.[1] These alternative approaches were replaced by the one acceptable method that there be immediate recognition;[2] a question then arose as to whether such amounts should be disclosed as an ordinary or an extraordinary component of income.

---

[1] *Accounting Research Bulletin No. 43*, chapter 15, paragraph nos. 6 and 8; *Accounting Principles Board Opinion No. 6*, paragraph no. 19.

[2] *Accounting Principles Board Opinion No. 26*, paragraph no. 20.

Initially, an early extinguishment qualified as extraordinary because of its infrequent occurrence.[3] But when the criteria of *extraordinary* were revised to require that the occurrence be both unusual and infrequent, an early extinguishment no longer qualified because it is not unusual for companies whose bonds are outstanding to engage in such a transaction.[4] However, a subsequent FASB pronoucement specifically mandates that early extinguishments of debt are to be treated as *extraordinary* determinants of income.[5]

In addition to the disclosure issue, a question exists whether a gain or loss should even be recognized immediately, especially when an early extinguishment is effected by exchanging new bonds for the old securities. Consider the case of Western Union, Inc. which once offered its bondholders $100 cash and $560 principal amount of a new 10¾ percent bond for each $1,000 principal amount of outstanding 5¼ percent bonds. It received about $62 million of the old securities, issued $35 million of new bonds, paid out $6 million cash, and thereby recognized approximately a [$62 million − ($35 million + 6 million =) $41 million =] $21 million gain in its earnings.

Such a situation could arise for any company whose outstanding bonds have an interest rate that is low relative to the current rate. From the point of view of Western Union bondholders, a 10¾ percent return on $560 is $60.20 which compares favorably with the ($1,000 × 5¼% =) $52.50 annual interest income on the older bonds. The reason they might exchange a $1,000 face value bond for one whose principal is only $560 is that the old bond's current market value would probably be close to $560 when the yield is 10¾ percent.

That the bond is trading at such a *deep* discount is attributable to the inverse relationship which exists between a bond's value and the prevailing market interest rate which was cited earlier. In this case, as the market rate increased from the 5 percent range to that of 11 percent, the value of the bond decreased, as expected. From the point of view of Western Union, paying the $6 million cash as part of the exchange package and committing itself to pay additional annual interest of [($35,000,000 × 10.75% =) $3,762,500 − ($62,000,000 × 5.25% =) $3,255,000 =] $507,500 might well be worthwhile in light of the resulting opportunity to recognize a $21,000,000 gain in its current income statement. In addition, there is the [$1,000 − ($560 + 100 =) $660 =] $340 of cash which Western Union saves on each of the old bonds which no longer need to be redeemed at maturity, that is, the $21,000,000 gain has a cash-flow dimension as well.

The very fact gains and losses must be recognized in their entirety during

---

[3] *Accounting Principles Board Opinion No. 9*, paragraph no. 21.

[4] *Accounting Principles Board Opinion No. 30*, paragraph no. 20.

[5] *Financial Accounting Standards Board Statement No. 4*, paragraph no. 9.

the period in which early extinguishments occur has therefore been questioned. It has been pointed out that such an approach ". . . fails to require recognition of the economic effects associated with an early extinguishment of debt designed to yield a profit, [that] such a payment . . . is essentially in every case a refunding at a higher cost of money (over the remaining original term) than that of the debt being prepaid, . . . that omission of a provision for this added interest cost overstates the profit in the year of prepayment and shifts the interest burden to future periods."[6] Another concern is that immediate recognition of a gain or loss may induce a company to produce a gain by borrowing money at high interest rates to pay off discounted debt bearing low rates. Alternatively, the knowledge that a loss would be recognized may discourage refunding even though it is economically desirable.

Convertible Bonds

When a corporation seeks to obtain long-term capital financing, it generally has two alternative avenues to pursue—debt capital or equity capital. In practice, however, there are a number of variations of each of these alternatives. One such variation is issuing preferred stock instead of common shares. The nature of this approach is that such stockholders are granted a preference with respect to dividends, but would typically not enjoy voting rights.

A variation of issuing conventional bonds is the offering of bonds convertible into shares of common stock. Such bonds are usually converted on the basis of a predetermined exchange formula, sometimes to be accompanied by a specified amount of cash, and perhaps involving certain time constraints. The issuing corporation might include the conversion privilege to incur a lower interest cost, to eventually increase its equity capital without immediate dilution of existing stockholders' interests, or merely to create an inducement for prospective investors to buy the bonds.

With respect to the issuance of convertible bonds, three important accounting ramifications result. They relate to earnings per share calculations, whether or not the conversion feature requires explicit issuance date accounting recognition, and how to account for the actual conversion into common shares.

With respect to earnings per share, a set of rules exists which has as one of its integral elements that, as a result of the importance of economic substance, the determination of earnings per share must include the effect of common stock equivalents (when dilutive) even though in legal form they are not currently outstanding shares of common stock. The specific charac-

---

[6] *Accounting Principles Board Opinion No. 26,* paragraph no. 22.

teristics required for a particular convertible bond to be included is beyond the scope of this volume; what is important is that the potential "equity capital" nature of convertible bonds is one of the critical factors to be considered when determining per-share amounts.

Issuance Date

The second area of concern is whether or not, when convertible bonds are issued, there should be immediate financial statement recognition of the potential *equity capital* nature of the bonds. In other words, should convertible debt securities be treated by the issuer solely as debt, or should the conversion option receive separate accounting recognition at the time of its issuance? At one time, the Accounting Principles Board required such recognition.[7] The rule was subsequently changed to apply only to debt securities which were themselves not convertible, but which contained detachable warrants which enabled the bondholder to purchase shares of the issuer's common stock.[8] The nature of the currently required accounting treatment is best explained through the use of an illustration.

Assume that 20-year bonds having a $10,000,000 face value are issued at a yield interest rate of 7 percent. The investment banking firm which assumed underwriting responsibility for the bond's issuance states that had the bonds not had a conversion privilege or, alternatively, detachable warrants, the interest rate would probably have been 9 percent. This variance of 2 percentage points would be the basis for accounting recognition. The interest savings of [$10,000,000 × (9% − 7% =) 2% = $200,000; $200,000 × 20 years =] $4,000,000 would be viewed as constituting the value of the conversion privilege or warrants. This reflects the belief that inherent economic value should be recognized.

Since the bondholder is viewed as acquiring a *call* on the issuer's stock, $4,000,000 of the proceeds would be accounted for as an element of the issuer's owners' equity. However, since the liability under the debt obligation is not reduced as a result of such attribution, there would be corresponding recognition as a discount and it would be amortized. Recall that a discount on outstanding debt arises when the face value of an issued bond exceeds the proceeds received when it was issued. Thus, in our example, each year's interest expense would include not only the ($10,000,000 × 7% =) $700,000 cash interest which accrues annually, but an additional ($4,000,000 ÷ 20 years =) $200,000 as well. The ($700,000 + 200,000 =) $900,000 total reflects the ($10,000,000 × 9% =) $900,000 interest cost which presumably would have been incurred had a conventional bond been

---

[7] *Accounting Principles Board Opinion No. 10;* paragraph nos. 8 and 9.

[8] *Accounting Principles Board Opinion No. 14;* paragraph no. 16.

issued, that is, one not having conversion rights or detachable warrants. The ($4,000,000) issuance date increase in owners' equity signifies that only $7/9$ of the 9 percent interest cost will result in reduced assets, thus benefitting the existing stockholders' equity.

Such accounting recognition applies only to bonds issued with detachable stock warrants; it does not apply to bonds which themselves are convertible into shares of stock. The difference between these two situations is that of the separability of the detachable warrants versus the inseparability of a conversion feature. Regarding the latter case, a debt security which is convertible is said to be "a complex hybrid instrument bearing an option, the alternative choices of which cannot exist independently of one another. The holder ordinarily does not sell one right and retain the other. . . . The two choices are mutually exclusive; for they cannot both be consummated."[9]

Another aspect of the rejected accounting treatment is that of the practical difficulty encountered in attempting to place a value on the conversion privilege as distinct from the bond itself. Recall that in our example it was assumed the investment banking firm which assumed underwriting responsibility had been able to make a judgment as to the interest savings, but this is easier said than done. In the absence of separate transactions, such values are not established in the marketplace, and as a result the value assigned is necessarily subjective. By contrast, detachable warrants often trade separately from the debt security such that the two elements of the security exist independently and thus lend themselves to being treated as separate securities.

Conversion Date

A third accounting ramification of convertible bonds is how to recognize the actual conversion into shares of stock. Once a convertible bond has been issued, whether or not to convert is a unilateral decision made by bondholders. Thus, although the issuer is necessarily a party to the ensuing transaction in the sense that it issues shares of stock in exchange for bonds and perhaps cash as well, the discretionary character of the exchange is for all intents and purposes limited to the bondholders. The important accounting question which arises is whether the issuer's relatively passive role in the conversion transaction should affect the manner in which the resulting accounting is effected. This matter is best discussed in context of the following example.

Assume a single convertible bond whose (accounting basis) book value on the conversion date is $800, that is, it appears in the issuing corporation's balance sheet at this amount. For purposes of this example, it makes no

---

[9] Ibid., paragraph no. 7.

difference whether the bond had generated proceeds equal to its $800 face value, or if its face amount is greater and it had been issued at a discount, or if its face amount is lower and that it had been sold at a premium. In any case, when accompanied by cash of $300, the bond is convertible into ten shares of the corporation's $5 par value common stock. Assume further that at the time of the conversion the market value of a share of the corporation's stock is $123, or $1,230 for the 10 shares, and that the market value of the bond is $970.

Exhibit 8–3 portrays three different approaches to accounting for the conversion transaction. Method A considers only the existing accounting-based amounts of the consideration received from the bondholder, that is, the $800 bond and $300 of cash—which totals $1,100. This $1,100 amount in turn becomes the accounting basis for recording the issuance of the ten shares of stock ($50 par value and a $1,050 premium to appear as Capital in Excess of Par Value). The nature of Method A is to yield neither a gain nor a loss.

Method B looks to the market value of the newly issued shares of stock as its focal point. The corporation receives cash of $300 and a reduction in a liability currently reflected in its balance sheet as $800, or a total considera-

Exhibit 8–3

Accounting for Conversion of Bonds into Stock

	Method		
	A	B	C
Issuer receives:			
Bond			
Carrying value	$ 800	$ 800	$800
Market value			970
Cash	300	300	
	$1,100	$1,100	
Issuer issues:			
Shares of stock			
Carrying value	1,100		
Market value		1,230	
	–0–		
Gain			**$170**
Loss		**$ 130**	

171

tion of $1,100. In exchange, it issues shares which presumably would have generated proceeds of $1,230 had they been sold for cash in a conventional stock issuance. Because it effectively realizes only $1,100 rather than the shares' $1,230 market value, the corporation sustains a ($1,230 − 1,100 =) $130 loss. [The shares would be recorded as follows: par value of $50 and Capital in Excess of Par Value of ($1,230 − 50 =) $1,180.]

Method C also uses a market value frame of reference, but it is the market value of the surrendered convertible bond which is the focus of its attention. The corporation receives cash of $300 as well as a bond whose current market value is $970, or total consideration of $1,270. When comparing this amount with the ($300 + 800 =) $1,100 carrying value, a $170 gain results. The gain is attributable to the fact the bond's ($970) market value exceeds its ($800) carrying value by $170. Had the company bought the bond for cash it would have incurred a cost $170 greater than the carrying value; since the bond was converted into stock, that additional cost will not be incurred. [The newly issued shares, in turn, have an accounting basis of ($1,100 − 170 =) $930 (which is par value of $50 and Capital in Excess of Par Value of $880).]

Method A is the only one of the three approaches permitted by generally accepted accounting principles. The reason why only this approach may be used is because it is the only method which results in the recognition of neither a gain nor a loss. That an enterprise may not recognize a gain or a loss resulting from changes in the market value of its own securities is attributable to the concept that an entity is accountable only for transactions to which it is a party. That investors in a corporation's stocks and bonds buy and sell its securities at prices which to them are good, bad, or indifferent is viewed as being of no direct consequence to the entity as such. The corporation is not engaged in the transaction, and neither its assets nor its liabilities are directly affected as a result.

To counter the theory underlying Method A, an effective case can be made on behalf of Method C whose nature is to recognize a gain or loss on the basis of the difference between the converted bond's market value and its book value; in our example, a ($970 − 800 =) $170 gain. One could argue that Method C embodies the method required for an early extinguishment of debt. Recall that when an issuer retires a bond prior to its maturity date, a gain or loss must be recognized on the basis of the difference between the debt's book value and the consideration tendered to effect its retirement. Inasmuch as this requirement applies without regard to how the issuer finances the extinguishment—issuance of new bonds, issuance of shares of its stock, or general corporate cash—the fact that shares are issued in context of a conversion should not in its own right preclude its being treated in a like manner. In other words, to assert that the issuer should not be permitted to recognize a gain or loss on the basis of investors trading its securities is not appropriate inasmuch as the entity itself is a party to the conversion transaction, albeit a relatively passive or involuntary one at best.

Method B can be supported on the basis of the early-extinguishment-of-debt theory as well. What appears in legal form to be one (conversion) transaction, in substance is effectively two distinct events, namely, an early extinguishment of debt and an issuance of capital stock. With respect to the latter, a corporation's owners' equity is generally increased by the amount of proceeds received in the marketplace. What this approach therefore suggests is that the accounting recognition should reflect the presumption that for the issuer to *receive* market-based proceeds on the issuance of its new shares, it must first *expend* an identical amount of cash to extinguish its outstanding debt.

It should be noted that the notion of there being in substance two transactions—on which both Methods B and C are based—is one which has relevance to Method A as well. When presenting a statement of changes in financial position, a question arises as to what disclosure if any are necessary for a conversion of debt securities to equity securities. Although this is a matter considered in light of broader issues considered in Chapter 11, we return again to our example keeping in mind that Method A is the only acceptable accounting approach.

Cash of $300 and a bond whose book value is $800 are exchanged for shares of stock resulting in an $1,100 increase in the issuer's owners' equity. The issuer's cash and working capital are increased by only $300 which means, in a technical sense, only the $300 amount would be portrayed as a source of cash or of working capital. However, the accounting requirement is that a source of funds of $1,100 results from the issuance of capital stock and $800 be included as a use of funds to retire convertible bonds. Thus, even though the total effect is only the net $300 cash received, the nature of the required disclosure appears to reflect the belief that although in legal form a conversion is but a single transaction, in substance it is effectively two distinct transactions.

INTEREST ON LONG-TERM DEBT

The expression *long-term debt* is used to signify receivables and payables whose maturity date will occur at least one year hence. Such obligations are payable in cash and are typically evidenced by a written document, although this is not necessarily always the case. The debt arises because the creditor had given the debtor either (1) cash, (2) cash involving a right or privilege as well, or (3) non-cash property, goods, or services. The issue in the following discussion is to determine what portion of the resulting, specified obligation is the debt's interest element as distinct from its principal.

In the case of a creditor giving a debtor cash only, an interest element is recognized by both parties at the time of the exchange only if the cash exchanged differs from the face value of the resulting obligation. When such a difference exists, it is accounted for as a premium or discount, and in turn is subject to amortization in the manner described earlier with respect to the issuance of bonds. When cash is the only consideration given by the creditor to the debtor, there is no need to impute interest.

The second situation is that of a creditor giving cash to a debtor, and receiving in exchange both the commitment to repay the loan as well as a right or privilege. For example, a customer lends money to a supplier and receives in exchange a promissory note as well as the right to purchase the debtor's merchandise at a reduced price. In this case, a discount is imputed by comparing the cash with the present value of the future payment(s). This requirement exists for both the creditor and debtor, and is illustrated with the use of the following example.

Tell Co. borrows $10,000 from its customer Rye, Inc. on December 1, 19x1 by issuing a promissory note due one year later; both companies' fiscal years correspond to the calendar year. Tell also grants to Rye the privilege of purchasing its merchandise at a cost less than the prevailing market price. Using the 10 percent interest rate we shall assume is what Tell would otherwise have to pay, the present value of $10,000 (compounded monthly) is $9,052. This in turn suggests the presence of a ($10,000 − 9,052 =) $948 discount, which is recorded by both Rye and Tell, as illustrated in Exhibit 8–4.

This $948 amount represents the interest implicit in the loan. In the case at hand, it manifests itself in the form of the right granted by the debtor to the creditor. Whereas interest is conventionally remitted in the form of a direct cash payment, in this instance it is conveyed through price reductions to be enjoyed by the creditor when purchasing goods from the debtor. The $948 discount is amortized, thus becoming an element of both the debtor's interest expense and the creditor's interest revenue. In our example, the amount to be amortized for the month of December is ($9,052.12 × 10% × $\frac{1}{12}$ =) $75.43, and this is reflected in journal-entry form in Exhibit 8–4.

Assume that on January 5, 19x2, Rye purchases from Tell merchandise having a standard invoice price of $2,300. However, because of the right Tell had granted to Rye, the latter is given a $200 price reduction. This means that as both parties record the transaction, $2,300 is the amount reflected as Purchases by the buyer and as Sales by the seller while $2,100 is recorded as the resulting payable and receivable. Because the $200 difference is merely the realization of the price reduction granted by the seller pursuant to the earlier $10,000 loan, it becomes the basis for adjusting Rye's Deferred Charge and Tell's Unearned Revenue balances, as illustrated in Exhibit 8–4.

Exhibit 8–4

Long-Term Debt

Creditor
Rye, Inc.

December 1, 19x1:		
Notes Receivable (N/R)	10,000	
Cash		10,000
Deferred Charge	948	
Discount on N/R		948
December 31, 19x1:		
Discount on N/R	75	
Interest Revenue		75
January 5, 19x2:		
Purchases	2,300	
Accounts Payable		2,100
Deferred Charge		200

Debtor
Tell Co.

Cash	10,000	
Notes Payable (N/P)		10,000
Discount on N/P	948	
Unearned Revenue		948
Interest Expense	75	
Discount of N/P		75
Accounts Receivable	2,100	
Unearned Revenue	200	
Sales		2,300

The third "interest on long-term debt" situation is the one whose accounting treatment presents a challenge. This is the case of long-term debt arising not from the conveyance of cash, but rather from the exchange of property, goods, or services. In exchange for such non-cash consideration, the debtor becomes obligated to remit to the creditor a specified amount of money, and the resulting promissory note contains either no stated interest, a stated interest which is unreasonably low, or a face value materially different from the current cash sales price for the same or similar item or different from the current market value of the note.

Initially, an effort is made to identify the implicit interest rate. This can be determined if either of the following two values is known:

The fair value of the item at the exchange date, which is the current cash sale price of the same or similar items.

The market value of the note at the exchange date, which is the proceeds that would be realized if it were discounted with an independent lender.

The resulting difference between the more readily determinable value and the face value of the note constitutes the *discount*.

Present value techniques are then applied to the discount to derive the note's implicit interest rate, and that rate then becomes the basis for amortizing the discount. In the event the implicit interest rate cannot be so determined, the present value of the note would be calculated by discounting all future payments at an imputed interest rate appropriate at the date the note is exchanged. It would be based on factors such as the debtor's credit standing; restrictive covenants; the collateral, payment, and other terms pertaining to the debt; and possible tax consequences for each party.

The following example presents an application of the implicit interest situation. On October 1, 19x5, Molly Co. sells land having a cost basis of $31,000 to Love, Inc. receiving in exchange a $50,000 promissory note. The note has no stated interest rate, and is payable at the end of four years. A professional appraiser determines the fair value of the land is $35,000; the resulting ($50,000–35,000 =) $15,000 difference is the discount. Assuming interest is compounded quarterly, reference to the appropriate present value table indicates an implicit interest rate of 9 percent. If it had not been possible to determine the fair value of the land, and if the market value of the note had also not been determinable, it would then have become necessary to impute an appropriate interest rate which would permit proceeding in the same manner described for the case of a derived implicit interest rate.

The October 1, 19x5 accounting recognition of the sale by both Molly and Love is set forth in Exhibit 8–5. Note the land is recorded by the buyer,

Exhibit 8–5

Accounting for Implicit Interest

Creditor
Molly Company

October 1, 19x5:		
Notes Receivable (N/R)	50,000	
Discount on N/R		15,000
Land		31,000
Gain on Sale		4,000
December 31, 19x5:		
Discount on N/R	788	
Interest Revenue		788
September 30, 19x9:		
Cash	50,000	
Notes Receivable		50,000
Discount on N/R	1,100	
Interest Revenue		1,100

Debtor
Love, Inc.

Land	35,000	
Discount on N/P	15,000	
Notes Payable (N/P)		50,000
Interest Expense	788	
Discount on N/P		788
Notes Payable	50,000	
Cash		50,000
Interest Expense	1,100	
Discount on N/P		1,100

Love, at its $35,000 fair value, and the $15,000 difference between this value and the $50,000 face value of the note is recorded as a discount on notes payable. If Love were immediately to prepare a balance sheet, the land would be reflected at its $35,000 fair value, and disclosure of the obligation would parallel that which applies to bonds payable (which had been discussed earlier in this chapter). The $50,000 payable is classified as a noncurrent liability and the $15,000 discount appears as a contra-account, as follows:

Noncurrent liabilities:	
Notes payable	$50,000
Less discount on notes payable	15,000
Net payable	**$35,000**

Molly Co. also recognizes a $15,000 discount, because it received a $50,000 note in exchange for an asset whose fair value was $35,000. Molly also uses the $35,000 fair value as the basis for measuring the gain it realizes on the sale of the land, namely, the $4,000 excess of the land's ($35,000) fair value over its ($31,000) cost basis. If Molly were to immediately prepare its balance sheet, its assets would include the following:

Noncurrent assets:	
Notes receivable	$50,000
Less discount on notes receivable	15,000
Net receivable	**$35,000**

Continuing with this example, assume the fiscal year of both companies ends on December 31. At this time, both Molly and Love will recognize ($35,000 × 9% × ¼ year = $787.50 or) $788 or interest during 19x5. For Love, this amount represents interest expense and, as indicated in Exhibit 8–5 entails amortizing the Discount on Notes Payable. For Molly, $788 is the interest revenue, resulting from amortizing its Discount on Notes Receivable. This interest recognition occurs throughout the four-year life of the obligation. The ensuing amount of both the net receivable and the net payable which would appear in Molly's and Love's respective December 31, 19x5 balance sheets is [$50,000 − ($15,000 − 788 =) $14,212 =] $35,788, and this amount increases systematically until it reaches $50,000 at the note's maturity date.

When the note matures on September 30, 19x9, Love remits $50,000 to Molly; the accounting entry for this transaction is set forth in Exhibit 8–5. In addition, the exhibit portrays the final adjustment made with respect to the related interest. Assuming each company records its adjustments at the end of each quarter, the amount applicable to the third quarter of 19x9 would be

(July 1's $48,899.76 × 9% × ¼ year = $1,100.24 or) $1,100. By virtue of making such recognition, the discount will have been fully amortized—as it should be as of the note's maturity date.

OWNERS' EQUITY

At its most fundamental level, the owners' equity of an enterprise is merely an arithmetic residual resulting from its assets being greater than its liabilities. This excess can have qualitative significance as well; for instance, one concept of solvency revolves around there actually being positive owners' equity.

A corporation's recorded owners' equity changes for many reasons. The most obvious factors relate to (1) the entity's transactions with its stockholders which are either investment or disinvestment transactions and (2) its operations, that is, the results of its revenue and expense transactions. With respect to the latter, the process of measuring earnings is so important that its many whys and wherefores are inevitably afforded attention distinct from Owners' Equity matters as such. Indeed, the net earnings amount of an income statement represents the only direct contact, as it were, with the owners' equity appearing in an enterprise's balance sheet.

It is therefore the investment and disinvestment transactions between stockholders and corporations which receive attention when discussing accounting for owners' equity. A number of these transactions are recorded in accordance with legal requirements. On the other hand, the treatment for certain other events and circumstances reflect considered accounting thought, and several such issues are examined below.

Retained Earnings

The medium that corporations use to provide their stockholders with a direct return on their investment is the dividend.[10] Dividends are usually distributed in the form of cash although other corporate assets might be dispensed as well. Preferred shares of stock invariably include a provision which states the amount of cash dividends to be distributed, but the shares held by common stockholders do not contain a specified dividend rate. Nevertheless, it is only when the corporation's board of directors decides to declare a dividend that shareholders receive one, with preferred shareholders receiving their predetermined amounts, and common stockholders the amount which the directors deem to be appropriate.

---

[10] Appreciation of shares' value as a medium is discussed later.

Because shareholders invest in a corporation's stock to earn a *return on* their investment rather than to receive a mere *return of* their investment, the company must in turn invest amounts provided by its stockholders in order to generate asset growth without an equal increase in its liabilities. If this effort is successful, income is earned; the growth in net assets manifests itself as earnings, and in turn becomes part of the retained earnings component of the corporation's owners' equity. Thus, when a portion of the enterprise's net asset growth is distributed to stockholders as a dividend, the amount of its retained earnings is thereby reduced as well. This reduction signifies that what had until then been a return to the corporation on *its* investment of stockholders' funds, is now being shared with those stockholders with the result they too can realize a return—on *their* investment.

The declaration of a cash dividend does not entail paying out retained earnings, because retained earnings is not something capable of being paid out. It is merely a measure of the portion of a corporation's cumulative asset growth resulting from profitable operations not yet distributed to stockholders. A corporation's ability to declare and pay a cash dividend depends on the level of its cash assets on hand and prospects for subsequent cash inflows and outlays, not on the size of its retained earnings balance. To the extent that the corporate statutes prohibit distributing dividends in excess of the entity's retained earnings balance, this amount becomes an upper limit. At the more substantive decision-making level, however, a corporation's board of directors is much more likely to consider a dividend's effect on the enterprise's capacity to fulfill existing cash obligations and its ability to make new commitments involving the disbursement of cash.

The size of a company's retained earnings balance implies nothing whatsoever about its cash balance. It may have almost no cash, or conversely, a corporation may have no retained earnings (or even a cumulative deficit) while concurrently having an enormous cash balance. Consider for example the newly founded corporation which has yet to earn any income but which, by virtue of selling shares of its common stock, already has a large amount of cash in the bank.

The absence of an inherent causality between an enterprise's cash and its retained earnings balances is attributable to the accrual concept of accounting. This concept states that when determining income by matching revenues and expenses, attention is *not* directed exclusively to cash inflows and cash outflows. Instead, it is the inflows and outflows of *all* assets and liabilities which provide the most comprehensive, and thus the most meaningful measure of an entity's performance. There is therefore no presumption an enterprise's income is at all related to its cash position.

In the parlance of business finance, this distinction has been expressed through the terms *profitability* and *liquidity*. Profitability pertains to the accrual-based results of an entity's operations, and liquidity refers to the company's ability to meet its cash obligations.

Cash Dividends

The traditional manner in which shareholders realize a return on their investment in an enterprise's stock is through receipt of a cash dividend. Although boards of directors of corporations are acutely aware of stockholders' expectations, when they consider making such a distribution, they must also be alert to its implications for the financial well-being of the enterprise itself. There may even be times when dividends are not distributed even though the corporation may have recently enjoyed record earnings and expects large amounts of income to be earned in the future.

In an environment where a corporation's outstanding shares of stock can be traded among investors with relative ease, it is understandable that the prevailing price of a share reflects the market's aggregate assessment of the entity's value. If one's orientation were to be limited to a strict interpretation of an enterprise's historical financial statements, it might be concluded the entity's value is that which is embodied in its recorded owners' equity. But in actual practice, it is the expected future returns on their present investment which stockholders use as their frame of reference. Thus, the current price of a publicly traded share of common stock is the composite value of the market's expectations regarding a future return on the investment in that particular stock.

If a corporation, in fact, has profitable operations of a magnitude which corresponds to the market's expectations, it might be assumed the company would distribute some of the net asset growth by declaring a cash dividend. This would enable existing shareholders to realize a return on their investment. However, the company may elect to distribute little or none of its assets to its stockholders, presumably because its directors believe that by retaining what would otherwise have been a cash dividend, the funds could be applied to further profitable use. For instance, a corporation which is likely to generate a 20 percent average return on assets may in effect say to its stockholders it is in *their* best interests to allow the company to reinvest the cash and proceed to probably earn a 20 percent return rather than distribute the cash dividend, with the knowledge it is highly unlikely that individual stockholders could invest their newly received cash and realize a comparable return on their investment.

Corporations, therefore, sometimes do not pay cash dividends even though the cash is technically available for distribution to the shareholders. When this happens, it is possible, even likely, the market will bid up the price of the company's outstanding shares of stock. In other words, if the market agrees the company has the ability to reinvest successfully what might otherwise have been a cash dividend, appreciation of the value of its shares might in fact result. Such capital appreciation is also a form of a return on stockholders' investment although until it is actually realized through the sale of the shares, it is considered to be only an unrealized holding gain, sometimes referred to by investors as a *paper profit*. Therefore, even though a cash dividend is the traditional medium through which stockholders receive a return on their investment, capital appreciation is considered to be a viable, if not superior, alternative medium by investors who are perhaps less risk-averse and/or less conservative in their investment outlook.

However, if the market expects a company will never pay cash dividends, in theory its shares of stock would be worthless because their salability assumes that at some point in time, the shareholders will receive a return for holding the stock rather than for selling it. There is an analogy here to a chain letter. Although people buy a chain letter because they feel they can sell it, ultimately someone will in fact not be able to sell it. If you fear you may turn out to be that unfortunate person, you would not buy the chain letter in the first place. And if everyone comes to the same conclusion, the persons now holding the letter would be holding a worthless piece of paper.

Stock Dividends

Thus, there is the expectation that cash dividends ultimately will be declared and distributed. However, sometimes a corporation, in lieu of or in addition to declaring a cash dividend, distributes additional shares of the same class of its stock to the existing stockholders. This type of distribution is called a *stock dividend*. The new shares are dispensed in a proportionately equal manner, e.g., each existing stockholder is given 10 percent additional shares. The declaration and distribution of a stock dividend is an accountable transaction from the point of view of the issuing corporation.

Its accounting nature is to transfer amounts already comprising the entity's owners' equity from retained earnings to the capital stock balance. The reduction in retained earnings reflects the dividend character of the transaction, and the increase in capital stock is required to disclose the existence of the newly issued shares of the corporation's stock. In the absence of a market value for the company's shares, the amount thus transferred corresponds to the new shares' aggregate par or stated value. However, if the company's shares do have a market value, retained earnings is reduced by the shares' market value. Since only the shares' par value is usually added to the capital stock balance, the resulting excess appears as Capital in Excess of Par similar to an issuance premium for which cash proceeds exceed par value.

At first glance, such accounting might be questioned on the basis that the corporation is recognizing the effect of the market's valuation of its shares—even though it is not party to the transaction which generates such a value. In other words, it would seem the only thing the enterprise does is distribute additional stock certificates to evidence its shareholders' ownership. Neither cash nor other assets are exchanged; indeed, the only transaction is a unilateral one, i.e., it lacks even the arm's length nature encompassed by the very term *transaction*.

In fact, the accounting treatment reflects an application of the concept of *substance over form*. What in legal form appears to be but a single transaction is in substance viewed as being two transactions: a cash dividend and the involuntary purchase of additional shares by existing stockholders. The corporation in effect distributes as a cash dividend precisely the amount that its recipients can reinvest in additional shares. Indeed, from the stockholders' vantage point, there are benefits. They generally pay no income tax on the receipt of their new shares, which would not have been the case had they received cash dividends and reinvested them. Another benefit is the avoidance of a fee which normally must be paid to a broker to purchase shares of stock.

Nevertheless, there are disadvantages. Since all shareholders automatically receive additional shares in proportion to their holdings, their relative equity is unchanged. Similarly, if stockholders seek liquid assets, the conversion of the new shares to cash will incur a transaction cost in the form of the fee paid to a broker to sell the shares. In addition, such a sale reduces their proportionate equity, which would not have been the case had a cash dividend been distributed in the first place.

What then are the substantive reasons for the board of directors of a corporation to declare a stock dividend? One reason is that it may be part of a strategy to conserve the corporation's cash. In the process of not declaring a cash dividend, or of declaring one whose amount is less than that which stockholders had expected, the directors may perceive a need to make a pacification gesture. Stockholders often think they are better off as a result of receiving a stock dividend. Even when stock is received in lieu of a cash dividend, there may be a tendency to believe they are at least as well off, and certainly no worse off. In light of such a mistaken notion, the board of directors can try to mitigate stockholders' disappointment in not receiving cash—at virtually no cost. The mistaken belief could be corrected with the recognition of the fact that real value would accrue to shareholders only if either the same dollar amount of cash dividends were still to be paid on each share as had been the case prior to receipt of the stock dividend, or if the market value per share were not to be reduced proportionately. With respect to the latter, why should the market believe a company's 11,000 shares of ownership have a different aggregate value from the 10,000 shares that had been outstanding before the issuance of 10 percent (i.e., 1,000) new shares?

The expectation the market will reduce the per-share value might also be one of the directors' motives, since this may make the shares more accessible to potential investors. In addition, the accounting reduction of the corporation's retained earnings might preempt future pleas for cash dividends from stockholders who incorrectly base their case solely on the size of that balance sheet amount.

Stock Splits

Somewhat similar to a stock dividend is the stock split. Whereas a stock dividend entails distributing additional shares to existing stockholders on the basis of an announced percentage, e.g., 10 percent, a stock split occurs when existing shares are exchanged for a greater number of new shares. For example, a 3-for-2 split means that on surrendering two shares of existing stock, the stockholder will receive three new shares in return. As a matter of arithmetic, a 3-for-2 split generates the same result as a 50 percent stock dividend; similarly, a 10 percent stock dividend yields the same outcome as an 11-for-10 split.

Because in a stock split the new shares have a proportionately reduced par value per share with no resulting difference in the aggregate par value, no accounting transaction is recorded. As was noted earlier, however, the stock dividend case does cause the aggregate par value to increase, and an accountable transaction results. Because stock dividends and stock splits have an identical effect on the number of shares outstanding, an accounting rule was established to distinguish between the two.

The applicable pronouncement states that the accounting recognition prescribed for the declaration of stock dividends does not apply when the underlying circumstances indicate ". . . that the transaction clearly partakes of the nature of a stock split."[11] In those instances in which the new shares are at least "20 percent or 25 percent of the number previously outstanding,"[12] the transaction is treated as a stock split and retained earnings is not reduced. A transaction in which the issuance of new shares is less than 20 percent or 25 percent of the existing outstanding shares would be recorded as though it were a stock dividend. This is another situation in which accounting recognition looks beyond the legal form of the transaction to the economic substance.

---

[11] *Accounting Research Bulletin No. 43*, chapter 7, paragraph no. 11.

[12] Ibid., paragraph no. 13.

Reserves

The lay definition of a *reserve* is that it is something stored for future use, or something reserved or set aside for a particular use, purpose or reason.[13] By contrast, use of the term "reserve" in accounting and financial reporting is intended to be limited to just one type of situation, namely, appropriations of retained earnings.

It was pointed out earlier that retained earnings is merely a measure of the cumulative net asset growth resulting from operations for which there has not been a compensating reduction in assets in the form of dividends. Because retained earnings is only a measure of some of the changes in an enterprise's assets and liabilities, it does not, in its own right, constitute or represent cash available for expenditures. However, inasmuch as the retained earnings balance reflects an entity's undistributed net asset growth, readers of financial statements might construe its very existence to suggest the corporation is thereby in a position to spend monies it would not have been able to had it not been for its record of profitable operations.

Such an assumption is unwarranted. Therefore, as a means of communicating its actual ability to spend, a corporation's board of directors may want to indicate that a portion of retained earnings has been appropriated, or earmarked as it were, for some specific purpose, such as plant expansion or the purchase of more efficient machinery and equipment. For example, the balance sheet might state that although retained earnings is $20,000,000 and its cash balance is $15,000,000, the company intends to spend $12,000,000 of the cash to expand the size of its plant. This, in effect, informs the reader that although the company could legally declare a cash dividend as high as $20,000,000, because of its plant expansion plans cash of only ($15,000,000 − 12,000,000 =) $3,000,000 would actually be available for dividends.

This is an example of a voluntary appropriation of retained earnings, that is, one which results from the company's board of directors exercising its own collective judgment. Another example of a voluntary appropriation is that of providing for a possible future decline in the market value of the company's merchandise inventory, which was discussed in Chapter 6. Its basic nature is that by communicating that subsequent periods' earnings could be adversely affected by a decline in inventory prices, the current retained earnings balance would be looked on in a somewhat different light.

Retained earnings appropriations can sometimes exist involuntarily. For example, when issuing bonds, a provision might be made which prohibits

---

[13] *Webster's Seventh New Collegiate Dictionary* (Springfield, Mass.: G. & C. Merriam Company, 1961), p. 730.

the company from reducing its retained earnings balance below a specified level. Such a restriction may be imposed to prevent the corporation from distributing a substantial amount of its cash as dividends, thereby possibly jeopardizing the bondholders' chances of receiving interest payments and the face value of the bonds at maturity. Although the restriction could be in a footnote, appropriating retained earnings might be viewed as being a more effective means of disclosure.

In all cases, whether the appropriation of retained earnings is voluntary or compulsory, once the crucial event occurs, the appropriated amount is reinstated in retained earnings proper. Thus, in our examples, when cash is disbursed to expand the plant or if the project is cancelled, when the decline in inventory prices happens or fails to materialize, and when the bond is redeemed, the segregation is no longer needed. Its balance is then transferred back to retained earnings, and additional disclosure is unnecessary.

Although a retained earnings appropriation is the only explicit situation that can justifiably be characterized as a reserve, there have been other instances in which the term "reserve" is used—much to the chagrin of contemporary American accountants. One such case is that of so-called valuation reserves. With respect to the balance sheet presentation of depreciable assets, it is a generally accepted practice to disclose both the assets' original cost and their accumulated depreciation. The latter amount had at one time been referred to as a *reserve* for depreciation; this is not considered to be desirable terminology since it could mislead the reader of financial statements into believing that funds have actually been set aside to provide for depreciation.

Another somewhat prevalent instance was that of liability reserves. This was merely a case of accountants using the term *reserve* to signify an estimated liability, viz., "reserve for income taxes," or to disclose a contingent liability through a "reserve for contingencies." Here too, the term *reserve* suggests a physical segregation of assets, which is not necessarily a true portrayal of the actual circumstances. As a result, to the extent that disclosure of such amounts is warranted in the first place, accountants now recognize use of the term *reserve* probably tends to be more a cause of misunderstanding than of clarification, and its use is therefore generally avoided.

In some countries there is the phenomenon of earnings reserves. This refers to the practice of unilaterally deciding to reduce a period's earnings by creating a reserve. Procedurally this involves making a charge against revenues in the current period's income statement, with the offsetting credit-balance reserve appearing in the end-of-period balance sheet. The objective of creating such a general reserve is to transfer income among fiscal periods. The motivation might be that if a "cushion" can be created during fiscal periods when business is thriving, in a subsequent period when there may be little prospect of attaining a satisfactory level of income, the cushion would be utilized to produce a larger amount of earnings. Although the use of general reserves is not permitted in the United States, it is not an uncommon practice in some other countries.

A variation of this idea is the secret reserve. Such a reserve exists when owners' equity is understated, and it manifests itself through an understatement of assets or an overstatement of liabilities. It occurs as a result of using methods and procedures which reflect accounting conservatism. An example would be using the LIFO method of inventory costing in a period of rising prices. Its nature is that the relatively higher, more current inventory costs have an immediate effect on earnings. They cause it and the resulting owners' equity to be understated relative to that which would be generated by other inventory costing methods. The balance sheet assets are understated by a like amount (assuming away income-tax effects) because the nature of the LIFO method is to reflect the end-of-period inventory in the balance sheet on a basis which reflects older, lower per-unit costs.

What happens therefore is that a company using accounting methods which cause its owners' equity to be understated relative to an alternative outcome might therefore be characterized as one having secret reserves. By extension, the notion of "secret reserves" is sometimes used by persons who believe the historical cost basis of accounting should be supplanted by a current value approach. Their reasoning would be that inasmuch as a cost-based system causes enterprises' assets and owners' equity to be understated, the resulting financial statements can be said to be characterized by secret reserves to an extent that they might actually be misleading. Unlike other "reserves," this one is a term, and is never recorded as an item in the accounts.

Treasury Stock

Treasury stock is the term used to denote a corporation's shares which had been outstanding but which were subsequently purchased by the corporation itself. If the shares have not been retired, they are viewed as being held in the company's treasury. The purchase of such shares is sometimes referred to as a *buy-back,* and it can be effected in two different ways. The corporation can acquire the shares through market transactions on a piecemeal basis through a brokerage firm and paying the going price. Alternatively, it can make a tender offer whereby it invites its stockholders to sell their shares directly to the corporation at a specified price.

The reasons a corporation might engage in a buy-back vary. In some cases, the purpose may be to retire the shares. In other cases, the company has plans to reissue the shares at a subsequent date. Such a reissuance could be through distribution to (1) employees who exercise stock options, (2)

187

investors on surrender of convertible senior securities which had been issued previously by the company, or (3) stockholders of another corporation as consideration with which to effect a business combination. The motivation to buy back its own shares might also relate to an intention to resell them. Such a course of action would necessarily reflect the belief that the proceeds to be realized subsequently will exceed the cost incurred to effect the buy-back in the first place. This type of reasoning is most likely to occur when the officers and directors of a corporation believe the shares' prevailing market price is too low and that not only will recovery occur but that it will be substantial as well.

While shares are in the treasury, there are fewer number of shares outstanding. This means that (1) less shares affect the company's earnings per share thus yielding a higher resulting amount, (2) less total cash is disbursed when the same cash dividend per share is declared than had been the case prior to the buy-back, and (3) the relative equity of each share still outstanding is increased.

The predominant approach to accounting for treasury stock is the cost method. It treats the cost of the treasury shares as a reduction of the corporation's owners' equity because the expenditure of the company's cash to effect the buy-back is viewed as being a diminution of the surviving stockholders' equity in the corporate assets. This is analogous to the case of a cash dividend whose declaration and payment result in the reduction of the enterprise's cash as well as a contraction of the stockholders' equity, because there is less corporate cash on hand in which there is equity. In the case of treasury stock, the reduction in the company's cash likewise results in less assets in which stockholders have equity. That diminished equity is therefore portrayed in the balance sheet as decreased owners' equity; it is generally shown as an explicit reduction from the amount which would otherwise have been the measure of the stockholders' equity.

Some companies that use the cost method disclose the cost of the treasury shares as an asset. In other words, instead of including the debit-balance amount as a reduction on the equities side of the balance sheet, it appears as a positive element on the assets side. This means of disclosure can be justified only in those instances when the express purpose of the buy-back is to use such shares to fulfill certain types of obligations, most notably an employee compensation commitment. In such a case, the shares might be viewed as tantamount to an economic resource having future service potential, and are therefore classified as assets. Although their legal form indicates a contraction of the entity's owners' equity, the economic substance underlying a particular buy-back can allow the cost of the shares to be disclosed among the assets of the corporation.

Although cash dividends are paid only on shares issued and outstanding,

188

the matter of stock dividends distributed on treasury shares is not as definitive. There may be a desire to preserve for the treasury shares a proportionate equity in anticipation of resale or other reissuance. For example, if one sixth of an enterprise's shares are in the treasury and as a result do not participate in a 10 percent stock dividend distribution, upon resale they will comprise a 15.4 percent interest as opposed to their original 16.7 percent equity. The stockholder originally having a 1 percent equity now has a 1.015 percent interest. On the other hand, had the stock dividend also been applied to the treasury shares, upon resale such shares would still comprise one sixth of the ownership equity while the original 1 percent stockholder emerges with only his or her same 1 percent interest.

The relative merit of the two points of view in terms of accounting theory must yield to legalistic constraints as well as business intent. The prescriptive role of accountants is to articulate to persons in positions of authority the accounting and financial ramifications of the different approaches; their descriptive function is to reflect what has transpired—in response to, or in spite of, their advice notwithstanding. Thus, regarding the circumstance at hand, it is the physical number of shares resulting from the stock dividend distribution that is critical, and which therefore governs the accounting. Stock splits are yet a different situation altogether. Because par (or stated) values change with no resulting effect on the aggregate par (or stated) value, treasury shares are affected by a split.

SUMMARY

In this chapter we have examined selected key elements relating to the Equities side of corporate balance sheets. Although there may be a tendency to view Assets as the active half of an enterprise's financial position while Equities are relegated to the status of being passive or reactive, in fact a variety of substantive issues do exist with respect to Equities.

In characterizing the complementing halves of a balance sheet, one accountant has observed its left side depicts those resources over which the entity's managers have command while the right side portrays those resources over which investors have command.[14] One might proceed to use such a categorization to argue that investors' equities are too critical to be afforded anything less than an incisive examination. However, the author believes the point that needs to be made is even more subtle. It is the very fact that in order to assure its existence as such, the corporation as a self-contained entity must interact with investors, that is, with its various present

---

[14] Louis Goldberg, *An Inquiry into the Nature of Accounting* (Sarasota, Fla.: American Accounting Association, 1965), pp. 162–74.

and prospective equityholders. If not for such interface, the matter of enterprise assets would be a moot one. It is in deference to this essential affinity that key elements of corporate equities have been given our considered attention.

Additional Readings

Anton, Hector R. "Accounting for Bond Liabilities." *The Journal of Accountancy* (September 1956), pp. 53–56.

Clancy, Donald K. "What Is a Convertible Debenture? A Review of the Literature in the U.S.A." *Abacus* (December 1978), pp. 171–79.

Collier, Boyd, and Carnes, Curtis. "Convertible Bonds and Financial Reality." *Management Accounting* (February 1979), pp. 47, 48, 52.

Cramer, Joe J., Jr. "The Nature and Importance of Discounted Present Value in Financial Accounting and Reporting." *The Arthur Andersen Chronicle* (September 1977), pp. 27–39.

Jacobsen, Lyle E. "Liabilities and Quasi Liabilities." In *Modern Accounting Theory*, edited by Morton Backer. Englewood Cliffs, N.J.: Prentice-Hall, Inc., 1966, pp. 232–49.

Ma, Ronald, and Miller, Malcolm C. "Conceptualizing the Liability." *Accounting and Business Research* (Autumn 1978), pp. 258–65.

Melcher, Beatrice. *Stockholders' Equity.* New York: American Institute of Certified Public Accountants, 1973.

Meyers, Stephen L. "Accounting for Long Term Notes." *Management Accounting* (July 1973), pp. 49–51.

Moonitz, Maurice. "The Changing Concept of Liabilities." *The Journal of Accountancy* (May 1960), pp. 41–46.

Paton, W. A. "Postscript on 'Treasury Shares'." *The Accounting Review* (April 1969), pp. 276–83.

Porterfield, James T. S. "Dividends, Dilution and Delusion." *Harvard Business Review* (November–December 1959), pp. 55–61.

Sprouse, Robert T. "Accounting for What-You-May-Call-Its." *The Journal of Accountancy* (October 1966), pp. 45–53.

Stern, Joel M. "Why Pay Dividends." *The Wall Street Journal* (July 10, 1978), p. 12.

Vatter, William J. *The Fund Theory of Accounting and Its Implications for Financial Reports.* Chicago: The University of Chicago Press, 1947.

9

Accounting for Business Combinations

Business combination is a term referring to two or more unrelated companies which, as a result of realigned ownership interests, become one enterprise. Business combinations are effected to attain any number of objectives. A company may seek horizontal integration which refers to combining with an enterprise engaged in a similar type of business, vertical integration which pertains to combining with a complementing company such as a supplier or distributor, or diversification whereby companies in unrelated industries combine in an effort to minimize their vulnerability to the economic health of relatively limited products or markets.

Companies with complementary strengths and weaknesses may combine to utilize their respective resources better. For instance, a highly research-oriented company, sensitive to the prospect of a liquidity crisis, may combine with a company whose business generates significant amounts of cash in relatively short time intervals. A company with an outstanding management team may combine with an enterprise in need of talented human resources. And invariably there are combinations effected simply because of the belief that "bigger is better" or what is sometimes referred to as "economies of scale."

Although there are many different ways a combination can be effected, a variety of legal avenues which might be used, and countless business and economic reasons for creating a combined enterprise, there are but three dimensions which warrant accounting attention. The first dimension is one of accounting measurement. This refers to the manner in which the assets, liabilities and owners' equity of the combined enterprise's constituent companies are accounted for. Two basic approaches exist: the purchase method

191

and the pooling of interests method. Several alternatives to these two approaches have received some attention as well, but they can properly be viewed more as variations than as alternatives having distinctly different orientations.

The second dimension is that of legal form. This pertains to the decision made by the constituent companies whether the combined enterprise is to operate as one legal entity or two. This is strictly a business decision and is not affected by which accounting measurement method is applied. Conversely, subsequent operation as one legal entity or two has no effect on which method of accounting measurement is appropriate in a particular set of circumstances.

The third dimension relates to financial statement disclosure. Addressed to the case of a combined enterprise operating as two legal entities, this dimension is concerned with how the combined nature of the affiliated companies' relationship is to be disclosed. On the one hand, each company could prepare only its own financial statements, or one set of consolidated financial statements could be prepared. The consolidated approach depicts the affiliated companies' financial position and operating results in a manner identical to that which would have resulted had the combined enterprise been operating in fact as one legal entity.

These three dimensions of business combinations are shown in Exhibit 9–1.

Exhibit 9–1
Accounting Dimensions of Business Combinations

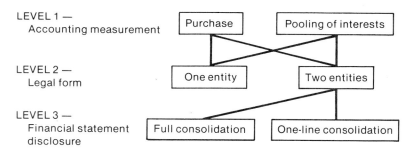

With respect to these three dimensions, the discussion in this chapter is addressed to the case of the combined enterprise which operates as one legal entity. The examination of pertinent issues is therefore limited to only those which relate to accounting measurement. The nuances which characterize the case of the combined enterprise operating as two legal entities are examined in the next chapter.

192

THE PURCHASE METHOD

One approach to accounting for a business combination is to view the transaction as a case of one company purchasing another company. The acquiring company is referred to as the *combinor* and the acquired company is called the *combinee*. Although the purchase is effected by the combinor company proper acquiring the assets and assuming the liabilities of the combinee, rather than being a transaction with the combinee company as such, it is made with the combinee's stockholders. In other words, the shareholders of the combinee company exchange their combinee shares of stock for consideration tendered by the combinor.

The consideration can be one, or a combination, of a variety of forms—cash, voting common stock, some other class or stock, or debt securities. Similarly, the value of the consideration may be equal to, less than, or greater than that of the combinee's recorded owners' equity. Our discussion is now directed toward obtaining an understanding of the nature of the purchase method of accounting for business combinations. In the course of this examination, the specific accounting implications of various types and amounts of consideration exchanged are addressed.

Asset Valuation

The first important characteristic to consider is that of asset valuation. Recall that in the case of a purchase of an individual asset, a buyer records an acquisition on the basis of its purchase price. At the moment the resource is traded, the bargained price is a measure of its current value. Thus, irrespective of what its cost basis may have been in the accounting records of the seller, the only relevant basis of accounting for a buyer is that of the price paid. As a result, each time an economic resource is bought, a new basis of accountability is created.

Using this accounting convention as its frame of reference, the purchase method of accounting for business combinations requires that the acquired assets and liabilities assumed be recorded to reflect the price paid to effect the purchase. The price paid is indicated by the current value of the consideration exchanged, and this amount can differ from that which appears as owners' equity in the combinee's balance sheet. This can happen because not only does market price per share usually vary from book value per share in the case of publicly-held companies' shares, but shareholders of privately held companies can also sometimes command greater compensation per share than that which the shares' book value alone would suggest.

Exhibit 9–2 presents pre-combination balance sheets of a combinor and a combinee. It assumes that the combinor gives $90,000 cash to the com-

Exhibit 9–2

Pre-combination Balance Sheets

	Combinor	Combinee
Cash	$300,000	$ –0–
Other assets	200,000	140,000
Total assets	**$500,000**	**$140,000**
Liabilities	$310,000	$ 59,000
Common stock	$100,000	$ 30,000
Capital in excess of par	2,000	12,000
Paid-in capital	$102,000	$ 42,000
Retained earnings	88,000	39,000
Owners' equity	$190,000	$ 81,000
Total equities	**$500,000**	**$140,000**

binee's stockholders as compensation for all of the outstanding combinee shares of stock. In exchange for the $90,000, the combinor obtains combinee assets having a book value of $140,000, and it assumes combinee liabilities in the amount of $59,000. Assuming that the stated amount of liabilities is fairly presented, one would conclude the reason $90,000 was paid for owners' equity having a book value of ($140,000 − 59,000 =) $81,000 is because the current value of the combinee's assets is ($90,000 − 81,000 =) $9,000 greater than its $140,000 book value.

It is apparent the purchase price in a business combination does not always equal the book value reflected in the combinee's pre-combination balance sheet. But it is also important to note that the purchase price itself may not necessarily correspond to the appraised current value of the underlying assets (less liabilities assumed). In the case at hand, assume that the particular assets' book values are as follows:

Asset A	$ 84,000
Asset B	36,000
Asset C	20,000
	$140,000

An appraiser, on the other hand, assigns the following current value amounts to the three assets:

194

Asset A	$ 70,000
Asset B	80,000
Asset C	50,000
	$200,000

The combinor was able to effect the purchase at an amount which attributed a ($90,000 purchase price plus $59,000 of liabilities assumed equals) $149,000 value to the assets. This sum is obviously at variance with both the $140,000 book value appearing in the combinee's balance sheet and the $200,000 current value provided by the independent appraiser.

Because the historical cost basis of accounting requires that asset valuation reflect the result of arm's length transactions, the combinor is precluded from recording the assets at the $200,000 amount. On the other hand, the purchase method of accounting for business combinations requires the combinee's assets be reflected in the post-combination balance sheet of the combined enterprise on the basis of the assets' implicit purchase price, that is, $149,000.

The resulting accounting question can be approached from another direction as well. Were the combined enterprise to record the combinee's assets as $200,000, there would then be an excess of current value over purchase price of ($200,000 − 149,000 =) $51,000. This would necessitate reducing the assets' recorded value by $51,000. The question which then arises is one of which asset(s) to reduce by $51,000. Instead of expressing the problem this way, the issue is expressed in terms of how—at the outset—the $149,000 shall be assigned to Assets A, B and C.

The approach used allocates the $149,000 purchase price on the basis of the assets' *relative* appraised values, as follows:

	Appraisal Value	Relative (appraisal) Value		Allocated Purchase Price
Asset A	$ 70,000	$\left(\dfrac{70}{200} =\right)$	35% × $149,000 =	$ 52,150
Asset B	80,000	$\left(\dfrac{80}{200} =\right)$	40% × $149,000 =	59,600
Asset C	50,000	$\left(\dfrac{50}{200} =\right)$	25% × $149,000 =	37,250
	$200,000			**$149,000**

For Asset A, although its $84,000 historical cost was ($84,000 ÷ 140,000 =) 60 percent of the three assets' total book value, its relative current value—based on the appraisal—is only ($70,000 ÷ 200,000 =) 35 percent. Applying this 35 percent measure of its relative value to the $149,000 purchase price paid for the three assets yields $52,150 as Asset A's cost basis to the combined enterprise.

To this point, it has been assumed that cash in the amount of $90,000 was given to combinee stockholders in exchange for their shares. Since $90,000 exceeds the combinee's $81,000 owners' equity by $9,000, the amount of Other Assets which appears in the post-combination balance sheet of the combined enterprise is $9,000 greater than the sum of the combinor's and combinee's pre-combination Other Assets. This can be seen in Exhibit 9–3. Column 1 indicates the combined enterprise accounts for $149,000—rather than the combinee's $140,000 book value—with the result that the post-combination balance sheet's $349,000 Other Assets exceeds the $340,000 sum of the combinor's ($200,000) and the combinee's ($140,000) pre-combination amounts by ($349,000 − 340,000 =) $9,000. Exhibit 9–2's second, third, and fourth columns depict the different results that occur when the purchase price exceeds the combinee's $81,000 book value by progressively higher amounts. And Column 5 sets forth the accounting result that occurs when the ($72,000) amount of the purchase price is less than the combinee's ($81,000) book value.

When the purchase method is used, it is the purchase price which becomes the combined enterprise's frame of reference for recording assets acquired and liabilities assumed. When having the benefit of current value data such as those that might be provided by a professional appraiser, the purchase price is allocated to the various affected assets and liabilities. This obligation also exists when the purchase price is less than the book value acquired. The combinor must determine what the underlying assets' and liabilities' values are, and proceed to account accordingly. Thus, in Exhibit 9–3's column 5, there is a ($140,000 − 131,000 =) $9,000 reduction in the combinee company's assets for which the combined enterprise is accountable. In concept, this is no different from the write-down of a particular asset while the aggregate value may be increasing, such as the earlier case of Asset A's $84,000 book value in the combinee's balance sheet being reduced to $52,150 in the combined enterprise's balance sheet.

Purchase Price in Excess of Current Value

As suggested in the previous section, the excess of purchase price over acquired book value is of no real accounting consequence as such. This is because it is only once the combinor ascertains the current value of the combinee's assets and liabilities and determines that it differs from the purchase price to effect the combination, that the excess must be dealt with, that

Exhibit 9–3

Cash Consideration

		Alternative Amounts of Cash			
(credit)	$90,000	$99,000	$162,000	$261,000	$72,000
Combination-date entry:					
Other assets	$149,000	$158,000	$221,000	$320,000	$131,000
Liabilities	(59,000)	(59,000)	(59,000)	(59,000)	(59,000)
Cash	(90,000)	(99,000)	(162,000)	(261,000)	(72,000)
Resulting combination-date balance sheet:					
Cash	$210,000	$201,000	$138,000	$ 39,000	$228,000
Other assets	349,000	358,000	421,000	520,000	331,000
Total	**$559,000**	**$559,000**	**$559,000**	**$559,000**	**$559,000**
Liabilities	$369,000	$369,000	$369,000	$369,000	$369,000
Common stock	100,000	100,000	100,000	100,000	100,000
Capital in excess of par	2,000	2,000	2,000	2,000	2,000
Retained earnings	88,000	88,000	88,000	88,000	88,000
Total	**$559,000**	**$559,000**	**$559,000**	**$559,000**	**$559,000**

is, an excess of either purchase price over current value or of current value over purchase price.

In discussing the latter situation, it was pointed out that because assets and liabilities cannot be reflected at amounts whose sum exceeds the combination's purchase price, an allocation procedure is used to ensure that purchase price is not surpassed. If the amount of the combinee's book value proper exceeds the purchase price, the excess would be the basis for reducing some assets' book value. The more typical case is that of an excess of purchase price over current value, and it is the subject of the discussion that follows.

We return to the earlier example in which $90,000 was the purchase price for owners' equity having an $81,000 book value. Since we had assumed the combinee's assets had a current value greater than their recorded historical cost, the combinee's assets of $140,000 are recorded by the combined enterprise at the purchase price amount paid by the combinor, i.e., $149,000. Assume now, however, that, instead of the assets having an appraised value in excess of the purchase price resulting in their being recorded at $149,000, the appraiser deems their current value to be only $145,000. In other words, the current value exceeds the book value by ($145,000 − 140,000 =) $5,000—but is less than the purchase price by ($149,000 − 145,000 =) $4,000. The issue that arises is how to account for the $4,000 excess.

Under the purchase method, this residual amount is included among the assets on the balance sheet of the combined enterprise. It is viewed as an intangible asset, and has been traditionally referred to as "goodwill." In this context it is assumed to be a measure of an economic resource which had not been reflected in the combinee's balance sheet. It presumably represents the value the combinor associates with certain qualities of the combinee which are not otherwise accounted for. Such qualities could relate to special technical skills, outstanding managerial competence, monopolistic or monopsonistic market position, trade names, established clientele, geographic location, or superior-quality merchandise, to name but a few.

Purchased goodwill is subject to amortization. In succeeding periods' income statements a portion of the goodwill's cost is charged, thereby reducing the asset's balance sheet carrying value. The amortization period may not exceed forty years, and unless the combined enterprise can justify using an alternative amortization method, it is to be effected by recognizing equal amounts each year.

Some accountants do not believe there should be formal recognition of such an excess as an asset; they advocate a reduction in either the combined enterprise's current earnings or in its owners' equity. This approach is based on the belief that "goodwill is not consumed in the generation of earnings and that attempted correlation to specific future benefits is inappropriate."[1] Furthermore, it has been argued that goodwill is not an asset because it is not a severable economic resource, that is, unlike other assets its lack of autonomy renders it incapable of being exchanged in an arm's length transaction.[2]

The contention that the cost of goodwill be accounted for as an immediate and direct reduction of the combined enterprise's owners' equity is based on a somewhat different point of view. The conventional interpretation of the purchase method of accounting for a business combination views the combinor company proper purchasing the combinee's stockholders' ownership interest. Alternatively, one could view the combination as a transaction between the stockholders of the combinor and the stockholders of the combinee—whereby the former group acquires the latter's equity interest in the combinee.

This point of view perceives the interests of the combinor and its stockholders as synonymous. Combinee assets and liabilities are recorded at their current (purchase price) values. The excess of purchase price over the current value of the owners' equity is viewed as a cost to be absorbed by the stockholders. Such cost to the stockholders is recorded by reducing their (owners') equity in the combined enterprise. "The value inherent in the goodwill element pertains to the stockholders and represents an advance expenditure on their behalf in anticipation of future earnings."[3] Thus, rather than representing the presence of an asset in the domain of the combined enterprise, the goodwill differential constitutes a decline in owners' equity because it is the cost to the stockholders of deriving future benefits as a result of the combinee's assets becoming part of the combined enterprise.

A third approach would recognize the excess of purchase price over current value acquired as an asset. But "since it is based on future earning power rather than being the cause of it, . . . it is inappropriate to amortize the asset to the income statement."[4] Therefore, a new owners' equity account is created to reflect the like amount, which in turn is removed from Retained Earnings. An example of this treatment is presented in Exhibit 9–4. Note that in Column 3, in addition to the emergent $4,000 goodwill which is

---

[1] FASB Discussion Memorandum, *Accounting for Business Combinations and Purchased Intangibles* (Stamford, Connecticut: Financial Accounting Standards Board, 1976) p. 53. Copyright © by Financial Accounting Standards Board, High Ridge Park, Stamford, Connecticut 06905, U.S.A. Reprinted with permission. Copies of the complete document are available from the FASB.

[2] Raymond J. Chambers, *Accounting, Evaluation and Economic Behavior* (Englewood Cliffs, N.J.: Prentice-Hall, Inc., 1966), p. 209.

[3] George R. Catlett and Norman O. Olson, *Accounting for Goodwill* (New York: American Institute of Certified Public Accountants, 1968) p. 90.

[4] John C. Burton, *Accounting for Business Combinations* (New York: Financial Executives Research Foundation, 1970), p. 88.

Exhibit 9–4

Goodwill Attributes

Based on pre-combination balance sheets appearing in Exhibit 9–2—and the assumptions that the purchase price is $90,000 cash and that the Other Assets of the combinee have a current value of $145,000.

(credit)	(1) Create Asset	(2) Reduce Owners' Equity	(3) Asset and Owners' Equity
Combination entry:			
Other assets	145,000	145,000	145,000
Goodwill	4,000		4,000
Retained earnings		4,000	4,000
Liabilities	(59,000)	(59,000)	(59,000)
Cash	(90,000)	(90,000)	(90,000)
ERFEP*			(4,000)
Annual amortization entry:			
Amortization expense	100		
ERFEP*			100
Goodwill	(100)		(100)

* Equity Representing Future Earning Power.

identical to the conventional approach (of Column 1), $4,000 is transferred from *permanent* Retained Earnings to the clearly-defined "Equity Representing Future Earning Power" (ERFEP) portion of the combined enterprise's owners' equity. Subsequent amortization of the asset balance is accompanied by a parallel reduction of the ERFEP balance.

The matter of accounting for purchased goodwill remains a controversial issue. That an excess of purchase price over the current value of the acquired owners' equity must be accounted for is a fact of life. The salient question is whether the amount in question is an asset or a reduction in owners' equity. However, the controversy is limited to the area of *purchased* goodwill, i.e., a company may not just decide that it has goodwill and then proceed to impute a value and include it as an asset in its balance sheet. Moreover, although the amount of purchased goodwill might appear to be a well-conceived and carefully-calculated amount, in fact it is merely the mathematical residual that emerges as a result of comparing the current value of a combinee's owners' equity with the purchase price negotiated between the combinor and the combinee's stockholders.

Resulting Owners' Equity

Another distinctive aspect of the purchase method relates to its effect on the owners' equity of the combined enterprise. Unless the combinor issues new shares of stock to the combinee's stockholders, the owners' equity of the combined enterprise is exactly the same as that of the combinor's prior to the combination. If the combinor does issue new shares, the paid-in capital portion of owners' equity will increase. But, in no case does the combined enterprise's retained earnings differ from the combinor's pre-combination balance. This reflects the accounting convention that a company's retained earnings balance increases as a result of profitable operations—and not as a result of a mere purchase—be it postage stamps, real estate, or another company. Exhibit 9–3 demonstrates this point. Note that for all five (Alternative Amounts of Cash) cases, the combined enterprise's resulting balance sheet yields an identical owners' equity, and that this owners' equity is also the same as the combinor's pre-combination owners' equity (depicted in Exhibit 9–2).

We shall now relax our assumption relating to the form of consideration used by the combinor to effect the combination. Instead of paying for the acquisition solely in the form of cash, assume that two-thirds (2/3) of the consideration is tendered through the issuance of combinor company shares of common stock and that one-third (1/3) is in the form of cash. Returning to the case in which $90,000 is the amount of consideration, ($90,000 × 2/3 =) $60,000 is tendered in stock and ($90,000 × 1/3 =) $30,000 through cash. Determining how many shares of combinor common stock represent the equivalent of $60,000 cash is based on the shares' market value, as follows.

If the market value per share is $120, then ($60,000 ÷ $120 =) 500 shares would be issued; if the per share value is $400, ($60,000 ÷ $400 =) 150 shares would be required. For purposes of our illustration, assume the market value per share is $300. Exhibit 9–5 identifies the resulting number of shares as well as the amount of cash needed to effect the combination for the same five alternative amounts of consideration to which the earlier "cash-only" illustration had been addressed. The allocation of amounts between *Common Stock* and *Capital in Excess of Par* reflects the assumption that par value per share is $100.

Exhibit 9–5

Two Alternative Payment Plans

	Cash Only	Combination of				
		2/3 Stock*		1/3 Cash		
		200 shares @ $300		$90,000 × 1/3		
A.	$ 90,000	$ 60,000	+	$30,000	=	$ 90,000
		220 shares @ $300		$99,000 × 1/3		
B.	$ 99,000	$ 66,000	+	$33,000	=	$ 99,000
		360 shares @ $300		$162,000 × 1/3		
C.	$162,000	$108,000	+	$ 54,000	=	$162,000
		580 shares @ $300		$261,000 × 1/3		
D.	$261,000	$174,000	+	$ 87,000	=	$261,000
		160 shares @ $300		$ 72,000 × 1/3		
E.	$ 72,000	$ 48,000	+	$ 24,000	=	$ 72,000

* The market value per share of the Combinor's common stock is $300.

We can now proceed to Exhibit 9–6 to observe the similarities and differences which exist between the earlier cash-only outcome and the 2/3 stock-1/3 cash case. With respect to the combination-date accounting entries, the amounts of Other Assets and Liabilities are identical, because the *form* of the consideration affects neither the amount of the purchase price nor the difference between the purchase price and the book value or current value of the combinee's owners' equity. The only variation that exists is that of cash being reduced for the full amount of the consideration versus one-third being a reduction in cash and two-thirds relating to the issuance of new shares. With regard to the resulting balance sheet of the combined enterprise, the noteworthy features are that the amounts of Other Assets are identical,

Exhibit 9–6

2/3 Stock—1/3 Cash Consideration

Alternative Amounts of Consideration

(credit)					
Stock =	$60,000	$66,000	$108,000	$174,000	$48,000
Cash =	30,000	33,000	54,000	87,000	24,000
Total =	**$90,000**	**$99,000**	**$162,000**	**$261,000**	**$72,000**

Combination date—entry:

Other assets	$149,000	$158,000	$221,000	$320,000	$131,000
Liabilities	(59,000)	(59,000)	(59,000)	(59,000)	(59,000)
Common stock	(20,000)	(22,000)	(36,000)	(58,000)	(16,000)
Capital in excess of par	(40,000)	(44,000)	(72,000)	(116,000)	(32,000)
Cash	(30,000)	(33,000)	(54,000)	(87,000)	(24,000)

Resulting combination date balance sheet:

Cash	$270,000	$267,000	$246,000	$213,000	$276,000
Other assets	349,000	358,000	421,000	520,000	331,000
Total	**$619,000**	**$625,000**	**$667,000**	**$733,000**	**$607,000**
Liabilities	$369,000	$369,000	$369,000	$369,000	$369,000
Common stock	120,000	122,000	136,000	158,000	116,000
Capital in excess of par	42,000	46,000	74,000	118,000	34,000
Retained earnings	88,000	88,000	88,000	88,000	88,000
Total	**$619,000**	**$625,000**	**$667,000**	**$733,000**	**$607,000**

and that Retained Earnings is $88,000 in all cases—despite the differing form of consideration and amount of consideration.

Combinee Earnings

If a business combination occurs *during* the fiscal year rather than at the beginning of the year, a question arises how to account for the combinee's pre-combination earnings. For example, assume the combinor's and combinee's earnings for the fiscal year, which is also the calendar year, are $60,000 and $24,000 respectively, income is earned uniformly during the year, and the combination occurs on October 1. The issue is the includibility in the combined enterprise's income of the combinee's ($24,000 × 9/12 =) $18,000 income earned prior to the combination.

Under the purchase method, the $18,000 is not included because it was not earned by the combined enterprise, that is, it was earned by the combinee prior to the combination, and is therefore conceptually no different from pre-combination income that may have been earned in preceding years. Equity in all such earnings accrued to the combinee's stockholders for which they are compensated by the combinor through greater consideration than would have been the case had such earnings not accrued. The combined enterprise did *not earn* the combinee's pre-combination income; it merely purchased equity in it, that is, in the asset growth it measures.

This can be viewed as similar to buying bonds between interest payment dates. The buyer compensates the seller for interest which had accrued and was therefore earned by the seller. The buyer thereby acquires equity in the interest which will be paid subsequently. It should also be viewed as being a part of the same principle discussed in the preceding section with respect to Retained Earnings. The combined enterprise does not include the combinee's pre-combination retained earnings in its retained earnings, nor can it include the combinee's pre-combination income of the current year in its current year income. In both cases, pre-combination earnings of the selling (combinee) company can have no effect on the purchaser's post-combination operating results. For informational purposes, APB Opinion No. 16 does require that for both the current and immediately preceding periods the combined enterprise ". . .include as supplemental information. . . results of operations on a pro forma basis. . . as though the companies had combined at the beginning of the period. . . (and) should as a minimum show revenue, income before extraordinary items, net income and earnings per share."[5]

---

[5] *Accounting Principles Board Opinion No. 16*, paragraph no. 96.

Summary

The four distinguishing characteristics of the purchase method relate to asset valuation, goodwill, retained earnings, and pre-combination combinee earnings. These four aspects could be further reduced to two distinctive features: valuation and retroactivity.

The purchase method's approach to valuation is to record the combinee company's assets at their current value, but not to exceed their (purchase price) cost. This reflects the belief that, irrespective of the value assigned by an appraiser, a combined enterprise may not record any asset at an amount which differs from what it encounters in an arm's length transaction, which is what a business combination accounted for by the purchase method is considered to be. The excess of (purchase price) cost over the current value of owners' equity acquired—traditionally referred to as "goodwill"—is an intangible asset and in turn is amortized as a determinant of annual income.

Retained earnings of a combined enterprise corresponds to the combinor's pre-combination retained earnings, while that of the combinee is not carried forward. Similarly, the combinee's income earned during the year of the combination but prior to the combination date is excluded from the combined enterprise's earnings for the year. This is viewed as being no different from the purchase of any other economic resource, namely, the buyer merely purchases the seller's equity in such resources even though the latter obtained such equity through earnings.

THE POOLING OF INTERESTS METHOD

The pooling of interests method is addressed to the same elements of business combinations as the purchase method. Two distinct corporate entities—referred to as the combinor and the combinee—enter into a business combination with the resulting entity known as the combined enterprise. Whereas the purchase method views the combinor as being the acquiring company and the combinee as the acquired (or selling) company, the pooling of interests approach attaches no significance to a party's being the acquiring or the acquired company. In fact, the terms "combinor" and "combinee" are specifically used because of their inherently neutral connotation. They merely distinguish between the two constituent companies whose combination results in one combined enterprise. The two constituents could have similarly been designated Companies A and B.

The theory underlying the pooling of interests approach is that a business combination marks the formal or physical unification of what is therewith construed to have been conceptually one entity. Stockholders of each constituent company agree to combine their equity interests. To effect such an objective, a new entity is created in the sense the stockholders can thereby pool their respective equities, and their sum can thus be reflected collectively. At a conceptual level, the constituent companies are not even parties to the combination per se. Yet, once the stockholding groups decide to pool *their* equity interests, the constituent companies do experience effects of the pooling. Specifically, because *stockholders'* equities are being combined, the related assets and liabilities are regrouped to form what is tantamount to a new accounting entity, i.e., the combined enterprise.

An important consideration underlying the pooling of interests approach is that the stockholders of the resulting combined enterprise in fact be the same parties that had owned the stock of the constituent companies. To implement this condition, the consideration the combinor gives to the combinee's stockholders should be combinor company voting common stock. If this were not the case, that is, if cash or bonds were to be tendered, the combinor company's stockholders would be effecting a purchase of—and not a pooling with—the combinee stockholders' interests.

Asset Valuation

Because the nature of the pooling of interests method assumes the combinor does not purchase the assets and liabilities of the combinee, the pooled assets do not have a new basis of accountability. There is no transaction on the part of either constituent company—each merely reflects in its accounting records the effect of its stockholders' new pooled interests.

From the point of view of the stockholders of the combined enterprise as well, there is no transaction involving assets per se. As a result, the combined enterprise values its assets on the very same basis they had been reflected in the constituent companies' pre-combination balance sheets, and this additivity (of asset book values) applies to liabilities as well.

Purchase Price in Excess of Current Value

Purchase price is measured by the current value of the shares of stock exchanged—the value of either the shares of the combinor or those of the combinee, whichever is deemed to be appropriate in a particular set of circumstances. Current value of the combinee's assets and liabilities can be determined in a manner similar to that occurring when the purchase method is used. Certainly such measures of value—of the consideration tendered and of the underlying assets and liabilities—are relevant in negotiating the terms of a business combination. They play a critical role, if only at an implicit or intuitive level, that is, even if definitive measurements are not made in formal sense.

There is no formal accounting recognition of either the purchase price value of the shares exchanged or the current value of the combinee's assets and liabilities. Thus, even though there may be an excess of purchase price over the current value of the combinee's owners' equity, it is not accounted for.

Resulting Owners' Equity

The pooling of interests method assumes the combinor issues new shares of its stock to the combinee's stockholders in exchange for their combinee shares. The only relevant shares of outstanding stock are therefore those of the combined enterprise, and these shares are owned by the former stockholders of both the combinor and the combinee. Inasmuch as the assets and liabilities of the combined enterprise are equal to the sum of the constituent companies' respective assets and liabilities, the combined enterprise's owners' equity will necessarily be equal to the sum of the constituent companies' respective owners' equity amounts as well. However, the amounts of particular elements comprising the combined enterprise's owners' equity will not necessarily correspond to the sum of the constituent companies' owners' equity components. Correspondence occurs only if the aggregate par value of the shares issued by the combinor to the combinee's stockholders equals that of the combinee's shares for which they are exchanged.

Before proceeding to consider case situations, attention is directed toward determining the combined enterprise's Retained Earnings. The basic rule is that the retained earnings of the combined enterprise may be as large as the sum of the constituent companies' retained earnings. The retained earnings of the combinor and the combinee are additive—because the mere pooling of stockholder interests has no effect as such on the amount of earnings which has in fact been earned by the combined enterprise albeit through its two constituent companies.

Recall that the nature of the purchase method precludes a combinor's retained earnings being affected by a business combination. The pooling of interests approach, on the other hand, is predicated on the belief that two companies which had previously operated as separate entities are merely pooling their interests. As their stockholders pool *their* ownership interests, the companies themselves pool their assets and liabilities. To the extent each constituent's excess of assets over liabilities results from prior periods' profitable operations, such amounts are accounted for as retained earnings— whether they operate individually as combinor and combinee or jointly as a combined enterprise. The particular circumstances which can prevent a combined enterprise from reflecting retained earnings equal to the sum of the constituent companies' retained earnings are set forth in an illustration below.

Illustrative Example

The nature of the pooling of interests approach is best understood when it is discussed in terms of differences between it and the purchase method. To facilitate making such comparisons, we shall use the same circumstances and data which comprised the case situation that appeared in the earlier examination of the purchase method. The combinor company effects a business combination by agreeing to buy all the shares of outstanding voting common stock of the combinee company. Payment is made by issuing combinor company voting common stock having a par value of $100 per share and a market value of $300 per share. The pre-combination balance sheets of the two constituent companies appear in Exhibit 9–7.

Exhibit 9–7

Pre-combination Balance Sheets

	Combinor	Combinee
Cash	$300,000	$ –0–
Other assets	200,000	140,000
Total assets	**$500,000**	**$140,000**
Liabilities	$310,000	$ 59,000
Common stock	$100,000	$ 30,000
Capital in excess of par	2,000	12,000
Paid-in capital	$102,000	$ 42,000
Retained earnings	88,000	39,000
Owners' equity	$190,000	$ 81,000
Total equities	**$500,000**	**$140,000**

Five different cases are set forth, each involving the issuance of a different number of combinor company shares; the number of shares issued are as follows:

(1) 300 shares
(2) 330 shares
(3) 540 shares
(4) 870 shares
(5) 240 shares

These five cases parallel those which earlier illustrated the nature of the purchase method. The amount of consideration tendered in each case corresponds to the "cash tendered" in the previous discussion, and this can be ascertained by multiplying the number of shares listed above by their $300 market value per share. For example, 300 shares @ $300 = $90,000 which is the amount of cash consideration in the first of the five cases appearing in Exhibit 9–3.

Each of the five cases comprising the illustrative example reflects a different amount of aggregate par value of the shares issued by the combinor company. Exhibit 9–8 identifies the relationship between each case's aggregate par value of combinor shares issued and the combinee's owners' equity components. The significance of these differences will become evident as we proceed to examine the five cases.

Exhibit 9–8

Par Value of Combinor Common Stock Issued to Combinee Shareholders: Alternative Amounts

(1) $30,000 is equal to Combinee's common stock par value:
                   300 shares @ $100 = $30,000

(2) $33,000 is greater than Combinee's common stock par value:
                   300 shares @ $100 = $30,000
    Less than Combinee's paid-in capital:
                   $30,000 + 12,000 = $42,000

(3) $54,000 is greater than Combinee's paid-in capital:
                   $30,000 + 12,000 = $42,000
    Less than Combinee's owners' equity:
                   $42,000 + 39,000 = $81,000

(4) $87,000 is greater than Combinee's owners' equity:
                   $42,000 + 39,000 = $81,000

(5) $24,000 is less than Combinee's common stock par value:
                   300 shares @ $100 = $30,000

The five cases are considered in terms of the accounting (entry) recognition of the combination by the combinor company. Note that the combinee merely credits all its asset balances and debits all its equities amounts, and ceases to be an accounting entity. The combination-date balance sheet that results for the combined enterprise is also presented for each of the five

Exhibit 9–9

The Pooling of Interests Method

	(1)	(2)	(3)	(4)	(5)
			Alternative Number of Shares		
(credit)	*300 Shares*	*330 Shares*	*540 Shares*	*870 Shares*	*240 Shares*
Combination date—entry:					
Other assets	140,000	140,000	140,000	140,000	140,000
Liabilities	(59,000)	(59,000)	(59,000)	(59,000)	(59,000)
Common stock	(30,000)	(33,000)	(54,000)	(87,000)	(24,000)
Capital in excess of par	(12,000)	(9,000)	2,000	2,000	(18,000)
Retained earnings	(39,000)	(39,000)	(29,000)	4,000	(39,000)
Resulting combination date balance sheet:					
Cash	$300,000	$300,000	$300,000	$300,000	$300,000
Other assets	340,000	340,000	340,000	340,000	340,000
Total assets	**$640,000**	**$640,000**	**$640,000**	**$640,000**	**$640,000**
Liabilities	$369,000	$369,000	$369,000	$369,000	$369,000
Common stock	$130,000	$133,000	$154,000	$187,000	$124,000
Capital in excess of par	14,000	11,000			20,000
Total paid-in capital	$144,000	$144,000	$154,000	$187,000	$144,000
Retained earnings	127,000	127,000	117,000	84,000	127,000
Total owners' equity	$271,000	$271,000	$271,000	$271,000	$271,000
Total equities	**$640,000**	**$640,000**	**$640,000**	**$640,000**	**$640,000**

cases. Refer now to Exhibit 9–9 which will be our focal point for the following discussion.

In Case 1 appearing in Column 1, the ($30,000) aggregate par value of the newly issued combinor shares equals that of the combinee's shares. Because the combinor increases its Common Stock balance by the same aggregate par value amount that had appeared in the combinee's pre-combination balance sheet, it carries over intact the combinee's other owners' equity components—($12,000) Capital in Excess of Par and ($39,000) Retained Earnings—as well. As a result, the combined enterprise's balance sheet corresponds to the sum of the constituents' pre-combination balance sheet amounts.

In Case 2, the aggregate par value of new combinor shares exceeds that of the combinee's shares by ($33,000 − 30,000 =) $3,000, but it does not exceed the sum of the combinee's pre-combination Paid-in Capital and the combinor's pre-combination Capital in Excess of Par.

As a result, $3,000 of the combinee's $12,000 pre-combination Capital in Excess of Par balance does not carry over to the combinor because, in effect, it has been reclassified. The result, as depicted in the combined enterprise's balance sheet, is that its ($144,000) Total Paid-in Capital is the same as the Case 1 outcome which means it is also equal to the sum of the constituents' pre-combination ($102,000 + 42,000 = $144,000) Total Paid-in Capital.

Case 3 reflects the combinor issuing shares whose aggregate par value exceeds not only that of the combinee company, but its Paid-in Capital as well. As a result of increasing the combinor's Common Stock by $54,000 rather than by the $30,000 which had been the combinee's Common Stock, ($54,000 − 30,000 =) $24,000 is transferred from the only other Paid-in Capital component that exists—the constituent companies' precombination Capital in Excess of Par amounts.

But the combinor's and combinee's balances were only $2,000 and $12,000 respectively, or a total of $14,000, which means that there is a ($24,000 − 14,000 =) $10,000 deficiency. As a result, $10,000 of the combinee's $39,000 pre-combination retained earnings is "reclassified" and only $29,000 is carried forward. The owners' equity section of the combined enterprise's balance sheet therefore contains no Capital in Excess of Par, and its $117,000 Retained Earnings is $10,000 less than the constituents' pre-combination $127,000 sum. However, its ($271,000) total owners' equity is identical with the sum of the pre-combination combinor's ($190,000) and the combinee's ($81,000) amounts.

In Case 4, the $87,000 aggregate par value of the newly issued shares exceeds the combinee's entire $81,000 pre-combination owners' equity. Because it exceeds the combinee's aggregate par value by ($87,000 − 30,000 =)

$57,000, an even greater amount of the constituents' pre-combination retained earnings is not carried over to the combined enterprise than had been the case in the immediately preceding set of circumstances. Not only will all of the constituents' ($2,000 + 12,000 =) $14,000 Capital in Excess of Par be reclassified, but ($57,000 − 14,000 =) $43,000 of pre-combination retained earnings becomes vulnerable as well. This means the full amount of the combinee's $39,000 pre-combination balance as well as ($43,000 − 39,000 =) $4,000 of the combinor's do not carry over to the combined enterprise. As a result, the $84,000 post-combination Retained Earnings is $43,000 less than the ($88,000 − 39,000 =) $127,000 sum of the constituents' pre-combination balances. But, as in all of the cases being considered, the same ($271,000) post-combination owners' equity emerges intact.

Case 5 represents a set of circumstances which differs from any of the preceding four cases. It reflects a situation whereby the ($24,000) aggregate par value of the shares issued by the combinor is less than that of the ($30,000 of the) combinee. Since the resulting $6,000 difference which had appeared as part of the combinee's Common Stock within its total Paid-in Capital does not represent par value, it is added to the combinor's Capital in Excess of Par. Thus, in the post-combination balance sheet, the combined enterprise's ($144,000) Paid-in Capital equals the sum of the combinor's ($102,000) and the combinee's ($42,000) pre-combination Paid-in Capital amounts. The full amount of the constituents' pre-combination retained earnings balances carries forward, and the combined enterprise has the same ($271,000) owners' equity, which also resulted in the other four cases.

Specifically with respect to the combined enterprise's owners' equity, the illustrative example provides several important insights. First, the post-combination owners' equity is equal to the sum of the constituents' pre-combination owners' equity (less the expenses of effecting the combination). Second, the constituents' individual amounts of Retained Earnings carry over to the combined enterprise in their entirety only if the newly issued shares' aggregate par value does not exceed the constituents' pre-combination Paid-in Capital sum. If it is in excess, the combined retained earnings is less than the constituents' sum by the amount of the excess (as depicted in Cases 3 and 4). Because the post-combination retained earnings may not exceed the pre-combination sum, if the newly-issued shares' aggregate par value is less than the forfeited combinee shares, the excess is added to the combined enterprise's Capital in Excess of Par (as illustrated in Case 5). Third, the amount of post-combination Capital in Excess of Par relative to the sum of the constituents' pre-combination Capital in Excess of Par amounts can be either greater (Case 5), less (Cases 2, 3 and 4) or equal (Case 1), depending on the relative amounts of aggregate par value of the new and old shares.

212

Combinee Earnings

Another difference between the pooling of interests and purchase methods—besides asset valuation, goodwill, and resulting owners' equity—is that of accounting for the combinee's earnings during the year of combination. For example, assume the combinor's and combinee's earnings for the calendar year fiscal year are $60,000 and $24,000 respectively, income is earned uniformly during the year, and the combination occurs on October 1. The issue is the includibility in the combined enterprise's income of the combinee's ($24,000 $\times$ 9/12 =) $18,000 income earned prior to the combination.

The retroactive nature of the pooling of interests method mandates that, similar to the carryover feature of retained earnings discussed in the preceding section, both constituents' earnings for the entire year comprise the net income of the combined enterprise. The pooling of interests concept assumes that rather than the combinor purchasing the combinee's owners' equity, two stockholder groups merely combine *their* interests. This suggests that as one homogeneous stockholder group, all of the post-combination stockholders have an interest in all earnings of the combined enterprise—both prospective and retrospective. Not only do they all have equity in the pre-combination income, they all are viewed as having had an interest in the earning of such income as well.

This same reasoning underlies the "additivity of asset values" feature as well. The presumption is that all the post-combination stockholders are viewed as having been the stockholders when the combined enterprise acquired what had heretofore been ostensibly combinor and combinee assets. This critical retroactivity aspect places an obligation on the combined enterprise to restate prior years' financial statements, which are presented for comparative purposes. Such restatement entails making a presentation which assumes the constituent companies had comprised the combined enterprise since their inception.

The accounting treatment of a combinee's pre-combination earnings is one of the primary reasons why a combinor might seek to use the pooling of interests method. When its results are considered in context of earnings per share and the dynamics of price earnings ratios, certain desirable outcomes may occur. An example is presented to demonstrate how a company might experience a threefold increase in the market value per share of its outstanding shares of common stock—by effecting four business combinations accounted for as poolings of interests.

A company has earnings of $50,000, 10,000 outstanding shares of stock, and therefore earnings per share (EPS) of $5. Assume that in the secondary securities market, investors are prepared to buy the company's shares for an amount eight times as large as EPS; 8 is the price-earnings ratio (P/E ratio). This means on the basis of its $5 EPS, the market value per share would be $40. The company then combines with another company which will be referred to as Combinee A. A has income during the year of $16,000, and a cash purchase price of $70,000 is negotiated. But in lieu of paying cash, the Combinor issues 2,000 new shares which, because their value is (2,000 @ $40 =) $80,000, creates a sufficiently attractive incentive for A's shareholders to accept stock instead of cash.

Refer now to Exhibit 9–10. The earnings of the combined enterprise is the sum of the combinor's $50,000 and the combinee's $16,000, for a total of $66,000. The combined enterprise's outstanding shares include the combinor's original 10,000 shares plus the newly issued 2,000 shares outstanding, for a total of 12,000 shares. The EPS increases to $5.50, and the market value per share would presumably rise to $44.

Soon afterward, the combinor effects a combination with Combinee B whose earnings during the year are $26,400. It is agreed that $88,000 is a fair purchase price, and, given a $44 market value per share, another 2,000 shares are issued. The resulting EPS is $6.60, and investors in the market,

Exhibit 9–10

Combinee Earnings

					Earnings per Share	Price Earnings Ratio	Market Price per Share
			$\dfrac{\$\ 50{,}000}{10{,}000}$	=	$5.00	× 8	= $ 40
A.	$16,000 +	50,000 =	$\dfrac{\$\ 66{,}000}{12{,}000}$	=	$5.50	× 8	= $ 44
	2,000[1] +	10,000					
B.	$26,400 +	66,000 =	$\dfrac{\$\ 92{,}400}{14{,}000}$	=	$6.60	× 10	= $ 66
	2,000[2] +	12,000 =					
C.	$39,600 +	92,400 =	$\dfrac{\$132{,}000}{16{,}000}$	=	$8.25	× 12	= $ 99
	2,000[3] +	14,000 =					
D.	$43,320[4] +	132,000 =	$\dfrac{\$175{,}320}{18{,}000}$	=	$9.74	× 13	= $126.62
	2,000 +	16,000 =					

[1] $80,000 ÷ $40 = 2,000 shares
[2] $88,000 ÷ $44 = 2,000 shares
[3] $132,000 ÷ $66 = 2,000 shares
[4] $198,000 ÷ $99 = 2,000 shares

impressed by such growth, might now be willing to pay an amount equal to 10 times earnings to acquire the combined enterprise's shares—with the result the market value per share would increase by ($66 − 44 =) $22 or ($22 ÷ 44 =) 50 percent in value.

The increase in market value per share means that 2,000 shares represent the potential for even more cash-equivalent when the combinor negotiates with Combinee C than had been the case earlier. Even though C has more earnings than B had had, and a higher purchase price therefore results (i.e., $132,000), the combination is effected with a like number of shares. The EPS increase to $8.25 triggers an even larger P/E multiple—of 12—and a market value per share of $99. The cycle repeats itself when the combinor pools its interests with Combinee D by issuing another 2,000 shares whose market value is (2,000 @ $99 =) $198,000. The resulting ($9.74 − 8.25 = $1.49; $1.49 ÷ 8.25 =) 18 percent increase in earnings per share causes even more optimism in the company's shares—with its P/E ratio now up to 13, and an increase in the combined enterprise's market value per share to $126.62—which is more than three times the value before the four combinations occurred.

It is not surprising therefore to understand why the retroactive nature of the pooling of interests method might sometimes be viewed as an attractive aspect of a business combination. Of course, the example did make an assumption about the behavior of the combinor's price-earnings ratio, namely, that investors would not discern the substance of what was happening. Yet, in practice there are instances of such reactions actually occurring.

Summary

Our examination of the pooling of interests approach to accounting for business combinations offered several important insights into its nature. First, irrespective of the market value of the shares issued by the combinor to effect a business combination, the combined enterprise's assets and liabilities are always equal to those of the constituent companies just prior to the combination. Second, precisely because the pooling of interests method does not formally account for assets', and liabilities' current value, the matter of accounting for goodwill (representing the difference between purchase price and the current value of the combinee's owners' equity) does not even present itself.

Third, although the owners' equity of the combined enterprise equals the sum of the constituents' pre-combination owners' equity, the amounts associated with its specific components can vary. Its key feature is that the retained earnings of the combined enterprise may be the sum of the constituents' balances, but this result does not occur in all cases. And fourth, the

215

earnings reported by the combined enterprise for the year during which the combination occurs includes both the combinor's and combinee's income earned throughout the year irrespective of whether the combination occurred on the first, last, or any other day of the year.

THE CHALLENGE OF IMPLEMENTATION

The purchase method has been criticized on several grounds. Some persons question the desirability of having a combined enterprise accounting for its assets on two different bases. The combinor's assets continue to be reflected on the basis of the historical cost incurred at the time they were originally acquired. The combinee's assets, on the other hand, are accounted for on the basis of their current value to the extent it is embodied in the combination's purchase price. Another concern of some accountants is that of the nature of the excess of purchase price over the current value of the combinee's owners' equity. Even those persons who maintain that the excess evidences the existence of a "goodwill" asset are confronted with the following question: If goodwill is a bona fide asset, why must a business combination occur in order to be able to formally recognize its existence?

With respect to the pooling of interests method, the following concerns have been expressed. First, it *does not* explicitly recognize the economic effects of a negotiated transaction between the buyer and the seller—the combinor and the combinee. Second, its assumption about the combination's retroactive nature may be unrealistic in the sense that the resulting accounting data reflect an "as if" state of affairs which does not portray circumstances as they actually were. And third, although the combined enterprise is arithmetically the sum of its constituent parts, a new entity is effectively created, for which a new cost basis is in order.

The ARB Criteria

Another dimension of the ensuing controversy revolves around defining the criteria which govern when each method may or may not be used. Initially, there had been four criteria that had to be met in order to use the pooling of interests method, and these were continuity of ownership, continuity of management, continuity of operations, and relative size.[6] And when all four were met, the combinor could use *either* the purchase method or the pooling of interests method; if they were not met, the purchase method had to be used. In addition to the concern that existed with respect to the existence of two alternative methods when the four criteria were met, there

_____
[6] *Accounting Research Bulletin No. 48*, paragraph nos. 5, 6.

were doubts about the meaningfulness of the first and fourth conditions, at both conceptual and implementational levels.

The continuity of ownership criterion related to the belief that in order to use the pooling of interests method, the stockholders of both the combinor and the combinee companies be the shareholders of the combined enterprise. The question that arose was whether this means all the combinee's stockholders had to receive shares of the combinor's stock, or whether some of the combinee shares could be exchanged for other forms of consideration. And if the latter route were permitted, what portion of combinee shares would not have to be traded for combinor stock and not thereby jeopardize the availability of the pooling of interests method.

With respect to the relative size condition, the reason for its existence presumably was related to the matter of *dominance*. If the relative size of the combinor and the combinee indicated the former was the dominant party, the combination was to be viewed as a purchase—by the dominant combinor of the dominated combinee. But if the relative sizes of the constituents indicated dominance was not present, the combination could qualify as a pooling of interests (if the other three criteria were met as well). At an applied level, the dimension whose relative size was evaluated was the number of combined enterprise shares of stock held respectively by the combinor's and combinee's stockholders. The more difficult question was deciding how large a percentage of combined enterprise stock could be owned by combinor shareholders and still not be viewed as constituting a dominant position. The official position was that ". . . where one of the constituent corporations is clearly dominant, for example, where the stockholders of one of the constituent corporations obtain 90 percent or 95 percent or more of the voting interest in the combined enterprise, there is a presumption that the transaction is a purchase rather than a pooling of interests."[7]

The lack of definitive rules resulted in accounting practices which were questionable. Perhaps the most infamous result was what became known as *partial pooling,* which refers to the following situation. A combinor, interested in using the pooling of interests method in accounting for a particular business combination, was precluded from doing so because of failure to meet the continuity of ownership test. For example, only 75 percent of the combinee shares were acquired by issuing combinor shares, with the remaining 25 percent of the combinee shares obtained by paying cash or issuing debt securities. Instead of accounting for the combination as a purchase, 75 percent of the combination was accounted for as a pooling of interests and 25 percent as a purchase. Although it is incongruous to use diametrically opposed approaches to account for different portions of the

---

[7] Ibid., paragraph no. 6.

same transaction, the practice was condoned, because the rules had failed to stipulate that *partial pooling* was not an acceptable compromise method.

The APB Conditions

The Accounting Principles Board (APB) issued its Opinion No. 16 in 1970. Perhaps the most subtle aspect of this pronouncement was its statement that the purchase and pooling of interests methods were not to be viewed as alternatives to one another. Instead, the nature of each combination's distinct set of circumstances would dictate which one method must be used in that particular case. A second feature of Opinion No. 16 was that the notion of *relative size* was deemed to be of no consequence, i.e., that a dominant combinor might be *purchasing* a dominated combinee would no longer be a relevant consideration. A third characteristic of the Opinion was that when the purchase method is used, any resulting excess of purchase price over the current value of owners' equity acquired—goodwill—would be recorded as an asset. This is noteworthy because an APB-commissioned Accounting Research Study had recommended such an excess should be charged immediately to the owners' equity of the combined enterprise.[8]

However, the most pervasive contribution of APB Opinion No. 16 was its establishment of the conditions which must be met in order to account for a business combination as a pooling of interests. The Securities and Exchange Commission (SEC) subsequently refined and made additions to the APB conditions which, for all intents and purposes, have become operational universally. The resulting (APB/SEC) conditions are set forth below:

- Each constituent must be autonomous; it cannot have been a subsidiary or division of another company within two years prior to the combination initiation date.
- Each constituent is independent of the other; more than a 10 percent intercorporate investment would preclude pooling.
- The combinee must be an operating company. This SEC-imposed condition would preclude pooling if the combinee has relatively nominal sales and expenses.
- The combination must be a single transaction or an "articulated" series of transactions completed in one year. Step-by-step acquisitions would preclude pooling.
- Voting common stock must be exchanged for substantially all the combinee's voting common stock; "substantially all" means at least 90 percent. This permits cash or other consideration to be exchanged for the remaining shares or they may continue outstanding as a minority interest.
- There can be no change in equity interest through new issuances, ex-

---

[8] Catlett and Olson, p. 90.

changes, retirements, and so forth, of voting common stock by either constituent within two years prior to the combination initiation date.

- There can be no treasury stock purchases for other than APB- or SEC-sanctioned purposes within two years prior to the merger initiation date. "APB- or SEC-sanctioned purposes" are described in a series of interpretations, but basically include shares acquired under a systematic pattern for stock option, compensation or bonus plans; conversion of convertible stock or debt; exercise of warrants; and recurring stock dividends. Certain "one-time" acquisitions are also acceptable. Acquisitions for specific purchase business combinations, to meet existing contingent share agreements from prior business combinations, or to settle a legal claim pursuant to the original issuance of shares are examples. Shares acquired for other purposes are called "tainted." A constituent company can hold up to ten percent tainted shares. The 10 percent is measured against the number of shares to be issued in the combination. For the combinee company, the measurement presumes a translation of treasury shares into equivalent shares of the combinor company based on the merger exchange ratio. Tainted shares become "untainted" after being held for two years.
- Each individual shareholder who exchanges his/her stock must receive a voting common stock interest in proportion to his/her relative voting common stock interest in the combinee before the combination.
- Shareholder voting rights must be unaltered after the combination.
- No contingencies relating to the combination may remain after consummation. For instance, subsequent payments to combinee shareholders contingent on earnings or market price behavior of the combined enterprise would preclude pooling.
- The combined enterprise may not agree to retire or reacquire any of the stock which is issued to effect the combination.
- There are no other special financial arrangements made for the benefit of former shareholders of a constituent company.
- There is no intention at consummation of the combination to sell a material part of the combined assets within two years.
- Another SEC-imposed requirement is that a major shareholder of either constituent company may not sell shares received in a combination until thirty days of combined operations have been completed and financial results have been disseminated to the public; failure to comply invalidates the use of pooling.

SUMMARY

Accounting for business combinations is one of the most complex areas of accounting, both in theory and in practice. It is a multi-faceted issue which deals with questions of valuation, whether or not to impute the existence of a goodwill asset, differentiating economic substance from legal form, relating stockholders' interests to those of a corporate entity, accounting retroactively for contemporary transactions, and establishing criteria to distinguish between different types of business combinations. Many of its "resolved" facets persist in posing valid conceptual questions such as: is dominance relevant, should the form of consideration influence the resulting accounting, is purchased goodwill more worthy of accounting than non-purchased goodwill, and do the APB/SEC criteria effectively accomplish the task for which they were established?

In this chapter, our attention has been directed exclusively to those business combinations whereby the combinor and combinee companies operate subsequently as a one-legal-entity combined enterprise. In practice, a combined enterprise can also operate as two or more legal entities; that is, each constituent retains its own legal identity. The accounting aspects of having the combined enterprise operate as separate companies, namely, the combinor and combinee as distinct entities but yet comprising the combined enterprise, are examined in the next chapter.

Additional Readings

Briloff, Abraham J. "Dirty Pooling." *The Accounting Review* (July 1967), pp. 489–96.

Burton, John C. *Accounting for Business Combinations.* New York: Financial Executives Research Foundation, 1970.

Catlett, George R., and Olson, Norman O. *Accounting for Goodwill.* New York: American Institute of Certified Public Accountants, 1968.

Eigen, Martin M. "Is Pooling Really Necessary?" *The Accounting Review* (July 1965), pp. 536–50.

Emery, Kenneth G. "Should Goodwill Be Written Off?" *The Accounting Review* (October 1951), pp. 560–67.

FASB Discussion Memorandum. *Accounting for Business Combinations and Purchased Intangibles.* Stamford, Conn.: Financial Accounting Standards Board, 1976.

Foster, William C. "The Illogic of Pooling." *Financial Executive* (December 1974), pp. 16–21.

Fotenos, James F. "Accounting for Business Combinations: A Critique of APB Opinion Number 16." *Stanford Law Review* (January 1971), pp. 330–46.

Gitres, David L. "Negative Goodwill Paradox." *The CPA Journal* (December 1978), pp. 45–48.

Harmon, David Perry, Jr. "Pooling of Interests: A Case Study." *Financial Analysts Journal* (March–April 1968), pp. 82–88.

Lauver, R. C. "The Case for Poolings." *The Accounting Review* (January 1966), pp. 65–74.

Sapienza, Samuel R. "Business Combinations." In *Modern Accounting Theory,* edited by Morton Backer. Englewood Cliffs, N.J.: Prentice-Hall, Inc., 1966, pp. 339–65.

Sapienza, Samuel R. "Distinguishing between Purchase and Pooling," *The Journal of Accountancy* (June 1961), pp. 35–40.

Schrader, William J.; Malcom, Robert E.; and Willingham, John J. "In Support of Pooling," *Financial Executive* (December 1969), pp. 54–63.

Snavely, H. Jim. "Pooling Should Be Mandatory." *The CPA Journal* (December 1975), pp. 23–26 and (April 1976), pp. 5–6.

Snavely, Howard J. "'Pooling' Is Good Accounting." *Financial Analysts Journal* (November–December 1968), pp. 85–89.

Wyatt, Arthur R. *A Critical Study of Accounting for Business Combinations.* New York: American Institute of Certified Public Accountants, 1963.

Wyatt, Arthur R. "Inequities in Accounting for Business Combinations." *Financial Executive* (December 1972), pp. 28–35.

10

Accounting for Intercorporate Investments

Corporations often invest in the securities of other corporations. Such securities can be either debt securities (bonds) or equity securities (shares of stock). Such investments are assets, and therefore are so disclosed in the investor's balance sheet. Whether a particular investment is categorized as a current asset or a noncurrent asset generally depends on two factors: management intent and the security's marketability. And depending on how the security is classified, there are different procedures for determining the investment's accounting basis which appears in the balance sheet.

DEBT SECURITIES

The cost of an investment in a bond includes transaction costs such as a brokerage fee incurred to effect the purchase. However, for purchases that occur between interest-payment dates, the accrued interest paid to the seller or issuer of the bond is not a cost of the investment. Instead, it is in effect the purchase of an interest receivable, namely, a payment for the interest earned by the seller, the equity in which is thereby sold to the new investor.

The cost of the investment may differ from the face amount of the obligation. This happens because of the inverse relationship that exists between the value of the bond and the market interest rate. This phenomenon was discussed in Chapter 8 when accounting for bonds was examined from the point of view of the issuing corporation. Since a particular bond may contain a nominal or coupon rate which differs from the prevailing market rate, an investor cannot be expected to invest an amount of money which equals the bond's face value. Instead, investors will pay a price which assures them their periodic interest revenue, fixed in absolute amount by the coupon rate, will represent a rate of return which corresponds to the investment date market interest rate.

The spread between the investment cost and the security's face value is a premium when the cost is larger, and a discount when the face value is larger. This amount does not appear as such in the balance sheet; rather, it is included in the composite amount reflected in the Investment account. Whether or not there is any formal accounting concern with the premium or discount subsequent to the investment date depends on how the bond is categorized in the balance sheet.

If the management of the investor company views the investment as being temporary in nature *and* the bond is readily marketable, it is classified as a current asset. If management does not expect to liquidate the investment prior to its maturity date; it is depicted as a long-term investment and grouped among the noncurrent assets. Bonds which are current assets are conventionally reflected in balance sheets at the lower of their cost or current market value. Accordingly, there is no direct concern with any purchase premium or discount.

The theory underlying the use of the lower-of-cost-or-market rule appears to reflect the general approach to valuing current assets. Receivables are reflected at their net realizable value by virtue of formally recognizing the expected impact of bad debt losses, and inventories are typically valued on a lower-of-cost-or-market basis. Indeed, the very premise for grouping certain assets as "current" is to emphasize their near-term realizability and utility as cash resources.

Debt securities that management does not expect to liquidate prior to their maturity or for which there is no readily accessible market in which to liquidate them are classified as long-term investment assets. The expectation of holding bonds till maturity calls for formal accounting for the purchase premium or discount. The presence of a premium or discount indicates the investor is earning interest at an effective rate which differs from the coupon rate. On the basis of only the cash interest received by an investor, interest revenue appearing in the income statement would not reflect the effective interest earned. This amount would reflect the true interest earned only if the bond had been purchased at its face value. Therefore, to enable the income statement to portray the effective interest earned, the premium or discount is amortized.

This process, in the case of a premium, involves reducing the asset amount down toward its maturity date value. Interest revenue is also reduced because the investment date interest rate was less than the coupon interest rate. Because the reduction in the investment asset is accompanied by interest revenue being reported at an amount less than that currently receivable, the favorable effect of cash interest on total assets is thereby dampened by the reduction in the investment asset's carrying value.

In the case of purchase discount, the required adjustment is effected by increasing the investment asset balance upward toward its maturity date value and reflecting this favorable movement as an addition to interest revenue disclosed in the earnings statement. This amortization represents the presence of the market interest rate exceeding the coupon interest; growth in the investment asset has the same positive effect on the investor as the growth in its cash balance resulting from receipt of the interest payment, and together they constitute the investor's interest revenue.

EQUITY SECURITIES

Corporations also invest in equity securities. When management expects to convert such securities into cash within a year (or the operating cycle whichever is longer) and there is a readily available market in which to effect the conversion, the investment is classified as a current asset. If either criterion is not met, the investment is reflected in the balance sheet as a noncurrent asset; in any case, the cost of the investment includes transaction costs.

There are three dimensions to the matter of accounting for investments in equity securities which warrant examination. The first of these is whether the investment has created a situation in which the investor is presumed to have the ability to exercise significant influence over the operating and financial policies of the company in which it has invested, which is called the investee. The other two considerations are whether a particular equity security is marketable, and whether or not management expects to convert its investment to cash within the time interval to warrant disclosure as a current asset. Depending on which, if any, of the three factors are present in a particular case, four distinct accounting results can occur. These different outcomes are depicted in Exhibit 10–1.

If the investment in voting common stock gives the investor the ability to exercise significant influence over an investee's operating and financing policies, the investment is not included among current assets—even if it is marketable. In addition, it is accounted for on the equity basis, an accounting method examined in depth later in this chapter. If significant influence is not present, the "marketability" criterion must be considered. Marketable means that sales price or bid-and-ask prices are currently available on a national securities exchange or in the over-the-counter market.[1] If the security is not

---

[1] Financial Accounting Standards Board Statement No. 12, paragraph no. 16. Copyright © by Financial Accounting Standards Board, High Ridge Park, Stamford, Connecticut 06905, U.S.A. Reprinted with permission. Copies of the complete document are available from the FASB.

marketable, it is classified as a noncurrent asset and is accounted for by the cost method of accounting which is described below.

The Cost Method

Under the cost method, when the investee company reports its earnings, there is no recognition in the investor's financial statements. When the investee distributes a cash dividend, the investor recognizes the dividend as revenue in its income statement. Dividend revenue is recognized as of the dividend's date of record, which may differ from the actual receipt of the cash.

The investee's declaration and distribution of a stock dividend or the occurrence of a stock split requires no formal recognition by the recipient investor (unless the dividend reduces the acquisition-date retained earnings). However, receipt of the additional shares of stock does require a memorandum notation since the original cost of the investment is thenceforth spread over a greater number of shares. This becomes important in identifying the cost per share when the shares are sold.

When an investor sells its investment in stock, a gain or loss occurs depending on whether the proceeds are greater or less than the cost of the

Exhibit 10–1
Classification of Investments in Equity Securities

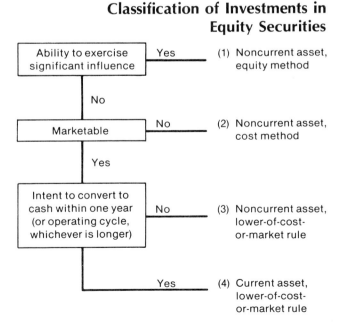

225

shares sold. Such a gain or loss is reflected in the investor's current income statement. If the investor purchases shares of the investee's stock at several different dates at various prices, on selling some of the shares a question arises as to which shares are being sold. The investor can use a specific identification method, the first-in first-out (FIFO) method, or the weighted-average approach. Whatever method is employed, it must be used consistently and appropriate supporting records should be maintained.

The Lower-of-Cost-or-Market Rule

Exhibit 10–1 notes that if the second criterion—marketability—is met, the lower-of-cost-or-market (LCM) rule is applied. However, presence of the third and final criterion—management intent regarding conversion to cash—suggests that even though at this point LCM applies in any case, there is still a distinction to be made in the resulting balance sheet disclosure. There are also different income reporting rules when applying LCM to the current and noncurrent portfolios—situations 3 and 4 in Exhibit 10–1.

The nature of the lower-of-cost-or-market method is that the aggregate cost and the aggregate market value are computed separately for each portfolio, and the lower amount for each portfolio appears on the balance sheet. The *aggregate* aspect means that the lower of cost or market is *not* determined for each individual security in the portfolio. Rather, the cost bases of the securities are added together, the market values of the securities are added together, and the lower of these two sums appears on the balance sheet.

The use of the aggregate approach can be questioned because of the "offset" effect which can occur. For example, consider a portfolio having these characteristics:

Equity Security	Cost	Market	Lower
X	$ 10,000	$12,000	$10,000
Y	40,000	15,000	15,000
Z	50,000	63,000	50,000
Total	**$100,000**	**$90,000**	**$75,000**

Under the required aggregate approach, $90,000, being lower than $100,000, emerges as the lower of cost or market. The individual securities approach, by adding each security's lower of cost or market amount, would yield a $75,000 result. The ($90,000 − 75,000 =) $15,000 difference between the two approaches reflects the fact that under the aggregate approach, the impact of security Y's ($40,000 − 15,000 =) $25,000 loss is offset by the gains of both security X's ($12,000 − 10,000 =) $2,000, and

226

security Z's ($63,000 − 50,000 =) $13,000. The impact of security Y's $25,000 loss mitigated by securities X's and Z's ($2,000 + 13,000 =) $15,000 gain is such that only a ($25,000 − 15,000 =) $10,000 *net* loss ($100,000 − 90,000 = $10,000) emerges.

This approach is justified on the grounds that application on an individual security basis would be unduly conservative and at variance with the "collective assets" manner in which enterprises generally view their investment in marketable equity securities.[2] However, the Financial Accounting Standards Board (FASB) requires supplemental disclosure, either in the body of the financial statements or in the accompanying notes, of the *gross* amounts "to inform as to the extent to which such offsets exist. . . ."[3] In our example, therefore, both the $25,000 gross unrealized loss and the $15,000 gross unrealized gain would be disclosed in a footnote.

In our examination in Chapter 6 of the lower-of-cost-or-market rule as it is applied to valuing inventories, it was noted that once the asset had been written down to market value, it could not be revalued upward in later financial statements if the market value subsequently increased. However, in applying LCM to marketable equity securities, if market value were to increase subsequent to a write-down, there is upward valuation so long as it does not exceed the original cost. Therefore, in evaluating separately the current and noncurrent portfolios, it is possible each could generate either a net unrealized loss (as is the case of inventory) or a net unrealized gain (which cannot occur with inventory).

As mentioned in our discussion of the cost method, gains and losses resulting from a sale of current or noncurrent marketable equity securities— realized gains and losses—are reflected in the income statement. However, when applying the lower-of-cost-or-market method, the financial statement disclosure of the unrealized gains and losses differs for the two portfolios. A *valuation allowance* contra-account to the respective current and noncurrent investment assets absorbs the entire balance sheet effect of unrealized gains and losses. Unrealized gains and losses relating to the current portfolio are reflected immediately in the income statement. Unrealized gains and losses pertaining to the noncurrent portfolio are not included in the income statement but are reflected in the owners' equity section of the investor's balance sheet.

Upon selling securities, as the cost of the securities is removed from the investment asset account, the cumulative net unrealized gain or loss likewise is removed from the valuation reserve. For the current portfolio, this cumulative amount had been previously included in income determination. For the

---

[2] Ibid., paragraph no. 31.
[3] Ibid.

noncurrent portfolio, unrealized gains and losses had not already appeared in earnings; therefore, upon realization the entire difference between cost and proceeds is reflected in the income statement.

With respect to the exclusion from income determination of unrealized gains and losses relating to the noncurrent portfolio, the FASB felt it could not deal with the issue on a piecemeal basis for purposes of establishing rules for marketable security securities.[4] In other words, there are larger issues involved which apparently would have unduly broadened the scope of the particular matter to be resolved. The general matter of introducing a current value basis of accounting universally—as opposed to selected instances—is examined in Chapter 13.

Indeed, the very establishment of the lower-of-cost-or-market requirement for marketable equity securities is an example of a selected instance in which current value is mandated. There is admittedly a significant conceptual shortcoming in the nature of the method inasmuch as market prices are valid only for purposes of writing cost *down* to market. That current prices are not equally reliable for valuation above the cost of assets is an inconsistency, the presumed virtues of conservatism notwithstanding.

The Equity Method

All investments in equity securities are recorded at cost. The accounting procedures employed subsequent to acquisition depend on whether or not the investor can exercise significant influence over operating and financial policies of the investee corporation. Significant influence is assumed to be present if the investor holds 20 percent or more of the investee's outstanding voting common stock. However, the specific circumstances must be examined. It is possible that significant influence may not be exercised by the investor in a particular case even if it holds greater than a 20 percent interest. Similarly, there may be situations in which significant influence can be exercised by the investor when there is less than 20 percent equity in the investee's outstanding shares. The 20 percent criterion in practice is therefore only viewed as a guideline to be applied in the absence of evidence to the contrary.

The Investment Account

We now consider the accounting practices that govern investments in stock when the investor can exercise significant influence over the affairs of the investee. Initially, we assume the investor forfeits cash to effect the investment; later, this assumption is relaxed and the accounting implications of non-cash exchanges will be considered.

---

[4] Ibid., paragraph no. 29(b).

In recording the investment at cost, there is no difference between the equity method and the cost method. However, once the initial investment is recorded, differences begin to occur. The first distinguishing characteristic is that the investor must examine the acquisition-date financial statements of the investee to determine the amount of the investee's owners' equity in which it has acquired equity. If the investment occurs at the very beginning of the investee's fiscal year, such a determination is relatively easy. A review of its balance sheet's owners' equity section will identify the amounts comprising the book value of the investee's common shares. If the investment occurs during the investee's fiscal year, it is necessary to take into consideration the earnings and dividends to date as well.

Excess of Cost over Book Value

It is essential that the investor compute the amount of book value acquired. It is only as a result of such a calculation that the investor can determine the amount of excess of cost over book value or excess of book value over cost. How such excesses are accounted for is a problem discussed later in light of its business combination overtones. The most likely reasons underlying an excess are that the investee's recorded assets or liabilities are misvalued and therefore need to be revalued and/or a heretofore unrecorded goodwill asset of the investee needs to be recorded.

In practice, an excess of cost over book value is usually associated with undervalued assets such as inventory, land, depreciable plant assets, or recorded intangible assets, with overstated liabilities, or with unrecorded goodwill. Similarly, an excess of book value over cost is typically associated with overvalued assets such as receivables, inventory, depreciable plant assets, or intangible assets, and/or may be attributable to understated liabilities.

Investee Earnings and Dividends

As the investee earns and reports its income, the equity method requires the investor to formally recognize its proportionate share of, that is, its equity in, such income. The basis for such recognition is the accrual concept; namely, since the investor exercises significant influence over the investee, the critical event is the investee's earning of income and not its subsequent decision to distribute a dividend. The manner in which the investor records its equity in investee earnings is by increasing the carrying value of the investment asset in its balance sheet and by recognizing Equity in Investee Income in its earnings statement.

If there had been an excess of purchase price over book value, the requirements discussed in context of business combinations apply here as well. This means that once assets and liabilities are revalued, the remaining ex-

229

cess, if any, is subject to amortization. At this juncture, attention is directed to an excess which is not allocable to particular assets and liabilities. Its amortization is effected by reducing both the Equity in Investee Income and the Investment in Stock amounts that would have been recorded solely on the basis of the investor's equity in the investee's reported earnings.

Because the investor's investment is recorded at cost and not at book value acquired, it includes the excess of cost over book value. Amortization of such an excess in a conventional business combination has the effect of reducing the acquiring company's earnings. To render a similar result in a *significant influence* intercorporate investment relationship, the investor's Equity in Investee Earnings must be reduced by the amount that would have been explicitly amortized in a true business combination. For example, on January 1, 19x4, PQR Co. bought a 40 percent interest in JKL, Inc. for $180,000 when PQR's owners' equity was $300,000. The excess of the cost over book value acquired of [$180,000 − ($300,000 × .40 =) $120,000 =] $60,000 is amortized over 40 years. If JKL reported income in 19x4 of $50,000, PQR would recognize in its earnings statement [$50,000 × 40% = $20,000; $20,000 − ($60,000 ÷ 40 years =) $1,500 =] $18,500 as its equity in JKL's income. This practice suggests that accountants impute a *business combination* character to intercorporate investments in which significant influence results. It also helps explain why the equity method is deemed to be the proper basis of accounting; namely, its nature is to simulate the result that would transpire had there been a genuine business combination.

When the investor receives a cash dividend from the investee, there is a decrease in its Investment in Stock. An effective way of understanding the underlying concept is to visualize such a transaction as one in which the investor is merely shifting its investment from a non-liquid state (long-term investment) to a liquid state (cash). Alternatively, recognize that the equity method's nature is such that all changes in an investee's owners' equity affect the carrying value of the investor's investment. Increases in the investee's owners' equity, such as profitable operations, cause an increase in the carrying value of the investor's investment. Decreases in the investee's owners' equity, resulting from the payment of cash dividends or from a net loss from operations, cause the carrying value of the investor's investment to decline.

The ongoing balance in the Investment in Stock account has been referred to as its carrying value. By no means does this amount purport to represent the current market value of the investment. Note also that in the investor's balance sheet, this carrying value is disclosed as a single amount. This means no explicit distinction is made between that portion which represents the investment's original cost and that part which represents the investor's equity in post-acquisition changes in the investee's owners' equity. Also, no explicit disclosure is made with respect to what portion of the investment's cost relates to the "excess of cost over book value" which is subject to continuing amortization.

Intercompany Sales of Merchandise

An investor corporation and investees in which it has a significant interest sometimes enter into transactions involving the purchase and sale of merchandise. Such transactions typically generate a profit for the seller. However, if the buyer had not yet resold the goods to an independent third party by the time its fiscal year ends, an accounting dilemma arises. Recalling that the equity method in effect perceives the investee to be an extension of the investor, it is inappropriate for the investor corporation to include in its income statement any profit that results from a transaction with the investee. Such a transaction is effectively a mere transfer of merchandise from one location within the company to another one within its sphere of influence. A transfer of this sort results in no realization of revenue by the company, and no profit is earned as a result. Profit recognized prior to its realization in a revenue transaction with an independent third party is therefore eliminated from the investor's income statement. For example, assume that an investee, XYZ, had a 19x1 income of $70,000 which includes that $4,000 profit it earned on a sale of merchandise to the investor during the year, merchandise which had not been resold by year-end. To recognize its 30 percent equity in XYZ's 19x1 earnings, the investor includes ($70,000 − 4,000 = $66,000; $66,000 × 30% =) $19,800 in its income statement.

When the investee sells merchandise to the investor, it is referred to as an *upstream* sale. The investor decreases its Equity in Investee Income by the amount of unrealized profit in order to exclude that part of the investee's reported earnings which, from the investor's point of view, was not income in which the investor has equity. Such equity does not exist because it did not result from a sale to an independent third party. The investor also removes the unrealized profit from its merchandise inventory to restore it to its historical cost basis.

Consider now the case of a *downstream* sale—when the investor sells merchandise to an investee which in turn was not resold by the end of the fiscal period. In this situation, it is the investor's own operating income which includes the unrealized intercompany profit. The investor therefore removes the unrealized profit from its reported earnings, and reflects a deferred credit on its balance sheet. This deferred credit discloses the profit whose recognition is deferred until realization occurs in a subsequent fiscal period through sale by the investee to a third party. When the merchandise is sold to a third party, the unrealized profit is transferred from the balance sheet to that period's earnings statement.

Note that when eliminating the effect of unrealized intercompany profit in inventory, it is the gross profit, and not the net profit, eliminated. Calculating the net profit per unit of merchandise is a very difficult undertaking which would require a number of somewhat arbitrary allocations. Because gross profit does not include selling and administrative costs, it is considered more suitable. It is important to correctly compute the amount of gross profit to be eliminated. Sometime the available information is expressed as a markup percent; such a percentage in turn might be expressed relative to either sales or cost of goods sold. An item having a cost of $80 which is sold for $100 has a $20 gross profit. The $20, in turn, can be viewed as being either a ($20 ÷ $80 =) 25 percent return on cost or a ($20 ÷ $100 =) 20 percent margin on sales.

Disinvestment

When the equity method is used, the procedures used to record a disinvestment are similar to those employed when the cost method is used. This means it is important to identify which shares are being disposed of so that the appropriate carrying value per share can be removed from the Investment account. An investor may use a specific identification, weighted average, or FIFO basis. The Investment account balance at any point in time reflects not the shares' cost but their carrying value as determined by the equity method. This aspect is obviously different from that which exists when the cost method is used. Accordingly, given the use of the equity method, the accountant removes from the Investment account the carrying value of the shares being sold, and not only the original cost of the shares.

The difference between the proceeds and the carrying value of the shares surrendered is a gain or loss to be recognized in the current income statement. The amount of the gain or loss would be different if the cost basis had been in effect, because the investor's equity in cumulative changes in the investee's owners' equity recognized by the equity method when they occur would all be combined in the determination of the gain or loss.

For example, the cost of the investment was $60,000, its carrying value increased by $15,000 during the first five years of the investment, and one-third of the shares were sold for $32,000 at the beginning of the sixth year. Under the cost method, there would be a [$32,000 − ($60,000 × 1/3 =) $20,000 =] $12,000 gain while the equity method would yield a [$32,000 − ($60,000 + 15,000 = $75,000; $75,000 × 1/3 =) $25,000 =] $7,000 gain. The cost method generates a gain $5,000 larger than that of the equity method. This is because under the equity method, the ($15,000 × 1/3 =) $5,000 increase in carrying value during the five-year period had already been reflected in the investor's earnings. Thus, only

$7,000 of the apparent $12,000 gain is a true trading gain, and this result occurs only when the equity method is used.

Changing to or from the Equity Method

Let us now consider what happens when circumstances necessitate changing the basis of accounting for long-term stock investments from the cost method to the equity method and vice versa. If an investor holds less than 20 percent of the investee's voting common stock, the cost method usually prevails. If the investor were to acquire additional shares causing its total interest to exceed 20 percent, it would usually begin to employ the equity method. Such a change in method is categorized as a change in accounting entity, and is accounted for on a retroactive basis.

The investor applies the equity method to the shares which had originally been accounted for by the cost method. The investor calculates the appropriate carrying value for the shares purchased earlier and converts the Investment in Stock account from the cost basis to the equity basis. The complementary effect on Retained Earnings recognizes what is in effect a correction of prior period earnings; an example follows.

On January 1, Odd Company buys 100 of Even Company's 1,000 voting common shares for $6,000 when Even's owners' equity is $50,000. During the next two years, Even earns $6,000 and $8,000 and on November 1 of each year, it declares dividends of $2,000. On January 1 of the third year, Odd buys 200 more shares of Even from existing stockholders at a cost of $18,400.

To apply the equity method retroactively to the 100 shares acquired during the first year, the following calculation is made.

	Year 1	Year 2	Total
Equity method:			
Earnings (10% equity interest)	$600	$800	$1,400
Amortization of excess	25	25	50
Total	$575	$775	$1,350
Cost method:			
Dividends (10% equity interest)	200	200	400
Adjustment required	**$375**	**$575**	**$ 950**

The amortization of the "excess of cost over book value" is based on cost of $6,000 less ($50,000 × 10% =) $5,000 or $1,000 amortized on a straight line basis over 40 years.

When the reverse situation occurs, namely, when an investor which had been correctly applying the equity method no longer exercises significant influence, the cost method becomes applicable. In this case, *no* retroactive adjustment is made since the equity method carrying value of the shares becomes the pertinent cost basis. But with the onset of the cost method, none of the investor's interest in subsequent changes in the investee's owners' equity will be reflected in its Investment account.

PARENT-SUBSIDIARY RELATIONSHIPS

When an investor has more than a 50 percent interest in the outstanding voting common stock of an investee, it is said to have a controlling rather than merely a significant interest. The investor corporation is then called the *parent* company and the investee is referred to as a *subsidiary* company, the result being a parent-subsidiary relationship. If the parent owns all the subsidiary's outstanding voting common stock, the subsidiary is a wholly-owned subsidiary. If the subsidiary is not wholly owned by the parent, the stockholders who own its remaining outstanding shares represent its *minority interest*. A parent and companies in which is has either a significant or a controlling interest comprise an affiliated group, and can be referred to individually as affiliates.

Recall that in Chapter 9, it was pointed out that when a business combination occurs, irrespective of whether it is measured for accounting purposes as a purchase or as a pooling of interests, two other dimensions must be considered. The first of these is the legal form through which the combined enterprise operates—as one legal entity or as two legal entities. Chapter 9 dealt exclusively with a one-entity outcome.

The two-entities approach occurs when one company owns all the outstanding voting stock of the other firm. The result is the same parent-subsidiary relationship that occurs once an investor's equity interest in an investee exceeds 50 percent. In other words, just as the parties to a true business combination can operate as two legal entities and not jeopardize their combined status, once an investor's equity interest gives it the identity of being a parent, a business combination can be said to have occurred. This means that once an investor also becomes a parent, the accounting approach moves out of the realm of an investment in marketable equity securities and into the domain of business combinations.

Although combined companies may operate as autonomous legal entities, they may also consolidate their financial statements with a result which corresponds to that which would have occurred had they actually operated as one legal entity. Thus, a parent prepares its financial statements on an unconsolidated basis only, which means the investment in its subsidiary is reflected in its balance sheet investment account and in its income statement Equity in Subsidiary Income account. Alternatively, the parent can also prepare a set of consolidated financial statements which includes in an explicit sense the subsidiary's assets, liabilities, revenues, and expenses as well.

There are always valid business reasons underlying a decision not to combine the two companies into one legal entity. It may be that the nature of the companies' respective organizational structures, personnel, product lines, or reputations necessitate that each constituent retain its own identity for operational purposes even though, from an ownership point of view, the two companies are really one. Such companies may therefore wish to operate as parent and subsidiary. In fact, there are instances in which a parent company may engage in no business per se but acts solely as a coordinative medium for the subsidiaries; such a parent company is called a *holding company.*

Another reason the merging companies may not combine into one legal entity is that the acquiring corporation may not own 100 percent of the other enterprise. It may wish only to exert control, or it may lack the cash needed to buy all the outstanding shares. Another cause for two legal entities to exist is that some of the acquired company's stockholders may be unwilling to surrender their shares to the acquiring company. As a result, the acquiring company may simply be prevented from acquiring the 100 percent interest needed to combine the two enterprises into one legal entity.

The existence of a parent-subsidiary relationship is in effect prima facie evidence that a business combination has occurred. Despite the presence of a minority interest, the parent has effectively consummated a business combination by virtue of exerting control over the subsidiary. The manner in which a company becomes a parent can vary. The parent may acquire shares from existing subsidiary company owners in the secondary securities market, or by extending an offer to the stockholders to tender their shares directly to the prospective parent at a designated price per share. Another method is to purchase an approrpriate number of shares directly from the prospective subsidiary itself.

In the discussion that follows, the parent-subsidiary relationships result from the parent acquiring its interest from existing stockholders by exchanging cash, which means that the purchase method of accounting applies. The nature of this approach is that the acquired company's assets are recorded by the acquiring company on the basis of the cash tendered. Thus, when a business combination occurs and the two companies operate subsequently as one legal entity, the acquiring company records the acquired company's assets, not at their former book value, but at an amount reflecting the purchase price it pays.

Similarly, when the combination occurs with the creation of a parent subsidiary relationship, the parent records its investment in the assets less the liabilities, that is, the owners' equity of the subsidiary on the basis of *its* cost. Its cost is measured by the amount of cash it pays to acquire its interest in the subsidiary. A company's ownership interest in another company by definition refers to its interest in that other company's owners' equity.

Note also that the investment in a subsidiary's stock involves the same accounting procedures that apply to investments in equity securities of non-subsidiaries. Therefore, these same procedures will now be considered from a business combination perspective. The equity method of accounting applies to an investment in a subsidiary the same way it is employed for less-than-controlled investees. However, since such an investment is not viewed as a business combination, we can better appreciate the accounting procedures used when the cost of the investment exceeds the investor's equity in the underlying book value of the investee's owners' equity.

In the case of an investment in which the investor has a *significant* interest in an investee, it was pointed out that any excess of cost over book value acquired was subject to the same allocations required when accounting for business combinations. This is true as well for investments in which a *controlling* interest exists. Now we can understand why this should be. Given that a parent-subsidiary relationship can be viewed as being a manifestation of a business combination, there should be consistent application of the equity method for significant investees as well.

Consolidated Financial Statements

Irespective whether a parent uses the purchase method or the pooling of interests method to record its investment in a subsidiary, the parent may consolidate its subsidiary's financial statements with its own. This option is generally left to the discretion of the parent company's management.

Accountants believe "there is a presumption that consolidated statements are more meaningful than separate statements and that they are usually necessary for a fair presentation. . . ."[5] Such statements permit the affiliated companies to portray their operating results and financial position as one economic entity, even though they are in fact two or more legal entities. In instances in which a subsidiary operates in a distinctly different industry from the parent, such as a manufacturing company with an insurance company subsidiary, consolidation may be inappropriate. Although consolidation is usually the preferred approach and most parent companies do prepare con-solidated financial statements, the only time a parent is required to consoli-date the financial statements of a subsidiary is when the subsidiary's principal

---

[5] *Accounting Research Bulletin No. 51*, paragraph no. 1.

business activity is leasing property or facilities to the parent or other affiliated companies. This requirement prevents a company which, rather than increasing its debt when acquiring plant assets, creates a subsidiary to contract the debt and not reflect it in the parent's balance sheet. The consolidation requirement recognizes that while in legal form there are two legal entities, the economic substance of the circumstances is such that it is tantamount to being the parent's debt, and it should be so disclosed.

As opposed to an unconsolidated balance sheet in which the parent's equity in the subsidiary's current owners' equity is summarized in the single noncurrent investment asset account, consolidation entails a greater degree of disclosure. In a consolidated balance sheet, the subsidiary's assets and liabilities are combined with those of the parent and therefore do not appear as a single or *net* Investment figure. When combining the parent's and subsidiary's account balances to prepare a consolidated balance sheet, intercompany amounts must be eliminated. The two most notable eliminations are intercompany debt—such as advances, payables, and bondholdings—and the very intercompany investment which effected the combination.

When the unconsolidated format is used, that is, when the parent's equity in the subsidiary's assets and liabilities is summarized in the single Investment amount reflecting equity method accounting, the presentation is sometimes called a "one-line consolidation." Similarly in the case of the earnings statement, there are differences between a consolidated approach and an unconsolidated presentation. Whereas in the latter case, the parent's equity in a subsidiary's earnings is presented as a single amount in the parent's income statement (Equity in Subsidiary Earnings), a consolidated income statement offers more extensive disclosure. The specific revenue and expense amounts comprising the subsidiary's net income are combined with the parent's corresponding amounts, and intercompany transactions are eliminated, most notably intercompany sales of merchandise, intercompany interest accruals, and gains and losses on intercompany sales of plant assets.

Before preparing consolidated financial statements, the parent and subsidiary each initially prepares its own set of financial statements. A worksheet is then prepared to consolidate these financial statements. The eliminations are generally made only on the consolidated worksheet, and not in either company's accounting journals or ledgers. This point impresses on us that the separate entities continue to maintain their respective accounting records on the basis of legal relationships with other companies which may include affiliated companies.

Before proceeding to examine conceptual issues and nuances surrounding consolidated statements, let us reiterate the nature and purpose of consolidated financial statements. Such statements portray the two or more legal entities as though they were one company. As a result, the presentation corresponds to what would have been the case had the acquiring company elected to combine the acquired company into itself, i.e., the same legal entity at the time the business combination occurred. Thus, consolidation procedures yield the same result that would have ensued had the parent-subsidiary organizational structure not been created, but that instead the two companies had operated as one entity, instead of two.

Elimination of Intercompany Investment

The most apparent elimination is the one concerned with the parent's investment in the subsidiary's voting common stock. The parent's unconsolidated balance sheet contains the investment among its noncurrent assets, and the subsidiary's balance sheet reflects in its owners' equity section the book value in which the parent has a controlling interest. Elimination therefore involves negating the effect of the investment on consolidated assets inasmuch as the consolidated entity cannot have an investment interest in itself. Similarly, the consolidated owners' equity cannot include amounts which represent outstanding shares held by the consolidated unit itself.

When the purchase method of accounting for business combinations is used and the purchase price equals book value acquired, the amount placed in the parent's investment account is the same as its equity in the subsidiary's owners' equity. But when there is an excess of purchase price over book value acquired, the amount recorded as the parent's investment exceeds that of the parent's equity in the subsidiary's *recorded* owners' equity. This means when consolidation is effected, a larger amount is eliminated from the parent's investment asset (with a credit) than is eliminated from the subsidiary's owners' equity (with a debit).

The resulting excess is the same amount which would have surfaced had the two companies operated as one legal entity since the combination date. And, as seen in the discussion of business combinations in Chapter 9, the excess is subject to an allocation procedure whereby only the excess of cost over the *current value* of recorded owners' equity is accounted for as an autonomous amount. Accordingly, each time consolidated statements are prepared and the investment elimination is made, the accountant identifies the particular assets and liabilities to be revalued and appropriate disclosure appears in the consolidated balance sheet. Note that this procedure is repeated each time consolidated statements are prepared because prior recognition as part of the consolidation process will not have been recorded in either company's own accounting records.

An additional problem arises if one of the assets revalued as of the combination date happens to be merchandise inventory which, in turn, has since been sold. For example, inventory with a recorded book value of $1,000 was deemed to have a current value of $1,300 at the combination date. If it is subsequently sold for $1,500, the subsidiary's income statement would reflect a ($1,500 − 1,000 =) $500 gross profit. But from a consolidated point of view, the consolidated income statement in the year of sale should reflect only a ($1,500 − 1,300 =) $200 gross profit—based on the *consolidated unit's cost basis* which is the combination date current value. Therefore, when eliminating the intercompany investment at the end of the period of sale, the ($1,300 − 1,000 =) $300 revaluation of inventory is reflected in the period's consolidated cost of goods sold, causing it to be $300 higher. In subsequent fiscal periods, the $300 difference will be a correction of that period's beginning consolidated retained earnings.

A problem also arises if one of the assets revalued as of the combination date is a depreciable plant asset. The subsidiary in subsequent periods will have been recording depreciation expense on the basis of *its* recorded original cost while for purposes of preparing a consolidated income statement, depreciation expense should be based on the combination date current value which is the cost basis to the consolidated enterprise. Therefore, when eliminating an intercompany investment, there can be ramifications for the consolidated statements' depreciation expense and accumulated depreciation amounts as well.

Consolidating the financial statements of a parent and subsidiary yields the exact same result had the combining companies decided to operate as one legal entity. To illustrate this, we will use the same data developed in the examination of business combinations in Chapter 9. We shall assume the excess of purchase price over book value results in revaluation of the subsidiary's "other assets," a consolidated balance sheet is prepared as of the combination date, and the only elimination necessary is that which relates to the intercompany investment.

Assume that Big Co. purchases for cash all of the shares of outstanding voting common stock of Small Co., and the companies will operate as two legal entities. The companies' pre-combination balance sheets appear as illustrated at the top of the following page (240), and, in addition, we shall consider five different amounts of cash paid by Big Co. to Small Co.'s shareholders: $90,000, $99,000, $162,000, $261,000, and $72,000. The accounting entries and balance sheet results discussed below are set forth in Exhibit 10–2.

In this "cash only" situation, Big Co.'s financial position is affected only to the extent it surrenders cash to acquire Small Co.'s assets and assume its liabilities. Because Big Co. issues no shares to effect the combination, its owners' equity accounts are not affected—either individually or collectively. Observe in Exhibit 10–2 that Section I identifies the accounting entry required when only Big Co. survives the combination, and that Section II sets forth the resulting balance sheet for each of the five amounts of cash ex-

Pre-combination Balance Sheets
(thousands of dollars)

	Big Co.	Small Co.
Cash	$300	$ 0
Other assets	200	140
Total assets	**$500**	**$140**
Liabilities	$310	$ 59
Common stock	100	30
Capital in excess of par	2	12
Paid-in capital	102	42
Retained earnings	88	39
Total owners' equity	190	81
Total equities	**$500**	**$140**

Exhibit 10–2

Accounting Entries and Resulting Balance Sheets

Purchase Method
(thousands of dollars)

	$90,000		$99,000		$162,000		$261,000		$72,000	
I. Acquisition entry:										
Other assets	149		158		221		320		131	
Liabilities		59		59		59		59		59
Cash		90		99		162		261		72
II. Resulting balance sheet:										
Cash	210		201		138		39		228	
Other assets	349		358		421		520		331	
Total	**559**		**559**		**559**		**559**		**559**	
Liabilities	369		369		369		369		369	
Common stock	100		100		100		100		100	
Capital in excess of par	2		2		2		2		2	
Retained earnings	88		88		88		88		88	
Total	**559**		**559**		**559**		**559**		**559**	

Exhibit 10–2 (*continued*)

	$90,000	$99,000	$162,000	$261,000	$72,000
III. Acquisition entry:					
Investment	90	99	162	261	72
Cash	90	99	162	261	72
IV. Resulting balance sheet:					
Cash	210	201	138	39	228
Investment	90	99	162	261	72
Other assets	200	200	200	200	200
Total	**500**	**500**	**500**	**500**	**500**
Liabilities	310	310	310	310	310
Common stock	100	100	100	100	100
Capital in excess of par	2	2	2	2	2
Retained earnings	88	88	88	88	88
Total	**500**	**500**	**500**	**500**	**500**
V. Elimination entry:					
Common stock	30	30	30	30	30
Capital in excess of par	12	12	12	12	12
Retained earnings	39	39	39	39	39
Other assets	9	18	81	180	9
Investment	90	99	162	261	72

VI. Resulting balance sheet—same as II above.

pended. If Small Co. is operated as Big Co.'s subsidiary, the latter's investment entry, depicted in Section III, summarizes the effect of the acquisition, and Section IV identifies the balance sheet outcome.

Section V portrays the investment elimination, which serves three purposes. It eliminates Big Co.'s investment balance, it eliminates Big Co.'s equity in Small Co.'s owners' equity amounts, and it recognizes explicitly the revaluation of the "other assets" in a manner which yields the same balance sheet—see Section II—that results had Big Co. and Small Co. actually become one legal entity.

241

Minority Interest

There is one other aspect of the purchase method that warrants our attention. If a parent company purchases less than 100 percent of the subsidiary's outstanding voting common stock, what effect if any will this have on the valuation procedures brought about by the presence of an excess of purchase price over book value acquired? Let us return to the Big Co.-Small Co. example. Assume that Big. Co. had paid $72,800 for 80 percent of Small Co.'s outstanding shares. This means that it acquired an 80 percent equity in Small Co.'s owners' equity or ($81,000 × 80% =) $64,800. Assume further, that examination of Small Co.'s assets indicates that land, whose book value of $12,000 has a current value of $50,000.

Upon preparing consolidated financial statements, the intercompany investment is eliminated and only an ($72,800 − 64,800 =) $8,000 revaluation is recognized because the consolidated entity records *its* land solely on the basis of *its* cost, the different presumed value of $50,000 notwithstanding. There is, however, another point of view which states that to recognize only the $8,000 revaluation is improper accounting even though that amount does reflect the effective equity of Big Co.'s stockholders in Small Co.'s land. But it simultaneously excludes the equity of Small Co.'s minority stockholders who are also equityholders to be reckoned with by the consolidated unit. If $8,000 is the equity of 80 percent of the pertinent stockholders, then ($8,000 ÷ 8 = $10,000; $10,000 × .20 =) $2,000 should be the amount of land revaluation to be recognized by the consolidated entity in which its minority stockholders have equity. In terms of formal consolidated worksheet recognition, there would be *two* entries as follows:

Common stock (30,000 × .8)	24,000	
Capital in excess of par (12,000 × .8)	9,600	
Retained earnings (39,000 × .8)	31,200	
Land	8,000	
Investment		72,800
Land	2,000	
Minority interest		2,000

Before considering the relative merits of the $2,000 revaluation, a comment is in order regarding the consolidated entity's balance sheet disclosure of a subsidiary's minority interest. Because a subsidiary is a legal entity, the equity of all its stockholders must be accounted for. By convention, the equity of the subsidiary's minority stockholders in its owners' equity is reflected as one composite amount on the equities side of the consolidated balance sheet. This summary amount represents the interest of the minority stockholders in the consolidated assets, and in theory should be identical with the amount of their interest in the subsidiary's assets.

Returning to the matter at hand, the issue is whether the land should reflect the equity of both the majority (Big Co.) and the minority (Small Co.) shareholders, or only that of the majority stockholders. Of course, if both were to be included, we would already have an example of a difference between the minority stockholders' equity that is reflected in the consolidated balance sheet and that which appears in the subsidiary's own balance sheet. But this observation alone should not be the criterion with which to examine the point of view's relative merits.

In fact, the theoretical issue is much more fundamental: whose financial statements are consolidated statements? Accounting theory has traditionally embraced a proprietary approach, namely, the assumption that there is a mutuality of interests between the firm and its stockholders. An alternative view has been in the direction of the pure-entity approach—one which reflects a belief that no one external group has any more attachment to or kinship with the entity than does any other external party. This distinction is relevant to the consolidated entity situation at hand.

A strict proprietary position would suggest that consolidated statements are prepared to reflect the interests and ownership perspective of the parent company's stockholders. Any other equityholder is perceived to be an external party whose interests in the consolidated entity are, from an accounting viewpoint, subservient to those of the parent's shareholders. The subsidiary's minority stockholders, not being part of the ownership group whose proprietary interests dominate, therefore do not warrant any special recognition of their "interest" in the revalued portion of subsidiary assets.

Advocates of a pure-entity orientation would maintain that the function of a consolidated presentation is not to depict the interests of parent company stockholders in a manner which effectively discriminates against any other equityholder. Rather, consolidation should employ methods which measure the interests of all equityholding parties in a comparable manner. Accordingly, if the consummation of a business combination through a parent company's purchase of a controlling interest warrants application of the purchase method of accounting and revaluation of assets, the interests in such revaluation of all benefitting stockholders—majority and minority—should be recognized. The fact that only the parent's stockholders are directly involved in the combination transaction should not result in only their interests being recognized. Since an independent transaction defines a new basis of accountability, to reflect the "majority" portion of an asset on a current cost basis and its "minority" portion on a historical cost basis not only discriminates among equityholders but also results in inconsistent asset valuation.

243

Parent-Subsidiary—Pooling of Interests

Recall that the business decision to operate the combining companies as one or two legal entities is made irrespective whether accounting measurement is effected by applying the purchase method or the pooling of interests method. We shall now consider the application of the pooling of interests method to business combinations effected through the creation of a parent-subsidiary relationship.

In the discussion of the pooling of interests method in Chapter 9, it was pointed out that one of its major characteristics was that the combined enterprise reflects all of its assets and liabilities, and hence its owners' equity, at the constituent companies' recorded book values. This means if a parent-subsidiary relationship is created, the parent records its investment at an amount equal to its share of the subsidiary's recorded owners' equity acquired. This is the case even if the current values of the subsidiary's assets and liabilities differ from their recorded book values. And this holds true even if the current value of the newly issued parent company shares given to the subsidiary company shareholders exceeds the book value of the assets and liabilities received in exchange.

When the parent records its investment in the subsidiary at an amount equal to the acquired book value, it is likely this amount will differ from the par (or stated) value of the parent company shares being issued. Typically, the investment amount exceeds the aggregate par value; any excess is reflected as Capital in Excess of Par on the parent's balance sheet.

Let us return to the Big. Co.-Small Co. example which first appeared in Chapter 9. The five case situations to be illustrated reflect different amounts of consideration given by Big Co. to Small Co. in exchange for all its shares. The par value of a Big Co. share is $100 and its market value is $300. The total market value of the shares issued is equal to the cash surrendered in this chapter's earlier example relating to the purchase method of accounting. The number of Big Co. shares tendered is 300, 330, 540, 870 and 240—in exchange for Small Co. shares having an aggregate par value of $30,000. The two companies' pre-combination balance sheets are as follows:

Pre-combination Balance Sheets
(thousands of dollars)

	Big Co.	Small Co.
Cash	$300	$ 0
Other assets	200	140
Total assets	**$500**	**$140**

Pre-combination Balance Sheets (*continued*)
(thousands of dollars)

	Big Co.	Small Co.
Liabilities	$310	$ 59
Common stock	100	30
Capital in excess of par	2	12
Paid-in capital	102	42
Retained earnings	88	39
Total owners' equity	190	81
Total equities	**$500**	**$140**

Had the combined companies operated as one entity, the accounting recognition and resulting balance sheet for each of the five situations, as set forth in Chapter 9, appear below:

	In Thousands of Dollars				
	300 Shares	330 Shares	540 Shares	870 Shares	240 Shares
Acquisition entry					
Other assets	140	140	140	140	140
Liabilities	59	59	59	59	59
Common stock	30	33	54	87	24
Capital in excess of par	12	9	2	2	18
Retained earnings	39	39	29	4	39
Resulting balance sheet					
Cash	300	300	300	300	300
Other assets	340	340	340	340	340
Total	**640**	**640**	**640**	**640**	**640**
Liabilities	369	369	369	369	369
Common stock	130	133	154	187	124
Capital in excess of par	14	11			20
Retained earnings	127	127	117	84	127
Total	**640**	**640**	**640**	**640**	**640**

If a parent-subsidiary relationship had been created, the investment would be reflected at an amount equal to the subsidiary's book value acquired. The accounting entry which the parent would make appears below for each of the five cases.

In Thousands of Dollars

	300 Shares	330 Shares	540 Shares	870 Shares	240 Shares
Investment	81	81	81	81	81
Retained earnings				4	
Capital stock	30	33	54	87	24
Capital in excess of par	51	48	27	2	57

In all the cases other than the one in which 870 shares are issued, there is an excess of book value acquired over the aggregate par value of Big Co. shares issued; this excess is reflected in Big Co.'s Capital in Excess of Par account.

However, when 870 shares are issued, the acquired ($81,000) owners' equity is *less* than the ($87,000) aggregate par value of the newly issued Big Co. shares by ($87,000 − 81,000 =) $6,000. Therefore, the Big Co. reduces its Capital in Excess of Par to the extent possible, which in this case is limited to its existing $2,000 balance. The remaining ($6,000 − 2,000 =) $4,000 is subtracted from Big Co.'s retained earnings.

The resulting Big Co. balance sheet for each of the five case situations appears below:

In Thousands of Dollars

	300 Shares	330 Shares	540 Shares	870 Shares	240 Shares
Cash	300	300	300	300	300
Investment	81	81	81	81	81
Other assets	200	200	200	200	200
Total	**581**	**581**	**581**	**581**	**581**
Liabilities	310	310	310	310	310
Common stock	130	133	154	187	124
Capital in excess of par	53	50	29		59
Retained earnings	88	88	88	84	88
Owners' equity	271	271	271	271	271
Total	**581**	**581**	**581**	**581**	**581**

Note that the total assets, total liabilities, and total owners' equity are the same in all five cases. The only difference among them lies in the amounts comprising the identical owners' equity totals.

Elimination of Intercompany Investment

The need to eliminate the intercompany investment—the parent's investment in its subsidiary's outstanding voting common stock—is as necessary when the pooling of interests method applies as when the purchase method is in effect. Recall that in the earlier discussion of the investment elimination in context of the purchase method of accounting, it was pointed out this particular elimination serves three purposes: it eliminates the parent's investment balance, it eliminates the parent's equity in the subsidiary's owners' equity accounts, and, when cost differs from book value acquired, it recognizes explicitly the revaluation of particular subsidiary assets and liabilities.

There are, however, two distinct differences to be aware of when the pooling of interests method is used. The first difference relates to allocating an excess of cost over book value acquired. When the purchase method is used, the investment amount contains such an excess. In a pooling of interests, however, the investment amount would not contain an excess, because a new cost basis does not emerge when the pooling of interests method is in effect.

The second difference relates to the need to eliminate the parent's equity in the specific amounts comprising the subsidiary's owners' equity. When the purchase method applies, the parent's equity in each of these accounts is eliminated, even, or especially, its equity in the subsidiary's combination date retained earnings. This aspect is particularly important because it reflects one of the key characteristics of the purchase method, namely, that the acquiring company cannot increase its retained earnings as a result of a business combination. Hence, to assure that the retained earnings reflected on the parent's unconsolidated balance sheet appears intact in the consolidated balance sheet, all its equity in the subsidiary's combination-date retained earnings is eliminated.

One of the features of the pooling of interests method, however, is that the surviving company's retained earnings can be as large as the sum of the constituent companies' retained earnings. Therefore, when eliminating a parent's investment that had been recorded as a pooling of interests, its equity in the subsidiary's combination-date retained earnings is not generally eliminated. There are, however, some cases in which a portion or all of the subsidiary's retained earnings is eliminated. These are the same situations identified and examined in Chapter 9's consideration of the pooling of interests method, namely, when the aggregate par value of the shares issued by the combinor exceeds the combinee's Paid-in Capital.

We shall now identify both the nature of the investment elimination for our five case situations and the resulting consolidated balance sheet for each. Although the cases' investment eliminations are examined individually, observe at this point the resulting balance sheets are identical to those which would have occurred had Big Co. and Small Co. operated as one legal entity.

When 300 shares are issued by Big Co., their aggregate par value of (300 @ \$100 =) \$30,000 is equal to that of Small Co.'s tendered shares. There-

	In Thousands of Dollars				
	300 Shares	330 Shares	540 Shares	870 Shares	240 Shares
Investment elimination					
Common stock	30	30	30	30	30
Capital in excess of par	51	51	41	12	51
Retained earnings			10	39	
Investment	81	81	81	81	81
Resulting consolidated balance sheet					
Cash	300	300	300	300	300
Other assets	340	340	340	340	340
Total	**640**	**640**	**640**	**640**	**640**
Liabilities	369	369	369	369	369
Common stock	130	133	154	187	124
Capital in excess of par	14	11			20
Consolidated retained earnings	127	127	117	84	127
Owners' equity	271	271	271	271	271
Total	**640**	**640**	**640**	**640**	**640**

fore, the elimination negates Small Co.'s par amount ($30,000) and the ($51,000) Capital in Excess of Par which Big Co. had recognized at the time of the combination for a total of $81,000—the same amount which is eliminated from Big Co.'s investment balance.

The issuance of 330 shares results in the aggregate par value of Big Co.'s shares ($33,000) exceeding that of Small Co. ($30,000) by $3,000. In order to yield a consolidated balance sheet whose Capital in Excess of Par is lower by the same $3,000 that its Common Stock exceeds the sum of the constituents' pre-combination aggregate par values, we eliminate not only the $48,000 Capital in Excess of Par which Big Co. recognized to record the combination, but also $3,000 of pre-combination Capital in Excess of Par or a total of $51,000.

In the case of 540 shares being issued, their aggregate par value ($54,000) exceeds that of Small Co.'s ($30,000) by $24,000. To compensate for the presence of this additional amount in the consolidated Common Stock par balance, we eliminate not only Big Co.'s $27,000 Capital in Excess of Par related to the combination, but also, if available, $24,000 of pre-combination Capital in Excess of Par. However, Big Co.'s and Small Co.'s pre-combination Capital in Excess of Par total of only ($2,000 + $12,000 =) $14,000 is still ($24,000 − 14,000 =) $10,000 less than needed. Therefore, $10,000 of pre-combination retained earnings is also eliminated with the result the consolidated retained earnings of $117,000 is less than the sum of the constituent companies' pre-combination retained earnings of ($88,000 of Big Co. and $39,000 of Small Co. =) $127,000 by $10,000.

If 870 shares had been issued, Big Co.'s new shares' aggregate par value ($87,000) exceeds that of Small Co.'s surrendered shares ($30,000) by $57,000. Observe that $6,000 of this $57,000 differential was already accounted for by Big Co. when, in the process of recording its investment in Small Co., it reduced its Capital in Excess of Par (by $2,000) and Retained Earnings (by $4,000 for a total of $6,000). Therefore, Capital in Excess of Par, which had a combined amount of ($12,000 + $2,000 =) $14,000 before the combination, has only ($10,000 + 2,000 =) $12,000 available to absorb the [$57,000 − ($4,000 + 2,000 =) 6,000 =] $51,000 amount.

As a result, an additional ($51,000 − 12,000 =) $39,000 of pre-combination retained earnings is eliminated together with the $12,000 elimination of Capital in Excess of Par. The $84,000 consolidated retained earnings which appears on the consolidated balance sheet is therefore less than the sum of the constituents' pre-combination retained earnings of $127,000 by $43,000. This can be seen as being all of the Small Co.'s $39,000 and $4,000 of Big Co.'s pre-combination retained earnings not carrying over to the surviving entity.

When Big Co. issues 240 shares, their ($24,000) aggregate par value is *less* than that of Small Co.'s ($30,000) tendered shares by $6,000. Although this $6,000 does not appear as part of the Big Co.'s Common Stock, it is still included in the paid-in capital segment of owners' equity. To assure that consolidated Capital in Excess of Par exceeds the sum of the constituents' ($2,000 + $12,000 =) $14,000 by $6,000, we eliminate only $51,000 of the $57,000 Capital in Excess of Par that Big Co. recognized when its investment was recorded. And the resulting balance sheet does indeed disclose Capital in Excess of Par of ($14,000 + 6,000 =) $20,000.

Our examination of the application of the pooling of interests method to parent-subsidiary relationships has been limited to three facets: the basis for recording the investment, the non-presence of an excess of cost over book value, and determination of the post-combination parent company's owners' equity. Another aspect which differs from the purchase method of accounting relates to the fact that a consolidated income statement includes the pre-combination earnings of the subsidiary. In other words, the "retroactive" characteristic discussed in Chapter 9 applies whether the combining companies operate as one or as two legal entities. It might also be noted it is possible to have a minority interest in the subsidiary's owners' equity even when the pooling of interests method is used; but such interest cannot exceed 10 percent without jeopardizing the parent's ability to use the method in the first place.

This marks the end of our discussion of the application of the pooling of interests method to a business combination when the constituent companies continue to operate as separate legal entities. We shall now examine several other topics relating to the equity method, parent-subsidiary relationships, and consolidated financial statements—whose accounting treatment and financial statement disclosure aspects are similar under both the purchase and the pooling of interests methods.

Minority Interest—General Considerations

Minority shareholders holding a subsidiary's voting common stock are a class of equityholders whose interest is disclosed when preparing consolidated financial statements. Since these stockholders have equity in the subsidiary's assets, once the subsidiary's assets are included among the consolidated assets, their interest is included in the consolidated balance sheet as well.

Whereas stockholders' equity is normally set forth in terms of a "capital stock, capital in excess of par value, and retained earnings" format, the equity interest of minority shareholders in consolidated assets is by convention summarized in one self-contained number. This dollar amount in turn is included as one of the (right side) equities in consolidated assets. But given the classical liabilities and stockholders' equity categorization of equities, the question arises where the minority stockholders' interest should appear. Again, by convention, the minority interest invariably appears in the gray area between consolidated liabilities and consolidated owners' equity.

Recall our earlier discussion with respect to recognizing a minority interest in the revaluation of assets which can occur when the purchase method of accounting is used and there is a difference between the purchase price paid by a parent and the book value of the acquired owners' equity. As was pointed out, the two critical points of view regarding the presence of minority shareholders reflect different perceptions of the relationship between the accounting entity and external parties; here too that same distinction must be considered.

The use of one summary amount and its exclusion from consolidated stockholders' equity reflects a proprietary perception of the accounting entity. Given the supremacy of the parent company stockholders' proprietary interest—which underlies the very preparation of consolidated financial statements—the equity interests of other parties, who are by definition external parties, are not a part of consolidated owners' equity and therefore do not warrant more than one-line summary disclosure. On the other hand, advocates of a pure entity orientation would maintain that the interests of all shareholders deserve like treatment so the minority interest in consolidated assets will be integrated with that of majority stockholders and included in consolidated owners' equity. An illustration of the disclosure differences appears below:

	Proprietary View		Pure Entity View
Liabilities		$ 30,000	$ 30,000
Minority interest		10,000	
Owners' equity			
Common stock	$20,000		$20,000
Capital in excess of par	10,000		10,000
Consolidated retained earnings	30,000		30,000
Majority interest			60,000
Minority interest			10,000
Consolidated owners' equity		$ 60,000	$ 70,000
		$100,000	$100,000

In the consolidated earnings statement, all the revenue and expense amounts are presented on a consolidated basis. This means the amounts appearing in the parent's and subsidiary's income statements are added together, with the exception of eliminated intercompany transactions such as sales and interest payments. The conventional—proprietary—approach refers to the resulting amount as combined income from which the minority interest in subsidiary earnings is subtracted to derive consolidated net income. The pure entity point of view would refer to the combined income as consolidated net income in which there are two interests—of the majority and minority stockholders.

In the context of our discussion of the minority interest, note that it is possible that minority shareholders' equity interest in a subsidiary can exceed that of the parent company's majority interest. Consider a case in which Company A has a 70 percent interest in Company B, and Company B has a 60 percent interest in Company C. Even though Company A has only a (70% × 60% =) 42 percent interest in Company C, by virtue of its controlling interest in Company B, Company A can exercise Company B's controlling interest in Company C. Company C is therefore a subsidiary and can be included in Company A's consolidated financial statements. But the minority interest in Company C is (100% − 42% =) 58 percent, which is the sum of Company C's minority's (100% − 60% =) 40 percent and Company B's minority's (100% − 70% = 30%; 30% × 60% =) 18 percent interests.

Unrealized Intercompany Inventory Profits

In our earlier discussion of the equity method and the manner in which an investor recognizes its share of an investee's income, the question of intercompany sales of merchandise was considered. It was pointed out if such goods had not been resold to a third party by the end of the fiscal period, any gross profit recognized by the seller must be eliminated because it was not yet realized by the consolidated entity. In the case of an upstream sale, the investor also eliminated the gross profit from its inventory asset account, and in the case of a downstream sale, the investor reflects a "deferred profit" credit in its balance sheet. In either case, the investor eliminates only that portion of the unrealized profit which corresponds to its interest in the investee's voting common stock, whether that interest is a controlling interest or only a significant interest.

When consolidated financial statements are prepared, however, the conventional practice is to eliminate the entire unrealized profit. In the case of a downstream sale, this is understandable since the parent by definition has 100 percent equity in the unrealized profit appearing in its earnings statement. But an upstream sale is different because minority shareholders have an equity interest in the profit contained in the subsidiary's earnings statement which from their point of view *is* realized because it was sold to another legal entity. The propriety of full elimination can therefore be questioned. To facilitate understanding, an example is presented as follows:

Parent Co. operating income	$100,000
Subsidiary Co. net income	$ 50,000
Intercompany profit—upstream sale	$ 10,000
Minority interest	30%

When the parent company applies the equity method, its resulting (unconsolidated) net income is determined as follows:

Parent's operating income		$100,000
Subsidiary's net income	50,000	
Parent's interest	× 70%	
	35,000	
Less intercompany profit ($10,000 × 70% =)	−7,000	28,000
		$128,000

When contemplating the same data for purposes of calculating consolidated net income, the identical result will occur. However, there is a noteworthy difference. The calculation can be effected two different ways both yielding the same ($128,000) amount that resulted on an unconsolidated basis. But, depending on whether there is full or partial elimination of the unrealized intercompany inventory profit, the amount of the minority interest in subsidiary earnings to be reflected in the consolidated income statement differs.

		100% Elimination		Partial (i.e., 70%) Elimination
Parent's operating income		$100,000		$100,000
Subsidiary's net income		50,000		50,000
Total		$150,000		$150,000
Less:				
Intercompany profit:				
	$10,000			
($10,000 × 70% =)			$ 7,000	
Minority interest:				
($50,000 − 10,000 = $40,000;				
$40,000 × 30%)	12,000			
($50,000 × 30%)			$15,000	
Total		$ 22,000		$ 22,000
Consolidated net income		**$128,000**		**$128,000**

Under partial elimination, the minority interest is $15,000, and under full elimination, it is $12,000. The ($15,000 − 12,000 =) $3,000, representing 30 percent of the $10,000 unrealized intercompany profit, also manifests itself in the asset section of the consolidated balance sheet. In other words, when the entire $10,000 is eliminated, it causes both the inventory asset and the minority interest on the equities side to be $3,000 less than if only 70 percent of the profit had been eliminated from the asset account. Understanding this phenomenon facilitates appreciating why the full elimination approach prevails in practice, as is explained below.

Consider again the distinction made regarding the proprietary and pure entity approaches to the relationship between an accounting entity and external parties. The partial elimination method of eliminating unrealized intercompany profits can be seen as reflecting a proprietary orientation. It states in effect that only the interest in the unrealized profit of the predominant parent company stockholders needs to be eliminated. The interests of the external minority shareholders need not be eliminated because they, as stockholders of a company which realized profit in a transaction with another entity, do have "legal" equity in such profit.

Advocates of a pure entity approach on the other hand would maintain that, given the existence of the consolidated enterprise as the pertinent focal point, all its stockholders should have their respective interests accounted for on a like basis. Thus, all the profit which from the vantage point of the consolidated unit is unrealized must be eliminated proportionately against the equities of both the majority and minority groups. And this would be so even if the minority stockholders' equity in subsidiary income depicted in the consolidated income statement does not correspond to their "legal" equity.

In the earlier discussion regarding the revaluation of subsidiary's assets as well as the matter of the disclosure of a minority interest in consolidated financial statements, it was observed that accounting practice in these areas reflects a proprietary orientation. In the case at hand, however, ARB No. 51 states that "the amount of intercompany profit or loss to be eliminated . . . is not affected by the existence of a minority interest."[6] The reason is offered—that it "is consistent with the underlying assumption that consolidated statements represent the financial position and operating results of a single business enterprise"[7]—could be applied to the earlier instances as well, but it isn't.

It is possible that the reason for the exception in the case of unrealized intercompany inventory profits stems from accountants' concern for conservatism and consistency. Given the choice, in our case example, of reducing the inventory asset by the full $10,000 or by (the 70%) $7,000, conservatism suggests eliminating the entire $10,000. More important, though, is the desire to reflect the inventory asset on a consistent basis; namely, that if some of the profit is eliminated, the other part of the profit should not remain. In addition, there may be a deterrent factor at hand as well. Consider the case of end-of-period inventory purchases from a less-than-wholly-owned subsidiary at a price in excess of the subsidiary's cost basis. Although such a transaction would affect the consolidated statements only through larger balance sheet amounts of inventory asset and minority interest, a parent company could exploit the "partial elimination" method to inflate its current assets, working capital, current ratio, and so forth. Requiring the full elimination approach precludes such possible abuse from occurring.

In concluding coverage of this subject, the following additional factors warrant mentioning. The principles described apply as well to intercompany profit in beginning-of-period inventory, and elimination in one period only on a consolidated worksheet must be reeliminated in subsequent periods if the inventory had not been sold in the interim. An unrealized intercompany inventory loss is also eliminated, as would be the case of an unrealized gain or loss on an intercompany sale of a plant asset. If the asset is a depreciable asset, subsequent recognition of depreciation expense in the buyer's income statement must be modified for consolidated purposes to reflect the fact the consolidated entity's depreciable base is that of the selling affiliate.

---

[6] Ibid., paragraph no. 14.

[7] Ibid.

Interperiod Tax Allocation

When an investor has either a controlling or a significant interest in the voting common stock of another corporation, one of the characteristics of the equity method is that the investor recognizes in its income statement its share of the investee's earnings. Recalling the discussion of interperiod tax allocation in Chapter 5, we are reminded of the need to accrue income taxes in those instances when the difference between taxable income and pretax accounting income is a timing difference. Consider therefore the case of the investor's recognition of the investee's income as it is earned by the investee in light of its not being subject to income taxation until a dividend is received from the investee.

The critical factor to consider is whether or not remittance of the investee's earnings in a taxable transaction will be postponed indefinitely. Taxes need not be accrued where evidence shows that remittance will not be forthcoming. In the case of an investor having only a significant interest, taxes should be accrued. But a parent company need not recognize such taxes if there is evidence to suggest the subsidiary's earnings will not be so transferred. The topic of interperiod tax allocation as it applies to intercorporate investments is complex, and to deal with it further is beyond the scope of this book.

COST METHOD, EQUITY METHOD, AND CONSOLIDATION—AN OVERVIEW

Let us refer once again to the proprietary and pure entity approaches to the accounting entity's relationship with external parties. Upon considering the cost method of accounting for intercorporate investments, one perceives pure entity overtones. The investor does not recognize its share of the investee's income as it is earned but instead must wait until dividends are received. The investor cannot assume its interests and those of the investee are mutually beneficial. The investor's relationship to the entity is in effect comparable to that of other external parties in that no special status is enjoyed. The underlying nature of the equity method is that what is good for the investee is good for the benefitting investor. Because of this mutuality of interests, the investor need not wait until benefits are realized in the form of dividend distributions; instead, benefits accrue to the stockholder as they accrue to the investee.

"Creation" of the consolidated entity is therefore viewed as a logical extension of the equity method. Indeed, its relative advantage over the equity method in unconsolidated form is the degree of disclosure it provides. The substantive measurements required to effect full consolidation are virtually identical to those made when the equity method is applied on an unconsoli-

255

dated basis, viz., "the difference between consolidation and the equity method lies in the details reported in the financial statements. Thus, an investor's net income for the period and its stockholders' equity at the end of the period are the same whether an investment in a subsidiary is accounted for under the equity method or the subsidiary is consolidated. . . ."[8]

It is therefore evident that given the presumed superiority of a consolidated presentation, in its absence the next best thing is the equity method. The presentation of consolidated financial statements, in lieu of those of the parent and its subsidiary(ies) on an unconsolidated basis, reflects the notion of the economic unity characteristic of a single company. It has been observed, "there is a presumption that consolidated statements are more meaningful than separate statements. . . ."[9] The desirability of recognizing only the legal form of various affiliated entities is superseded by the economic substance benefit which results from a consolidated presentation.

Thus, we observe the equity method and consolidated financial statements reflect a proprietary orientation. In turn, when preparing consolidated statements, the methods with which a minority interest is disclosed and assets sometimes revalued also appear to reflect proprietary overtones. The one instance in which the proprietary approach is not evident is in the requirement there be full, rather than partial, elimination of unrealized profits, gains, and losses resulting from intercompany sales of inventory or plant assets.

And of course we do not want to lose sight of the fundamental premise underlying parent-subsidiary relationships, namely, that a business combination has been effected. It is this focal point which governs the accounting procedures used even for less-than-wholly-owned subsidiaries— consolidated *and* unconsolidated. It is also the theme underlying the applicability of the equity method to intercorporate investments when only a significant—and not a controlling—interest exists; such relationships can be viewed as quasi-business combinations.

Additional Readings

Blum, James D., and Jensen, Herbert L. "Accounting for Marketable Securities in Accordance with FASB Statement No. 12." *Management Accounting* (September 1978), pp. 33–41.

Lynch, Thomas Edward. "Accounting for Investments in Equity Securities by the Equity and Market Value Methods." *Financial Analysts Journal* (January– February 1975), pp. 62–69.

---

[8] *Accounting Principles Board Opinion No. 18,* paragraph no. 19.

[9] *Accounting Research bulletin No. 51,* paragraph no. 1.

Moonitz, Maurice. "Accounting for Investments in Debt Securities." In *Essays in Honor of William A. Paton,* edited by Stephen A. Zeff, Joel Demski, and Nicholas Dopuch. Ann Arbor, Mich.: The University of Michigan Graduate School of Business Administration Division of Research, 1979, pp. 57–72.

Moonitz, Maurice. *The Entity Theory of Consolidated Statements.* Brooklyn, N.Y.: The Foundation Press, 1951.

Perry, Kenneth W. "Intercompany Profits and ARB 51." *The Accounting Review* (July 1963), pp. 626–28.

Petri, Enrico. "Income Reporting and APB Opinion No. 18." *Management Accounting* (December 1974), pp. 49–52.

Petri, Enrico. "Sales to Controlled Corporations." *Management Accounting* (August 1973), pp. 42–44.

Storey, Reed K., and Moonitz, Maurice. *Market Value Methods for Intercorporate Investments in Stock.* New York: American Institute of Certified Public Accountants, 1976.

Walker, R. G. "International Accounting Compromises: The Case of Consolidation Accounting." *Abacus* (December 1978), pp. 97–111.

11

The Funds Flow Dimension of Accounting

$\mathbf{A}$ccounting has been defined "as the process of identifying, measuring and communicating economic information to permit informed judgments and decisions by users of the information."[1] Accountants identify two types of economic information worthy of measurement and communication. The first type of information is that which relates to financial position as of a particular point in time. *Financial position* is measured by considering the cost of the entity's economic resources and the amount of its obligations to creditors with the result the remaining amount becomes a measure of its owners' equity. Information about financial position is communicated through publication of a balance sheet.

The second type of information relates to activity during a particular time interval, or more specifically, information about an entity's performance over a period of time. *Performance* has traditionally been measured in terms of earnings, which involves accrual accounting, revenue realization criteria, and the matching principle. The results of this measurement process are communicated through an earnings statement which sets forth the entity's various revenues and expenses. The excess of revenues over expenses is a measure of earnings; it has been suggested that revenue is a measure of accomplishment, and expense a measure of effort.[2] To the extent accom-

---

[1] Committee to Prepare a Statement of Basic Accounting Theory, *A Statement of Basic Accounting Theory* (Sarasota, Fla.: American Accounting Association, 1966), p. 1.

[2] W. A. Paton and A. C. Littleton, *An Introduction to Corporate Accounting Standards* (Sarasota, Fla.: American Accounting Association, 1940), p. 15.

plishment exceeds effort, there is success (i.e., income); and if effort exceeds accomplishment, there is failure (i.e., loss).

Analysis of financial statements had traditionally emphasized the balance sheet. This position statement offered an insight into the entity's present measurable resources and its prospective obligations. As such, it provided information regarding capital structure, solvency, and relationships among its various components. The earnings statement played a relatively second- ary role such that one could observe the income statement's role was to serve as a link between two balance sheets.

With the emphasis in the 1960s on performance, earnings-per-share, price-earnings multiples, glamour stocks, and go-go mutual funds, there was a shift in orientation from balance sheet to earnings statement analysis. Concern ranged from the income statement's *bottom line* all the way to de- tailed *quality of earnings* assessments. The changed orientation could be described as one in which earnings statements were paramount, and balance sheets were merely a link between successive periods' income state- ments.

As the American economy entered a recessionary period during the late 1960s, a phenomenon which continued into the 1970s as well, a number of major corporations found themselves with liquidity crises. Much publicity was afforded such companies' situations. One of the many questions asked centered around the adequacy of such companies' financial statements. Why had their balance sheets and income statements not given advance indica- tion of the impending crises? Furthermore, if the nature of these financial statements was such that information of this sort would not generally surface in financial statements, what changes in financial statement disclosure might overcome this deficiency?

The income statement, in fact, has a rather limited scope as far as even *performance* is concerned. It purports only to explain the effect of operations on but one balance sheet account—the retained earnings account. The in- come statement offers no insight into how or why any of the other balance sheet amounts changed during the year. The reason for this is the income statement uses measurement rules which have no direct association with cash receipts and disbursements. Indeed, a company can report earnings but have no cash on hand, or a firm can add no earnings in a period but have a considerable amount of cash in its bank account.

Cash can be obtained through sources other than operations, most nota- bly by borrowing, by selling shares of stock or by selling non-cash assets. Similarly, a company may use cash to pay obligations not directly associated with transactions affecting current operations. A company may expend cash to pay a cash dividend, buy treasury stock, reduce debt, or purchase capital assets. Transactions such as these are certainly accounted for, and their

259

resulting effect on the entity's asset, liability, and owners' equity accounts does appear implicitly in the firm's balance sheet.

The magnitude of these inflows and outflows of funds is not reflected explicitly in the one traditional performance financial statement—the earnings statement. This points out the somewhat limited scope of the income statement.

Official Pronouncements

The Accounting Principles Board (APB) had been aware of the need to introduce an additional financial statement which would offer some of the insights not already provided by balance sheets and income statements. It commissioned the preparation of research study which was subsequently published,[3] and in a 1963 pronouncement it stated that an appropriate financial statement "should be presented as supplementary information in financial reports (but) the inclusion of such information is not mandatory."[4]

Relatively few companies accepted the APB recommendation, and of those companies which did prepare the new statement, only in some instances was the statement included in the scope of the independent CPA's audit report. The Securities and Exchange Commission (SEC) subsequently introduced a rule that required inclusion of a funds statement when submitting a registration statement to the Commission, and in 1970 it further required its inclusion in the annual Form 10–K filing.[5]

In 1971, the APB, in its Opinion No. 19, established a requirement that a statement of changes in financial position be prepared as a basic financial statement.[6] What this means relative to our earlier definition of accounting is that accountants thus identified a second dimension of performance which warrants communication. Measurement is effected by determining the nature and amounts of an entity's various sources and uses of funds, and communication occurs through the preparation of an autonomous financial statement.

The term *funds* denotes either cash or some other form of liquidity which might be measured. To lay persons, *funds* is a term used interchangeably with *cash;* in corporate finance, *funds* is occasionally used to denote all an enterprise's financial resources. Therefore, *funds* is a term which should be used only when there is common understanding of its particular context. The accountant, seeking to prepare a statement of changes in financial position,

---

[3] Perry Mason, *"Cash Flows" Analysis and the Funds Statement* (New York: American Institute of Certified Public Accountants, 1961).

[4] *Accounting Principles Board Opinion No. 3,* paragraph no. 8.

[5] *SEC Accounting Series Release No. 117;* October 14, 1970.

[6] *Accounting Principles Board Opinion No. 19,* paragraph no. 7.

must first inquire how the company wishes to define *funds*. Although cash, the universal medium of exchange, might appear to be the focal point to adopt, most companies use the working capital approach for purposes of preparing the statement of changes in financial position.

Current Assets and Current Liabilities

Accountants group assets and liabilities into homogeneous categories. Assets are typically placed into current, long-lived, and long-term investment classes. The *current asset* category consists of those assets management reasonably expects to convert into cash within one year or the operating cycle, whichever is longer. An operating cycle is the time interval encompassing the initial disbursement of cash to acquire inventory, the processing and sale of inventory, and the subsequent collection of cash. Current assets include cash, receivables, marketable securities, inventories and prepaid expenses.

Accounts receivable and notes receivable which are collectible within the applicable time period are included as current assets net of an allowance for doubtful accounts and therefore are reflected at their net realizable value. Marketable securities include both debt and equity securities issued by other corporations or by governments. Not only must they have a ready market, but there must also be a reasonable expectation they could be converted to cash within the designated time interval. Bonds which management expects to hold until they mature several years later or stocks being accounted for with the equity method would therefore be excluded. Inventories, by definition, are current assets, and this is the reason for the special provision for an operating cycle in excess of one year. In industries such as timber, whiskey, and tobacco, the aging process exceeds one year. In order to assure that such inventories are designated *current,* the definition so provides.

Prepaid expenses are items such as rent, insurance, or advertising for which payment is made prior to the time the service is performed. Such expenditures therefore are assets because they represent economic resources having future service potential. As the service is received, that is, as their future service potential decreases, amounts are systematically transferred to the income statement and classified as expenses. That such prepayments should be categorized as current assets is questionable since they, unlike other current assets, have no future cash inflow consequences; that is, management cannot convert these prepayments into cash within a year or for that matter, at any future date. "Prepaid expenses are not current assets in the sense they will be converted into cash but in the sense, if not paid in advance, they would require the use of current assets during the operating cycle."[7] In practice, prepaid expenses tend to be immaterial in size, and in

---

[7] *Accounting Research Bulletin No. 43,* chap. 3A, paragraph no. 4.

many cases companies do not include such expenditures among their current assets at all.

Liabilities are categorized into two classes: current and noncurrent. The criterion for classification as a current liability is that the obligation can be expected to require the use of resources classified as current assets. Included in current liabilities are accounts payable, notes payable, dividends payable, accruals payable, revenue received in advance, and that portion of long-term liabilities which matures within the designated time period.

Because current assets are defined as those assets which management reasonably expects to convert to cash within a year (or operating cycle, whichever is longer) and current liabilities are those obligations which will be due within the same time frame, the excess of current assets over current liabilities represents the cushion, as it were, with which management can work—the liquid assets that are not committed to specific existing liabilities. This excess is called Working Capital.

To understand the analytic potential of working capital data, consider the following table:

| | December 31 | | Working Capital |
	19x2	19x1	Increase (decrease)
Current assets	$170	$100	$ 70
Current liabilities	80	30	(50)
Working capital	**$ 90**	**$ 70**	**$ 20**

During year 19x2, current assets grew by $70 and current liabilities increased by $50; as a result, working capital grew by ($70 − 50 =) $20. In an absolute sense, there is ($90 − 70 =) $20 more working capital at the end of 19x2 than there had been one year earlier. This could represent useful information, and given that balance sheets usually have subtotals for their various asset and liability categories such a table could be constructed on the basis of only the comparative balance sheets. However, observe that when considering the data in a relative, rather than an absolute, dimension, a somewhat different result can occur. The ratio of current assets to current liabilities as of December 31, 19x1 is ($100 ÷ 30 =) 3.3 and one year later it is ($170 ÷ 80 =) 2.1. Thus, even though the amount of working capital increased during the year from $70 to $90, or $20, the company had been *relatively* more liquid at the beginning of the year because its current assets then were more than three times as large as its current liabilities, versus only slightly more than twice as plentiful one year later. This apparent anomaly can be attributed to the fact, although current assets increased by $70 and current liabilities grew by only $50, current assets' increase was ($70 ÷ 100 =) 70 percent while that of current liabilities was ($50 ÷ 30 =) 167 percent. Not only does this reference to the relative changes suggest the importance of multi-dimensional analysis, but it also points out the need to explain *how and why* the various "current" accounts' balances changed during 19x2.

Working Capital

Recall that the basic accounting equation is

$$Assets = Equities \qquad (1)$$

and that this is conventionally expanded to

$$Assets = Liabilities + Owners' Equity. \qquad (2)$$

We can proceed even further by observing that

Current Assets + Noncurrent Assets
= Current Liabilities + Noncurrent Liabilities + Owners' Equity   (3)

Upon subtracting Noncurrent Assets and Current Liabilities from both sides of the equation, we derive

Current Assets − Current Liabilities = Noncurrent Liabilities
+ Owners' Equity − Noncurrent Assets   (4)

And since working capital is measured by subtracting current liabilities from current assets, equation (4) is restated as follows:

Working Capital = Noncurrent Liabilities
+ Owners' Equity − Noncurrent Assets   (5)

Observe that in equation (5) all of the balance sheet's current accounts are on the left side of the equation and all of its noncurrent accounts are to the right of the equal sign.

We can now proceed to discover what characteristics a particular transaction must have in order to cause a change in working capital. The first candidate is a transaction involving only current accounts such as purchasing supplies inventory on account or collecting cash on a trade receivable. Such transactions affect only the left side of equation (5) (hereafter, "the equation"), only causing shifts among particular current accounts but with no net effect on working capital as such. Therefore, a transaction involving only current accounts neither provides nor uses working capital.

The second candidate is a transaction affecting only noncurrent accounts, that is, only accounts appearing on the right side of the equation. An example of such a transaction would be purchasing land with a long-term mortgage loan, or bonds being converted into stock. Only particular account balances on the right side of the equation are affected, and there is no effect on either the right side total or the left side total. Therefore, a transaction involving only noncurrent accounts has no net effect on working capital. There will be a discussion later regarding the matter of disclosing such transactions despite their having no net effect.

The third and final candidate is the transaction which involves at least one current account *and* at least one noncurrent account. Given that there are three different kinds of noncurrent accounts on the right side of the equation, each of which can either increase or decrease as a result of a transaction involving it and a current account, there are six different transactions which involve at least one current *and* one noncurrent account, as depicted below.

Change in a Noncurrent Account	Sample Transaction	Effect on Working Capital
1. Increase noncurrent liabilities	Issue bonds for cash	Increase
2. Increase owners' equity	Issue stock for cash	Increase
3. Decrease noncurrent assets	Sell land for cash	Increase
4. Decrease noncurrent liabilities	Retire bonds for cash	Decrease
5. Decrease owners' equity	Buy treasury stock	Decrease
6. Increase noncurrent assets	Buy land for cash	Decrease

Note that the six sample transactions do not necessarily involve *cash* as the affected current account. For instance, the *increase noncurrent liabilities* example could just as well have been "purchase inventory by issuing a promissory note due in eighteen months;" the *decrease owners' equity* example could have been "declare cash dividends;" and *increase noncurrent assets* example might have been "buy truck by issuing 90-day note." In all of these cases, the transaction consists of one current *and* one noncurrent account.

The three transactions which cause an increase in working capital to occur are viewed as *sources* of working capital; the three transactions which result in a decrease in working capital represent *uses* of working capital. The financial statement presentation in the form of a statement of changes in financial position identifies the three types of sources and the three types of uses. Sources exceed uses by an amount exactly equal to the increase in working capital. If there had been a decline in working capital during the period, this is evidenced by uses exceeding sources by the same amount.

Working Capital from Operations

As an example of an increase in owners' equity being a source of working capital, the issuance of stock for cash was cited. Consider now that profitable operations also affect an entity's owners' equity through an increase in its retained earnings. Whether the occurrence of net income *also* represents a

264

source of working capital depends on the types of asset and liability accounts that were affected. This can be explained by recalling the nature of a company's earnings.

Net income is a mathematical residual which occurs when subtracting expenses from revenues. Revenues, in turn, are a measure of an increase in assets such as cash or accounts receivable (or they reflect a decrease in liability account balances). Expenses are a measure of a decrease in assets or creation of the liability to reduce assets in the future. Hence, net income is a measure of the growth of an entity's assets net of liabilities, which, in turn, is referred to as its owners' equity.

Although net income is the valid basis for measuring the change in total assets and liabilities resulting from operations, it does not necessarily follow that it is also the appropriate basis for measuring the change in *current* assets and *current* liabilities resulting from operations. In fact, net income would serve the latter function as well if all the period's revenues represented only increases in current assets and decreases in current liabilities, *and also* if all of the period's expenses represented only decreases in current assets and increases in current liabilities.

In the typical earnings statement, however, there are revenue and expense amounts which do *not* represent a change in a current account. As a result, the earnings of the period are not also the measure of working capital provided by operations. In fact, there are twelve types of transactions included in the determination of net income which have no effect on working capital.

This does not detract from an entity's obligation to measure and communicate the extent to which its operations were either a source or a use of working capital during each fiscal period. What it does require is there be recognition of only those income statement components which affect working capital in order to identify the working capital impact. In practice, the reported net income is used as a starting point; the accountant adds to it or subtracts from it those amounts which will convert the reported earnings into the amount of working capital provided by, or used by, operations. The twelve items which require adjustment of the net income are identified below.

> (1)   Depreciation expense entails increasing the pertinent depreciable asset's *allowance for depreciation* contra-account, an accounting entry having no impact on current accounts; in other words, there is no current outflow of working capital although reported net income is reduced. The related working capital effect was recognized as a use of working capital when the original expenditure's resulting current liability was created. Therefore, to neutralize the presence of depreciation expense in net earnings, the depreciation is added back to reported income; a similar adjustment is necessary for depletion expense as well.

265

(2) Amortization of intangible assets involves reducing the carrying value of the related noncurrent asset. The reasoning which leads to an adjustment therefore is identical to that of depreciation expense; the amortization expense is added back to net income.

(3) Loss from write-down, retirement or abandonment of a noncurrent asset has no effect on working capital; therefore, the amount of the loss is reinstated in earnings.

(4) Deferred compensation, pension and retirement accruals which create long-term liabilities do not affect current accounts. Therefore, any related charges to income are added back to calculate the working capital equivalent.

(5) Deferred income taxes included in income tax expense but which are not currently payable because of timing differences between financial and tax accounting create a deferred balance. This is typically not classified as a current item, and because the deferred portion of the expense has no working capital impact it is added back to reported income.

(6) Deferred investment tax credits are amounts whose favorable effect is reflected in earnings statements in periods other than those in which there was a reduction in taxes paid. Although properly included for income measurement, there is no working capital effect. To neutralize its favorable effect on earnings, the amount of prior period credit thus deferred is subtracted from reported income to derive working capital.

(7) Compensating employees by distributing shares of newly issued shares or treasury stock is not a use of working capital. Although compensation in this form is properly recognized as an expense, it must be reinstated in reported earnings to compute working capital generated by operations. The issuance of new shares increases a noncurrent owners' equity account(s), and reissued treasury shares reduce an account whose working capital effect was recognized as a use of working capital when the shares were purchased.

(8) Equity in the income or loss of an investee in which there is a controlling or significant interest not accompanied by a cash dividend requires adjustment because there was an effect only on the investor's *noncurrent* investment asset account with no working capital impact whatever. To the extent cash dividends were received or accrued, no adjustment is necessary. The accountant therefore subtracts from reported income the investor's equity in *undistributed* earnings (and adds its equity in an investee's reported loss). For example, if Bird, Inc. includes in earnings its $20,000 equity in its unconsolidated subsidiary's, Gail Co.'s, earnings and receives a $6,000 dividend, only ($20,000 − 6,000 =) $14,000, equal to the undistributed profit which is the net increase in the investment asset's carrying value, must be adjusted.

(9) A gain or loss on early extinguishment of debt must be removed from net income. It is already included implicitly in the statement of changes in financial position because the amount expended to extinguish debt is included

as a use of working capital, and this amount already reflects the gain or loss. For example, if a bond having a book value of $50,000 is extinguished early through an expenditure of $48,000, it is the latter amount which appears as a use of working capital. Since the ($50,000 − 48,000 =) $2,000 gain is already included by virtue of the use being recorded as $48,000 and not $50,000, it is subtracted out to neutralize its presence in reported earnings.

(10) Amortization of the discount or premium on *issued* debt securities is reflected as an element of interest expense in measuring income. The nature of this recognition entails reducing the premium or discount account which is a component of noncurrent liabilities; hence, it has no effect on working capital. Adjustment is also required for amortization of an imputed discount relating to payables having a life exceeding one year. In the case of a discount, the amortized amount is added to net income; for an issuance premium, the amortization is subtracted from reported earnings.

(11) Amortization of discount or premium on *purchased* debt securities being held until maturity is included in interest revenue when calculating earnings. Since it involves adjusting the noncurrent investment asset account, no current accounts are affected. Similarly, adjustment is necessary for amortization through interest revenue of an imputed discount on receivables with a life exceeding one year. The amount of discount amortization is subtracted from reported earnings, and the amount of amortized premium is added to net income to derive working capital provided by operations.

(12) Gains and losses on the disposition of noncurrent assets are included in the determination of net income. In the case of a gain, the proceeds exceed the book value of the sold asset, and is the amount of the current assets received that represents a source of working capital. Assume that land with a book value of $50,000 is sold for $70,000. If $70,000 appears in the statement of changes in financial position as an autonomous source of working capital, failure to remove the $20,000 gain from net income would result in double counting. Therefore, to neutralize the presence of the gain in earnings, the amount is subtracted; conversely, in the case of a loss, the amount is added back.[8]

In recent years, some companies' statements of changes in financial position have included alternative methods of dealing with this problem of double counting. One approach is to leave the gain or loss intact in earnings, and to show as an autonomous source of working capital only that portion of the proceeds which recovers book value, in our example, the $50,000. However, the situation becomes somewhat awkward when there is a loss; consider the following illustration. If land with a book value of $50,000 is

---

[8] If the disposition of a long-lived asset is effected through an exchange, that is, by obtaining an asset or assets other than cash, or by receiving a combination of current and noncurrent assets, the adjustment that would result would be based on the pertinent working capital effects.

sold for $44,000, this approach would identify $50,000 as a source of working capital concurrent with the $6,000 loss intact in earnings. To isolate book value from a gain or a loss may be desirable for measuring earnings, but when only flow of funds is being depicted, one can only speculate as to what purpose is being served.

Yet another approach sometimes used in practice is to include the entire proceeds in the determination of working capital provided by operations. This means that the reported gain or loss amount is converted into one which reflects the recovery of book value as well. This is effected by adding the amount of book value to the gain or loss. This too might be questioned inasmuch as the sale of a long-lived asset is not one of the typical transactions which comprise operations, despite the inclusion of such gains and losses when determining income. Moreover, it can be argued that sales of capital assets are significant enough to warrant disclosure as an autonomous source of working capital, and should not be relegated to the status of a mere adjustment of reported earnings.

To summarize, operations are usually a source of working capital.[9] The extent to which operations in fact cause working capital to increase depends not only on the size of net income, but also on whether all of the components of net income affect current asset and current liability accounts. Those revenue and expense amounts which do not fully reflect changes in working capital must be excluded from the calculation of working capital provided by operations. Although this could be done easily if the income statement were reconstructed in its entirety, the more typical case is for a company simply to add to or subtract from its reported earnings those amounts which would not have been included had *working capital provided,* not *net income,* been the calculation's objective from the outset.

An additional comment is in order with respect to the adjustment necessary to neutralize the presence of the depreciation expense component of net income. Companies often identify the depreciation add-back as the first adjustment to reported earnings, and for a manufacturing enterprise it is likely that the amount of its annual depreciation is relatively large. Readers are sometimes inclined to observe merely that depreciation appears in the statement of changes in financial position as a positive factor in arriving at working capital provided by operations. As such, it is an amount whose existence arithmetically causes the resulting working capital amount to be larger than it would have been otherwise. It is therefore concluded that depreciation is an alternative source of working capital, similar to earnings

---

[9] *Operations* would not be a source of working capital if the period's net loss were large enough to exceed the non-working capital amounts that are added back to it.

268

and the issuance of securities. This is a wrong impression, and it needs clarification.

Accounting for depreciation is a means of allocating to benefitting fiscal periods the cost of tangible capital assets in a systematic and rational manner. Under generally accepted accounting principles, depreciation accounting is a process of allocation, *not* of valuation, through which the productive effort (expense) to be matched with productive accomplishment (revenue) for fiscal periods is measured. Depreciation accounting, therefore, is concerned with the timing of the consumption of the service potential embodied in the cost of tangible capital assets; depreciation charges neither recover nor create funds. Revenue-producing activities are the sources of funds from operations: if funds-producing revenues exceed funds-reducing expenses during a fiscal period, funds are available to cover expenditures other than these expenses; if such revenues do not exceed such expenses, funds are not made available no matter how much, or how little, depreciation is charged. In other words, depreciation expense reduces reported earnings without involving a direct outflow of working capital.

Depreciation can only have an *indirect* effect on funds. First, depreciation charges affect reported income and hence may affect managerial decisions such as those regarding pricing and dividends. Second, depreciation charges affect taxable income and thus the amount of income taxes accrued in the year of deduction with the result there is an after-tax funds benefit attributable to the tax deductibility of depreciation. Third, to the extent depreciation is included as a recoverable cost in cost-plus type of contracts, a contractor can recover its original outlay expenditure.

Cash Provided by Operations

When a company uses cash as its measure of funds, the same conceptual issues discussed regarding working capital again present themselves. However, the matter is complicated by the fact that invariably every account balance appearing on the accrual-based income statement requires adjustment. The nature of a cash dimension is that the accountant seeks to derive an amount which represents the excess of cash inflow over cash outflow or vice versa. This means the analysis is restricted to only that portion of revenues and expenses which represents cash flows. The creation of a receivable or a payable, for instance, has no immediate cash consequences.

As an example, if rent expense for a year is $5,000 and the prepaid rent account balance decreased by $400 during the period, only ($5,000 − 400 =) $4,600 of cash was disbursed for rent during the year, because debits to the prepaid account evidencing cash payments were smaller than credits to the account which represent expense recognition. Similarly, if a particular period's sales were $80,000 and receivables decreased by $3,000 during the period, cash collections from customers are ($80,000 + 3,000 =) $83,000 because credits to the receivable account representing cash collections were $3,000 larger than the debits which represent charge sales.

Consider also the following data of a company which buys and sells merchandise to determine the amount of cash it paid its suppliers during Year 2.

	End of Year Balances	
	Year 1	Year 2
Merchandise inventory	$19,000	$26,300
Trade accounts payable	$ 8,200	$ 3,300
Cost of goods sold		$55,300

First observe that Cost of Goods Sold is an accrual derived account which by itself offers no insight into the amount of cash expended during Year 2. Its cash counterpart would be the amount of cash disbursed to the company's suppliers; in order to determine that amount, we must first determine the dollar amount of the year's purchases. Thus, the ($26,300 − 19,000 =) $7,300 increase in inventory relative to the given cost of goods sold indicates that purchases during Year 2 had been ($55,300 + 7,300 =) $62,600 since an increase in inventory means that the cost of goods *purchased* exceeded the cost of goods *sold*.

Now that the amount of purchases has been determined, its *cash* dimension can be computed. The ($8,200 − 3,300 =) $4,900 decrease in trade accounts payable suggests that debits to this account representing cash disbursements exceeded credits which reflect purchases. The result is that $4,900 is the amount by which cash payments exceeded purchases, and disbursements to suppliers were therefore ($62,600 + 4,900 =) $67,500.

What can be seen in these examples is that depicting an accrual-based earnings statement in terms of its cash equivalent requires adjustment of virtually every component of net income. Although some persons try to estimate cash-flow from operations by neutralizing the effect of only depreciation expense, such an approach is unacceptable since it ignores all the other elements of earnings not similarly stated in their cash dimension. Even in those instances in which the conversion from net income to its cash counterpart is calculated correctly, there is a possibility that readers of a statement of changes in financial position may impute to this cash amount some quasi-earnings characteristics. To preclude such a misleading conclusion from happening, the accountant must be very careful not to suggest that the cash result is in any way a substitute for accrual-based net income.

Approaches Used in Practice

According to *Accounting Trends and Techniques,* an annual survey of the published financial statements of 600 publicly-held corporations, approximately 93 percent of the companies in its 1977 sample use the working capital approach.[10] Some of the companies that do not define *funds* as working capital use "cash" as the measure of funds. Another approach is to define funds as the sum of cash and those marketable securities which are classified as current assets. The underlying thinking is that the very marketability of such securities makes them effectively as liquid as cash itself; indeed, such investments are often made only as a temporary use of idle cash.

The Objectives of Funds Flow Analysis

The purpose of the statement of changes in financial position is to offer an insight not otherwise available from either an earnings statement or a balance sheet. As a performance report, the income statement offers information which relates to only one aspect of financial position, namely, retained earnings. And although retained earnings is implicitly a measure of growth in the entity's assets less liabilities resulting from operations (and net of dividends), examination and evaluation of net income or even the elements comprising net income provide little, if any, information about an enterprise's sources and uses of funds.

The statement of changes in financial position, on the other hand, identifies quite explicitly the nature and amount of these various sources and uses. Indeed, it may be useful for an interested external user of a company's financial statements—stockholder, creditor, supplier, competitor, employee, and so forth—to know what sources a company has turned to historically to obtain the *funds* to meet its obligations.

Whether or not financing through the creation of additional debt is significant relative to other sources is important. On the one hand, it indicates the company historically has had access to such outlets; yet, it suggests that over-reliance on this source could result in its soon being exhausted. The extensive use of financing by issuing equity securities might indicate the borrowing option no longer exists; it also portrays a situation in which existing stockholders' proportionate interest is diluted, and/or, to retain their relative equity positions, the shareholders must invest more funds in the corporation.

Whether or not operations themselves constitute a significant source of funds is an important factor to consider. It can be argued that ultimately

[10] George Dick and Richard Rikert, *Accounting Trends & Techniques* (New York: American Institute of Certified Public Investments, 1978), p. 344.

funds from operations must sustain the enterprise. Yet, during particular intervals, operations can be expected to be a relatively inconsequential source of funds; indeed, they might even represent a use of funds. Consider a development-stage company or an established enterprise heavily engaged in research and product development, whose current operations generate small amounts of funds relative to management's expectations for the long-run. It is useful to know the extent to which operations currently affect funds, and to be made aware of the resulting need for other sources to be considered.

The manner in which a company uses funds can be revealing as well. Whether the company uses surplus funds to increase its cash dividend, reduce its debt, or expand its productive capacity can disclose a great deal about its managerial philosophy. Indeed, persons with specialized interests, such as creditors seeking to have the amount of indebtedness reduced or stockholders desirous of more cash dividend income, can assess the company's approach to these issues during pertinent prior periods—without having to reach explicit conclusions about management behavior in general.

Therefore, the types of insights that can be obtained that are not otherwise available include the amount expended to acquire new capital assets and the proceeds realized from the disposition of older fixed assets, the extent to which new long-term debt was incurred and the amounts of existing noncurrent obligations that were liquidated, the proceeds from new issuances and the cost of purchasing its own shares to be resold or retired. These kinds of insights instill a dynamic quality into the otherwise static amounts that appear in an enterprise's balance sheet.

Preparation of the Statement

To identify the various sources and uses of funds, the accountant evaluates each account appearing in a company's balance sheet whose change during the period had an effect on funds. Thus, if funds are defined as working capital, the statement of changes in financial position identifies the various sources and uses underlying increased or decreased working capital. This means the statement will disclose those changes in noncurrent accounts which simultaneously caused a change in a current account. The aggregate change in noncurrent accounts is necessarily equal to the aggregate change in the current accounts.

Accordingly, if the accountant examines each noncurrent account's change during the period and isolates its effect on current accounts, there will be a basis for determining the presence of either a source or a use of working capital. And if successful in reconciling the change in each noncurrent account with its resulting impact on a current account, the accountant will have derived a listing of all the sources and uses underlying the change in working capital.

For example, although a company's land account may have increased from $20,000 to $50,000 during the year, it does not necessarily follow the net increase of ($50,000 − 20,000 =) $30,000 occurred because cash was expended and there was a $30,000 use of working capital. Analysis by the accountant may reveal that land, having a cost basis of $5,000, was sold for cash of $7,000, and that cash of [$50,000 − ($20,000 − 5,000 =) $15,000 =] $35,000 was expended to acquire additional land. In this case, the $7,000 proceeds from the sale of land is a source of working capital, and the $35,000 a use of working capital.

Consider another illustration in which a company's noncurrent Notes Payable account balance decreased from $100,000 to $70,000 during Year 1. Examination by the accountant indicates that during Year 1 a $10,000 promissory note due in Year 4 was created to borrow cash from a bank, and a $40,000 note included in Year 1's beginning-of-year balance was due to be repaid in the middle of Year 2. The $40,000 obligation was correctly classified as a noncurrent liability at the beginning of Year 1 because its due date was to occur more than one year later. However, at the end of Year 1, there is *less* than one year until maturity, which means the $40,000 noncurrent liability must be reclassified as a current liability. The reclassification—a reduction in a noncurrent liability and an increase in a current liability—constitutes a use of working capital. Recall that when working capital is defined as the measure of funds, there need not be a cash transaction in order to effect a change in funds. Therefore, the ($100,000 − 70,000 =) $30,000 decline in noncurrent liabilities is the manifestation of two phenomena which appear in the statement of changes in financial position—a $10,000 source of working capital (inflow of cash) and the $40,000 use of working capital (increased current liability).

In summary, when working capital constitutes funds, the challenge facing the accountant is one of being able to portray in a statement of changes in financial position each change in a noncurrent account in terms of its being a source or a use of working capital or both. The internal check for this procedure is that the net change in total noncurrent accounts' balances must equal the net change in total current accounts' balances. The difference between the sources and the uses of working capital must equal the change in working capital manifested in the current asset and current liability accounts.

When a company adopts *cash* as its measure of funds, the same type of challenge faces the accountant, at least at the conceptual level. The difference that emerges at the practical level is that the change in every *non-cash* account on the balance sheet is examined in an effort to explain the change

273

in the cash account balance. This means that even current accounts, other than cash itself, are analyzed to discern the extent to which their respective end-of-period balances, being greater or less than those of the beginning of the period, individually constitute a source or a use of cash. And if a company were to depict its funds flow in a format other than working capital or cash—and discretion is permitted—the same conceptual framework prevails. This means that at the applied level the accountant examines the non-funds accounts to determine if their increases and decreases constitute sources and uses of funds.

The Total Resources Concept

When funds are defined as working capital, a source of funds or a use of funds occurs only from transactions which affect at least one current account *and* at least one noncurrent account. A transaction involving only current accounts may affect the amount contained in each account, but it has no impact on aggregate working capital. Similarly, a transaction involving only noncurrent accounts, such as the purchase of land by issuing a promissory note due in two years, has no effect on working capital, that is, there is no change in working capital as a result of the transaction. But there is one other dimension that must now be mentioned.

It is true that a transaction involving only noncurrent accounts does not affect working capital. This is borne out by the arithmetic nature of the accounting equation underlying balance sheets. However, the basic objective of the statement of changes in financial position is to offer insights into an enterprise's overall financing and investing activities.

The purchase of a plant asset by creating a mortgage payable, or the conversion by bondholders of bonds into stock, are events worthy of portrayal in the statement of changes in financial position. The issuance of a long-term debt obligation to acquire land can be viewed as being in effect two discrete financing transactions: borrowing cash by creating a noncurrent liability, and using cash to purchase land. Similarly, the conversion of debt into equity can be seen as being effectively two financing transactions: issuing shares of stock for cash, and using cash to reduce long-term debt.

Because such transactions constitute bona fide financing transactions of the variety depicted in the statement of changes in financial position had they been effected differently, they too are identified in the statement. This is an example of how economic substance prevails over legal form. Even though in form there was ostensibly a single transaction, the accountant looks to the economic substance and imputes the presence of two distinct transactions. This recognition, solely for purposes of providing optimal disclosure in the statement of changes in financial position, results in an equal amount por-

274

trayed as a source of funds and as a use of funds. They, in turn, offset one another in an arithmetic sense with no net effect on the period's increase or decrease in working capital.

In our example, if the land had cost $100,000, the statement of changes in financial position would identify the creation of the $100,000 liability as a source of funds, and the purchase of land costing $100,000 as a use of funds. And in the other case, if the converted bonds had a book value of $500,000, the statement would list the issuance of capital stock as a $500,000 source of funds and the reduction in bonds payable outstanding as a $500,000 use of funds. Note that the total resources concept applies not only to the working capital format, but to *cash* and other formats as well.

Structure of the Presentation

There are several aspects of the formal presentation of the statement of changes in financial position which warrant our attention. First, three approaches are used in practice to identify the excess of sources over uses, or of uses over sources. Using an example where sources exceed uses by $20,000, the three methods of presentation encountered in practice are as follows:

	Method 1		Method 2		Method 3	
Sources:						
Operations	$25,000		$25,000		$25,000	
Stock issues	75,000		75,000		75,000	
Total		$100,000		**$100,000**		**$100,000**
Uses:						
Retire bonds	$65,000		$65,000		$65,000	
Buy land	15,000		15,000		15,000	
Total		$ 80,000	$80,000			
Increase in working capital		**$ 20,000**	20,000		20,000	
Total				**$100,000**		**$100,000**

Method 1 isolates the increase in funds by depicting it as truly an excess. Method 2 adds the excess to the lesser sum ("uses" in our illustration) while Method 3 does not even present a subtotal of the lesser sum but instead seems to suggest some degree of homogeneity between the excess and the amounts comprising the lesser sum. Observe that if highlighting the excess is a major function of the presentation, Method 1 best achieves this purpose. If the excess per se is not to stand out and thereby possibly distract readers from

275

examining the particular sources and uses amounts, Methods 2 or 3 would probably best achieve that goal.

A second aspect of providing accounting information about sources and uses of working capital is that of disclosing the amounts by which particular current asset and current liability account balances changed during the period. The statement of changes in financial position identifies the noncurrent accounts whose changes during the period caused working capital to change. Given such information, it is also considered desirable to disclose how the aggregate change in working capital manifested itself, that is, the extent to which each of the company's current accounts was affected by transactions involving noncurrent accounts. As a result, a schedule identifying the effect on working capital of the change in each element of working capital is often presented in conjunction with the statement of changes in financial position. When the cash format is used, a special schedule is not needed to disclose the change in the single cash account. When a format other than working capital or cash is used, an appropriate supplemental schedule of this sort can be prepared; indeed it would appear to be particularly useful in such cases to convey to the reader the nature of the distinctive format being used.

Another noteworthy aspect of the formal presentation relates to the disclosure of funds provided by operations. Operations are usually a source of funds and are the first listed source. The initial amount listed in the derivation of *funds provided by operations* is Net Income before Extraordinary Items as it appears in the earnings statement. Adjustments to this amount such as for depreciation and amortization of discount or premiums are then disclosed individually with a resulting subtotal representing the funds provided by operations before consideration of extraordinary items. At this point, the amount of Extraordinary Items, as it appears in the earnings statement, is entered followed by adjustments to neutralize the presence of components having no funds consequences. The resulting subtotal is combined with the earlier subtotal to yield the total funds provided by operations.

One additional matter warranting attention is that the title, *statement of changes in financial position,* is the recommended title. Therefore, one rarely encounters the titles that had existed previously such as statement of funds flow, statement of sources and applications of working capital, or cash flow statement. Similarly, it is important that there be disclosure of how the company defines *funds* in context of the formal presentation of the statement.

Significance of the Statement of Changes in Financial Position

Many companies, including well-known corporations, experienced liquidity crises during the late 1960s and into the 1970s. Although the imminence of these problems may have been apparent to the companies' internal managers, external parties often were not aware of the prospective danger until a point of no return had been reached. It was largely as a reaction to this phenomenon that the statement of changes in financial position finally came to be required.

The statement complements the accrual-based earnings statement whose stated purpose is to measure profits. An enterprise's ability to pay its bills cannot be discerned merely by examining net income. The statement of changes in financial position discloses the dynamic dimension of financial position as distinct from knowing only what financial position is at given points in time; indeed, learning about changes in financial position implicitly assumes some degree of familiarity with the components of financial position proper.

What in effect is part of a return to balance sheet basics in turn spawned yet another interest, that of balance sheet reform. As balance sheets received increasing attention, there arose the matter of their possibly containing "excess weight"—in the form of account balances of dubious conceptual justification. Among the balance sheet components subject to this type of scrutiny were purchased goodwill, organization costs, research and development expenditures, and deferred income taxes. Some of these matters were subsequently considered by the Financial Accounting Standards Board, and in several instances reforms resulted.

The message conveyed by the statement of changes in financial position has had other ramifications as well. The chairman of the board of one major corporation suggested his company's deteriorating profit condition conveyed a false impression about its performance and thus of its prospects, and stated the firm did not have a cash problem but rather a bookkeeping problem relating to its huge investment in plant and inventory. Such an assertion can mislead persons who do not appreciate the distinction between any enterprise's dual needs to be profitable and liquid. Investments eventually must yield returns. This is as much a fact of life for a corporate manager responsible for capital budgeting as it is for an individual investing money in securities, a new automobile, a college education, or a two-week vacation trip. Ultimately, total returns must exceed total costs; to measure these factors only in terms of their liquidity aspects for a particular time interval is shortsighted.

To utilize funds flow analysis as a substitute for profitability analysis is a fallacy. Merely because funds flow had been on the sidelines for so long does not mean that it should now supplant income analysis. The key point is that these two types of analysis complement one another. One is concerned with profitability, the other with liquidity. One seeks to identify the transactions which caused the firm's owners' equity to change, the other identifies the effect of all pertinent transactions on the firm's ability to pay its bills. One is concerned with matching a particular period's revenues and expenses as part of its desire to document growth or decline in the long-run, the other seeks to summarize a particular interval's events in terms of its ability to meet its obligations in the short-run.

Funds flow analysis thus plays an interesting role within the fabric of accounting theory and financial reporting. Conceptually it is a logical result of applying the accounting equation—to do more than prove that a balance sheet is in balance. There is very little controversy about the statement of changes in financial position per se other than that which is raised periodically by someone who proposes a refinement in the statement's presentation. But there are some persons who would maintain that funds flow analysis can empirically be shown to be of more consequence than that provided by traditional earnings data. And there are persons who believe that truly comprehensive analysis of funds should not be limited to an artificial format such as working capital or cash, but that only the flow of all monetary amounts can offer the needed insight. But at the present time, the statement of changes in financial position as described in this chapter is a generally accepted feature of financial accounting.

Additional Readings

Anton, Hector R. *Accounting for the Flow of Funds.* Boston: Houghton Mifflin Co., 1962.

Coleman, Almand R. "Restructuring the Statement of Changes in Financial Position." *Financial Executive* (January 1979) pp. 34–42

Giese, J. W., and Klammer, T. P. "Achieving the Objectives of APB Opinion No. 19." *The Journal of Accountancy* (March 1974), pp. 54–61.

Gilman, Stephen. "Accounting Principles and the Current Classification." *The Accounting Review* (April 1944), pp. 109–16.

Heath, Lloyd C. *Financial Reporting and the Evaluation of Solvency.* New York: American Institute of Certified Public Accountants, 1978.

Hirschman, Robert W. "A Look at 'Current' Classifications." *The Journal of Accountancy* (November 1967), pp. 54–58.

Jaedicke, Robert K., and Sprouse, Robert T. *Accounting Flows: Income, Funds, and Cash.* Englewood Cliffs, N.J.: Prentice-Hall, Inc., 1965.

Mason, Perry. *"Cash Flow" Analysis and the Funds Statement.* New York: American Institute of Certified Public Accountants, 1961.

Merrill, Walter W. "The Statement of Changes in Financial Position Cash Format Is Far Easier to Understand." *Massachusetts CPA Review* (November–December 1973), pp. 23–26.

Moonitz, Maurice. "Reporting on the Flow of Funds." *The Accounting Review* (July 1956), pp. 378–85.

Nurnberg, Hugo. "APB Opinion No. 19—Pro and Con." *Financial Executive* (December 1972), pp. 58–70.

Park, Colin. "Funds Flow" in *Modern Accounting Theory,* edited by Morton Backer. Englewood Cliffs, N.J.: Prentice-Hall, Inc., 1966, pp. 301–19.

Seed, Allen H., III. "Utilizing the Funds Statement." *Management Accounting* (May 1976), pp. 15–18.

12

Financial Reporting and Changing Prices: Part 1

A 1936 book entitled *Stabilized Accounting*[1] examined the effect of inflation on the dollar and on the meaningfulness of accounting data. It in turn proposed that accountants recognize such effects when preparing financial statements. The accounting profession was reluctant to pursue this avenue primarily because it appeared to represent a deviation from the time-honored historical unit-of-money basis of recording transactions, and because the degree of inflation in any given year was seen as not sufficiently material in size to warrant modifying the existing accounting model.

An Accounting Principles Board-commissioned research study[2] was published in 1963 in which the issue of accounting for changes in the *general* price-level was discussed. Note that this is quite different from the separate matter of measuring and disclosing *price changes unique to particular assets* as suggested when comparing their historical and current values. This distinction is examined in depth in the ensuing sections of this chapter. In 1969, the APB set forth a definitive framework and a workable system with which companies could prepare financial statements reflecting the effect of changes in the general price level.[3] The pronouncement stated that such financial

---

[1] Henry W. Sweeney, *Stabilized Accounting* (New York: Harper & Row, 1936).

[2] Staff of the Accounting Research Division, *Reporting the Effects of Price-Level Changes* (New York: American Institute of Certified Public Accountants, 1963).

[3] *Accounting Principles Board Statement No. 3.*

statements were not to be a substitute for traditional statements; and that information extracted from them were neither prohibited nor required, but they were a permitted supplement. The nature of the measurement process was viewed not as a deviation from the historical cost basis, but rather a mere restatement of it.

The argument that inflation in a given year was not significant enough to justify restatement lost much of its force when double-digit inflation befell the American economy several years later. The Financial Accounting Standards Board in 1974, therefore, considered the matter of disclosing the effects of inflation. An exposure draft of a proposed Statement was circulated during 1975 with the hope a final resolution would be effected by the end of that year. The FASB proposal stated that price-level adjusted statements should be prepared essentially in accordance with the APB's 1969 approach. But rather than publishing these statements as such, companies would publish specified key accounting data as a required supplement to their (unadjusted) historical financial statements.

In March, 1976, the Securities and Exchange Commission adopted a rule requiring footnote disclosure of certain financial data reflecting current replacement cost.[4] Applicable to registrants whose qualifying assets exceeded $100 million and which comprised more than 10 percent of total assets, such disclosures were required only in such companies' annual Form 10-K submissions to the SEC. Current replacement cost data had to be disclosed for inventories, cost of goods sold, cost of plant assets, and depreciation expense, and the required information did not have to be audited. Although the SEC's pronouncement stated that it was not intended to preempt the FASB resolution of the general price-level changes issue, the FASB shortly thereafter did decide to postpone indefinitely further consideration of its proposed Statement citing the SEC action as only one of several factors that affected its decision.

In September 1979, the Financial Accounting Standards Board published Statement No. 33 entitled, "Financial Reporting and Changing Prices,"[5] which applies to publicly held companies that have inventory and gross plant assets amounting to more than $125 million or total assets exceeding $1 billion. The pronouncement identifies disclosures that are to be presented as supplementary information in published annual reports. The disclosures relate to the effect on the company's financial statements of both general price inflation and the current cost of its inventory and plant assets.

---

[4] *Accounting Series Release No. 190.*

[5] *Financial Accounting Standards Board Statement No. 33* (Stamford, Conn.: Financial Accounting Standards Board, 1979). Copyright © by Financial Accounting Standards Board, High Ridge Park, Stamford, Connecticut 06905, U.S.A. Reprinted with permission. Copies of the complete document are available from the FASB.

Specific aspects of the FASB requirements are discussed at appropriate points in both this chapter and Chapter 13.

CHANGES IN THE GENERAL PRICE LEVEL

When the purchasing power of the dollar changes, the prices of most if not all goods and services within the economy are affected. Government economists measure this effect by identifying a representative collection of goods and services whose aggregate price is used to represent the average price for goods and services of the economy at large. One year is designated the base period year and a price index number of 100 is assigned to it.When the general price level of any other year is determined, it is also expressed in terms of a price index number. The relationship between any two years' index numbers identifies the relative purchasing power of the dollar between the two years. The following examination of changes in the general price level is directed exclusively to the case of increasing prices; in a period of deflation, differences would be in the opposite direction, but the concepts would be the same.

Price Index Numbers

Assume the index number for 19x1 is 100 and by the end of 19x2 it had increased to 110. This means that what on the average had cost $100 in 19x1 would have a price of $110 at the end of 19x2. The purchase of the same goods would on the average require $10 more in 19x2 than in 19x1 because the dollar is less valuable, that is, its purchasing power has declined. Accordingly, if a parcel of land had been purchased by a company on January 1, 19x1 for $500 it can be said the cost of the land restated to reflect the purchasing power of end-of-19x2 dollars would be $550 as based on the following computation: $500 × (110 ÷ 100 =) 1.1 = $550. The 1.1 amount is called the conversion factor. This would be the case irrespective of whatever amount an appraiser would assign as its December 31, 19x2 current value. Assume now the land was sold on January 1, 19x3 for $620; even though the apparent gain on the sale is ($620 − 500 =) $120, ($550 − 500 =) $50 of the gain is merely the result of price inflation, and the restated gain is only ($620 − 550 =) $70.

Pursuing this example one step further, instead of selling the land, assume that on January 1, 19x3 the company purchased a second parcel of land at a cost of $800, and that by the end of 19x3, the price index number had risen to 132. The amount of December 31, 19x3 dollars that represents the equivalent of the ($500 + 800 =) $1,300 actually paid is calculated in the following illustration:

Purchase Price	Date of Purchase	Index Number	Conversion Factor	Purchase Price Restated to Dec. 31 19x3 Dollars
$ 500	Jan. 1, 19x1	100	132 ÷ 100 = 1.32	= $ 660
$ 800	Jan. 1, 19x3	110	132 ÷ 110 = 1.2	= $ 960
$1,300				$1,620

This could be taken to mean that if the parcels of land purchased at the beginning of 19x1 and 19x3 had been bought at the end of 19x3, they would have required an expenditure of $1,620. This statement is valid, however, only if one assumes the declining purchasing power of the dollar affected the price of the two parcels of land in the same manner it affected the average goods and services in the economy at large.

Before proceeding to discuss how accounting would incorporate price index numbers into the preparation of financial statements, recall the manner in which economists use such measures in national income analysis. When comparing the gross national product (GNP) of two years, the economist is interested in determining *real* growth rather than just growth in nominal terms. This means that by isolating that portion of a subsequent year's higher GNP attributable to an increase in the general price level, there is an opportunity to measure the change that occurs irrespective of fluctuating price levels. This is called using *constant* dollars rather than *nominal* dollars.

Returning to the earlier example, assume that instead of land purchased for $500 in 19x1 and sold for $620 in 19x3, these same amounts pertain to a country's gross national product expressed in billions of dollars. The apparent growth in GNP, based solely on the absolute dollar change, is ($620 −500 =) $120 billion. To measure GNP's real growth, the economist restates the $620 billion in terms of 19×1 dollars, viz., $620 × (100 ÷ 110 =) .909 = $564 billion. The real growth in GNP is therefore the difference between $564 billion and $500 billion, or $64 billion in 19×1 dollars.

The difference in approaches used by the accountant and by the economist lies solely in the choice of years whose dollars constitute the standard of measurement. The 1969 APB model and the subsequent FASB pronouncement sought to express dollar amounts in terms of current purchasing power, or what is refferred to as *constant dollars,* based on the purchasing power prevailing during the last quarter or the last month of the current year. Therefore, for 19×2 the accountant would restate 19×1's $500 as the equivalent of $550 dollars having December 31, 19×2 purchasing power. The economist, on the other hand, would restate 19×2's $620 in terms of the equivalent 19×1 purchasing power with $564 being the number of dollars which could have purchased in 19×1 what $620 actually did buy on December 31, 19×2.

In summary, the economist and the accountant use price index numbers for similar purposes, namely, to identify the effect of changes in the general price level. The economist restates later years' data to reflect the dollar's purchasing power of some prior year, because of an interest to measure growth relative to the earlier year. The accountant would restate prior years' data to reflect the dollar's current purchasing power, because financial statement readers seek to make decisions in terms of the dollar's current relative worth. Certainly, accounting data could be restated in the same manner that economists use, and the right to do so has been so advocated.[6] For purposes of explication, however, all subsequent examples use the approach set forth by the FASB.

Monetary and Nonmonetary Items

The example in the previous section assumed that *land* was the asset purchased and sold. Land is a *nonmonetary* asset because its price—its cash equivalent—is not fixed. Because it is not fixed, the price can and does vary such that it is affected by changes in the general price level. As opposed to this, *monetary* assets are those whose amounts are fixed by contract or otherwise in terms of numbers of dollars regardless of changes in prices. Cash and receivables are monetary assets, and most other assets are nonmonetary.

The distinction between monetary and nonmonetary items is applicable to the equities side of the balance sheet as well. Payables for which the amount owed is fixed in terms of numbers of dollars regardless of changes in prices are monetary liabilities. Other "right side" amounts such as revenue received in advance and owners' equity balances are nonmonetary. Note that the designation of an amount as monetary or nonmonetary occurs irrespective of whether it is a current or noncurrent account.

We shall consider first the effect of upward changes in the general price level on nonmonetary items and how a financial reporting system would respond to and account for such changes. The determination that the purchase of a nonmonetary asset would incur a greater dollar cost in the current period than what had actually occurred in a prior period is not an accountable event. However, the asset balance would be restated, but only to the extent of the change in the general price level. Consider the earlier example in which land which cost $500 in 19x1 had increased in value to $620

---

[6] *Common-Sense Accounting in an Era of Persistent Inflation—A Position Paper*, (New York: Price Waterhouse & Co., 1977). pp. 9–10.

by the end of 19x2, and was still on hand as of that date. Since we had determined that 550 December 31, 19x2 dollars are the equivalent of 500 19x1 dollars, the asset is only restated to $550. The remaining ($620 − 550 =) $70 is not accounted for because it does not relate to the general price change.

Even though the asset is restated, there is no recognition in the 19x2 earnings statement; the company does not realize any benefit merely because inflation has occurred. The offsetting credit is therefore reflected implicitly in restated owner's equity because, as a nonmonetary item, it too must be restated in terms of 19x2 dollars.

If the land were to be sold for $620 in 19×3, a year during which we shall initially assume there was no inflation, the gain on the sale would be $70, which is the excess of the proceeds from the sale expressed in current dollars ($620) over its cost basis expressed in constant dollars ($550). In terms of journal-entry recognition, consider the following:

Land	50	
Owners' Equity		50
To restate land in 19x2—pro forma.		
Cash	620	
Land		550
Gain		70
Sale of land in 19x3.		

It is apparent that eventually the entire $120 spread between the $620 sale price and the $500 original cost becomes part of owners' equity. But the important factor to consider is that only $70 flows through the income statement because it is only this amount which represents the gain not caused by price inflation.

Taking this example one step further, instead of assuming there was no inflation in 19x3, consider the outcome if the index number for 19x3 had been 132. The resulting journal entries are presented below:

Land (500 × .1)	50	
Owners' Equity		50
To restate land in 19x2 − pro forma.		
Land [550 × (132 ÷ 110 =) 1.2 = 660;		
660 − 550 =]	110	
Owners' Equity		110
To restate land in 19x3 − pro forma.		
Cash	620	
Loss	40	
Land (500 + 50 + 110 =)		660
Sale of land in 19x3.		

In this case, the effect of inflation was so severe that by accepting $620 for the land, the company did not even recover its original cost, in terms of equivalent purchasing power. We thus observe the effect of inflation on a nonmonetary asset is that the carrying value of the asset increases, owners' equity increases, and income is unaffected.

In the case of *monetary* assets and liabilities, the asset or liability itself is not restated because the very nature of being monetary is that the stated amount is fixed. However, whereas inflation has no immediate gain or loss effect on nonmonetary assets, its effect on monetary accounts is one that does require immediate earnings statement recognition. Companies holding cash or receivables are adversely affected by inflation because the declining purchasing power of the dollar causes the asset held to be less valuable. For example, if someone holds $1,400 of cash from 19x1 when the price index is 100 until 19x2 whose index number is 110, the $1,400 in 19x2 can only buy $(100 \div 110 = .909$ or) 91 percent of the goods and services that could have been bought in 19x1. The accountant would recognize an inflation loss of $[\$1,400 \times (110 \div 100 =) 1.1 = \$1,540; \$1,540 - 1,400 =] \$140$ in the 19x2 earnings statement. This $140 is the amount of purchasing power lost by holding the $1,400 in cash rather than having bought a nonmonetary asset when it could still have been obtained for $1,400 versus the $(\$1,400 \times 1.1 =) \$1,540$ it on the average would cost in 19x2.

On the other hand, owing money—monetary liabilities—during inflation results in an inflation gain. This happens because the dollars subsequently used to reduce the debt have less purchasing power than when the obligation was initially created. By being able to borrow $600 in 19x1 and paying it back in 19x3 during which time the price index increased from 100 to 132 results in a realized gain of $[\$600 \times (132 \div 100 =) 1.32 = \$792; \$792 - 600 =] \$192$. Had the creditor required that repayment be effected in 19x3 with dollars having the same purchasing power the original $600 had had in 19x1, the debtor would have to remit $792. Being able to pay only the $600 generates a $(\$792 - 600 =) \$192$ savings for the borrower, and this is referred to as an inflation gain;[7] it is sometimes also referred to as a purchasing power gain, or more descriptively as a gain from the decline in purchasing power.

CHANGES IN SPECIFIC PRICES

Until now, our discussion has been limited to measuring the effect of changes in the general price level. The underlying assumption of restatement

---

[7] Recognize that a portion of the "gain" may be offset by the presence of a high interest rate which was charged in anticipation of the price inflation.

is that historical cost data are retained albeit in a somewhat different form, namely, in terms of the current purchasing power of the dollar. An important aspect of the resulting disclosures is that nonmonetary items are still *not* reflected at their current value.

It would be unusual for the current value of a particular nonmonetary asset to be exactly the same as the amount corresponding to its historical cost restated to reflect the change in the general price level. Typically, the current value of such an asset differs from its original cost for both of two reasons: general price changes *and* specific price changes. A specific price change refers to the unique circumstances—location, technical sophistication, supply and demand phenomena, and so forth—affecting a particular nonmonetary asset. Since it is difficult if not impossible to identify what contribution to total value is provided by particular factors, only composite values are usually calculated and used.

Differences of opinion exist among accountants as to what method to use and which external markets to refer to when making such determinations. Although the nature, ramifications, and relative merits of the various points of view are examined in Chapter 13, we can note that the two basic viewpoints are those which advocate *realizable value* and those which advocate *replacement cost. Realizable value* refers to the sum that would be realized in non-distress liquidation, and *replacement cost* is the amount it would cost to replace the asset with a comparable item. To help appreciate that these two resulting amounts can and typically do differ,consider the case of determining the current value of one's used car. On the one hand, the purchase of an identical automobile might cost $2,200; on the other hand, the sale of the car at hand might realize only $1,900. Replacement cost is an *entry* price and realizable value is an *exit* price.

The traditional historical cost basis of accounting does not restate financial statements to reflect the effect of inflation. However, under the 1979 model set forth by the FASB, financial statements would be restated to reflect the impact of inflation, albeit initially only by very large corporations in order to provide certain supplementary disclosures. Similarly, when the historical cost basis of accounting is supplanted by a system which uses current values as its focal point, there are also two approaches to accounting for the effect of changes in the general price level. One method is *not* to recognize such changes because the current value data themselves implicitly reflect the price changes wrought by inflation; this is the *current value/nominal dollar* approach.

To illustrate, assume a parcel of land is purchased for $250 in 19x6 when the price index is 120, its end-of-year current value is $325, and it is sold in 19x7 for $340 when the price index is 150. Assume that the current value basis is used in lieu of historical costs, and there is no explicit concern with measuring inflationary effects. The accountant recognizes a ($325 − 250 =) $75 holding gain in 19x6 and a ($340 − 325 =) $15 holding gain in 19x7. Such gains and losses are recognized immediately in the income statement, and the nonmonetary asset in the balance sheet is updated to reflect current value. With respect to monetary assets and liabilities, no gains and losses are recognized because the isolated effects of inflation *per se* are not accounted for under the current value/nominal dollar approach.

The second approach to current value accounting does take into account the measurable effects of changes in the general price level; this is the *current value/constant dollar* method. The nonmonetary assets in the balance sheet are reflected at their current value. But that portion of the change in value attributable to changes in the general price level is not recognized as a determinant of income as was the case when restating historical cost data for inflationary effects. Only that portion of the change which can be attributed to a change in the asset's specific price is reflected in the earnings statement. And when there is restatement, the gain or loss resulting from monetary items' exposure to inflation is also included in the income statement.

Rather than present an isolated illustration of the *current value/constant dollar* approach, the following sections introduce comprehensive examples which, in addition to illustrating the various approaches, are also the basis for making a comparison among the approaches.

A FRAME OF REFERENCE

It should be recognized that we are dealing with two different approaches to accounting valuation: historical costs and current values. The distinction between the historical cost and current value bases revolves around whether current valuations should supplant the recorded historical costs of non-monetary assets. When the current value approach prevails, the resulting value changes appear immediately in the income statement.[8] In addition, each approach may or may not explicitly recognize the effect of changes in the general price level. When the impact of inflation *is* accounted for, there is a restatement of the data generated by the basic approach—restated historical costs or restated current values. The nature of restatement is different for monetary and nonmonetary items. The restatement of nonmonetary items is

---

[8] This would be the case under the *financial capital* concept—but not under a *physical capital* approach; see FASB Discussion Memorandum, *Conceptual Framework for Financial Accounting and Reporting: Elements of Financial Statements and Their Measurement.* (Stamford, Connecticut: Financial Accounting Standards Board, 1976), pp. 123–43. Copyright © by Financial Accounting Standards Board, High Ridge Park, Stamford, Connecticut 06905, U.S.A. Reprinted with permission. Copies of the complete document are available from the FASB.

reflected in the balance sheet but is not an explicit factor in earnings determination; note, however, that revenues and expenses are nonmonetary in nature and are therefore restated in their own right. The restatement of monetary items appears in the income statement as an inflation gain or loss.[9]

An appreciation of the nature of the various approaches and the differences among them can be achieved by studying the examples presented below. An essential first step is to recognize the four methods of accounting with which we shall be concerned:

1. *Historical Costs:* Not restated for general price-level changes, i.e., nominal dollars

2. *Historical Costs:* Restated for general price-level changes, i.e., constant dollars

3. *Current Values:* Not restated for general price-level changes, i.e., nominal dollars

4. *Current Values:* Restated for general price-level changes, i.e., constant dollars

In the exhibits which accompany the following examples, the results generated by these four methods are set forth in columns, numbered 1 through 4. In the interest of brevity, the related narrative will often refer to a particular method by its column number.

Nonmonetary Asset—Income Statement Effect

Refer now to Exhibit 12–1. In this example, we are concerned with *land,* a single, nonmonetary asset bought and sold over a two-year period. During the first year, there is a change only in the asset's specific price; in the second year there is a change only in the general price level. The income statement effect alone is considered in this illustration. Column 1 depicts the conventional method whereby historical costs are *not* restated for general price level changes. A ($2,500 − 2,000 =) $500 gain upon sale is therefore recognized in 19x2.

Column 2 illustrates the restatement of historical costs to reflect changes in the general price level. The price level rose in 19x2, as indicated by the increase in the price index number from 100 to 140. The cost of the land expressed in 19x2 purchasing power is [$2,000 × (140 ÷ 100 =) 1.4 =]

---

[9] Note, however, that when one year's financial statements are presented in a subsequent year for comparative purposes, all of their amounts, i.e., even monetary items, are restated to reflect the purchasing power in which the subsequent year's financial statements are expressed.

Exhibit 12–1

Nonmonetary Asset—Income Statement Effect

Date	Event	Amount	Price Index
January 1, 19x1	Purchase land	$2,000	100
December 31, 19x1	Market value	$2,500	100
December 31, 19x2	Sale of land	$2,500	140

	(1)	(2)	(3)	(4)
	Historical Cost		Current Value	
	Nominal Dollars	Constant Dollars	Nominal Dollars	Constant Dollars
19x1 Net income	–0–	–0–	$500[3]	$ 500[3]
19x2 Net income (loss)	$500[1]	$(300)[2]	–0–	$(1,000)[4]
19x1 Net income restated in 12/31/x2 dollars				700[5]
Two-year net income (loss)	**$500**	**$(300)**	**$500**	**$ (300)**

Supporting computations:
[1] $2,500 − 2,000 = $500
[2] $2,000 × (140 ÷ 100 =) 1.4 = $2,800; $2,800 − 2,500 = $300
[3] $2,500 − 2,000 = $500
[4] $2,500 × 140 ÷ 100) 1.4 = $3,500; $3,500 − 2,500 = $1,000
[5] $500 × (140 ÷ 100 =) 1.4 = $700

$2,800. This ($2,800 − 2,000 =) $800 restatement does not result in gain or loss recognition. But when the land is sold for $2,500, a $300 loss is recognized to reflect the excess of the ($2,800) restated cost basis over the ($2,500) sale price.

In Column 3, the current value basis of accounting is presented with no explicit recognition of the effect of general price level changes. Instead, its concern is solely with aggregate changes in current value. Because 19x1's end-of-year value is ($2,500 − 2,000 =) $500 greater than the original cost, a $500 gain is recognized. In 19x2, there is no additional change in the value of the land, and no gain or loss arises. Note that the cumulative, two-year gain is the same for Current Value/Nominal Dollars (Column 3) as it is for Historical Cost/Nominal Dollars (Column 1). The difference between these two approaches is one of timing, namely, when to recognize the $500 gain. The historical cost method requires recognition only when it is realized in a sale transaction, and the current value system recognizes gains and losses whenever the external marketplace indicates a change in value.

Column 4 presents the current value approach *with restatement* of previously recorded amounts to reflect the effect of changes in the general price level. The 19x1 result is similar to what occurred in Column 3 because there is no change in the general price level in 19x1. However, in 19x2 when there is price inflation, it is necessary to restate the ($2,500) beginning-of-year value to ($2,500 × 1.4 =) $3,500. It is this ($3,500) amount which is matched with the ($2,500) sales proceeds to yield a gain or loss—in this case, a $1,000 loss. This states, in effect, that given the $2,500 beginning-of-year value and the 19x2 inflation, it would require 3,500 end-of-year dollars to compensate for disposing of the land. Because 1,000 less end-of-year dollars are received, a $1,000 loss results.[10]

Before comparing the cumulative result of the Current Value/Constant Dollar approach (Column 4) with that of the Historical Cost/Constant Dollar approach (Column 2), recognize that Column 4's $500 19x1 gain and its $1,000 19x2 loss are not additive because they are not expressed in dollars of comparable purchasing power. To compensate for this deficiency, 19x1's $500 gain is restated in terms of 19x2's year-end purchasing power, and it yields a ($500 × 1.4 =) $700 gain. Column 4's two-year result is the difference between a $1,000 loss and a $700 gain or a net $300 loss—identical to that of Column 2.

The reason for the variation between Columns 2 and 4 is exactly the same as that which explained the difference between Columns 1 and 3; namely, it is a timing difference. The historical cost system, despite its being restated in Column 2, does not recognize gains or losses until they are realized in an arm's length transaction. The current value approach, even when recognizing inflation, still records gains or losses in value prior to realization on sale so long as the change is not attributable to inflation, and in our case the $500 increase in value occurred in 19x1 when there was no change in the general price level.

In summary, Columns 1 and 2 are alike because neither recognizes gains and losses resulting from changes in current values, which is a key feature of the historical cost approach. Columns 3 and 4 are similar because, not burdened by historical cost rules, they recognize value changes as they occur. But Columns 1 and 3 also have the common characteristic that the effects of inflation are not explicitly recognized, and Columns 2 and 4 parallel each other as they both do account for changes in the general price level. The $500 income recognized in Columns 1 and 3 exceeds the $300 loss of Columns 2 and 4 by $800. This difference is attributable to the inflation that

---

[10] With respect to the Gain on Land, there exists the matter of separating the "realized" gain from the "unrealized" (holding) gain. This issue is not considered in this chapter; it will, however, be discussed in Chapter 13.

occurred during 19x2, since $800 is the amount of the total price change which results from the change in the general price level. In Columns 1 and 3, because this $800 is not isolated, it is included in earnings, i.e., the resulting $500 income. In Columns 2 and 4, however, where the $800 restatement is isolated, it is not a component of earnings, hence, the $800 difference resulting in a $300 loss.

Nonmonetary Asset—Balance Sheet and Income Statement Effects

We now proceed to an illustration in which concurrent changes in both specific and general prices are examined in terms of both balance sheet valuation and the effect on earnings. In addition, although the general price-level increases continuously over a five-year period, the current value of the one nonmonetary land asset fluctuates. In Exhibit 12–2, the four-column configuration of the preceding example is again used.

Land is purchased on January 1, 19x1 for $10,000 when the index num-

Exhibit 12–2

Nonmonetary Asset—Balance Sheet and Income Statement Effect (five years)

Date	Event	Amount	Price Index
January 1, 19x1	Purchase land	$10,000	100
December 31, 19x1	Market value	$10,500	100
December 31, 19x2	Market value	$14,000	110
December 31, 19x3	Market value	$13,000	110
December 31, 19x4	Market value	$11,000	132
December 31, 19x5	Sale of land	$15,000	165

	Historical Cost		Current Value	
	(1) Nominal Dollars	(2) Constant Dollars	(3) Nominal Dollars	(4) Constant Dollars
Balance sheet asset:				
December 31, 19x1	$10,000	$10,000	$10,500	$10,500
December 31, 19x2	10,000	11,000[1]	14,000	14,000
December 31, 19x3	10,000	11,000	13,000	13,000
December 31, 19x4	10,000	13,200[2]	11,000	11,000
December 30, 19x5	10,000	16,500[3]	15,000	15,000

292

Exhibit 12-2 (*continued*)

	Historical Cost		Current Value	
	(1) Nominal Dollars	(2) Constant Dollars	(3) Nominal Dollars	(4) Constant Dollars
Income statement:				
19x1 income	–0–	–0–	$ 500[5]	$ 500
19x2 income	–0–	–0–	3,500[6]	2,450[10]
19x3 income (loss)	–0–	–0–	(1,000)[7]	(1,000)[7]
19x4 income (loss)	–0–	–0–	(2,000)[8]	(4,600)[11]
19x5 income (loss)	$5,000	$(1,500)[4]	4,000[9]	1,250[12]
Five-year income (loss)	**$5,000**	**$(1,500)**	**$5,000**	**$(1,500)**[13]

Supporting computations:
[1] $10,000 \times (110 \div 100 =) 1.1 = \$11,000$
[2] $11,000 \times (132 \div 110 =) 1.2 = \$13,200$
[3] $13,200 \times (165 \div 132 =) 1.25 = \$16,500$
[4] $16,500 - 15,000 = \$1,500$
[5] $10,500 - 10,000 = \$500$
[6] $14,000 - 10,500 = \$3,500$
[7] $14,000 - 13,000 = \$1,000$
[8] $13,000 - 11,000 = \$2,000$
[9] $15,000 - 11,000 = \$4,000$
[10] $14,000 - [\$10,500 \times (110 \div 100 =) 1.1 =] 11,550 = \$2,450$
[11] $13,000 \times (132 \div 110 =) 1.2 = 15,600; 15,600 - 11,000 = \$4,600$
[12] $15,000 - [\$11,000 \times (165 \div 132 =) 1.25 =] 13,750 = \$1,250$
[13] 19x1: $500 \times (165 \div 100 =) 1.65 =$ $ 825
      19x2: $2,450 \times (165 \div 110 =)1.5$ =   3,675
      19x3: ($1,000) $\times (165 \div 110 =) 1.5$ =   (1,500)
      19x4: ($4,600) $\times (165 \div 132 =) 1.25$ =   (5,750)
      19x5:   1,250
                                                 $(1,500)

ber depicting the general price level is 100. The land is sold on December 31, 19x5 for $15,000 when the index number in 165. The balance sheet amounts are presented as of each December 31 except for 19x5. In this one instance, the account balance provided is that which existed just prior to the sale; in the exhibit, the date used is December 30. Column 1 indicates that the land's original $10,000 cost appears on all subsequent balance sheets and that a ($15,000 − 10,000 =) $5,000 gain is recognized upon sale in 19x5.

In Column 2, observe that neither a gain nor a loss appears in an income statement until 19x5 which is the year of sale. But the amounts pertaining to land in successive balance sheets do vary in response to changes in the general price level, as based on the indicated supporting computations. Note that since Column 2 represents application of the historical cost system, despite its being restated for inflationary changes the land's current value data are not accounted for. The $1,500 loss recognized in the year of sale is the difference between the ($15,000) proceeds which represent 19x5 purchasing power and the ($16,500) *restated* cost basis reflecting like purchasing power.

The third column uses current values. Since the effects of general price level changes are not isolated from other changes in value, the given market value amounts appear in each year's balance sheet and the entire change in value is presented as a gain or loss in each year's earnings statement. Observe also that Columns 1 and 3 again generate an identical five-year effect on income with individual years' differences attributable to the same timing phenomenon referred to in the earlier discussion (of the data contained in Exhibit 12–1).

The machinations of Column 4's Current Value/Constant Dollar approach warrant patient year-by-year analysis. Because there is no inflation in 19x1, all of that year's ($10,500 − 10,000 =) $500 increase in market value results from a specific price change and is, therefore, recognized in the earnings statement. But in 19x2, the ($14,000 − 10,500 =) $3,500 increase in value does not appear in the income statement in its entirety.

That portion of the increase which arises because of a change in the general price level is not recognized as a gain because it is merely a restatement of the beginning-of-year land account balance. Had there only been an increase in the general price level, the balance sheet asset would have increased from $10,500 to [$10,500 × (110 ÷ 100=) 1.1=] $11,550, an increment of ($11,550 − 10,500 =) $1,050. Because $1,050 of the total $3,500 increased value is merely the result of the inflation-induced restatement, it is only the remaining ($3,500 − 1,050 =) $2,450, attributable to the specific price change, that is recognized as a determinant of earnings.

Note, however, that the balance sheet reflects the entire $14,000 current value, that is, even that portion not included in the income statement. So long as the current value basis is in effect, the full value appears in the asset account. When restatement for the effects of inflation is superimposed on current valuation, only the income statement is precluded from disclosing the entire change in value.

In 19x3, the market value declined to $13,000 and this amount is reflected in the balance sheet. Because there is no change in the general price level (viz., the same index number in 19x2 and 19x3), the full ($14,000 − 13,000 =) $1,000 decrease appears as a loss in 19x3's income statement.

In 19x4, there is a further decline in value and the resulting $11,000 value appears in the year-end balance sheet. However, there is an increase in the general price level in 19x4, and this means it is necessary to analyze the factors underlying the ($13,000 − 11,000 =) $2,000 change in value.

To isolate the effect of inflation, the $13,000 beginning-of-year balance is restated to [$13,000 × (132 ÷ 110 =) 1.2 =] $15,600, and the resulting ($15,600 − 13,000 =) $2,600 restatement does not appear in the income statement. However, on comparing the restated beginning-of-year value with the actual end-of-year value — both expressed in terms of end-of-year purchasing power—a ($15,600 − 11,000 =) $4,600 loss emerges; a summary follows:

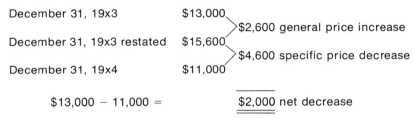

December 31, 19x3	$13,000	
		$2,600 general price increase
December 31, 19x3 restated	$15,600	
		$4,600 specific price decrease
December 31, 19x4	$11,000	
$13,000 − 11,000 =		$2,000 net decrease

While the balance sheet asset decreases by the net $2,000 change, only the $4,600 specific price decrease appears in 19x4's income statement.

In 19x5, in light of the $15,000 sale date current value, the increase over the beginning-of-year balance is ($15,000 − 11,000 =) $4,000. The inflationary effect is [$11,000 × (165 ÷ 132 =) 1.25 = $13,750; $13,750 − 11,000 =] $2,750, which means that ($4,000 − 2,750 =) $1,250 is the specific price change which appears in 19x5's income statement.

As was the case in the illustration contained in Exhibit 12–1, the cumulative, five-year income statement effect of Columns 2 and 4 are identical. In the situation at hand, this is demonstrated with the aid of supporting computation No. 13 wherein the gains and losses of 19x1 through 19x4 are restated in terms of December 31, 19x5 purchasing power to foster additivity among the five years' amounts. The two columns' aggregate results are alike because in neither case are the income statements affected by changes in the general price level. The individual years' amounts vary because of timing differences caused by the diverse nature of the historical cost and current value bases of accounting.

Monetary Assets and Liabilities—Gains and Losses from General Price-Level Changes

The nature of monetary assets and liabilities, that is, cash, receivables and payables whose amounts are expressed in a fixed number of dollars, precludes specific price changes occurring, because of their "fixed number of dollars" character. However, they *are affected* by changes in the general price level. For a number of dollars to remain fixed while their underlying purchasing power declines means that as a result of inflation, less valuable dollars are (1) on hand, (2) receivable, or (3) payable than had been the case when the dollars were originally obtained or the obligation created.

To appreciate the impact of inflation on monetary assets and liabilities, refer to Exhibit 12–3. The example covers one year, and price index numbers are given for January 1, December 31, and the average for the year. In addition, the conversion factors with which pre-December 31 amounts are restated to December 31 purchasing power are provided. The six cases are derived from two different January 1 balance sheets. One has an excess of monetary assets over monetary liabilities of ($1,000 − 700 =) $300, which is called a *net monetary asset;* the other has an excess of monetary liabilities over monetary assets of ($1,200 − 1,000 =) $200, which is a *net monetary liability.*

An inflow of monetary items results from transactions which increase monetary assets or decrease monetary liabilities with no effect on a monetary asset such as making charge or cash sales. An outflow of monetary items results from increasing monetary liabilities or decreasing monetary assets while not affecting monetary liabilities such as incurring expenses or buying assets payable in cash. It is assumed that inflows and outflows occur uniformly during the year; and six resulting year-end monetary positions emerge.

To determine the company's gain or loss from the exposure of its monetary items to changes in the general price level, a restatement of the year-end monetary position is computed. The resulting amount does not appear in any financial statement. Instead, its purpose is to identify what the year-end monetary position would have been had the company and parties with whom it has monetary relationships—debtors, creditors, and the nation's central bank—provided bilaterally for adjustments in numbers of dollars to neutralize the devaluation effect of the rising general price level.

Refer to Column 1 whose January 1 $300 net monetary assets are restated as $363. Monetary inflows ($4,500) and monetary outflows ($4,000) during the year are restated to $4,950 and $4,400 respectively with a resulting restatement of year-end net monetary assets of $913. On comparing this with the actual $800 year-end net monetary assets, $113 emerges as the *inflation loss on net monetary items.* This means that had the company provided contractually that the numbers of dollars reflect equivalent inception-date purchasing power, that is, had the effect of inflation been neutralized—or had there been no inflation at all—the purchasing power of its year-end net monetary assets would have been $113 larger than is actually the case. In other words, as a result of inflation, its monetary assets exceed its monetary

Exhibit 12–3

Monetary Assets and Liabilities—Gains and Losses from General Price-Level Changes

Date	Price Index	Conversion Factor (to 12/31)
January 1, 19x1	100	(121 ÷ 100 =) 1.21
Average during 19x1	110	(121 ÷ 110 =) 1.1
December 31, 19x1	121	

January 1, 19x1 Balance sheet

Monetary assets	$ 1,000	
Nonmonetary assets	1,000	
Total	**$ 2,000**	
Monetary liabilities	$ 700	$ 1,200
Nonmonetary liabilities	500	200
Owners' equity	800	600
Total	**$ 2,000**	**$ 2,000**

	(a)	(b)	(c)	(d)	(e)	(f)
1/1/x1 Net monetary assets (liabilities)	$ 300			$(200)		
19x1 monetary inflows	4,500			4,500		
19x1 monetary (outflows)	(4,000)	(4,900)	(5,300)	(3,900)	(4,200)	(5,000)
12/31/x1 Net monetary assets (liab.)	$ 800	$(100)	$(500)	$ 400	$ 100	$(700)
1/1/x1 Net monetary assets (liabilities) restated (i.e., × 1.21)	$ 363	$ 363	$ 363	$(242)	$(242)	$(242)
Monetary inflows restated (i.e., × 1.1)	4,950	4,950	4,950	4,950	4,950	4,950
Monetary outflows restated (i.e., × 1.1)	(4,400)	(5,390)	(5,830)	(4,290)	(4,620)	(5,500)
12/31/x1 Net monetary assets (liabilities) restated	$ 913	$(77)	$(517)	$ 418	$ 88	$(792)
Inflation gain (loss) on net monetary items	**$(113)**	**$(23)**	**$ 17**	**$(18)**	**$ 12**	**$ 92**

liabilities by $113 less purchasing power than would have happened had there been no inflation, or if its effects had been neutralized as a result of prior arrangement.

The same steps are used in the other five columns as well, and we can proceed to examine the underlying dynamics, namely, what types of circumstances generate gains or losses. The following table summarizes the results of the six different situations.

Case	January 1	December 31	Outcome
1.	Net Monetary ASSET	Larger Net Monetary ASSET	Loss
2.	Net Monetary ASSET	Net Monetary LIABILITY	Loss
3.	Net Monetary ASSET	Net Monetary LIABILITY	Gain
4.	Net Monetary LIABILITY	Net Monetary ASSET	Loss
5.	Net Monetary LIABILITY	Net Monetary ASSET	Gain
6.	Net Monetary LIABILITY	Larger Net Monetary LIABILITY	Gain

In Case 1, a loss occurs because a larger amount of net monetary assets became exposed to inflation during the year than had existed as of January 1. In Case 2, a loss occurs even though the company is in a net monetary liability situation at year-end. The loss, however, results from the magnitude of the earlier exposure relative to the changed circumstances as of December 31. This is borne out in Case 3 when the movement toward a net monetary liability position was more pronounced (to $500 versus to $100) during the year (and larger as of December 31), with the result that a gain occurs.

Case 4 depicts a beginning-of-year net monetary liability which, as a result of monetary flows during the year, becomes a net monetary asset as of December 31, and this movement results in a loss. Yet, Case 5 also illustrates a change to a net monetary asset position at year-end but because its magnitude is less than that of the preceding case (to $100 rather than to $400), a gain results. And certainly in Case 6, a gain occurs as the size of the January 1 net monetary liability increases during the year.

It is apparent that in a period of inflation, it is more desirable to be in a net monetary liability position than to be in a net monetary asset position. Individuals and companies would prefer to pay their debts with less valuable dollars than they had borrowed, but with respect to payments from their debtors, an opposite desired outcome is sought. When restating financial statements to reflect the effect of changes in the general price level, recognition of a gain or loss resulting from exposure of monetary assets and liabilities is therefore essential.

The issue of monetary items' exposure to gains and losses exists also with respect to fluctuation in foreign currency exchange rates. The notion of a strengthening or weakening dollar relative to a particular foreign currency parallels the case of strengthening or weakening purchasing power of the dollar. Foreign currency exchange rates are the counterpart of price index numbers' conversion factors. Just as a company anticipating inflation is well-advised to be in a net monetary liability position, an American corporation expecting a foreign currency to weaken relative to the dollar is similarly well-advised to be in a net monetary liability position, that is, to have its foreign currency denominated monetary liabilities exceed foreign currency denominated monetary assets. Other aspects of the inflation and foreign exchange situations are examined in Chapter 14.

Monetary and Nonmonetary Assets—Balance Sheet and Income Statement Effects

We now proceed to an example which integrates the various features of accounting for general and specific price changes. The exhibits which follow illustrate the approach taken by the historical cost and current value bases of accounting under both the nominal dollar and the constant dollar approaches. Both the assets and equities sides of the balance sheet are presented, both monetary and nonmonetary assets appear, and important income statement effects are provided as well.

The example covers a three-year period, and the general price-level increases each year; each year is depicted as a separate exhibit. At the beginning of 19x1, stock is issued for cash, and 25 percent of the cash is used immediately to purchase land. A portion of the land is sold at the end of the second year and the remainder is sold one year later. We shall examine each year in terms of the four different systems of accounting with which we were concerned in the earlier examples. Exhibit 12–4 identifies the four approaches' accounting results for the first year.

Under the historical cost basis of accounting in which there is no restatement to reflect the effect of changes in the general price level (Column 1), the balance sheet amounts portray their original transaction basis and there is no effect on income. However, when there is restatement for changes in the general price level (Column 2), the land's ($500) cost is restated to [$500 × (125 ÷ 100 =) 1.25 =] $625. The monetary asset *cash* is not restated but an inflation loss is included in the income statement. The loss is a result of holding the ($1,500) beginning-of-year cash during a period of inflation; the equivalent of the 1,500 beginning-of-year dollars is ($1,500 × 1.25 =) $1,875 having year-end purchasing power. There is,

Exhibit 12–4

Monetary and Nonmonetary Assets—Balance Sheet and Income Statement Effects

Date	Event	Amount	Price Index
January 1, 19x1	Issue stock for cash	$2,000	100
January 2, 19x1	Purchase land	500	100
December 31, 19x1	Market value of land	800	125
December 30, 19x2	Sell 40% of land	460	150
December 31, 19x2	Market value of land	1,200	150
December 30, 19x3	Sell land	1,800	165

	(1)	(2)	(3)	(4)
	Historical Cost		Current Value	
19x1	Nominal Dollars	Constant Dollars	Nominal Dollars	Constant Dollars
12/31/x1 Balance sheet:				
Cash	$1,500	$1,500	$1,500	$1,500
Land	500	625[1]	800	800
Total	**$2,000**	**$2,125**	**$2,300**	**$2,300**
Capital stock	$2,000	$2,500[2]	$2,000	$2,500[2]
Retained earnings	—0—	(375)	300	(200)
Total	**$2,000**	**$2,125**	**$2,300**	**$2,300**
19x1 Income statement:				
Inflation (loss)		$(375)[3]		$(375)[3]
Holding gain			$300[4]	175[5]

Supporting computations:
[1] $500 × (125 ÷ 100 =) 1.25 = $625
[2] $2,000 × (125 ÷ 100 =) 1.25 = $2,500
[3] $1,500 of cash × (125 ÷ 100 =) 1.25 = $1,875; $1,875 − 1,500 = $375
[4] $800 − 500 = $300
[5] $800 − [500 × (125 ÷ 100 =) 1.25 =] 625 = $175

therefore, a ($1,875 − 1,500 =) $375 loss due to inflation, i.e., to reflect the fact that an additional $375 is needed at year-end to purchase goods and services whose cost had been $1,500 at the beginning of the year.

In Column 3, changes in market value are used and there is no recognition of the effect of changes in the general price level. Thus, land appears in the balance sheet at $800, and the ($800 − 500 =) $300 increase in its value is a gain in the income statement. Column 4's approach also reflects land at its current value, but only the [$800 − ($500 × 1.25 =) $625 =] $175 not attributable to changes in the general price level appears in the income statement. In addition, earnings are affected by the same $375 inflation loss that was recognized in Column 2.

The illustration now proceeds to the following year during which the price index number increases from 125 to 150, 40 percent of the land is sold at year-end for $460, and the market value of the remaining land is $1,200 as of December 31. Refer now to Exhibit 12–5.

In Column 1, a [$460 − ($500 × .4 =) $200 =] $260 gain on sale is recognized in the earnings statement. With respect to Column 2, recall that the December 31, 19x1 restated cost of land was ($500 × 1.25 =) $625. It, in turn, is restated to [$625 × (150 ÷ 125 =) 1.2 =] $750 to reflect the effect of the change in the general price level during 19x2. On hand at year-end is 60 percent of the $750 which is why land appears in the balance sheet as ($750 × .6 =) $450. The $160 gain on the sale of 40 percent of the land is the difference between the $460 proceeds and the ($750 × .4 =) $300 restated cost of the sold land.

The 19x2 inflation loss is based on the company holding $1,500 of cash during the entire year. Since inflation occurs throughout 19x2, the year-end purchasing power of the $1,500 is less than it had been at the beginning of the year. Therefore, [($1,500 × 1.2 =) $1,800; $1,800 − 1,500 =] $300 is the loss from holding a monetary asset in a period during which there was an increase in the general price level. Retained earnings is based on both the beginning-of-year deficit—negative retained earnings—restated to reflect end-of-year purchasing power, and 19x2's income which is explained in supporting computation No. 8 in the exhibit.

In Column 3, the December 31 land is reflected at its $1,200 current value, and the income statement includes the increase in land value during the year. This $860 increase is the amount by which the ($1,660) sum of the ($460) value of the sold parcel and that of the ($1,200) remaining land exceeds the ($800) beginning-of-year value.

Column 4's income statement reflects the same ($300) inflation loss that appeared in Column 2. In addition, it contains that portion of the ($860) increase in land value not attributable to a change in the general price level. Had there been only a change in the general price level, the $800 beginning-of-year land value would have been restated to ($800 × 1.2 =) $960. Therefore, since its actual value was ($460 + 1,200 =) $1,660, the ($1,660 − 960 =) $700 difference is recognized as a gain in the earnings statement.

Recall that in the earlier examples concerned with nonmonetary assets

Exhibit 12–5

Monetary and Nonmonetary Assets—Balance Sheet and Income Statement Effects

	(1)	(2)	(3)	(4)
	Historical Cost		Current Value	
19x2	Nominal Dollars	Constant Dollars	Nominal Dollars	Constant Dollars
12/31/x2 Balance Sheet:				
Cash	$1,960[1]	$1,960[1]	$1,960[1]	$1,960[1]
Land	300[2]	450[4]	1,200	1,200
Total	**$2,260**	**$2,410**	**$3,160**	**$3,160**
Capital stock	$2,000	$3,000[5]	$2,000	$3,000[5]
Retained earnings	260	(590)[8]	1,160[10]	160[12]
Total	**$2,260**	**$2,410**	**$3,160**	**$3,160**

19x2 Income statement:				
Gain on land	$ 260[3]	$ 160[6]	$ 860[9]	$ 700[11]
Inflation (loss)		$(300)[7]		$(300)[7]

Supporting computations:
[1] 12/31/x1 of $1,500 + 460 = $1,960
[2] 12/31/x1 of $500 × .6 = $300
[3] $460 − ($500 × .4 =) $200 = $260
[4] $625 × .6 = $375 × (150 ÷ 125 =) 1.2 = $450
[5] 12/31/x1 of $2,500 × (150 ÷ 125 =) 1.2 = $3,000
[6] $460 − [$625 × .4 = $250; $250 × (150 ÷ 125 =) 1.2 =] $300 = $160
[7] 12/31/x1 of $1,500 × (150 ÷ 125 =) 1.2 = $1,800; $1,800 − 1,500 = $(300)
[8] Retained earnings (deficit) 12/31/x1 .... $(375)

Restated to 12/31/x2: $375 × (150 ÷ 125 =) 1.2 .... $(450)
19x2 Net loss ($300[7] − 160[6] =) .... $(140)

$(590)

[9] $460 + 1,200 = $1,660; $1,660 − 800 (of 12/31/x1) = ... $860
[10] 12/31/x1 of $300 + 19x2 income of $860[9] = $1,160
[11] $460 + 1,200 = 1,660; $1,660 − [800 × (150 × 125 =) 1.2 =] $960 = $700
[12] Retained earnings (deficit) 12/31/x1 .... $(200)

Restated to 12/31/x2: $200 × (150 ÷ 125 =) 1.2 = ... $(240)
19x2 net income ($700[11] − 300[7] =) .... $ 400

$ 160

only (Exhibits 12–1 and 12–2), the cumulative earnings of the approaches presented in Columns 1 and 3 were identical, as well as those depicted in Columns 2 and 4. In the case at hand, however, comparison of the respective retained earnings balances as of the end of either 19x1 or 19x2 does not yield such a result because the nonmonetary asset has not been liquidated yet. In other words, the earlier conclusion regarding comparisons of a column with another column is appropriate only for an interval with only monetary assets on hand at both its beginning and its end. When a nonmonetary asset exists also, the cumulative earnings patterns vary among the four approaches because all the "catch-up" factors for which there are timing differences have not yet occurred. Refer now to the results of 19x3, which appear in Exhibit 12–6, with which the example concludes—and not unexpectedly with the sale of the remaining parcel of land.

In Column 1, the income statement contains a $1,500 gain based on the excess of the ($1,800) proceeds from the sale of land over its [($500 × .6 =) $300] original cost. Retained earnings is the ($1,760) sum of 19x2's ($260) and 19x3's ($1,500) gains on sales of land.

Column 2's income statement reflects the adverse effect of the beginning-of-year's ($1,960) cash being subjected to inflation during 19x3: a [$1,960 × (165 ÷ 150 =) 1.1 = $2,156; $2,156 − 1,960 =] $196 inflation loss. In addition, there is a $1,305 gain on the sale of the remaining parcel of land—based on the excess of the ($1,800) proceeds over its [($450 × 1.1 =) $495] restated cost basis. The resulting retained earnings—as explained in supporting computation No. 7 in the exhibit—is based on both 19x3's earnings and the ($590) December 31, 19x2 deficit restated to December 31, 19x3 purchasing power.

In Column 3, a ($600) gain appears in the income statement reflecting the increase in the current value of the land from $1,200 as of December 31, 19x2 to the $1,800 realized on the date of sale. The $1,760 year-end retained earnings reflects the gains from land value increases which appeared in the income statements of 19x1 ($300), 19x2 ($860), and 19x3 ($600). At this point, note that the retained earnings in Columns 1 and 3 are identical.

Column 4's income statement contains the same ($196) inflation loss that appears in Column 2. Its recognition of the gain resulting from appreciation of the land's value is limited to that portion of the increase not associated with the change in the general price level. The value increment is ($1,800 − 1,200 =) $600, but since ($1,200 × 1.1 = $1,320; $1,320 − 1,200 =) $120 relates to the effect of inflation, only ($600 − 120 =) $480 flows through the income statement. The ($460) year-end retained earnings, as derived in supporting computation No. 11 in the exhibit, is the result of combining 19x3's income with the December 31, 19x2 retained earnings restated to dollars expressed in end-of-19x3 purchas-

Exhibit 12–6

Monetary and Nonmonetary Assets—Balance Sheet and Income Statement Effects

	(1)	(2)	(3)	(4)
	Historical Cost		Current Value	
19x3	Nominal Dollars	Constant Dollars	Nominal Dollars	Constant Dollars
12/31/x3 Balance sheet:				
Cash	**$3,760**[1]	**$3,760**[1]	**$3,760**[1]	**$3,760**[1]
Capital stock	$2,000	$3,300[4]	$2,000	$3,300[4]
Retained earnings	1,760[3]	460[7]	1,760[9]	460[11]
Total	**$3,760**	**$3,760**	**$3,760**	**$3,760**
19x3 Income statement				
Gain on land	$1,500[2]	$1,305[5]	$ 600[8]	$ 480[10]
Inflation (loss)		$ (196)[6]		$ (196)[6]

Supporting computations:

[1] 12/31/2 of $1,960 + 1,800 = $3,760
[2] $1,800 (Proceeds) − 300 (cost) = $1,500
[3] 12/31/x2 of $260 + 19x3 income of $1,500 = $1,760
[4] 12/31/x2 of $3,000 × (165 ÷ 150 =) 1.1 = $3,300
[5] $1,800 − [12/31/x2 of $450 × (165 ÷ 150 =) 1.1 =] 495 = $1,305
[6] 12/31/x2 of $1,960 × (165 ÷ 150 =) 1.1 = $2,156; $2,156 − $1,960 = $196

[7] Retained earnings (deficit) 12/31/x2	$ (590)
Restated to 12/31/x3 : $590 × (165 ÷ 150 =) 1.1	$ (649)
19x3 income : $1,305[5] − 196[6] =	$1109
	$ 460

[8] $1,800 − 12/31/x2 of 1,200 − $600
[9] 12/31/x2 of $1,160 + 600 = $1,760
[10] $1,800 − [$1,200 × (165 ÷ 150 =) 1.1 =] $1,320 =

[10]	$480
[11] Retained earnings 12/31/x2	$160
Restated to 12/31/x3 : $160 × (165 ÷ 150 =) 1.1 =	$176
19x3 income (480[10] − 196[6] =)	$284
	$460

ing power. And as expected, the retained earnings amounts produced by Columns 2 and 4 are identical.

SUMMARY

To establish a context for understading the relative merits of the three alternatives to the traditional historical cost basis, several examples were presented. Some general observations are now provided to summarize the various features and machinations of, and similarities and distinctions among, the different approaches.

The following table identifies which financial statements—the balance sheet and/or the income statement—reflect amounts different from the traditional historical cost/nominal dollar basis of accounting.

	Nonmonetary Items	Monetary Items
Historical Cost/Constant Dollars	Balance sheet*	Income statement
Current Value/Nominal Dollars	Balance sheet *and* income statement	Neither
Current Value/Constant Dollars	Balance sheet *and* income statement	Income statement

* Recognize, however, that all of the income statement amounts themselves would be restated in terms of end-of-year purchasing power.

Under the *Historical Cost/Constant Dollar* approach, nonmonetary amounts are restated in the balance sheet. Since the restatement merely depicts the number of dollars having balance-sheet date purchasing power equal to that underlying the original transaction-date dollars, no gain or loss as such occurs and there is no explicit income statement effect.[11] Income statements are affected by the restatement portion of nonmonetary assets only when the assets' future service potential is exhausted—in a sale or through transformation into "expense" status. With respect to monetary items, however, their being amounts expressed in a fixed number of dollars precludes their being restated in the balance sheet. And because this very "fixed dollar" nature in a period of changes in the general price level results in a gain or loss, the effect is disclosed in the income statement.

When the *Current Value/Nominal Dollar* approach is used, the current value of nonmonetary assets is disclosed in the balance sheet, and the resulting holding gain or loss—although technically unrealized until an arm's-length transaction occurs—is included in the current income statement. The nature of monetary assets and liabilities precludes their having a current value different from their original transaction basis; there is, therefore, no balance sheet effect. There is no income statement consequence either because, unlike the "constant dollars" case, the effect of changes in the general price level is not accounted for.

Under the *Current Value/Constant Dollar* approach, the current value of nonmonetary assets appears in the balance sheet. That portion of a value change attributable to changes in the general price level does not affect current earnings. This means that only the remaining portion of the value change—deemed to be a measure of the *specific* price change—appears as a

305

gain or loss in the current income statement. Regarding monetary items, since their nature precludes recognizing a balance sheet amount different from their original transacted amount, any inflation-induced gain or loss in their purchasing power is included in the current period's earnings.

Given an exposure to the nature of, and differences among, the four distinct approaches to asset valuation and income measurement, we are ready to consider the relative merits of measuring the effects of general and specific price changes at a conceptual level to identify salient issues, points of contention, and implications for users of financial statements. These matters are examined in Chapter 13.

Additional Readings

FASB Research Report. *Field Tests of Financial Reporting in Units of General Purchasing Power.* Stamford, Conn.: Financial Accounting Standards Board, 1977.

Gay, William C., Jr. "Inflation, Indexation and Violation of Human Rights." *Price Waterhouse Review* (1978, vol. 23, no. 2), pp. 20–29.

Jones, Ralph Coughenour. "Financial Statements and the Uncertain Dollar." *The Journal of Accountancy* (September 1935), pp. 171–97.

King, Alfred M. "Price-Level Restatement: Solution or Problem?" *Management Accounting* (November 1976), pp. 16–18.

Paton, William A. "Measuring Profits under Inflation Conditions: A Serious Problem for Accountants." *The Journal of Accountancy* (January 1950), pp. 16–27.

Roehm, Harper A., and Castellano, Joseph F. "Inflation Accounting: A Compromise." *The CPA Journal* (September 1978), pp. 38–47.

Seed, Allen H, III. *Inflation: Its Impact on Financial Reporting and Decision Making.* New York: Financial Executives Research Foundation, 1978.

Shank, John K. *Price Level Adjusted Statements and Management Decisions.* New York: Financial Executives Research Foundation, 1975.

Staff of the (AICPA) Accounting Research Division. *Reporting the Financial Effects of Price Level Changes.* New York: American Institute of Certified Public Accountants, 1963.

Stickney, Clyde P., and Green, David O. "No Price Level Adjusted Statements, Please (Pleas)." *The CPA Journal* (January 1974), pp. 25–31.

Sweeney, Henry W. *Stabilized Accounting.* New York: Harper & Brothers, 1936.

Tierney, Cecelia. "Price-Level Adjustments—Problem in Perspective." *The Journal of Accountancy* (November 1963), pp. 56–60.

Wilcox, Edward B., and Greer, Howard C. "The Case against Price-Level Adjustments in Income Determination." *The Journal of Accountancy* (December 1950), pp. 492–504.

13

Financial Reporting and Changing Prices: Part 2

Chapter 12 introduced the topic of accounting for general and specific price changes. It suggested that in fact there are two accounting questions that need to be resolved. There is the matter of what attribute should be measured in financial statements, and there is the separate question of how the attribute should be measured. The two attributes that can be measured are *historical cost* and *current value,* and measurement can be effected with either *nominal dollars* or *constant dollars.*

The objective of this chapter is to examine these issues in terms of their underlying nature—their presumed benefits and their alleged deficiencies. At the outset, there is an analysis of the traditional historical cost basis. It is followed by a discussion of the relative merits of measuring cost data with constant dollars, as distinct from the traditional nominal dollar approach. The current value basis of accounting is then examined, culminating in a discussion of contemporary financial reporting applications.

THE HISTORICAL COST BASIS OF ACCOUNTING

The traditional approach to accounting focuses on historical exchange prices. The adjective *historical* refers to the fact that subsequent to the date a particular resource is acquired, it is reflected in financial statements at its original cost. This means the basis at which it first came into the entity's realm of accountability. Cost is a foregoing, a sacrifice to obtain a reciprocal benefit, and it is measured by the exchange price reflecting a transaction between independent parties. Cost is the basis on which accountants have traditionally recorded the value of economic resources. At the time of an exchange, cost is assumed to be identical with value; it is, therefore, viewed as being an objective measure of value received.

The primacy of valuation in the historical cost basis of accounting can be understood in light of its relationship with other principles of accounting. First, the *realization* concept of accounting suggests that only transactions between distinct parties shall be accounted for, and at amounts which reflect agreed-upon historical exchange prices. Second, *matching* of revenues and expenses, rather than mere valuation of an enterprise's owners' equity at two dates, is predicated on the notion that comparing benefits received with their related costs is the most meaningful way to measure earnings. Third, the cost basis has the quality of being internally *consistent,* that is, once cost is recorded, it becomes the basis of disclosure in all subsequent financial statements. Fourth, *objectivity* is one of the attributes of the cost basis. To rely on periodic valuation which reflects economic resources' current worth introduces subjectivity, and a decline in the disclosures' reliability. And finally, the cost basis in periods of rising prices yields more *conservative* balance sheet amounts than does a system which recognizes current values.

Criticism of the Traditional Cost Approach

One of the criticisms of the traditional historical cost basis focuses on the issue of *homogeneity.* It is argued that dollars which appear in financial statements are only representations of the more fundamental notion of current purchasing power. A reader of financial statements assumes that data between years are comparable. Indeed they are comparable insofar as it is the *number* of dollars being accounted for. But, in fact, users of accounting data want to be able to assume that the values implied by "dollars," that is, the purchasing power underlying dollars of different periods, is constant as well.

Historical cost accounting in units of money does not provide this kind of comparability. Consider the question of whether you would prefer to have four apples or five apples. Many persons would immediately indicate a preference for five apples, because they assume all nine apples are of equal size. The cautious individual would not indicate a preference until the relative sizes of the nine apples were known. The analogy to the stable-dollar assumption of accounting is obvious: different years' financial statements reflecting dollars of different purchasing power are not comparable, and to the extent that preparers and users of such data assume that they are comparable, they operate with invalid premises.

The homogeneity question goes even beyond interperiod comparability of financial statements. Even within a particular period, costs which had arisen in prior periods but which were capitalized because related revenues had not been generated yet are matched with current revenues. For instance, when goods purchased in 19x1 are only sold in 19x3, they are an inventory asset at the end of 19x1 and 19x2; as part of 19x3 cost of goods sold, they are matched with 19x3 revenues to determine 19x3 income. If the *value* of 19x1 dollars is different from that of 19x3 dollars, the matching process becomes one similar to that of the proverbial mixing of apples and oranges—or for that matter yen, pesos, francs and dollars.

A second alleged shortcoming of the historical cost basis is that in addition to yielding dollars having different underlying values, the amounts which appear in the financial statements offer little if any insight into current values. Admittedly, the amounts do portray the number of dollars expended at the time cost was incurred, and this information could possibly be useful to persons interested solely in stewardship aspects of a company's management. But in an age of publicly held enterprises, absentee ownership, and lay investors for whom *value*—currently and prospectively—might be of paramount importance, exposure to historical cost-based accounting data is comparable to operating an automobile using the rear-view mirror and not the front-facing window.

A third criticism of historical cost accounting focuses on its requirement that an arm's length transaction with external parties is effectively a prerequisite for accountability. If there is no transaction as such, there is no basis for accountability. (Admittedly, the accrual principle might be viewed as a modification of this premise inasmuch as it mandates recognition of certain economic events even though a formal, physical transaction as such does not occur.) In any case, the *transaction* requirement is viewed by some as reflecting a rather unworldly approach to economic phenomena. Its exclusion of environmental influences—notably changes in particular resources' value as evidenced by activity in pertinent marketplaces—is seen as being a parochial attitude toward measuring and disclosing the effects of important accountable phenomena.

Other perceived deficiencies in the historical cost basis include its failure to conform to classical economics' approach to value and income measurement, and more generally that it does not provide a relevant basis for assessing the current value of the enterprise as whole. In addition, it does not provide the cash-flow orientation that present and prospective stockholders seek in light of their dividend income and capital appreciation investment objectives, although this is a purpose of providing a statement of changes in financial position.

From an internal management point of view, a company presumably allocates its resources and prices its goods and services on the basis of existing and expected circumstances and states of nature. Accounting data biased in favor of depicting sacrifices made by prior periods' managers offer little insight for future-directed decision making.

A final major objection to the historical cost basis of accounting points to the distortions it may foster in governmental taxation of income. Although tax statutes do not necessarily reflect accounting rules used for financial reporting, income taxes are in fact based largely on the same historical cost data. Companies, therefore, pay taxes on income which, because of the matching principle, reflects many costs sustained in prior periods whose current replacement requires incurring relatively higher costs. Were the base on which taxes are computed to reflect current, rather than historical, costs, less taxes would accrue and there would be larger after-tax cash flow to finance the higher replacement costs. But because the existing system imposes taxes on the basis of older, invariably lower costs which results in higher taxable income, after paying relatively higher taxes the after-tax cash flow is lower. Thus, when visualizing the actual taxes paid in light of high replacement costs which will be incurred henceforth, it has been argued the impact of income taxation is significantly larger than what a historical cost-based system of taxation would seem to suggest. Opponents of the traditional approach would maintain that were there to be modifications for financial reporting purposes, there might then be an opportunity to introduce change in the tax area as well.

Support for the Traditional Cost Approach

Supporters of the traditional historical cost basis of accounting tend to base a large part of their position on the system's compatibility with other generally accepted accounting principles. Indeed, in an earlier discussion in Chapter 3, it was pointed out that many of the fundamental principles of accounting support or are supported by, companion principles. The particular elements which "justify" adherence to the historical cost basis already specifically cited in this chapter are the realization concept, the matching principle, interperiod consistency, the objectivity criterion, and the doctrine of conservatism. Opponents of the historical cost basis question the validity of *objectivity* and *conservatism,* and they dispute the meaningfulness of matching unlike dollars.

At an even more fundamental level, historical cost supporters point out that the traditional function of accounting precludes deviating from historical costs. To use current value-based measurement rules, they assert, is inappropriate since accounting does not, and should not, strive to present information about the current value of either particular assets or the enterprise at large. To the extent such information is deemed to be useful, it could be disclosed "outside" of an enterprise's financial statements.

Moreover, to disclose what an asset would cost today when in fact it was purchased a decade earlier at a lower price is of questionable usefulness. Similarly, to identify the current value rather than that which had actually been expended previously might be interesting, but it would be of little if any consequence once the asset is already owned and paid for. And to suggest that presently constituted earnings measurement should be supplanted by a system which recognizes the fluctuation of values on the basis of transactions not directly involving the entity raises unwarranted questions about the proven reliability of the traditional approach to realization of revenues, gains, and losses. To gauge the number of dollars an owned asset would yield if it were disposed of in a non-duress sale would violate the spirit, if not the essence, of the going-concern assumption because liquidation, albeit of a non-distress nature, is not the kind of transaction into which a going concern typically enters. This line of reasoning can be countered by observing that although the notion of a going concern relates to the enterprise at large, there is continual turnover of particular resources.

Apparent Deviations from the Cost Basis

Before analyzing the various approaches proposed as substitutes for the traditional historical cost basis of accounting, several instances of apparent deviations from historical costs will be examined. The first is the last-in, first-out (LIFO) system of assigning inventory costs to a period's operations and to the end-of-period inventory asset balance. The nature of this costing method is to treat the most recent (unit) costs of purchased and manufactured merchandise as the cost of the goods sold during the period. Concurrently, the (unit) costs of the merchandise on hand at the beginning of the period become the basis for determining the end-of-period inventory on hand. The result is that the amount reflected in the income statement is approximately the current replacement cost of the goods sold and *not* necessarily the actual historical cost of the units sold. Indeed, as pointed out in the discussion in Chapter 6, the effect of LIFO on income is particularly pronounced in periods of rising prices. As to its being a deviation from historical cost, it should be recognized that all of the amounts comprising cost of goods sold and inventory on hand do in fact reflect historical costs in the sense they are all based on historical exchange prices resulting from arm's length transactions.

A second apparent departure from the historical cost basis is the required use of the lower-of-cost-or-market method for valuing inventory (see Chapter 6) and marketable equity securities (see Chapter 10). The nature of this method is to reflect the asset at current value when it is less than the historical cost basis. The resulting loss attributable to inventory and marketable equity securities classified as current assets is recognized immediately in the earn-ings statement even though it is technically not realized until an actual sale is effected. This deviation is defended on the grounds that there has been a loss of economic benefit and, therefore, in the interests of accounting conser-vatism, the presumed objectivity quality of the cost basis is superseded by the relative subjectivity of a current value. If market values exceed historical costs, however, upward adjustments are not permitted, except for written-down marketable equity securities and then not to exceed the original histor-ical cost.

A third apparent deviation from strict historical cost accounting is the requirement that the equity method of accounting be used when a company has either a controlling or qualifying significant investment interest in another corporation. As described in Chapter 10, although the initial investment is recorded on the basis of its cost, the equity method prescribes that the investor's balance sheet investment reflect its proportionate share of the investee's undistributed earnings. The equity method is defended on the grounds it is a logical extension of the accrual method of accounting; that is, the equity method results not from a deviation from the cost basis but rather from an event recognizable as revenue, in effect a type of receivable or a claim on the investee's equity.

A fourth apparent departure from historical cost is the requirement that when a business combination is recorded as a purchase (as opposed to being accounted for as a pooling of interests), the excess of purchase price paid over the owners' equity acquired is assigned to particular assets and liabilities on the basis of their fair values. Accordingly, some of the assets and liabilities of the combined enterprise are reflected in subsequent balance sheets on the basis of their value as of the combination date rather than their original cost. In this situation, however, a new arm's length transaction has in fact occurred. As is the case in the purchase of any asset, the currently negotiated price supersedes any prior basis of valuation. The valuation prob-lem for accountants arises in a business combination once the aggregate value has been agreed on; it is usually only then that valuation of the com-binee's individual assets and liabilities occurs. It is, therefore, in this con-text that the fair value of the aggregate assets must be allocated to individual assets; that is, it is the cost incurred by the combinor—which is by definition that date's current value—that is assigned to the combinee's assets and liabilities.

The final apparent deviation from historical cost occurs in certain non-monetary transactions, a subject examined in Chapter 7. The relevant feature of this apparent exception is that accounting for such transactions is gener-ally based on the fair value of the assets or services involved. However, rather than being a departure from the historical cost basis, it represents "the only method consistent with the accounting principle that an asset acquired should be reported at its cost as measured by the fair value of the asset relinquished to acquire it."[1] By virtue of being an accountable transaction with cash the *only* missing element in a pure exchange, the cost is measured by direct reference to the value of the goods or services—rather than have the cash transferred be the intermediary measure.

Thus, although there are five possible aspects of the traditional accounting model that ostensibly depart from strict historical cost accounting, each can be justified, and in most of the instances it can be demonstrated that what in form appears to be a departure, in substance is not the case at all.

ACCOUNTING FOR CHANGES IN THE GENERAL PRICE LEVEL

A balance sheet restated to depict the effect of changes in the general price level reflects monetary assets and liabilities at their recorded amounts. Nonmonetary items, on the other hand, are restated to reflect the purchasing power of the dollar as of the balance sheet date. Recognize, however, that the purchasing power of some earlier base period is used in the publication of *national income* data, and has been proposed by some as an option that should be available to individual companies as well. The amounts comprising an income statement are nonmonetary because they are, in effect, component elements of the nonmonetary retained earnings appearing in the balance sheet. Therefore, because of their nonmonetary nature, they too are restated in terms of the end-of-year general price level.

In the examples appearing in Chapter 12, index numbers were used to restate dollar amounts representing different price levels. In the case of revenues, expenses, gains, and losses appearing in an earnings statement, index numbers and their resulting conversion factors are used as well. For those amounts which are assumed to occur uniformly during the year such as sales revenue and salaries expense, the conversion factor is derived by relating the year-end index number to that which reflects an average for the year. For example, if the beginning-of-year index number is 100 and the end-of-year index is 121 and there was 10 percent inflation during each half of the year, the average index is computed to be 110.

The Case for Accounting for Changes in the General Price Level

The case for restating historical cost data to recognize changes in the general price level is a multifaceted one. Perhaps its most important contention is that failure to restate can, and invariably does, cause financial state-

---

[1] *Accounting Principles Board Opinion No. 29,* paragraph 15.

ments to be misleading. Earnings can be overstated in a period of inflation because revenues reflecting the current price level are matched with expenses expressed in dollars which do not reflect the current price level. Only if expense dollars are restated in terms of the equivalent number of current dollars, would a valid measure of earnings be forthcoming.

This relates to the fundamental premise that one should not use a varying unit of measure. In the same sense that yen and pesos are not additive because they are different units of measure, dollars having different purchasing power are not additive. In those instances in which unlike units of measure are treated as if they were alike, the results become distorted and meaningless. This notion underlies the distinction between *nominal* dollars and *constant* dollars. The *"nominal* dollars" approach refers to unlike dollars being treated as though they were alike on the basis of their bearing the same name "dollar." The *"constant* dollars" approach refers to unlike dollars being restated into units having a fixed purchasing power, that is, purchasing power at a common point in time such as the end of the current fiscal year or the base period used in calculating the price index.

Income taxes are assessed on the basis of earnings amounts *not* restated for inflation. When restated earnings are lower than conventional income, business enterprises are effectively taxed on non-existent profits—non-existent in the sense that taxable income is based on numbers of dollars rather than their underlying purchasing power.

Inflated after-tax income, in turn, can motivate stockholders to expect sizable cash dividends. Such dividends may not be feasible, however, because a greater number of dollars must be expended to replace the resources whose service potential was exhausted in the process of generating revenues—even if the replacement price were only to reflect an increase corresponding to the change in the general price level. Inflated earnings data also encourage employees to clamor for higher remuneration when, in fact, the apparent income is needed to replenish assets to maintain a constant level of operating capacity.

The high reported income caused by failure to restate its underlying components poses yet another problem. In an era when companies are increasingly concerned with avoiding liquidity crises and with being able to obtain long-term infusions of capital, it is difficult to reconcile the adverse effect of inflation with companies' earnings reports. The uninitiated may not understand that despite significant amounts of reported earnings, a particular company may be in a precarious liquidity state or may encounter investor resistance when it seeks to issue debt or equity securities. Were earnings data restated to reflect the actual inflationary circumstances in which a company operates, it might be easier to relate an enterprise's liquidity and access-to-capital predicaments to its actual earnings experience.

Another reason for restatement relates to interperiod comparability of financial statements. Recall our earlier reference to the effort made by economists to express national income data in constant dollars so that interyear variations might represent *real* increases or decreases in gross national product and related measures of economic activity. Accounting data, as presently constituted, are retrospective rather than prospective in nature. This suggests that trend information consisting of various periods' accounting data which is an important feature of financial statement analysis should be based on dollars having common purchasing power.

Supporters of a system which recognizes the effect of changes in the general price level also point out that the resulting restatement of accounting data does not compromise the historical cost basis of accounting. As demonstrated by Chapter 12's examples, constant dollars merely express historical cost dollars in terms of purchasing power in effect as of a particular balance sheet date.

Other points advanced by supporters of restatement include the belief the effect of changes in the general price level would be more readily appreciated if there was restatement. It is said that readers of financial statements assume that dollar amounts are homogeneous when, in fact, differences in underlying purchasing power indicate they are not. In summary, if the accounting model is to continue to be a comprehensive medium through which economic data are identified, measured and communicated, it is said there must be explicit, integrated recognition of the impact of a phenomenon as real as changing price levels.

The Case against Accounting for Changes in the General Price Level

Opponents to accounting for changes in the general price level maintain that, the term *restatement* notwithstanding, the nature of the procedures required to account for changes in the general price level is a departure from the traditional historical cost accounting model. They also argue that because legal precedents and principles of taxation are based on a system having no restatement provisions, it would be naive and wasteful to modify the financial reporting model only to have it operate separate from the taxation model. The counter argument is that with the implementation of a restatement system, there would be basis for modifying the legal and taxation applications as well.

Some opponents of restatement assert that the index numbers underlying the restated dollar amounts are merely estimates of average price behavior in the economy at large and that restatement is, therefore, inconsistent with the exactness which permeates the existing accounting system. Advocates of

315

restatement, however, offer as a counter argument the assertion that, in fact, estimates already pervade the historical cost approach. An allowance for doubtful accounts is based on an estimate, the system for depreciating plant assets is based on several estimates, and the recognition of loss contingencies requires conjecture about future outcomes. So the *estimate* quality of restating historical cost data should not, in their opinion, be viewed as tainting an otherwise sound system.

Another argument advanced by opponents of restatement is that inflation in any particular year in the United States has typically not been of sufficient size to warrant modification of existing accounting practices, and that the double digit inflation experienced in the 1970s was a relatively temporary aberration attributable to an especially acute energy crisis. In response to this argument, supporters of restatement maintain that even if inflation in a particular year is immaterial in size, the cumulative effect of general price changes over several years does tend to be significant and, therefore, warrants restatement. Opponents of restatement also advance the argument that rather than restating all the data comprising financial statements, the nature, magnitude and impact of inflation could be disclosed adequately as supplementary information rather than in the basic financial statements. This, in fact, was the approach advanced by the Financial Accounting Standards Board in its Statement No. 33, issued in September 1979.[2]

A back-to-basics type of argument contends the stable-dollar assumption conveys the traditional belief that it is not in the realm of accounting and thus of financial statements to identify, measure, and communicate the effects of changes in purchasing power over time. Indeed, the phenomenon of a changing price level is, in its own right, difficult enough for laymen to understand and for economists to explain. Sensitizing accounting data to the occurrence of inflation and deflation would increase rather than mitigate the extent of existing misunderstanding and confusion.

Perhaps the most potent point raised by opponents of restatement is that the nature of the resulting accounting data would affect the manner in which companies structure their business affairs. Because gains and losses on monetary assets and liabilities are recognized during a period of changing price levels, being in a net monetary liability position is an attractive stance during inflation, and an inflation gain can ensue. An opposite effect tends to occur when a net monetary asset situation prevails.

Given this knowledge about the resulting accounting effects, a company anticipating inflation can create a net monetary liability position and with it

---

[2] *Financial Accounting Standards Board Statement No. 33* (Stamford, Conn.: Financial Accounting Standards Board, 1979). Copyright © by Financial Accounting Standards Board, High Ridge Park, Stamford, Connecticut 06905, U.S.A. Reprinted with permission. Copies of the complete document are available from the FASB.

an inflation gain. Were it not for the inflation gain wrought by restatement, the company might well have elected to liquidate some of its debt. Conversely, the prospect of being required to recognize an inflation loss may well cause managers to act defensively and possibly opt for that avenue which yields the "best" accounting result.

The counter argument is that the resulting accounting does indeed convey a message, and this message should motivate managers to react meaningfully to an expected change in the general price level. The very emergence of an inflation gain when an enterprise is in a pronounced net monetary liability position tells an important story. It dramatizes the point that in anticipation of a period of inflation, hedging against prospectively less valuable dollars can be effected by borrowing today's dollars expecting to subsequently repay with less valuable dollars, that is, dollars having less purchasing power. Disclosure of such a phenomenon apprises readers of the presence and impact of general price changes. It also alerts them to the fact the enterprise and its managers should be evaluated in light of what means are employed to anticipate and to react to inflation or deflation.

THE CURRENT VALUE BASIS OF ACCOUNTING

In Chapter 12 a distinction was made between the historical cost and current value bases of accounting. It was pointed out that under either basis it is possible to restate the data to reflect the effect of changes in the general price level; that is, historical cost amounts can be presented in either nominal dollars or constant dollars, and the same choice exists for current value data. Distinct from the issue of appropriate measuring unit is the question of the attribute to be measured—historical cost or current value. Under the historical cost/nominal dollar approach, the effect of neither general nor specific price changes appears in financial statements. Under the historical cost/constant dollar approach, only the impact of changes in the general price level is reflected in financial statements. If the current value/nominal dollar approach is used, the separate effects of general and specific price changes cannot be discerned. But when the current value/constant dollar approach is used, specific price changes are differentiated from general price changes. A specific price change is that portion of the change in its value not attributable to changes in the general price level.

Whereas Chapter 12 considered the nature of restatement, attention is now directed toward the matter of what should be the attribute to be measured, that is, a current value basis of accounting or the historical cost basis of accounting. The question of whether or not to superimpose restatement on the current value basis—to distinguish between the effects of general and

317

specific price changes—is considered *after* examining some of the fundamental conceptual issues which relate to the current value basis proper.

An Illustration

One attribute of current value that might be measured is the replacement
cost of economic resources. In simplified form, this is done by estimating the
cost that would be incurred currently to obtain an asset with the equivalent
productive capacity as that which is already owned. The nature of this
approach is illustrated in Exhibits 13–1 and 13–2.

Exhibit 13–1 deals with a particular year's income statement and Exhibit
13–2 presents the end-of-year balance sheet results. The background information and data underlying these exhibits are as follows. The beginning-of-
year inventory's historical cost was $2,500 and its replacement cost at that
date was $2,800. During the year, purchases were $5,000, and sales totaled
$14,000. The end-of-year inventory's historical cost basis is $3,000 and its
replacement cost is $3,400. The FIFO method of inventory costing is used,
and the date-of-sale replacement cost of the goods sold was $5,600. Ma-
chinery was purchased at the beginning of the year for $11,000, and it was
depreciated on a straight-line basis with no anticipated salvage value at the
end of its expected five-year useful life. A few days after its acquisition, the
company learned that the replacement cost of the machinery had risen to
$13,000. There was no change in the general price level during the year.
Other expenses of $4,000 resulted in immediate cash disbursements.

Since the income statement based on historical costs is relatively uncomplicated, the ensuing discussion is directed toward the earnings statement
that contains replacement cost data. The $5,600 cost of goods sold is based
on the given date-of-sale replacement cost of the inventory sold. To reconcile
the $1,100 difference between this amount and the $4,500 cost of goods sold
generated by the historical cost basis, consider the following:

	Historical Cost	Replacement Cost	Difference
Beginning inventory	$2,500	$2,800	$ 300
Purchases	+5,000	5,000	
Increase in replacement cost of goods available for sale		+1,200	+1,200
Cost of goods available for sale	$7,500	$9,000	$1,500
Ending inventory	-3,000	-3,400	-400
	$4,500	$5,600	$1,100

318

Exhibit 13–1

Replacement Cost Income Statement

		Historical Cost	Replacement Cost
Sales		$14,000	$14,000
Cost of goods sold		4,500[1]	5,600[3]
Gross profit		$ 9,500	$ 8,400
Depreciation expense		$ 2,200[2]	$ 2,600[4]
Other expenses		4,000	4,000
Total		$ 6,200	$ 6,600
Net income		**$ 3,300**	
Current operating income			$ 1,800
Realized holding gain:			
On (sold) inventory	$1,100[5]		
On (depreciated) machinery	400[6]		
Total			$ 1,500
Realized income			$ 3,300
Unrealized holding gain:			
On (growth in) inventory	$ 100[7]		
On (undepreciated) machinery	1,600[8]		
Total			$ 1,700
Replacement cost income			**$ 5,000**

Supporting computations:
[1] $2,500 + 5,000 = $7,500; $7,500 − 3,000 = $4,500
[2] $11,000 ÷ 5 years = $2,200
[3] Given
[4] $13,000 ÷ 5 years = $2,600
[5] $5,600 − 4,500 = $1,100
[6] $2,600 − 2,200 = $400
[7] ($3,400 − 2,800 =) $600; $600 − ($3,000 − 2,500 =) $500 = $100
[8] (13,000 − 2,600 =) $10,400; $10,400 − ($11,000 − 2,200 =) $8,800 = $1,600

This schedule points out that besides the $300 difference between the beginning-of-year inventory's original cost and its replacement cost, during the year there was an additional $1,200 cost appreciation—of units on hand at the beginning of the year and/or of merchandise purchased during the year. Of the resulting ($300 + 1,200 =) $1,500 increase, $400 is contained in ending inventory, and ($1,500 − 400 =) $1,100 is associated with units that were sold.

Exhibit 13–2
Replacement Cost Balance Sheet

	Historical Cost	Replacement Cost
Cash	$ 6,000	$ 6,000
Inventory	3,000	3,400
Current assets	$ 9,000	$ 9,400
Machinery	$11,000	$13,000
Accumulated depreciation	(2,200)	(2,600)
Plant assets	$ 8,800	$10,400
Total assets	**$17,800**	**$19,800**
Paid-in capital	$ 4,500	$ 4,500
Retained earnings	13,300	15,300
Total equities	**$17,800**	**$19,800**

Depreciation expense is based on the machinery's replacement cost so that the earnings statement depicts the cost of using an asset in terms of its current cost. Inventory is used when merchandise is sold, and a depreciable asset is used as it experiences physical deterioration and technological obsolescence—such uses occurring as part of the revenue generating process. When current costs are measured, the use of resources such as inventory and depreciable assets is measured in terms of the number of dollars that must be expended to replace the used resource.

In an income statement based on replacement cost data, the amount that remains after expenses are subtracted from revenues is called *current operating income*. It is the income that results when current revenues are matched with replacement costs. It is the amount looked on by some as a measure of disposable income. When current costs exceed past costs as is usual, current operating income is less than the net income that appears in a historical cost earnings statement. This is because only the unfavorable aspect of higher replacement costs has been considered—unfavorable in the sense that more dollars will be required to replace the asset whose service potential has been exhausted.

Holding Gains

It should be recognized that there is a favorable factor to consider as well. Despite the fact that the cost of subsequent purchases exceeds that of past purchases, the company does benefit from having acquired the assets previously at a lesser amount than would be the case today. This, in turn, leads us to the earnings statement's recognition of *holding gains*. This section of the income statement identifies the gains or losses which accrue to the company as a result of merely holding assets while their replacement cost increases or decreases. To better appreciate the favorable aspect being depicted, the expression *cost savings* might be more descriptive than *holding gain*.

Realized holding gains are those gains and losses which relate to a portion of an asset whose exhausted service potential appears in the same earnings statement as a cost of generating revenue, that is, as a determinant of current operating income. The realized quality of the $1,100 holding gain relating to inventory is the difference between the historical cost and replacement cost of the goods sold. And with respect to the machinery, because one-fifth of its cost is depreciated during the period, 20 percent of its ($13,000 − 11,000 =) $2,000 cost appreciation, or $400, is recognized as a realized holding gain.

On adding the realized holding gain to the current operating income, the resulting sum is referred to as *realized income*. This is the amount the company actually realized during the period. It was observed earlier that current operating income includes the unfavorable effect of prospectively incurring replacement costs which exceed historical cost, and that the realized holding gain identifies the favorable aspect of cost appreciation. It is also the very same cost appreciation whose unfavorable and favorable aspects are afforded particular attention at different points in the determination of earnings.

The dollar amount of the Realized Income appearing in the replacement-cost earnings statement is identical with the amount of Net Income generated by the historical cost basis of accounting. However, the distinctive aspect of the replacement-cost approach is that it identifies the existence of cost appreciation. It does so in a manner which effectively isolates its retrospective impact—actually incurring a historical cost which is less than what would have subsequently been the case—and its prospective effect, that is, having to absorb a higher cost in an actual subsequent replacement than had previously been the case.

Unrealized holding gains are the holding gains—perhaps more descriptively, the cost savings—that relate to that portion of assets whose service potential has not yet been exhausted. In the exhibit, both inventory and machinery on hand at year-end are assets whose service potential had not yet been fully reflected as an expense.

With respect to inventory, its historical cost is $3,000 and its replacement cost is $3,400. This means that ($3,400 − 3,000 =) $400 is the ending inventory's unrealized holding gain. Because there was also an unrealized holding gain in the period's beginning inventory of ($2,800 − 2,500 =) $300, only the ($400 − 300 =) $100 not previously recognized appears in this period's earnings statement. This result might be more understandable upon considering the following:

1.	Cost appreciation of inventory on hand at beginning of the period ($2,800 − 2,500 =)	$ 300
2.	Cost appreciation during the period of goods available for sale (derived)	+1,200
3.	Total cost appreciation of goods available for sale	$1,500
4.	Cost appreciation of inventory on hand at end of the period ($3,400 − 3,000 =)	− 400
5.	**Cost appreciation of goods sold during the period** ($5,600 − 4,500 =)	**$1,100**

Since $1,200 (line 2) is the amount of the holding gain that occurred during the period, and $1,100 (line 5) is that portion of the period's holding gain which has been realized, the remaining ($1,200 − 1,100 =) $100 is the unrealized holding gain for the period.

Regarding machinery, realization occurs only when the asset's underlying service potential has been exhausted in the process of generating revenue. Since 20 percent of the machinery's cost basis has been depreciated, 20 percent of its ($13,000 − 11,000 =) $2,000 holding gain, or $400, is viewed as having been realized. Because 80 percent of the machinery has yet to be depreciated, the remaining 80 percent of the $2,000 holding gain, or $1,600, appears in the earnings statement as an unrealized holding gain.

The ($100 + 1,600 =) $1,700 total unrealized holding gain is added to the realized income, and the resulting sum is referred to as Replacement Cost Income. This amount is also referred to as Business Income, Economic Income, or Earned Income. This measure of income identifies the enterprise's net increase in owners' equity resulting from *both* its operations *and* changes in the replacement cost of the economic resources underlying its owners' equity.

General Observations

The $3,200 sum of the $1,500 realized holding gain and the $1,700 unrealized holding gain is a measure of the increase in the assets' replacement cost during the current period—$1,200 relating to inventory and $2,000 pertaining to machinery. The ($1,500) holding gain realized is evidenced by its appearance in the earnings statement not only as a component in deriving Realized Income but in the determination of Current Operating Income as well. This occurs by virtue of cost of goods sold and depreciation expense reported at amounts larger than their respective historical costs. The ($1,700) unrealized holding gain, because it has yet to affect any period's Current Operating Income, causes the pertinent assets appearing in the replacement cost balance sheet to be reflected at amounts which exceed those reflected in a balance sheet prepared under the historical cost basis of accounting.

Refer now to Exhibit 13–2. The inventory and machinery asset amounts differ between the historical cost and replacement cost bases, and both the machinery proper and its related accumulated depreciation are affected. On the equities side of the balance sheets, there is a ($15,300 − 13,300 =) $2,000 difference between the respective amounts of retained earnings. There is also a ($19,800 − 17,800 =) $2,000 difference between the balance sheets' total assets.

The question that arises is why do the two balance sheets' respective amounts of retained earnings differ by $2,000 if the period's unrealized holding gain is only $1,700? The answer lies in the fact the $1,700 amount is a measure of the current period's holding gain while the $2,000 higher amount in the replacement cost balance sheet is a measure of the *cumulative* unrealized holding gain related to assets on hand. The ($2,000 − 1,700 =) $300 difference relates to, and is, therefore, explained by, the ($2,800 − 2,500 =) $300 unrealized holding gain in the inventory on hand at the beginning of the period.

Its relevance to the issue at hand (the FIFO method of inventory costing notwithstanding) can be appreciated by referring to the following data:

1.	Cost appreciation of inventory on hand at beginning of the period ($2,800 − 2,500 =)	$ 300
2.	Cost appreciation during the period of goods available for sale (derived)	+1,200
3.	Total cost appreciation of goods available for sale	$1,500
4.	Cost appreciation of inventory on hand at end of the period ($3,400 − 3,000 =)	− 400
5.	**Cost appreciation of goods sold during the period** **($5,600 − 4,500 =)**	**$1,100**

Of the $1,100 holding gain which is realized, $300 was lodged in beginning inventory because it had arisen in a prior period and had, therefore, been previously recognized as being unrealized; this $300 is realized in the current period. It follows that only ($1,100 − 300 =) $800 of the gain realized in the current period actually occurred during this period. Since a $1,200 gain did occur this year, and since $800 of it was also realized during the period, the remaining ($1,200 − 800 =) $400 is unrealized as of the end of the period. In other words, even though $400 is the cumulative unrealized holding gain in ending inventory, there was an unrealized holding gain of $300 in beginning inventory, and only the ($400 − 300 =) $100 unrealized holding gain increment appears as an unrealized holding gain in the current replacement cost earnings statement. The full $400 unrealized holding gain does appear in the resulting balance sheet, however.

The Benefits of the Current Value Basis of Accounting

Perhaps the most basic argument advanced in support of the current value basis of accounting is that economic resources and obligations depicted in financial statements should be presented on a basis that facilitates predictions of future operating results. Investors in a company's equity securities seek future cash flow returns on their investment—in the form of cash dividend distributions, capital appreciation, or both. To forecast the likelihood of particular future outcomes, information as chronologically close as possible to such future dates is needed. Since the present is closer to the future than the past is, information about values, relationship, circumstances, and environmental factors in effect as of the balance sheet date emerges as the most appropriate input for investors to obtain and thereby to be able to use.

In addition, the "direct" nature of the current value basis is deemed to be significant. Direct reference to "market" data is considered to be superior to the strict "transactions" nature of the historical cost basis of accounting which is characterized by allocations, estimates, and amortizations. In other words, even though the current value approach is based to a considerable extent on estimates, estimates are also a characteristic of the historical cost approach. What then distinguishes the current value approach (from the historical cost approach) is its focal point being current market phenomena rather than transactions-based data of the past.

A replacement cost based earnings statement can provide new information. Information about holding gains and losses, realized and yet-to-be realized portions of such changes in value, and the disclosure of current operating income based on the replacement cost, rather than historical cost, of expenses are said to provide a better explanation of changes in an enterprise's owners' equity than does the mere matching of current revenues with expenses which reflect historical costs.

Implementation of the current value basis of accounting, in the opinion of

324

many of its supporters, also reduces the need to be concerned explicitly with the accounting implications of changes in the general price level. One of the primary features of restating historical costs to reflect the effect of changes in the general price level is to dramatize the impact of uncontrollable external phenomena on an enterprise's operating results and financial condition. Rather than using index numbers designed to reflect economy-wide average price movements of heterogeneous goods and services, current value data, computed individually for particular assets or classes of relatively homogeneous assets, are likely to be more meaningful if only because their nature embraces all external factors, that is, both specific and general price change phenomena.

A somewhat related point is that current values are more homogeneous than historical costs. Under a historical cost system, the dollar amounts appearing in a company's financial statements are not homogeneous because they pertain to amounts of cost at different acquisition dates. Thus, a dollar amount purporting to measure the cost of several parcels of owned land is merely the arithmetic sum of different acquisition amounts. Moreover, it is difficult, if not impossible, to make meaningful intercompany comparisons. That the dollar amount of one company's cost of fixed assets is twice that of another company's could be as much the result of costs incurred in the *same* period for *different* assets as it could relate to costs incurred for the *same* assets acquired in *different* periods. By using current values, all assets are reflected in terms of a common, current value, regardless when they were acquired.

Perhaps the most important benefit provided by the current value basis of accounting is that which can be dramatized by the following illustration. A person received a valuable wristwatch as a gift; a short time later, the wristwatch is lost and its owner is without the means of determining what the time of day is: what is the dollar amount of the loss? From a purely historical cost point of view, the answer would be there was no monetary loss because the owner of the lost watch had incurred no accountable historical cost to acquire it.[3] But from a current value perspective, the dollar loss of the wristwatch is measured by the monetary cost that is incurred to replace it. The value of the old watch is determined *not* by the sacrifice made to acquire it; rather it is based on the amount that would be expended to replace it.

The Measurement of Current Value

Until this point in our discussion, reference to the measurement of current value has been in terms of the replacement cost approach. *Replacement cost*

---

[3] In fact, even the historical cost system would require that gifts be recorded at their fair value.

is a basis which assigns a value to economic resources in terms of dollar amounts that would be paid currently for equivalent, but not necessarily identical, items. If there has been a change in the underlying technology since a particular plant asset had been acquired, there would be a difference between its replacement cost and its reproduction cost. Replacement cost may be a more meaningful amount to use because a company would be more likely to replace it with a technologically superior item than to reproduce the exact same asset it has on hand. This distinction suggests there are very real practical problems to be encountered when such a system is implemented. In addition, the cost of professional appraisals is an aspect of replacement cost accounting which companies may not be especially interested in incurring. There are, however, other possible means of measuring current value, two of which are considered below. They are realizable value and discounted future cash flows.

As an alternative to using the "entry" price approach represented by a replacement cost basis of accounting, it is possible to measure value in terms of "exit" prices. One of the ways to express such a value is to estimate the realizable value of particular resources. This is done by measuring assets and liabilities in terms of dollar amounts that would be realized or paid in the course of non-duress liquidation. Earnings for a particular period is the difference between the beginning-of-period and end-of-period exit prices other than changes related to stockholders' investment or withdrawals that occurred during the period. This approach identifies an enterprise's opportunity cost because, in effect, it measures the cost sustained, that is, the benefit foregone, by holding its economic resources rather than obtaining their current cash equivalent.

At an intuitive level, one might expect an asset's replacement cost and realizable value to coincide. Actually, these two measures of value are based on the dynamics of two different markets: an input market and an output market. To illustrate how even at a relatively personal level one can encounter variation, consider the following situation.

In an effort to determine the current value of his three-year old automobile, a person painstakingly visits various used-car lots. He determines that a similar make-and-model car manufactured in the same year as his own, with identical optional equipment and in comparable condition, would now cost $1,800. On the other hand, on presenting his car to the proprietor of a used-car dealership, he is offered only $1,300. What is the current value of the automobile—its $1,800 replacement cost or the $1,300 realizable value? This illustration can be extended further when one considers that as a result of placing a classified advertisement in a newspaper, the resulting sale directly to a consumer might yield an amount greater than the $1,300 offered by the used car dealer.

The historical cost basis of accounting reflects the notion that at the moment an economic resource is exchanged, its cost and current value are equal, that is, *cost* is the measure of *value*. Purchasers of economic resources are prepared to incur a particular cost for desired goods or services because they perceive the cost to be equal to the present value of the expected future benefits to be derived from it. A business enterprise experiences such future benefits in the form of cash flows, whose measurement yields a second "exit" price approach to measuring current value. Rather than expressing exit price by identifying the value of an enterprise's assets and liabilities in terms of what is currently realizable, the *discounted future cash flows* concept of current value seeks to place a value on the present value of expected *future* cash outcomes. With respect to determining earnings for a period, a result similar to the other exit price approach emerges. Income is the change in the present value of future cash flows, including the effect of revised expectations. It is similar in form to the realizable value method in that revenues and expenses are not set forth in the traditional format which characterizes the historical cost and replacement cost methods.

Although the discounted future cash flows method may be attractive at a theoretical level, practical application can be very difficult. Many estimates must be made about future outcomes, the current value of an enterprise at large invariably exceeds the sum of individual assets' (less liabilities') current value, and earnings for particular periods are not necessarily explained in terms of the traditional component-oriented revenue and expense framework.

Relationship with Traditional Accounting Principles

The three alternative methods of measuring current value that have been identified are replacement cost, realizable value, and discounted future cash flows. It could be argued that it is first necessary to demonstrate the need to supplant the historical cost basis of accounting with a system which measures current values, then to determine which of the three cited methods of measuring current value should be used. On the other hand, if none of the three methods (nor some other method) proves satisfactory, efforts to abandon historical cost data will have been in vain. Therefore, in this section the three methods of quantifying current values are examined in terms of major elements of the traditional accounting model. Our objective is to determine which of the alternatives have characteristics incompatible with elements of the existing accounting model.

One of the assumptions underlying financial accounting is that the business entity will operate indefinitely. The very nature of the realizable value concept of current value is to assign value to assets and liabilities on the basis of the amount that would currently be received in an orderly liquidation. To base a valuation method on an assumption of liquidation is said to contradict the traditional assumption of continuity, or going concern. However, this argument can be countered with the assertion that while the assumption of going concern relates to the entity at large, particular assets and liabilities are liquidated in the normal course of events.

Another element of existing financial accounting is that recognition of gains or losses requires realization in the form of an arm's length transaction with an independent party. Although income measured by all three methods can include the effect of many, if not all, changes in value of assets and liabilities, income statements generated by the realizable value and discounted future cash flows methods make no distinction between portions of holding gains and losses which are either realized or unrealized. It was also observed that, the presence of such differentiation notwithstanding, even the unrealized holding gain or loss becomes part of replacement cost based income and owners' equity.

The conventional approach to income measurement prescribes that revenues be matched with expenses incurred to generate those revenues. This suggests that not only should measurement of income be effected on this basis, but also that the resulting earnings data be communicated in a like manner. As opposed to this scheme is that of the realizable value and discounted future cash flows methods whereby income is merely the change in an enterprise's value other than the portion attributable to capital investment and withdrawals.

Objectivity is the attribute of the historical cost basis of accounting which suggests notions of verifiability, freedom from bias, and the gathering of evidential matter. Many people argue that assigning current values is inconsistent with the principle of objectivity, with the implication that the integrity or fairness of the resulting accounting data is necessarily compromised.

However, there are counter arguments. First, *objectivity* as an accounting criterion should not be treated as an absolute concept. Instead, it should be viewed in terms of a continuum with objectivity and subjectivity situated at opposite ends of the spectrum. Furthermore, even the historical cost basis of accounting cannot be assumed to reside at the extreme point on the "objective" side of the continuum. Even, or especially, under the historical cost system, there are a variety of instances requiring professional judgment to resolve certain issues. Certainly, one could observe that discretion is an inevitable part of any basis of accounting measurement. Although there can be no doubt that movement to a current value basis of accounting would result in a rating which moves toward the "subjective" portion of the continuum, the offsetting benefit provided by more insightful current value data may more than compensate for the sacrifice of objectivity.

328

CONTEMPORARY APPLICATIONS

To summarize, there are four possible avenues that could be pursued with respect to a valuation basis of accounting:

Historical Cost/Nominal Dollars
Historical Cost/Constant Dollars
Current Value/Nominal Dollars
Current Value/Constant Dollars

Were the Current Value basis of accounting to be adopted using either nominal dollars or constant dollars, there arises the question of how to measure current value. The three alternatives discussed in this chapter are replacement cost, realizable value, and discounted future cash flows.

Different measurement schemes yield different insights. One important study reached the following general conclusions. Historical cost is appropriate for describing a past aspect of all assets and liabilities, that is, the sacrifices incurred to acquire assets and the benefits received when creating liabilities. Replacement cost may be the best means for measuring the benefits of long-term assets held for use rather than sale. Replacement cost may be particularly appropriate when significant price changes or technological developments have occurred since the assets were acquired. Realizable value may be a reasonable substitute for measuring the potential benefit or sacrifice of assets and liabilities expected to be sold or discharged in a relatively short time. Discounted cash flow quantifications, while directly relevant to prediction, are often difficult to assign to individual assets and liabilities. The discounted cash flow method, however, may be useful for measuring potential benefits for groups of related assets such as operating subsidiaries and divisions for which no independent market value exists.[4]

Not unexpectedly, in those instances when a current value basis of accounting has been applied to all elements of financial statements, an eclectic approach resulted. For example, short-term accounts receivable would be reflected on a realizable value basis, other monetary assets and liabilities on a discounted future cash flows basis, marketable securities on the basis of market prices, inventories on either a replacement cost or realizable value basis, land at its realizable value, and depreciable plant assets at their replacement cost.

Much time and effort has been invested by theoreticians and practitioners in debating which one measure of current value, if any, has universal applicability. Perhaps, given the more realistic possibility or inevitability of someday having to adopt an eclectic approach to current value, the question

[4] Study Group on the Objectives of Financial Statements, *Objectives of Financial Statements* (New York: American Institute of Certified Public Accountants, 1973), p. 43.

would be reduced to which measurement scheme most effectively depicts particular components of companies' financial position. Superimposed on such deliberations is the additional issue of whether or not to restate the basic—historical cost or current value—accounting data to reflect the effect of changes in the general price level, that is, whether the measuring unit should be nominal dollars or constant dollars.

Restatement of accounting data to reflect changes in the general price level is, in a period of price inflation, a response to the decreased value of money. As a result, an inflation gain or loss is recognized to report the effect of the inflation on a company's *monetary* assets and liabilities. The current value basis of accounting, on the other hand, does recognize explicitly gains and losses from changes in value of *nonmonetary* assets (and liabilities) as components of income.

A system which integrates both of these features would provide the additional benefit of isolating that segment of nonmonetary assets' increased value attributable to changes in the general price level. The remaining portion of the change in value is the specific price change, and is included in earnings. Persons who advocate use of the current value/nominal dollar approach contend that the only pertinent measure of value is that generated for particular assets. Once such a value is obtained, to speculate on what the value might have been had there only been economy-wide price inflation is irrelevant because a particular asset does not experience general price changes per se; it sustains only specific changes in its value.

Although it might appear that the matter of restating basic accounting data to reflect changes in the general price level can lead to distinctly different points of view when considered alternatively in context of the current value basis or the historical cost basis of accounting, it must be recognized that the objective of restatement is different from that of current value. Restatement is an issue of whether the measuring unit should be nominal dollars or constant dollars. Current value accounting, on the other hand, relates to determining what attribute it is that should be measured. The whys and wherefores are multi-faceted in nature, and needless to say the implications for financial reporting are monumental.

FASB STATEMENT NO. 33

In September 1979, the Financial Accounting Standards Board published Statement No. 33 entitled, "Financial Reporting and Changing Prices,"[5]

---

[5] *Financial Accounting Standards Board Statement No. 33* (Stamford, Conn.: Financial Accounting Standards Board, 1979). Copyright © by Financial Accounting Standards Board, High Ridge Park, Stamford, Connecticut 06905, U.S.A. Reprinted with permission. Copies of the complete document are available from the FASB.

which applies to publicly-held companies that have inventory and gross plant assets amounting to more than $125 million, or total assets exceeding $1 billion. The pronouncement identifies disclosures that are to be presented as *supplementary* information in published annual reports. This means that the approximately 1,300 qualifying corporations continue to prepare their

Exhibit 13–3

Statement of Income from Continuing Operations Adjusted for Changing Prices

For the Year Ended December 31, 19x1
In Thousands, the Constant Dollar Is
Average 19x1 Purchasing Power

Income from continuing operations, as reported in the income statement		$28,506
Adjustments to restate historical costs to constant dollars:		
Cost of goods sold	$6,191	
Depreciation, amortization and depletion expense	5,376	$11,567
Income from continuing operations, in historical cost/constant dollars		$16,939
Adjustments to reflect the difference between general price changes and changes in current costs:		
Cost of goods sold	$2,304	
Depreciation, amortization and depletion expense	4,971	$ 7,275
Income from continuing operations, in current cost/constant dollars		**$ 9,664**
Gain from decline in purchasing power of net monetary items		**$ 1,324**
Increase in current cost of inventories, and property, plant, and equipment held during the year*		$31,652
Effect of increase in general price level		22,254
Excess of increase in current cost over increase in the general price level		**$ 9,398**

* At December 31, 19x1, current cost of inventory was $93,660 and current cost of property, plant, and equipment, net of accumulated depreciation, was $115,295.

basic financial statements in the traditional manner, that is, on a historical cost/nominal dollar basis. However, they must also provide the following disclosures that are stipulated by Statement No. 33.

- Income from continuing operations—on a historical cost/constant dollar basis.
- Inflation gain or loss, i.e., the purchasing power gain or loss on monetary items.
- Income from continuing operations—on a current value/constant dollar basis.
- Inventory and plant assets on a current value/constant dollar basis.
- Changes in the current value/constant dollar amounts of inventory and plant assets.
- Five-year comparison of selected historical cost and current value data— expressed in constant dollars.

In terms of the framework presented in Chapter 12 and in this chapter, the FASB has opted for Column 2 and Column 4 type of supplementary disclosures. It should also be noted that according to Statement No. 33, *current value* is measured by the current cost of the assets owned by the company and not the cost of other assets that might be acquired to replace the owned assets. Furthermore, Income from Continuing Operations on both the historical cost/constant dollar basis and the current value/constant dollar basis is not based on a restatement of all earnings statement components. Instead, only the cost of goods sold and depreciation/amortization/depletion expense amounts are restated, i.e., no adjustments are required for other revenues, expenses, gains, and losses. See format illustration in Exhibit 13–3.

SUMMARY

Financial reporting of the effect of changing prices is probably the most perplexing challenge facing accountants, business executives, financial analysts, and persons charged with promulgating financial reporting standards. Certainly the accounting questions it raises are profound, at both the conceptual and applied levels. Much of the scholarly literature on the subject is of an advocative nature, i.e., enlightened persons presenting points of view which they believe are worthy of universal acceptance. Research endeavors on the subject have typically identified the differential effect on financial statements that would result under various approaches to the issue. Piecemeal disclosures provided by certain large corporations in their annual SEC filings since 1976 notwithstanding, there has not been any definitive evidence to suggest that departure from the historical cost/nominal dollar basis of accounting is or is not warranted.

The appearance of FASB Statement No. 33 can therefore be viewed as being a rather momentous development. It represents a determined effort by the Financial Accounting Standards Board to deal directly with issues that should have been resolved previously. Yet, the Board has approached the matter with justifiable caution; indeed Statement No. 33 is more of an experiment than the ultimate truth. It applies only to very large, publicly-held corporations, and its required disclosures are presented as a supplement to the basic financial statements which continue to be prepared in accordance with existing generally accepted accounting principles. But it is an important first step: it challenges the qualifying companies to prepare new data, it invites users of financial accounting to modify their analytical approach, and it offers standard setters and researchers an opportunity to reevaluate fundamental accounting and financial reporting issues with a frame of reference that had not been available previously.

Additional Readings

AICPA Task Force on Conceptual Framework for Accounting and Reporting. *The Accounting Responses to Changing Prices: Experimentation with Four Models.* New York: American Institute of Certified Public Accountants, 1979.

Anthony, Robert N. "A Case for Historical Costs." *Harvard Business Review* (November–December 1976), pp. 69–79.

Backer, Morton. *Current Value Accounting.* New York: Financial Executives Research Foundation, 1973.

Baxter, W. T. *Accounting Values and Inflation.* Maidenhead, Berkshire, England: McGraw-Hill Book Company (U.K.) Limited, 1975.

Bedford, Norton M. "Relationships among Income Measurements." In *Essays in Honor of William A. Paton,* edited by Stephen A. Zeff, Joel Demski, and Nicholas Dopuch. Ann Arbor, Mich.: The University of Michigan Graduate School of Business Administration Division of Research, 1979, pp. 139–55.

Bedford, Norton M., and McKeown, James C. "Comparative Analysis of Net Realizable Value and Replacement Costing." *The Accounting Review* (April 1972), pp. 333–38.

Chambers, R. J. "NOD, COG, and PuPu: See How Inflation Teases!" *The Journal of Accountancy* (September 1975), pp. 56–62 and (February 1976), p. 41.

Chippindale, Walter, and Defiese, Philip L., ed. *Current Value Accounting: A Practical Guide for Business.* New York: Amacom, 1977.

Davidson, Sidney, and Weil, Roman L. "Inflation Accounting: What Will General Price Level Adjusted Income Statements Show?" *Financial Analysts Journal* (January–February, 1975), pp. 27–31, 70–84.

Edwards, Edgar O., and Bell, Philip W. *The Theory and Measurement of Business Income.* Berkeley and Los Angeles: University of California Press, 1961.

Frank, J. W.; Kealey, T. F.; and Silverman, G. W. *The Effects and Significance of*

333

Replacement Cost Disclosure. New York: Financial Executives Research Foundation, 1978.

Friedman, Lawrence A. "An Exit-Price Income Statement." *The Accounting Review* (January 1978), pp. 18–30.

Hale, David. "Inflation Accounting and Public Policy around the World." *Financial Analysts Journal* (September–October 1978), pp. 59–72.

Ijiri, Yuji. "A Defense for Historical Cost Accounting." In *Asset Valuation and Income Determination,* edited by Robert R. Sterling. Houston: Scholars Book Co., 1971, pp. 1–14.

Kohler, Eric L. "Why Not Retain Historical Cost?" *The Journal of Accountancy* (October 1963), pp. 35–41.

Largay, James A., III., and Livingstone, John Leslie. *Accounting for Changing Prices.* New York: John Wiley & Sons, Inc., 1976.

Lassman, Daniel A., and Weil, Roman L. "Adjusting the Debt-Equity Ratio." *Financial Analysts Journal* (September–October 1978), pp. 49–58.

Lee, T. A. *Income and Value Measurement: Theory and Practice.* Baltimore: University Park Press, 1972.

Mautz, R. K. "A Few Words for Historical Cost." *Financial Executive* (January 1973), pp. 23–27.

McCarthy, George D., and Healey, Robert E. "The Economics of Valuing A Company." *Price Waterhouse Review* (Winter 1971–72), pp. 13–21.

McDonald, Daniel L. *Comparative Accounting Theory.* Reading, Mass.: Addison-Wesley Publishing Company, Inc., 1972.

Paton, William A. "Cost and Value in Accounting." *The Journal of Accountancy* (March 1946), pp. 192–99.

Peloubet, Maurice E. "Is Value an Accounting Concept?" *The Journal of Accountancy* (March 1935), pp. 201–209.

Revsine, Lawrence. *Replacement Cost Accounting.* Englewood Cliffs, N.J.: Prentice-Hall, Inc., 1973.

Rosenfield, Paul. "Current Replacement Value Accounting—A Dead End." *The Journal of Accountancy* (September 1975), pp. 63–73.

Scott, George M. *Research Study in Current-Value Accounting Measurement and Utility.* New York: Touche Ross Foundation, 1978.

Sprouse, Robert T., and Moonitz, Maurice. *A Tentative Set of Broad Accounting Principles for Business Enterprises.* New York: American Institute of Certified Public Accountants, 1962.

Sterling, Robert R. "Relevant Financial Reporting in an Age of Price Changes." *The Journal of Accountancy* (February 1975), pp. 42–51.

Sterling, Robert R. *Theory of the Measurement of Enterprise Income.* Lawrence, Kansas: The University Press of Kansas, 1970.

Touche Ross & Co. *Current Value Accounting: Economic Reality in Financial Reporting.* New York: Touche Ross & Co., 1975.

14

Accounting
for the Translation
of Foreign Currency

Many American companies are multinational, and the financial statements of these companies must take into consideration accounting differences caused by the international nature of the business. In the case of the company whose international involvement is limited to that of creditor-debtor relationships denominated in foreign currency, there is a need to determine the effect of fluctuations in currency exchange rates. When an American company has either a controlling or a significant interest in a foreign company's voting common stock, the investee's foreign currency financial statements must be translated into U.S. dollars.

When translating foreign financial statements, there is also a need to reconcile differences between the foreign country's accounting standards and those that prevail in the United States. Indeed, the Financial Accounting Standards Board has stated that before translation, foreign statements to be included in an enterprise's financial statements should first be prepared in conformity with U.S. generally accepted accounting principles and then be translated into dollars.[1] Although there does exist an organization called the International Accounting Standards Committee which issues pronouncements whose objective is to foster uniform accounting standards among nations, considerable differences exist between countries' accounting practices which will probably continue. Such variations in financial statement preparation can pose a problem for American parent companies desirous of

---

[1] *Financial Accounting Standards Board Statement No. 8*, paragraph no. 10. Copyright © by Financial Accounting Standards Board, High Ridge Park, Stamford, Connecticut 06905, U.S.A. Reprinted with permission. Copies of the complete document are available from the FASB.

integrating their foreign subsidiaries' statements with their own and for persons who themselves read financial statements of enterprises located in different countries of the world.[2]

FOREIGN CURRENCY EXCHANGE RATES

A foreign currency exchange rate expresses the relationship between the currencies of two different countries, and the rate can be expressed in terms of either currency. For instance, one could express the relationship between the U.S. dollar and a *hub*, which is the currency of an imaginary foreign country called Bostonia, either as 2.5 dollars per hub, H 1 = $2.50—or as .4 hubs per dollar, $1 = H .4.

Foreign currency exchange rates fluctuate in response to business, economic, and international trade phenomena, or because a particular country's government unilaterally mandates that the official exchange rate be changed. If the currency exchange rate between dollars and hubs were to change from H 1 = $2.50 to H 1 = $3.00, this would evidence a weakening of the dollar relative to the hub inasmuch as the cost to buy one hub has increased from $2.50 to $3.00. Alternatively, this can be viewed as a strengthening of the hub relative to the dollar since only H .33 rather than H .40, is needed to buy one dollar.

If this change in the currency exchange rate had been effected by formal action of the American government, it would be referred to as a devaluation, because the dollar's value relative to the hub has been decreased, i.e., it has been devalued. On the other hand, if the change had been the result of an official action on the part of the Bostonian government, it would be called a revaluation or perhaps more descriptively, an upvaluation—as the hub's value relative to the dollar has been increased.

FOREIGN CURRENCY TRANSACTIONS

Receivables and payables are denominated in a foreign currency if their amounts are expressed in terms of a fixed amount of foreign currency. Assume that on December 20, 19x1, an American company purchases land in Bostonia for H 10,000, and that it expects to liquidate the resulting payable on its due date thirty days later. If the debt is denominated in terms of the 10,000 hubs, the buyer must use dollars to purchase the 10,000 hubs. Alter-

---

[2] An example of a publication which identifies the nature of such differences is *Guide for the Reader of Foreign Financial Statements*—Second Edition, published by Price Waterhouse & Co. in 1975.

natively, the seller may be willing to accept the equivalent number of dollars, that is, the amount whose conversion would yield 10,000 hubs.

Because the buyer is an American company, it accounts for all of its transactions in terms of U.S. dollars. As a result, given the December 20, 19x1 exchange rate of H 1 = $2.50, it records the purchase of land costing (H 10,000 @ $2.50 =) $25,000. This amount measures both the Land asset and the Accounts Payable liability. Eleven days later marks the end of the buyer's fiscal year and an obligation to prepare financial statements. Assuming that the currency exchange rate as of December 31 had become H 1 = $3.00, there is an obligation to reflect the effect of this change, but only to the extent that it has consequences for the buyer.

Because the liability is denominated in hubs, more dollars would be expended to acquire the 10,000 needed hubs were the debt to be paid on December 31. The dollar cost would be (H 10,000 @ $ 3 =) $30,000—which is ($30,000 − 25,000 =) $5,000 more than that recorded previously as the buyer's liability. The nature of the $5,000 is that it is a foreign currency exchange loss—sustained because of the fluctuating exchange rate. The new rate reflects a weakening of dollars relative to hubs—as more dollars are needed to acquire hubs than had been the case even a few days earlier. Had the American company expended $25,000 while the earlier rate was still in effect, it would have avoided the $5,000 loss. But since the dollars to buy the 10,000 hubs are to be expended on the due date, the recorded liability is increased from $25,000 to $30,000, and the resulting $5,000 loss is included in 19x1's income statement.

The $25,000 amount recorded as the cost of the Land asset is not affected by a new exchange rate. This is because it is not a monetary item; that is, its amount is not expressed in a fixed number of either dollars or hubs. The amount of proceeds that will be generated upon its sale is not fixed, and certainly not denominated in a particular currency. The relevant amount of its cost is $25,000 because that was the equivalent dollar amount at the only time its cost is measurable, namely, when it was purchased. The recorded cost of any asset is generally not subject to revision if a different price emerges subsequent to its acquisition.

In pursuing this example, assume that when the buyer remits 10,000 hubs to the seller on January 19, 19x2 the exchange rate has again changed: to H 1 = $2.80. This means that when the 10,000 hubs are acquired on the due date, their cost would be (H 10,000 @ $2.80 =) $28,000—and not the $30,000 which is the recorded liability as of December 31, 19x1. The resulting ($30,000 − 28,000 =) $2,000 savings is reflected as a foreign currency exchange gain in 19x2's earnings statement. Questions have been raised regarding the propriety of recognizing a $5,000 loss in 19x1 and a $2,000 gain in 19x2. It has been argued that foreign currency exchange gains and losses should not be recognized until they are realized, in the case at hand, a ($28,000 − 25,000 =) $3,000 foreign currency exchange loss upon its realization in 19x2. This matter is discussed later.

A similar accounting result occurs when receivables are denominated in a foreign currency. For example, assume an American company sold merchandise to a Bostonian company at a price of H 400 when the exchange rate was H 1 = $2.80; the revenue and receivable are both recorded in the amount of (H 400 @ $2.80 =) $1,120. If the exchange rate had risen to H 1 = $3.20 as of the date the 400 hubs are collected, a foreign currency exchange gain of [H 400 @ ($3.20 − 2.80 =) $.40 =] $160 would be recognized. This gain signifies that the date-of-sale dollar equivalent of H 400 had been $1,120 while the collection date dollar equivalent is (H 400 @ 3.20 =) $1,280, a favorable difference of $160. The foreign currency exchange gain results from the dollar's weakening relative to the hub; because the dollar is relatively weaker, the American creditor benefits from the receivable having been denominated in terms of the stronger (hub) currency.

In summary, when a transaction is denominated in a foreign currency, it is measured in dollars on the basis of the currency exchange rate on the transaction date. Those elements of the transaction which are monetary in nature, that is, whose sum is expressed in a fixed amount of foreign currency—such as receivables, payables and (foreign) cash—can be the basis for recognizing accounting gains and losses when subsequent exchange rate fluctuations occur.

In light of the fixed nature of monetary amounts, a new foreign currency exchange rate signifies that the number of dollars which is the equivalent of the denominated foreign currency differs from that which had initially been recorded. Inasmuch as the monetary asset or liability has a different dollar value than had been the case previously, the new exchange rate has either a favorable or unfavorable effect on the American company. This result, in turn, is recognized immediately as a foreign currency exchange gain or loss. Such recognition is made as of the date financial statements are prepared even though the gain or loss is not yet realized—and may never be realized if there should be a reverse fluctuation before the monetary asset or liability is actually converted into U.S. dollars.

Although this monetary-nonmonetary distinction is the basis for the method of accounting for foreign currency which is acceptable for financial reporting purposes in the United States, other approaches exist as well. Because consideration of such alternatives is best effected after having acquired an appreciation of present practice, the following section describes the existing method's nature and some of its subtleties. With such understanding, one will be in a better position to appreciate and evaluate other approaches.

FOREIGN CURRENCY FINANCIAL STATEMENTS

As a perspective with which to approach foreign currency financial statements, the same monetary-nonmonetary distinction used when translating foreign currency transactions applies here as well. Monetary assets and liabilities are translated on the basis of the foreign currency exchange rate in effect as of the balance sheet date, and nonmonetary items are reflected in financial statements at the exchange rate that existed when the pertinent transaction occurred.[3]

Although an American company may engage in foreign operations through media such as branch offices, joint ventures, or purchased subsidiaries, the focal point in this section is an American parent company that creates a foreign subsidiary corporation. The nature of the accounting differences which arise when the foreign entity ownership interest is purchased subsequent to its inception is addressed at a later juncture.

To introduce the nature of the process of translating foreign currency financial statements, an illustrative example is provided. Assume that on January 1, 19x1 an American company creates a subsidiary corporation in the country of Bostonia. Bostonia's currency is *hubs* which are signified by the letter "H"; thus, 12 hubs expressed numerically is H 12. The creation of the subsidiary entails issuing capital stock in exchange for cash. It is further assumed that three other assets—Inventories, Land, and Machinery—as well as a Payables balance appear in the foreign subsidiary's balance sheet as of the end of its first day of business. The exchange rates between dollars and hubs are as follows:

$$\text{January 1, 19x1} - \text{H 1} = \$.80$$
$$\text{December 31, 19x1} - \text{H 1} = \$1.00$$
$$\text{19x1 average} - \text{H 1} = \$.90$$

This pattern reflects a weakening of the dollar relative to the hub—as ($1.00 − .80) = $.20; $.20 ÷ .80 =) 25 percent more dollars must be expended to buy a hub at year-end than had been the case twelve months earlier.

Column 1 in Exhibit 14–1 contains the January 1, 19x1 balance sheet amounts expressed in hubs. The dollar equivalent, which appears in Column 3, is derived by applying to each hub-based amount the .80 rate which

---

[3] An exception mandated by the *temporal method* is introduced in a later section.

Exhibit 14-1

Foreign Currency Financial Statements

	(1)	(2)	(3)	(4)
	Hubs (H)		Dollars ($)	
	Jan 1, 19x1	Dec. 31, 19x1	Jan. 1, 19x1	Dec. 31, 19x1
Balance sheet:				
Cash	H 2,200	H 2,500	$ 1,760[1]	$ 2,500[2]
Inventory	2,800	4,500	2,240[1]	4,050[3]
Land	5,000	7,000	4,000[1]	5,800[4]
Machinery (net)	10,000	9,000	8,000[1]	7,200[1]
	H20,000	**H23,000**	**$16,000**	**$19,550**
Payables	H 1,000	H 3,000	$ 800[1]	$ 3,000[2]
Common stock	19,000	19,000	15,200[1]	15,200[1]
Retained earnings		1,000		1,350[5]
	H20,000	**H23,000**	**$16,000**	**$19,550**

Income statement (credit):	19x1	19x1
Sales	H(25,000)	$(22,500)[3]
Inventory, January 1	H 2,800	$ 2,240[1]
Purchases	20,000	18,000[3]
Inventory, December 31	(4,500)	(4,050)[3]
Cost of goods sold	H18,300	$ 16,190
Depreciation expense	1,000	800[1]
Other expenses	4,700	4,230[3]
Foreign currency exchange (gain)		(70)[5]
	H24,000	$ 21,150
Net (income)	**H(1,000)**	**$(1,350)**

Supporting computations:

[1] Based on $.80 exchange rate of Jan. 1, 19x1
[2] Based on $1.00 exchange rate of Dec. 31, 19x1
[3] Based on $.90 exchange rate of average for 19x1
[4] H 5,000 × $.80 exchange rate of Jan. 1, 19x1 = $4,000
    H 2,000 × $.90 exchange rate average for 19x1 = +1,800
$5,800

[5] Derived amount—see narrative discussion.

expresses the January 1, 19x1 relationship between dollars and hubs. Because January 1 is both the balance sheet date and the date on which all of the underlying transactions occurred, this one common rate is used to translate monetary and nonmonetary amounts alike.

Column 2 depicts the end-of-year balance sheet as well as the income statement for 19x1. It is assumed that sales and the accrual of "other expenses" occur uniformly during the year. The FIFO basis of inventory costing is used, and the machinery is being depreciated at a rate of 10 percent annually—with no expected salvage value at the end of its useful life. No foreign exchange gain or loss appears in the hub-based income statement because all of the subsidiary's monetary transactions during the year were denominated in hubs; and income tax aspects are ignored.

Column 4 presents the subsidiary's December 31, 19x1 financial position and operating results for the year then ended, in terms of their dollar equivalent. Because Cash and Payables are monetary items, they are translated on the basis of the current, i.e., December 31 exchange rate of H 1 = $1. Inventory costing H 20,000 and land costing H 2,000 were purchased during the year when the exchange rate was H 1 = $.90. The land which had been purchased on January 1 at a cost of H 5,000 is translated at its historical rate of H 1 = $.80. Therefore, as indicated in supporting computation no. 4, the resulting U.S. currency equivalent is $5,800 for land.

With respect to Machinery reflected on a net-of-accumulated depreciation basis, the H 9,000 balance is translated at its historical, that is, January 1, currency exchange rate of H 1 = $.80. Common Stock is also translated on the basis of its historical H 1 = $.80 exchange rate. The dollar equivalent of the year-end Retained Earnings in a purely procedural sense might be viewed as being merely the dollar amount needed to make the balance sheet balance. However, in this illustration, the $1,350 amount can be calculated independently—and its very derivation offers an important insight into the dynamics of foreign currency translation. However, because any end-of-period retained earnings is affected by the net income of the period then ended, we must first consider the 19x1 income statement.

With respect to the translation of 19x1's income statement, purchases are translated at their historical H 1 = $.90 rate, as are sales and other expenses, because of the assumption that they occur uniformly during the year. The beginning-of-period inventory is translated at H 1 = $.80, which was the exchange rate when it was acquired on January 1. Given the assumption regarding the FIFO method of inventory costing, the end-of-period inventory is based on the H 1 = $.90 exchange rate applicable to 19x1's purchases. Depreciation expense is translated by using the appropriate historical exchange rate; which is the H 1 = $.80 rate in effect at the time the depreciable asset was acquired.

Exchange Gains and Losses

Foreign currency exchange gains and losses measure the effect of fluctuation in the currency exchange rate on those assets and liabilities whose inherent nature exposes them to its vicissitudes. An appreciation of the distinction between monetary and nonmonetary components of an enterprise's financial position suggests that it is precisely because a foreign subsidiary's monetary assets and liabilities are sums denominated and expressed in a fixed amount of foreign currency that they are affected by a change in the exchange rate. It is, therefore, the impact of such a change on monetary items which produces a gain or loss.

Refer now to Exhibit 14–2. Column 1 identifies the foreign subsidiary's January 1 monetary position. The excess of the H 2,200 monetary asset Cash over the H 1,000 monetary liability Payables yields a net monetary asset of H 1,200. Whereas the foreign currency exchange rate till this point has been expressed in terms of dollars, observe that it can be expressed in terms of hubs as well:

	Exchange Rate in terms of	
	Dollars	*Hubs*
January 1	H 1 = $ .80	$1 = H 1.25
December 31	H 1 = $1.00	$1 = H 1.00

In this case, it is the calculation, H 1 ÷ $.80 = 1.25 which yields the $1 = H 1.25 result.

The change from H 1 = $.80 as of January 1 to H 1 = $1.00 as of December 31 is $.20, or 25 per cent of January 1's H 1 = $.80 rate. Thus, the value of the dollar relative to the hub decreased during the year by 25 percent, because, whereas a hub could have been purchased with $.80 at the beginning of the year, $.20 more dollars are needed to buy a hub at the end of the year. On the other hand, the value of the hub relative to the dollar increased 20 percent during the year because 20 percent less hubs—H 1.00 instead of H 1.25—are needed at year-end to buy one dollar than was needed to buy a dollar twelve months earlier.

A favorable outcome results for an American company which, through its Bostonian subsidiary, is in a net monetary asset position with respect to amounts denominated in a relatively stronger foreign currency—in our example, favorable to the extent of (H 1,200 × $.20 =) $240. But this assumes that its January 1 H 1,200 net monetary asset position remains intact throughout the year, and this is not the case at all. By December 31, the H 2,200 Cash monetary asset had risen to H 2,500, or a H 300 change, and

342

Exhibit 14–2

Foreign Currency Exchange Gain/Loss: Direct Calculation

	(1)	(2)	(3)	(4)
			\multicolumn{2}{c}{Change in}	
	January 1	December 31	Hubs	Dollars
Cash	H 2,200	H 2,500	H 300	
Payables	1,000	3,000	2,000	
Net monetary asset	H 1,200			
Net monetary liability		H 500		
Change			H 1,700	
Upvaluation of hub:				
Dec. 31: H 1 = $1.00				
Jan. 1: H 1 = $ .80				
$ .20				
$.20 × ½ =	$ .20	×	$ .10	
	$240	less	$170 =	
Foreign currency exchange gain				**$70**

the H 1,000 Payables monetary liability had increased to H 3,000, or a H 2,000 change. As a result, the company is in a H 500 *net monetary liability* position at year-end.

The change from net monetary assets of H 1,200 to net monetary liabilities of H 500 is one of (1,200 + 500 =) 1,700 hubs. Because this change is assumed to have occurred uniformly during the year, it can be said that on the average it occurs during a period of a ($.20 × ½ =) $.10 upvaluation of the hub. Therefore, the movement into a net monetary liability position reduced what would otherwise have been a $240 gain. The amount of this reduction is (H 1,700 × $.10 =) $170, with the result that the foreign currency exchange gain for the year is ($240 − 170 =) $70.

It is important to note that the foreign currency exchange gain or loss is based solely on the exposure of a company's monetary assets and monetary liabilities. It is only such assets and liabilities that are exposed to the vicissitudes of foreign currency exchange rates, because it is only such items whose sums are expressed in a fixed amount of foreign currency. Because nonmonetary amounts comprising financial statements are translated at their historical transaction date foreign currency exchange rate, they are not affected by subsequent fluctuations.

To return to the end-of-period Retained Earnings which appears in the dollar-based balance sheet, the $1,350 amount can be traced directly to the year's income statement. The income statement, in turn, was prepared with relative ease because the one amount having the potential to be very troublesome, if not impossible, to calculate—the foreign currency exchange gain—was a surmountable problem because of the illustration's simplifying assumptions. In practice, however, the foreign currency exchange gain or loss is not so readily determinable, which means that net income cannot be computed and ending retained earnings cannot be calculated as they were in our illustration.

What happens, therefore, is that the amount of retained earnings which appears in an end-of-period balance sheet is that which allows its total equities to be equal to its total assets. In turn, this dollar sum, the given beginning-of-period retained earnings (so derived at the end of the preceding period), and the dollar equivalent of the current period's declared dividends become the basis for calculating the period's net income amount. The difference between this sum and that which represents income before consideration of the period's foreign currency exchange gain or loss then becomes the measure of such a gain or loss. This procedure is demonstrated in Exhibit 14–3 which portrays data for our illustration's following year.

Column 1 of the Exhibit identifies those dollar amounts the company's accountant will have been able to compute on the basis of pertinent foreign currency exchange rates. Note that the balance sheet amounts for ending retained earnings and total equities cannot be directly determined, and that the amounts for foreign currency exchange loss, net income, and ending retained earnings are also not directly determinable in the statement of income and retained earnings.

Column 2 demonstrates how these non-determinable amounts can be derived in an indirect manner. On the basis of the balance sheet's total assets being $40,000, the same amount is entered as total equities. As a result, ending retained earnings emerges as $12,800, and it is also entered as the sum amount in the statement of income and retained earnings. This total, together with the $2,000 amount of dividends declared enables us to obtain the ($12,800 + 2,000 =) $14,800 amount which, in turn, represents the sum of beginning retained earnings and the period's net income. The preceding period's $1,350 ending retained earnings balance is the current period's beginning balance, which means that ($14,800 − 1,350 =) $13,450 is the amount of the current period's net income. Upon comparing it with the $16,000 Income before Foreign Currency Exchange Gain or Loss which appears in Column 1, ($16,000 − 13,450 =) $2,550 emerges as the amount of the Foreign Currency Exchange Loss.

Exhibit 14–3

Foreign Currency Exchange Gain Loss: Indirect Calculation

Balance sheet:	(1)	(2)
Total assets	**$ 40,000**	**$ 40,000**
Payables	$ 12,000	$ 12,000
Common stock	15,200	15,200
Retained earnings	?	12,800
Total equities	**?**	**$ 40,000**

Statement of income and retained earnings (credit):		
Sales	$(50,000)	$(50,000)
Cost of goods sold	$ 25,000	$ 25,000
Depreciation expense	3,000	3,000
Other expenses	6,000	6,000
Total	$ 34,000	
Income before foreign currency exchange gain or loss	$(16,000)	
Foreign currency exchange loss	?	2,550
Total		$ 36,550
Net income	$?	$(13,450)
Beginning retained earnings	(1,350)	(1,350)
Total	$?	$(14,800)
Less dividends declared	2,000	2,000
Ending retained earnings	**$(?)**	**$(12,800)**

Current versus Historical Exchange Rates

As a general rule, monetary assets and liabilities are translated on the basis of the exchange rate prevailing at the end of the current accounting period. In contrast to this current exchange rate, nonmonetary items are translated by using the exchange rate which existed when the underlying transaction occurred. Thus, nonmonetary assets are translated on the basis of the exchange rate on their acquisition date, and nonmonetary liabilities and components of invested capital are measured in terms of the exchange rates in effect when they entered the company's realm of accountability. The nonmonetary revenue, expense, gain, and loss items comprising the income statement are similarly translated on the basis of their historical exchange rates, namely, those which existed at the time of the pertinent transactions. When circumstances so justify, a weighted average historical exchange rate may be used.

The method of translating both foreign currency transactions and foreign currency financial statements that was prescribed by the Financial Accounting Standards Board in 1975 is called the Temporal Method. It is similar to the monetary-nonmonetary distinction, but it does have one additional feature which is now examined. It requires that those nonmonetary items already reflected in companies' financial statements at their current value—rather than at their historical cost—are to be translated on the basis of the current exchange rate rather than their historical acquisition date exchange rate.

In effect, the temporal method asserts it is incongruous for merchandise or a marketable equity security which, as a result of the application of the lower-of-cost-or-market method, is already expressed at its current value in a foreign currency to be translated into dollars at the exchange rate which existed when the company originally incurred a cost to acquire the asset. Precisely because its cost basis is no longer relevant—since it is reflected now at its current value—there is no reason why the related historical exchange rate should have any relevance either. Similarly, were other nonmonetary items to appear in financial statements on a current value basis, they too would be translated with the current exchange rate.

A resulting problem posed by the use of the lower-of-cost-or-market method is whether to apply it to the foreign currency amounts first and then translate the lower amount into domestic currency, or to first translate and then select the lower of translated cost or translated market. Exhibit 14–4 sets forth the different outcomes.

In Case 1, Market is lower than Cost—in terms of both hubs and dollars—so that the $3,500 amount is used. In Case 2, however, the larger variance between the historical and current foreign currency exchange rates causes an outcome whereby the market value is lower than cost when expressed in hubs but is higher than cost when measured in dollars. Because the FASB prescribes that "translated historical cost shall be compared with translated market,"[4] the following anomalous situation results. The very same asset is reflected at its current market value in the Bostonian sub-

---

[4] *Financial Accounting Standards Board Statement No. 8,* paragraph no. 46. Copyright © by Financial Accounting Standards Board, High Ridge Park, Stamford, Connecticut 06905, U.S.A. Reprinted with permission. Copies of the complete document are available from the FASB.

Exhibit 14–4
Lower of Cost or Market

	Cost		Market	
	Hubs	Dollars	Hubs	Dollars
Case 1:				
Historical rate:				
H 1 = $4	H 1,000	$4,000		
Current rate:				
H 1 = $5			H 700	$3,500
Case 2:				
Historical rate:				
H 1 = $4	1,000	4,000		
Current rate:				
H 1 = $6			700	4,200
Case 3:				
Historical rate:				
H 1 = $4	1,000	4,000		
Current rate:				
H 1 = $3			1,200	3,600

sidiary's hub-based balance sheet and at its historical cost in the American parent's dollar-based balance sheet.

In Case 3, the foreign subsidiary uses the historical cost sum because its H 1,000 amount is less than its H 1,200 market value. But note that the foreign currency exchange rate at the balance sheet date is H 1 = $3— rather than the historical H 1 = $4 rate. As a result, the market value expressed in dollars is $3,600, which is less than the $4,000 dollar-based historical cost amount. Because it is the lower of translated cost or translated market which must appear in the American parent's financial statements, the $3,600 market value is used even though the foreign subsidiary reflects the inventory on the basis of its lower historical cost.

Intercompany debt between an American company and its foreign affiliate reflected in foreign currency on the affiliate's balance sheet is translated to its reciprocal dollar amount, that is, equal to that which already appears in dollars in the American company's balance sheet. A subsidiary's or significant investee's investment date nonmonetary items are translated on the basis of the investment date exchange rate, and not the rate in existence when the affiliate first reflected the amounts in its financial statements.

When translating a foreign currency income statement into dollars, those amounts that pertain to nonmonetary balance sheet items are translated at the same rate, viz., depreciation expense. Revenue and expense transactions with the American parent or an American affiliate are translated to an amount equal to that which was recorded reciprocally by the American counterpart. Although our examination of translating foreign currency financial statements has been in context of proceeding to prepare consolidated financial statements, the procedures are as applicable to the case of merely wanting to apply the equity method of accounting for intercorporate investments. The foreign statements are first translated, then the equity method is applied.

A final aspect of accounting for the effect of fluctuating foreign currency exchange rates might be characterized as one of "timing." There is an accounting rule which states that when there are post-balance sheet date ". . . events that provide additional evidence with respect to conditions that existed at the date of the balance sheet and affect the estimates inherent in the process of preparing financial statements, . . . the financial statements should be adjusted for any changes in estimates resulting from the use of such evidence."[5] The question that arises is whether or not a government-imposed devaluation of currency after the end of a company's fiscal period, but before its financial statements are issued, warrants adjusting those amounts which were already translated on the basis of the balance sheet date foreign currency exchange rate.

This issue had been particularly important early in 1973 as many American companies were preparing financial statements for their 1972 calendar year. The United States government devalued the dollar in February 1973, and in the view of some observers this action was merely a formal recognition of what had in effect already been a de facto devaluation, namely, that the official devaluation simply recognized the protracted deterioration of the value of the dollar. The accounting approach is now better defined as a result of the FASB rule that ". . . statements shall not be adjusted for a rate change that occurs after the date of the financial statements."[6]

---

[5] Statement on Auditing Standards No. 1, *Codification of Auditing Standards and Procedures* (New York: American Institute of Certified Public Accountants, 1973), paragraph no. 560.03.

[6] *Financial Accounting Standards Board Statement No. 8*, paragraph no. 34. Copyright © by Financial Accounting Standards Board, High Ridge Park, Stamford, Connecticut 06905, U.S.A. Reprinted with permission. Copies of the complete document are available from the FASB.

THE GENERAL PRICE LEVEL CONNECTION

In Chapter 12, attention was devoted to the issue of accounting for changes in the general price level. It was pointed out that price inflation signifies a deterioration of the purchasing power of the dollar. Because money is only as valuable as its purchasing power, significant accounting ramifications became apparent. Most notably, amounts of dollars pertaining to transactions at different points in time may have different purchasing power, and thus different value. Dollars having different value are not homogeneous and are, therefore, not additive. To prepare financial statements containing dollar amounts reflecting different purchasing power is viewed by some persons as being tantamount to the proverbial mixing of apples and oranges.

It is with this same conviction—that unlike items are not additive—that accountants also face the question of translating foreign currency. The same conceptual inconsistency that would characterize Bostonian hubs being added to and subtracted from U.S. dollars is related to the possibility that U.S. dollars having 1980 purchasing power are being added to or subtracted from U.S. dollars having 1954 purchasing power. Dollars having different purchasing power pose the same conceptual challenge as do amounts expressed in different nations' currencies.

To understand the similarities, an illustration is presented. The circumstances are those which had served as the basis of Chapter 12's discussion of the balance sheet and income statement effects of inflation on monetary and nonmonetary assets. The example covers a three-year period, and the general price level increases each year. At the beginning of 19x1, common stock is issued for cash, and a part of the cash is used immediately to purchase land. A portion of the land is sold at the end of the second year and the remainder is sold one year later. Both the assets and equities sides of the balance sheet were considered, both monetary and nonmonetary assets appeared, and important income statement effects were pointed out as well. These effects were set forth in a separate exhibit for each of the three years, and they are reproduced in Exhibit 14–5 to which we shall now refer.

As of the end of 19x1, the nonmonetary land and capital stock amounts are restated to reflect the year's inflation, and the 19x1 income statement reflects the inflation loss that results from holding the monetary cash asset during an inflationary period. As of the end of 19x2, the amount of cash had risen because of the cash proceeds from the sale of land, and the remaining land and capital stock are restated to reflect 19x2's inflation. The income statement for the year includes an inflation loss to reflect the effect on holding cash of an increase in the general price level. The income statement also contains the gain on the sale of land, which is the difference between the

Exhibit 14–5

Accounting for Changes in the General Price Level

Date	Event	Amount	Price Index
January 1, 19x1	Issue stock for cash	$2,000	100
January 2, 19x1	Purchase land	500	100
December 31, 19x1			125
December 30, 19x2	Sell 40% of land	460	150
December 30, 19x3	Sell remaining land	1,800	165

Balance sheet:

	1/2/x1	12/31/x1	12/31/x2	12/31/x3
Cash	$1,500	$1,500	$1,960[4]	$3,760[10]
Land	500	625[1]	450[5]	
	$2,000	$2,125	$2,410	$3,760
Capital stock	$2,000	$2,500[2]	$3,000[6]	$3,300[11]
Retained earnings	–0–	(375)[3]	(590)[9]	460[14]
	$2,000	$2,125	$2,410	$3,760

Income statement:

	19x1	19x2	19x3
Inflation (loss)	$(375)[3]	$(300)[7]	$(196)[12]
Gain on sale of land		$ 160[8]	$1,305[13]

Supporting computations:
[1] $500 × (125 ÷ 100 =) 1.25 = $625
[2] $2,000 × (125 ÷ 100 =) 1.25 = $2,500
[3] $1,500 of cash × (125 ÷ 100 =) 1.25 = $1,875; $1,875 − 1,500 = $375
[4] 12/31/x1 of $1,500 + 460 = $1,960
[5] $625 × .6 = $375; $375 × (150 ÷ 125 =) 1.2 = $450
[6] 12/31/x1 of $2,500 × (150 ÷ 125 =) 1.2 = $3,000
[7] 12/31/x1 of $1,500 × (150 ÷ 125 =) 1.2 = $1,800; $1,800 − 1,500 = $300
[8] $460 − [$625 × .4 = $250; $250 × (150 ÷ 125 =) 1.2 =] $300 = $160
[9] Retained earnings (deficit) 12/31/x1 $(375)

Restated to 12/31/x2: $375 × (150 ÷ 125 =) 1.2 $(450)
19x2 Net loss ($300[7] − 160[8] =) (140)
$(590)

[10] 12/31/x2 of $1,960 + 1,800 = $3,760
[11] 12/31/x2 of $3,000 × (165 ÷ 150 =) 1.1 = $3,300
[12] 12/31/x2 of $1,960 × (165 ÷ 150 =) 1.1 = $2,156; $2,156 − 1,960 = $(196)
[13] $1,800 − [12/31/x2 of $450 × (165 ÷ 150 =) 1.1 =] $495 = $1,305
[14] Retained earnings (deficit) 12/31/x2 $(590)

Restated to 12/31/x3: $590 × (165 ÷ 150 =) 1.1 = $(649)
19x3 Net income: 1,305[13] − 196[12] = 1,109
$460

proceeds received and its restated cost basis. The ending retained earnings balance is the sum of the restated beginning retained earnings and the earnings statement's ($300 − 160 =) $140 net income.

In the illustration's third and final year, the sale of the remaining land further increases the cash on hand, and the nonmonetary capital stock is restated to reflect the year's inflation. The income statement has the same components as that of the preceding year with different amounts of course, and the end-of-year retained earnings is also derived in a manner similar to that of a year earlier.

Each of the three years resulted in an inflation loss. To determine the cumulative inflation loss for the three-year period, the three loss amounts cannot merely be added, because each is expressed in terms of dollars having different purchasing power. To effect additivity, therefore, it is necessary to restate each loss amount in terms of the purchasing power prevailing at a common point in time, that is, that all of the amounts be measured in constant dollars. The following table demonstrates how the cumulative loss is determined if it were to be measured in dollars having purchasing power equal to that of dollars at the end of the three years, i.e., December 31, 19x3; or that at the beginning of the three-year period, i.e., January 1, 19x1.

	Inflation Loss	Measured in 12/31/x3 Dollars	Measured in 1/1/x1 Dollars
19x1	$375	$\times \frac{165}{125} = \$ 495$	$\times \frac{100}{125} = \$300$
19x2	$300	$\times \frac{165}{150} = \$ 330$	$\times \frac{100}{150} = \$200$
19x3	$196	$= \underline{196}$	$\times \frac{100}{165} = \underline{119}$
		$1,021	**$619**

To appreciate the parallel between accounting for changes in the general price level and accounting for foreign currency, these same data are now used to represent Bostonian hubs (H), with the objective to translate these amounts into the equivalent number of U.S. dollars ($). The numbers which were cast as price index amounts now signify foreign currency exchange rates. Indeed, as indicated below, the exchange rate expressed in terms of hubs uses the same amounts which comprise the price index numbers. And when it is desirable to express the exchange rate in terms of dollars—as is the case at hand—it is merely the inverse amount which is used (e.g., $1.00 ÷ H 1.25 = $.80).

	Price Index	Exchange Rate in Terms of	
		Hubs	Dollars
January 1, 19x1	100	$1 = H 1.00	H 1 = $1.00
January 2, 19x1	100	$1 = H 1.00	H 1 = $1.00
December 31, 19x1	125	$1 = H 1.25	H 1 = $ .80
December 31, 19x2	150	$1 = H 1.50	H 1 = $ .67
December 31, 19x3	165	$1 = H 1.65	H 1 = $ .606

Before proceeding to demonstrate the situations' similarity in terms of amounts appearing in financial statements, an overview discussion of the conceptual parallels is in order.

Using 19x2 as a focal point, in the general price level case, the purchasing power of the year-end dollar is weaker than that of a year earlier inasmuch as $150 is needed to buy what could have been bought earlier for only $125. In the foreign currency case, the year-end hub relative to the dollar is weaker than what had been the case at the beginning of the year. This is demonstrated by the fact that at year-end H 1.50 is needed to buy $1 as compared to the beginning-of-year cost of H 1.25. In the general price level case, even though money is measured in amounts of dollars, it is purchasing power which is its essential ingredient; as a result, its changing value affects a company in real terms. In the foreign currency case, even though foreign currency is measured in amounts of dollars, it is the relative strength of the foreign currency in which monetary assets and liabilities are denominated which is the key consideration, and it is their changing relative value which affects an American company in real terms.

In the general price level situation that was depicted, the company was in a net monetary asset position—since cash was its only monetary item. As a result, inflation during each of the three years generated an adverse effect, as indicated by each year's income statement recognition of an inflation loss. The loss was determined by examining the effect of inflation on monetary items in the balance sheet. Recall that while nonmonetary amounts were restated, it was the inherent *fixed number of dollars* nature of monetary items which precluded their being restated as well. The inflation loss, in effect, identified the amount of restatement which would have been recorded had the monetary sum, in fact, been nonmonetary. Thus, it identifies the loss sustained as a result of having held cash rather than a nonmonetary asset such as land.

With this orientation in mind, refer now to Exhibit 14–6. The circumstances described at the top of the exhibit are the same as that of the earlier illustration. The December 31, 19x1 balance sheet expressed in dollars entails translating each hub-based amount at its appropriate foreign currency

Exhibit 14–6

Accounting for Foreign Currency

			Exchange Rate in Terms of	
Date	Event	Amount	Hubs	Dollars
January 1, 19x1	Issue stock for cash	H 2,000	$1 = H 1.00	H 1 = $1.00
January 2, 19x1	Purchase land	H 500	$1 = H 1.00	H 1 = $1.00
December 31, 19x1			$1 = H 1.25	H 1 = $ .80
December 31, 19x2	Sell 40% of land	H 460	$1 = H 1.50	H 1 = $ .67
December 30, 19x3	Sell land	H 1,800	$1 = H 1.65	H 1 = $ .606

Balance sheet:

	1/2/x1	12/31/x1	12/31/x2	12/31/x3
Cash	$1,500[1]	$1,200[4]	$1,307[6]	$2,279[11]
Land	500[2]	500[2]	300[7]	
	$2,000	**$1,700**	**$1,607**	**$2,279**
Capital stock	$2,000[3]	$2,000[3]	$2,000[3]	$2,000[3]
Retained earnings	–0–	(300)[5]	(393)[10]	279[14]
	$2,000	**$1,700**	**$1,607**	**$2,279**

Income statement:

	19x1	19x2	19x3
Foreign currency exchange (loss)	$(300)[5]	$(200)[8]	$(119)[12]
Gain on sale of land		$107[9]	$791[13]

Supporting computations:

[1] H 2,000 − 500 = H 1,500; 1,500 × 1.0 = $1,500

[2] H 500 × 1.0 = $500

[3] H 2,000 × 1.0 = $2,000

[4] H 1,500 × .8 = $1,200

[5] (H 1,500 × 1.0 (of 12/31/x1) = $1,500; 1,500 − $1,200[4] = $300

[6] H 1,500 + H 460 = H 1,960; H 1,960 × .67 = $1,307

[7] H 500 × .6 = H 300; H 300 × 1.0 = $300

[8] (H 1,500 × .8 =) $1,200; $1,200 − (H 1.500 × .67 =) $1.000 = $200

[9] H 460 × .67 = $307; $307 − (H 500 × .4 = H 200; H 200 × $1.0 =) $200 = $107

[10] ($300)[5] + ($200)[8] + $107[9] = $(393)

[11] H 1.500 + H 460 + H 1.800 = H 3,760; H 3,760 × .606 = $2,279

[12] $1,307[6] − (H 1,960 × .606 =) $1,188 = $119

[13] H 1,800 × .606 = $1,091; $1,091 − (H 300 × 1.0 =) $300 = $791

[14] $(393)[10] + $(119)[12] + $791[13] = $279

exchange rate. The one monetary amount, cash, is translated on the basis of the current H 1 = $.80 exchange rate, while the nonmonetary land and capital stock balances are translated at the historical H 1 = $1 exchange rate. With respect to the income statement, the $300 foreign currency exchange loss measures the effect of the hub-denominated cash's exposure to the weakening of hubs relative to dollars.

The balance sheet as of the end of 19x2 depicts the increased amount of hub-denominated cash (H 1,500 + H 460 = H 1,960) translated into dollars on the basis of the current (year-end H 1 = $.67) exchange rate. The remaining land and the (original) capital stock continue to be translated at their historical (H 1 = $1) exchange rate. The foreign currency exchange loss appearing in the income statement results from applying the same procedures as those of the preceding year. The gain on the sale of part of the land is the difference between the cash proceeds translated at the historical, that is, transaction date (H 1 = $.67) exchange rate and the cost basis of the land translated at its historical (H 1 = $1) exchange rate. The end-of-period retained earnings is a nonmonetary item; it is, therefore, merely the sum of the previous year's ending balance already expressed in dollars and the current year's ($200 − 107 =) $93 net income which is also already expressed in dollars. At the end of the third year, the hub-denominated cash is translated into dollars at the current (H 1 = $.606) exchange rate. And the remaining balance sheet and income statement balances are translated in a manner similar to that of one year earlier.

It is no coincidence that for each year, the amounts of the inflation loss and the foreign currency exchange loss are identical. The inflation loss of each year (summarized in Exhibit 14–5) and the foreign currency exchange loss for each year are reproduced in the table below.

	Inflation Loss (from Exhibit 14–5)	Foreign Currency Exchange Loss (from Exhibit 14–6)
19x1	$300[a]	$300[d]
19x2	$200[b]	$200[e]
19x3	$119[c]	$119[f]

[a] $1,500 × (125 ÷ 100 =) 1.25 = $1,875; $1,875 − 1,500 = $375; $375 × (100 ÷ 125 =) .8 = $300

[b] $1,500 × (150 ÷ 125 =) 1.2 = $1,800; $1,800 − 1,500 = $300; $300 × (100 ÷ 150 =) .67 = $200

[c] $1,960 × (165 ÷ 150 =) 1.1 = $2,156; $2,156 − 1,960 = $196; $196 × (100 ÷ 165 =) .606 = $119

[d] H 1,500 × 1.0 = $1,500; $1,500 − 1,200 = $300

[e] H 1,500 × .8 = $1,200; $1,200 − (H 1,500 × .67 =) $1,000 = $200

[f] H 1,960 × .67 = $1,307; $1,307 − (H 1,960 × .606 =) $1,188 = $119

Being in either a net monetary asset position in the general price level case when the purchasing power of the dollar weakened relative to the number of dollars held, or in a net monetary asset position in the foreign currency case when the value of the hub, in which currency its transactions are denominated, weakened relative to dollars in which it measures its financial position and operating results caused the company to suffer.

The parallel is that with respect to foreign exchange, accounting takes amounts denominated in a foreign currency and measures them in terms of the domestic currency. In the case of accounting for changes in the general price level, accounting takes numbers denominated in *numbers* of nominal dollars, and measures these amounts in terms of constant dollars. Thus we have foreign currency measured in equivalent dollars, and numbers of nominal dollars measured in constant (purchasing power) dollars, respectively.

In the changing price level case, under inflation it is desirable to be in a net monetary liability position. Given that inflation signifies that the equivalent purchasing power value of the nominal dollars is weakening, debtors prefer to repay their debts with weakened, that is, less valuable dollars—as opposed to having remitted earlier when greater purchasing power made the same number of dollars relatively more valuable. In the foreign exchange situation, the relative weakening, i.e., devaluation, of a foreign currency in which receivables and payables are denominated, means that the American company which is in a net monetary liability position benefits because its U.S. dollars will liquidate more debt now than would have been the case had the devaluation not occurred.

Thus, inflation yields the same effect as does devaluation of a foreign currency. Debtors whose obligations are denominated in nominal dollars in the inflation case and in weaker foreign currency in the foreign exchange case are in a desirable position. This is so because receivables and payables are liquidated with dollars having less purchasing power value in the inflation case, and with devalued currency in the foreign exchange case. And, needless to say, those conditions attractive to a debtor are undesirable for a creditor. Similarly, price deflation, that is, increased purchasing power of the dollar or a relative strengthening of the foreign currency in which monetary amounts are denominated, would be looked upon favorably by creditors and unfavorably by debtors.

These observations are summarized in the following table:

	Weakened by Devaluation OR Inflation, Respectively	*Strengthened by Upvaluation OR Deflation, Respectively*
Net monetary assets	Loss	Gain
Net monetary liabilities	Gain	Loss

355

By identifying the conditions which result in the recognition of a gain or loss, the table dramatizes the need to be sensitive to both changing price levels and fluctuating exchange rates. In anticipation of particular business trends or economic developments, it may be possible to position a company's monetary assets and liabilities in a manner which minimizes its exposure to an undesirable economic outcome.

ALTERNATIVE METHODS OF ACCOUNTING

The Temporal Method became a requirement for American companies in 1975, and its fundamental orientation is to focus on the distinction between financial statements' monetary and nonmonetary amounts. Monetary items are translated on the basis of the currency exchange rate in effect as of the balance sheet date, and most nonmonetary amounts are reflected at the currency exchange rate which existed when the underlying transaction occurred. The distinctive temporal feature entails also using the balance sheet date currency exchange rate to translate nonmonetary amounts which are already measured in terms of their balance sheet date current value.[7]

An important aspect of the FASB's requirements is that as currency exchange rates fluctuate, the resulting gain or loss is recognized immediately as an ordinary element of income. This result has provoked some concern among business executives and accountants of companies whose earnings thereby became particularly susceptible to fluctuating foreign currency exchange rates. Before examining some of the specific issues surrounding this matter, characteristics of two alternative approaches that had been used prior to 1976 are described.

The *current-noncurrent method* uses both the current balance sheet date exchange rate and historical exchange rates. The criterion used to determine which rate is to be applied for a particular amount is that of how it is classified for financial statement disclosure purposes. Current assets and current liabilities are translated on the basis of the current exchange rate, and all other financial statement amounts are measured in terms of their historical exchange rates. When exchange rates fluctuate, a foreign currency exchange gain or loss is computed. The specific manner in which it is disclosed is not implied by the method proper; as a general rule, however, most companies using this method did not recognize gains and losses as immediate determinants of income in the manner prescribed by the FASB in 1975. The FASB rejected this method because it felt the current-noncurrent distinction had no inherent relevance for currency translation despite its usefulness in measuring changes in financial position; its translation of long-term and short-term

---

[7] Ibid., paragraph nos. 123–125.

receivables and payables at different exchange rates was viewed as being particularly questionable, as was its like treatment of receivables and inventory.

The other alternative method that had been used by some companies prior to the FASB ruling is one which translates all amounts on the basis of the currency exchange rate in effect as of the balance sheet date. The FASB viewed it as being unacceptable because its underlying nature ". . . to retain the foreign currency as the unit of measure stems from the belief that the foreign statements represent the most meaningful presentation of a foreign operation and that translation should preserve the relationships in those statements."[8] But because the dollar is the unit of measure for American companies, "if assets and liabilities that are measured at past prices in foreign statements are translated at the current rate and included in dollar financial statements, the dollar financial statements depart from historical-cost-based accounting because inventory, property, plant, equipment, and other assets normally carried at cost are reflected at varying dollar amounts resulting from changes in rates."[9]

The following table summarizes the differences between the monetary-nonmonetary, current-noncurrent, and current rate methods.

	Foreign Currency Translation Rates		
	Monetary-Nonmonetary Method	Current-Noncurrent Method	Current Rate Method
Cash, current receivables, current payables	Current	Current	Current
Other current amounts	Historical	Current	Current
Noncurrent receivables, noncurrent payables	Current	Historical	Current
Other noncurrent amounts	Historical	Historical	Current

Note, however, that the prescribed temporal method can be viewed as a variation of the monetary-nonmonetary approach as it applies the current exchange rate to those amounts which are already measured in terms of their balance sheet date current value.

The most controversial aspect of accounting for the translation of foreign currency transactions and foreign currency financial statements is the requirement that a foreign currency exchange gain or loss be recognized in the period when the exchange rate change occurs. Opposition to immediate earnings statement recognition centers around the argument that until a gain

---

[8] Ibid., paragraph no. 84.

[9] Ibid., paragraph no. 134.

or loss is realized in an arm's length transaction, its recognition may be premature inasmuch as it may be negated by subsequent exchange rate fluctuation.

Moreover, it is asserted that immediate income statement recognition of a substantial gain or loss can have the effect of distorting net income in the sense that users have difficulty in discerning critical patterns and relationships which would otherwise be more readily apparent. It has also been suggested that in light of the potential gyrations in reported income that could occur, companies invariably introduce appropriate defensive measures. For instance, the managers of a company with significant foreign currency exposure may structure its financial affairs as a response to what in effect is its short-term financial reporting exposure, which may actually be inconsistent with the company's best business interests in the long-run.

The FASB requirement that there be immediate income statement recognition of a gain or loss can be defended in the following manner. The question of realization is not really more of an issue in this instance than it is in certain other cases where the accrual principle is similarly applied. "Conservatism is a way of dealing with uncertainty and is intended to avoid recognizing income on the basis of inadequate evidence that a gain has occurred. The Board believes that a rate change . . . provides sufficient objective evidence . . . to warrant changes in the dollar carrying amounts. . . ."[10] With respect to the potential gyrating effect on earnings, ". . . the Board rejected the implication that a function of accounting is to minimize the reporting of fluctuations. Past rate changes are historical facts, and the Board believes that users of financial statements are best served by accounting for the changes as they occur. It is the deferring or spreading of those effects, not their recognition and disclosure, that is the artificial process. . . . In the Board's opinion, readers of financial statements will not be confused by fluctuations in reported earnings caused by rate changes."[11]

SUMMARY

Prior to the mid-1970s, accounting for foreign currency was a subject which received relatively little attention by regulatory bodies. October 1975 marked the issuance of FASB Statement No. 8 which established measurement and disclosure requirements. The effect of this pronouncement was to create financial reporting rules significantly more definitive than had been the case previously.

Criticism of the Statement revolves around its allegedly misleading results

---

[10] Ibid., paragraph no. 190.
[11] Ibid., paragraph nos. 198–199.

and the effect it has on the way business executives make decisions. Concern at a theoretical level focusses on the realization principle of accounting and on the meaningfulness of using translation rates based on whether an item was categorized as monetary or nonmonetary in nature. To the extent that the Financial Accounting Standards Board maintains that Statement No. 8 is consistent with accounting theory while critics question this conclusion, there are differences of opinion that reflect alternative perceptions of the pertinent theoretical considerations. However, this would not be addressing the same issue as that which is raised in the argument that reconsideration of the Statement is warranted because of the economic consequences that allegedly result from its application.

Additional Readings

Choi, Frederick D. S., and Mueller, Gerhard G. *An Introduction to Multinational Accounting.* Englewood Cliffs, N.J.: Prentice-Hall, Inc., 1978.

Cooper, Kerry; Fraser, David R.; and Richards, R. Malcolm. "The Impact of SFAS #8 on Financial Management Practices." *Financial Executive* (June 1978), pp. 26–31.

Dukes, Roland E. *An Empirical Investigation of the Effects of the Statement of Financial Accounting Standards No. 8 on Security Return Behavior.* Stamford, Conn.: Financial Accounting Standards Board, 1978.

Evans, Thomas G.; Folks, William R., Jr.; and Jilling, Michael. *The Impact of Financial Accounting Standards No. 8 on the Foreign Exchange Risk Management Practices of American Multinationals: An Economic Impact Study.* Stamford, Conn.: Financial Accounting Standards Board, 1978.

FASB Discussion Memorandum. *Accounting for Foreign Currency Translation.* Stamford, Conn.: Financial Accounting Standards Board, 1974.

Hayes, Donald J. "Translating Foreign Currencies." *Harvard Business Review* (January-February 1972), pp. 6–18.

Lorensen, Leonard. *Reporting Foreign Operations of U.S. Companies in U.S. Dollars.* New York: American Institute of Certified Public Accountants, 1972.

Norr, David. "Improved Foreign Exchange Disclosure for the Investor," *Financial Analysts Journal* (March–April 1977), pp. 17–20.

Peat Marwick Mitchell & Co. *A Survey of the Economic Impacts of FASB Statement No. 8, "Accounting for the Translation of Foreign Currency Transactions and Foreign Currency Financial Statements"* New York: Peat Marwick Mitchell & Co., 1977.

Rosenfield, Paul. "General Price-Level Accounting and Foreign Operations," *The Journal of Accountancy* (February 1971), pp. 58–65.

Rudnitsky, Howard. "How Companies Cope." *Forbes* (January 23, 1978), pp. 43–44.

Rule, John E. "The Practical Business Effect of Exchange-Rate Fluctuations." *The Arthur Andersen Chronicle* (September 1977), pp. 63–75.

Seidler, Lee J. "An Income Approach to the Translation of Foreign Currency Financial Statements," *The CPA Journal* (January 1972), pp. 26–35.

Shank, John K.; Dillard, Jesse F.; and Murdock, Richard J. *Assessing the Economic Impact of FASB No. 8.* New York: Financial Executives Research Foundation, 1979.

Steinhauer, Walter R. "Confusing Encounter." *Price Waterhouse Review* (1976, No. 3), pp. 20–27.

Watt, George C.; Hammer, Richard M.; Burge, Marianne. *Accounting for the Multinational Corporation.* New York: Financial Executives Research Foundation, 1978.

Facets
of Accounting
Disclosure

In addition to serving an important measurement function, accounting is also concerned with providing adequate financial statement disclosures. Such disclosures are not limited to displaying summary numbers in the financial statements proper; footnotes and supplementary schedules are other media used to disclose relevant information.

Changes in the way business is conducted are often the basis for introducing modifications to, and the expansion of, traditional accounting approaches. Such changes can have accounting measurement implications, financial reporting disclosure implications, or both. Accounting issues whose predominant effect is in the realm of accounting measurement were discussed in earlier chapters, e.g., business combinations, general price level changes, and foreign currency translation. Those accounting matters whose primary nature revolves around financial statement disclosure—although they usually have important measurement aspects as well—are examined in this chapter.

THE NEED FOR PERSPECTIVE

Bottom line is an expression which in recent years has become part of the vernacular. It, along with "operating in the red" and "other side of the ledger" are examples of accounting jargon that play an integral role in the popular parlance. *Bottom line* is based on the accounting convention that on subtracting expenses from revenues, the resulting residual—either net income or net loss—by necessity appears as the bottom line of the income

361

statement. To the extent revenues depict accomplishment and expenses represent effort, income is a measure of success or alternatively, loss is a measure of failure.

To lay persons, this income or loss is viewed as a shortcut or summary evaluation of the results of an enterprise's operations. It is a concise means of communicating whether performance was good or bad, satisfactory or unsatisfactory, worthy or unworthy of replication, and so forth. In turn, it becomes the basis for overlooking particular underlying circumstances or environmental constraints, and ignoring the uncontrollable or non-discretionary factors imposed on persons responsible for generating a particular type of outcome. It might even be observed that *bottom line* personifies the mentality that focuses on ends while overlooking the pertinent means needed to achieve such ends.

It is ironic that lay persons have glorified the expression *bottom line* in a manner that runs counter to its substantive financial reporting nature. Informed readers of financial statements are not so naïve to assume a single amount is the all-purpose instrument with which to evaluate an enterprise's performance. Not only are many of the revenue and expense elements of earnings based on managers' and accountants' estimates, but there is also the more fundamental need to identify an appropriate perspective and frame of reference.

The amount appearing on the bottom line of an income statement is merely an arithmetic residual. In its own right, it has no qualitative significance; it merely summarizes in arithmetic terms the net result of various substantive amounts categorized as revenues, expenses, gains and losses. Knowledgeable users of income statements focus their attention on these important underlying factors. By considering such "gross" amounts, an understanding of the enterprise's various activities can be obtained. And more important, because these amounts relate to particular aspects of the overall earnings endeavor, they can provide a meaningful basis for effecting evaluations in light of a variety of benchmark criteria.

This leads to the important matter of perspective. To contemplate either a $10,000 net income or a $200,000 sales revenue figure without an appropriate frame of reference offers no insight as such. Analogously, to be told that someone's brother weighs 30 kilograms provides no meaningful information unless it is accompanied, for instance, by a statement of the brother's age. Were one to be told the brother is four years old, the weight information would signify that the youngster is considerably overweight. On the other hand, if the boy is 16 years old, the cited weight would suggest a case of being substantially underweight.

With respect to financial statements, the kind of contextual or benchmark

362

information that can be useful include the current period data of other comparable companies, the same company's data for prior years, and the expected outcome for the company projected prior to the beginning of the period. In addition, relationships within a set of financial statements can offer insights, such as relating sales to total assets, or liabilities to owners' equity. The function of such analysis is to focus on critical interdependencies. Ratios are useful because it is their nature to relate two different amounts to each other.

Of all the numbers generated by an accounting system, the net income or net loss amount invariably receives most attention. Because users of accounting information do place emphasis on this one amount, accountants are particularly careful in measuring and disclosing it. Its importance and limitations can be demonstrated by the following example.

A person is considering the purchase of 100 shares of common stock either of Company A, which consistently has annual earnings in the $1,000,000 range, or of Company B, whose income each year tends to be in the area of $200,000. Which situation appears to be more attractive? Assume the person initially puts aside consideration of factors such as investment objectives, growth potential, and other nonquantitative issues. If the decision is to be made solely on the basis of the historical earnings patterns—which is not to say that such an approach is the one right approach or for that matter that it has many or any "right" aspects about it—which company's shares should be acquired?

Before proceeding, one additional bit of information is needed, namely, the number of each company's shares of stock that are outstanding. If Company A, which earns $1,000,000 each year, has 100,000 shares outstanding, its earnings per share (EPS) is ($1,000,000 ÷ 100,000 =) $10. If Company B, with only about one-fifth the annual income were to have only 4,000 shares of its stock outstanding, its earnings per share would be ($200,000 ÷ 4,000 =) $50. Thus, although on the basis of aggregate net income data alone Company A would appear to be the more profitable company, once the data are seen in a different perspective, it becomes evident it may well be Company B has the more attractive earnings.

Investors are understandably interested in relating a company's historical earnings to the market value of its shares. Since both data can be expressed in a common dimension, earnings expressed on a per-share basis has supplanted the aggregate dollar amount of earnings as the most frequently cited measure of an enterprise's performance. Relating earnings to market value provides a rate of return type of measure, viz., $8 earnings per share divided by $40 market value per share results in a 20 percent return on investment. In practice, however, the generally accepted mode of expression is the inverse amount; thus, dividing the $40 market value per share by the $8 earnings per share yields a price-earnings ratio of five to one, which would be referred to as a P/E ratio of 5.

This ratio is considered a communicator of investors' perceptions about particular companies' outstanding shares of stock. One may hear statements such as "a particular individual will not purchase a stock having a P/E ratio of more than six" or "investors expect large future earnings for a certain company as indicated by its shares' high P/E ratio of 25." The latter statement in particular is noteworthy because it suggests investors are generally prepared to pay a price for a stock they feel is warranted based on their expectations with respect to future earnings. In other words, because only *past* earnings data are actually available, they perforce become the basis on which a P/E ratio is expressed. But, in practice, each investor must make his or her own assessment of future earnings and act or react accordingly. The very fact all investors are making their own estimates about future income levels is characteristic of risk-taking, which is, of course, an essential ingredient of the private enterprise system.

EARNINGS PER SHARE

Because of the importance of earnings per share (EPS), the procedures used in its calculation are designed to preempt any misstatement. Without specific rules, EPS could be manipulated through its denominator and also through its numerator. Specifically, a company may have a financial structure which would result in a particular number of shares appearing in its EPS denominator. This legal form aspect notwithstanding, accounting requires there be recognition of the underlying economic substance of the financial structure which may in turn yield a more conservative earnings per share outcome.

The existence of such possibilities has, in turn, precipitated an amalgam of rules—do's and don'ts—with which accountants make the necessary EPS calculations. Although one might be critical of the conceptual or theoretical substance underlying its required computational scheme, the rules that now exist were created to respond to what were or might have been rampant incidents of substandard and misleading disclosures of vital earnings-based data. Rather than describe all its details, selected key aspects of the resulting schema are discussed below in a conceptual context.

To achieve consistency between earnings and outstanding shares, the number of shares included in the EPS calculation is based on a weighted average number of shares outstanding during the period. When prior years' EPS amounts are presented for comparative purposes, and there had been a stock dividend or split in the interim, the earlier amounts must be restated to their current equivalent shares outstanding. For example, assume that 19x1 earnings of $10,000 had been divided by 2,000 outstanding shares to yield EPS of $5, and that there was a 2 for 1 stock split in 19x3; when presenting prior years' data for comparative purposes in 19x3, the 19x1 EPS would be restated as ($10,000 ÷ 4,000 =) $2.50. As a result, the earlier year's EPS is based on the comparable number of post-split shares—the same dimension as the current year's shares already expressed on a post stock split basis.

A two-tier approach is used whereby two EPS measures often are disclosed: primary earnings per share and fully diluted earnings per share. One of the key elements of the underlying computations is determining whether any of the company's senior outstanding securities qualify for inclusion as a common stock equivalent, a notion used solely for purposes of calculating EPS.

"A common stock equivalent is a security which is not, in form, a common stock, but which usually contains provisions to enable its holder to become a common stockholder and which, because of its terms and the circumstances under which it was issued, is in substance equivalent to a common stock."[1] Because of the importance of the underlying economic substance, the determination of primary earnings per share of common stock includes the effect of such *equivalents* (when dilutive) even though in legal form they are not currently outstanding shares of common stock.

In addition, there can also be a required ". . . pro-forma presentation which reflects the dilution of earnings per share that would have occurred if *all* contingent issuances of common stock that would individually reduce earnings per share had taken place. . . ."[2] This second tier *fully diluted* amount encompasses factors not included in the earlier notion of common stock equivalents. The additional disclosure requirement is an example of an instance in which the economic substance consideration—any and *all* potential dilution of existing common stockholders' equity interest—is assumed to be more pervasive an aspect than that indicated by only the legal form of ownership interests.[3]

The types of securities that could qualify for recognition in the EPS denominator include convertible preferred stock, convertible debenture bonds, stock options, and stock warrants. Whether a particular security qualifies depends on whether certain conditions are met. If a security's potential common shares are included in the denominator of the EPS calculation, there must be consistency in the numerator as well. This means if a convertible

---

[1] *Accounting Principles Board Opinion No. 15,* paragraph no. 25.

[2] Ibid., paragraph no. 15.

[3] The fully diluted amount need not be disclosed if it represents less than 3 percent additional dilution. (See Ibid., paragraph no. 14 and footnote no. 2).

debenture is recognized as "converted," the related interest cost included in net income for the period must be neutralized. In other words, if a debenture is viewed as common stock for denominator purposes, it should not be treated as a debt security for numerator purposes. As the resulting shares are added to the denominator, the interest expense, net of its income tax effect, is simultaneously added to the numerator.[4]

The reason for including such potential shares in EPS calculations is that holders of such instruments are perceived to be affected by fluctuations in the market value of the common shares which are actually outstanding. The nature of such persons' relationship to the company is that they have the *potential* to share in earnings, to the same extent a current stockholder does. Their potential return is not fixed by either a predetermined preferred dividend rate or an interest rate. They have the potential to experience the same rights and risks existing residual shareholders experience, and this potential can be realized by unilateral action on the part of the individual—and not the company.

In summary, the measurement and disclosure of earnings per share is one of the most important aspects of accounting and financial reporting. EPS is viewed by some if not many investors as a concise, well-defined indication of a company's performance, and one which can be related to the market value of the corporation's outstanding shares of common stock. However, perceptive users of financial statements recognize that an understanding of a company's performance requires analysis more comprehensive than the mere contemplation of a single ratio result. Noteworthy also is the fact that the determination and dissemination of earnings per share data is not required for companies whose securities are not publicly traded.[5]

RESULTS OF OPERATIONS

Prior to 1966, there was no uniformity among companies' financial statements with respect to disclosing the results of operations. The primary point of contention centered on where in a company's financial statements should there be disclosure of the effect of extraordinary gains and losses. This refers to a transaction whose nature indicates it was not demonstrably a determinant of current income; examples included asset writeoffs, gains and

---

[4] If the resulting EPS exceeds what it would otherwise have been, it is called *anti-dilutive* and it would be ignored altogether.

[5] *Financial Accounting Standards Board Statement No. 21,* paragraph nos. 12 and 13. Copyright © by Financial Accounting Standards Board, High Ridge Park, Stamford, Connecticut 06905, U.S.A. Reprinted with permission. Copies of the complete document are available from the FASB.

losses from foreign currency fluctuation, and gains and losses resulting from a condemnation action.

Two schools of thought existed. One advocated a *current operating* approach which maintained that the income statement should include only those factors which affect current operations. These are items readers can assume are not unique to the period in question, but are likely to occur in subsequent periods as well. All gains and losses which did not qualify as operating items were accounted for as direct charges or credits to retained earnings. The all-inclusive method, on the other hand, argued for including in the earnings statement all types of gains and losses irrespective of whether they were ordinary or extraordinary. This point of view was based on the concern that not including all such items as determinants of income would have the effect of their not being given the attention they warranted.

A 1966 Accounting Principles Board pronouncement[6] resolved the controversy. It required that all items be included in the income statement, but it stipulated that there be two categories of income determinants: ordinary and extraordinary. To qualify as extraordinary, the gain or loss had to be either unusual in nature or infrequent in occurrence. These are terms whose connotations were refined six and one half years later by a pronouncement whose primary function was to state that to qualify as extraordinary, instead of being *either* unusual *or* nonrecurring, the item in question had to be *both* unusual *and* nonrecurring.[7] Whether an item is usual or unusual depends on the nature of the enterprise's business. To be unusual, it would have to be abnormal and unrelated to the company's ordinary and typical activities; *nonrecurring* refers to an event or transaction of a type not reasonably expected to recur in the foreseeable future.

Thus, the loss resulting from a Florida citrus crop damaged by frost is unusual because frost damage is not a normal characteristic of the citrus growing business.[8] Similarly, if a warehouse chain realized a gain or loss on the sale of unneeded contiguous land bought routinely in the event expansion would be warranted is unusual because gains and losses on the sale of land is not a typical activity of the warehousing industry. However, neither of these two examples would qualify as extraordinary because in neither case is the gain or loss necessarily a nonrecurring event. The citrus grower is located geographically in an area which experiences frost from time to time, and the warehouse company purchases extra property from time to time, so the test of infrequent occurrence is not met.

---

[6] *Accounting Principles Board Opinion No. 9.*

[7] *Accounting Principles Board Opinion No. 30,* paragraph no. 20.

[8] The examples contained in this and the following two paragraphs are based on the *Accounting Interpretation of APB Opinion No. 30* issued by the American Institute of Certified Public Accountants in November, 1973.

Consider the case of a highly diversified corporation which, for the first time, sells investment securities from its portfolio, or the case of a company which relocates its plant for the first time in 20 years with no plans to do so again. In both these instances, even though the event occurs infrequently as far as the particular company is concerned, neither situation can be characterized as being unusual in nature. It is not unusual for a company owning investment securities to sell a portion of its portfolio, nor is it unusual for companies having plants to relocate a plant.

Because classification as an extraordinary item requires it be both unusual in nature and infrequent in occurrence, only a few situations qualify. Some examples follow:

(1) A tobacco crop destroyed by a rare hailstorm
(2) The sale by a steel fabricating company of the only land it owns acquired for since-abandoned expansion purposes
(3) An oil refinery destroyed by an earthquake

In addition to such sets of circumstances which must be considered in light of the prescribed criteria, there are two items always reflected in an income statement as extraordinary items. The first is the realization of the tax benefit resulting from an operating loss carryforward. When a corporation sustains an operating loss with which it may reduce subsequent years' income tax payments, unless the company's management expects to realize the future benefits beyond any reasonable doubt (discussed in Chapter 5), the subsequent realization is recognized as an extraordinary credit to income. The other mandated extraordinary item is the gain or loss that results from an early extinguishment of debt (discussed in Chapter 8). Even though such a transaction is not unusual for a company having outstanding debt securities, the resulting gain or loss is treated as an extraordinary item for financial reporting purposes.[9]

Although the matter of determining what constitutes an extraordinary item is ostensibly one of disclosure, an important measurement aspect exists as well. When disclosing an extraordinary gain or loss, it is reflected on a net of income tax basis. This is explained by the example which appears in Exhibit 15–1. The company in question incurs income tax charges equal to 45 percent of its taxable income, its taxable income is equal to accounting income, and the only extraordinary item is a $30,000 gain.

Column A demonstrates the income statement format whereby the $58,500 income tax expense (line 4) represents the tax accrual equal to 45

---

[9] *Financial Accounting Standards Board Statement No. 4,* paragraph no. 8. Copyright © by Financial Accounting Standards Board, High Ridge Park, Stamford, Connecticut 06905, U.S.A. Reprinted with permission. Copies of the complete document are available from the FASB.

Exhibit 15–1

Intraperiod Tax Allocation

		A	B
1.	Sales	$400,000	$400,000
2.	Expenses	−300,000	−300,000
3.	Income before income taxes	$100,000	$100,000
4.	Income taxes	− 58,500	− 45,000
5.	Income before extraordinary items	$ 41,500	$ 55,000
6.	Extraordinary gain	+$ 30,000	30,000
7.	Income taxes		− 13,500
8.	Net extraordinary gain		+$ 16,500
9.	**Net income**	**$ 71,500**	**$ 71,500**

percent of the total pre-tax earnings of (line 3's $100,000 plus line 6's $30,000 equal to) $130,000. Its nature is (1) to disclose the income tax expense as one self-contained amount and (2) to portray the extraordinary gain intact as $30,000. This is *not* permitted by generally accepted accounting principles.

By contrast, Column B illustrates an earnings statement presentation which conforms with generally accepted accounting principles. Its nature is to allocate the $58,500 income tax accrual between its ordinary and extraordinary components. The 45 percent tax rate applied to the $100,000 ordinary income produces a $45,000 tax (line 4), and the 45 percent tax rate applied to the $30,000 extraordinary gain yields a $13,500 tax (line 7). The sum of the $45,000 and $13,500 tax amounts is the same $58,500 which had appeared autonomously in Column A (line 4). The Column B approach exemplifies *intraperiod tax allocation* as it allocates within the period's earnings statement the total income tax which accrued. The superiority of its presentation to that of Column A is the meaningfulness of both the ordinary and extraordinary components of income being reflected on a like, net-of-income-tax basis.

An additional aspect of the related disclosure requirement is that the income statement must display:

(1) Income before extraordinary items per share,
(2) Extraordinary items per share, and
(3) Earnings per share.

Items which are either "unusual and recurring" or "usual and nonrecurring" are also identified, but not in the expanded manner required for extraordinary items.

The correction of errors in the financial statements of a prior period—those resulting from mathematical mistakes, mistakes in the application of accounting principles, or oversight or misuse of facts which existed at the time the financial statements had been prepared—are accounted for as direct adjustments of the (subsequent) period's beginning retained earnings.

SEGMENTS OF A BUSINESS ENTERPRISE

Although business combinations were by no means an unheard of phenomenon prior to 1960, many of the combinations which began to occur with frequency during the Sixties were distinctive. Whereas those of an earlier era were apt to be characterized by vertical or horizontal integration, diversification became a widespread practice in these more recent corporate combinations.

Two specific ramifications for financial reporting emerged. First, because of the accounting preference for preparing the financial statements of a parent corporation and its subsidiary companies on a consolidated basis, readers of such financial reports were usually unable to appreciate the relative contribution made by each segment of the overall enterprise. This situation can exist even if diversification is not effected through the operation of subsidiaries which are legal entities in their own right. The mere existence of divisions or well-defined product lines within one autonomous legal unit can also raise the question of whether and how to disclose the effect of distinct parts of the aggregated whole.

The second issue stimulated by the 1960's proliferation of business combinations is that of accounting for discontinued operations. This matter became particularly important in the 1970s when a number of corporations divested themselves of some of the acquisitions made in the preceding decade. In some cases, only a portion of an acquired business would be discontinued while in other instances an entire company would be sold. Questions therefore arose as to what measurement and disclosure rules were to be applied in different situations.

Segment Reporting

The importance of segment reporting in financial accounting was aptly stated by the Financial Accounting Standards Board as follows:

> The broadening of an enterprise's activities into different industries or geographic areas complicates the analysis of conditions, trends, and ratios and,

therefore, the ability to predict. The various industry segments or geographic areas of operations of an enterprise may have different rates of profitability, degrees and types of risk, and opportunities for growth. There may be differences in the rates of return on the investment commitment in the various industry segments or geographic areas and in their future capital needs.[10]

Persons who advocate that such disclosures be made maintain that the various segments of an enterprise have different risk characteristics and hence different implicit price-earnings ratios, and disclosure affords investors an opportunity to evaluate the ability of a diversified company's management to allocate resources. Especially in the case of business combinations, data are provided which permit judgments to be made as to whether the expected benefits of a particular combination were, in fact, realized. In a more macro or aggregated sense, the availability of such data facilitates intra-industry comparisons among companies. Such information would not routinely be obtainable if the five leading companies in a particular industry were all subsidiaries of corporations whose consolidated financial statements concealed their subsidiaries' individual operating results and financial position. Related to this is the belief that one of the elements which can foster competition and, in turn, benefits to consumers is that of available information. Access to financial data of segments allows prospective entrants into an industry to evaluate the relative desirability of becoming a competitor.

Opponents of formal segment reporting offer arguments as well. The confidentiality of segment data is such that its disclosure could jeopardize a company's future profitability. In addition, the practical difficulties and related costs of accumulating such data may be significant Moreover, the knowledge that disclosures are required could prove to be a disincentive for management to experiment and be innovative. There is also the problem of defining a segment. For example, shall the automobile manufacturer concentrate on each automobile model (Nova versus Impala), each family of automobiles (Chevrolet versus Buick), each type of vehicle (cars versus trucks), or an even broader concept (vehicles versus household appliances)?

An eloquent case against segment reporting is that which is known as the "chop suey" argument.[11] It maintains that when consuming a platter of chop suey and thereupon extending appropriate accolades to the chef, one does not customarily inquire as to its recipe or ingredients: because the only consid-

---

[10] *Financial Accounting Standards Board Statement No. 14*, paragraph no. 59. Copyright © by Financial Accounting Standards Board, High Ridge Park, Stamford, Connecticut 06905, U.S.A. Reprinted with permission. Copies of the complete document are available from the FASB.

[11] Howard C. Greer, "The Chop Suey Caper," *The Journal of Accountancy* (April 1968), pp. 27–34.

eration of consequence is the pleasure or displeasure provided by the dish taken as a whole. In other words, the decision to recommend the dish to friends or to order it again in a subsequent visit to the restaurant is influenced by one's overall satisfaction—not on the basis of knowing what its ingredients happen to be. Similarly, on receiving the aggregated results of a diversified enterprise, information as to its underlying whys and wherefores is said to be an inappropriate, if not an irrelevant, issue.

The FASB has set qualitative guidelines as to what comprises a segment, and has also established quantitative tests to assure that particular companies' number of segments is appropriate.[12] A reportable segment must meet only one of the following three tests: its revenue is at least 10 percent of total revenue, its identifiable assets comprise at least 10 percent of total assets, or its operating profit or loss is at least 10 percent of the dollar amount of the operating profit of the profitable segments or the operating loss of the unprofitable segments, whichever is larger. If the test was usually met in the past and is expected to be satisfied in the future, its not being met in a particular year does not exempt that year from the disclosure requirement. The opposite is true as well, that is, there is no reporting requirement if the test is met in a particular year with no similar past experience or expectation in the future.

To assure that the designated reportable segments comprise a substantial portion of the company's total activity, the sum of the reportable segments' revenue must represent at least 75 percent of the enterprise's total revenue. If this 75 percent test is not satisfied, the company must further refine its definition of segments until the 75 percent test is met. At the other extreme, if the number of reportable segments exceeds ten, combining segments into more broadly defined segments is appropriate. If the company operates exclusively or predominantly in one particular industry—when its revenue, operating profit or loss *and* identifiable assets *all* represent 90 percent of the company's total (revenue, operating profit or loss and assets)—the disclosures are not required, but the industry is identified.

For segments so defined, three types of data are disclosed: revenue, operating profit or loss, and identifiable assets. Operating profit or loss is measured by the difference between revenue and operating expenses; operating expenses not directly related to particular segments are allocated on a "reasonable" basis. Items which do not affect the determination of operating profit or loss include interest costs, income tax charges, discontinued operations, extraordinary items, and the effect of changes in an ac-

---

[12] *Financial Accounting Standards Board Statement No. 14*, paragraph nos. 15–19; segment reporting is required only for companies whose securities are traded publicly. Copyright © by Financial Accounting Standards Board, High Ridge Park, Stamford, Connecticut 06905, U.S.A. Reprinted with permission. Copies of the complete document are available from the FASB.

counting principle. Identifiable assets can include both tangible and intangible assets. A particular asset need not be used exclusively by the segment; assets used jointly by two or more segments are allocated to each. Assets used for general corporate purposes, such as cash and marketable securities, are not subject to allocation.

The information presented regarding reportable segments includes the types of products and services of each segment; the basis of accounting for intersegment sales or transfers; the nature and amount of any unusual or infrequent income statement items; each segment's depreciation, depletion and amortization expense; capital expenditures; equity in unconsolidated affiliates whose operations are vertically integrated with it as well as their geographic areas; and the effect on each segment of a change in an accounting principle. This information can be presented within the body of the financial statements, entirely in footnotes or in a separate schedule (which is an integral part of the financial statements). The information must be set forth in dollar amounts and must be reconciled to the pertinent amounts appearing in the financial statements of the total entity.

Several conceptual matters warrant consideration. First, in an attempt to render segment data which purport to reflect their autonomous or disaggregated nature, certain "natural" problems arise. The matter of allocating indirect costs is no less a serious matter—conceptually and procedurally—in this milieu than it has been for decades in the price renegotiation, armed services procurement regulations, and cost accounting standards contexts.

A direct cost is one that is incurred for the exclusive benefit of a single cost objective. Although the total enterprise constitutes a single cost objective, each of its reportable segments becomes a separate cost objective when disaggregation occurs. While a cost incurred by a company for which benefits accrue to several of its reportable segments is a direct cost to the total enterprise, it is an indirect cost to each of the benefitting segments—indirect because no one segment is the exclusive beneficiary. A meaningful basis is, therefore, selected to allocate such indirect costs to the various segments.

Another problem is that of intersegment sales transactions. Understandably, the selling segment seeks to recognize the resulting revenue on the basis of market prices, while the buying segment prefers to have the transaction recorded on the basis of its cost to the overall enterprise, i.e., the selling segment's cost basis. This problem of *transfer pricing* is difficult to resolve, and is beyond the scope of this volume. In measuring and disclosing segments' revenues, these intersegment sales are added to those made to unaffiliated customers. Because the amounts which represent intersegment sales are not based on uniform guidelines, they may be arbitrary and even distortions of the actual underlying circumstances.

In addition to disclosures relating to a company's operations in different

373

industries, information is also required regarding an enterprise's foreign operations and export sales, and sales to its major customers. Revenues, operating profit or loss, and identifiable assets are identified separately for foreign and domestic operations. The foreign-versus-domestic breakdown is required either if the foreign operations' revenues comprise at least 10 percent of total revenue or if the identifiable assets of the foreign operations represent at least 10 percent of total assets. When foreign operations are so reported, they must be disclosed by geographical area for those regions whose revenues or whose identifiable assets constitute at least 10 percent of the company's total.

The identity of the particular geographical areas encompassed by the foreign operations is set forth. The information is presented in absolute dollar terms, and the data are reconciled with related amounts appearing in the company's financial statements. If sales by its domestic operations to customers in foreign countries constitute at least 10 percent of total company sales, the dollar amount is disclosed in the aggregate and by geographical area.

The requirement regarding information about major customers applies if at least 10 percent of the company's total revenue results from sales to any single customer. In this case, the amount of revenue derived is disclosed for each qualifying customer. The rule applies also to sales to governments (domestic government agencies or foreign governments), and the company also identifies which of its industry segments made the sales.

In summary, it may be useful to consider the Financial Accounting Standards Board's response to the charge that its rigorous amalgam of measurement and disclosure rules constitutes an unwarranted extension of the scope of existing accounting practice. The FASB likens the resulting data to those which comprise the statement of changes in financial position. The analogy lies in the fact the segment-oriented information is simply a rearrangement of a company's consolidated financial statements in the same sense the statement of changes in financial position is a rearrangement of data already encompassed by the reporting entity's balance sheet and income statement. And it is in this sense that the segment reporting requirement "in the Board's judgment . . . does not go beyond or enlarge the boundaries of accounting."[13]

Discontinued Operations

The disposal of a business *segment* raises several accounting questions. At a definitional level, a segment of a business operation is viewed as a compo-

---

[13] Ibid., paragraph no. 64.

nent of an entity whose activities represent a separate major line of business or class of customer, as distinguished from other disposals of assets incident to the evolution of its business such as the disposal of *part* of a line of business. The accounting rules relating to discontinued operations apply only to *segments* such as:

(1) a diversified company selling its only electronics division,
(2) a meat company selling its significant interest in a professional football team,
(3) a communications company selling all its radio stations, and
(4) a food distributor selling its wholesale operation while retaining its institutional sales operation.

The disposal of an operation which does not qualify as a *segment* of a business operation receives no special earnings statement treatment, and is accounted for within the ordinary/extraordinary framework which was discussed earlier. Two examples of disposals which do not conform to the definition of a segment follow:

(1) a silver mining company selling one of its foreign subsidiaries while continuing to maintain like operations in other locations—this is merely a refinement of its intact product line, and
(2) a diversified company selling one of its two furniture manufacturing divisions—this is the disposal of only a part of a line of business.[14]

In those cases which qualify as disposals of a segment of a business, special income statement treatment is provided. Rather than designation of being either an ordinary or an extraordinary determinant of income, gains and losses related to discontinued operations are portrayed as an autonomous component of net income. One's initial reaction would be that the gain or loss would be based simply on the difference between the proceeds realized and the recorded carrying value of the assets thereby relinquished. Actually, although the resulting sum does properly measure the gain or loss on the disposal proper, there is another aspect to consider.

The discontinued operation may have earned revenues and incurred expenses during the year until the disposal date. The question that arises is where such revenues, expenses, and the resulting income or loss should appear in the earnings statement. On the one hand, such data might not warrant being isolated; on the other hand, it may be important to distinguish between

---

[14] The examples contained in this and the preceding paragraphs are based on the *Accounting Interpretation of APB Opinion No. 30* issued by the American Institute of Certified Public Accountants in November, 1973.

revenues and expenses that relate to continuing operations as opposed to those which pertain to the discontinued portion of the business. Such disclosure would identify those amounts which, as a result of the disposal, are not expected to recur in subsequent periods. And if such disclosure were to be made, it might be appropriate to present it in conjunction with the disposal gain or loss proper.

An illustration of the three approaches is presented in Exhibit 15–2. The circumstances depicted are that the company in question had sales of $2,000,000 and expenses (other than income taxes) of $1,590,000 during a particular year. $25,000 of the resulting pretax income is attributable to a segment of the business discontinued during the year. The $25,000 income is based on revenues and expenses of $240,000 and $215,000 respectively; in addition, the disposal resulted in a $30,000 gain. Income tax aspects are not considered in the exhibit, that is, all of its amounts are presented on a pre-tax basis.

Exhibit 15–2

Discontinued Operations

	A	B	C
Sales	$2,000,000	$1,760,000	$1,760,000
Expenses	1,590,000	1,375,000	1,375,000
	$ 410,000	$ 385,000	$ 385,000
Discontinued operations:			
Sales		$ 240,000	
Expenses		215,000	
Income		+$ 25,000	$ 25,000
Gain on disposal	+ 30,000	+ 30,000	30,000
			+$ 55,000
Net income	$ 440,000	$ 440,000	$ 440,000

Refer now to the exhibit. Column A reflects the point of view that the $25,000 of income resulting from operations which have since been discontinued need not be isolated in the earnings statement. Column B does segregate the pertinent portion of income, and there is explicit disclosure of the underlying revenues and expenses. Neither of these approaches is acceptable. Column C is the method prescribed by generally accepted accounting principles. It isolates the $25,000 income without identifying the causal revenues and expenses, then proceeds to combine it with the $30,000 gain on disposal to generate a total $55,000 effect of the discontinued operation.

The provisions of intraperiod tax allocation are applied. This means the various amounts are disclosed on a net-of-income-taxes basis. Exhibit 15–3 presents the income statement format that results if a 40 percent tax rate had been applied and if there had also been a $60,000 extraordinary loss. The five asterisked items on the income statement would be reflected on a per-share basis as well.

Exhibit 15–3

Discontinued Operations and an Extraordinary Item

Revenues	$1,760,000	
Expenses	1,375,000	
Income from continuing operations before taxes		$385,000
Provision for income taxes		154,000
Income from continuing operations		$231,000*
Discontinued operations:		
Income from operations of Division Q (less applicable taxes of $10,000)	$ 15,000	
Gain on disposal of Division Q (less applicable taxes of $12,000)	18,000	33,000*
Income before extraordinary items		$264,000*
Extraordinary loss (less applicable taxes of $24,000)		36,000*
Net income		**$228,000***

* To be disclosed on a per-share basis as well.

ALTERNATIVE ACCOUNTING METHODS

Although it might appear that there are many instances for which different accounting methods are available, in some cases the nature of the circumstances dictates which particular method should be used. Examples include business combinations, tax loss carryforward benefit, and long-term leases. In other transactions and circumstances, no one accounting method is required to the exclusion of all others, for instance, inventory costing, investment tax credit, and depreciation.

Disclosure of Accounting Policies

There is a requirement that financial statements be accompanied by a description of the enterprise's significant accounting policies.[15] Such disclosure typically appears as a preamble to the financial statements' footnotes or as the very first footnote. The disclosure of which of several existing acceptable alternatives is being used is but one of three types of situations requiring citation.

The second kind of circumstances which warrants disclosure is that of accounting principles and methods peculiar to the enterprise's particular industry. Such disclosure is required even if the accounting practice is common in the specialized industry. Examples include:

(1) accounting for unconsolidated intercorporate investments on a *cost basis* by a company in the jurisdiction of the Federal Communications Commission whose "uniform system of accounts" so requires,

(2) a tobacco or whiskey producer defining working capital in terms of a greater-than-one-year time horizon because of a prolonged aging process unique to its inventory, and

(3) a diversified company applying accounting practices to its insurance company subsidiary unique to, and acceptable for, insurance companies.

The third type of situation includible in a company's summary of significant accounting policies is the use of unusual or innovative applications of generally accepted accounting principles. This is the least encountered situation of the three; an illustration of what it refers to follows. During the period when the equity method of accounting for intercorporate investments was deemed to apply only to a parent company's interest in a subsidiary, there were instances when an investor would use the equity method to account for even 50 percent ownership of another corporation's outstanding shares. Because the application was new, different, and not explicitly sanctioned by previous practice, it would have necessitated inclusion in the summary of significant accounting policies had the disclosure requirement already been in effect.

The formal summary-type format adds a certain structure to financial statement presentation. Since many of its disclosure elements had been included in footnotes prior to the emergence of the requirement in 1972, its contribution was to establish a generally accepted medium of communication. Readers of financial statements are given the pertinent information at an appropriate juncture and, more importantly, it sets forth in this one location insights which need not therefore be repeated in subsequent footnotes

---

[15] *Accounting Principles Board Opinion No. 22*, paragraph no. 8.

which deal with some of the more technical aspects of particular financial statement amounts.

It is noteworthy that the disclosures need not identify *why* one method was selected while others were rejected. Moreover, there is no requirement that there be disclosure of what accounting effect would have resulted had an alternative method been used.

The Big Bath

A 1970 article in one of the popular, weekly newsmagazines described the following phenomenon:

> During an economic crunch such as the one now under way, when the stock slump has depressed many a corporation's shares while profits are tumbling, business is taking something of a bath anyway. Many corporate leaders then decide to make the bath "really bad and clean up all our accounts" . . . writing off those bad results that you have been hiding for years. After all, if your stock is down 50 per cent already, how much worse can it get?[16]

This practice is referred to as the *big bath,* and it tends to happen during a year when a company is already experiencing reduced profits. Alternatively, it is not an uncommon practice during the first year of the administration of a new management team, typically one which had virtually no direct association with its predecessors. In both of these cases, there may be an inclination to cast the current year's financial data in as unfavorable light as possible, for two reasons. On the one hand, it is an opportune time to relieve asset carrying values of questionable amounts which may have accumulated over time. On the other hand, subsequent years are thereby placed in an excellent position to have their operating results look good by comparison.

A big bath can be effected in a number of different ways. As alluded to earlier, writing off asset amounts which no longer reflect the resources' expected future service potential is one means. Assets which at one time were particularly vulnerable candidates for such writedowns included capitalized research and development costs, and purchased goodwill. As a result of the issuance of new pronouncements, however, non-reimbursable research and development expenditures are no longer even accounted for as assets, and goodwill must be amortized on a systematic basis over a period not to exceed 40 years.

Another means of effecting a big bath is to change an accounting principle, such as switching from the straight-line depreciation method to an accelerated method. This medium had also been exploited, but a subsequent

---

[16] "The Big Bath," *Newsweek,* July 27, 1970; pp. 54, 57.

pronouncement[17] imposed such rigorous measurement and disclosure rules on accounting changes that prospective users of the big bath technique are now more wary of engaging in its practice. The nature of how accounting changes are reflected in financial statements is examined in the next section of this chapter.

Other developments since the early 1970s have also lessened the incidence of *big bath* accounting. In addition to the new rules in the areas of research and development costs and purchased goodwill, more definitive standards regarding loss recognition have been promulgated with respect to foreign currency exposure, contingent events, and the decline in marketable equity securities' current value. With respect to accounting changes per se, the number of situations for which acceptable alternative methods even exist has been decreased. At a more subtle level, the formalization of interim reporting requirements—to be discussed in a later section of this chapter—has had the effect of diverting some attention away from annual data. This, in turn, has stimulated different comparison frames of reference, thus placing an obligation on companies to "own up" to their operating results four times each year, rather than just once annually.

The more stringent definition of what constitutes an extraordinary gain or loss, and the isolated measurement of a gain or loss from discontinued operations, have had an effect as well. When the rules were less rigorous, there may have been a tendency to accumulate loss amounts and make a one-time big-bath recognition with the impact dampened by virtue of its being labeled "extraordinary" in the year the loss first appears in the earnings statement. But when referred to for comparative purposes in subsequent years, it would be the lower "after extraordinary items" measure of income which would become the focal point—so that the interyear change would appear to be relatively more favorable. The more demanding nature of what now constitutes "extraordinary" results in the incidence of significantly fewer extraordinary items, and thus less of an incentive to effect a "big bath." The requirement that the effect of gains and losses from discontinued operations be segregated in the income statement, rather than being classified as *extraordinary*, also reduces companies' flexibility in emphasizing or deemphasizing the occurrence of losses on segment disposals.

Thus, the imposition of more definitive rules which offer less discretion to reporting entities than had been the case previously may have indirectly contributed to the containment of the big-bath phenomenon. Especially when viewed in conjunction with the general trend toward requiring more extensive disclosures, it may well be that the ease of effecting, and traditional

---

[17] *Accounting Principles Board Opinion No. 20,* paragraph nos. 18, 19, and 21.

benefits derived from, such practices may be more a historical happening than a contemporary problem.

Accounting Changes

There are four types of accounting changes:

(1) change in accounting principle,
(2) change in accounting estimate,
(3) change in accounting entity, and
(4) correction of an error in prior periods' financial statements.

A *change in an accounting principle* occurs when one method is selected to replace another one which had also conformed to generally accepted accounting principles; an example would be changing from the straight-line method of depreciation to the sum-of-the-years' digits method. A *change in an accounting estimate* is one which relates to a numerical assumption made in the process of implementing a particular accounting principle. An example would be changing from eight years to six years the estimated useful economic life of a depreciable asset.

A *change in an accounting entity* occurs when the parameters of the accounting entity differ from those which had existed previously. When a business combination is accounted for as a pooling of interests, the combined enterprise is viewed as though it had been one company retroactively, and this means that the one company is a changed entity from each of its individual predecessors. A *correction of an error* in prior periods' financial statements results from mathematical mistakes, mistakes in the application of accounting principles, or oversight or misuse of facts that existed at the time the financial statements had been prepared. An example would be the failure to record depreciation expense relating to a fleet of motor vehicles.

In describing how and why each of these types of accounting changes is measured and disclosed in financial statements, attention is directed toward Exhibit 15–4. The objective of the exhibit is to convey an understanding of the various financial reporting approaches that exist with respect to accounting changes. At the top of the diagram, a basic question is asked: Should the effect of the accounting change be recognized on a retrospective basis? An answer of "no" yields the approach reflected in Cell A, that is, such a change is accounted for only on a prospective basis. A "yes" response generates a second question: How should the prior years' results be changed? One approach, signified by Cell B, is that prior years' earnings statements are restated. The other approach is that the cumulative effect is reported in the current period's financial statements, either as a direct adjustment of the

Exhibit 15–4

Accounting Changes

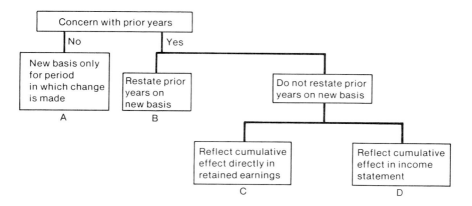

beginning-of-period retained earnings, Cell C, or in the current period's income statement proper, Cell D.

The overriding concern in the area of accounting changes is that of consistency, namely, that accounting principles and procedures be applied on a basis consistent with that of the preceding period. Therefore, not only is there an implicit presumption that the new accounting basis is preferred, but it is imperative that there be adequate disclosure as to its nature and effect as well.

A change in accounting principle is measured and disclosed in conformity with the Cell D approach. This means that if the cumulative effect of the change is reflected in the current year's earnings statement, it appears as a separate item, after extraordinary gains and losses, in both dollars and per-share amounts. This manner of accounting gives readers an opportunity to react to such a change in the same income statement context in which it had originally appeared. However, for three specific kinds of changes in accounting principle—a change from the LIFO method of inventory costing to another method, a change in the method of accounting for long-term construction-type contracts, and a change to or from the "full cost" method of accounting which is used in the extractive industries—the more extensive (Cell C) retroactive restatement is required. The reasoning behind these three exceptions relates to such changes' pervasiveness, that is, their nature is that they invariably cause a substantial amount of profit or loss to be recognized in the period of the change which, in fact, is attributable to several periods.

The concern for fostering interperiod comparability is also the basis for a requirement that even for those changes in accounting principles for which there need only be income statement disclosure of the cumulative effect, there is also supplemental disclosure of the "pro forma" effects of retroactive application. However, the Financial Accounting Standards Board pronouncements which require a company to change from an existing accounting principle to one mandated by the Board generally stipulate that the cumulative effect be treated as a direct adjustment of the period's beginning retained earnings. Some have questioned the validity of prescribing disclosure requirements for FASB-mandated changes in accounting principles that are different from those that apply to comparable changes which are initiated by the reporting entity itself.

A change in an accounting estimate is accounted for on a current and prospective basis only—Cell A in Exhibit 15–4. To appreciate the nature of this approach, consider the following example. An asset purchased in January, 19x1 for $10,000 is expected to have a ten-year depreciable life and no salvage value when it is then retired from service. It is depreciated on a straight-line basis—$1,000 per annum—but late in 19x4, a revised estimate indicates the asset's useful economic life is now expected to be only a total of eight years.

The following chart indicates two possible approaches to accounting for the change.

	Method A	Method B
19x1	$ 1,000	$ 1,000
19x2	1,000	1,000
19x3	1,000	1,000
19x4	{ 750	
	{ 1,250	1,400
19x5	1,250	1,400
19x6	1,250	1,400
19x7	1,250	1,400
19x8	1,250	1,400
	$10,000	**$10,000**

Method A assumes that once the estimated life is revised in 19x4, there should be an immediate correction of the three preceding years' earnings. Since an eight-year economic life would have required a $1,250 annual depreciation charge, underdepreciation during the first three years necessitates a ($1,250 − 1,000 = $250; $250 × 3 years =) $750 correction of the January 1, 19x4 retained earnings. As a result of this one-time correction, each of the remaining five years, 19x4 through 19x8, recognizes depreciation expense of $1,250. This method had been acceptable at one time; however, once the practice of direct corrections of retained earnings was curtailed, Method A ceased to be a valid approach.

Method B is the only acceptable approach. Since (3 years @ $1,000 =) $3,000 had already been depreciated, the remaining ($10,000 − 3,000 =) $7,000 is expensed over the remaining (8 − 3 =) 5 years; therefore, each of the subsequent five years is charged with ($7,000 ÷ 5 years =) $1,400. This approach reflects the belief that the total amount of $750 by which 19x1, 19x2, and 19x3 earnings are overstated is offset by the ($1,400 − 1,250 = $150; $150 × 5 years =) $750 understatement which will occur during the remainder of the asset's expected useful life. In effect, it says that over the full eight-year life of the asset, the proper amount of depreciation will have been recorded even though particular years' amounts are misstated.

The nature of a change in an accounting entity is such that retroactive restatement—depicted by Cell B—is required. The new relationship between what had previously been two distinct entities needs to have its financial position and operating results set forth in light of a relevant frame of reference. Envisioning the predecessor entities on a unified basis permits interperiod comparisons to be made for the combined enterprise. The specific disclosures are made in the year of the change, and in subsequent periods they need not be repeated.

The correction of an error in prior periods' financial statements is accounted for in accordance with Cell C in the diagram. Although it is important that such errors be corrected, disclosure of the correction as a determinant of the current period's income is deemed inappropriate. The correction is recorded as an adjustment of the current period's beginning retained earnings; if the prior period's income statement is presented for comparative purposes, its amounts in question would be restated. The correction of an error differs from a change in an accounting estimate in that a change in an estimate comes about as a result of access to better, i.e., improved, information subsequent to the conclusion of the period.[18]

INTERIM REPORTING

By convention, financial statements are prepared for dissemination to external parties on an annual basis. However, publicly held companies are also required to issue financial reports every three months; *interim reporting*

---

[18] Besides the correction of an error and a mandated change in accounting principle, the only other direct adjustment of beginning retained earnings is that which results from the realization of income tax benefits of a precombination operating loss carryforward of a subsidiary whose acquisition had been recorded by the purchase method of accounting (*FASB Statement No. 16*, paragraph no. 11).

is the term which encompasses the preparation and distribution of such quarterly reports. Although at a conceptual level, nothing suggests that three month intervals are any more or less meaningful than interim periods comprising two months or four months, quarterly reporting has in fact, become institutionalized; some of its accounting ramifications, therefore, warrant attention.

The value of quarterly reporting lies in its timeliness. For present and prospective stockholders and creditors to make decisions regarding their ongoing relationship with an enterprise, there is a continual need to be aware of changes in its financial position and operating results. In an era in which a myriad of exogenous factors affect companies' profitability and stability, timely insights are a particularly important aspect of the accounting and financial reporting environment. Although the fairness of quarterly reports need not be attested to by an independent auditor, limited reviews by CPAs are sometimes conducted. Large publicly held companies are required by the Securities and Exchange Commission to include in their annual reports selected data relating to each of the year's four quarters.

One of the issues in accounting for interim periods concerns the extent to which such financial reporting must conform to, and be compatible with, the existing financial reporting framework. In turn, there arises the philosophical question whether each interim period is a self-contained time interval, or whether it is merely an integral part of the longer, i.e., annual, period. Differences between the two approaches manifest in matters such as when to recognize accrued vacation pay and how to disclose adequately portions of the annual provision for income taxes.

In 1973, the Accounting Principles Board "concluded that each interim period should be viewed primarily as an integral part of an annual period."[19] Vacation pay is accrued so that each period absorbs its due share of the year's total cost. Income tax for the year is estimated in advance and an effective rate is derived for purposes of determining each quarter's proportionate share of the annual tax. Extraordinary gains and losses are disclosed in the same manner prescribed for annual reports, and the determination of materiality is affected by income for the full year and not that of only the interim period. Complete financial statements are not required. The required data include sales, income tax, extraordinary items, net earnings, earnings per share, seasonal factors, contingent items, and significant changes in financial position. Users of quarterly reports have as possible frames of reference the following data:

(1) the corresponding quarter of prior years,
(2) a prior quarter(s) of the current year,

---

[19] *Accounting Principles Board Opinion No. 28*, paragraph no. 9.

(3)   cumulative (quarterly) data for the current year and for prior years, and

(4)   the financial statements of the prior year(s).

Thus, the state of affairs in interim reporting is that although each quarter represents a fiscal period, it exists as a part of the whole, that is, it is an integral part of the total fiscal year. There is a widespread belief that interim financial information has an effect on the prices of publicly traded securities, which suggests that investors do avail themselves of such data. It is, therefore, not surprising that rule-making bodies in both the public and private sectors continue to direct much attention to the subject of interim financial reporting.

SUMMARY

In an era of accountability, consumerism, and "telling it like it is," accounting information is increasingly the focal point of persons seeking to obtain insights into the structure and practices of business enterprises. All the disclosure requirements described in this chapter have been promulgated since 1965, thus indicating the extent to which change has occurred in recent decades. *Disclosure* assumes that pertinent information worthy of communication has been duly identified, and the underlying accounting measurements are appropriate in the circumstances. Although there is a conceptual distinction between measurement and disclosure, at the practical, implementational level, they are decidedly complementary to one another.

This summary is as applicable to the entire volume as it is to its final chapter. *Accounting and financial reporting* has come a long way in the last 50 years, indeed, in the most recent two decades. Its role in the private enterprise system is an ever-expanding one, and its importance to both a corporation's managers and its stockholders is ever-increasing. *Accounting and financial reporting's* responses to the many challenges with which it is and will continue to be confronted will be monitored by more interested parties than had ever been the case previously. If this volume has, in fact, provided its readers with the insight to appreciate the nature and ramifications of such issues and developments, its objective will have been achieved.

Additional Readings

American Institute of Certified Public Accountants Committee on Social Measurement. *The Measurement of Corporate Social Performance.* New York: American Institute of Certified Public Accountants, 1977.

Beaver, William H. "Current Trends in Corporate Disclosure." *The Journal of Accountancy* (January 1978), pp. 44–52.

Bedford, Norton M. *Extensions in Accounting Disclosure*. Englewood Cliffs, N.J.: Prentice-Hall, Inc., 1973.

Briloff, Abraham J. *More Debits Than Credits*. New York: Harper & Row Pubs., Inc., 1976.

Briloff, Abraham J. *Unaccountable Accounting*. New York: Harper & Row Pubs., Inc., 1972.

Chambers, R. J. "Stock Market Prices and Accounting Research." *Abacus* (June 1974), pp. 39–54.

Cook, James S., Jr.; Davidson, Lewis F.; and Smith, Charles H. "Social Costs and Private Accounting." *Abacus* (December 1974), pp. 87–99.

Dyckman, Thomas R.; Downes, David H.; and Magee, Robert P. *Efficient Capital Markets and Accounting: A Critical Analysis*. Englewood Cliffs, N.J.: Prentice-Hall, Inc., 1975.

FASB Discussion Memorandum. *Financial Reporting for Segments of a Business Enterprise*. Stamford, Conn.: Financial Accounting Standards Board, 1974.

FASB Discussion Memorandum. *Interim Financial Accounting and Reporting*. Stamford, Conn.: Financial Accounting Standards Board, 1978.

Foster, George. *Financial Statement Analysis*. Englewood Cliffs, N.J.: Prentice-Hall, Inc., 1978.

Greer, Howard C. "The Chop Suey Caper." *The Journal of Accountancy* (April 1968), pp. 27–34.

Hawkins, David F., and Campbell, Walter J. *Equity Valuation: Models, Analysis and Implications*. New York: Financial Executives Research Foundation, 1978.

Hepworth, Samuel R. "Smoothing Periodic Income." *The Accounting Review* (January 1953), pp. 32–39.

Herwitz, David R. "The Risk of Liability for Forecasting." In *Objectives of Financial Statements—Selected Papers*, vol. 2. New York: American Institute of Certified Public Accountants, 1974, pp. 247–73.

Horngren, Charles T. "Increasing the Utility of Financial Statements." *The Journal of Accountancy* (July 1959), pp. 39–46.

Lev, Baruch. *Financial Statement Analysis: A New Approach*. Englewood Cliffs, N.J.: Prentice-Hall, Inc., 1974.

Mautz, R. K. *Effect of Circumstances on the Application of Accounting Principles*. New York: Financial Executives Research Foundation, 1972.

Peloubet, Maurice E. "Is Further Uniformity Desirable or Possible." *The Journal of Accountancy* (April 1961), pp. 35–41.

Rappaport, Donald. "Materiality." *Price Waterhouse Review* (Summer 1963), pp. 26–33.

Savage, Linda, and Siegel, Joel. "Disposal of a Segment of a Business." *The CPA Journal* (September 1978), pp. 32–37.

Schiff, Michael. *Accounting Reporting Problems—Interim Financial Statements.* New York: Financial Executives Research Foundation, 1978.

Sprouse, Robert T. "Chop Suey, Chain Stores, and Conglomerate Reporting." *The Journal of Accountancy* (April 1968), pp. 35–42.

Stern, Joel M. "Annual Reports and Stock Prices." *The Wall Street Journal* (January 29, 1979), p. 16.

CASES

Boston Harbor Scrolls

A recent discovery of documents, yet to be authenticated but tentatively known as the Boston Harbor Scrolls, indicates that the founding fathers may have addressed themselves to the matter of accounting principles. It seems that subsequent to the drafting of a certain well-known Declaration, there was a debate dealing with some of the basic concepts and conventions of accounting. Excerpts from the minutes of one such historic session are presented below.

John: "As far as inventory is concerned, I say we should allow both FIFO and LIFO."

Ben: "But by sanctioning LIFO, we would be permitting tea leaves left over from the Boston Tea Party to be carried in twentieth century balance sheets at 1773 prices!"

Tom: "Of course we would. We simply justify it on grounds of conservatism. In fact we'll justify the lower-of-cost-or-market rule on the basis of conservatism as well."

Ben: "You're a fine one to advocate conservatism; we all thought you were a real authentic liberal."

James: "Speaking of the Tea Party, should we regard the loss of tea as being an ordinary or extraordinary loss?"

John: "And whatever way you go, will it be disclosed on a net of tax basis?"

Tom: "Now that you mention such unheard of things as taxes, why not also require footnote disclosure of the social cost effect of polluting Boston Harbor?"

James: "What's this I hear about footnotes? Did we attach any footnotes to the Declaration of Independence? No siree; anything worth mentioning we include in the body of the statement."

Patrick: "Back to the central point, all this chatter about FIFO and LIFO, you know, assumes the cost basis of accounting will remain supreme. Are we truly prepared to burden future generations with such a convention?"

John: "I happen to think the historical cost basis is very important because, if for no other reason, the word 'historical' will cause accountants forever and ever to be reminded of the importance of us, their historical roots."

Ben: "Why would anyone not be content with the cost basis anyway?"

Tom: "It is possible that in future generations, the current values of assets might differ significantly from their original cost."

James: "We could always introduce depreciation procedures to take care of that. Take, for instance, Faneuil Hall, which dates back some thirty odd years to 1742. You could estimate a useful economic life of 50 or 60 years and thereby reduce its net carrying value on subsequent balance sheets."

Tom: "But suppose your estimate is wrong. Just suppose Faneuil Hall, or even the State House, which was built back in 1713, were to survive their estimated useful lives, and even be used in the very, very distant future such as the nineteenth or twentieth centuries, what happens then to your depreciation accounting?"

James: "We could call such a situation a change in accounting estimate and concern ourselves only with its prospective effect by depreciating lesser amounts once we determine its life is going to be longer than our original expectations."

Ben: "Not to mention that depreciation would apply only to resources experiencing obsolescence or physical deterioration. What about the decline in value of natural resources such as a well-known cherry tree? Are any of us prepared to play with a hot potato like depletion accounting?"

Patrick: "Forget the isolated cases of depreciable and depletable assets. What relevance does historical cost have in a period of inflation?"

John: "No Pat, I think we can assume away inflation on the basis of

390

being immaterial. This is the New World; there's no way too many dollars would ever be chasing too few goods. We've got all the natural resources we need for centuries and centuries."

Tom: "Since we're talking about rules that would be applied many years down the road, let me raise this question. I've got some plans for us to go out and annex some property which would become known as Louisiana. How would such an acquisition be accounted for? And based on your answer, recognize that it would be referred to by all future accountants as either the Louisiana Purchase or the Louisiana Pooling of Interests!"

Ben: "And would the accounting be affected by whether the acquired entity becomes a state or whether it remains a self-contained territory?"

James: "I think we should adopt a method whereby the investor's equity in changes in the investee's net worth be accounted for whether or not there is consolidation. In fact, such an approach might just be called the equity method."

Patrick: "But suppose such affiliated entities are halfway around the world where they have different currency and an unusual political environment. We would have to translate the financial data into their dollar equivalent. It would be very difficult to do this if there were to be fluctuations in currency exchange rates, not to mention major devaluations."

John: "Are these problems any different from those resulting from arm's length transactions with foreign enterprises like when an American owes or is owed money payable in foreign currency?"

Tom: "Not to change the subject gentlemen, but consider for a moment whether persons practicing as accountants should be certified."

Ben: "By whom?"

Tom: "Perhaps by the state, perhaps by a panel of peers."

John: "On what basis would such licensing be granted?"

Tom: "How about a combination of educational background, field experience, and a rigorous written examination?"

John: "If we go about this in the right way, accountants might even be considered to be members of a profession."

Tom: "Just like doctors and lawyers."

Ben: "They might even be entitled to a confidential relationship with clients which could become meaningful in a courtroom."

Tom: "Speaking of courts, wouldn't they also be susceptible to malpractice suits?"

Ben: "In theory you're absolutely right, but in practice it'll never happen. Believe me, I have prophetic vision. . . ."

Questions

1. What is the accounting justification for disclosing LIFO-based inventory costs in balance sheets at amounts reflecting price levels of many years ago?
2. What is accounting conservatism, what purpose does it serve, and what should its function be?
3. What accounting principles and conventions would influence the manner in which financial statements would disclose a loss as momentous as that of the Boston Tea Party?
4. What are social costs, how are they measured, and what disclosure rules exist with respect to corporate financial statements?
5. What are the different types of footnote disclosures that are generally presented in conjunction with corporate financial statements, and what is the relationship between each category and the financial statements proper?
6. Is the expression "historical cost basis" in fact an adequate characterization of the traditional accounting model?
7. What areas of accounting other than "depreciation" entail the use of estimates, and what should happen when it is subsequently discovered that an estimate had been wrong?

Case 1–2

Case of Cause and Effect

The September 1976 issue of *Financial Executive* contained an article bearing the title "Accounting to Whom for What," authored by Walter B. Wriston, Chairman of Citicorp.

> If the current direction in which the accounting profession is headed is followed to its logical extreme, the impact in our country over time on unemployment, on state and municipal financing, on home financing from savings-and-loan associations, on obtaining insurance coverage, and on the ability of banks and the financial intermediaries to stick with their customers during the next recession, will be far more important than any new technical triumphs or disasters we encounter along the way.

If lenders are to be required to reprice their long-term financial assets to market value each month-end with the resultant offset against earnings, they will obviously be strongly motivated to purchase only securities with very short maturities, which are relatively unaffected by changes in interest rates.

The political explosion which will occur when the 50 governors and the thousands of mayors across the country come to learn that by a stroke of the pen their long-term school bonds or general-obligation bonds have suddenly become unattractive to any institutional purchaser will be heard far and wide. The needs of states and municipalities to continue to finance themselves will not go away in the foreseeable future, and an accounting rule that would force them to issue only short-term obligations would create an unsound financial pattern, which is just the reverse of what is called for by sound practice. If an accounting change drives a business decision in the wrong economic direction, we should stop and examine it before plunging ahead to create a situation that will exacerbate the already difficult position of many states, cities and municipalities.

. . . Things that we now take for granted, like the ability to obtain adequate insurance coverage for our families and our businesses, could well be adversely impacted. Should the current accounting trends continue and be applied generally, it might well become increasingly difficult to obtain insurance coverage every time interest rates rose in response to some shift in monetary or fiscal policy. The so-called Kenny ratio, that is, the annualized premium written as a multiple of an insurance company's net worth, would gyrate wildly if statutory surplus were computed in accordance with current-value accounting. This result would occur because if current-value concepts applied to long-term bonds as well as equities, they would have to be written up and down as markets changed. In high-rate environments, as long-term bonds fell in the marketplace and the book net worth of the company shrank or even evaporated, you or I might be unable to get insurance coverage on our homes, our cars or our lives. Available insurance coverage might be frozen or even shrink because many regulators look at this ratio as one means of determining how much insurance may safely be written by a given company. An accounting rule which would have this effect is unacceptable to our society.

Testimony presented to the Securities and Exchange Commission in March 1978 on behalf of The Committee to Permit Small Producers to Compete in Energy Exploration included the following statement.

If successful-efforts accounting were required, most of these companies would report substantially lower earnings and retained earnings. Depending on their success rates and the extent of their current drilling activity in relation to their established earnings base, the majority will show earnings reductions of 25–50 percent. Those companies that are increasing their commitments to exploratory drilling most rapidly will suffer even larger declines in earnings.

The extent to which significant reductions in reported earnings will change strategies for future drilling is uncertain. Shareholders in these companies tend to be aggressive investors who are interested in growth potential. And among the smaller and middle-sized companies ownership is frequently dominated by the company founder or his heirs, who also are interested in growth. Moreover, the larger independents tend to be followed by security analysts who are knowledgeable about the industry: hence there may be greater understanding of the fact that a change in accounting standards does not influence the essential values in a company. Most of these companies rely for their outside financing on bank debt, for which commitments are generally made on the basis of reserves valuation rather than on the balance sheet and income statement. These factors may make these companies somewhat less sensitive to earnings restatement than other types of organizations.

Nevertheless, we believe reduced earnings will have a noticeable impact on drilling efforts, with the impact varying for companies of different size. Small companies that have limited access to public or institutional financing may readjust their programs only modestly even though their financial statements will probably show the greatest impact. Medium-sized companies, which attract a broader and less sophisticated investor group, will readjust to a greater extent since their investors will place greater reliance on price-earnings ratios and other common yardsticks of corporate performance. They will also exhibit a tendency toward greater management of earnings by adjusting their drilling effort as the extent of success for earlier efforts becomes known. The larger independent companies will tend to display some of the same maturity characteristics of those companies already operating on successful efforts, and some will not show a large income statement effect.

The impact of FASB-19 on the specialized independents as a group can be summarized as follows:

- Some companies will moderate their commitments to exploratory drilling, and others will find it more difficult to justify projected increases in drilling activity.
- New entrants to exploratory drilling will be discouraged.
- Drilling emphasis will shift to safer prospects, and to development drilling.

We estimate that the specialized independents will reduce their commitments to exploratory drilling by perhaps 10–20 percent below the level which would occur if full-cost accounting were utilized. This estimate derives both from direct comments made to us in the course of our interviews, as well as by an indication of the extent to which such a reduction would influence reported earnings. As an example, if a typical specialized independent drilling company with an exploration budget of $20 million now reports earnings of $15 million per year on a full-cost basis, we estimate that their reported earnings on a successful-efforts basis would be about 40 percent lower, i.e., $9 million. If the level of exploration activity is reduced to $17 million, the corresponding reduction in reported earnings would be about one-third; this level may be more tolerable to some risk-oriented managements, although others will regard it as much too high.

In an August, 1978 address, Oscar S. Gellein, then a member of the Financial Accounting Standards Board, offered the following thought.

> On a previous occasion I observed that financial reporting is more like a barometer than a rainmaker. The barometer produces a reading for someone else to use in assessing the prospects of storm or clemency. The barometer has an impact if it causes someone to buy an umbrella, or not to buy an umbrella, or if someone invokes the power on high to prevent a storm, or sends a rainmaker up to seed the clouds. The barometer is useful to those with adverse interests if it describes what it purports to show and measures that accurately—that is, if it is neutral. But suppose those who designed the barometer decided that the public interest would be served better if forebodings of storm were minimized and, accordingly, a bias toward clemency was built into the calibrations of the barometer. Surely, it is reasoned, an improved expectation of sunshine would be for the public good. The difficulty is that some would get wet because they did not have umbrellas, others would beseech for rain not knowing that it was on its way, clouds would be seeded needlessly, and worst of all, some persons would not duck into storm cellars or batten down the hatches soon enough to protect against imminent storm. And so it is with financial reporting.

Questions

1. To what do you attribute the increasing importance of socio-economic aspects of accounting rules?
2. What have traditionally been the predominant considerations used by rule-making bodies in accounting, and what do you think the relevant factors should be?
3. With respect to the general matter of promulgating accounting standards, what should be the role of persons who do not have a formal accounting background?
4. If the socio-economic implications of accounting were to play an increasingly important role in the standard-setting process, what improvements or deficiencies could be expected to occur?
5. If the socio-economic ramifications of accounting rules were to become a primary consideration on the part of standard setting bodies such as the FASB, and all existing accounting doctrines and practices would as a result be subject to reexamination, which conventions and rules would you expect to see placed on the active agenda of the FASB?

Sun Oil Company

The Sun Oil Company was ranked in the "Fortune 500" for 1968 as 42nd in revenues, 28th in assets and 21st in reported profit.

Included in the July, 1969 issue of Sun's monthly newsletter to its Sunoco credit card holders were the following two paragraphs:

> Sun Oil Company's tax bill last year amounted to 8.9 per cent of gross revenues. The direct tax burden on Sun was $160.6 million, almost equaling the Company's net income of $164.4 million.
>
> Also last year, Sun collected from customers an additional $384.9 million in taxes on the products it sold, and it paid over to governments another $48.6 million in taxes withheld from its employees' wages. The scorecard on who got what from Sun's operations:

Taxes turned over to governments	$594.2 million
Wages, salaries, and benefits to employees	315.0 million
Cash & stock dividends to stockholders	163.3 million

Sun's 1968 consolidated statement of income and earnings employed in the business, as it was presented in the company's Form 10-K submitted to the Securities and Exchange Commission in 1969, appears below. Although the statement contained a number of references to footnotes, only Note 6 is reproduced herein.

Consolidated Statement of Income and Earnings Employed in the Business For the Year Ended December 31, 1968
(in thousands of dollars)

Revenues:	
Sales and other operating income	$1,778,183
Other income:	
Gain on sale of fixed assets	3,045
Dividends	2,549
Interest	14,842
Miscellaneous, net	2,592
	1,801,211

Costs and expenses:	
Costs and operating expenses	1,091,664
Selling, general and administrative expenses	209,967
Taxes, other than income taxes	91,587
Intangible development costs	54,898
Depreciation, cost depletion and retirements	110,554
Interest and debt expense	16,170
Minority interest	(1,419)
	1,573,421
Income before provision for income taxes and extraordinary items	227,790
Provision for income taxes:	
Federal	44,290
Foreign and other	19,070
	63,360
Income before extraordinary items	164,430
Extraordinary items:	
Gain on sale of Avisun Corporation, net of taxes of $5,700,000	22,432
Preoperating expenses for Great Canadian Oil Sands, Limited and reserve for losses in foreign operations	(22,432)
Net income	164,430
Earnings employed in the business at January 1, as previously reported	
Sun Oil Company	141,977
Sunray DX Oil Company	410,177
Adjustment to conform accounting policies	(142,050)
Earnings employed in the business at January 1, as restated	410,104
Cash dividends:	
Sun Oil Company—preferred stock, $.513 per share	9,490
Sun Oil Company—common stock, $.94 per share	25,208
Sunray DX Oil Company—common stock before merger, $1.125 per share	20,778
Stock dividends:	
Sun Oil Company common stock—6%	107,792
	163,268
Earnings employed in the business at December 31	**$ 411,266**

Consolidated net income per common share outstanding at December 31, 1968, after assuming a full year's dividend requirements on preferred stock $4.59

Consolidated net income per common share outstanding at December 31, 1968, and assuming full conversion of preferred stock $4.16

Note 6—*Taxes:*

Taxes, other than income taxes, charged to income in 1968 are as follows (in thousands of dollars):

Capital stock and franchise	$ 2,002
Social security	9,666
Crude oil and natural gas production	48,572
Ad valorem	24,730
Import duties, transportation, excise and miscellaneous	3,384
Gasoline, lubricating oil, use and sales	3,233
	$91,587

In addition to the taxes shown above, direct sales and excise taxes, including State and Provincial gasoline and lubricating oil taxes were paid or accrued in the amount of $384,944,000 which were collected and were not included in the statement of income.

Investment tax credits of $11,182,000 have been applied as a reduction of Federal income tax expense in 1968.

The provision for income taxes includes deferred amounts of $33,262,000 the most significant portions of which result from additional deductions for past service pension costs and accelerated depreciation allowable currently for tax purposes.

Questions

1. What are the factors that motivate a company to share financial data with its customers?
2. Are the assertions made by Sun in the letter to its customers valid, and consistent with what appears in its financial statements?
3. Are the amounts cited in Sun's letter to customers determinants or distributions of income?
4. What was Sun's effective Federal income tax rate during 1968?
5. What accounting measurement and financial disclosure differences would you expect to see between Sun's 1968 presentation and that of the current year?

Case 2–1
Cohen Commission

The Commission on Auditors' Responsibilities was an independent study group the American Institute of Certified Public Accountants (AICPA) established in 1974 to examine the problems and controversies confronting CPAs in their role as independent auditors. The chairman of the study group was the late Manuel F. Cohen, and the group was in turn referred to as the Cohen Commission. The Commission's report was published in 1978, and an excerpt from that document appears below.

A major part of the auditor's present role is to evaluate whether the information presented by the company adequately portrays its financial position and earnings and the related uncertainties surrounding their measurement. That responsibility should be retained. The auditor should not attempt to reduce uncertainty by predicting the outcome of future events. However, under current requirements, some prediction is inevitably involved in deciding whether to express a "subject to" qualification. The auditor should be expected to evaluate the information presented and decide whether financial statement users are given enough information to make their own evaluation of the outcome of uncertainties. The present audit reporting requirements for uncertainties are inconsistent with the auditor's accepted role in expressing an opinion; they may confuse users; and they may create false expectations. Also, a "subject to" qualification provides little or no protection for an independent auditor.

The need to consider whether to qualify may cause the auditor to devote too little attention to evaluating the adequacy of disclosure of uncertainties. Users of financial statements need enough information to make their own evaluation of uncertainties, and they are not served by a reporting requirement that diverts the auditor's attention from evaluating the disclosure of uncertainties to highlighting the existence of some uncertainties.

For the foregoing reasons, the audit requirement to express a "subject to" qualification when financial statements are affected by material uncertainties should be eliminated. The auditor would still be required to express a qualified or adverse opinion because of a departure from generally accepted accounting principles when he does not agree with management's evaluation of the uncertainty, or when the information disclosed does not adequately reflect the considerations bearing on the potential outcome and management does not make the required adjustments or disclosures. In combination with improvements in financial accounting standards for the disclosure of uncertainties, eliminating the requirement should improve understanding of both the effect of uncertainties on financial statements and the auditor's responsibility when uncertainties exist.

One of the most significant uncertainties that can cause a "subject to" qualification under present reporting requirements is doubt about a company's ability to continue operations. When this occurs, the recoverability and classification of most asset amounts and the amounts and classification of many liabilities are called into question. In these circumstances, financial statements based on the assumption of liquidation may more adequately portray the company's financial position.

The conditions that cause doubt about a company's ability to continue operations usually include some combination of recurring operating losses, serious deficiencies in working capital, inability to comply with the terms of loan agreements, or difficulty in obtaining sufficient financing. A single lawsuit may be sufficient to cause a going-concern uncertainty if an unfavorable outcome would jeopardize continued operations.

A distinguishing feature of a going-concern uncertainty is the extreme consequence of unfavorable resolution. The implications of eliminating the audit requirements to express a "subject to" qualification when significant uncertainties exist are highlighted by consideration of going-concern uncertainties.

There is no reason to believe independent auditors are more able to predict whether a company will liquidate than they are able to predict the outcome of other uncertainties. In fact, research has shown that an analysis of financial statements, using certain simple financial ratios, is a better indicator of a company's future prospects than noting whether the auditor had expressed a qualified opinion or an unqualified opinion.

A qualified opinion expressing doubts concerning a company's ability to continue as a going concern is not intended to be a prediction of liquidation, but many financial statement users apparently view it as such. Creditors often regard a "subject to" qualification as a separate reason for not granting a loan, a reason in addition to the circumstances creating the uncertainty that caused the qualification. This frequently puts the auditor in the position of, in effect, deciding whether a company is able to obtain the funds it needs to continue operating. Thus, the auditor's qualification tends to be a self-fulfilling prophecy: The auditor's expression of uncertainty about the company's ability to continue may make the company's inability a certainty.

An unqualified opinion is not a guarantee that a company will continue operations, but the general practice of giving "subject to" qualifications for going-concern uncertainties may create that impression. If uncertainty about a company's ability to continue operations is adequately disclosed in its financial statements, the auditor should not be required to call attention to that uncertainty in his report.[1]

The Auditing Standards Executive Committee of the AICPA in turn issued an exposure draft of a proposed Statement on Auditing Standards (SAS). A perti-

---

[1] *The Commission on Auditors' Responsibilities: Report, Conclusions and Recommendations* (New York: American Institute of Certified Public Accountants, 1978), pp. 28–30. Copyright © 1978 by the American Institute of Certified Public Accountants, Inc.

nent paragraph appearing in the cover letter attached to the exposure draft appears below:

> The proposed Statement provides that the auditor would not modify his opinion because of a contingency if he concludes that the accounting and financial reporting for that contingency is in conformity with generally accepted accounting principles; however, he would not be precluded from declining to express an opinion on financial statements because of the possible effect of a contingency on the going concern assumption. If the auditor concludes that an accrual for or disclosure of a contingency is not in conformity with generally accepted accounting principles, he would express a qualified opinion or an adverse opinion because of the departure from generally accepted accounting principles.[2]

The views of two different interested parties to the AICPA's proposal aptly portray an alternative point of view. First, there appears below four paragraphs excerpted from the submission of one respondent.

> We are opposed to elimination of the "subject to" opinion when there is a question of whether the going concern assumption is appropriate. We are not convinced by the Cohen Commission's argument that the independent auditor's issuance of a qualified opinion in this situation is a "prediction of liquidation." Some companies which receive such an opinion do fail, but not as a result of the independent auditor's going concern qualification—and many survive. A "subject to" opinion in this situation is not a prediction of the future failure of the company, but rather a recognition that the company's survival is dependent upon certain factors which cannot be measured at the report date (e.g., a major reorganization or cash infusion).
>
> The key question in such cases should not be whether there are adequate disclosures related to the company's ability to continue as a going concern. The important issue is whether the financial statements should be prepared in conformity with generally accepted accounting principles which contemplate the continuation of the company as a going concern or whether liquidation accounting principles are called for. As noted by the Cohen Commission, "There is no reason to believe independent auditors are . . . able to predict whether a company will liquidate . . ." Accordingly, we believe it is important for the auditor to communicate this significant uncertainty about the basis of accounting used. At present this can be done best by means of a "subject to" qualification.
>
> The Exposure Draft would require the independent auditor to choose between an unqualified opinion (which could create an impression that a company is trouble-free when major uncertainties exist about its continuation) or a

[2] *Proposed Statement on Auditing Standards: Auditor's Report When There Are Contingencies*—Exposure Draft, October 31, 1977 (New York: American Institute of Certified Public Accountants, 1977).

disclaimer of opinion in those situations where there is a question whether the company is a going concern. In our view, this judgment would place the independent auditor squarely in the position of a "predictor of continuation or liquidation."

We disagree with the Cohen Commission's conclusion that "the need to consider whether to qualify may cause the auditor to devote too little attention to evaluating the adequacy of disclosure of uncertainties." Our experience has been that consideration of a "subject to" qualification focuses more attention on the disclosure by management, outside counsel and independent accountants. Thus, we are concerned that elimination of the "subject to" opinion may result in less care being exercised in the evaluation of contingencies by these parties.

A summary of the position taken by another interested party is presented below:

> We strongly disagree with the conclusions expressed in the AICPA exposure draft. In our view, the adoption of the proposed SAS would eliminate an important service provided by auditors—alerting readers of financial statements to significant uncertainties facing a company. It would also force auditors to express an unqualified opinion on financial statements even though the auditors might have serious reservations regarding whether the financial statements under examination, even with footnote disclosures, adequately portray the financial position and results of operations of the company.
>
> The AICPA press release announcing the issuance of the exposure draft emphasized the position taken in the proposed SAS that, if footnote disclosure of an uncertainty is adequate, there is no conceptual reason for the auditor to issue a "subject to" opinion. But what about the reader of the financial statements who traditionally looks to the auditors' report to alert him to significant uncertainties facing the company? What must he do in the future? In its November 4, 1977 report on the issuance of the exposure draft, *The Wall Street Journal* stated in the opening paragraph that "the professional association of auditors proposed elimination of a familiar 'red flag' investors look for in corporate financial reports." We agree. It would be a serious disservice to the investment community as well as to independent auditors to eliminate this warning signal from auditors' reports.
>
> In the same press release referred to above, an AICPA spokesman stated that the proposed SAS is a "direct response" to a recommendation contained in the Report of Tentative Conclusions of the AICPA-sponsored Commission on Auditors' Responsibilities (Cohen Commission) issued earlier this year. The Cohen Commission based this recommendation on its belief that the current form of "subject to" opinion requires an auditor to be an originator or interpreter as well as a reporter of financial information that goes beyond what that Commission envisions the auditor's basic role to be.
>
> We fully agree with the Cohen Commission's conclusion that an auditor should not be an originator or interpreter of financial information. These are

properly the roles of management. In our view, however, the issuance of a "subject to" opinion does not require the auditor to be either. If the disclosure of uncertainties in the financial statements is inadequate, the auditor should be expected to take exception in his or her report to the adequacy of such disclosure. Furthermore, the auditor cannot and should not be expected to predict the ultimate resolution of such uncertainties. The "subject to" qualification is not a prediction of the future outcome but merely a recognition that the uncertainty is so significant that its potential effect on financial position and results of operations could be material and cannot be measured at the current time.

Questions

1. Does citation of uncertainties in the auditor's report cast the CPA in either an advocate or a forecaster role, or both? Is this "good" or "bad"?
2. What are the kinds of circumstances that would raise "going concern" questions?
3. What are the prospective financial implications for a company which receives a "subject to" opinion from its independent auditor?
4. What circumstances would you expect an auditor to encounter to necessitate disclaiming an audit opinion altogether?
5. Should a company receive an unqualified opinion from its auditors if its financial statements fairly reflect the poor state of the company's health?
6. Should uncertainties alone mean that a company's financial statements will receive a qualified audit opinion?
7. What is the auditor's responsibility when a client refuses to disclose in footnotes to the financial statements the presence of uncertainties?
8. If CPAs were precluded from rendering "subject to" audit opinions, what effect, if any, might this have on the financial reporting environment?

Case 2–2
Ingleside, Inc.

Ingleside, Inc. was a diversified manufacturing company that had been founded in 1942 by Ben Light. By 1979, the company was operating four plants in addition to its base of operations in Baltimore, Maryland, with two of the locations being outside of the United States. In 1979, Mr. Light was serving as chairman of the board and as Ingleside's chief operating officer.

A CPA firm was engaged each year to conduct an audit, and each year's examination had resulted in an unqualified opinion. It was a record of which the board of directors was proud, and the board was equally pleased with the company's impressive earnings trend. Ingleside's fiscal year ended each December 31.

On March 2, 1980, the independent CPA, Fred Ronald, sent a letter to Ben Light to indicate that complications had arisen in the course of the 1979 audit. The problems were categorized as relating to "subsequent events," and their specific nature was set forth in the letter. On March 4, Mr. Light received from Ingleside's controller a memorandum which (1) identified the accounting rules relating to subsequent events, and (2) summarized the particular circumstances that existed with respect to Ingleside's financial statements for 1979. The text of the controller's memo follows:

That a corporation's fiscal year ends on a particular day is the result of discretion of its board of directors. Although companies' fiscal years may correspond to some logical juncture in its seasonal pattern, the year-end date does nevertheless become institutionalized as far as the company's accounting and financial reporting cycle is concerned.

An important aspect of such a cycle is the notion of cutoff procedures. This entails being sure that transactions that occur just before and just after year-end be recorded in the proper year, that is, the old year or the new year. As a result, an integral part of an independent auditor's responsibility is to determine that end-of-year transactions have in fact been recorded in the appropriate period.

However, there exists also the problem of disclosing the effects of subsequent events. The following five paragraphs are taken from the pertinent pronouncement of the American Institute of CPAs.[1]

An independent auditor's report ordinarily is issued in connection with historical financial statements that purport to present financial position at a stated date and results of operations and changes in financial position for a period ended on that date. However, events or transactions sometimes occur subsequent to the balance-sheet date, but prior to the issuance of the financial statements and auditor's report, that have a material effect on the financial statements and therefore require adjustment or disclosure in the statements. These occurrences hereinafter are referred to as 'subsequent events.'

Two types of subsequent events require consideration by management and evaluation by the independent auditor.

---

[1] Statement on Auditing Standards No. 1, *Codification of Auditing Standards and Procedures* (New York: American Institute of Certified Public Accountants, 1973). Copyright © 1973 by the American Institute of Certified Public Accountants, Inc.

The first type consists of those events that provide additional evidence with respect to conditions that existed at the date of the balance sheet and affect the estimates inherent in the process of preparing financial statements. All information that becomes available prior to the issuance of the financial statements should be used by management in its evaluation of the conditions on which the estimates were based. The financial statements should be adjusted for any changes in estimates resulting from the use of such evidence.

The second type consists of those events that provide evidence with respect to conditions that did not exist at the date of the balance sheet being reported on but arose subsequent to that date. These events should not result in adjustment of the financial statements. Some of these events, however, may be of such a nature that disclosure of them is required to keep the financial statements from being misleading. Occasionally such an event may be so significant that disclosure can best be made by supplementing the historical financial statements with pro forma financial data giving effect to the event as if it had occurred on the date of the balance sheet only, in columnar form on the face of the historical statements.

Subsequent events affecting the realization of assets such as receivables and inventories or the settlement of estimated liabilities ordinarily will require adjustment of the financial statements because such events typically represent the culmination of conditions that existed over a relatively long period of time.

Summarized below are the six sets of circumstances that have been identified as possibly having an effect on the company's 1979 financial statements.

1. In applying lower-of-cost-or-market procedures to its year-end portfolio of marketable equity securities, depressed market prices resulted in the recognition of a loss in the company's income statement. A February 28 review of the portfolio indicates that a further reduction in value has occurred.
2. With respect to litigation in which it is the defendant, on February 24 the company reached an agreement with the plaintiff to settle for an amount different from that which had previously been recorded in its accounts.
3. On February 11 the company was informed by two of its customers that because of bankruptcy in one case and a fire two days earlier in the other instance, the company will probably never to able to collect two material "trade accounts receivable" amounts it is owed.
4. On January 4 the company successfully issued 100,000 previously unissued shares of common stock. 40,000 of the shares were sold in the primary securities market, and the remaining shares constituted the consideration with which the company thereby effected a business combination to be accounted for as a purchase.
5. In 1975 Ingleside, Inc. and the Gila County Department of Economic Development entered into an agreement which called for Ingleside to expend funds to construct a new plant. Gila County would then buy the

completed plant from the company and grant it exclusive use of the facility. On January 26, 1980, Gila County remitted the agreed-upon sum, using the proceeds of an industrial development bond.

6. On February 4 the government of one of the two foreign countries in which Ingleside operates a fully consolidated subsidiary devalued its currency in response to the protracted deterioration in value that had been experienced relative to other currencies. Ingleside's auditor determined that the effect of this action would be to increase the amount of the company's foreign currency exchange loss that had been calculated as of December 31, 1979.

Questions

1. For each of the six independent sets of circumstances, what type of disclosure, if any, is called for? You are to assume that the amounts are material in each case, and that the auditor's report is to be issued on March 12 for the fiscal year ending December 31, 1979.
2. What disclosure obligations exist for Ingleside, Inc. or for Mr. Ronald, with respect to the subsequent discovery of facts existing at the date of the auditor's report, that is, discoveries that might occur subsequent to March 12?

Case 2–3
Universal General, Inc.

Universal General, Inc. was a highly diversified company having interests in the natural resources, transportation, high-technology electronics, textiles, pharmaceuticals, and entertainment industries. The breadth of its business interests was so vast that one student of the conglomerate phenomenon of the 1960's referred to Universal General as a "mutual fund with smokestacks." The company's consolidated revenues had exceeded $2 billion every year since 1969, annual earnings ranked consistently among those of the top 200 American companies, and in 1978, its investment in operating assets exceeded $1 billion.

It had been a long-time practice of the Federal Trade Commission (FTC) to collect consolidated income data from companies with assets over $10 million as well as from a sampling of smaller companies. The resulting statistics were used to compile the Commission's quarterly financial report for manufacturing companies, segregated into 31 industries.

A problem which came to the fore in 1972 centered around large, highly diversified corporations whose reported income was usually an aggregate of several different industries. The information in the FTC's quarterly financial report was said to have become meaningless as the nature of conglomerate companies' financial statements resulted in an "information loss."

The FTC investigated the problem by surveying nine leading conglomerates whose assets had grown from $2 billion to near $17 billion between 1960 and 1969. The nine companies had acquired 348 other companies, most of which were in unrelated industries. In October 1973, the Commission proposed that companies should report their profit and sales on a line-of-business basis. A proposal of that magnitude had to be approved by the Office of Management and Budget; as a result, it forced the FTC to be more specific in its proposed requirements.

FTC officials decided to require reporting companies to break down their data within more than 400 product lines. The Commission claimed this would only require corporations to submit information which they already had. However, the new proposal was not easily accepted by the business community. Business representatives claimed the reporting requirements would be overly expensive and could damage the basic competitive system. The FTC promised to release the data only in aggregated form, thus protecting the identity of the corporations. The business representatives, in turn, were skeptical since they did not believe the FTC could prevent an information leak.

In March 1974, the FTC formally adopted the requirement, and asked the nation's 500 largest manufacturing companies to submit data by individual product line. Since the FTC sought information on research and advertising expenditures as well, it was decided to phase the program in over a two year period.

Congress had authorized the FTC to acquire information from 500 companies, but it recommended the requirement be limited to 345 companies during the initial year. The FTC began seeking information broken down into some 219 manufacturing segments of the economy. However, the FTC met stiff opposition from the business community and found the proposal back in the hands of Congress. The proposal was further modified to encompass only 250 companies, and this was passed by the House of Representatives. The Senate believed this would exclude too many large corporations, and it voted to allow 500 companies to be queried; this was eventually also passed by the House and sent to the White House for Presidential approval.

The funding for the FTC proposal was but a small part of a major agricultural appropriations bill. On August 8, 1974, President Nixon vetoed the bill in order to control inflation, and the FTC did not have formal approval of its funding. Despite the veto, the agency began implementing the plan by using funds available to it with the expectation of a definitive appropriation in the near future. This was not an unfounded hope since President Nixon had not cited the FTC proposal in his veto message, having focused instead on the other aspects of the bill being inflationary.

When the proposal was implemented, Universal General and several other companies filed a class-action petition to prevent the FTC from acquiring information pertaining to the profitability of their lines of business. The corporations contended that the line-of-business inquiry went beyond the Commission's authority to obtain information of American businesses. As a minimum, the plaintiffs sought to have the FTC delay action for at least four months, to enable them to analyze the new data-request form. During the four months, they would begin to accumulate the necessary information and to develop data on costs and time needed to comply with the FTC demands.

In January 1975, a suit was filed in a Federal district court on behalf of 12 affected companies charging that disclosure of the information would cause irreparable injury as well as violate their Fourth Amendment right to due process. The suit asked for an injunction against the FTC to prohibit implementation of its proposal, and this request was denied. The FTC, in the judge's opinion, was seeking to identify noncompetitive markets for law-enforcement purpose, i.e., possible antitrust violations which could only be identified by line-of-business reports.

As of January 1975, only 197 of the 345 companies receiving FTC requests for line-of-business data had furnished the required information; 129 companies including Universal General had refused and the rest were granted extensions. A Federal judge issued an order requiring the 129 non-responding companies to show cause for their neglect to comply. However, the very next day another Federal judge ruled the FTC had improperly adopted its line-of-business program, and he temporarily blocked the FTC from seeking such reports from seven companies.

A July 1977 ruling by a Federal judge upheld the FTC's right to obtain the information, and the corporations appealed the ruling. Prior to receiving the decision of the appeals court, concern arose regarding the administration of the program. Transfering its administration to the Department of Commerce's Census Bureau was proposed since it was the opinion of some businessmen that that agency would be better able to keep the information confidential.

In July 1978, the appeals bench upheld the lower court's ruling backing the FTC. Several major corporations then appealed to the Supreme Court. In November 1978, the Supreme Court upheld the lower court ruling, and thus paved the way for the FTC to carry out the program. Although the case then appeared to be closed as far as the courts were concerned, some businessmen indicated that they would still prefer to transfer the authority to the Census Bureau; presumably because it had a better relationship with business than did the FTC. The courts and the FTC apparently questioned whether the Census Bureau could gather the necessary information and analyze it for possible antitrust violations.

Questions

1. What conflicts exist between the need of individual companies to disseminate their financial statements (microeconomic data) and society's need to have economy-wide financial reports (macroeconomic data) in terms of what the private costs and benefits are versus the societal or social costs and benefits?
2. What economic consequences can be expected to result from the FTC's line-of-business disclosure rules, and how could these be demonstrated—identified and measured—by the FTC and by the companies required to participate?
3. What reporting conflicts can result from different disclosure standards being required by different governmental agencies? Cite examples—actual and potential.
4. What constraints exist or should exist with respect to permitting a governmental agency to exercise its administrative prerogative to obtain data from private enterprises?
5. What predictive ability can be associated with the financial data of entities whose parameters are broader than or narrower than those of legally constituted corporations?
6. What are the implications of the line-of-business case for the promulgation of accounting standards by an autonomous rule-making body in the private sector, or those set forth by an agency of the Federal government?

Case 3–1
Tommy Toys, Inc.

Tommy Toys, Inc. was a privately held manufacturing company whose sales volume had grown 10 percent to 15 percent during each of the past five years; revenues currently amounted to nearly $200,000,000 annually. Tommy's top management has been concerned exclusively with producing merchandise en masse and selling the goods as rapidly as possible. As a result, virtually no attention had been given to establishing any degree of sophistication in its internal control system.

The company's officers realized that one of the ramifications of its attitude and the resulting state of affairs was the effect on the company's auditability. In particular, the CPA firm that was engaged to render an audit opinion as of each year-end had to conduct an examination far more extensive than would have been the case had the company's internal control system been better conceived, or for that matter, even if there had been a greater degree of adherence to that semblance of a system which already existed. As a consequence, the dollar cost of Tommy's annual audit was considerably larger than that which would have been incurred if its systems and procedures had been in better condition.

The company's officers were resigned to having an annual audit performed by an independent CPA, and indeed they had a great deal of confidence in the technical competence of the CPA firm that had been engaged since the company's inception. Yet, they were extremely skeptical about investing significant sums of money to create and in turn to implement formal, well-defined accounting and administrative controls. Such a system appeared to them to be a distraction, one which had the potential of slowly but surely becoming an end, rather than being a means to an end.

The company's relative newness together with its rapid expansion had caused enormous amounts of money to be invested in plant and machinery. The substantial amounts of depreciation charges which appeared on Tommy's income statement together with material sums expended for advertising and product development resulted in annual reported earnings being less than that which a casual observer might expect.

The company's president and vice-president of finance had discussions on several occasions with the CPA firm's personnel regarding the measurement of annual income. When discussing the matter of selecting accounting methods, the CPAs were always careful to point out the conceptual pros and cons of the various acceptable approaches. Interestingly, of all the determinants of the company's earnings that were addressed, the one cost conspicuous by its absence had been that of the annual audit fee. The dollar amount of the audit fee happened to be material relative to Tommy's reported income which was an expected occurrence in light of the circumstances referred to earlier.

For the company's fiscal year ending on December 31, 1979, the CPA firm's personnel concluded their examination on February 18, 1980. The CPA firm's audit opinion was dated February 24, 1980, and information about completion of the audit work, billing by the CPA firm and remittances by Tommy Toys, Inc. follows.

410

Audit Work

June 5–22, 1979	25%
November 14–30, 1979	45
January 21–28, 1980	10
February 7–18, 1980	20
	100%

Billing

March 20, 1979	25%
June 20, 1979	25
September 20, 1979	25
December 20, 1979	25
	100%

Payments

April 30, 1979	20%
July 15, 1979	20
October 19, 1979	20
January 31, 1980	20
March 6, 1980	20
	100%

Questions

1. What are the reasons a privately held company would be interested in having a full-fledged audit performed by an independent CPA?
2. Does a company's failure to have an effective internal control system preclude its receiving an unqualified audit opinion?
3. If Tommy Toys, Inc. were to commission its CPA firm to design an internal control system for its exclusive use, would such an engagement jeopardize the firm's "independent auditor" status vis-a-vis Tommy?
4. How should a company account for the cost it incurs to design, introduce, and refine its new, comprehensive internal control system?
5. In what period(s) should Tommy Toys recognize the expense of the 1979 audit fee?
6. In what period(s) should Tommy's CPA firm recognize the revenue from the 1979 audit fee?
7. What criteria would you expect a company such as Tommy Toys to use in selecting from among acceptable alternative accounting principles?

411

Once upon a time there was a small group of financiers. These financiers formed two investment trusts. One investment trust was called the American Trust and the other was called the National Trust. Each trust started business with a paid-in capital of one million dollars comprising its sole assets and net worth. Each trust had numerous small stockholders, but the management of each was controlled by the small group of financiers. Each trust proposed to operate by investing its capital in small amounts among a large number of listed securities, buying such securities when they were considered cheap and selling them when their market price had appreciated so much that they were no longer considered attractive. Dividends were to be immediately reinvested.

Very soon after the formation of the two investment trusts, a crash in the stock market gave each of them an opportunity to invest all of its capital in sound securities at low prices. This each did and the American Trust invested its capital in exactly the same securities at exactly the same prices as did the National Trust. The stock market then started up and continued to go up for the next four years.

Now the financiers who controlled each of these trusts not only understood the investment trust business but also understood accounting principles. They were keenly aware of the opportunities presented to financiers by modern accounting procedure and they decided to enrich themselves at the expense of the public by taking full advantage of these opportunities. They therefore laid their plans with this in view.

By December 31 of the first year of operation both the American Trust and the National Trust had fared exactly alike because their investments were the same. Dividends had not amounted to much because the securities purchased had very small yields, but the appreciation in the market value of these securities had amounted to an average of 20 percent of their cost. Accordingly on December 31 the American Trust was ordered to sell all of its securities in order to "realize" its profit and was ordered to reinvest the proceeds in other securities. The investment manager of the American Trust pleaded in vain that other securities could not be more desirable than those already owned, but the financiers were firm. The investment manager therefore had no choice except to obey orders, and the securities on hand were sold and other securities were purchased.

* From Kenneth MacNeal, *Truth in Accounting* (Houston: Scholars Book Co., 1970— originally published in 1939), pp. 9–15. Reprinted with permission.

On January 1, the small group of financiers requested a well-known firm of certified public accountants to prepare a balance sheet and income statement for the past year for each of the two trusts controlled by it. This firm of certified public accountants was respected by everybody for its incorruptible integrity, and for the ability of its staff. Financial statements certified by it were accepted without question by bankers and individuals all over the world. This firm of certified public accountants made an audit of both trusts, and a certified balance sheet and a certified profit and loss statement for each trust were prepared by it and delivered to the financiers.

The profit and loss statement of the American Trust disclosed that it had earned $30,000 from dividends and had earned $200,000 from realized profits on the securities it had sold. This amounted to $230,000 or 23 percent of its capital stock. Its balance sheet disclosed that it had securities to a value of $1,230,000 and no liabilities. These securities were described as valued at "cost or market whichever is the lower."

The profit and loss statement of the National Trust disclosed that it had earned $30,000 from dividends and that it had no other earnings whatever. Its earnings as certified therefore amounted only to 3 percent on its capital stock. Its balance sheet disclosed that it had securities to a value of $1,030,000 and no liabilities. These securities were described as being valued at "cost or market whichever is the lower." It is true that there was a footnote on the balance sheet stating that the present market value of these securities was $1,230,000, but most of the public did not pay much attention to this and looked chiefly at the total of the assets which was distinctly shown as $1,030,000, and at the surplus which was distinctly shown as $30,000. The few people who did see and understand the footnote disregarded it because, they said, the appreciation of $200,000 was only a paper profit and could not be considered until it had been realized by being converted into cash, because a decline in the security market might wipe it all out in no time. Also, earnings were clearly shown in the profit and loss statement as only $30,000 without any qualification whatever.

Now, of course, as soon as the certified financial statements of the American Trust and of the National Trust were mailed to stockholders and printed in the newspapers, everybody learned that the American Trust had earned 23 percent on its capital stock during the year whereas the National Trust had earned only 3 percent on its capital stock. The price of the American Trust stock therefore rose sharply as many investors rushed to buy it, and the price of the National Trust stock dropped sharply due to selling by disappointed stockholders.

But the small group of financiers knew that, although the American Trust had earned 23 percent on its capital stock, the National Trust had also really earned 23 percent on its capital stock. It was intelligent enough to see that a

413

decline in the security market which would wipe out the 20 percent un-realized profit of the National Trust would also wipe out the 20 percent realized profit of the American Trust and that therefore the unrealized profit was just as safe as the realized profit. So the small group of financiers sold a large part of its holdings of American Trust stock at high prices and bought additional stock of the National Trust at very low prices.

By December 31 of the next year both trusts had earned an additional $30,000 from dividends and each had a further unrealized profit of $200,000 in its securities. So this time the National Trust was ordered to sell all of its securities and to invest the proceeds in the same securities that the American Trust owned. This was done and the profit of $200,000 for the current year plus the profit of $200,000 for the previous year was duly realized. The assets of the National Trust were now identical with those of the American Trust. The market value of each was $1,460,000. The two trusts were exactly alike and each owned exactly the same quantities of the same securities with a total market value of $1,460,000.

On January 1 the same widely known and trusted firm of certified public accountants was requested to prepare balance sheets and profit and loss statements for the past year for each of the two trusts. When this had been done the profit and loss statement of the American Trust disclosed that it had earned $30,000 from dividends and had no other earnings whatsoever. Its earnings as certified therefore amounted only to 3 percent on its capital stock. Its balance sheet disclosed that it had securities to a value of $1,260,000 and no liabilities. These securities were described as being valued at "cost or market whichever is the lower."

The profit and loss statement of the National Trust, however, disclosed that it had earned $30,000 from dividends and had earned $400,000 from realized profits on the securities it had sold. This amounted to $430,000 or 43 percent on its capital stock. Its balance sheet disclosed that it had securities to a value of $1,460,000 and no liabilities. These securities were described as being valued at "cost or market whichever is the lower."

Now, of course, as soon as the certified financial statements of the American Trust and of the National Trust were mailed to stockholders and printed in the newspapers, everybody learned that the American Trust had earned only 3 percent on its capital stock during the past year whereas the National Trust had earned 43 percent on its capital stock during the same period. The price of American Trust stock therefore dropped sharply due to selling by disappointed stockholders and the price of National Trust stock rose sky high as investors rushed to buy it.

But the small group of financiers knew that the American Trust had really earned 23 percent on its capital stock during the past year although its earnings were certified as only 3 percent and it also knew that the National Trust had earned only 23 percent on its capital stock during the past year although its earnings were certified as 43 percent. Also, it was intelligent enough to realize that a decline in the security market which would wipe out the 20 percent unrealized profit of the American Trust would also wipe out the same amount of the realized profit of the National Trust because each trust owned exactly the same quantity of exactly the same securities. Therefore the unrealized profit of the American Trust was obviously just as safe as the realized profit of the National Trust. In fact there was no difference whatever between them. It was clear to the small group of financiers that each trust now possessed exactly $1,460,000 of the same securities, and that each had started with exactly $1,000,000 in money two years ago. Neither trust had received anything except profits earned in the ordinary and usual course of its business. Therefore, each trust must have made exactly the same amount of money since its formation, and the practice of the accountants in recognizing realized profits as earnings but in refusing to recognize unrealized profits as earnings must have been pure hokum. So the small group of financiers bought back at low prices the American Trust stock it had sold at high prices a year ago and bought more in addition. Then it sold at high prices the National Trust stock it had bought at low prices a year ago and sold more in addition.

The profits to the financiers on these transactions were far greater than they could have hoped to make merely from dividends on their stock. So they continued the process year after year and never failed to make a killing because they knew that the accounting firm would always maintain that unrealized profits were not earnings. And they have become exceedingly wealthy and respected, and no one has ever ventured to criticize them because the trusted firm of accountants has certified every one of their financial statements and everyone is convinced that such a firm would never certify a fraudulent or deceptive profit and loss statement or balance sheet.

Questions

1. Did the CPA firm properly carry out its professional responsibilities?
2. What accounting principles caused/allowed the described circumstances to occur?
3. What function does the "lower-of-cost-or-market" rule serve with respect to accounting for investment securities?
4. Given that the fable was written in 1939, what effect have subsequent official pronouncements had on resolving the dilemma described in the fable?
5. What do you believe should be the accounting and financial reporting rules for unrealized profits?

March 1978 marked the fourth anniversary of the appointment of Dr. D. Nathan Bass as senior editor of the journal *Social Scientifica*. Dr. Bass's own educational background had been in the areas of English and Journalism, but as a result of his present occupation, he was considered to be rather well-versed in matters relating to the social sciences.

Social Scientifica was a journal published by a non-profit organization whose funding came from subscription sales and financial support from a charitable foundation. Although scholarly in its orientation, the primary objective of the twelve-year-old publication was to describe and evaluate developments in the social sciences in terms understandable to lay persons. Indeed *Social Scientifica* was well-received by its readers as well as by social scientists desirous of having their research findings disseminated to a large audience.

During its formative years, almost all of the material published in *Social Scientifica* had encompassed the areas of sociology, psychology, and anthropology. However, for the past four or five years, its articles had begun to include the subjects of political science and economics as well. And as one thing led to the next, Dr. Bass recently began to receive manuscripts dealing with business and accounting topics. The editors in turn decided to approach such submissions with caution. Part of this concern resulted from their recognition that innate to any body of knowledge are a galaxy of technical expressions, subtle definitions, jargon, and inherent nuances which may have distinctive connotations in different kinds of circumstances.

When a manuscript dealing with one of these subjects was received, Dr. Bass identified its potentially troublesome sections, and proceeded to seek the counsel of someone considerably more familiar with the area than he. Several such submissions that arrived in March and April 1978 dealt with the nature of and developments in the field of accounting. The tentative conclusions Dr. Bass reached were that although the articles appeared to be informative and well-articulated, he needed to obtain an "outside" opinion as to the validity of the following five items contained in the manuscripts. These items should be viewed as being independent and unrelated to one another, inasmuch as they appeared in different authors' articles.

---

* AICPA adapted.

Item A

The function of financial accounting is to measure a company's net earnings for a given period of time. An income statement will measure a company's true net earnings if it is prepared in accordance with generally accepted accounting principles. Other financial statements are basically unrelated to the earnings statement. Net earnings would be measured as the difference between revenues and expenses. Revenues are an inflow of cash to the enterprise and should be realized when recognized. This may be accomplished by using the sales basis or the production basis. Expenses should be matched with revenues to measure net earnings. Usually, variable expenses are assigned to the product, and fixed expenses are assigned to the period.

Item B

Financial statement analysis involves using ratios to test past performance of a given company. Past performance is compared to a predetermined standard, and the company is evaluated accordingly. One such ratio is the current ratio, which is computed as current assets divided by current liabilities, or as monetary assets divided by monetary liabilities. A current ratio of 2 to 1 is considered good for companies; but the higher the ratio, the better the company's financial position is assumed to be. The current ratio is dynamic because it helps to measure fund flows.

Item C

Accounting is a service activity. Its function is to provide quantitative financial information intended to be useful in making economic decisions about and for economic entities. Thus, the accounting function might be viewed primarily as a tool or device for providing quantitative financial information to management to facilitate decision making.

Item D

Financial statements developed in accordance with generally accepted accounting principles, which apply the conservatism convention, can be free from bias or can give a fair presentation with respect to continuing and prospective stockholders as well as to retiring stockholders.

Item E

If the value of an enterprise were to be determined by the method which computes the sum of the present values of the marginal (or incremental)

417

expected net receipts of individual tangible and intangible assets, the resulting valuation would tend to be less than if the value of the entire enterprise had been determined in another way, such as by computing the present value of total expected net receipts for the entire enterprise (i.e., the resulting valuation of parts would sum to an amount that was less than that for the whole). This would be true even if the same pattern of interest or discount rates was used for both valuations.

Question

Critique each of the five items in sequence, by directing your attention to those statements which are invalid, explaining why the reasoning is incorrect and how it might be rectified.

Case 4-1

Wisconsin Electric Power Company

In the 1977 Annual Report of the Wisconsin Electric Power Company (henceforth, the Company), the president's letter began with the following four paragraphs:

> By just about any standard, 1977 was a year of encouraging progress for Wisconsin Electric Power Co., its stockholders, its customers and its employes.
>
> Revenues increased by 13.1 percent and continued progress was made in efforts to control expenses and improve operating efficiency. Earnings per share of common stock increased from $3.19 in 1976 to $3.36 in 1977, despite the issuance of 1.6 million shares of new common stock in late 1976.
>
> Common stock dividend payments increased to $2.09 per share in 1977, up 5.6 percent over the previous year. This increase continues a trend which has seen per share dividend payments climb by 36 percent in the past five years.
>
> Growth in earnings indicates that Wisconsin Electric will continue to be an attractive investment—as it must be if we are to finance the major energy projects we face in the years ahead.

The Company's Summary of Significant Accounting Policies stated with respect to revenues that "meters are read and accounts are billed monthly. Utility revenues were recognized at time of billing until January 1, 1977 at which time the method of recognizing revenues was changed as prescribed by PSCW (Public Service Commission of Wisconsin), (see Note A)." Note A entitled "Accrued Utility Revenues," appeared as follows:

Effective January 1, 1977 the Company and its subsidiaries began recording as revenue the monthly increase or decrease in the estimated amount accrued for utility service rendered but not billed (accrued utility revenues). Previously, revenue was recognized at the time of billing in accordance with industry practice. As prescribed by PSCW, accrued utility revenues of $52 million (before income taxes) at December 31, 1976 were recorded as a deferred credit and are being amortized to income in equal annual amounts over a ten year period which began in January 1977. This amortization as well as subsequent changes in accrued utility revenues will be considered in determining revenue requirements in future rate proceedings. The accounting change increased 1977 net income by $2,500,000, or $0.14 per share of common stock.

Additional information about the Company is presented below:

	1977	1976	1975
Net income ($000)	68,195	60,130	49,011
Preferred stock dividend requirement ($000)	7,088	7,088	7,088
Net income applicable to common stock ($000)	61,107	53,042	41,923
Number of shares, end-of-year (000)	18,276	18,175	16,514
Average number of shares (000)	18,213	16,642	16,481
Earnings per share	$3.36	$3.19	$2.54

Questions

1. What is the significance of the president's words "despite the issuance of 1.6 million shares of new common stock in late 1976?"
2. Is the new approach to accounting for revenues a better application of generally accepted accounting principles than the previous method?
3. What purpose is served by the creation of a deferred credit balance, and where should it appear in the Company's financial statements?
4. Do you believe the president's letter portrays fairly the Company's earnings performance? If not, what changes do you recommend?
5. Should it be the independent CPA's responsibility to monitor consistency between the client's financial statements and representations made elsewhere in its Annual Report?
6. What effect, if any, should the adoption of the PSCW-sanctioned method have on the independent CPA's audit opinion?

Cheryl Academy offered home-study courses to prepare qualified men and women for careers as para-executives. Persons completing the course of study were able to obtain employment as office managers, administrative assistants, and executive secretaries. Although Cheryl Academy was located in an office complex in a large metropolitan area, all its revenues were earned from fees remitted by students who enrolled in its correspondence courses. Cheryl's certificate program encompassed 12 courses and the courses were completed at the students' own pace. Generally, of those 60 percent of the students who completed the entire program, it took an average of two years to complete all the prescribed courses.

Students were charged $2,700 for the program: $1,500 was due when the registration agreement was signed and three $400 payments were due 2, 8, and 14 months later. The Academy viewed the $2,700 contract price as comprising a $300 initial registration fee and $200 tuition per course. Students who did not complete the program could obtain a refund of $100 per waived course, not to exceed a total of $1,000. Cash inflows from fee collections occurred uniformly during the year as did cash outlays relating to expenses and refunds. Cheryl's variable costs were $40 per student per course, and $30 to process each new registrant.

Cheryl Academy had been founded in 1956 by Ms. Z. Y. Cheryl. Ms. Cheryl and members of her immediate family had been the sole stockholders (owning 96 percent and 4 percent respectively) until July 18, 1979 at which time the company was sold to a major textbook publisher. A portion of the consideration given to the previous stockholders was treated by the new owner as being compensation to Ms. Cheryl in exchange for her agreement—set forth in writing—not to operate a competing correspondence school, or to be associated in any way with any other commercial home study or on-site educational institution. The non-competition agreement would remain in effect for 8 years. Ms. Cheryl proceeded to establish a consulting firm through which she was able to share her expertise with professional societies and trade associations interested in creating continuing education programs for their members.

Questions

1. When should Cheryl recognize the revenue embodied in the $2,700 fee it charged for its complete course of study?
2. In light of the alternative approaches that might be used to recognize

revenue, how should Cheryl deal with the issue of matching revenues and expenses?
3. How should Cheryl account for (1) implicit interest, (2) refunds, and (3) bad debts?
4. What different approach, if any, would you take if instead of a school offering a program consisting of a finite number of courses, the company in question was a health spa which earned revenue from subscribers who buy contracts to use its facilities for time periods ranging from 6 months to 3 years?
5. How should the non-competition agreement be accounted for by the new owner and by Ms. Cheryl?

Case 4–3
Metro-Goldwyn-Mayer, Inc.

Metro-Goldwyn-Mayer, Inc. (MGM) was a major motion picture and television program producer, and it owned and operated the MGM Hotels in Las Vegas and Reno, Nevada. MGM owned what it believed to be the most valuable motion picture library in the world, never having sold a single negative. Important revenues are derived from its library through theatrical reissue and television licensing.

The company's 1977 Annual Report relating to the fiscal year ending August 31, 1977 contained the following information in its Summary of Accounting Policies:

> The Company is reporting revenue from television licensing agreements entered into after August 31, 1972, along with related costs, in the accounting period in which the agreement is executed, provided certain conditions of sale have been met, including availability for broadcast.
>
> For all license agreements entered into on or before August 31, 1972, the revenue and related costs are recognized proportionately over the contract term. The consolidated statements of income reflect the following from such agreements (in thousands, except for per share amounts):

	1977	1976
Revenue	$4,836	$7,521
Net income	$2,090	$3,756
Net income per share	$ .15	$ .27

Earnings per share for 1977 were $2.35; and for 1976, it had been $2.24 before a $.25 extraordinary item relating to prior years' tax refund claims.

In April, 1978 MGM announced it had signed a contract with CBS Inc. licensing its film *Gone With The Wind* to the television network for 20 years for $35 million. MGM stated it anticipated the license revenue would be reported over four consecutive fiscal years beginning in the fourth quarter of fiscal 1978. Payments by the licensee were to be made in five consecutive annual installments beginning in September 1978.

MGM's interim report for the second quarter of its 1978 fiscal year contained the following information:

> Subsequent to the end of the quarter, we announced that MGM will receive the largest license fee ever paid by a network for a single film in the history of television. MGM's most famous picture *Gone With The Wind* has been licensed to CBS for an unprecedented $35,000,000 for a term of 20 years.
>
> The license revenue will be reported over three (in lieu of four as initially anticipated) consecutive annual installments, commencing in the fourth quarter of fiscal 1978. Payment of the license fee by CBS will be made in five consecutive equal annual installments, commencing in September 1978.
>
> *Gone With The Wind,* generally acknowledged as the most popular motion picture of all time, drew the largest audience for a theatrical film in the history of television when first shown on network television in November 1976. It is estimated that the movie was watched, all or in part, by 162 million people during the two nights of its presentation. In 1977, the American Film Institute named *Gone With The Wind* as the "greatest American film of all time."
>
> MGM has retained worldwide rights to future theatrical releases of *Gone With The Wind* as well as Canadian and foreign television rights. The film is currently in major theatrical reissue in Italy and Japan, where it is doing excellent business, and is also being exhibited in many other territories throughout the world.

MGM's 1978 Annual Report included the following disclosure in the President's Report.

> Two important steps were taken by the Company in fiscal 1978 which will have a significant impact in future periods.
>
> In an unprecedented agreement providing for the largest license fee ever paid for a single film, MGM licensed United States network television rights to *Gone With The Wind* to CBS for $35,000,000. Income from this license will be recognized in the first quarter of fiscal 1979. The Company retains the valuable worldwide theatrical and foreign television rights to the film.
>
> On August 14, 1978, we advised that the MGM Executive Committee would investigate Atlantic City, New Jersey in order to determine its potential for a major hotel/casino. On October 9, 1978 we announced jointly with Hilton Hotels Corporation that an agreement had been entered into for the

acquisition of property in Atlantic City with each company planning to develop its own hotel/casino complex on a portion of the land.

The 1978 Annual Report also contained the following information:

Quarterly Financial Information
For the Years Ended August 31, 1978 and 1977
(in thousands except per share amounts)

	Operating Revenues*	Operating Income*	Net Income	Per Share Earnings†
1977				
First Quarter	$ 71,757	$13,500	$ 7,375	$ .49
Second Quarter	75,432	12,614	6,335	.43
Third Quarter	74,333	14,771	7,449	.50
Fourth Quarter	71,489	21,654	12,029	.82
1978				
First Quarter	$ 74,522	$15,757	$ 8,215	$ .56
Second Quarter	92,605	19,362	9,607	.66
Third Quarter	106,920	25,989	13,074	.90
Fourth Quarter	127,359	33,913	18,445	1.27

* Reclassified (See note 1 to Financial Statements). [Merchandising revenues, formerly classified as "interest and other income, net," was reclassified as filmed entertainment operating revenues.]

† Adjusted to reflect 5% stock dividend with record date of November 22, 1977.

Common Stock Prices and Cash Dividends Per Share
For the Years Ended August 31, 1978 and 1977

	Common Stock Price*		Cash Dividends Paid Per Share*
	High	Low	
1977			
First Quarter	$13.875	$11.625	$.219
Second Quarter	18.125	13.000	.238
Third Quarter	21.875	16.625	.238
Fourth Quarter	23.875	18.750	.238
1978			
First Quarter	$23.375	$19.750	$.238
Second Quarter	28.625	23.375	.275
Third Quarter	37.625	25.750	.275
Fourth Quarter	54.750	33.500	.275

* Adjusted to reflect 5% stock dividend with record date of November 22, 1977. The principal market for the Common Stock of the Company is the New York Stock Exchange.

In October 1978, MGM's board of directors (1) approved a 2-for-1 stock split of shares outstanding on January 9, 1979, (2) declared a 5 percent stock dividend payable December 22, 1978, and (3) instituted a new dividend policy to be implemented in January, 1979 whereby the quarterly cash dividend would be 15¢ per share.

MGM's interim report for the first quarter of its 1979 fiscal year disclosed the following information as part of the President's Report.

First Quarter Highlights
Three Months Ended November 30
(in thousands, except per share amounts)

	1978	1977	Percent Increase
Operating revenues	$143,395	$74,522	92%
Net income	$ 26,016	$ 8,215	217%
Earnings per share	$ 1.70	$ 0.53	221%

Net income for the first quarter of the 1979 fiscal year, ended November 30, 1978, increased 217 percent to $26,016,000, or $1.70 per share, on operating revenues of $143,395,000.

For the quarter ended November 30, 1977, MGM reported net income of $8,215,000, or 53 cents per share, on operating revenues of $74,522,000.
. . .

Results for the first quarter of fiscal 1979 include $14,821,000 of net income, equal to 97 cents per share, and $29,545,000 of operating revenues recognized from the licensing of network television rights of Gone With The Wind to CBS. The $35,000,000 to be received by MGM under the license is the largest fee ever paid for a single film in the history of television. MGM has retained valuable worldwide theatrical rights, foreign television rights, and certain other ancillary rights to Gone With The Wind.

Questions

1. How would the agreement which MGM made with CBS during "fiscal 1978 . . . have a significant impact in future periods" as stated in that year's President's Report?
2. What disclosure should MGM make regarding the Gone With The Wind licensing agreement in the financial statements included in (1) its Quarterly Report for the first quarter of 1979, (2) its Annual Report for 1979, and (3) Annual Reports for subsequent years during which CBS has exclusive domestic exhibition rights to the film?

3. Why did the interim report for the first quarter of the 1979 fiscal year contain $29,545,000 of revenue and $14,821,000 of net income resulting from the *Gone With The Wind* agreement when $35,000,000 continued to be reported as the licensing fee to be paid by CBS to MGM?
4. What recognition should MGM give to previously expensed costs that had been incurred to produce *Gone With The Wind* several decades earlier—which would have been deferred and matched against the CBS license fee revenue had MGM anticipated that the latter would in fact occur?
5. What accounting differences should there be between MGM's agreement with NBC for one showing of *Gone With The Wind* during the 1976 calendar year, and the CBS contract which provided for an unlimited number of broadcasts over a 20-year period?
6. At what dollar amount should *Gone With The Wind* be reflected in MGM's balance sheet?
7. How should CBS, Inc. account for its contract with MGM relating to *Gone With The Wind*?

Case 5–1
Zymco Electronics Company

Zymco Electronics Company was a manufacturing company whose sales and earnings last year were approximately $50 million and $4 million respectively. Up until three years ago, the company's product line had encompassed electric hand tools, electronic games, adding machines, and pocket calculators. However, in response to the well-entrenched hair grooming trend toward the so-called natural look, Zymco then proceeded to develop, produce, and market a relatively low-cost hot-air comb and brush kit, called the "Zymkit." These units had an average retail price of less than $18, and were sold in supermarkets and drugstores throughout the United States, Canada and Western Europe; units sold were as follows:

3 years ago	45,000
2 years ago	75,000
Last year	120,000
Current year:	
Jan.–Sept.	90,000
Oct.–Dec.	50,000*
Next year	165,000*

* Projected.

As a result of receiving complaints from Zymkit customers about various features of the unit, Zymco instituted a comprehensive testing program during March of the current year. The tests' initial findings indicated that as many as 60 percent of Zymkits already in circulation had the potential of posing a health hazard to their users. It was therefore decided in late September to recall all the outstanding units, and to either rectify the problem or provide the customer with a new replacement model. An extensive, follow-up review of pertinent specifications, production records, and quality control reports disclosed the following remedial action was warranted.

All the units sold to date would require physical examination by Zymco technicians. About 30 percent of the units would need to have only a single part replaced, and as many as 20 percent of the Zymkits would require replacement of the entire unit. Although it was expected that the problem would not recur, Zymco could not be absolutely certain that the new part would in fact be durable over an extended period of time.

Costs associated with the current year's handling of 170,000 recalled Zymkits were as follows:

Engineering—diagnostic and remedial	$ 85,000
Publicity, postage and handling	$255,000
Replacement of parts and entire units	$680,000

It was expected that 10,000 additional "recalled" units would be handled during the next fiscal year. The 80,000 completed Zymkits that had not been sold as of September 30 would be examined before customers would have access to them, and ¾ of these units were expected to be available for retail sale well before year-end.

Questions

1. What are the financial reporting and disclosure requirements relating to a product recall?
2. How should Zymco Electronics account for the cost of the Zymkit recall?
3. What are the accounting and financial disclosure requirements with respect to the cost of a possible *future* recall?
4. How do a current year's financial statements reflect corrections of prior periods' accounting data?
5. How should a company account for future losses contingent on warranty claims submitted by its customers which the company expects to honor?

426

Case 5–2
American Electric Power Company

Electric power companies engaged in interstate transmission of power are regulated by the Federal Power Commission (FPC). Regarding deferred income taxes, the FPC attempts to employ a policy which is flexible between particular case situations such that its point of view may be compatible with that of the respective state commissions. Accordingly, the FPC permits the use of both "flow through" and "normalization."

With regard to the point of view which calls for normalization, a question arises. By its very nature, that portion of the normalized tax obligation deferred to future years is assumed to represent the presence of cash not yet paid to the government and thus still in the company's domain. Had a flow through approach been employed, the lower tax expense on the income statement would result in larger "retained earnings." But when normalization is used, there is a question where to locate the balance sheet disclosure of deferred taxes.

In its Accounting Series Release (ASR) No. 85, which is applicable to regulated and unregulated companies alike, the Securities and Exchange Commission (SEC), stated that

> . . . any financial statement filed with this Commission which designates as earned surplus (or its equivalent) or in any manner as a part of equity capital (even though accompanied by words of limitation such as "restricted" or "appropriated") the accumulated credit arising from accounting for reductions in income taxes resulting from deducting costs for income tax purposes at a more rapid rate than for financial statement purposes will be presumed by the Commission to be misleading or inaccurate despite disclosure contained in the certificate of the accountant or in the footnotes to the statements, provided the amounts involved are material.[1]

This position reflected the SEC's belief that it is improper to charge income with an item required for the proper determination of net income and concurrently to credit retained earnings.[2] It should not be inferred that the SEC requires normalization; it merely prohibits including the deferred amount in the stockholders' equity section of the balance sheet. Its ASR No. 86 states "it was not the Commission's intention . . . to make mandatory the use of deferred tax accounting beyond the requirements of generally accepted accounting principles."[3]

---

[1] *Accounting Series Release No. 85,* paragraph no. 10.

[2] Ibid., paragraph no. 4.

[3] *Accounting Series Release No. 86,* paragraph no. 1.

When the SEC announced its intent to introduce what was to become the aforementioned ASR No. 85, hearings were held at which time various points of view were enunciated. One point of view was that the deferred credit amount ". . . constitutes a reserve against which increased future taxes resulting from higher current depreciation deductions are to be charged; such a reserve is no more a part of equity capital than is the reserve for depreciation."[4] On the other hand, it was asserted that

> . . . since there is no present tax cost or liability for the deferred tax provided (there being only a future tax cost at some later date), the deferred-tax credit arising from such normalization belongs to the stockholders and should be included in the equity capital rather than a reserve account that implies provision for a current tax cost.[5]

The plight of bondholders was introduced;

> . . . a requirement that such accumulations be classified a 'reserve' or a 'deferred liability' or as 'deferred taxes' could well lead . . . bond holders to the erroneous conclusion that the accumulations represent a claim upon assets prior to the claims of bond holders, although, in fact, there is no real liability likely to arise until long after the maturity of all the outstanding bonds.[6]

The interests of consumers were cited when it was pointed out

> . . . that to the extent of such amount, the utility has cost-free equity capital available for investment in plant and results in lower rates than they would otherwise enjoy for many thousand rate payers.[7]

Officers of the American Electric Power Company (AEP) contended that if a utility does not utilize normalization procedures, by use of book depreciation charges which are less than tax depreciation amounts, the tax benefits flow through to stockholders' equity accounts. Therefore, when normalization is employed, the benefits it generates should also flow through to stockholders' equity.[8] In support of this contention, the following comments were introduced at the SEC hearings:

> Income equal to the normalizing charge has actually been received, but no expense has been incurred in the current fiscal period in connection with the receipt of that income. The income has been retained for use in the business.[9]

---

[4] United States Securities and Exchange Commission, "Official Report of Proceedings before the Securities and Exchange Commission," Docket No. S7–178, April 8 and 10, 1959, 13 (unpublished).

[5] Ibid., 26–27.

[6] Ibid., 56–57.

[7] Ibid., 147.

[8] Ibid., 198.

[9] Ibid., 199.

. . . the real effect of the normalization charge is merely to delay the recognition of earnings in the income statement, but those earnings have been, in fact, received.[10]

. . . normalizing an income account neither creates nor destroys income. It merely fixes the time when income which has actually been received is recognized in the income account. Charges made to earned surplus restricted and credited to income when taxes are increased in later years cannot operate to reduce total earned surplus or total equity. They can merely serve to turn earned surplus restricted into earned surplus unrestricted. Finally, . . . the normalizing charge equal to the tax reduction cannot be a current cost and it cannot measure a liability. It can only serve to channel earnings, which otherwise would have appeared as net income after taxes, directly into surplus and thus into equity.[11]

The case for normalizing the income account is based not on the premise that a current cost is involved, but rather on the desirability of equalizing tax costs as between present and future generations of consumers.[12]

Specifically with regard to the operations of AEP, it was contended that

. . . during the past several years, we have had substantial help from the amount in restricted surplus as a basis of maintaining our equity ratios. It has therefore served the same purpose as newly created capital. It has enabled us to sell more low cost debt securities than would otherwise have been possible and has served to reduce Federal income taxes and capital costs. This substantial help in financing has redounded to the benefit of both investors and consumers.[13]

AEP submitted an exhibit which identified the alleged effect of its debt (to asset) ratio on annual charges required to carry investment. It suggested that as the debt ratio rises from 45 percent to 60 percent, the annual charges as a percent of original investment decline from 9.77 percent to 8.40 percent, with the attendant benefits accruing to the consumer. AEP, in turn, offered the following argument:

The Holding Company Act provides that holding company systems be regulated by the SEC to protect "investors, consumers and the general public." The subject Notice fails to include 'consumers' in stating that "the Commission considers that the action thus taken is necessary or appropriate in the public interest or for the protection of investors . . ." The consumers have apparently been overlooked in this instance . . . Inasmuch as income taxes are operating expenses for utilities, the resulting reduction in operating expenses redounds entirely to the consumers. The reduction in capital costs also benefits the

---

[10] Ibid., 200.
[11] Ibid., 202–203.
[12] Ibid., 228.
[13] Ibid., 228.

consumers . . . The restricted earned surplus method of accounting for deferred taxes protects and enhances such interests. We submit, therefore, that the Commission cannot appropriately take the proposed action [ASR No. 85] which, as we have shown, would adversely, and in material respects, affect both consumers and investors.[14]

In February, 1960, the SEC issued ASR No. 85 prohibiting the controversial deferred credit from being included in the owners' equity section of corporate balance sheets. Later in 1960, an AEP subsidiary company (Kentucky Power Company) filed an application with the SEC regarding a proposal to issue and sell up to $40,000,000 of unsecured notes. Included in the owners' equity section of its balance sheets were amounts identified as "Earned Surplus Restricted for Future Federal Income Taxes." Such a presentation did not conform to the ruling set forth by the SEC in its ASR No. 85; hearings were scheduled.

AEP contended that inclusion of the deferred credit among its liabilities would cause its debt ratio to be four (4) percentage points higher (57.7 percent versus 53.7 percent) than would have occurred had the credit been contained in the owners' equity section of the balance sheet.[15] AEP maintained that imposition of the SEC point of view would have an adverse effect on its bond ratings because it would

> . . . in effect . . . require an increase in common equity and a concommitant decrease in debt . . . [resulting] in a substantial increase in the cost of capital and taxes . . . [having] an adverse effect on rates charged for its services and would thus impose an unnecessary and unwarranted burden on consumers and that such a result would be inconsistent with the proper protection of consumers which is one of the primary objectives of the Act.[16]

A compromise between AEP and the SEC was reached. It called for revised financial statements with the disputed amount to be identified as an independent category,

> Accumulated Amount Invested in the Business Equivalent to Reduction in Federal Income Taxes Resulting from Accelerated Amortization and Liberalized Depreciation Which Is Recorded as Earned Surplus Restricted for Future Federal Income Taxes in Accounts Maintained Pursuant to State Regulatory Requirements.[17]

---

[14] Arthur Andersen & Co. SEC *Administrative Policy Re: Balance-Sheet Treatment of Deferred Income-Tax Credits,* Vol. V (Chicago: Arthur Andersen & Co., 1961), 339–340.

[15] Ibid., 43.

[16] Ibid., 44.

[17] Ibid., 45.

Thus, for purposes of formal financial statements, the principle set forth in ASR No. 85 was upheld. However, for purposes of its consideration of the adequacy of the utility's financial structure, ". . . the Commission will give due weight to the existence of the accumulated tax reduction and its size in determining appropriate capitalization ratios."[18] Noteworthy is the SEC's acknowledgement that in context of its own analysis,

> . . . the accumulated tax reduction may properly be regarded as a deferred credit to income in that it represents a source of enhancement of future income by way of mitigation, for financial accounting purposes, of a future expense—namely, income tax expense. It will thus furnish the basis for future accretions to unrestricted earned surplus.[19]

AEP's president stated that ". . . if the term victory were to be used, I think it might be said that the electric consumer . . . was the victor. He won recognition in that his interest—the consumer's interest—was recognized as being equally important along with that of the investor and the public."[20]

Questions

1. What are advantages and disadvantages of using accelerated depreciation procedures, and are they as applicable to a public utility as they are to a nonregulated company?
2. Does the advantage of employing accelerated depreciation procedures for income tax purposes accrue to a public utility's customers, or to the company itself and ultimately to its stockholders?
3. Do identical income tax savings result when using either normalization or flow-through; and to the extent that any tax benefit occurs, how is it reflected in the company's financial statements?
4. Given the conventional distinction between an entity's liabilities and its stockholders' equity, where would you classify a company's (credit balance) deferred taxes balance? Why?
5. If timing differences between a company's financial accounting and income tax accounting were to yield a *debit* balance, where should the resulting amount appear in its balance sheet?

---

[18] Ibid.

[19] Ibid.

[20] Paper read by Philip Sporn before a group of financial analysts and other representatives of the financial community in the clubroom of the New York Society of Financial Analysts, February 2, 1961 (appears in the Subject File of Arthur Andersen & Co.).

Mason Company operated several plants at which limestone was processed into quicklime and hydrated lime. The Russell Plant, where most of the equipment was installed many years ago, continually deposited a dusty white substance over the surrounding countryside. Citing the unsanitary condition of the neighboring community of Glentown, the pollution of the Glen River, and the high incidence of lung disease among workers at Russell, the state's Pollution Control Agency ordered the installation of air pollution control equipment. Also, the Agency assessed a substantial penalty, which was used to clean up Glentown. After considering the costs involved, which could not have been reasonably estimated prior to the Agency's action, Mason decided to comply with the Agency's orders, the alternative being to cease operations at Russell at the end of the current fiscal year. The officers of Mason agreed that the air pollution control equipment should be capitalized and depreciated over its useful life, but they disagreed over the period(s) to which the penalty should be charged.

Mason's Green Plant caused approximately as much pollution as Russell. Green, however, was located in another state, where there was little likelihood of governmental regulation, and Mason had no plans for pollution control at that plant. One of Mason's officers, Mr. Grove, said that uncontrolled pollution at Green constituted a very real cost to society, which was not recorded anywhere under current practice. He suggested this "social cost" of the Green Plant be included annually in Mason's income statement. Further, he suggested that measurement of this cost was easily obtainable by reference to the depreciation on Russell's pollution control equipment.

Questions

1. Should the cost of the Russell Plant penalty be accounted for as a retroactive adjustment of prior periods' earnings, as an expense of the current year, or should it be capitalized and amortized over future fiscal years? Explain.
2. Is Mr. Grove correct in stating that costs associated with Green's pollution are entirely unrecorded?
3. Evaluate Mr. Grove's proposed method of measuring the annual "social cost" of Green's pollution.

* AICPA adapted.

4. Discuss the merit of Mr. Grove's suggestion that a "social cost" be recognized by Mason.

5. What disclosure requirements should exist for a company and for its independent auditor if they are aware of pollution violations by the company which are punishable by fines, but of which the environment protection authorities are as yet unaware?

Case 6–1
International Whisket Corporation

An October 1973 essay in *The Wall Street Journal* offered some comments about inventory accounting practices, and several of its paragraphs are presented below.

> If inflation qualifies as foul economic weather, then sharp surges in the wholesale price index this year have been among the best "foul weather friends" corporate profits have had.
>
> Solely because inflation boosted the value of corporate inventories, second quarter profits were enriched $21 billion; inventory profits accounted for more than 16% of the $108 billion annual rate at which profits were running at mid-year.
>
> That may have looked great to investors scanning the bottom line, but a growing amount of securities research is focusing on how soon the piper must be paid for that segment, at least, of robust earnings performance. . . .
>
> Where prices of vital goods climb spectacularly, the FIFO method can bring sharp pressures to bear on profit margins even before inflation rates begin to ease.
>
> For example, Tampax Inc. has taken a clobbering in over-the-counter trading in recent weeks. The stock, which is a widely held "growth" favorite and has traded as high as 131½ this year, fell nearly 12 points last week as analysts continued to lower their estimates of 1973 earnings to the $2.50-to-$2.60 a share range. In 1972, Tampax earned $2.33 a share. The stock was quoted yesterday at 86½ bid. Although other factors, including an eroding market share, are involved, the main negative analysts see is that Tampax is a major user of cotton, which has about tripled in cost this year. Because the company is on a FIFO basis, its inventory profits advantage is being offset by its need to replace inventories at higher costs. "Gross profit margins will come under increasing pressure as higher-cost cotton finds its way into the cost of goods sold," says one analyst.

In May 1974 *The Wall Street Journal* contained the following news article.

Inventory profit from foreign oil should continue to have an impact on earnings of Mobil Oil Corp. for the rest of the year, officials said.

But Rawleigh Warner Jr., chairman, told the annual meeting here that Mobil is unable to determine, at this point whether overall earnings for the remaining quarters "will hold up to anywhere near" the level of the previously reported $258.6 million in the first quarter.

When it reported first quarter profits last week, Mobil cited inventory gains from foreign oil as a factor in the 66 percent increase in overall earnings from a year earlier. Other international oil companies also had major inventory profits in the first quarter as a result of the sharp increases in prices of foreign oil posted by the producing governments at the beginning of the year.

But unlike some of the other internationals, Mobil utilizes what it calls an average cost inventory accounting method in its foreign operations. Income is charged with an average of current cost and historic cost. In the first quarter, Mobil said, if it had charged foreign income with current costs only, its earnings would have been lower by about $90 million.

After the annual meeting, a Mobil official said use of this accounting system should continue to give the company inventory gains from foreign oil for each of the remaining three quarters. William P. Tavoulareas, president, estimated the gains should run each period at about the same rate as the $90 million of the first quarter, "assuming there aren't any major changes in prices or volumes" of foreign oil.

In August 1974 *The Wall Street Journal* published an editorial entitled, "The FIFO Crisis." That editorial is presented in its entirety below.

The current surge of inventory profits is causing a crisis that is not only economic but political and social as well. And while the typical business critic is unlikely ever to discover this particular crisis, it is a textbook example of the critics' theme that social problems result from narrow-minded profit-maximizing.

Say that International Whisket Corp. makes a $1.50 whisket out of $1 worth of fishfeathers. When the price of fishfeathers jumps from $1 to $2 a bale, International has to raise the price of its whisket to $2.50. After all, it wants to stay in business, and knows that as soon as it sells the whisket it will have to turn around and pay $2 for its next bale of fishfeathers.

However, International has a supply of fishfeathers that it bought at $1. So until this supply runs out, it is selling $2.50 whiskets made out of $1 fishfeathers. Obviously it can show a profit of $1.50 instead of the usual $.50. Yet at the same time, after it buys its next bale of fishfeathers, International has only $.50 to spend on dividends, new whisket mills and other traditional uses of profit.

With the current double-digit inflation, precisely this has been going on throughout American industry. Business is reporting "record profits," but a great deal of these profits are as illusory as International Whisket's extra $1.

434

Estimates of inventory profits range as high as 40 percent of all current profits. The "record profits" give business a black eye in some minds, and give labor leaders a bit of rhetoric to back up wage demands. But this distortion is the smallest part of the problem.

The biggest part is that the corporate income tax is based on total profits, so the inventory profits artificially swell federal revenues. This disguises the government's bad economic management; since budget deficits are not as bad as they might be, Congress feels freer to spend. But if commodity prices stabilize, and fishfeather futures have been acting strangely, the inventory profits may vanish overnight. This means federal revenues would collapse, the budget deficits would soar and inflation would be further stimulated.

Beyond that, it seems some companies are themselves being fooled by illusory profits. The president of International Whisket looks at his books, sees profit swelling to $1.50, and starts handing out lush bonuses, increasing the dividend and agreeing to fat wage settlements. When the inventory profits vanish, or even when it's time to buy the next bale of fishfeathers, there is loud talk about a "corporate liquidity crisis," bank loans soar, and the Fed rushes in to bail everyone out by flooding them with money and further stimulating inflation.

The American business community could have prevented this crisis entirely. The crisis is purely and simply an artifact of the accounting practice nearly all major corporations follow in accounting for inventory—first in, first out. It would have been prevented if corporations had instead chosen the permissible alternative—last in, first out. If International Whisket had scrapped FIFO and put itself on LIFO, when it sold a $2.50 whisket it would charge to expenses $2 worth of fishfeathers and would show a profit of $.50, which is of course the more meaningful figure.

Amazingly, most corporations have chosen FIFO even though LIFO is clearly in their own best interest. Under FIFO, International Whisket has to pay tax on $1.50, which comes to $.75. Its cash in hand is the $1 recovery on fishfeathers plus the $.75 left after tax, or $1.75. To buy the $2 fishfeathers it has to scrape up $.25 somewhere.

Under LIFO, International pays tax on only $.50, which comes to $.25. Its cash in hand is $2 recovery on fishfeathers plus $.25 left after tax, or $2.25. It can buy the $2 fishfeathers and still have $.25 left to spend on dividends and whisket mills.

If International nonetheless decides it is willing to pay the extra $.50 to Uncle Sam for the privilege of being on FIFO, it will be making the same decision most American corporations have. The privilege of FIFO is that International gets to write in its annual report that instead of making $.50 pretax and $.25 after tax, it made $1.50 pretax and $.75 after tax.

Now, somewhere you may find a sophisticated defender of FIFO who will argue that the higher reported earnings boost the price of International's stock and thus its borrowing power, so in the end it comes out ahead. Do your stocks go up when the company gives away company resources? In fact, if the stock market is anywhere near as efficient as the academic research shows, the

435

impact of a change from FIFO to LIFO will be felt solely in the earnings multiple; the share price will stay the same.

Executive bonuses are another matter, being tied to whatever is written in the annual report. Executive egos, given the mystique of the business culture, often seem to like the bonuses to be tied solely to the one figure of earnings per share. And perhaps the greatest lesson of the FIFO crisis is that this mystique is misplaced, that business serves both itself and society better if it looks not simply at reported earnings but at the underlying health of the business enterprise.

With respect to the relative popularity of the three primary methods of determining inventory cost, data for the 600 industrial and commercial corporations whose annual reports comprise the annual *Accounting Trends and Techniques* survey are presented through "percent" amounts in the following chart:

	Number of Disclosures	FIFO	Average Cost	LIFO	Other	Total
1972	920	41%	26%	16%	17%	100%
1973	927	43	25	16	16	100
1974	1,054	36	22	29	13	100
1975	1,044	36	23	30	11	100
1976	1,059	37	22	31	10	100
1977	1,066	37	21	31	11	100
1978	1,048	37	21	33	9	100

Questions

1. What is the effect of a decreasing rate of inflation on the profit reported by companies using FIFO, LIFO, or a weighted average method of inventory costing?
2. To what factors do you attribute companies' selection of an inventory costing method?
3. With respect to a company which uses a particular inventory costing method, should it be required, permitted, or forbidden to disclose what the inventory cost and resulting profit would have been had an alternative method been adopted?
4. Under what circumstances should a company be allowed to change its method of inventory costing, and what financial disclosure requirements, if any, should apply?
5. What disclosures, if any, should Tampax have made in its 1972 financial statements with respect to the presence of inventory profits?

6. In light of the typically opposite balance sheet and income statement effects of FIFO and LIFO, can you envision a system which embraces the desirable features of both of these methods?

Case 6–2
United States Steel Corporation

By 1977 the United States Steel Corporation had established itself as a diversified materials producer. In the steel business, its investment of capital was centered heavily on replacement and modernization projects. In its various nonsteel businesses, investment was for expansion of facilities and for new product lines. In 1977 the sales revenue of the nonsteel businesses was $3 billion, approximately 30 percent of total revenues.

One of the company's perceived strengths for the future was its extensive raw material reserves. Owned or leased iron ore properties in the United States in grades subject to beneficiation were estimated early in 1978 to be adequate to produce approximately 4.2 billion net tons of iron ore concentrates. In Canada, mining rights covered additional proven reserves equivalent to approximately 1.8 billion net tons of recoverable high-grade iron ore concentrates. A major thrust of U.S. Steel's mid-Sixties plan was the development and expansion of the industrial chemical and agricultural chemical businesses. The plan also contemplated further diversification into a broad range of minerals on a worldwide basis, the formation of an engineering and consulting business, and the formation of a realty business to develop already owned or newly acquired real estate for sale or lease.

The material that follows is taken from U.S. Steel's Form 10–K SEC submission for the fiscal year ended December 31, 1977.

	In Millions	
	1977	1976
From the Consolidated Statement of Income:		
Cost of products and services sold	$7,944.5	$6,720.1
Wear and exhaustion of facilities	372.0	308.6
Income	137.9	410.3
Income per common share (in dollars)		
Primary	$ 1.66	$ 5.03
Fully diluted	$ 1.66	$ 4.90

	In Millions	
	1977	1976
From the Consolidated Balance Sheet:		
Inventories	$1,254.8	$1,387.1
Property, plant and equipment (net)	5,724.2	5,279.2
Total assets	9,914.4	9,167.9
Total ownership (assets less liabilities)	5,141.7	5,129.0
Total current assets	3,040.3	2,791.2
Total current liabilities	1,712.5	1,637.4

From the Summary of Principal
Accounting Policies:

Inventories—Since 1941, the cost of inventories has been determined primarily under the last-in, first-out (LIFO) method which, in the aggregate, is lower than market.

From the Notes to Financial Statements:

	In Millions	
	December 31	
Inventories	1977	1976
Raw materials	$ 401.0	$ 543.9
Semi-finished products	372.6	372.2
Finished products	263.4	270.4
Supplies and sundry items	212.5	178.5
Construction contracts in progress	126.6	160.8
Less invoices rendered	(121.3)	(138.7)
Total	**$1,254.8**	**$1,387.1**

December 31, 1975 inventory balance was $1,170.7 million.

Under the LIFO method, current acquisition costs are estimated to exceed the inventory value at December 31, 1977, as shown above by approximately $1,580 million.

The net of construction contracts in progress less invoices rendered includes $12.1 million in 1977 and $28.4 million in 1976 related to contracts for which cumulative costs exceed invoices rendered and $(6.8) million in 1977 and $(6.3) million in 1976 applicable to contracts for which cumulative invoices rendered exceed cumulative costs.

For the effect on income of the penetration of LIFO inventory layers see page 18.

The pertinent material that appeared on page 18 follows:

During the five year period (1973 through 1977), there were quantity reductions in many LIFO inventory pools—a common and frequent occurrence in U. S. Steel. Inventory liquidations occur generally as a consequence of planned inventory programs to support changes in process technology, customer product specifications, and market conditions, and because of the discontinuance of product lines. A computation of the effect of LIFO quantity reductions was made in conformance with the Internal Revenue Service procedure. Included in costs of products and services sold and income before taxes were credits from inventory liquidations of $88.2 million in 1977, $55.9 million in 1976, $58.3 million in 1975, $85.1 million in 1974, and $87.5 million in 1973. These benefits were more than offset by the lag in price increases needed by U.S. Steel to offset continuing cost increases.

From *Estimated Replacement Cost Information—(unaudited)*:

Inventories

For LIFO inventories, current acquisition costs were applied to year-end inventory quantities. Non-LIFO inventories are reflected at current actual cost. This estimate of current replacement cost, which excludes the cost reduction of own-produced inventories that would result from the more efficient replacement facilities, is approximately double the historical cost amount reflected in the balance sheet. Sufficient calculations of cost benefits were made to establish that cost reduction from facility replacements would be substantial. This subject is further discussed under Cost of Products and Services Sold.

Cost of Products and Services Sold

This replacement cost estimate represents the historical cost of products and services sold adjusted to a replacement cost basis for the LIFO inventories used and reduced for the rental cost of leased facilities that were capitalized in developing fixed asset replacement costs. The resultant amount, not adjusted to reflect the productivity and efficiency gains that would be realized from the use of new facilities, is approximately the same as the historical costs reflected in the income statement.

It would be entirely impractical to currently fully engineer and evaluate the eventual replacement of the Corporation's entire productive capacity, since future product markets and plant locations are unknown. The timing of such replacements would necessarily extend far into the realm of undeterminable future technology and economic conditions. However, sufficient calculations of cost benefits were made to determine that they would be substantial. Based on studies that have been made, U. S. Steel management believes that the cost savings from completely replacing present capacity over the years would at least offset the additional depreciation from the significantly increased investment.

439

Summary of Replacement Cost Data (in billions)

	Assets Subject to Replacement Cost Disclosure				Total Amount per Financial Statements	
	Estimated Re-placement Cost		Present Recorded Cost			
	1977	*1976*	*1977*	*1976*	*1977*	*1976*
At year-end:						
Inventories	$ 2.8	$ 2.8	$ 1.3	$1.4	$ 1.3	$ 1.4
Property, plant, and equipment						
Gross	$41.3*	$36.0	$11.4*	$9.1	$12.5	$11.9
Net	14.1*	11.0	4.7*	3.4	5.7	5.3
For the year:						
Cost of products and services sold	$ 8.0	$ 6.7	$ 7.9	$6.7	$ 7.9	$ 6.7
Depreciation (wear and exhaustion of facilities)	$ .8†	$ .6	$ .4†	$ .2	$ .4	$ .3

* Included in 1977 gross are $4.3 estimated replacement cost and $2.0 present recorded cost for mineral resource associated productive plant and equipment and for locations outside North America and European Economic Community which are not included in 1976 replacement cost disclosures. Likewise, net includes $2.8 and $1.1 for these items.

† Included in 1977 are $.1 estimated replacement cost depreciation and $.1 present recorded cost depreciation for mineral resource associated productive plant and equipment and for locations outside North America and European Economic Community which are not included in 1976 replacement cost disclosures.

Questions

1. What was the effect of U.S. Steel's use of LIFO on its 1976 and 1977 net income, and on both years' end-of-period owners' equity and working capital?
2. How would a subsequent year's earnings be affected by sales of U. S. Steel's product which was significantly greater than or less than that year's production output?
3. What would be U. S. Steel's replacement cost basis earnings per share, and what would be the effect on its "return on equity" based on its historical cost earnings and the replacement value of its assets?
4. Given the following general price-level (GNP Deflator) index numbers,

1941	47.2	1966	113.9
1946	66.7	1971	141.4
1951	85.6	1976	195.6
1956	94.0	1977	206.4
1961	104.6		

what observations can be made with respect to U. S. Steel's inventory balances?

5. What portion of U. S. Steel's Form 10–K disclosures should also be included in the 1977 Annual Report that is sent to its quarter of a million shareholders?

Case 6–3
Lockheed Aircraft Corporation*

At the beginning of the 1970s, Lockheed Aircraft Corporation was the United States' largest defense contractor, and it was also in the process of developing a major commercial airplane known as the L–1011 TriStar. Commencing in 1969, Lockheed suffered a number of major financial setbacks. The two most publicized related to the C–5A military transport airplane and the L–1011 commercial transport airplane, but there were other very serious financial losses involving an aborted helicopter project, the development of a missile motor, and some shipbuilding contracts. These problems raised major questions as to Lockheed's financial position and results of operations.

The L–1011 TriStar airplane project was a vast and complex undertaking. The first year of substantial expenditures was 1968 ($45 million), and the program was expected to continue into the late 1980s—a span of approximately two decades. It was estimated that both expenses and revenues during this period would exceed $10 billion, and that 300 or more airplanes would be delivered. The program was complicated technically and economically. It was affected by many events, including one of the largest bankruptcies in the history of the United Kingdom, that of Rolls Royce Ltd., and a major

---

* Much of the information in this case study is derived from a discussion of the Lockheed TriStar project and the related accounting published by Lockheed's auditors, Arthur Young & Company, in 1977. Reprinted by permission, from *Professional Responsibilities in a Time of Change*. Arthur Young & Company's Response to "The Accounting Establishment," a special edition of *The Arthur Young Journal,* Spring/Summer 1977, pages 42–44, 52. Copyright © 1977 by Arthur Young & Company.

financial crisis in the airlines industry, including the customers for the L–1011. This latter crisis was triggered by the direct impact of the energy crisis on the cost of flying airplanes and the indirect impact of the energy crisis on the economy of the world and thereby on the market for air travel. These events were of course, unforeseen at the time the program was launched, and other unforeseen developments, either favorable or unfavorable could surface by the time the program is ended.

It has been the experience of the aircraft industry like many other industries, that the early production units of an item have a direct cost greatly in excess of the direct cost of later units, and that, when an airplane program continues at approximately level production under relatively stable economic conditions, the cost per airplane reduces steadily and continuously to the end of the program. This phenomenon is called the "learning curve." If the production rate changes drastically, or if surrounding economic conditions change, the trend may temporarily reverse (go up) but can be expected to reverse again (go down) after conditions stabilize. During the early history of the L–1011 program, there were three major disruptions.

The first disruption, and the most dramatic, resulted from the bankruptcy of Rolls Royce Ltd., the supplier of engines for the L–1011. The development cost of these engines so far exceeded the expectations of Rolls Royce that it was forced into bankruptcy and stopped work on the engine. As a result, Lockheed interrupted production of the L–1011 in January 1971 and did not fully resume until November 1971, after Rolls Royce had been recapitalized and had resumed production.

The second disruption resulted from an outbreak of production inefficiencies. A change was made in the management of the plant responsible for the L–1011 final assembly, and thereafter costs resumed their downward trend. This disruption occurred during the period of approximately July to November 1973.

The last disruption was caused by a marked decrease in the number of airplanes produced per month as a consequence of the difficulties of the customer airlines (both as to financing and as to load factors), which caused the airlines to stretch out previously scheduled deliveries. The extent of this condition can be briefly illustrated by the number of airplanes delivered, as follows: 1974—41, 1975—25, and 1976—16. These stretch-outs started to affect production costs about a year earlier than they affected deliveries.

The first two of these three disruptions had a heavy impact on labor hours and, to the extent that overhead was variable, a corresponding impact on overhead. The last disruption had only a modest impact on labor hours, but it increased the overhead rate per hour because hours were down and much of the overhead was fixed.

Another pervasive aspect of airplane programs in general is that research and development costs represent a larger proportion of the cost of sales than is generally true in higher volume manufacturing industries. The L-1011 program was no exception. For the purposes of this discussion, it will be convenient to consider Lockheed's investment in the L-1011 as falling into three categories:

1. Hard inventory costs.
2. Start-up costs.
3. Research and development (R&D) costs.

Hard inventory costs are the costs of labor and material, together with a proration of factory overhead. Most such costs are collected by association with an airplane "lot"—a predetermined group of airplanes—and then prorated to individual airplanes within the lot. A smaller portion of costs is collected in larger cost centers and then prorated to lots. Thus, lot costs and individual airplane costs are determined with reasonable accuracy, not with absolute precision.

Start-up costs consist primarily of two elements. The first element is the cost of creating the jigs and special tools necessary for the manufacturing process; much of this is a one-time cost occurring early in the program. Smaller amounts of such costs are incurred later in the program and are also included in this category. The second element of start-up costs is an allocation of the high production costs of the earlier airplanes. Start-up costs are spread over the estimated life of the program.

The largest component of Lockheed's research and development (R&D) expense is engineering salaries and related overhead. The category also includes other items relating to the development and testing of the airplane. Like tooling costs, R&D expense is incurred primarily at the beginning of the program but continues at a reduced rate throughout the program.

Lockheed had been recording start-up costs as assets since before World War II. McDonnel Douglas Corporation had a similar asset (classified as a current asset) on its balance sheet with respect to the similar airplane, the DC-10. The Boeing Company had a similar asset on its balance sheet with respect to the 747. These costs have been carried as an asset by Lockheed because it was expected that they would probably be realized through L-1011 sales. Until the last quarter of 1974, it was Lockheed's accounting practice to initially charge to inventory all three categories of cost. In December 1974, in response to FASB Statement No. 2, the R&D costs were retroactively charged to expense of the years in which they were incurred. This had a $280,000,000 net-of-tax adverse effect on shareholders' equity. This left the hard inventory costs and the start-up costs in inventory.

For each of the years beginning with 1969, Lockheed spelled out, in notes to its financial statements, the uncertainties in its financial position and results of operations. For each of those years, the auditor's report refers to such notes, and the audit opinion was subject to those uncertainties; that is, the opinion was not a "clean" opinion. For instance, in a note to its 1974 financial statements the company expressed the view that ". . . over the remaining term of the program, margins are expected to increase and result in recovery of the initial planning and tooling costs and of unrecovered production costs of previously delivered aircraft and provide a program gross profit," and set forth, in some detail, the reasons why, in its view, that expectation was uncertain.

As of December 31, 1974, 97 aircraft had been delivered. Lockheed's Form 10-K submitted to the SEC stated that "studies indicate a TriStar program of 300 aircraft should recover the December 29, 1974 inventory and provide a gross profit . . . [and that] deliveries in 1975 are expected to be in the range of 25 to 30; in subsequent years of the program, annual production and deliveries are expected in the range of 12 to 14 aircraft."

The last paragraph of the auditor's report relating to the 1974 financial statements read as follows:

> In our opinion, subject to the outcome of the matters described in the second and third preceding paragraphs, the statements mentioned above present fairly the consolidated financial position of Lockheed Aircraft Corporation at December 30, 1973 and December 29, 1974 and the consolidated results of operations and changes in financial position for the years then ended, in conformity with generally accepted accounting principles applied on a consistent basis during the period after restatement of the consolidated financial statements for 1973 to give retroactive effect to the change with which we concur, in the method of accounting for development costs as described in Note 2 to the consolidated financial statements.

The alluded to change is that of conforming with the FASB Statement No. 2, and the referred to "third preceding paragraph" of the report appeared as follows:

> The Company's studies indicate that the carrying value of its L–1011 TriStar inventories will be recovered and that gross profit will be realized over the remainder of the program. As discussed in Note 5, future sales and cost of sales of the L–1011 TriStar program will be affected by a number of factors, the effects of which have been estimated by the company in accounting for the program. We believe these estimates are reasonable; however, because of uncertainties inherent in such estimates, the ultimate impact of the factors referred to above cannot be presently determined.

444

Selected data from Lockheed's 1974 financial statements appear below:

Inventories:		
TriStar related:		
Start-up costs	$549,800,000	
Hard costs	185,300,000	
	$735,100,000	
Other	157,400,000	$ 892,500,000
Total current assets		1,277,700,000
Total assets		1,634,100,000
Total current liabilities		775,900,000
Total liabilities		1,607,600,000
Retained earnings (deficit)		(63,900,000)
Total shareholders' equity		26,500,000
Net earnings for the year		23,200,000

Questions

1. How do you think Lockheed should account for the $549,800,000 initial planning, tooling, and unrecovered production start-up costs?
2. What are the ramifications of the alternative accounting approaches for Lockheed's liquidity, solvency, and profitability?
3. To what extent is your reaction to the issue at hand affected by the (1) quality of Lockheed's recoverability forecasts and (2) the possible effect of its accounting resolution on Lockheed's ability to continue as a going concern?
4. Do you agree with the CPA firm's interpretation of its audit role and responsibility? Explain.

Case 7–1
Boothe Computer Corporation

In 1972 Boothe Computer Corporation reported to the Securities and Exchange Commission (SEC) that, as a result of a disagreement over presentation of its 1971 financial results, its former CPA firm had been replaced by another public accounting firm. This was one of the first disputes involving a major company to be disclosed to the public as the result of an SEC rule requiring corporations in its jurisdiction to report when the reason for a change in auditors was due to disagreements over accounting and auditing matters. The breach between Boothe and its former CPAs related to the audit opinion received relative to its 1971 financial statements. The CPA firm had decided it could not give the company an unqualified opinion, but it was prepared to issue a "subject to" opinion; the new auditor, however, indicated it would provide an unqualified opinion based on the facts available at the time.

Boothe Computer Corporation leased computer equipment to customers, and purchased substantially all of its System 360 equipment from International Business Machines Corporation (IBM). The equipment was shown as an asset on Boothe's balance sheet while it was being rented to lessees. The leases were based on different kinds of contracts which often included provisions that would require Boothe to take the computers back before the cost of the equipment was fully recovered by the rental payments collected to date.

The displaced CPA firm's concern was based on the fact that if existing contracts were to be cancelled, Boothe's rental revenue would decline significantly and the value of its System 360 portfolio would fall to levels below the equipment's depreciated cost basis. Such an outcome was a distinct possibility since IBM was then in the process of marketing a new series, the System 370, which would be more powerful and possess many more capabilities. The prior independent auditors, therefore, maintained that the new series of equipment raised uncertainties whether Boothe would be able to recover its substantial investment in the System 360 equipment. Since these CPAs were unable to measure the potential write-down, but yet considered the uncertainty to be very important, they planned to issue an audit opinion saying the statements were presented fairly subject to the effect of the outcome— which cannot now be determined—of future events with respect to rental revenues the computer equipment will produce.

Boothe's officers vehemently disagreed with the CPAs' position and even denied there were important uncertainties about the company's future. Boothe maintained that even if one were to assume decreased rental demand for its equipment arising from the new computer models, sufficient revenues based on the facts then available would be generated to recover the company's investment in its System 360 portfolio. And since the decision regarding the recoverability of its investment was judgmental in nature, Boothe and its former CPA firm severed their long-time relationship in a professional manner.

In 1973, the successor independent auditors issued a qualified audit opinion on Boothe's 1972 financial results. The qualification was based on Boothe's ability to recover the investment in its System 360 equipment as well as its ability to maintain adequate financing. The company's net loss in 1972 amounted to $37,700,000 from continuing operations primarily due to a $34,300,000 increase in its depreciation charge for the year, an increase

446

that was recorded in order to reduce the book value of its computer equipment. And since the 1972 loss reduced Boothe's owners' equity, agreements were made with major private lenders that provided, in part, for the waiver through January 31, 1974, of defaults based on the reduced owners' equity. In consideration for the agreements, equipment having a book value of $88,600,000 was pledged as collateral, and certain cash restrictions were imposed as well.

Two of Boothe's largest competitors in leasing IBM System 360 equipment were Leasco Corporation and Greyhound Corporation. All three companies had rental equipment as of the end of 1972 whose original cost was around a quarter of a billion dollars, and which generated revenues during 1972 of about $50,000,000. All three companies recognized depreciation expense on a straight-line basis with an expected useful life of ten years. Whereas Boothe's computer leasing constituted more than 80 percent of its total revenues, its two competitors' computer leasing activity represented a significantly smaller percentage of their revenues. Leasco's and Greyhound's annual reports also cited the potential impact of the newer System 370 on the revenue-generating potential of the System 360 equipment to which they had made a significant investment commitment. And although both companies acknowledged the likelihood of experiencing reduced income from their respective leasing operations, neither company characterized its circumstances in as drastic a manner as that which was presented by Boothe. All three companies engaged the same firm of CPAs, and both Leasco and Greyhound received unqualified audit opinions.

Questions

1. Is a "subject to" opinion in effect a disclaimer of opinion?
2. Boothe Computer's 1972 letter to the SEC emphasized the notion of "based on the facts known today" while the displaced auditors' letter to the SEC referred to "the accuracy of forecasted future results." What are the relative merits of using each of these criteria?
3. Did the auditor's qualified opinion on the 1972 financial statements result from the manner in which Boothe effected the reduction of its computer portfolio, i.e., through an additional depreciation charge? Is this an acceptable or desirable means of effecting an intended reduction?
4. Other than the matter of the "recoverability of the cost of some or all of a company's assets," what are the other types of accounting and auditing disagreements that might be the basis for the termination of an auditor-client relationship?
5. In September, 1977, the SEC proposed that companies should (1) state their reasons for switching to a new auditor rather than only stating

whether there was any disagreement, and (2) state whether auditor changes were approved or disapproved by their audit committees or, in the absence of an audit committee, by their full boards. What are the relative merits of such a proposal, and what other aspects of an auditor-client relationship should be disclosed?

Case 7–2
Unifashion, Ltd.*

The board of directors of Unifashion, Ltd. recently made a major policy decision, namely, that the apparel manufacturer would shift its emphasis in marketing from basic, or simply constructed garments, to fashion oriented garments. In a fashion garment, elements of style, body construction, and color are paramount whereas in a basic garment, style, construction, and color are more uniform.

The change had a profound effect on the manufacturing operation. When the company was involved in the manufacture of basic garments, efficiencies were obtained through long production runs and simplicity of body construction. This enabled each sewing machine operator to perform a few of the many operations involved in the manufacture of the garment on an assembly-line basis. In a fashion business, however, there were many more and different styles which generally do not lend themselves to long production runs; therefore, it became imperative for the operators to develop the necessary skills to perform many different operations rather than the few previously performed on a repetitive basis.

To develop these skills meant that substantial sums of money would have to be expended in a retraining effort since the operators, who were paid on a piece-rate basis, would have to be paid at their average earnings rate during their period of training, despite the fact they would not be producing finished garments at that rate.

Management did not believe it could successfully enter the fashion market if it had to include the entire amount of retraining expenses in inventory standard costs, and price garments on that basis. If, on the other hand, these retraining costs were not included in the standard cost of the fashion garments, then the company would have to absorb the entire cost of this entry into a new market in one year since it was the company's policy to charge or

* Adapted from: R. K. Mautz, *Effect of Circumstances on the Application of Accounting Principles* (New York: Financial Executives Research Foundation, 1972), pp. 70–71.

credit to expense any variations between manufacturing standards and actual costs of production. It was not deemed prudent, however, to burden that year's production with a cost which would produce little benefit in that year, but could produce substantial benefits in future years.

The decision was made, therefore, to capitalize retraining costs and to amortize them over a period of three years. The three-year period was used since it approximated the company's employee turnover experience, and it was believed that amounts expended for retraining in the first year would have value as long as the employees who had been retrained were still in the employ of the company.

Questions

1. What are the recurring types of circumstances that cause a company to adopt a "policy to charge or credit to expense any variations between manufacturing standards and actual costs of production?"
2. Is the expenditure made by Unifashion for retraining a capitalizable cost?
3. Given that Unifashion had proceeded to treat the expenditure as the purchase of an asset, evaluate the propriety of the amortization approach it proposed to use.
4. Identify other types of "managerial accounting" nuances which can affect a company's approach to its financial accounting and reporting responsibilities.

Case 7–3
Atlanta Falcons

In 1974 the Atlanta Falcons professional football team was engaged in an income tax refund suit which had the potential of affecting the market value of professional teams in all sports. The lawsuit pertained to the tax shelters available to owners of professional athletic teams. In 1966 the Falcons paid $8,500,000 to join the National Football League, and the resulting litigation was to determine if the amount paid could be written off for tax purposes. A victory for the government could have far reaching effects on professional sports since it would make league expansion and development riskier and potentially less lucrative.

Among the witnesses involved in the trial were experts testifying as to the dollar value of "superstars" and average football players. The main issue in dispute was the basis for allocating the $8.5 million between the franchise itself and the portion applicable to the 42 players who were selected from other teams in the league's expansion draft. Five Smiths Inc., the team's corporate owner, treated $50,000 as the franchise payment, and most of the remainder, approximately $7.7 million, as payment for the players' contracts.

The key issue was "allocation" since the franchise right could not be depreciated because of its indefinite useful life. "Depreciating" players' contracts had begun in baseball where such contracts are bought and sold for cash, a practice that now pervades all professional team sports.

Five Smiths assigned a useful life of 5¼ years, resulting in a $1.5 million deduction in each tax year. The first two years' resulting losses were $506,000 and $581,000 respectively. "Cash flow" was about $1,000,000 each year. The owners of Five Smiths were able to use these losses to offset profits from their other interests.

The Internal Revenue Service had determined the value of the player contracts to be $1,000,000, thus disallowing $1,300,000 of the $1,500,000 deduction. However, the government subsequently decided that none of the $8.5 million was depreciable. The government argued that Five Smiths joined an exclusive class acquiring a number of substantial and valuable monopoly rights forming a single mass asset with an indefinite life. It pointed out that only 23 of the 42 players eventually played for the team, and that many of the 19 unsuccessful players' contracts were sold for the nominal $100 waiver price. Furthermore, it argued that the $50,000 value for the franchise was unreasonable if only because the Falcon's share of the league's network television revenue would be $1,200,000 per year.

The defendant, in turn, claimed that $1.4 million of the $8.5 million should be allocated to television rights, and that it be depreciated on that basis. The government countered that television rights have an indefinite life and are therefore not depreciable. The defendant also sought to present evidence that the $201,000 assigned to each player was reasonable.

Questions

1. What service-potential benefits did the owners of the Falcons acquire via the franchise purchase?
2. Is the cost of obtaining a franchise to operate a team as part of a professional sports league an amortizable asset?

3. How would accrual accounting be applied to the case of a team signing an athlete to a seven-year, no-cut contract
   a. with a substantial front-end bonus payment as well as provision for salary payments to be disbursed ratably over a 20-year period, and
   b. for the player's own career development, he will for the first two years of his contract perform for a (minor league) farm team owned and operated by the (parent) team?
4. What are the monetary costs and monetary benefits attributable to human resources in enterprises other than professional sports organizations?
5. How are manufacturing-oriented concepts such as capital budgeting and standard costs applicable to accounting for human resources?
6. What "asset" characteristics would have to be present to justify balance sheet recognition of human resources?
7. Since salaries and wages are the means with which a person's services are "acquired," what are the relative merits of imputing "human asset" values on the basis of such remuneration, and what are the problems?

Case 8–1
Pacific Northwest Bell Telephone Company

During August 1978, the market for debt securities—the bond market—experienced a decreasing supply of new corporate issuances. Only $1,000,000,000 of fresh company bonds were scheduled for sale in August, a relatively low amount compared to both the $2,100,000,000 sold in the previous month and the monthly average of $1,500,000,000 for the first seven months of 1978.

Since the lack of supply had been generating an increase in bond prices, it was expected a new $150,000,000 issue of Pacific Northwest Bell Telephone Company bonds would be priced to yield 8.9 percent or less, which was considerably less than what had been the prevailing rate of 9.05 percent for similarly high-rated bonds issued by other American Telephone & Telegraph Co. subsidiaries during the preceding week. There were no newly issued bonds available, a distinctly different situation from the usual case of an undistributed "inventory" approximating $80,000,000.

As it turned out, Pacific Northwest Bell's 40-year debenture bonds were issued to yield 8.75 percent.

Questions

1. What are the causes and effects of "a decreasing supply of new corporate bonds?"
2. In what sense could a decreasing supply of new corporate bonds result in very expensive terms, that is, which terms and expensive for whom?
3. If the debentures in question had yielded the same 9.05 percent available on comparable bonds issued a week earlier, what would its accounting ramifications have been?
4. In the case at hand, what individual effects, if any, resulted from the bonds' (1) credit rating, (2) pre-printed 8¾ percent coupon rate, and (3) 40 year life?
5. What post-issuance activity in the bond market would create an incentive for an early extinguishment of outstanding debt securities?

Case 8–2
Baystate Corporation*

On January 1, 1980 Baystate Corporation issued for $1,106,775 its 20-year, 8 percent bonds, which have a maturity value of $1,000,000 and pay interest semiannually on January 1 and July 1. Bond issue costs were not material in amount. The following are three presentations of the long-term liability section of the balance sheet that might be used for these bonds at the issue date:

1. Bonds payable (maturing January 1, 2000)	$1,000,000
Unamortized premium on bonds payable	106,775
Total bond liability	**$1,106,775**

---

* AICPA adapted.

2. Bonds payable—principal (face value $1,000,000, maturing January 1, 2000)	$ 252,572*
Bonds payable—interest (semiannual payment $40,000)	854,203†
Total bond liability	**$1,106,775**
3. Bonds payable—principal (maturing January 1, 2000)	$1,000,000
Bonds payable—interest ($40,000 per period for 40 periods)	1,600,000
Total bond liability	**$2,600,000**

* The present value of $1,000,000 due at the end of 40 (six-month) periods at the yield rate of 3½% per period.

† The present value of $40,000 per period for 40 (six-month) periods at the yield rate of 3½% per period.

Questions

1. Explain why investors would pay $1,106,775 for bonds which have a maturity value of only $1,000,000.
2. Discuss the conceptual merit(s) of each of the date-of-issue balance sheet presentations shown above for these bonds.
3. Assuming that a discount rate is needed to compute the carrying value of the obligations arising from a bond issue at any date during the life of the bonds, discuss the conceptual merit(s) of using for this purpose:
   a. The coupon (nominal) rate.
   b. The effective (yield) rate at date of issue.
4. If the obligations arising from these bonds are to be carried at their present value computed by means of the current market rate of interest, how would the bond valuation at dates subsequent to the date of issue be affected by an increase or a decrease in the market rate of interest?

Case 8–3
L. C. Limited

L. C. Limited was a specialty manufacturing company that was founded in 1947 by members of the Logan and Cook families. It produced components for television sets and phonograph equipment, and by 1979 its annual sales had reached $19,000,000. Its voting common stock was owned by 38 persons with no individual holding more than 10 percent. The corporation's preferred stock was owned by employees, customers, suppliers, and some of its common stockholders. L. C.'s CPA firm had been issuing an unqualified audit opinion for 22 consecutive years.

At L. C.'s 1980 stockholders' meeting, the question of "going public" was raised and several issues having accounting and financial reporting consequences were included in the discussion that followed. One issue related to establishing the company's aggregate and per-share values. Another matter discussed was that of the implications of the "conservative" nature of L. C.'s accounting policies. The third issue discussed dealt with the company's plans to expand by opening a new plant in the town of Brookville. The decision to operate at this particular location was significantly affected by an inducement provided by the municipality's government. L. C. would be given outright ownership of a recently abandoned factory complex for the nominal cost of $100. The company in turn would be committed to creating 200 new jobs of which a minimum of 50 percent were to be filled by the local citizenry. The property's value was appraised to be $1,200,000, 90 percent of which was associated with the building whose expected useful life was estimated to be 40 years; L. C. estimated, however, that it would incur costs of about $200,000 to renovate the building.

The December 31, 1979 balance sheet of L. C. Limited was as follows:

Cash	$ 45,000	Current liabilities	$ 112,000
Receivables	211,000	Mortgage payable	428,000
Inventory	368,000	Convertible debt	300,000
Building	800,000	Preferred stock (@ $1)	120,000
Machinery	972,000	Common stock (@ $10)	100,000
Accumulated		Capital in excess of par	119,000
depreciation	(419,000)	Retained earnings	798,000
Total assets	**$1,977,000**	**Total equities**	**$1,977,000**

Questions

1. What is the book value of the company's assets and what is the book value per share of common stock?
2. What is the significance of these book value amounts and what are and should be their financial reporting disclosure requirements?
3. What is a reserve, and what kinds of reserves if any are permitted by existing accounting rules?
4. What are secret reserves, and what effect do they have on a company's financial statements?
5. What effect if any would ownership of the Brookville factory complex have on the company's financial statements during the ensuing 40 years?

Case 9–1
Drake Industries, Inc.

During the latter part of December, the board of directors of Drake Industries, Inc. was in the process of deciding what course of action to pursue with respect to a prospective merger with the Robin Carpet Company. Negotiations between the two companies' officers had been amiable, and both groups were prepared to proceed. The one issue still in need of resolution was that of the consideration to be given to Robin's stockholders. The fiscal year of both companies corresponded to the calendar year, and the merger was to be consummated on December 31.

One approach would be for Drake to give Robin's stockholders cash in the amount of $10,000,000; the alternative plan would require Drake to issue 800,000 of its $2 par value shares. In either case, Drake would receive in exchange all of Robin's 1,000,000 outstanding shares. An appraisal of Robin's assets indicated that the current value of its inventory was $24,000,000 while that of its land was $16,000,000. Other than the matter of the nature of the consideration to be exchanged, the Drake/Robin combination would qualify for treatment as a pooling of interests.

Combination Date Balance Sheets
(in thousands)

	Drake	Robin
Cash	$110,000	$ 3,000
Receivables	20,000	7,000
Inventory	30,000	19,000
Current assets	$160,000	$29,000
Land	40,000	6,000
Total	**$200,000**	**$35,000**
Payables	$120,000	$26,000
Common stock	$ 4,000	$ 4,000
Capital in excess of par value	1,000	1,000
Retained earnings	75,000	4,000
Owners' equity	$ 80,000	$ 9,000
Total	**$200,000**	**$35,000**
Additional data		
Earnings per share	$ 2.50	$2.25
Market value per share	$15.00	$9.50

Questions

1. What are the ramifications for the combined enterprise's combination-date balance sheet and for its year-of-combination earnings per share under pooling of interests and purchase accounting, respectively?
2. How would your answer to the previous question be affected by each of the following different assumptions, which are to be treated independently?
   a. Instead of "land," Robin's plant asset was machinery whose remaining depreciable life is estimated to be 8 years.
   b. In lieu of exchanging cash or stock, Drake would issue convertible debentures.
   c. The cash payment would be $7,000,000, rather than $10,000,000.
   d. The appraised value of the inventory and land had been $10,000,000 and $12,000,000 respectively.
   e. Robin's earnings per share for the year was $1.75, rather than $2.25.
   f. The market value per share of Drake's shares had been $17 instead of $15.
   g. The par value per share of Drake's shares had been $8 instead of $2.
3. Which accounting method would you as a stockholder in the Robin Carpet Company prefer? Why?

Case 9–2
Vincent Enterprises, Ltd.

Vincent Enterprises, Ltd. was in the process of effecting a business combination with Summer Stores, Inc. The officers of both companies were determined to structure the exchange transaction in such a manner to assure accounting recognition as a pooling of interests. Although these officers did not understand what a pooling of interests was either conceptually or at a practical level, they knew it required compliance with a series of definitive conditions and that its use would be beneficial to all parties concerned. Vincent and Summer had 60,000 and 20,000 shares of voting common stock outstanding respectively; Vincent proposed to acquire all of Summer's shares in exchange for 8,000 of its shares.

A joint committee was given the responsibility to consider the various factors which could affect the companies' ability to qualify for the pooling of interests method. In recognition of the likelihood the Vincent/Summer combination would be the first of many similar transactions in the future, the committee decided to also address itself to possible circumstances which may not actually have been relevant to the present situation, but whose clarification would enhance the officers' general understanding of the pertinent issues.

The committee proceeded to identify 8 different situations which were likely to arise in either the Vincent/Summer merger or in one of the succeeding combinations. To facilitate the discussion among themselves and possibly with an outside expert, the committee decided to designate Vincent and Summer in each case as the combinor and combinee companies respectively. The eight sets of mutually exclusive circumstances are set forth below.

a. Summer had been Vincent's less-than-wholly-owned subsidiary until 16 months ago at which time Vincent sold all of its Summer shares in the secondary securities market.

b. Summer had owned 5,000 Vincent shares for several years prior to the proposed combination.

c. Vincent did not plan to dissolve Summer; instead Summer would continue to exist as an autonomous legal entity such that Vincent would be the parent company and Summer would be its subsidiary.

d. Vincent would acquire 78 percent of Summer's shares today, and the remaining shares 2½ years hence—both through the exchange of its voting common shares.

e. All except 3 Summer stockholders are willing to exchange their shares for those of Vincent. The 3 dissidents held a total of 1,600 Summer shares, and indicated that they would part with these shares only for cash.

f. To effect the combination, Vincent would issue to Summer stockholders a new class of common stock—having the same voting rights as its original common shares, the only variation being that in the event of dissolution, holders of the new issue would receive an amount equal to the shares' par value plus a liquidation premium.

g. Although Summer's stockholders would own only 11.8 percent of the combined enterprise's outstanding shares, Summer's assets and sales would constitute approximately 20 percent and 30 percent respectively of those of the combined enterprise.

h. The par value of Vincent's and Summer's shares were $10 and $1 respectively, and neither company had "capital in excess of par value"—thus precluding all of Summer's $82,000 retained earnings being carried forward to the balance sheet of the combined enterprise.

Questions

1. What are the benefits—and costs—of having a business combination qualify for "pooling of interests" accounting recognition?

2. Irrespective of the official rules that may now be in effect, state whether

you believe "pooling of interests" is or is not a valid accounting method. Why?

3. Given that "pooling of interests" is mandated as being an acceptable accounting method, what criteria do you believe should be met in order for a business combination to qualify for "pooling" treatment (irrespective of the actual criteria that are now in effect)?

4. Assume you are the outside expert engaged by the joint committee of Vincent's and Summer's officers; state your opinion in light of existing rules as to how each of the eight mutually exclusively situations would affect the combined enterprise's ability to use the "pooling of interests" method.

Case 9–3
Atlantic Richfield Company

The February 13, 1978 issue of *Barrons,* in an article entitled "Copper Bulls," contained the following observation about the Atlantic Richfield Company (ARCO).

> ARCO reported that its newly acquired Anaconda unit made a pre-tax contribution of $88 million "based on acquisition cost" in 1977. Anaconda was acquired for 60 percent of its book value. Atlantic Richfield is amortizing in excess of $550 million, the difference between what it paid for Anaconda and the latter's stated book, and a good chunk of this is being amortized over a five-year stretch against Anaconda's mineral interests. This treatment of "negative good will" generates "earnings" but, of course, no cash flow.

Atlantic Richfield's 1977 Annual Report contained the following paragraph in its "financial review" section:

> The (Atlantic Richfield) Company completed a major step toward its goal of diversification into other mineral resources by acquiring The Anaconda Company on January 12, 1977. Atlantic Richfield issued approximately eight million shares of common stock valued at $420 million plus $260 million in cash to acquire this major copper, aluminum and uranium producer. The recording of the Anaconda purchase in Atlantic Richfield's accounts reflects the economic value of the entity acquired as determined by the arms-length acquisition. Atlantic Richfield's total investment was allocated to the various operating

segments on the basis of the present value of the expected future earnings of those operations. In addition, inventories and land were recorded based on current values while all known liabilities and commitments, such as unfunded vested pension benefits, were recognized.

The company's comparative Consolidated Balance Sheets included among its December 31, 1976 "Investments and Long Term Receivables" the following item:

Affiliated companies accounted for on the equity method:
The Anaconda Company   S274,292,000

In its Statement of Changes in Capital Accounts, the following account increases were reported for 1977:

Common stock:
    Acquisition of Anaconda $ 40,483,000
Capital in excess of par value of stock:
    Acquisition of Anaconda $380,545,000

The company's Consolidated Statement of Changes in Financial Position 1977 and 1976 listed the following item as an "Application" of working capital:

	1977	1976
Consolidation of The Anaconda Company:		
Net property, plant, and equipment	$590,370,000	
Long term debt	(394,223,000)	
Investment in The Anaconda Company	(274,292,000)	268,661,000
Other (net)	(13,166,000)	

In addition, in an analysis of changes in working capital, it was indicated that in 1977 working capital acquired from Anaconda was $610,119,000.

Footnote 17 to its financial statements was entitled, "Merger With The Anaconda Company," and it stated the following:

On January 12, 1977, The Anaconda Company was merged into a wholly owned subsidiary of the Company. The merger was accounted for as a purchase. Atlantic Richfield's equity in the net assets of Anaconda exceeded its investment of approximately $700,000,000 by approximately $530,000,000. This excess was allocated to Anaconda assets acquired and liabilities assumed and resulted in lower costs, principally depreciation of Anaconda assets.

Prior year condensed financial information of Anaconda (thousands of dollars):

	1976
Net current assets	$ 377,009
Property, plant and equipment—net	1,144,675
Long term debt and capitalized lease obligations	(502,006)
Other noncurrent assets—net	196,256
Net assets	$1,215,934
Sales	$1,481,143
Net income	$ 16,703

Pro forma combined results of operations excluding purchase accounting adjustments of Atlantic Richfield and Anaconda for 1976 as though the acquisition had taken place on January 1, 1976 are as follows (thousands of dollars except per share data):

	1976
Combined sales and operating revenue	$10,398,430
Combined net income	581,611
Earned per share	4.77

ARCO's 1977 Form 10–K disclosure of its combination with Anaconda provided an expanded version of the first paragraph of footnote 17 that had appeared in its Annual Report (while the second paragraph was identical) as follows.

On January 12, 1977, the Anaconda Company was merged into a wholly owned subsidiary of the Company pursuant to a Plan and Agreement of Reorganization dated July 26, 1976. In connection with the merger Atlantic Richfield issued approximately 8,085,000 shares of common stock valued at approximately $420,407,000 and paid approximately $97,000,000 in cash. Atlantic Richfield had previously acquired on March 31, 1976, 27 percent of Anaconda common stock in a cash tender offer for approximately $167,000,000. On July 1, 1976, Atlantic Richfield purchased $100,000,000 principal amount of Anaconda 8 percent conditionally convertible debentures.

The merger was accounted for as a purchase. Atlantic Richfield's equity in the net assets of Anaconda exceeded its investment of approximately $700,000,000 by approximately $530,000,000. This excess was allocated to Anaconda assets acquired and liabilities assumed and resulted in lower costs, principally depreciation of Anaconda assets.

Atlantic Richfield's Consolidated Statement of Income for 1976 includes its 27 percent interest in Anaconda's earnings from April 1, 1976 amounting to $8,337,000. During 1976 Atlantic Richfield received approximately $2,700,000 in dividends from Anaconda.

Questions

1. Why do you think the previous stockholders of Anaconda were willing to accept an amount that was significantly less than their company's indicated owners' equity?

2. What are the component elements of the "approximately $700,000,000" investment cost referred to in Footnote 17?
3. How did Atlantic Richfield account for the difference between its investment cost and the net assets acquired?
4. Was there "negative goodwill": How and where should its presence be disclosed?
5. Reconcile Anaconda's net current assets $377,009,000 amount that appears in Footnote 17 with the $610,119,000 figure included in the addendum to Atlantic Richfield's consolidated statement of changes in financial position.
6. What is the significance of the $88,000,000 pre-tax contribution of Anaconda cited in the *Barron's* article?

Case 10–1
Stateside Chemical Corporation*

Stateside Chemical Corporation acquired all the outstanding common stock of Morgan Minerals, Ltd.; the acquisition was effected on July 1, 1979. As consideration for the purchase, Stateside gave the stockholders of Morgan $550,000 of cash and 500,000 shares of its previously unissued common stock in exchange for all of the outstanding stock of Morgan Minerals. Stateside's stock had a $1 par value per share and a quoted market value of $2.50 per share both before and after the acquisition of Morgan. Both companies' fiscal years corresponded to the calendar year.

---

* AICPA adapted.

The balance sheet of Morgan Minerals as of June 30 was as follows:

Assets

Current assets:

Cash		$120,000	
Accounts receivable		240,000	
Inventories		210,000	$ 570,000

	Cost	Allow-ance for Depre-ciation	Book Value	
Fixed assets:				
Property A	$ 310,000	$160,000	$150,000	
Property B	370,000	170,000	200,000	
Property C	480,000	180,000	300,000	
Property D	250,000	150,000	100,000	
	$1,410,000	$660,000	$750,000	$ 750,000
				$1,320,000

Equities

Accounts payable		$ 470,000
Stockholders' equity:		
Common stock—authorized and outstanding:		
500,000 shares of $1.00 par value	$500,000	
Capital in excess of par value	100,000	
Retained earnings	250,000	850,000
		$1,320,000

All receivables were considered collectible. Inventories were stated at cost, which was also equivalent to replacement cost. Properties B, C, and D were appraised at $600,000, $800,000, and $200,000, respectively. An engineer of the Stateside Corporation estimated the properties of Morgan Minerals would have a ten-year useful life from July 1, 1979, with no salvage value at the end of that period. Both companies used the straight-line method of depreciating their assets. On July 3, 1979, Morgan's Property A was sold for $500,000.

For the six months ended December 31, 1979, Morgan reported net income of $450,000, which included the gain from the sale of Property A, and depreciation of $55,000. Morgan's balance sheet as of December 31, 1979 was as follows:

Assets

Current assets:
Cash		$390,000	
Accounts receivable		355,000	
Inventories		260,000	$1,005,000

	Cost	Accumu-lated Depre-ciation	Book Value	
Fixed assets:				
Property B	$ 370,000	$188,500	$181,500	
Property C	480,000	204,000	276,000	
Property D	250,000	162,500	87,500	
	$1,100,000	$555,000	$545,000	545,000
				$1,550,000

Equities

Accounts payable			$ 250,000
Stockholders' equity:			
Common stock		$500,000	
Capital in excess of par value		100,000	
Retained earnings		700,000	1,300,000
			$1,550,000

Questions

1. What alternative acccounting measurement and financial reporting avenues are available to Stateside with respect to its July 1, 1979 transaction, what are their respective ramifications, and which course of action do you recommend be adopted?
2. What accounting basis (dollar amounts) should Stateside assign to Properties A, B, C, and D?
3. How should Stateside account for Morgan's income earned between July 1, 1979 and December 31, 1979?
4. What differences in circumstances would have to exist to necessitate accounting for goodwill or for negative goodwill?
5. What accounting recognition of the June 30, 1979 transaction should be made by Morgan?

The Hertz Corporation, its subsidiaries, and independent licensees engaged principally in the business of renting and leasing automobiles and trucks to customers in the United States and in many foreign countries. Collectively they operated what Hertz believed was the largest rent-a-car business in the world and the second largest full service truck leasing and renting business in the United States. Hertz and its subsidiaries and licensees collectively operated, during 1977, approximately 185,000 automobiles and trucks, at over 4,300 locations, including service at approximately 1,400 airports in approximately 2,000 cities in the United States and more than 100 other countries. At December 31, 1977 an aggregate of 178,700 automobiles and trucks were operated. Other activities of the company included the rental, lease, and sale of construction and materials handling equipment, leasing of office, and business equipment, and the operation of an airport terminal and hotel services.

Foreign operations accounted for approximately 14 percent of consolidated operating revenues during 1977, and assets related to those operations represented approximately 10 percent of consolidated assets as of December 31, 1977. While foreign operations resulted in losses in the years 1971 through 1974, those operations had been increasingly profitable since 1975, based on implementation of a program which entailed consolidation of locations, more extensive and redirected marketing efforts, and improved fleet utilization.

In accordance with its policy of offering current year or the previous year's model automobiles to its rent-a-car customers, Hertz ordinarily disposed of its rent-a-car fleet after an average period of approximately one year. Automobiles leased to customers were disposed of after the expiration of each lease. In the case of trucks, the period of ownership by Hertz was ordinarily from three to five years for leased trucks and three years for transient rental trucks.

On October 20, 1977, Hertz executed loan agreements (the "Loan Agreements") with ten insurance companies providing for the borrowing by Hertz of an aggregate amount of $50 million, to be represented by 8¾ percent Senior Subordinated Promissory Notes due October 1, 1997 (the "Notes"). Pursuant to such agreements, Hertz borrowed $25 million on October 25, 1977 and $25 million on December 15, 1977, and in each instance, issued Notes to the lenders equal in principal amount to the sums borrowed. The Notes provided that interest on unpaid principal was payable on April 1 and October 1 in each year at the rate of 8¾ percent per annum and that $3.3 million of principal had to be prepaid annually commencing October 1, 1983 through and including October 1, 1996 with the final principal payment of $3.8 million due at maturity on October 1, 1997. The Notes were redeemable at the option of Hertz at their principal amount, plus accrued interest, plus a premium of 8¾ percent of the principal amount redeemed, which premium reduced annually after October 1, 1978, provided that no optional redemption be made prior to October 1, 1987 as part of or in anticipation of a refunding operation by Hertz or an affiliate where the indebtedness incurred in connection with such refunding has either an interest rate or an effective interest cost below 8¾ percent per annum. As of December 31, 1977, $50 million principal amount of the Notes was outstanding.

RCA Corporation, Hertz's parent, charged Hertz for general administrative services. These charges amounted to $2.3 million in 1977, $2 million in 1976 and in 1975, and $1.6 million in 1974 and in 1973. In the normal course of its business, Hertz leased and rented vehicles to RCA and its subsidiaries, and obtained certain communications equipment and services from those corporations. All such leases, rental services, and other charges were at competitive rates.

Hertz and its domestic subsidiaries were included in the consolidated federal income tax return of RCA. Pursuant to an arrangement with RCA, Hertz provided for current and deferred taxes as if it filed a separate consolidated tax return with its domestic subsidiaries; except that if any items were subject to limitations in Hertz's consolidated return calculations, such as foreign tax credits, investment tax credits, capital losses, and net operating losses, such limitations were determined on the basis of the entire RCA consolidated group. To the extent items which would be subject to limitation at Hertz's consolidated return level were not limited in the RCA consolidated return, Hertz received credit for such items.

During the past five years, Hertz paid dividends to RCA as follows (in millions): 1977—$29.4, 1976—$20.5, 1975—$16.0, 1974—$7.0, and 1973—$7.8. It was Hertz's intention to continue to pay dividends to RCA after taking into account Hertz's earnings, capital requirements, and future prospects, retaining such amounts as it deemed appropriate to maintain a proper capital structure. Dividends paid in prior years reflected this policy. Administrative charges made to Hertz, the settlement of tax payments or benefits, and any dividends declared by Hertz to RCA, were settled in cash between Hertz and RCA.

The Hertz Corporation's parent company, RCA Corporation, prepared consolidated financial statements (Exhibits 1, 2, and 3), which included the accounts of RCA Corporation and its majority-owned subsidiaries except for

RCA Credit Corporation and Electron Insurance Company. Selected data from RCA's December 31, 1977 financial statements appear below:

Sales and other revenue	$5,923,400,000
Net profit for year	247,000,000
Retained earnings—end of year	920,500,000
Current assets	2,376,400,000
Current liabilities	1,400,200,000
Total assets	4,351,700,000
Shareholders' equity	1,430,300,000

Exhibit 1

THE HERTZ CORPORATION AND SUBSIDIARIES
1977 Consolidated Statement of Income
(thousands)

Revenues from continuing operations:	
Car rental	$491,273
Truck leasing and rental	256,982
Car leasing	49,807
Construction equipment rental and sales	22,940
Other	16,418
	837,420
Expenses:	
Direct operating	421,741
Depreciation of revenue earning equipment	164,763
Selling, general and administrative	83,865
Interest	38,361
	708,730
Income before income taxes	128,690
Provision for taxes on income	68,690
Net income	**$ 60,000**
Cash dividends	**$ 29,400**

NOTES TO CONSOLIDATED STATEMENT OF INCOME

(a) The Corporation operates in the United States and in foreign countries. The operations within major geographic areas are summarized as follows (in thousands):

Revenues

United States	$ 718,829
Europe	90,349
Other	28,242
Total	$ 837,420

Income Before Income Taxes

United States	$ 111,100
Europe	17,626
Other	(36)
Total	$ 128,690

Total Assets at December 31

United States	$ 936,241
Europe	79,277
Other	28,719
Total	$1,044,237

(b) Depreciation of revenue earning equipment includes the following:

Depreciation of revenue earning equipment	$ 173,225
Less adjustment of depreciation upon disposal of the equipment	(22,700)
Rents paid for vehicles leased	14,238
Total	$ 164,763

(c) The provision for taxes on income consists of the following:

Current:	
Federal	$ 24,387
Foreign	6,731
State and local	6,872
Total	37,990
Deferred:	
Federal	25,804
Foreign	1,896
State and local	3,000
Total	30,700
Total	$ 68,690

Exhibit 2

Consolidated Balance Sheet at December 31, 1977 and Consolidated
Reinvested Earnings for the Year Ended December 31, 1977
(thousands)

Assets

Cash	$ 9,405
Receivables, less allowance for doubtful accounts ($3,132):	117,671
Inventories, at lower of cost or market	7,542
Prepaid expenses and other assets	13,105
Contracts receivable for equipment and vehicles leased, net	93,379
Revenue earning equipment, at cost	
Vehicles	898,786
Less accumulated depreciation	(206,691)
Other equipment	44,490
Less accumulated depreciation	(10,398)
Total revenue earning equipment	726,187
Property, equipment and intangibles at cost	
Land, buildings and leasehold improvements	76,171
Service equipment	49,370
	125,541
Less accumulated depreciation	(52,286)
	73,255
Franchises, concessions and leaseholds, net of amortization	2,656
Cost in excess of net assets of acquired subsidiaries, net of amortization	1,037
Total property, equipment, and intangibles	76,948
	$1,044,237

Liabilities and Shareholder's Equity

Accounts payable	$ 58,571
Accrued salaries and other compensation	10,952
Other accrued liabilities	50,929
Accrued taxes	37,205
Debt	526,064
Public liability and property damage	34,815
Deferred taxes on income, principally related to depreciation	110,300
Commitments and contingencies	
Shareholder's equity:	
Common stock, $1 par value, authorized and issued 1,000 shares	1
Additional capital paid-in	37,697
Reinvested earnings—	
Balance beginning of year	147,103
Net income	60,000
Dividend	(29,400)
Balance end of year	177,703
Total shareholder's equity	215,401
	$1,044,237

Exhibit 3

Consolidated Statement of Changes in Financial Position
Year Ended December 31, 1977
(thousands)

Source of cash:	
Net income	$ 60,000
Expenses not requiring outlay of cash—	
Depreciation of revenue earning equipment	164,763
Depreciation of property and equipment	10,327
Deferred taxes on income	30,700
Total from operations	265,790
Decrease in inventories	547
Increase in public liability and property damage	1,123
Increase in accrued liabilities	951
Increase (decrease) in debt—	
Proceeds from sale of subordinated debt	50,000
Other, net	32,547
Total	350,958

Application of cash:

Investment in revenue earning equipment—	
Purchases	598,717
Less: Net book value of equipment sold	(318,684)
Net increase	280,033
Increase in contracts receivable for equipment and vehicles leased, net	16,762
Additions to property, equipment and intangibles, net	10,869
Increase in receivables	6,428
Increase in prepaid expenses and other assets	385
Decrease in accounts payable	8,563
Decrease in accrued taxes	7,717
Cash dividends	29,400
Total	360,157
Net decrease in cash	**$ 9,199**

Excerpts from
NOTES TO FINANCIAL STATEMENTS

Revenue Earning Equipment—these assets are used in the rental of vehicles and construction equipment, the leasing of automobiles under closed-end leases where the disposition of the vehicles upon termination of the lease is for the account of the Corporation, and the leasing of trucks principally under full service maintenance agreements which provide for a fixed time charge plus a mileage charge. Revenue is recorded when it becomes receivable, and expenses are recorded as incurred. Aggregate minimum future rentals for vehicles leased at December 31, 1977 are receivable approximately as follows (in millions): $155 in 1978, $111 in 1979, $66 in 1980, $35 in 1981, $23 in 1982 and subsequent years. In addition, contingent rentals, primarily based on mileage, are charged under certain leases. These contingent rentals amounted to approximately $68 million and $65 million for the years 1977 and 1976, respectively. Vehicles held for lease at December 31, 1977 amounted to $264 million (net of accumulated depreciation of $122 million).

Depreciation, amortization, maintenance, and retirements—the provisions for depreciation and amortization are computed on a straight line basis over the estimated useful lives of the respective assets, as follows:

Revenue earning equipment:	
Vehicles—	
Automobiles	3 to 4 years
Trucks	3 to 8 years
Other equipment	2 to 15 years
Buildings	20 to 25 years
Leasehold improvements	Term of lease
Service vehicles	3 to 4 years
Other service equipment	2 to 10 years
Franchises, concessions and leaseholds	5 to 20 years
Cost in excess of net assets of acquired subsidiaries	15 to 40 years

470

Depreciation of revenue earning equipment is intended to reduce book value of equipment over the period of use by the Corporation and its subsidiaries to an amount that approximates market value at the date of sale. Upon disposal, the difference between the remaining book values and the net proceeds from sale, due to variances from the original market value estimate, is reflected as an adjustment of depreciation. The Corporation and its subsidiaries follow the practice of charging maintenance and repairs, including the costs of minor replacements, to maintenance expense accounts. Costs of major replacements of units of property are charged to property and equipment accounts and depreciated on the basis indicated above. Gains and losses on dispositions of property and equipment are included in income as realized.

Revenue Earning Equipment and Property and Equipment

The consolidated balances by major classes of revenue earning equipment and property and equipment are as follows:

	December 31, 1977 (in thousands)
Revenue earning equipment—	
Vehicles—	
Automobiles	$497,255
Trucks	401,531
	898,786
Other equipment	44,490
	943,276
Less—Accumulated depreciation	217,089
Total	$726,187
Property and equipment	
Land	$ 6,321
Buildings	12,441
Leasehold improvements	57,409
Service equipment	49,370
	125,541
Less—Accumulated depreciation	52,286
Total	$ 73,255

Debt and Reinvested Earnings:

Debt of the Corporation and its subsidiaries is as follows:

	December 31, 1977 (in thousands)
Revolving credit notes, 1977, 7¾%; 1976, 6%	$ 51,000
Notes payable (including commercial paper in millions: 1977, $95.5; 1976, $72.5), average interest rate: 1977, 6.6%; 1976, 4.8%	115,500
Promissory notes—	
5½%, due 1978 to 1981 in millions:	
$4.5 per year to 1980; $6.5 in 1981	20,000
5¼%, due 1979 to 1985 in millions:	
$2.1 per year to 1982; $3.1 in 1983 and 1984; $1.2 in 1985	15,800
5⅞%, due 1979 to 1985 in millions:	
$4.5 per year to 1981; $5.5 in 1982; $6.5 in 1983; $7.5 in 1984; $2.5 in 1985	35,500
10½%, due 1978 to 1990 in millions:	
$2.4 per year to 1984; $2.7 in 1985; $.6 per year 1986 to 1989; $.5 in 1990	22,400

11¼%, due 1978 to 1990 in millions:	
$3.6 per year to 1984; $3.8 in 1985; $1.5 per year 1986 to 1989; $1.4 in 1990	36,375
Sinking Fund debentures, 8⅞%, due 1982 to 2001 in millions: $2.4 per year 1982 to 2000; $4.4 in 2001	50,000
Subordinated promissory notes—	
Senior 8¾%, due 1983 to 1997 in millions; $3.3 per year to 1996; $3.8 in 1997	50,000
Senior 5½%, due 1979 to 1980 in millions: $1.5 per year	3,000
Junior 5½%, due 1979 to 1983 in millions: $.8 per year to 1982; $2.8 in 1983	6,000
Revolving bank loans (in millions: $19.6), commercial paper (in millions: $9.0), and other debt of subsidiaries, average interest rate: 8.4%	120,489
	$526,064

The aggregate amounts of maturities of debt, in millions, exclusive of revolving credit notes of $51.0 are as follows: 1978, $173.8 (including $144.1 of commercial paper, demand loans, and revolving bank loans of subsidiaries); 1979, $36.2; 1980, $41.6; 1981, $23.0; 1982, $19.5; after 1982, $181.0.

The aggregate of notes payable including commercial paper and revolving bank loans, exclusive of revolving credit notes, on a monthly basis, averaged $129.3 million and $96.5 million during 1977 and 1976, respectively, with a weighted average interest rate of 6.5 percent and 7.1 percent, respectively. The maximum amounts of such borrowings during 1977 and 1976 were $153.5 million and $131.7 million, respectively.

Under the terms of the Revolving Credit Agreement, the Corporation may borrow up to $150 million through April 15, 1981. Any amount then outstanding would be converted into four-year term notes payable in monthly installments. Each note issued under the Revolving Credit Agreement bears interest at a rate per annum equal to the current prime rate of The First National Bank of Chicago from time to time in effect. The Corporation is required to pay an annual commitment fee of ½ percent on any unused portion of the commitment and has agreed to maintain compensating balances equal to 11.7 percent of the total commitment and 10 percent of the outstanding borrowings in excess of $50 million.

In connection with certain borrowings at December 31, 1977, including those under the Revolving Credit Agreement, the Corporation and its subsidiaries were required to maintain compensating balances to a maximum of $17.7 million; unused lines of credit aggregated approximately $257 million at December 31, 1977.

The terms of the Corporation's loan agreements limit the payment of cash dividends. At December 31, 1977, approximately $44.4 million of the consolidated reinvested earnings were free of such limitations.

Debt of subsidiaries includes approximately $83 million, which is secured by contracts receivable for equipment and vehicles leased and mortgaged property.

MANAGEMENT'S DISCUSSION AND ANALYSIS OF THE CONSOLIDATED STATEMENT OF INCOME—1977 versus 1976

Revenues

For the seventh year in a row, the Corporation achieved higher revenues from continuing operations. Such revenues increased to $837.4 million in 1977 from $780.5 million in 1976. The record revenues were achieved despite the fact that the Corporation's car transport service operations, which generated revenues of $31.4 million in 1976, were sold in early 1977 and are not reflected in 1977 revenue (or expense) data. The revenue improvement is primarily attributable to gains in domestic car rental operations, due to greater travel activity.

Expenses

Total expenses increased to $708.7 million in 1977 from $690.5 million in 1976. In analyzing the comparative increase in expenses, consideration must be given to the fact that 1976 included expenses of $30.1 million attributable to the car transport service operations mentioned above, which have been sold. Direct operating costs of all other operations increased due to the higher volume of business, although the rate of increase has been minimized due to operational efficiencies; depreciation of revenue earning equipment increased due to higher prices for new automobiles and trucks, an expanded 1977 fleet and an increase in the number of vehicles leased; selling, general and administrative expense increased primarily due to greater sales promotion activity; and interest expense increased due to the higher debt levels required to finance the Corporation's larger and more expensive fleet.

Income From Continuing Operations Before Income Taxes

Income from continuing operations before income taxes increased to $128.7 million in 1977 from $90.0 million in 1976. This increase resulted from the revenue and expense factors noted above.

Provision For Taxes On Income

The provision for taxes on income in 1977 was $20.9 million higher than 1976, primarily due to increased income on continuing operations before income taxes.

Questions

1. What criteria should a parent company use with respect to whether or not to include particular subsidiaries in its consolidated financial statements?
2. What business reasons can you offer to explain RCA's 100 percent ownership of The Hertz Corporation, and why would the combined companies be operated as a parent-subsidiary relationship?
3. Under what circumstances would the financial statements of RCA's wholly owned subsidiary Hertz Corporation be made available to the general public?
4. Identify specific Hertz data—accounts and amounts—that should be set forth explicitly in the body of RCA's consolidated
   a. balance sheet

473

b. earnings statement

c. statement of changes in financial position

5. What footnote disclosures should RCA make with respect to Hertz?

6. Should RCA disclose the amount of the dividends and the general administrative services fee it received from Hertz?

7. Would Hertz's "rental vehicles" asset qualify for inclusion among RCA's current assets or as part of its "plant and equipment" category?

Case 10–3
Crane Company

Crane Company was engaged in manufacturing and selling fluid and pollution control equipment, building products, and aerospace equipment in the United States and abroad, and in distributing fluid and pollution control building products at wholesale; in the manufacture and sale of steel and steel products; and in the wholesaling and manufacture of sash, door, and millwork products. Crane's products as a whole had primary application in the industrial, construction, and building industries, and as such were dependent upon numerous unpredictable factors including changes in market demand, general economic conditions, residential and commercial building starts, energy exploration, and energy allocations during times of scarcity. 1977 was the fourth consecutive year in which Crane's sales exceeded $1 billion, and as of December 31, 1977 its total assets and shareholders' equity were $837 million and $330 million respectively. Net income in 1977 was $66,171,000, a 38 percent increase over the preceding year's $47,959,000.

The President's and Chairman's letter to Shareholders, which appeared in Crane's 1975 Annual Report, contained the following information.

> During 1975 the Company offered to purchase shares of common stock of The Anaconda Company tendered, up to a maximum of 5,000,000 shares (approximately 22.6 per cent of the outstanding Anaconda common stock). The ratio of exchange is $20.00 principal amount of Crane Co. 8 per cent Subordinated Sinking Fund Debentures due December 1, 1985, for each share of Anaconda common stock tendered. As of December 31, 1975, 3,282,401 shares had been accepted and $65,648,000 principal amount of subordinated debentures had been issued.
>
> The cost of each Anaconda share is the $20.00 principal amount of debentures exchanged, commission of $.80 paid to brokers, and $.20 in other tender offer costs, for a total of $21.00 per common share.

This amount includes $3.60 per share of original issue discount which resulted from the $100 of principal amount of subordinated debentures initially trading at a market price of $82.00, or $18.00 of discount for every five shares of The Anaconda Company. Since December 31, the exchange offer has been extended and 836,679 additional shares have been tendered to date and $16,733,600 additional debentures were issued.

The closing price for a share of Anaconda common stock the day before Crane's August, 1975 announcement of its tender offer, was $15.125.

A footnote appearing in Crane's 1975 Annual Report stated the following:

Long-term debt was increased by $96,907,000 during 1975, principally by the issuance under an exchange offer of 8 percent Subordinated Sinking Fund Debentures due 1985 of $65,648,000 principal amount for The Anaconda Company common stock and by the negotiation of a $30,000,000 unsecured five-year senior term loan. Original issue debt discount of $11,817,000 on the 1985 debentures is included with Investments and Other Assets and is being amortized over the term of this debt.

In March, 1976, Crane completed its tender offer whereby it acquired a (cumulative) total of 4,120,230 shares of Anaconda common stock, comprising approximately 18.7 percent of Anaconda's outstanding shares. A footnote appearing in Crane's 1976 Annual Report disclosed the 1976 ". . . issuance of $16,757,000 of 8 percent Subordinated Sinking Fund Debentures due 1985 in exchange for an additional 837,829 shares . . . (having an) original issue debt discount of $3,016,000."

A related development in March, 1976 was the announcement by the Atlantic Richfield Company (ARCO) that it sought to acquire 6,000,000 shares of Anaconda common stock. ARCO's tender offer, to pay $27 cash per share (a $5 premium above the previous day's closing price) or a total of $162,000,000 was effected later that month, thus giving ARCO a 27 percent equity interest in Anaconda. Soon thereafter, on July 6, 1976, ARCO announced its intent to effect a business combination with Anaconda. ARCO offered to exchange $6 and one-quarter of an ARCO share for each tendered share of Anaconda. Inasmuch as ARCO shares would be experiencing a 2-for-1 stock split payable two months later, the exchange rate would become $6 and one-half of an ARCO share for each tendered Anaconda share. On January 12, 1977, ARCO consummated the business combination; closing stock prices of the two companies were as follows:

	Anaconda	ARCO
July 2, 1976	$29.125	$104.00
January 11, 1977	$29.25	$ 56.625
January 12, 1977	$28.25	$ 54.875
January 13, 1977	$32.375	$ 54.375

Atlantic Richfield market price per share amounts by quarter during 1977 were as follows: First, 50—58.25; Second, 52—62.875; Third, 50—60.75; Fourth, 48.75—54.125.

Crane's 1977 Annual Report contained in the consolidated income statement "Miscellaneous—net" Other Income of $26,441,871. An asterisked footnote reference at the bottom of the page disclosed the following:

> The year 1977 included the following non-recurring transactions:
> a) A cash dividend of $24,721,000, a realized gain of $4,541,000 on 260,115 Atlantic Richfield common shares sold and an unrealized gain of $22,968,000 on 1,800,000 Atlantic Richfield common shares, for a total gain of $52,230,000 as a result of the Atlantic Richfield/Anaconda merger.
> b) A provision of $26,291,000 principally for unfunded pension liabilities for operations being phased out or relocated.
> c) The net income from these transactions was $28,389,000, or $2.78 per share.

Three pertinent footnotes included in Crane's 1977 "Financial Review and Accounting Policies" appeared as follows:

Long-Term Investments

Long-Term Investments are valued, in the aggregate, at the lower of cost or market.

In early 1977 the company exchanged 4,120,230 common shares of The Anaconda Company (cost $71,577,000) for 2,060,115 Atlantic Richfield common shares in a tax-free exchange. As required by Accounting Principles Board Opinion No. 29, the company assigned a market value of $47.50 to each Atlantic Richfield share retained (see . . . "Consolidated Statement of Income"). Overall, 560,115 Atlantic Richfield common shares were sold during 1977.

Details of Long-Term Investments are as follows:

	In Thousands	
	1977	1976
Atlantic Richfield Company 1,500,000 common shares	$71,250	$71,577
Asarco, Inc., 564,000 common shares	8,611	—
Deferred income taxers on unrealized gain—net	(5,125)	—
	$74,736	$71,577

Miscellaneous—Net

	Components (in thousands)	
	1977	*1976*
Non-recurring transactions—net	$25,939	$13,738
Gain on investments—net	4,924	668
Gain (loss) on disposal of capital assets—net	(1,605)	1,880
Minority interest	(1,116)	(1,680)
Loss on foreign exchange adjustments	(1,166)	(1,514)
Loss on repurchase of debentures	(470)	(675)
Other	(64)	(79)
	$26,442	$12,338

Income Taxes (excerpt):

Income taxes on non-recurring transactions were a credit of $2,450,000 for 1977 and a charge of $5,072,000 for 1976.

A relevant paragraph from the President's and Chairman's letter (in the 1977 Annual Report) appeared as follows:

Early in 1977 Crane reported two non-recurring transactions. First, an after-tax gain of $41,570,000 resulted from the Atlantic Richfield/Anaconda merger; second, an after-tax provision of $13,181,000 was provided principally for unfunded pension liabilities relating to operations phased out or relocated. These transactions increased 1977 net income by $28,389,000 of $2.78 per share. In 1976 there were two non-recurring transactions, which increased net income by $8,148,000 or 78 cents per common share.

Selected portions of Crane's 1975, 1976, and 1977 consolidated balance sheets and consolidated statements of changes in financial position appear in Exhibit 1.

Exhibit 1

CRANE COMPANY

	1975	1976	1977
Consolidated Balance Sheet			
Investments and other assets:			
The Anaconda Company, cost of			
common shares	$57,105,259	$71,576,716	—
Atlantic Richfield Company, 1,500,000			
shares			$71,250,000
Unamortized debt discount on			
8% debentures	$11,711,644	$11,375,050	$ 9,002,664
Long-term debt:			
Subordinated debentures:			
8% Sinking fund debentures			
due 1985, 10% due annually			
commencing December 1, 1976	$59,083,200	$65,922,600	$57,682,600
Consolidated Statement of Changes in Financial Position			
Sources of funds:			
Operations:			
Net income	$63,607,793	$47,958,777	$66,171,165
Amortization of debt discount	$ 105,000	$ 3,352,778	$ 2,372,386
Decrease in long-term investments	N/A	N/A	$18,466,716
Application of funds:			
Investment in The Anaconda Company	$57,105,259	$14,471,457	—

Questions

1. Did the manner in which Crane accounted for its acquisition and holding of shares of Anaconda common stock reflect good accounting?
2. Was Crane's accounting for and financial disclosure of its 8 percent sinking fund debentures in conformity with generally accepted accounting principles?
3. What is your assessment of the manner in which Crane accounted for the exchange of Anaconda shares for those of Atlantic Richfield?
4. What disclosures of the pending Anaconda/Atlantic Richfield combination would have been appropriate in Crane's 1976 Annual Report?
5. What changes would you introduce to make Crane's financial disclosures more understandable and responsive to the needs of external parties?

Case 11–1
Zuber Imports, Inc.

Zuber Imports, Inc. was a closely held company engaged in importing manufactured merchandise from the Far East and Western Europe for wholesale and retail sale in the United States. The firm's four officers—Mr. Peace, president; Ms. Queen, executive vice-president; Mr. James, vice-president for sales; and Mr. Jakes, vice president for finance—had assembled for their monthly meeting to discuss, among other things, the company's preliminary year-end financial results. Inasmuch as Zuber Imports had a great deal of potential foreign currency exchange loss exposure and for several years had been in a 4-to-1 debt-to-equity ratio range, the officers' attention was as always focused on possible implications for the company's liquidity. Ever aware of the officers' concern, the chief accountant provided the following "ballpark" data for their consideration.

Earnings Statement

Sales	$54,000,000	
Equity in subsidiary income	5,000,000	
Total		$59,000,000
Cost of goods sold	$34,000,000	
Depreciation	6,500,000	
Income taxes	3,500,000	
Other expenses	14,000,000	
Total		$58,000,000
Net income		**$ 1,000,000**

Selected Balance Sheet Amounts

	January 1	December 31
Cash	$ 1,800,000	$ 2,200,000
Current assets	7,300,000	10,600,000
Total assets	20,000,000	23,000,000
Current liabilities	2,000,000	5,300,000
Total liabilities	16,000,000	18,000,000

One-third of the sales were credit sales, and collections during the year on accounts receivable were $14,000,000. Merchandise inventory decreased during the period by $2,100,000; and accounts payable (trade) and deferred taxes payable increased by $4,400,000 and $1,400,000 respectively. The subsidiary declared no dividends, the company maintained no prepaid ex-

479

pense accounts, and its year-end accruals payable balance was $1,100,000 less than it had been 12 months earlier.

Mr. Peace:	As you know, I always look first at the bottom line, and that million dollar figure looks pretty good to me. After all, it's the first time we've ever hit that magic number.
Ms. Queen:	I don't want to be the party pooper, but when you consider the million dollars in light of our sales, it's less than 2 percent.
Mr. Jakes:	I'd argue that we should look at the million in light of our total assets, and it's a lot less than what could be earned in a savings account.
Mr. Peace:	OK, OK . . . your points are well taken, but let's zero in on our real nemesis, liquidity.
Mr. James:	I can quickly see a deterioration in working capital. In fact, it looks like it's fallen from more than 3-to-1 all the way down to 2-to-1.
Mr. Peace:	But that's no problem, because the universal rule of thumb is that 2-to-1 is a good ratio.
Ms. Queen:	If you want to start talking ratios, it wasn't too many meetings ago when our little group sat around this very same table bemoaning the bad state of the company's debt burden. And someone said that the debt-to-equity ratio was the most effective way of assessing the reasonableness of our debt. So how do we stand with that ratio?
Mr. James:	You're absolutely right. In fact, it appears the ratio is not nearly as bad as it had been this time last year.
Mr. Jakes:	But hold on for a minute, ratio or no ratio, our debt is now $2 million larger than it had been one year ago.
Ms. Queen:	Not to mention there was more than a $3 million increase in current liabilities, and doesn't that mean it will have to be paid off quicker than if it had not been a current liability?
Mr. Peace:	Let's get back to this income statement for a moment. I still can't get over the fact that we finally earned a million dollars.
Ms. Queen:	Be that as it may, do we really have a million dollars more cash to spend?
Mr. James:	I sure don't think so; it looks to me like we've got a half million less cash at year-end, not a full million more.
Mr. Peace:	But you forgot about the depreciation. Cash-flow is what really matters, and you get that by adding depreciation to the income, and that gives us 7½ million bucks.

Mr. James: That doesn't sound right to me.

Mr. Jakes: The fact of the matter is that depreciation did not affect cash this period.

Ms. Queen: So why is it in the income statement in the first place?

Mr. Jakes: It's there because Generally Accepted Accounting Principles say it has to be there.

Mr. Peace: That may be fine for getting a CPA to certify the statements, but it doesn't mean that for our purposes we can't focus our attention on cash-flow; after all, it's cash-flow that makes a business go.

Mr. James: I'm still just not comfortable with that. You can't meet a payroll with depreciation. I just don't see why it's at all relevant.

Mr. Jakes: That's precisely the point. Because it's not relevant we neutralize its existence by adding it to net income, and that gives us cash-flow.

Ms. Queen: Take a look at this income statement again if you will. I notice there is a $5 million item called Equity in Subsidiary Income. If I'm correct in assuming this relates to our investment in that Japanese factory deal, let me then remind you we didn't receive any dividends from them at all this past year. So what bearing does that have on our cash position?

Mr. Jakes: Your point is well-taken; it has no effect whatsoever.

Mr. Peace: So what does that mean?

Mr. James: To me, it would seem to mean it ought to be handled just like depreciation.

Mr. Peace: Well, that's super. It means that cash-flow therefore becomes 1 million plus 6½ million plus 5 million for a grand total of 12½ million.

Mr. Jakes: No, no! It's similar to depreciation, but its effect is in the opposite direction.

Mr. James: Why should that be?

Mr. Jakes: Because it had had an opposite effect on the derivation of net income.

Mr. Peace: So, should we just ignore the 5 million, and say that cash-flow was 7½ million?

Mr. Jakes: I'm afraid not. It means the 5 million should be subtracted from the 7½ million.

Ms. Queen: But that gets us all the way down to 2½ million.

Mr. Peace: I was afraid you were going to say that.

Mr. James: It appears to be right though.

Mr. Queen:	Are we to conclude therefore that our cash-flow was the 2½ million then?
Mr. Peace:	I'd sure like to see the 13½, but somehow the 7½ million seems right to me.
Mr. James:	Frankly, I have trouble with all these adjustments in the first place . . . so I think we ought to live with the million dollar bottom line amount. After all, if our accountant was willing to stop there, why should we be any different?

Questions

1. What was Zuber Imports, Inc.'s cash-flow from operations?
2. Was the company more liquid at year-end than it had been twelve months earlier?
3. How do you reconcile the apparent inconsistencies generated by working capital analysis and debt-to-equity ratio results?
4. What liquidity-oriented disclosures should be included in published financial statements?
5. What rule(s) of thumb would you advise Zuber Imports' officers to use as they assess financial statement data in the future?
6. Are such rules of thumb valid?

Case 11–2
Global Tool Corporation

Global Tool Corporation had throughout its 80-year history always been a closely-held company; the stockholders, however, recently decided the corporation should "go public." As a result, its financial statements would subsequently receive significantly wider distribution. An important ramification of this latter aspect was it therefore became necessary to train a small group of persons to be capable of responding to outside parties' inquiries about Global Tool.

An important phase of the training program was to enable these individuals to answer questions regarding the company's financial accounting policies and practices. Such persons were already knowledgeable about the nature of Global Tool's accounting system as well as familiar with "generally accepted accounting principles." The primary function of this phase of the exercise was to enhance the individuals' ability to articulate the company's financial accounting policies and practices in an informed, coherent, and unambiguous manner.

The training program module dealing with the company's statement of changes in financial position placed particular attention on eight matters which occurred during the previous two years. The eight cases selected for special attention represented items which did not tend to appear on a recurring basis in most corporations' statements of changes in financial position; hence, they were the most likely candidates for inquiries from outside parties.

A brief description of each of the items is reproduced below, and the program participants were instructed to examine each item independently. Each person was to consider each situation in terms of its nature, its effect on the company's funds position, and the manner in which that effect would be disclosed in the statement of changes in financial position.

a. The $114,000,000 increase in the company's Investments in Affiliated Companies balance during the year was attributable to the following factors. $85,100,000 was expended to acquire new equity of which $14,000,000 was effected through the issuance of a 60-month note. A $10,000,000 (carrying value) block was sold for $18,500,000, equity in affiliates' earnings was $49,600,000 (less $1,400,000 amortization of investments' goodwill component), and cash dividends received totaled $9,300,000.

b. During the year, the company wrote off $2,700,000 of its accounts receivable, and at year-end it recognized bad debt expense of $3,100,000.

c. Sales of (plant assets) land and building yielded cash proceeds of $3,500,000, a reduction in the long-term portion of the related mortgages of $867,000 and a gain of $1,600,000.

d. Five years earlier, the company had established a provision amounting to $50,000,000 resulting from a decision to eliminate unproductive elements of its business operations. Charges against this reserve in the current year amounted to $7,250,000.

e. The unexpended portion of $68,000,000 in long-term funds borrowed during the year for plant expansion (being held by a trustee) was $17,000,000 as of year-end.

f. During the year, the company entered into new contracts with several of its key officers. Among other provisions, the new agreements called for minimum salary levels over the next five years, life insurance, and stock options. As a result, the total amount of the company's commitment under the contractual formula was $1,750,000 as of year-end, and it was charged to the year's operations.

g. During the year the company effected two business combinations. In one instance, it issued new shares of stock (par value of $30,000, market value of $4,200,000), and in the other case it tendered treasury shares (par value $10,000, cost basis $675,000, and market value $1,440,000).

h. There were three reasons for the $41,000,000 decrease in the company's long-term debt. $7,000,000 was reclassified as a current liability to reflect that it would mature five months after year-end, $23,000,000 was retired before maturity at a cost of $14,000,000, and there had been no related unamortized issuance premium or discount. An $11,000,000 reduction was attributable to holders of convertible debentures tendering their securities together with $8,200,000 of cash in exchange for shares of the company's common stock (par value of $150,000, market value of $23,000,000).

Questions

1. In light of Global Tool's belief the eight items included in its training module were non-recurring matters, identify those components of the statement of changes in financial position which tend to appear on a regular, ongoing basis.
2. What is the nature of the "all resources" approach to preparing a statement of changes in financial position, what purpose does it serve, and which of the Global Tool situations suggest its applicability?
3. What is the conceptual difference between the "working capital" and the "cash" approaches to preparing a statement of changes in financial position, and what implementational variations between these two approaches would occur in disclosing the eight Global Tool situations?
4. What responses would you prepare for each of the eight items if you were one of the persons participating in the Global Tool training program?

Case 11–3
Centex Corporation

The roots of Centex Corporation, dating back to 1950, were deeply imbedded in the nation's housing industry. The founding philosophy of the Company was to become one of the nation's leading multi-market builders, to be achieved through the development of the company's homebuilding subsidiaries, Fox & Jacobs, Inc. operating in Dallas, Fort Worth and Houston, and Centex Homes Corporation with homebuilding operations in the metropolitan areas of San Francisco, Miami, Chicago, Denver, Washington, D.C., Baltimore, Minneapolis, and in northeastern New Jersey.

Since the early 1960's, Centex, through the operations of its other subsidiaries, branched out into other fields creating a strong base of operations in general construction, cement and related products, and energy resources. The general construction activities included a variety of major construction projects in the public as well as private sector. Office buildings, hospitals, educational facilities, military housing, and wastewater treatment plants were among the primary areas of the company's general construction work. Cement and related products operations included three cement plants; related products included aggregate and readymix operations and the production of concrete pipe, brick, and chemical additives for concrete. Energy resources activities included oil and gas exploration and development in the Southwestern and Southern states of Texas, Oklahoma, Mississippi, Louisiana and the offshore waters of Texas and Louisiana, and the intrastate purchase, transportation, and sale of natural gas. The Company became active in oil and gas operations late in its 1975 fiscal year and since that time substantially expanded its exploration and development activities. Its energy activity also included coal mining and processing to assure an ongoing supply of this energy source to the Company's cement plants and to serve as a base for broadening energy activities.

The Company's revenue for the year ended March 31, 1978 was $645,683,000, net earnings were $29,099,000, and earnings per share was $2.00. Centex's consolidated balance sheets as of March 31, 1978 and 1977 appear as Exhibit 1, and its consolidated statement of changes in financial position for the year ended March 31, 1978 appears as Exhibit 2.

Exhibit 1

CENTEX CORPORATION AND SUBSIDIARIES
Consolidated Balance Sheets

	March 31, (in thousands)	
	1978	*1977*
Assets		
Cash	$ 14,379	$ 19,336
Restricted certificates of deposit	10,305	16,552
Notes and accounts receivable		
Trade receivables	45,446	34,428
Construction contracts	20,108	18,595
Notes and contracts receivable	17,570	16,775
Inventories		
Housing projects	221,428	147,697
Land held for development and sale	112,564	113,426
Cement and related products	7,904	5,631
Oil and gas properties, net	43,830	26,286
Investments in and advances to joint ventures	6,280	6,195
Property and equipment, net	76,213	45,673
Other assets and deferred charges	11,564	7,654
	$587,591	**$458,248**
Liabilities and Stockholders' Equity		
Notes payable	$135,609	$ 78,710
Payables and accruals		
Accounts payable and accrued liabilities	92,133	78,276
Federal income taxes	—	16,815
Long-term debt	149,919	114,658
7% senior subordinated convertible debentures	2,600	3,300
Deferred income taxes	48,258	36,276
Minority stockholders' interest	3,861	1,836
Stockholders' equity		
Common stock, $.25 par value; authorized shares, 25,000,000; issued at March 31, 1978 and 1977, 14,560,205 and 14,554,006, respectively, including 20,000 shares of treasury stock	3,640	3,639
Capital in excess of par value	45,449	45,388
Retained earnings	106,122	79,350
Total stockholders' equity	155,211	128,377
	$587,591	**$458,248**

Exhibit 2

CENTEX CORPORATION AND SUBSIDIARIES
Consolidated Statement of Changes in Financial Position
For the Year Ended March 31, 1978

Source of funds:
Operations
Net earnings $ 29,099
Add (deduct) items not requiring (providing) funds
Depreciation, depletion and amortization 10,173
Equity in earnings of joint ventures and
unconsolidated subsidiary (in excess of) less
than distributions (1,993)
Deferred income taxes 12,897

50,176
Increase in notes payable 56,899
Increase in long-term debt 35,261
Decrease in restricted certificates of deposit 6,247
Decrease in cash 4,957
Increase in minority interests 2,025
Decrease in land held for development and sale 862
Decrease (increase) in investments in and advances to
joint ventures 557
Common stock issued 62
$157,046

Use of funds:
Increase in housing projects $ 73,731
Additions to property and equipment, net 35,964
Increase in oil and gas properties 22,293
Increase (decrease) in receivables 13,326
Decrease in payables and accruals 3,873
Cash dividends 2,327
Increase (decrease) in cement and related products
inventories 2,273
Prepayment on debentures 700
Other changes, net 2,559
$157,046

Selected excerpts from the Notes to the Consolidated Statements are presented below:

A. SIGNIFICANT ACCOUNTING POLICIES

Consolidation

The consolidated financial statements include the accounts of Centex Corporation and subsidiaries (the Company), after the elimination of all significant intercompany balances and transactions. The Company did not consolidate its wholly-owned mortgage company which has financial operations dissimilar to those of the consolidated group. At March 31, 1978, the mortgage company had assets of $20,935,000, primarily receivables for mortgages insured by U.S. government agencies, and liabilities of $18,870,000. Results of operations are not significant. The Company carries its investment in this subsidiary on the equity basis.

Revenue Recognition

Revenue from single-family projects is recognized as homes are completed, required down payments are received and title passes. The balance of the purchase price is received at or shortly after closing. Revenue from sales of condominium units, in projects requiring a construction period of more than nine months, is reported on the percentage-of-completion method. However, no revenue is recognized until 50 percent of the units are sold and 25 percent of estimated construction costs are incurred.

Revenue from long-term construction contracts is recognized on the percentage-of-completion method based on the costs incurred relative to total estimated costs. Full provision is made currently for estimated losses, if any. Billings are rendered monthly on construction contracts, including the amount of retainage withheld by the customer until completion of the contract. As general contractor, similar retainage is withheld from each subcontractor. Retainages of $6,997,000 in construction contracts receivable and $7,391,000 in accounts payable at March 31, 1978, are substantially receivable and payable within one year. General operating and research and development expenses associated with general contracting operations are expensed as incurred. Claims are recognized as income only when an agreement for payment is reached with the customer.

Sales of commercial parcels associated with housing projects are generally made on terms and reported as revenue only when an adequate down payment has been received. Sales of recreational land are reported on the installment method of accounting.

Notes and contracts receivable are collectible over periods extending to approximately fourteen years, with $6,637,000 being due within one year.

Inventory Capitalization and Cost Allocation

Housing projects and land held for development and sale are stated at the lower of cost or market, including capitalized interest and real estate taxes. Direct construction costs together with project and regional overhead are included in the cost of housing projects. Proportionate costs are included in the consolidated statement of earnings as related revenues are recognized.

Interest costs are capitalized in housing projects and land held for development and sale based on actual borrowings from outside lenders. This industry practice appropriately recognizes interest as an integral cost of land development and housing construction. Had the Company continually expensed interest as incurred, net earnings would have been reduced $2,261,000 in 1978 ($.15 per share) and $881,000 in 1977 ($.06 per share).

Inventory of cement and related products is stated at average cost, not in excess of market, which includes material, labor and plant overhead.

C. NOTES PAYABLE, LONG-TERM DEBT AND DEBENTURES
Notes Payable

The Company's notes payable include $121,550,000 and $66,110,000 at March 31, 1978 and 1977 under a $130,000,000 in 1978 and $110,000,000 in 1977 unsecured line of credit extended by several banks to a subsidiary which loans funds to Centex subsidiaries, under certain restrictions, for land acquisition, development and construction. The loan agreement provides, among other things, that (1) the loans shall bear interest at the banks' prime rate, which was 8 percent at March 31, 1978; (2) loans made to subsidiaries shall be secured; and (3) the banks have the right to call for collateral. The line of credit matures each year at June 30 and is subject to renewal and revision at that time.

Long-Term Debt

Long-term lines of credit for $60,500,000 expiring from 1979 to 1982 have been established primarily for land acquisition and development. At March 31, 1978, $50,354,000 of available credit had been borrowed. This and other long-term debt is summarized below.

	March 31, (in thousands)	
	1978	1977
Lines of credit at ¼ to 2% over prime due from 1979 to 1982, collateralized by land, land development and stock of subsidiaries	$ 50,354	$ 41,302
5 to 11% mortgage notes, maturing at various dates to 2001, collateralized by land, land development, property and equipment and certificates of deposit	70,584	35,072
8 to 10½% notes maturing at various dates to 1982, collateralized by oil and gas properties and certificates of deposit	16,103	23,031
5½ to 6.4% mortgage bonds, payable annually to 1981, collateralized by property and equipment	2,660	3,640
6 to 10½% unsecured notes, maturing at various dates to 1987	8,015	8,148
Noninterest bearing unsecured notes, maturing at various dates to 1985	2,203	3,465
	$149,919	$114,658

489

Maturities of long-term debt during the next five years are: 1979—$62,983,000; 1980—$19,693,000; 1981—$13,416,000; 1982—$23,074,000; 1983—$5,468,000. Payments on certain long-term debt may be accelerated as land is released. Weighted average interest rates on long-term debt were 8.4 percent in 1978 and 7.6 percent in 1977.

Debentures

The 7 percent Senior Subordinated Convertible Debentures are convertible into common stock at $16.50 per share. The Company may redeem the debentures in whole or in part at face value. Semi-annual principal prepayments of $350,000 are required.

Arrangements and Restrictions

In connection with the lines of credit described above, the Company has informal arrangements with the banks for maintenance of defined average compensating balances. During 1978 and 1977, the average balances maintained were approximately $18,100,000 and $15,500,000, not including funds for uncleared transactions. The Company has complied with these informal arrangements.

Under the most restrictive covenants of the debt agreements, the Company is prohibited from, among other things, (1) declaring or paying annual cash dividends in excess of 25 percent of the prior year's consolidated net income or 25 percent of the preceding four quarters' net income, (2) allowing consolidated tangible stockholders' equity and subordinated debt, as defined, at any time to be less than $100,000,000, and (3) making purchases, redemptions or other acquisitions of any shares of the Company's common stock. The Company has obtained the necessary waivers of the restrictive covenants which would prohibit the purchase of its stock from the Murchison interests as described in footnote (J).

Questions

1. Was Centex Corporation more, less, or equally liquid as of March 31, 1978 in comparison to its position one year earlier?
2. In light of Centex's statement of changes in financial position's use of the expressions "source of funds" and "use of funds," what do you perceive to be the company's definition of "funds?"
3. Recast Centex Corporation's statement of changes in financial position using the format most frequently encountered in corporate annual reports.
4. What factors might explain the reason for Centex's distinctive approach to reporting its changes in financial position?
5. Are the terms "funds flow statement" and "statement of changes in financial position" synonymous? Which of these (or some other) should be the preferred approach?

Case 12–1
Nonmon, Inc.

On January 1, 19x1 Nonmon, Inc. was created. Shares of common stock were issued that same day for cash. $20,000 of these proceeds was used immediately to purchase land. Nearly four years later, on December 31, 19x4, the land was sold for $18,500.

The company's fiscal year corresponded to the calendar year, and at each year-end the land's current value was determined by a professional appraiser, as follows:

December 31, 19x1	$22,000
December 31, 19x2	$23,000
December 31, 19x3	$18,000

Once the land was sold, some the company's officers expressed the view that the effect on each of the intervening four years of these changes in value should be reflected in financial statements prepared on a pro forma basis.

However, when the officers contemplated the matter further, they realized that general economy-wide price changes had also been occurring during the four-year period. As a result, they believed it would not be at all purposeful to proceed with their plan. In particular, they became concerned when the published general price level index numbers were collected and plotted, as follows.

	Index Number	Percentage Change
January 1, 19x1	110	
December 31, 19x1	132	(22 ÷ 110 =) 20% increase
December 31, 19x2	99	(33 ÷ 132 =) 25% decrease
December 31, 19x3	121	(22 ÷ 99 =) 22% increase
December 31, 19x4	100	(21 ÷ 121 =) 17% decrease

The concern was especially evident with respect to 19x2 and 19x4 when the appraised value of the land increased despite a decrease in the general price level, and in 19x3 when the land's appraised value declined while there was a concurrent increase in the general price level. Nonmon's officers suspected that it would be useful to see what interactive effects if any might be imputed.

As the officers probed further into the data's various nuances, they became more and more uncertain as to the merit of their efforts. A point was reached where the only land-related amounts in which the officers had any confidence were its $20,000 cost which appeared in the intervening balance sheets and the $1,500 loss on sale of land which was a determinant of 19x4's earnings.

Questions

1. What are pro forma financial statements, and what purpose do they serve?
2. In context of the historical-cost basis of accounting restated to reflect the effect of changes in the general price level,* what was Nonmon's (a) gain or loss from price fluctuations and (b) gain or loss on the sale of land?
3. If the company's officers wanted to have data reflecting only appraised values, i.e., not restated to reflect changes in the general price level, what amounts would appear in each year's pro forma financial statements?
4. Given that the change in the appraised value of Nonmon's land in most years appeared to run counter to the direction of changes in the general price level,† prepare an analysis which identifies the concurrent effect of both specific and general price changes for each of the four years. Should appraisal values and changes in the general price level be the same, or at least be consistent?

* To facilitate use of computations, assume that a year's general price level change occurs at the very beginning of the year.
† Ibid.

Case 12–2
Philip N. Thropist

Philip N. Thropist was approached by a professional fund raiser to present a substantial cash gift to his alma mater. Phil agreed tentatively to make such a contribution with the understanding that one-fifth of the total amount would be remitted at the end of each of the next five years. Phil was particularly pleased with the stretch-out feature of the agreement since he had a keen appreciation of the time-value-of-money concept. Indeed, he had even contemplated placing into a certificate-of-deposit-type savings account at the local savings bank that amount which would grow and provide the means to make the five payments.

In the process of thinking about the gift he would be presenting to his alma mater, Phil thought about old times, recalling among other things, that when he graduated from college he had done two quirky things. During his last semester on campus, Phil had purchased about 100 paperback books at an average cost of $1.00 apiece. Regrettably, practically all of the volumes remained untouched in his study. The other thing Phil had done was to take the first $100 he earned after graduation, exchange it at a bank for a crisp new $100 bill, and retain it in a shoe box in his attic. Not only was the amount of the bill the same as the cost of the books bought, but it too had remained untouched in the intervening years.

Returning to the present, several days before making a firm final commitment to the fund raiser, Phil was having lunch with his accountant, Joe Mahoney. Joe mentioned he had recently attended a somewhat technical lecture in which the speaker had voiced some provocative opinions about coping with inflation. Phil indicated he agreed that it was an important topic, and that he was sorry he hadn't been present as well. Joe, in turn, told Phil that he had picked up a copy of the talk as he left the lecture hall, and that he'd be pleased to pass it on to Phil.

Pertinent paragraphs of the speech follow.

Within the general price level restated financial statement, the purchasing-power gain or loss on monetary items is of little value and is probably a financial redundancy given the efficiency of the credit markets. Further, including a purchasing-power gain or loss may lead to dangerous financial management decisions and also may unintentionally mislead the less sophisiticated users of financial statements.

If cash or other monetary items are held during a period of inflation, a loss in purchasing power occurs. Monetary liabilities, however, generate a gain in purchasing power because the money owed declines in value during inflation. It takes less purchasing power to pay off the debts. Monetary assets and liabilities, then, bring about real losses or gains as a direct result of inflation, i.e., losses or gains in purchasing power. Stopping at this point greatly oversimplifies the issue and presents a misleading picture. No recognition in general-price-level-adjusted financial statements is given to the efficiency of credit markets in compensating lenders by providing them with a "real" rate of return over and above the prevailing rate of inflation.

Most of the time creditors are compensated for lending money in times of inflation because of the "inflation premium" they receive. This fact arises because lenders generally have at least as much information about expected future inflation rates as borrowers, and will demand a higher interest rate to compensate them during inflationary periods.

The recommended procedure for computing monetary gains or losses over-states the gain from holding debt and overstates the loss from holding interest-bearing monetary assets during an inflationary period. Thus, much, if not all, of a company's apparent gain from holding debt may be offset by the high interest payments it will be making to support this outstanding debt. And, the apparent loss from holding monetary assets may be offset to some extent by the interest earned on these items. It should be noted here that interest expense is a tax deductible item for most firms and that interest earned is a taxable item; however, interest expense and interest revenue get an additional loading when restated for the changes in the general price level.

Under the accounting restatement proposals, it is desirable to be in a net monetary liability position in a period of inflation. Managers may structure the company's financial position in reaction to its short-term inflation exposure, which may actually be inconsistent with the firm's best business interest in the long run. In an attempt to maximize restated accounting income, financial managers would have a strong incentive to increase debt. This increase in debt would probably be done at precisely the wrong time in the business cycle since a highly inflationary period is nearly always followed by, or is coincident with, an economic downturn. The firm will then have been enticed into taking on high-cost debt at a time when it will probably be most difficult for the firm to make the high-cost interest payments. The result is a greater risk of financial insolvency.

Recognition of monetary gains in the general-price-level-adjusted net income may enable a company to show profits even though its cash position is deteriorating. In the extreme, it could happen that a nearly bankrupt company may present a favorable general-price-level-adjusued net income figure. This could conceivably happen because purchasing power gains are not realized cash inflows. The misleading picture this presents to the less sophisticated reader of financial statements is quite apparent.

Questions

1. Assuming that what had cost $1 when Mr. Thropist graduated from college would on the average cost $3 currently, what is the economic effect of his having bought 100 paperback books and retained the crisp $100 bill? Prepare today's balance sheet adjusted to reflect the effect of changes in the general price level.
2. What would be the financial effect on Mr. Thropist and on his alma mater if the annual rate of inflation exceeded the interest rate being earned by the certificate-of-deposit bank account?
3. Compare and contrast the effect of inflation on the following four companies for whom "percent" data are provided, and express your response in terms of the kind of industry each company would appear to typify.

	A	B	C	D
Cash and receivables	50%	15%	15%	80%
Inventories	30	5	25	5
Plant assets	20	80	60	15
Total assets	100%	100%	100%	100%
Monetary liabilities	40%	70%	40%	50%
Owners' equity	60	30	60	50
Total equities	100%	100%	100%	100%

Case 12–3
Indiana Telephone Corporation

The 1976 Annual Report of Indiana Telephone Corporation (ITC) included in its Summary of Significant Accounting Policies the following explanation of the company's financial statement presentation.

In the accompanying financial statements, amounts measured by dollars disbursed at the time of the expenditure are shown in "Column A—Historical Cost." Amounts in "Column B—Historical Cost Restated to Current Purchasing Power" have been restated in terms of the price level at December 31, 1976, as measured by the Gross National Product Implicit Price Deflator.

Since 1969, the Corporation has followed the methods set forth in Statement No. 3 of the Accounting Principles Board of the American Institute of Certified Public Accountants in determining the amounts set forth in Column B, except that, contrary to Statement No. 3, the effects of price-level changes on long-term debt and preferred stock have been reflected as income in the year in which the debt and preferred stock are retired and not refinanced. The Accounting Principles Board took the position that all such amounts should be taken into income in the year of price-level change. The Corporation's management believes that the position of the Accounting Principles Board does not result in a proper determination of income for the period. The caption "Unrealized Effects of Price-Level Changes" recognizes the excess of adjustments on the Statements of Assets over the adjustments of the Common Shareholders' Interest, prior to any income taxes which would be paid upon the realization of these unrealized effects. . . .

Dollars are a means of expressing purchasing power at the time of their use. Conversion or restatement of dollars of differing purchasing power to the purchasing power of the dollar at the date of conversion results in all dollars being treated as mathematical likes for the purpose of significant data. The resulting financial statements recognize the changes in price levels between the periods

495

of expenditure of funds and the periods of use of property. Accordingly, the results of operations, assets, and other data available for use by management and other readers of financial statements provide important information and comparisons not otherwise available.

No one would attempt to add, subtract, multiply, or divide marks, dollars, and pounds. The failure to change the title of the monetary unit may be partially responsible for this violation of mathematical principle. This conceals the fact that mathematical unlikes are being used and, therefore, unfortunate results have been produced by present generally accepted accounting principles. . . .

The amount for consolidated telephone plant in service, on a replacement cost basis, did not differ significantly from that shown in the accompanying financial statements under Column B—Historical Cost Restated to Current Purchasing Power. In addition, accumulated depreciation and current depreciation expense computed on a replacement cost basis, were not significantly different from corresponding amounts shown under Column B.

The Corporation cautions that neither replacement cost nor the amounts shown under Column B represent the current value of existing telephone plant. In addition, amounts computed as replacement costs and those derived by restating historical cost in terms of current purchasing power may not always produce similar results.

Although all of ITC's financial statements were presented on both Column A and Column B bases, only selected amounts are reproduced herein as exhibits. Exhibit 1 presents five-year comparative "revenues, expenses, and earnings" data, and Exhibit 2 identifies the components, by nature and amount, of nonoperating items for 1975 and 1976. ITC's balance sheet data were presented in the company's statement of assets and statement of capital; and summary amounts are identified in Exhibit 3.

ITC's Annual Report included the four-paragraph text of the report received from the company's independent auditor. The first paragraph contained the CPA's standard reference to the scope of the audit examination. The second paragraph reiterated the presence of an uncertainty which had already been cited in a Note to the financial statements, which in turn would be the basis of a qualified audit opinion. The text of the remaining two paragraphs appears below:

In our opinion, subject to the effect of such adjustment, if any, as may be required as a result of the matter referred to above, the accompanying financial statements shown under Column A present fairly the financial positions of Indiana Telephone Corporation and subsidiary and of Indiana Telephone Corporation as of December 31, 1976 and 1975, and the results of their operations and the changes in their financial position for the years then ended, in conformity with generally accepted accounting principles consistently applied during the periods.

Exhibit 1

INDIANA TELEPHONE CORPORATION
Corporate* Revenues, Expenses, and Earnings
1972 through 1976

Historical Cost

	1976	1975	1974	1973	1972
Operating revenues	$16,451,913	$14,829,524	$13,506,367	$12,494,685	$11,732,962
Operating expenses—					
Depreciation	3,238,835	2,957,700	2,631,584	2,295,252	2,053,700
Other	6,381,564	5,793,050	5,384,238	4,421,117	4,235,777
Operating taxes	3,011,790	3,001,981	2,715,683	2,830,985	2,748,174
Operating income	3,819,724	3,076,793	2,774,862	2,947,331	2,695,311
Net income	2,670,745	2,537,064	2,023,718	2,312,169	2,126,274

Historical Cost Restated to Current Purchasing Power

	1976	1975	1974	1973	1972
Operating revenues	$16,777,776	$16,013,783	$16,158,286	$16,532,543	$16,373,889
Operating expenses—					
Depreciation	4,799,599	4,566,083	4,328,144	3,907,085	3,624,150
Other	6,501,237	6,263,533	6,463,279	5,862,009	5,914,211
Operating taxes	3,107,719	3,215,377	3,226,768	3,730,869	3,823,481
Operating income	2,369,221	1,968,790	2,140,095	3,032,580	3,012,047
Net income	1,019,467	1,714,369	1,186,955	2,006,376	2,155,065
Indices:					
GNP—Implicit Price Deflator					
(1972 = 100)	133.8	127.3	116.4	105.8	100.0
Consumer Price index					
(1972 = 100)	136.1	128.7	117.9	106.2	100.0

* Corporate, as opposed to consolidated.

Exhibit 2

INDIANA TELEPHONE CORPORATION
Corporate* Nonoperating Income and Expenses
1975 and 1976

	Column A Historical Cost		Column B Historical Cost Restated to Current Purchasing Power	
	1976	1975	1976	1975
Operating income	$3,819,725	$3,076,793	$2,369,221	$1,968,790
Nonoperating (income) and expenses:				
Interest on long-term debt	$1,902,842	$1,203,919	$1,940,532	$1,300,062
Other deductions	259,948	225,902	256,211	236,220
Allowance for funds used during construction	(103,652)	(158,835)	(105,705)	(171,519)
Undistributed earnings of subsidiary	(412,953)	(395,582)	(86,656)	(434,957)
Other income	(467,170)	(160,121)	(476,424)	(172,908)
Federal income taxes	(2,700)	(140,489)	(2,753)	(151,708)
Gain from retirement of long-term debt through operation of sinking funds	(16,181)	(23,548)	(16,502)	(25,429)
Price-level gain from retirement of long-term debt	—	—	(137,531)	(150,552)
Gain from retirement of preferred stock through operation of sinking funds	(11,154)	(11,517)	(11,375)	(12,437)
Price-level gain from retirement of preferred stock	—	—	(37,834)	(36,057)
Price-level (gain) loss from monetary items	—	—	27,791	(126,294)
Total nonoperating (income) and expenses	$1,148,980	$ 539,729	$1,349,754	$ 254,421
Net income	$2,670,745	$2,537,064	$1,019,467	$1,714,369

* Corporate, as opposed to consolidated.

Exhibit 3

INDIANA TELEPHONE CORPORATION
Summary of Corporate* Statements of Assets and Capital
December 31, 1975 and 1976

	Column A Historical Cost		Column B Historical Cost Restated to Current Purchasing Power	
	1976	1975	1976	1975
Statements of assets				
Telephone plant (net)	$40,399,935	$36,958,967	$56,041,003	$53,970,721
Current assets	$ 7,709,385	$ 7,157,213	$ 7,737,117	$ 7,647,749
Current liabilities	6,585,953	7,034,291	6,585,953	7,427,325
Net working capital	$ 1,123,432	$ 122,922	$ 1,151,164	$ 220,424
Other	$ 4,435,693	$(1,134,071)	$ 3,254,028	$(2,078,495)
Total investment in telephone business	**$45,959,060**	**$35,947,818**	**$60,446,195**	**$52,112,650**
Statements of capital				
Long-term debt	$24,719,750	$16,766,430	$24,719,750	$17,703,238
Preferred stock	1,598,000	1,629,400	1,598,000	1,720,440
Common shareholders' interest	19,641,310	17,551,988	19,042,516	18,627,834
Unrealized effects of price-level changes	—	—	15,085,929	14,061,138
Total investment in telephone business	**$45,959,060**	**$35,947,818**	**$60,446,195**	**$52,112,650**

* Corporate, as opposed to consolidated.

In our opinion, however, subject to the effect of such adjustment, if any, as may be required as a result of the matter referred to above, the accompanying financial statements shown under Column B more fairly present the financial positions of Indiana Telephone Corporation and subsidiary and of Indiana Telephone Corporation as of December 31, 1976 and 1975, and the results of their operations and the changes in their financial position for the years then ended, as recognition has been given to changes in the purchasing power of the dollar, on the basis explained in Note 1(a).

Questions

1. Given that Indiana Telephone's practice to not prepare a conventional balance sheet was unrelated to its disclosure of "restated" accounting data, to what do you attribute its presentation of separate statements of assets and capital (which are summarized in Exhibit 3)?
2. With what factors or circumstances do you associate Indiana Telephone's Column A/Column B mode of financial statement presentation, and what purpose is served by adopting such an approach?
3. What would be the effect of using Column B data to compute the following Indiana Telephone financial ratios for 1976?
   Earnings per common share.
   Debt to equity ratio.
   Return on average common equity.
   Dividend payout ratio.
4. What are the reasons for, and ramifications of, the differences between ITC's Column B method and the approach recommended by the Accounting Principles Board in 1969; and is the company's policy defensible? Why was ITC permitted to use an approach different from that set forth by the APB?
5. How do you reconcile ITC's 1976 $27,791 price-level loss from monetary items with its tenfold increase in working capital during the year?
6. What generalizations can be made about the effect of price inflation on capital-intensive companies?
7. When and how should a company recognize in its financial statements the effect of gains and losses resulting from changes in the general price level?

Nickel Smelting Company*

During the Korean War the United States Government established a large program of stockpiling materials considered to be strategic to the prosecution of the War and the defense of the country. In 1953 the Government entered into a long-term contract with The Nickel Smelting Company for the development of a substantial nickel deposit owned by it, but heretofore unused. Under the terms of the contract the Company was to build the smelter with capital funds advanced by the Government.

The smelter was built during 1953–54, and began producing in quantity in 1955. Initial construction costs were $21,000,000, and an additional $1,800,000 was spent during 1955–56 for replacements and improvements, all of which were capitalized.

The Government purchased virtually the entire output of the years 1955–1960 as it was obligated to do under the contract. The agreed upon price was computed to permit the Company to recover its out-of-pocket costs of production plus an "amortization payment" of approximately 26¢ per pound of nickel. The amortization payment was used by the Company to repay the Government's capital advance.

The Company did not charge depreciation as such in its accounts or report depreciation in the financial statements. In lieu thereof it considered the amortization payments as depreciation and reduced the book value of the plant in such amounts. By December 31, 1960 all amortization payments had been made; thus the book value of the plant had been reduced to zero.

Under the terms of the contract the Company had the right to acquire clear title to the Plant by making a "residual payment" computed by the application of a specified formula. The Company exercised its right on January 1, 1961, paying the formula-computed price of $1,700,000. This amount was recorded on its books as the cost of the plant on that date.

Before making the payment the Company had the plant appraised by a qualified appraisal company. The latter computed the reproduction cost new to be $19,647,693. Experienced depreciation reduced this amount to a current depreciated value of $11,921,233. The appraisal company made a financial analysis of the operating results of this and other smelting companies and their future prospects. It determined the fair market value of the plant to be $9,440,000. It then reduced the "cost" amount ($11,921,233) because of certain enumerated risk factors by 10 percent, and expressed the

* Howard W. Wright, "A Case of Valuation," *The Accounting Review,* American Accounting Association (July, 1966), pp. 559–560.

opinion that the fair value of the plant was $10,730,000 on December 31, 1960.

An accountant who was involved in certain aspects of the case made a rough estimate of the depreciated cost of the plant. He applied the Internal Revenue Service's depreciation guideline rates by classes of buildings and equipment to the acquisition costs of assets by years of acquisition. These rough computations indicated a depreciated cost value of approximately $11,500,000 on December 31, 1960.

Late in 1960 the Company insured the smelter for $16,514,000. During 1961 the State Tax Commission appraised the plant at $18,794,480, while in the same proceedings the Company advanced a valuation of $11,723,598. Subsequent negotiations resulted in an agreement that the smelter had a value of $15,113,240 on January 1, 1961.

Questions

1. Are cost-based data more objective and subject to less variation than appraisal-based amounts?
2. How are each of the following notions relevant, if at all, to Nickel Smelting Company's circumstances?
   a. substance over form
   b. arm's length transaction
   c. out-of-pocket cost
   d. interperiod consistency
   e. accounting verifiability
3. What is the value of the smelter?
4. What should be the smelter's accounting basis? Explain.

Case 13–2
Old Line Trading, Inc.

Old Line Trading Inc. was a manufacturing and wholesaling company that specialized in souvenirs for sale to tourists visiting historical sites. Its only assets were cash, inventory and machinery; it had no receivables because all its sales were for cash. Old Line used a calendar year for financial reporting, and there was no general price-level increase (inflation) during 1978 and 1979. Cost of Goods Sold (FIFO-based), Depreciation, Salaries, and Income Taxes were the only expenses on the company's income statement.

As of December 31, 1978, cash was $125,000 and liabilities (payable in cash) were $65,000. As of January 1, 1978, its inventory's cost basis and market value had both been $15,000. Its machines had had a (net) book value of $60,000 and an expectation they would last six more years at which time there would be no salvage value. If Old Line had had to replace the machines with comparable machinery, it would have cost $66,000; this latter increment in value can be presumed to have occurred in January 1978.

The cost of inventory purchased (for cash) in 1978 was $300,000 and the cost basis of the December 31 inventory was $25,000. The replacement value of the goods sold in 1978 was $276,000; sales revenue was $600,000; and because of lower demand for, and excess supply of, conventional souvenirs, the December 31, 1978 replacement value of the inventory on hand was $8,000.

During 1979, Old Line Trading purchased (for cash) merchandise costing $350,000, sold for $750,000 goods whose original cost was $320,000, and had ending inventory whose historical cost of $55,000 was equal to its current replacement cost. In addition, Old Line's management knew that the replacement value of the goods sold during 1979 was $298,000.

Old Line's historical-cost financial statements appear below:

Income statement:

	1978	1979
Sales	$600,000	$750,000
Beginning inventory	$ 15,000	$ 25,000
Purchases	300,000	350,000
Ending inventory	25,000	55,000
Cost of goods sold	$290,000	$320,000
Gross profit	$310,000	$430,000
Depreciation expense	10,000	10,000
Salaries expense	150,000	170,000
Income tax expense	50,000	80,000
Net earnings	**$100,000**	**$170,000**
Balance sheet:		
Cash	$125,000	$275,000
Inventory	25,000	55,000
Machinery (net)	50,000	40,000
	$200,000	**$370,000**
Liabilities	$ 65,000	$ 65,000
Owners' equity	135,000	305,000
	$200,000	**$370,000**

503

Questions

1. Prepare replacement cost basis income statements for 1978 and 1979 as well as each year's end-of-period balance sheet.
2. Reconcile for each year the following three amounts:
   a. Unrealized net holding gain or loss
   b. Excess of Replacement Cost Income over Net Earnings
   c. Difference between Total Assets in the Historical Cost and the Replacement Cost balance sheets
3. What would be the financial statement consequences of using the lower-of-cost-or-market method of inventory pricing?
4. As a result of the changed value of its nonmonetary assets during the two-year period, what benefit or loss accrued to Old Line in a practical business sense, and in terms of the effect on its financial reporting results?

Case 13–3
Ernst & Whinney

During the 1970s debate as to the relative merit of retaining, restating, or supplanting historical cost accounting data, one proposal advanced was particularly novel in its resolution of the issues at hand. The suggested method was referred to by its proponents as a "current cost depreciation" approach in which *depreciation* should be read to include depreciation, depletion, and amortization of long-lived tangible assets. An excerpt from the proposed method follows.*

> We have long recommended LIFO accounting for inventories as a partial solution to the problem of inflation. LIFO has a twofold effect. By bringing the most recent costs incurred into cost of goods sold, to be matched with current revenue dollars, a more understandable net income figure results than would otherwise be obtained during a period of inflation. In addition, because LIFO is accepted for tax purposes, it has positive financial benefits to the companies which adopt it. The immediate cash flow advantages of LIFO through reduced income taxes help a company bear the financial burden of inflation.
>
> During periods of inflation, depreciation on a historical cost basis understates, in terms of current dollars, the cost of replacing depreciable property consumed through operations. To compensate for this, and to prevent capital

* *Accounting Under Inflationary Conditions* (Cleveland: Ernst & Ernst [subsequently renamed—Ernst & Whinney], 1976), pp. 5–7. Reprinted with permission.

erosion, proposals have been made to "restate" assets and depreciation on a replacement cost or some other basis.

None of the present proposals, in our judgment, has a realistic expectation of the dual benefits of LIFO adoption—both income statement and positive cash flow effects. Proposed accounting adjustments for depreciation tend to reduce reported income, thereby decreasing the company's relative ability to obtain capital and credit, without any compensating improvement in cash flow. Rather than helping effected companies bear the burden of inflation, such restatement levies an additional burden. Something more than this is needed.

Briefly stated, we urge acceptance of increased depreciation for both income tax and financial reporting purposes so that affected companies retain more cash to permit acquisition of replacement assets at higher prices.

. . . Insofar as accounting technique is concerned, the procedure is uncomplicated and readily understood. It provides that:

1. The property and associated accrued depreciation accounts would be maintained on a historical cost basis with no necessary change in method of computation or estimate of life.
2. Depreciation charged against income for both book and tax purposes would be computed on historical cost restated to current dollars by application of selected indices acceptable to the Treasury Department.
3. Accrued depreciation in excess of historical cost depreciation would be credited to a special account in the shareholders' equity section of the balance sheet which would accumulate during inflation and decrease during deflation.
4. As long as reinvestment occurs, there would be no attempt to recapture the restated depreciation for either book or tax purposes. Gain or loss on retirement or sale of a capital asset would be calculated on the basis of historical cost amounts.
5. The amount and method of determining restated depreciation would be disclosed by footnote.

. . . The following simplified illustration presents the essentials of current cost depreciation. Assume a company with the following balance sheet on December 31, 1976. Its accounts are kept in accordance with generally accepted accounting principles.

Other assets	$400,000	Other liabilities	$285,000
		Taxes payable	15,000
Properties and equipment	500,000		
Less depreciation	−200,000	Shareholders' equity:	
	300,000	Capital stock	200,000
		Retained earnings	200,000
	$700,000		$700,000

The company's income statement for 1976 includes the following:

Revenues	$1,000,000
Other costs	850,000
Depreciation	50,000
	900,000
	100,000
Federal income tax	50,000
Net income	$ 50,000

To apply current cost depreciation in this situation, assume that the properties and equipment are being depreciated over 10 years, and that the cost indices appropriate to those assets have gone up an average of 40 percent since the assets were acquired. The current cost of the assets, therefore, is $700,000, and depreciation at a 10 percent rate for the current year is $70,000. An income statement for 1976 using current cost depreciation would appear as follows:

Revenues	$1,000,000
Other costs	850,000
Depreciation	70,000
	920,000
	80,000
Federal income tax	40,000
Net income	$ 40,000

This company's year-end balance sheet for 1976 under current cost depreciation would appear as follows:

Other assets	$400,000	Other liabilities	$285,000
		Taxes payable	5,000
Properties and equipment	500,000		
Less depreciation on a		Shareholders' equity:	
historical cost basis	−200,000	Capital stock	200,000
	300,000	Retained earnings	190,000
		Accumulated current	
		cost depreciation	20,000
			410,000
	$700,000		$700,000

Questions

1. Is the LIFO inventory costing method an effective means of accounting for the effects of inflation?
2. What role should ease of calculation and ease of understanding have in determining what accounting methods shall be acceptable?
3. Does the proposal compromise any of the elements of historical cost accounting?

4. With respect to generating support for adopting the proposed method, what differences in opinion could be expected from corporations, stock-holders, financial analysts, the Federal government, and practicing CPAs?
5. What are the accounting characteristics and the financial reporting ramifications of the amounts that would be added to an entity's share-holders' equity as a result of adopting the proposed method?
6. What cash-flow costs or benefits, if any, are likely to occur as a result of adopting the proposed method?
7. Is the proposed method equitable and socially desirable?

Case 14–1
Columbus-San Charter Enterprises*

Alas, so much confusion about the effects of floating the U.S. dollar and the ensuing foreign currency revaluations! I feel fortunate in being en-lightened by my good friend Christopher Columbus-San about the whole affair. Chris is a shipping magnate with worldwide interests. I ran into him on the train the other day, and I asked him how the foreign currency situation affected his business.

"Best thing that could happen," he said.

"Tell me about it."

"Well, I own three ships—the Nina, the Pinta and the Santa Maria. I bought them in Japan in 1492 and they were on my books at a cost of 3600 Japanese yen; that was the equivalent of $10.00 U.S. just before the revalua-tion. They have a ten-year remaining life and the charter rate is 360 yen per year; that's $1.00 per year U.S."

"So what!"

"So, you numbskull, I was barely breaking even before the revaluation. Look at these figures:

	Japanese Yen	U.S. Dollar Translation (before revaluation)
Yearly charter rate	Y360	$1.00
Cost depreciation	360	1.00
Profit	Y—	$ —

---

* Edward R. Noonan, "The Nina, Pinta, Santa Maria," World (Winter, 1972), pp. 28–29. Reprinted with permission.

"But now my accountant says I can make some money," Chris said cheerfully.

"Oh lucky for you, Chris. How does it work?"

"Easy, the ship charter rate is still Y360 per year but now it translates into $1.10 U.S.," Chris continued patiently. "It's simple, look at the figures:

	Japanese Yen	U.S. Dollar Translation (after 10% assumed revaluation)
Yearly charter rate	Y360	$1.10
Cost depreciation	360	1.00
Profit	Y—	$ .10

"Um, that's great, I'll bet the stockholders will be happy!"

"Yes, but that is only true for the Santa Maria. The Nina and the Pinta are not doing as well." He seemed depressed.

"Why is that?" I asked.

"Because I owe money on those ships; look:

	U.S. $ Equivalents			
	Nina	Pinta	Santa Maria	Total
Before revaluation:				
Cost (depreciated)	$10.00	10.00	10.00	30.00
Debt (repayable in Yen)	$10.00	5.00	—	15.00
After revaluation:				
Debt	$11.00	5.50	—	16.50
Debt revaluation adjustments	$ 1.00	.50	—	1.50

"Too bad, I see you have to take that $1.50 loss, but at least you can make it up on the $.10 profit from each of the ship charters."

"You don't understand," Chris raised his voice. "The $1.50 is not a loss, it is an added cost of my ships, like this:

	U.S. $ Equivalents			
	Nina	Pinta	Santa Maria	Total
Cost (historical)	$10.00	10.00	10.00	30.00
Debt revaluation adjustments	1.00	.50	—	1.50
Total	**$11.00**	**10.50**	**10.00**	**31.50**

"So I make some money; see:

	Nina	Pinta	Santa Maria	Total
Yearly charter rate	$1.10	1.10	1.10	3.30
Depreciation (historical plus debt revaluation adjustments)	1.10	1.05	1.00	3.15
Profit	**$ —**	**.05**	**.10**	**.15**

"I'm confused, Chris. What does the debt have to do with the cost?"

"Well my accountant says that if I'm not making any money in yen, I should not be allowed to show a profit to my U.S. stockholders."

"That makes sense, but you still show some profits. Why doesn't your accountant insist on showing no profits?"

"He can't, because the books won't balance."

"Why not? Just make all the ship costs $11.00 like the Nina!"

"No, that violates historical cost accounting principles, which are embodied in cement at the moment; and it would mean adding $3.00 to the ship costs, whereas the debt adjustments total only $1.50."

"OK, but couldn't you credit capital for the other $1.50? Then the books would balance."

"True, but I can't do that either, because only securities holders contribute to capital, not governments. Besides the accountants will not let us write up the cost unless there is a long-term debt revaluation adjustment."

"I see, so the accountants don't want you to make money on the ship charters; you don't want to lose money on the debt revaluation; so it's a compromise: 50 : 50, right?"

"Wrong! Accountants do not compromise, they judge fair presentation under current conventions!!"

"Now I get it, they can't change historical cost accounting principles for the ship costs; they feel obligated to show the debt as a liability translated at current rates; and it's only fair to present half a story when you can't tell the whole story."

"At last, you're with it!" Chris was exasperated.

"Thanks, Chris, I feel enlightened. . . ."

"Oh, just one more thing, how does it work with the oil tankers operating in Indonesia that you bought with Swiss franc debt which was loaned to your German subsidiary operating out of Panama?"

Questions

1. What was the *financial* effect on Columbus-San Charter Enterprises of the change in the value of the dollar relative to the yen?
2. What *accounting* results would occur under contemporary financial accounting standards?
3. What currently is, and what do you believe should be, the respective effect on Columbus-San Charter Enterprise's profits of (1) the ships' purchase price having been denominated in yen, (2) its debt being repayable in yen, and (3) its charter rate being denominated in yen?
4. What changes in accounting rules would increase the likelihood of the company being able to report profits in the future?
5. What recommendations can you make that would result in financial reporting of changes in foreign currency exchange rates that would be acceptable to investors, financial executives of multinational corporations, and persons concerned with having internal consistency in accounting rules?

Case 14–2
Charles River

Minus, Ltd. had been created on January 2, 1974, in the country of Charles. The currency in Charles is the River, signified by the symbol "R." Minus has had 1,000 shares of common stock outstanding since its inception, these shares having been issued at a 66⅔ percent premium over their par value. On January 1, 1975 Plus Corporation purchased 600 of those shares in the secondary securities market for an amount of dollars equal to Minus, Ltd.'s book value. Since the nation of Charles has had a long and amiable relationship with the United States, its accounting principles and practices correspond to those generally accepted in the American business community. The companies' financial statements for the 1979 fiscal year (corresponding to the calendar year) appear in Exhibits 1 and 2.

Minus. Ltd.'s year-end inventories consisted of goods bought during the second half of the year. Its merchandise inventory reflected market value lower than the R50,000 cost basis, and supplies inventory was carried at historical cost. There were no intercompany profits in either the beginning or ending inventory. Prepaid Rent and Revenue Received in Advance balances reflected fourth and third quarter cash transactions respectively; neither of these accounts nor Supplies Inventory had existed before 1979. Sales, and

Exhibit 1

Balance Sheets
December 31, 1979

(credit)	Plus Dollars ($)	Minus Rivers (R)
Cash	$ 18,000	R 20,000
Accounts receivable	30,000	42,000
Allowance for bad debts	(6,000)	(8,000)
Merchandise inventory	60,000	40,000
Supplies inventory	10,000	9,000
Prepaid rent	7,000	2,000
Investment in Minus	128,100	–0–
Advance to Minus	24,000	–0–
Machinery	400,000	80,000
Allowance for depreciation	(220,000)	(16,000)
Organization costs	28,000	6,000
	$ 479,100	R 175,000
Accounts payable	$(17,000)	R(10,000)
Accrued liabilities	(28,000)	(15,000)
Due to plus	–0–	(7,000)
Bonds payable–current	–0–	(2,000)
Bonds payable–noncurrent	(100,000)	(38,000)
Revenue received in advance	(18,000)	(10,000)
Pension accrual	(42,000)	(12,000)
Deferred taxes	(20,000)	(1,000)
Preferred stock	(50,000)	(8,000)
Common stock	(100,000)	(3,000)
Capital in excess of par	(15,000)	(2,000)
Retained earnings	(89,100)	(67,000)
	$(479,100)	R(175,000)

those expenses which could not be identified with particular balance sheet accounts, occurred uniformly during the year unless otherwise indicated. The beginning-of-year merchandise reflected the December 31, 1978 market value, which was less than the original cost.

Minus, Ltd.'s preferred shares had been issued on July 1, 1974 for proceeds equal to their par value. Deferred taxes arose for the first time in 1979, and reflected a timing difference related to the depreciation of machinery

511

Exhibit 2

Combined Statement of Earnings and Retained Earnings
For the Year Ended, December 31, 1979

(credit)	Plus Dollars ($)	Minus Rivers (R)
Sales		
to Minus	$(112,000)	–0–
to others	(490,000)	R(202,000)
Beginning inventory	50,000	18,000
Purchases		
from Plus	–0–	35,000
from others	414,000	90,000
Ending inventory	(60,000)	(40,000)
Salaries expense	120,000	60,000
Rent expense	22,000	6,000
Supplies expense	2,000	1,000
Depreciation expense	20,000	8,000
Interest expense	10,000	2,000
Income tax expense	4,000	4,000
Net income	$(20,000)	R(18,000)
Beginning retained earnings	(61,000)	(51,000)
Dividends declared (and paid)	10,000	2,000
Ending retained earnings	**$(71,000)**	**R(67,000)**

purchased during that year. "Organization" costs were incurred in January 1974, and were not being amortized. The bonds had been issued on July 1, 1979 at their face value and they carried a 10 percent coupon rate. During 1979 Plus received "River" dividends from Minus, and the equivalent $4,200 sum constituted the only amount recorded in its Investment in Minus account during the year.

There follows a listing of transactions involving Minus's machinery:

January 1, 1974	R65,000 purchase
September 15, 1976	15,000 sale
January 2, 1977	10,000 purchase
April 1, 1979	20,000 purchase
	R80,000 balance

Listed below are the pertinent foreign exchange rates:

	Dollars per River
December 31, 1973	3.0
December 31, 1974	2.8
December 31, 1975	2.9
December 31, 1976	3.0
December 31, 1977	3.6
December 31, 1978	3.2
December 31, 1979	4.0

Excerpts from two pertinent paragraphs of FASB Statement No. 8 appear below.[1]

From paragraph No. 168

In practice, however, the exchange gain or loss is usually determined at the close of a period by translating both the ending balance sheet and income statement accounts at the rates required by the translation method (that is, current or historical rates for assets and liabilities and weighted average rate for most revenue and expenses). When the translation is completed and the net income less dividends in dollars is added to the beginning dollar balance of retained earnings, the sum of those amounts will usually not equal the ending dollar retained earnings shown in the translated balance sheet. The difference is the exchange gain or loss from translating foreign statements.

From paragraph No. 41

If a business combination with a foreign operation is accounted for by the purchase method, assets and liabilities that are translated at historical rates shall be translated at the rates in effect when the enterprise acquired its interest in the assets or liabilities. Thus, assets and liabilities of a foreign operation at the date of its acquisition shall be adjusted to their fair values in local currency and then translated at the rate in effect at the date of acquisition.

Questions

1. What useful purpose, if any, is served by translating Minus Ltd.'s financial statements into U.S. dollars if its parent company has no intention of preparing consolidated statements?
2. Without actually performing the calculations referred to in paragraph 168 of FASB Statement No. 8, would you expect Plus Corp. to have experienced a gain or a loss from foreign currency exchange in 1979?

---

[1] *Financial Accounting Standards Board Statement No. 8,* paragraph nos. 168 and 41. Copyright © by Financial Accounting Standards Board, High Ridge Park, Stamford, Connecticut 06905, U.S.A. Reprinted with permission. Copies of the complete document are available from the FASB.

3. Calculate the dollar amount of the gain or loss from foreign currency exchange by using the approach described in paragraph 168 of FASB Statement No. 8; you are to make the following assumptions.
   a. To calculate "average" and "end-of-quarter" exchange rates, there is a linear progression between each year's beginning and ending exchange rates.
   b. With respect to "depreciation," translated dollar amounts are proportionately equal to those expressed in rivers.
   c. Minus, Ltd.'s translated January 1, 1979 dollar balance of retained earnings was $184,100.
4. If Minus, Ltd.'s December 31, 1979 merchandise inventory had had a cost basis of R41,000 (instead of R50,000), what would be the translated dollar amount of the goods on hand?

Case 14–3
Yashica Company

An excerpt from a 1975 survey[1] revealed the following differences between accounting principles and reporting practices in the United States and Japan[2]:

	United States	Japan
Consolidated financial statements only are prepared for shareholders of a parent company	Majority	Not permitted
Parent company financial statements only are prepared for shareholders of a parent company	Not permitted	Majority
Investments in unconsolidated subsidiaries are carried on an equity basis	Required	Minority
Investments in less than 50% owned companies, where there is no joint venture relationship but where the investee is effectively controlled or significantly influenced, are carried on an equity basis	Required	Minority

---

[1] Price Waterhouse International, *A Survey in 46 Countries: Accounting Principles and Reporting Practices,* 1975.

[2] Ibid., topic nos. 210, 212, 230, and 105.

In May 1974, the chairman of Yashica Co., a Japanese-based camera manufacturer, publicly accused his company of "window-dressing" its financial statements as a result of having shipped excess goods to foreign subsidiaries. Such a practice would have the effect of inflating sales and profits of the parent company while accumulating the unsold merchandise elsewhere.

Shortly thereafter, trading of Yashica shares was suspended and inquiries were made concerning the validity of the comments. Sales had reportedly risen to $69,200,000 for the year ending March 31, 1974 as compared to $60,800,000 a year earlier: nearly a 14 percent increase. The chairman asserted that $13,600,000 of the current year's sales was "forcible transfer of inventory" to overseas subsidiaries. If these transfers had not been made, Yashica would have had earnings of $623,000 instead of $2,300,000—compared to year earlier income of $1,200,000.

The ensuing investigation found the statements of Yashica Co. were not window dressed. Its external auditor stated there may have been some transfers of inventories at the end of the accounting period, but they reflected a genuine transfer of merchandise and the resulting profit was duly taxed in Japan. The auditors acknowledged they couldn't investigate the company's motive for inventory transfers and therefore were unable to determine whether or not they were "forcible." The investigation revealed, however, that Yashica's domestic and foreign subsidiaries had above average inventory levels.

In 1977, the Japanese government issued new regulations affecting approximately 600 of its publicly traded companies requiring them to prepare and disseminate their financial statements on a consolidated basis. The rule was to apply to parent companies and enterprises in which they had more than a 50 percent ownership interest.

Questions

1. What are the accounting ramifications of a parent company engaging in "forcible transfers of inventories" to domestic and to foreign subsidiaries under each of the approaches (cited in the opening paragraph of the case)?
2. What differences in pricing policies of Japanese companies that sell their products in domestic and in foreign markets would be likely to result from the accounting requirements introduced in 1977?
3. What avenues for "window dressing," other than inventory transfers, are available to a parent company operating under the type of accounting rules that existed in Japan in 1974?

4. What are the relative advantages and disadvantages of the three accounting approaches from the point of view of a parent company's officers as well as that of its present and prospective stockholders?
5. What additional accounting requirement(s) would render the revised Japanese approach comparable to that which prevails in the United States, and what are the relative merits of the two approaches?

Case 15–1
Abigail Industries

Abigail Industries was a closely held diversified corporation when, in 1979, its owners contemplated "going public." Although the company's financial statements had been audited practically since its inception 35 years earlier, the board of directors recognized that more comprehensive accounting and financial disclosure rules would apply were the corporation to become a publicly held enterprise.

Abigail's president believed one of the major reasons the company had been able to operate so profitably in certain industries was its not having been required to make public disclosures regarding the individual performance of its seven lines of business. He recognized, however, that from a recordkeeping standpoint, generating segment data would pose no problem because the lines' identities were very well-defined, each operated with managerial autonomy, there were no intersegment sales, and virtually no "common" costs to speak of. Data relating to the seven divisions' revenues, profits, and identifiable assets appear below (in millions of dollars):

	Revenue	Earnings	Identifiable Assets
Apparel manufacturing	8	.7	6
Commuter airline	17	.8	25
Home study school	9	.7	2
Motels	40	3.5	32
Life insurance	13	2.9	2
Limousine service	7	.7	6
Rugs/tapestry manufacturing	6	.7	7
	100	10	80

Questions

1. What are the differences in accounting measurement and financial reporting disclosures between a closely held private corporation and one which is publicly held?
2. What are the reasons for and against being required to make segment disclosures? Prepare your answer in terms of both the societal and individual firm dimensions.
3. If Abigail were to "go public,"
   a. how should it define its segments,
   b. what are the maximum and minimum number of segments for which Abigail would provide accounting data, and
   c. what are the segment dollar amounts that it would be required to disclose?
4. What is the effect on Abigail's disclosure requirements of the fact that the seven product lines are operated as subsidiaries vs. divisions vs. departments?
5. What would be the effect on a company's segment disclosures of intersegment sales and common costs?
6. Relative to segment disclosure requirements currently in effect, what alternative approaches do you propose to be worthy of consideration?

Case 15–2
Gary Merchandising Company

Gary Merchandising Company had until recently been a family-owned business whose annual sales during the past four years had grown from $8 million to nearly $20 million. The company's product line consisted of leisure time products such as table-top games, sports equipment, and record albums. The firm has been particularly successful lately in its effort to promote the sale of reissued "golden oldie" records which had been very popular during the 1950's.

As a result of having recently "gone public," Mr. Franklin, the company's newly hired chief accountant apprised Gary's president, Mr. Steele, of the need to prepare and disseminate interim financial data for each of the fiscal year's four quarters; the company's fiscal year corresponds to the calendar year. The president, in turn, indicated he was prepared to delegate authority for this task to Mr. Franklin. Although not one to shirk his responsibilities, Mr. Franklin responded by bringing to the chief executive's attention the fact that the compilation of interim data entailed to some extent the use of some personal discretion, and it would be appropriate for the company's president to be the one to make such policy judgments. Mr. Steele's reply was that although he was surprised to hear that accounting even allowed for a non-accountant's input, he would be willing to comply with Mr. Franklin's request. In this regard, Mr. Steele directed the chief accountant to set forth in writing the various nuances of interim reporting relative to annual reporting, and to identify those discretionary matters for which a policy decision would have to be made.

Mr. Franklin decided to categorize the elements to be included in his report in terms of the materials-labor-overhead framework with which he was acquainted in his previous position with a large manufacturing company. Those items which did not fit into any of the three categories were designated as "other;" the pertinent portion of Mr. Franklin's report appeared as follows.

Materials-related

1. One of Gary's prime suppliers grants a "quantity" discount based on cumulative calendar-year purchases, for which the company usually qualifies for August through December purchases.
2. Inclement winter weather in the Northeast caused a delay in incoming deliveries of merchandise from a New England supplier, forcing Gary during the first quarter to "dip into" LIFO layers which reflect significantly lower unit costs than those incurred currently. Subsequent deliveries will allow the year-end inventory's LIFO layers to be unaffected.
3. Effective October 1, the company is increasing by 8 percent the unit sales price of virtually all its merchandise.
4. The June 30 merchandise inventory's excess of historical cost over current market value is not expected to prevail as of the end of the year.

Labor-related

5. At the beginning of the year, the company projects the amount of accrued pension expense for the year, and such estimates have typically been within 5 percent of the actual amount.
6. The company traditionally gives its management personnel a year-end bonus equal to 6 percent of each individual's annual salary.
7. Gary has a profit-sharing plan for its non-management personnel. This year, at the end of the first two quarters, the company estimated the "accrued" amounts that would be payable the following January, but a strike-induced third quarter loss was of such magnitude that no year-end profit sharing is likely to occur after all.
8. All employees are required to take their vacations between July 10 and August 7.

Overhead-related

9. During the second and third quarters the company incurs landscaping and gardening costs.
10. Heating costs are incurred during the months of November through March.
11. Air conditioning units are operated only during the months of July and August.
12. Major repair work and annual maintenance activity occurs during April and May.
13. The property tax rate increased as of July 1 from $80,000 to $100,000 per July 1-to-June 30 tax year.

Other

14. The company receives from its CPA firm progress billings relative to the annual audit fee; equal amounts are paid during July, September, November and the following January.
15. During August, the company discovers that an employee had embezzled a material amount of cash during June, and that recovery is highly unlikely.
16. Based on both a fixed beginning-of-year budgeted amount and an early December estimate of income expected to be earned during the year, the company disburses charitable contributions throughout the year although 75 percent of the gifts are tendered in December.
17. Estimated equal Federal income tax payments are made four times a year; the exact amount due is not determinable until year-end, and the pre-tax income is not identical for all four quarters.

Questions

1. What financial reporting differences are there between publicly held and privately held companies?
2. What types of personal discretion are sanctioned by accounting, and in this regard what differences exist between interim and annual financial reporting?
3. With respect to interim reporting and the potential to exercise personal judgment, what motivational differences would you expect to encounter among company presidents, accountants, and investors?
4. Concerning interim financial data, do you believe a company's independent auditor should attest to their fairness, at least be involved in some other limited manner, or serve in no capacity at all?
5. What do you recommend should be Gary Merchandising Company's method of accounting for each of the situations identified in Mr. Franklin's report?

In his capacity as senior editor of the journal *Social Scientifica*, Dr. D. Nathan Bass had responsibility for reviewing manuscripts submitted by authors seeking to have their ideas exposed to a highly respected professional and lay readership. Although *Social Scientifica* had originally limited its scope to papers relating to sociology, psychology, and anthropology, in 1978 it had expanded its range to include the fields of political science and economics as well.

Many of the papers dealing with the two new topics tended to address highly specialized topics and they invariably contained material which was extremely technical. As a result, in 1980, Dr. Bass and his associate editors decided to emphasize the publication of articles which had interdisciplinary content. One of the first submitted manuscripts that appeared to be consistent with the new policy was entitled "Annualized Quarterly Earnings," and the abstract accompanying that paper is reproduced below.

How useful is a financial forecast made at the beginning of a year once subsequent events and transactions begin to occur? For instance, given a calendar year company, assume that a forecast were published on January 2. Events occurring during the first quarter—disclosed in the March 31 quarterly report—may impair if not negate the meaningfulness of the original forecast such that for all intents and purposes no viable predictive tool would be available for the remaining nine months of the year.

Consider therefore the possibility of interim financial data serving as a means of updating the beginning-of-year forecast. This would be effected in a manner similar to that which is already used to measure and disclose the national economy's gross national product (GNP) and related national income data. Although a particular year's actual GNP is not determined until after its component twelve months have ended, estimates of the annual data are meticulously computed each quarter. Such amounts are adjusted to reflect seasonal variations and in turn are annualized in order to generate a meaningful approximation of GNP for the full year. Each quarter's data in effect serve as revision factors for the annual measure.

A major feature of the resulting data is that they are adjusted to reflect seasonal factors. Equally noteworthy is that by virtue of annualization, they are always presented in a uniform dimension. These attributes are as applicable to the accounting data of individual business enterprises as they are to the economy at large. A fringe benefit is that the nation's macroeconomic *and* microeconomic measures of performance would be expressed in common form.

This is how the system would work. At the beginning of the year, an earnings forecast would be published. At the end of the first quarter, the actual results for the three months would be adjusted to reflect seasonality and would in turn be annualized. The emergent amounts would be in effect a revised forecast of the annual earnings statement. This step would be repeated at the end of the second and third quarters, and at year-end the actual earnings statement would be prepared and disseminated.

Each succeeding quarter's revision of the annual estimate presumably would be more reliable than that of its predecessor. This is so because each successive estimate has the benefit of an additional three months of actual data from which to derive an annual estimate. An important feature of this system is that differences between one estimate and its successor data would constitute critical immediate disclosure of the effect of that quarter's events and transactions on the variance between the beginning-of-year forecast and actual annual earnings.

Questions

1. Is the publication of financial forecasts consistent with the notion that in a private enterprise economy the burden of risk should be borne by the party which stands to derive the resulting benefit?
2. If companies were permitted to publish financial forecasts, how extensive and precise should the disclosures be?
3. What involvement, if any, should its independent auditor have in a corporation's preparation of forecasted financial data?
4. Does the proposed system have merit at the conceptual level?
5. Is the proposed system responsive to the traditional arguments against published financial forecasts?
6. What problems do you envision in the implementation of such an approach, and what provisions could be introduced to make it more amenable to implementation?

Index of Cases

Subject Index

*This book has been set in 10 and 9 point Optima,
leaded 2 points. Chapter numbers are Serif Gothic
Bold outline and chapter titles are 24 point Optima Bold. The size of the type page is 27 by 42
picas.*